COLLECTED LETTERS OF
Samuel Taylor Coleridge

S. T. Coleridge

Mr Coleridge sat to me for this sketch about 1826

From a drawing of Samuel Taylor Coleridge made by Charles R. Leslie in 1818 and now in the possession of Mr. A. H. B. Coleridge

COLLECTED LETTERS OF

Samuel Taylor Coleridge

EDITED BY

EARL LESLIE GRIGGS

VOLUME V

1820–1825

OXFORD
AT THE CLARENDON PRESS
1971

Oxford University Press, Ely House, London W. 1

GLASGOW NEW YORK TORONTO MELBOURNE WELLINGTON
CAPE TOWN SALISBURY IBADAN NAIROBI DAR ES SALAAM LUSAKA ADDIS ABABA
BOMBAY CALCUTTA MADRAS KARACHI LAHORE DACCA
KUALA LUMPUR SINGAPORE HONG KONG TOKYO

PRINTED IN GREAT BRITAIN
AT THE UNIVERSITY PRESS, OXFORD
BY VIVIAN RIDLER
PRINTER TO THE UNIVERSITY

PREFACE

Of the many persons who have so generously contributed to my work, I am especially indebted to Mr. A. H. B. Coleridge, great-great-grandson of Samuel Taylor Coleridge, for permission to publish the letters. Mr. Coleridge, who controls the copyright of all unpublished manuscripts of Coleridge, has been most helpful from the beginning of this undertaking. It is a pleasure, too, to acknowledge my indebtedness to Lord Latymer, to whom this work is dedicated; to Professor Herbert B. Hoffleit of the University of California, Los Angeles, for a critical reading of the Greek and Latin passages in the letters; to Dr. B. A. Rowley of the University of East Anglia, for bibliographical information concerning German literature and philosophy; to Mr. W. Hugh Peal for many kindnesses and for giving me permission to make use of his valuable collection of Coleridge manuscripts; to Mr. T. C. Skeat, Keeper of Manuscripts, and Mr. J. P. Hudson of the Department of Manuscripts, British Museum, for help in the solution of textual and bibliographical problems and for patience in answering many inquiries; to the late William A. Jackson, Librarian of the Houghton Library, Harvard, for expert assistance; to Mr. Robert G. Vosper, Librarian, University of California, Los Angeles, for granting me special library privileges, and to Mr. Everett T. Moore, Assistant Librarian, Mr. Wilbur J. Smith, head of the Department of Special Collections, Mr. James R. Cox, head of the Circulation Department, Mrs. Frances J. Kirschenbaum of the Reference Department, and Mr. David Bishop and Mr. Don Reed of the Biomedical Library for bibliographical and other assistance; to Dr. Lawrence C. Powell, Director of the Clark Memorial Library, University of California, Los Angeles, and to his staff for many courtesies; to Dr. Donald C. Davidson, Librarian, University of California, Santa Barbara, for generous co-operation; and to the late Helen Darbishire, who will be remembered not only for her significant contributions to scholarship but also for her unfailing kindness to fellow scholars.

I owe a debt of gratitude, too, to the following persons: Mr. F. B. Adams, Jr., Mr. John Alden, Professor James F. Beard, Mr. P. R. Beaven, Mr. John Beer, Mr. Morchard Bishop, Sir Basil Blackwell, Mr. Carey Bliss, Mr. Charles S. Boesen, Mr. T. H. Bowyer, Professor H. Glenn Brown, Professor Henry J. Bruman, Mr. Herbert Cahoon, Mr. Kenneth Neill Cameron, Mr. Eric C. Chamberlain, Mr. W. A. Charlotte, Miss Nesta Clutterbuck, Mr. D. F. Cook, the Rev. C. Edward Crowther, Mr. Bertram R. Davis, Mr. A. J. F. Doulton,

Miss Emily Driscoll, Mr. Malcolm Elwin, Mr. David V. Erdman, Mr. Harry Fairhurst, Mr. M. H. Fisch, Miss Phyllis M. Giles, Professor Jonas C. Greenfield, the late J. L. Haney, Professor George H. Healey, Mr. R. H. Highfield, Mr. S. H. Horrocks, Miss Susan M. Hove, Mr. Sidney C. Hutchison, Rabbi Richard Israel, Professor Frederick L. Jones, Professor William F. Kahl, Dr. Paul A. Lacey, Professor D. J. Lindberg, Mr. G. E. Logsdon, Mr. T. Lyth, Professor E. L. McAdam, Jr., Mr. James G. McManaway, Professor William H. Marshall, Dr. W. S. Mitchell, Miss Winifred A. Myers, Miss Eleanor L. Nicholes, the Rev. Luther E. Olmon, Mr. W. A. Pantin, Mrs. J. M. Patterson, Mr. O. Pentelow, Mr. Carl H. Pforzheimer, Jr., Mr. F. N. L. Poynter, Mr. Mark Reed, Mr. F. W. Roberts, Mr. H. C. Schulz, Mr. C. M. E. Seaman, Miss Adelaide M. Smith, Professor Eli Sobel, Professor Charles Speroni, Mr. John C. C. Taylor, Mr. D. H. Varley, Dr. Lucyle Werkmeister, Mr. F. P. White, Mr. D. Whiteman, Mr. R. S. Woof, Sir James Wordie, and Dr. Louis B. Wright.

Noi non potemo perfetta vita avere sanza amici (Dante). As in the past I have called on my friends, so in the future I shall continue to request and know I shall receive invaluable assistance in the new edition of *The Complete Poetical Works of Samuel Taylor Coleridge* which I am preparing for the Clarendon Press.

I gratefully acknowledge the courtesy of the librarians and the trustees of the following institutions for making available to me the Coleridge autograph letters in their collections: Bibliothèque Municipale, Nantes; Birmingham University Library; Bodleian Library; Boston Public Library; Bristol Central Library; British Museum; Brown University Library; Central Library, Auckland, New Zealand; Columbia University Library; Cornell University Library; Dove Cottage, Wordsworth Museum; Fitz Park Museum, Keswick; Folger Shakespeare Library; Harvard College Library; Historical Society of Pennsylvania; Huntington Library; Indiana University Library; Jesus College Library, Cambridge; John Rylands Library; Knox College Library; Liverpool Public Libraries (Hugh Frederick Hornby Art Library); Longmans, Green & Co.; McGill University Library; Maine Historical Society; Massachusetts Historical Society; Montana State University Library (the H. W. Whicker Collection); National Library of Scotland; New York Public Library (Berg Collection and Arents Collections); The Carl H. Pforzheimer Library; Pierpont Morgan Library; Princeton University Library; Public Library of New South Wales, Sydney, Australia; Royal Institution of Cornwall; Rugby School; Rush Rhees Library, University of Rochester; State University of Iowa; Swedenborg Society; Texas Christian University Library;

Preface

University College Library, London; University Library, Cambridge; University of California Library, Santa Barbara; University of Kansas Library; University of Liverpool Library; University of Newcastle upon Tyne Library; University of Pennsylvania Library; University of Texas Library; University of York Library; Victoria University Library, Toronto; Wedgwood Museum; The Wellcome Historical Medical Museum; Dr. Williams's Library; Wisbech Museum and Literary Institute; and Yale University Library. I am likewise indebted to the Syndics of the Fitzwilliam Museum, Cambridge, and to the Delegacy of the University of London King's College.

I gratefully acknowledge, too, the generosity of the following persons in making available to me the manuscript letters of Coleridge in their possession: the late Miss Bairdsmith, the late Professor R. C. Bald, Mr. Gordon T. Banks of Goodspeed's Book Shop, the late Oliver R. Barrett, Mr. Foster W. Bond, Mr. H. T. Butler, Lady Cave, Lord Charnwood, Mrs. Sadie Spence Clephan, the late M. G. D. Clive, Mr. A. H. B. Coleridge, Dr. Basil Cottle, Professor Earl Daniels, Mrs. W. K. Denison, Francis Edwards Ltd., the late T. S. Eliot, Mr. C. Geigy-Hagenbach, Mrs. R. L. Grigg, Professor F. W. Hilles, Mr. Henry Hofheimer, Mrs. Phyllis Coleridge Hooper, Sir Geoffrey Keynes, Mrs. Valerie W. Lucas, the Earl of Lytton, owner of the Lovelace Papers, Professor Thomas O. Mabbott, Mr. Thomas F. Madigan, the late Sir John Murray, the late C. K. Ogden, Mr. James M. Osborn, Professor W. A. Osborne, Mr. W. Hugh Peal, the late Arthur Pforzheimer, Mr. Reynolds Rathbone, the late Mrs. E. F. Rawnsley, Mr. Walter T. Spencer, Mrs. J. L. Staufer, Mrs. W. M. Sweeny, Mr. Robert H. Taylor, Mr. W. T. Trimble, Professor Robert C. Whitford, Mr. Jonathan Wordsworth, and the late Charlton Yarnall.

I take particular pleasure in acknowledging the painstaking work of my assistants, Miss Kay Wong (now Mrs. Howe C. Fong), Miss Sandra J. Yee, Miss Barbara Joanne Meek, and Miss Kathi Schurter.

This edition of Coleridge's *Letters* has been made possible for me through the generosity of the Regents of the University of California in the form of liberal grants by the Research Committees in Los Angeles and Santa Barbara.

My greatest debt of all is to my wife.

E. L. G.

University of California
Santa Barbara

CONTENTS

LIST OF ILLUSTRATIONS

LIST OF LETTERS

List of Letters

(xvii)

List of Letters

List of Letters

Appendix B

Additional Letters (1795–1831) identified by *a* or *b* following the Letter Number; and Certain Letters in Volumes I–VI now reprinted from MS.

(xxvii)

List of Letters

ABBREVIATIONS AND PRINCIPAL
REFERENCES

Abbreviations

Aids to Reflection	Coleridge, S. T.: *Aids to Reflection in the Formation of a Manly Character on the several grounds of Prudence, Morality, and Religion: illustrated by select passages from our Elder Divines, especially from Archbishop Leighton*, 1825, 1831
Alaric Watts	Watts, Alaric A.: *Alaric Watts. A Narrative of His Life*, 2 vols., 1884
Biog. Lit.	Coleridge, S. T.: *Biographia Literaria*, . . . 2 vols., 1817; ed. H. N. Coleridge, 2 vols., 1847; ed. J. Shawcross, 2 vols., 1907. (Unless otherwise indicated references are to the Shawcross edition.)
Campbell, *Life*	Campbell, J. D.: *Samuel Taylor Coleridge, a Narrative of the Events of His Life*, 1894
Campbell, *Poetical Works*	Campbell, J. D., ed.: *The Poetical Works of Samuel Taylor Coleridge*, 1893
Chambers, *Life*	Chambers, E. K.: *Samuel Taylor Coleridge: A Biographical Study*, 1938
Church and State, The	Coleridge, S. T.: *On the Constitution of the Church and State, according to the Idea of Each; with aids toward a right judgment on the late Catholic Bill*, 1830, 2nd edn. 1830 (cited)
D.N.B.	Stephen, Leslie, and Lee, Sidney, eds.: *The Dictionary of National Biography*, 22 vols., reprinted 1937–8
E. L. G.	Griggs, E. L., ed.: *Unpublished Letters of Samuel Taylor Coleridge*, . . . 2 vols., 1932
Early Rec.	Cottle, Joseph: *Early Recollections; chiefly relating to the late Samuel Taylor Coleridge*, . . . 2 vols., 1837
Gillman, *Life*	Gillman, James: *The Life of Samuel Taylor Coleridge*, 1838
John Hookham Frere	Festing, Gabrielle: *John Hookham Frere and His Friends*, 1899
Lamb Letters	Lucas, E. V., ed.: *The Letters of Charles Lamb, to which are added those of his sister, Mary Lamb*, 3 vols., 1935
Later Years	De Selincourt, E., ed.: *The Letters of William and Dorothy Wordsworth: the Later Years*, 3 vols., 1939
Letters	Coleridge, E. H., ed.: *Letters of Samuel Taylor Coleridge*, 2 vols., 1895
Letters, Conversations and Rec.	Allsop, Thomas, ed.: *Letters, Conversations and Recollections of S. T. Coleridge*, 1836, 1858, 1864 (cited)

List of Abbreviations

Letters from the Lake Poets	[Coleridge, E. H., ed.] *Letters from the Lake Poets . . . to Daniel Stuart*, 1889
Letters Hitherto Uncollected	Prideaux, W. F., ed.: *Letters Hitherto Uncollected by Samuel Taylor Coleridge*, 1913
Letters of Hartley Coleridge	Griggs, G. E. and E. L., eds.: *Letters of Hartley Coleridge*, 1936
Life of Joseph Blanco White	Thom, J. H., ed.: *The Life of the Rev. Joseph Blanco White, written by himself; with portions of his Correspondence*, 3 vols., 1845
Literary Remains	Coleridge, H. N., ed.: *The Literary Remains of Samuel Taylor Coleridge*, 4 vols., 1836–9
Memoir of H. F. Cary	Cary, Henry: *Memoir of the Rev. Henry Francis Cary,* . . . 2 vols., 1847
Memorials of Coleorton	Knight, Wm., ed.: *Memorials of Coleorton, being Letters . . . to Sir George and Lady Beaumont,* . . . 2 vols., 1887
Middle Years	De Selincourt, E., ed.: *The Letters of William and Dorothy Wordsworth: the Middle Years,* 2 vols., 1937
Nineteenth-Century Studies (Cornell)	Davis, H., DeVane, W. C., and Bald, R. C., eds.: *Nineteenth-Century Studies*, 1940
Poems	Coleridge, E. H., ed.: *The Complete Poetical Works of Samuel Taylor Coleridge,* . . . 2 vols., 1912
Poetical Works	*The Poetical Works of S. T. Coleridge, including the Dramas of Wallenstein, Remorse, and Zapolya,* 3 vols., 1828, 1829 *The Poetical Works of S. T. Coleridge,* 3 vols., 1834
Rem.	Cottle, Joseph: *Reminiscences of Samuel Taylor Coleridge and Robert Southey,* 1847, 1848 (cited)
Robinson on Books and Their Writers	Morley, Edith J., ed.: *Henry Crabb Robinson on Books and Their Writers,* 3 vols., 1938
Southey Letters	Warter, J. W., ed.: *Selections from the Letters of Robert Southey,* 4 vols., 1856
Table Talk	[Coleridge, H. N., ed.] *Specimens of the Table Talk of the late Samuel Taylor Coleridge,* 2 vols., 1835, 1836
Theory of Life	Watson, Seth B., ed.: *Hints towards the Formation of a more comprehensive Theory of Life. By S. T. Coleridge,* 1848
Wise, Bibliography	Wise, T. J.: *A Bibliography of . . . Samuel Taylor Coleridge,* 1913

INTRODUCTION

I

THE letters in these volumes provide an invaluable record of the personal life and intellectual preoccupations of Coleridge from the year 1820 until his death in July 1834 and complete the self-portraiture begun in the correspondence of his early and middle years. The present letters, over half of which are now published for the first time, show especially his concern with the questions of moral and religious philosophy, reveal the nature of the friendships which he found so necessary and rewarding, and disclose the hopes and aspirations which sustained him, as well as the frustrations and sorrows which beset him. Although old age came upon him prematurely and ill health often incapacitated him, still these closing years brought him a measure of peace such as he had never known. Except for holiday excursions to the seaside, usually to Ramsgate, a tour of Belgium, the Rhineland, and Holland in 1828, a heartbreaking journey to Oxford in 1820, a pleasant one to Cambridge in the year before he died, and occasional visits to London or near by, Coleridge 'sat on the brow of Highgate Hill' reading, writing, and talking. Befriended by his neighbours, cheered by the visitors who called to pay him homage, and dedicated to the pursuit of knowledge, he became the sage of Highgate. If only a fraction of what he wrote during the last fourteen and a half years of his life reached publication, his major works, *Aids to Reflection*, 1825, *On the Constitution of The Church and State*, 1830, *Confessions of an Inquiring Spirit* published posthumously in 1840, and three editions of his *Poetical Works*, 1828, 1829, and 1834, as well as occasional contributions to *Blackwood's Magazine* and various Literary Annuals, indicate that he was far from being 'the sole unbusy thing' described in one of his poems.

By 4 January 1820, the date of the first letter in these volumes, Coleridge had been for several years an established and beloved member of the Gillman household at Highgate—indeed, his arrival there in April 1816 marked a turning-point in his life. The years of wandering from place to place were over. He had found at last what was to be his permanent home for the rest of his life. There was now much to be thankful for. Although he was troubled by his indebtedness to the Gillmans, he no longer had to fret over the annual premium for his Assurance Policy, his friend Green having arranged to pay it each year. It is unlikely, too, that he was able

Introduction

to contribute much financial assistance to his wife and daughter, Sara, at Keswick, but Mrs. Coleridge had long received the remaining half of the Wedgwood annuity. His three children he could speak of as 'unmingled blessings'. His elder son, Hartley, had been elected Probationary Fellow of Oriel College, Oxford, in April 1819, and his future seemed assured. His younger son, Derwent, was soon to be entered at St. John's College, Cambridge.

Coleridge could not have had more zealous and loyal friends than James and Anne Gillman, who accepted him as an intimate member of the family, extended hospitality to Hartley and Derwent, and welcomed Mrs. Coleridge and Sara when they first visited Highgate in 1823. 'I trust', Coleridge wrote to Derwent some years before making his Will, 'that I shall shortly be able to add—that whatever may be the state of my personal engagements to the Gillmans at the time of my death (& to no one else am I indebted) the whole proceeds of this Assurance Policy will be held sacred, to your Mother & Sister, & secured beyond all dependency on the will or feelings of any person.' With the full agreement of the Gillmans, Coleridge conscientiously fulfilled his intention, and in his Will he made specific provision for his family. The Will, which is as unique and Coleridgean as anything he ever wrote, is dated 17 September 1829 and the Codicil 2 July 1830. Both were witnessed by Mrs. Gillman. The full text of these documents is included in Volume VI, Appendix A.

Ever ready with encouragement and kindness, the Gillmans treated Coleridge's problems as their own. Nowhere is their affection better exemplified than in the crisis over Hartley Coleridge. On 30 June 1820 the benumbing news reached Highgate that Hartley's appointment as a Fellow of Oriel College, Oxford, would not be confirmed at the expiration of his probationary year in October. The decision was based mainly on the charge of intemperance. 'Sottishness' was the opprobrious term employed, a word which Coleridge found 'too mortifying' even to transcribe. Fortunately, the Gillmans were at hand to soothe and console the anguished father. 'Yesterday', Mrs. Gillman wrote to Allsop on 1 July 1820, Coleridge 'was convulsed with agony, tho' at first he was calm. In the evening he was tranquil, as he is today tho' of course remains deeply affected. His God & his Books are his refuge. . . . He is now going to walk with me, and I think we shall succeed in diverting his mind from this sad subject, until he must of *necessity* go into it fully.' She also explained that Derwent had already gone to Oxford 'to bring back his Brother here. . . . Mr C will then see what can be done to re-instate him.' On 7 August, however, she was far less sanguine: 'Mr Coleridge is, I grieve to say, very poorly; he has not as heretofore rallied—the affair of Hartley will I fear never be overcome.'

Fully realizing the serious consequences for Hartley if he were deprived of his Oriel fellowship, Coleridge devoted the last half of the year 1820 mainly to his son's affairs. How futile his efforts were is shown by his letter to Lockhart of December:

> It pleased God to afflict me most heavily by the unexpected & most cruel & unjust persecution of my eldest Son at Oxford, just as I had supposed him settled in independence for a course of years at least & with the fairest prospects—I was stunned scarcely less by the suddenness of the Blow than by it's weight. I hurried here & there—went to Oxford—made every inquisition, & every attempt—& succeeded only in obtaining decisive proofs of what in fact I had never doubted nor possibly could doubt, that my Son had been most cruelly wronged & then calumniated.

For the next two years Hartley remained in London and tried to support himself by his pen. Though free from 'all *active* bad', his growing intemperance, a tendency to run off under stress and conceal his whereabouts, and his 'Idiocies, Neglects, Provocations, and Promise-breach' finally convinced Coleridge that whatever else was to be done, 'London he must not live in'. Undoubtedly, Gillman's 'unweariable Kindness' influenced Hartley to depart for Ambleside late in the year 1822. He remained in the North for the rest of his life, and father and son never saw one another again. Coleridge, however, never ceased to be concerned about his son's welfare, and in one of his later letters he remarked: Hartley 'is seldom, an hour together, out of my head, and still less often *off* my heart'.

During the eighteen years Coleridge lived with the Gillmans at Highgate, he did everything in his power to serve them. In 1816 he wrote the *Theory of Life* expressly for Gillman's benefit, and he continually endeavoured to foster his friend's professional career. To the Gillmans he dedicated *The Friend* of 1818. 'If at the time, I published the Friend in Volumes', he later wrote, 'I had reason . . . to express what I did express in my Dedication of the Work to Mr and Mrs Gillman, what must I not say now, after eight years' unremitted Love & Affection, and hourly occasions to experience & venerate their worth!' Coleridge was always willing to share in the domestic problems inevitably facing the household. He wrote letters of advice to James, the elder son. He tutored Henry, the younger son, and succeeded in placing him at Eton College, though dismissal followed not long afterwards. To one of his correspondents he declared that he regarded Gillman's 'active and more than *dis*interested Friendship . . . as more honorable to me than all the Laurels on Parnassus could have been, tho' Apollo himself had

Introduction

woven and presented the Wreaths. No one, who has more than a
surface acquaintance either with him or me, is ignorant that my
Interests have at all times been as dear to him as his own, and in
fact more anxiously looked after.' And in his Will in 1829, Coleridge
paid special tribute to 'James & Anne Gillman, my more than
Friends, the Guardians of my Health, Happiness, and Interests,
during the fourteen years of my Life that I have enjoyed the proofs
of their constant, zealous, and disinterested affection, as an Inmate
and Member of their family'.

Lovable and affectionate, tolerant and placable, humble and for-
giving, Coleridge basked in the warmth of friendship. Whatever his
faults, 'he never did a mean thing', as the late Herbert Read so
pertinently remarked. If he felt the need of compassion and understanding on the part of those whom he loved—'In Sympathy alone
I found at once Nourishment and Stimulus'—he was always ready
to sacrifice his own interests to the aspirations and welfare of another. So it was that he turned aside from his own work to assist a
Hebrew scholar, an editor of Bacon, a Scottish preacher, a Swedenborgian, a rising surgeon, or a former housemate. 'Be assured',
he wrote to Gioacchino de' Prati, an Italian patriot whom he had
met only a month earlier, 'that whatever I could do for a brother,
I will do for you.' So, too, in 1828 he reported: 'I have with a sick
heart been all this day trotting about to make up, guinea by guinea',
twenty pounds to save Mrs. Morgan 'from God knows what.'

Long before 1820 a number of Coleridge's early friendships had
been broken off or had lapsed through a separation of many years.
'To feel the full force of the Christian religion', Coleridge wrote in
1818, 'it is perhaps necessary, for many tempers, that they should
first be made to feel, experimentally, the hollowness of human
friendship, the presumptuous emptiness of human hopes.' By 1826,
however, he had learned from his 'Philosophy' that 'selfless Reason
is the best Comforter, and only sure friend of declining Life', and
he could recall his former friendships without bitterness.

> And though thou notest from thy safe recess
> Old Friends burn dim, like lamps in noisome air,
> Love them for what they are; nor love them less,
> Because to thee they are not what they were.

Neither time nor disparity of temperament altered the friendship between Coleridge and Charles Lamb. Begun during their
school-days at Christ's Hospital, surviving a temporary alienation in 1798, the bond between them was lifelong. Lamb's humour
could be biting and sarcastic, but Coleridge was always ready to
forgive. 'When you know the *whole* of him', he wrote to Allsop in

1820, 'you will love him spite of all oddities & even faults—nay, I had almost said, *for* them'; and in December of the same year, he indicated the extent of his affection: 'We have loved each other from earliest manhood—& he has a right on many accounts to be borne with by me, even in cases that in any other friend I could not have borne without resentment.' Only a few of Coleridge's letters to Lamb survive. Lamb's letters, along with others he especially treasured, Coleridge kept in a packet labelled, 'Literae Sacerrimae'.

With his arrival at Highgate, Coleridge quickly drew around him a whole new circle of friends, among them John Hookham Frere, Hyman Hurwitz, Joseph Henry Green, H. F. Cary, C. A. Tulk, Charles and Mrs. Aders, and Thomas Allsop.

Coleridge first met Frere, diplomat, poet, and translator, in 1816, and immediately a warm friendship began. 'I assure you', he wrote to Murray, 'I regard the day, when I first saw Mr Frere, among the most memorable Red Letter Days of my Literary Life.' Four years of the closest intimacy followed. Frere seems to have taken the place formerly occupied by Wordsworth in Coleridge's mind and heart, and it was particularly unfortunate that his wife's health made it necessary for him to leave England at the end of the year 1820 and establish a permanent residence in Malta.

In September 1825 Frere returned to England for a year's visit, and cordial relations with Coleridge were resumed. 'It is a great delight to me to be any where with you', Coleridge wrote to him, 'and more than so . . . it is a source of Strength, and a renewal of hope.' And to Lady Beaumont he exclaimed, 'O! how many many reasons I have to think of him with Esteem, Admiration, and grateful Love!'

Before he returned to Malta in 1826, Frere obtained from Lord Liverpool a 'positive promise' to provide Coleridge with a sinecure of £200 a year. During the negotiations early in 1827, Liverpool suffered a paralytic stroke, and 'King George the IVth gave the place to another'. The case was brought to the attention of Canning, but 'Enteritis cried, Veto'. Canning died on 8 August 1827, and his death ended all hope of a sinecure. 'Had Lord Liverpool's promise & intention been realized', Coleridge wrote to Derwent, 'I should have made over half to your Mother.'

Even when Frere was in far-away Malta, Coleridge continued to revere him. In his Will he bequeathed to Gillman his most cherished possession, 'the Manuscript volume' containing three plays of Aristophanes translated and presented to him 'by my dear Friend & Patron, the Honorable John Hookham Frere'. For his part, Frere never forgot the obligation he felt for having been 'especially benefited' by his close association with Coleridge at Highgate. In 1839,

a year before his *Aristophanes. A Metrical Version of the Achar-
nians, the Knights, and the Birds* was published by Pickering, he
directed that the profit from 'half the impression (250 copies)'
should be paid to Gillman, 'who is entitled to all kindness from the
lovers of learning, and particularly from me, in this instance'. Long
after Gillman's death, Frere asked his brother to ascertain whether
Mrs. Gillman had 'profited by the sale of the Aristophanes'.

Little has been known of Coleridge's relations with Hyman
Hurwitz, master of the Hebrew Academy at Highgate and later
professor of Hebrew in the University of London, but a series of
hitherto unpublished letters reveals a long and significant friendship. Coleridge considered himself fortunate to have discovered 'by
mere chance of neighborhood' such 'a sound Oriental Scholar, &
a profound Hebraist', and through his intimacy with Hurwitz, his
'Christian Neighbor of the Jewish Persuasion', he discovered what
he had not before imagined, 'that a learned, unprejudiced, & yet
strictly *orthodox* Jew may be much nearer in point of faith & religious principles to a learned & strictly orthodox Christian, of the
Church of England, than many called Christians'.

Coleridge translated two Hebrew Dirges written by Hurwitz, and
prior to the publication of the latter's *Vindiciae Hebraicae; or a
Defence of the Hebrew Scriptures, as a Vehicle of Revealed Religion*,
he read the work 'sentence by sentence'. Hurwitz's *Hebrew Tales*,
too, owed much to Coleridge, who not only suggested the preparation of the work but corrected the manuscript and contributed
three *Specimens of Rabbinical Wisdom, selected from the Mishna*
which had earlier appeared in *The Friend*. He further assisted Hurwitz with two works on the Hebrew language. He also wrote to
Henry Brougham recommending Hurwitz's appointment to the
University of London.

The genial friendship between Coleridge and Hurwitz was a truly
remarkable one. It brought together two men differing in race,
training, and religious affiliation. If Coleridge seems to have been
unduly willing to forward his friend's career, Hurwitz made available to him an expert knowledge of the Hebrew Scriptures and led
him to a deeper understanding of them.

Coleridge's association with Thomas Allsop, a young business-
man in London, began in 1818. Allsop's devotion, occasional financial help, and willingness to be of service soon caused both Coleridge
and the Gillmans to regard him in the role of a dutiful son. Although
Allsop was a frequent guest at Highgate, Coleridge addressed to
him a larger number of letters than to any other correspondent
represented in the present volumes. The letters to Allsop served as
an 'Escape Valve' in which Coleridge could disburden himself of

whatever was 'bubbling and steaming' in his mind at the moment. In contrast to conversation, he explained to Allsop, 'letters are more permanent, and an epistolary correspondence perhaps more endearing—like all marks of remembrance in absence'. As a result, these letters provide an invaluable record of Coleridge's life during the Highgate period.

Two years after Coleridge's death, Allsop published anonymously his *Letters, Conversations, and Recollections of S. T. Coleridge*. Scarcely a letter was printed without omissions, and others were omitted altogether. Since, however, most of the manuscripts of the letters to Allsop included in this edition have come to light, the many outpourings which Coleridge dashed off spontaneously and without reserve can now be read as they were written.

Among the visitors who called at Highgate with some regularity were Basil Montagu and Edward Irving, 'the super-Ciceronian, ultra-Demosthenic Pulpiteer of the Scotch Chapel in Cross Street, Hatton Garden'. They usually came on Thursday. Thus in 1824 Coleridge established the 'Thursday Conversation Evenings' or 'Attic nights' as he called them, and the Gillmans issued a 'general invitation to . . . London & Suburban Acquaintances for Thursday Evenings, a humble sort of Conversazione'. Sometimes the guests were numerous. On one occasion there were in attendance 'two Painters, two Poets, one Divine, an eminent Chemist & Naturalist, a Major, a Naval Captain & Voyager, a Physician, a colonial Chief Justice, a Barrister and a Baronet'. Coleridge delighted in these meetings, which he once jocularly termed '*One*versazioni'. Gregarious by nature and a monologist *par excellence*, he seldom failed to leave on his auditors a vivid impression of his extraordinary intellectual powers and conversational ability. Increasing ill health forced him to abandon these 'Attic nights' in 1829, but there was no cessation of hospitality. 'Thursday nights are over now', he told Frere's nephew in December 1830, 'but any night whether Thursday or not I shall be most happy to see you.'

In January 1823 Sara Coleridge, then twenty years of age, arrived for a visit at Highgate. Coleridge was delighted with his beautiful and talented daughter, whom he had not seen since 1812. She 'is a good & lovely Girl', he wrote in 1824, '& every thing (save that her Health is delicate) that the fondest & most ambitious Parent could pray for. The young men, & some of their elders, talk in raptures of her Beauty.' Coleridge was equally enthusiastic about her intellectual activities: 'She is exceedingly industrious, has gained 130£ by a translation of the History of the Abipones in two volumes from the Latin of a German Jesuit, and is now compiling a Biography of the Chevalier Bayard.' It has been said that 'her father looked down into her eyes, and left in them the light of his own'. After Coleridge's death and that of her husband she became a distinguished editor of her father's works.

Derwent, after dallying away his undergraduate years at Cambridge, gladdened his father's heart by taking orders—'My dearest and right reverend Boy', Coleridge began a letter after his son's ordination to the priesthood in July 1827. Even towards Mrs. Coleridge his attitude softened. In August 1832 he was pleased to stand beside her at the christening of their daughter's second child, as evidence that their incompatibility did not extend to their parental relations. 'Bating living in the same house with her', he said, 'there are few women, that I have a greater respect & *ratherish* liking for, than Mrs C.'

Coleridge's last years were immeasurably brightened by the devotion of his nephew and son-in-law, Henry Nelson Coleridge, who married Sara Coleridge in 1829. He assisted Coleridge in the preparation of the second edition of *Aids to Reflection*, which was issued in 1831. 'I have quite confidence enough in your taste & judgement', Coleridge wrote to him in 1830, 'to give you a Chart Blanch for any amendments in the style.' It is no exaggeration to say that the *Poetical Works* of 1834 would not have seen the light of day if Henry Nelson Coleridge had not been at hand to prod, cajole, and coax, so that this, Coleridge's last edition of his poems, would be as definitive as possible. He was the only member of the family who visited Coleridge during his final illness, and after his uncle's death, he dedicated, as far as health and legal duties permitted, the remaining eight years of his own life to fostering Coleridge's posthumous reputation. Too little, perhaps, has been made of his efforts to preserve for posterity the multitudinous fragments of Coleridge's fertile genius.

Mainly through the influence of Basil Montagu, in March 1824 Coleridge was elected a Royal Associate of the recently founded Royal Society of Literature. As Royal Patron, George IV provided the Society with an annual grant of 1,100 guineas from the King's Privy Purse. The plans developed by the Society for the expenditure of this fund were as follows. The sum of 100 guineas was to be used each year by the Council of the Society to purchase two gold medals for presentation to distinguished British and foreign literati. The Council was also to elect ten Royal Associates, each of whom was to receive 100 guineas annually, with the obligation of reading a yearly essay before the Society.

On 6 May 1824 Coleridge was introduced to the Society as a Royal Associate, and in his formal Address on that occasion, he said he received the appointment 'with glad and grateful feeling, as powerfully confirming me in the assurance, that I had not mistaken my vocation'. He then went on to remark:

Men of Letters may be distinguished into two classes—of which the first and far more numerous have it for their Object to distribute and popularize the stores of knowlege already existing, and devote their talents to the instruction and entertainment of the Many. And these men . . . may rationally look for their own remuneration to the Public in whose service they labor. . . . But in every age and country there is, or ought to be, a smaller class, consisting of those who labor in the service of Science itself, for the enlargement of it's precincts or the deepening of it's foundations: and who must needs narrow the circle of their immediate influence and diminish the number of their readers in exact proportion to the success of their attempts. And to whom shall such men look for support and patronage, but to the lawful Representative of THE NATION, contra-distinguished from the People, as the Unity of the Generations of a people organized into a State—that is, to the King, or the Sovereign.

The 'annual stipend' attached to his appointment as Royal Associate, Coleridge continued, 'would enable me to employ my whole time in the completion of that System of Truths respecting Nature, Man, and Deity, evolved from one Principle'.

On 18 May 1825 Coleridge delivered before the Society a lecture, *On the Prometheus of Æschylus; an Essay, Preparatory to a series of Disquisitions respecting the Egyptian in connection with the Sacerdotal Theology, and in contrast with the Mysteries of ancient Greece,* and in 1827 he forwarded to the Secretary, Richard Cattermole, a brief outline of a second lecture. It was never given. Several of the Royal Associates, however, delivered no lectures at all.

Early in May 1831, almost a year after the accession of William IV, the Royal Associates were notified by Cattermole that the annual grants hitherto derived from the Privy Purse of George IV were to be discontinued. Coleridge quite rightly regarded as a 'life annuity' the hundred guineas which he had regularly received each year since his election as a Royal Associate in 1824. This sudden and unexpected withdrawal of his annual grant was overwhelming. It represented his only certain income. He consulted various friends as to what he should do and decided to apply to Lord Brougham, the Chancellor. Sotheby, who was on 'good terms' with Brougham, offered to act as intermediary. On 19 May, therefore, Coleridge addressed a letter to Sotheby enclosing one for Brougham. Neither letter has come to light. Certainly Coleridge believed that his annuity should be honoured during his lifetime, as were all those then appearing on the Pension List, and he hoped that if his case were properly presented, Brougham would recognize the validity of his application.

Sotheby lost no time in delivering Coleridge's letter and conferring with his friend Brougham, and on 26 May he sent Coleridge 'a trumpet *note* of gratulation' in which he enthusiastically exclaimed: 'I have succeeded beyond my Hopes tho' not beyond your Merits! Yet my Hopes were high, when I applied in your behalf to men of such cultivated minds as the Chancellor and Lord Grey [the First Lord of the Treasury]. . . . For your further gratification I copy Lord Brougham's letter to me.'

My dear Sir
Lord Grey has taken a very kind interest in our Friend Coleridge's Affair; and he has found 200£ which he can and will forthwith apply to his use. Let him have ½ each year.

yrs &c H. B.

Shocked by Sotheby's letter, which gave his 'poor intellects a touch of the *Staggers*', Coleridge realized that he had been wholly misunderstood. Both Brougham and Sotheby believed that his poverty was such as to demand immediate relief. Thus in lieu of a life annuity, he was offered an 'eleemosynary Grant' from the Treasury. Brougham did not reply to Coleridge's letter of 19 May. It was, of course, a thoughtless blunder on the part of Sotheby to send a copy of Brougham's curt note, with the offensive condition —'Let him have ½ each year'. Coleridge expressed his bitterness in a letter of 27 May to his son-in-law, Henry Nelson Coleridge, and sought his advice:

Now all I can make out of this communication is that as a compensation for a life annuity of One Hundred Guineas in connection with a title of Honor, suddenly taken away from me the very week when the 105£ should have been delivered to me, Lord Grey makes me a present of two hundred pound; but this to be entrusted into my hands in two installments, with a year's interval—so that on the supposition that a hundred pound would suffice to prevent me from starving for 12 months, I have a *respite* of a full year, before my deposition in the Work-house— For (as in my letter to Lord Brougham I distinctly stated) the 105£, due to me on May 1. 1831, formed the means, on which I had been authorized to rely, of defraying my Board &c from May 1. 1830. . . . Do you perceive any possibility that I have misconceived Mr Sotheby's note?

After conferring with his son-in-law and the Gillmans on Saturday morning, 28 May, Coleridge decided that 'it would be much better at once to write to Sotheby, and modestly decline the offered boon'. Although illness and a depression of spirits caused him to delay doing so until 3 June, he remained firm in his conviction that he could not accept the £200 grant from the Treasury without a 'sense of degradation'.

Meanwhile, Coleridge's friends had been active in his behalf. Lamb applied through Grey's brother-in-law, Edward Ellice, secretary to the Treasury, and reported the success of his intercession to Highgate. According to Lamb, Ellice 'expressly said that the thing was renewable three-yearly'. Joseph Hardman, a friend of Coleridge, asked Thomas Pringle to intercede. Pringle took up the matter with James Mackintosh, Colonel Fox (probably C. R. Fox, equerry to Queen Adelaide), and Samuel Rogers. On 26 May, Rogers called on Grey and next day reported to Pringle: 'The work is done for Coleridge. He is still to receive his annuity.' Pringle informed Hardman, who replied on 28 May: 'I shall have the pleasure of leaving your note with Mr. Coleridge this afternoon.' Coleridge knew, however, that Sotheby's information was not only official but correct. If the King's Ministers had entertained any thought of an annuity, Sotheby would have been informed.

In his letter of 3 June, Coleridge asked Sotheby to communicate the following message to Brougham and Grey:

I beg leave thro' you to convey, both to the L. Chancellor and Lord Grey, my grateful acknowlegement of the prompt attention, which my case has received from their Lordships, and my due appreciation of the humane desire, evinced by them, to prevent or obviate the *immediate* distress or embarrassment, in which the sudden Withdrawal and unforeseen Extinction of the honor and honorarium of a Royal Associate of the Royal Society of Literature might otherwise involve me, by a private Grant from the Treasury of 200£:—but that I beg leave most respectfully to decline it. This . . . is all, I presume, that it is necessary for me, or that it would be becoming in me, to say to their Lordships.

'To *You*', Coleridge explained to Sotheby, 'I seem to myself to owe a statement of the reasons that have actuated me to this decision.' He then revealed his irritation over the proposed mode of dispensing the £200, 'a moiety of which was (if I understand Lord Brougham's note aright) to be entrusted to me immediately, . . . the other 100£ to be held in reserve by you, & bestowed on me the year following', and went on to say:

I cannot but find a most essential difference between a private donation from Lord Grey, and a public honor and stipend conferred on me by my Sovereign in mark of approval of the objects and purposes to which I had devoted and was continuing to devote the powers and talents entrusted to me. . . .

To Lord Brougham I did not indeed hesitate to avow my Poverty. But grievously have I been misunderstood, if I have been supposed to plead that Poverty, for itself and independent of it's Causes, as the ground of my application. I avowed it because I knew it to have been not only a blameless but an honorable Poverty—. . . the effect and result of an entire and faithful dedication of myself to Ends and Objects, for the realization and attainment of which I was constrained to believe myself *especially* fitted & therefore *called.* . . .

Coleridge concluded his explanation to Sotheby as follows:

The issues of our life are with God! . . . but if I dared trust my own presentiments, I should hold it not improbable, that this 200£ would suffice to *bury* me as well as to sustain me while alive. But even on the assumption, that some such sum *must* be received by me from some quarter, . . . yet there is in my estimation a wide difference between receiving it from . . . *Friends* . . . and accepting the same sum, in the dark as it were, from a Stranger who neither knows or thinks aught of me but my wants, and on the score of the want exclusively, without reference to or recognition of any merit, has been induced to concede it as an eleemosynary Grant.

Before posting his letter to Sotheby, Coleridge suddenly discovered that the London newspapers had taken up the plight of the Royal Associates and particularly his own case. 'I have this minute', he added in a postscript to his letter of 3 June, 'seen a paragraph from the Magazine, called the Englishman, in the Times of To Day—& another in yestermorning's Morn. Chronicle.' Coleridge was in no way responsible for this publicity. As he explained to Sotheby, on learning 'some month ago' that an article on the 'Suppression of the R. S. L.' had been proposed by the publishers of the *Englishman's Magazine*, Coleridge 'instantly' informed Hardman through Gillman that 'any such article *could* do no good, and *might* work injuriously'—but at all events, as a '*personal* favor' he '*intreated*' that his name should not be introduced.

Despite Coleridge's warning, the June 1831 number of the *Englishman's Magazine* contained a rambling article entitled 'Extraordinary Case of the Royal Associates of the Royal Society of Literature'. It was certainly written by Joseph Hardman, who had obtained detailed information concerning the Society from the secretary, Richard Cattermole. Hardman begins with a brief history of the Society, gives the names of the ten Royal Associates, points out that they have hitherto received one hundred guineas each from the 'annual bounty' paid to the Society by 'the late King', notes that four of them are 'dependent for their subsistence on the paltry pittance which they receive from the funds of the Society', and exclaims: 'Intimation has actually been given on the part of the Crown, to Mr. Coleridge and his brother Associates, that they must expect their allowances "very shortly" to cease. . . . And this too, at a time when . . . the Pension List has been sacredly preserved in all its entireness of political infamy.' Reminding

Brougham that he is 'the official keeper of the royal conscience', Hardman calls upon him to 'prevent his patriotic master [William IV] from being *unconsciously* guilty of committing an action so unworthy of the dignity of the beloved sovereign of Britain', who 'can personally know nothing whatever of the matter'. But 'there can be no excuse for the Chancellor if he do not immediately interfere, and hinder a miserable attempt at economy'. The writer also exhorts Lord Grey, who had 'once declaimed most indignantly' against 'the Scotch' for their ungenerous treatment of Burns, to prevent the English from incurring a similar reproach. He notes, too, how little 'the Crown has ever done for the advancement of science or literature in Britain'.

A writer in *The Times* of 2 June took the author of this article to task for 'assuring the world, as an official authority', that the pensions of one class only, those 'doled out . . . in acknowledgment of literary and scientific eminence, . . . are one and all to be discontinued', and indignantly protested: 'What! take away from such men as Coleridge, Mathias, Ouseley, Roscoe, Sharon Turner, and a few others . . . the wretched pittance of 100£ per annum, . . . and in the case of some among them the only support of their declining years. . . . The charge is false. The King's Ministers know nothing of it. Lord BROUGHAM assuredly does not.' The writer admitted that the scandalously extravagant Pension List had not been overhauled by the present Government, as had been generally expected; instead, it had been preserved in its entirety, and its continuance justified as 'a point of honour', since the pensioners had '*understood*' that their pensions were for life. In conclusion the writer quoted extensively from the article in the *Englishman's Magazine*.

After having called at the Ministry, the same writer returned to the subject in *The Times* of 3 June:

We did no more than justice to His MAJESTY'S Ministers, in expressing our total disbelief of any concern . . . on their part in the harsh . . . discontinuance of the pensions bestowed during the former reign on gentlemen distinguished by their eminence in the literary world. We are now assured, and on the best information, that 'His MAJESTY'S Ministers are entirely guiltless of the act'.

It is further known that Lord GREY, on finding that Mr. COLERIDGE had lost, through the exercise of an authority distinct from that of the King's *responsible* servants, the pittance on which he had hitherto existed, has agreed to grant him an annuity equal to that withdrawn from him, though issuing out of a fund which is only temporary. This conduct does honour to Lord GREY, and we trust that his Lordship will have nerve and generosity to put the colleagues of Mr. Coleridge also on some less miserable footing than that to which a treatment similar to what he has experienced must ere now have reduced them.

The truth is, that the pensions were supplied by order of GEORGE IV. from the Privy Purse, over which, as it is well understood by Parliament, no person has authority but the King himself. However, if we are not mistaken, the act, which was a *blunder*, will in one way or other be repaired. The press is a powerful protector of the destitute.

Thoroughly aroused by this embarrassing publicity and by the 'strange misstatement' that Lord Grey had granted him 'an annuity', Coleridge determined to take definitive action. Gillman, who agreed with him, immediately sent the following letter to *The Times*, where it appeared on 4 June 1831:

Sir,—In consequence of a paragraph which appeared in *The Times* of this day, I think it expedient to state the fact respecting Mr. Coleridge as it actually is. On the sudden suppression of the Royal Society of Literature, with the extinction of the honours and annual honoraria of the Royal Associateships, a representation in Mr. Coleridge's behalf was made to Lord Brougham, who promptly and kindly commended the case to Lord Grey's consideration. The result of the application was, that a sum of 200£., the one moiety to be received forthwith, and the other the year following, by a private grant from the Treasury, was placed at Mr. Coleridge's acceptance; but he felt it his duty most respectfully to decline it, though with every grateful acknowledgment of the prompt and courteous attention which his case had received from both their Lordships.

I remain, Sir, yours respectfully,

Highgate, June 3. JAMES GILLMAN.

Gillman's communication to *The Times* settled the matter as far as Coleridge was concerned. Sotheby, however, called at Highgate soon after receiving the letter of 3 June from Coleridge, made him a gift of £50, and attempted to persuade him that 'the receiving of an eleemosynary grant in commutation for an honor was an exaggerated interpretation of the fact', and that he 'might take it without any sense of degradation'. Sotheby also won from him a promise to write a letter of explanation to Brougham. Coleridge did so on 13 June, but the letter has not come to light. On 14 June, he sent Sotheby a letter, in which he explained 'that in declining the Grant of 200£ . . . from the Treasury', he 'was actuated by no feeling of pride or vanity', and justified his original decision: 'The next day [after your visit to Highgate] I received a communication from a friend, who had just seen a letter from Col. Fox on the subject & which placed it out of doubt, that the grant had been both applied for & granted *exclusively* in consideration of my *Want*—of my *distressed* situation.'

An aftermath followed. In the July 1831 number of the *Englishman's Magazine*, Hardman renewed his attack on Grey and Brougham. He also pointed out: 'The heads of the Royal Society of Literature have made a formal appeal to the Premier, and their representations were heard with an attention, ominous, we trust, of the only measure befitting an administration professing a proper deference to the popular voice. It may be readily believed that a Grey and a Brougham are guiltless of projecting this miserable piece of thrift, but it will be difficult to exonerate them, . . . if they fail to repair the injury it has inflicted.' Nothing came of the appeal by the Royal Society of Literature; neither the Grey Ministry nor the Crown provided an annuity for any one of the Royal Associates.

Unknown to Coleridge, Stuart applied in his behalf on 19 July 1831 to the Earl of Munster, the son of William IV: 'To cast into Beggary at the Close of Life, a Man who by his writings has shed a lustre on the age he lives in, would be a reproach to the Nation. In declining years . . . he could not calculate on the loss of a Provision which seemed to have been settled for his Life.' Stuart, however, received from Munster only the discouraging reply that the late King's 'income *doubl'd* my Father's' and that his present Majesty 'could not be expected to be saddl'd with the Private Largesses of his Predecessor'.

Thus for the third time Coleridge failed to obtain the security of an income payable during his lifetime. In each case circumstances beyond his control intervened. On 10 January 1798 Thomas and Josiah Wedgwood gave him a life annuity of £150, but Josiah added a restrictive clause: 'We mean the annuity to be independent of every thing but the wreck of our fortune.' Tom Wedgwood died in 1805, but in his Will he provided for the payment of his share of the annuity, £75 annually. In November 1812 came an unexpected blow when Josiah Wedgwood reported to Coleridge that 'for some time' his expenses had exceeded his income and asked whether he was 'bound in honor' to continue paying the £75 annually, his half of the annuity. Coleridge graciously agreed that Wedgwood need not continue to do so. In 1826 Frere had obtained from Liverpool the promise of a £200 sinecure for Coleridge. As the letters show, Liverpool was stricken with paralysis and Canning, who would have carried out the promise, died before anything was accomplished. Coleridge's application to Brougham in 1831 to obtain an annual remuneration to replace the annuity which he had received since 1824 from the Royal Society of Literature brought only embarrassment and humiliating publicity. Three months before his death, Coleridge picturesquely remarked that he had not been worth a shilling in the world 'since King William the Fourth took my poor gold chain of a hundred links—one hundred pounds—with those of nine other literary veterans, to emblazon d'or the black bar across the Royal arms of the Fitzclarences'.

Coleridge's own statements indicate that he associated the beginning of his addiction to opium with the ill health which he suffered during the first year of his residence at Keswick, particularly in the spring of 1801. Thereafter, Coleridge made many futile efforts to break the habit. (See Introduction to Volume III of these *Letters*.) In 1816 he settled with Gillman in order to be under the constant supervision of a physician. As E. H. Coleridge has pointed out, Gillman never claimed to have cured Coleridge of his opium addiction. A new letter of Monday, 24 June 1816 (Letter 1013*a* printed in Appendix B of Volume VI of this edition) indicates the procedure which Gillman adopted. 'On Wednesday night about an hour before bed time', Coleridge wrote to Morgan,

I was taken as by surprize, with a sensation of indefinite *Fear* over my whole Frame; but it was not accompanied with any craving for Laudanum, and I fought up against it and went to bed. I had a wretched night —and next morning the few drops, I now take, only increasing my irritability, about noon I called on G. for the performance of *his* part of our mutual Engagement, & took enough and *barely* enough (for more, I am certain, would have been better) to break the commencing Cycle before the actual Craving came on.—To day I am much better.

Coleridge, however, considered the daily allowance to be insufficient, and he found a means of surreptitiously obtaining additional supplies of laudanum from T. H. Dunn, a chemist at Highgate and later in Tottenham Court Road, to whom from 1824 to 1833 he addressed the eleven letters appearing in these volumes. The notes to certain of these letters contain excerpts from an autobiographical account written in old age by S. T. Porter, Dunn's assistant for five years from 1824 to February 1829. Coleridge was already well established as a customer at Dunn's chemist shop when Porter came there as an apprentice.

According to Coleridge, laudanum temporarily lost 'all its anodyne powers' during a serious illness in 1832, and for a brief time he felt no 'craving' for 'the Poison, which for more than 30 years' had been 'the guilt, debasement, and misery' of his existence. On 7 April 1832 he remarked to Green: 'It is now 5 weeks since I have taken Laudanum. . . . But I have no sign or symptom of revalescence. . . . I am daily weaker & weaker.—Scarce able indeed to sit up for 3 or 4 hours in the 24.' Undoubtedly, the worsening of his health was due to the temporary 'abstraction' of laudanum. During these weeks, however, under Gillman's direction Coleridge was taking 'in the course of the 24 hours two grains of Acetate of Morphium'. On 17 May Coleridge again reported to Green: 'I do not feel the slightest wish or craving for the Laudanum; nor do I believe, that it would even alleviate my sufferings. But yet I grieve for the too apparent failure of the experiment.' This plan to leave off laudanum had not been approved by either Gillman or Green. Coleridge continued to take the drug during the short remainder of his life. The last letter to Dunn, which was written on 14 August 1833, contains a promise to pay 'the total amount' of his indebtedness.

Like Wordsworth, Southey, Scott, and other prominent authors, Coleridge contributed to several Literary Annuals, a curious fashion of the day. His contributions have long since been identified, but the story of his unhappy experiences with the editors of these rival publications has not hitherto been told. The letters in these volumes, especially those to Alaric A. Watts, editor of *The Literary Souvenir*, F. M. Reynolds, editor of *The Keepsake*, S. C. Hall, editor of *The Amulet*, and Charles Aders, a friend of long standing, now make it possible to disentangle the complicated details. Two examples may be cited here. The first issue in 1828 of *The Bijou*, edited by W. Fraser and published by Pickering, contained five of Coleridge's unpublished compositions which were to appear in the 1828 edition of the *Poetical Works*. Fraser first printed them in *The Bijou* without Coleridge's permission or knowledge and inserted a false statement in his preface: 'Mr. Coleridge, in the most liberal manner, permitted the Editor to select what he pleased from all his unpublished MSS.' Nor was any 'pecuniary acknowlegement . . . afterwards proferred'. Among the compositions was the poem *Youth and Age*, a copy of which Coleridge had previously sent to his friend Watts for publication in *The Literary Souvenir* for 1828. The 'resentment' which Watts felt on discovering that *Youth and Age* was also to appear in another Annual provoked him to state in his preface: 'I can only say, that I received it from the author, as a contribution to the Literary Souvenir.'

In 1826, through the mediation of 'an old acquaintance', Coleridge sent S. C. Hall several compositions for *The Amulet: The Improvisatore*, three short poems, and three letters of 1799 describing his Brocken tour. (In October 1835 Hall contributed these Letters, 280–2, to the *New Monthly Magazine*.) Hall published *The Improvisatore* in *The Amulet* for 1828, but he reduced the remuneration agreed upon from £20 to £10. The three short poems did not appear in that annual until 1833. The three letters of 1799 Hall 'rejected & sent back', but 'not without having taken a copy', and he neglected to seek Coleridge's consent when he printed large extracts from them in *The Amulet* for 1829. This 'not very reputable' conduct, 'if Honesty be a necessary ingredient of Repute', led to a new source of embarrassment for Coleridge. In 1828 Reynolds had offered Coleridge £50 for contributions to *The Keepsake* for 1829, with the provision that he publish in no other annual except *The Literary Souvenir*, a previous arrangement having been made with Watts. Reynolds later took advantage of Coleridge, as he did of Scott, Southey, and Wordsworth. But enough of 'these Reptilities', as Coleridge called them. It may be added, however, that in 1833 Coleridge contributed twelve compositions to *Friendship's Offering* for 1834, all but one of them previously unpublished. No untoward circumstance marred his association with Thomas Pringle, the editor, a personal friend and Highgate neighbour.

In 1823 Coleridge hoped to have an edition of his poems published under Murray's 'umbrageous Foliage', but the condition imposed—that H. H. Milman was 'to omit, what he pleased, and to make what corrections and additions, *he* might think desirable'— put an end to further negotiations. In August 1828 a three-volume edition of *The Poetical Works of S. T. Coleridge, Including the Dramas of Wallenstein, Remorse, and Zapolya* was published by Pickering. Prepared under Gillman's supervision and for his benefit, the work was 'sold off' by October. In 1829 a revised edition appeared, and by July 1832 the preparation of the *Poetical Works* of 1834 was already under way. The task of making this edition as complete as possible was made less onerous for Coleridge by the co-operation of his wife and by the untiring efforts of his son-in-law, Henry Nelson Coleridge.

During his later years Coleridge composed a handful of poems. Some are nostalgic and personal, some occasional, others meditative, religious, or abstract. The youthful spirit of the earlier poems has been replaced by a quiet, almost mournful acceptance of the limitations age had brought in its place. *Youth and Age*, which Coleridge wrote when he was fifty years old, he considered the best of his later poems. Despite his regret for lost youth, he was not yet ready to surrender to old age:

> Life is but thought: so think I will
> That Youth and I are house-mates still.

A 'premature warm and sunny day, antedating Spring', in February 1825 'called forth' the sad but beautiful poem, *Work without Hope*, and in a letter to Lady Beaumont of March of the following year Coleridge echoed in prose the mood of his poetic lines.

Tho' I am at present sadly below even *my* Par of Health or rather Unhealth, and am the more depressed thereby from the consciousness, that in this yearly resurrection of Nature from her winter sleep, amid young leaves and blossoms and twittering nest-building Birds, the sun so gladsome, the breezes so with healing on their wings, all good and lovely things are beneath me, above me, and every where around me—

and all from God—while my incapability of enjoying or at best languor in receiving them, is directly or indirectly from myself.

Lady Beaumont felt that Coleridge had neglected his poetic muse, and after talking with him on the subject during a visit to Highgate in 1828, she wrote to him in protest: 'Let me remind you of our last conversation wherein you said that metaphysics so far from deadening the spirit of imagination had added new wings from the power of contrast, and the last specimen you read is a proof of your not having deceived yourself. Do not let the last rays sink for want of exertion, and give Fancy its full play. . . . Hundreds will feel their purest thoughts kindle into life by the powers of that precious gift you have received. Do not throw it away.'

Deeply affected by this exhortation, Coleridge scribbled a note in a blank space in her letter. Again the harp and breeze are used figuratively, as in *The Eolian Harp.*

Lady B. in this letter urges me to resume Poetry.—Alas! how can I? —Is the power extinct? No! No! As in a still Summer Noon, when the lulled Air at irregular intervals wakes up with a startled *Hush*-st, that seems to re-demand the silence which it breaks, or heaves a long profound Sigh in it's Sleep, and an AEolian Harp has been left in the chink of the not quite shut Casement—even so—how often!—scarce a week of my Life shuffles by, that does not at some moment feel the spur of the old genial impulse—even so do there fall on my inward Ear swells, and broken snatches of sweet Melody, reminding me that I still have that within me which is both Harp and Breeze. But in the same moment awakes the Sense of *Change without*—Life *unendeared.* The tenderest Strings no longer thrill'd.

In order to poetic composition I need the *varied* feeling—Thought charmed to sleep;* and the too great *continuity* of mind broken up, to begin anew, with *new*-power seeking & finding *new* themes.

[* Thought's brief and genial Sleeps, that nourish Thought. Note by S. T. C.]

Wordsworth once said that if Coleridge's 'energy and his originality had been more exerted in the channel of poetry, an instrument of which he had so perfect a mastery, . . . he might have done more permanently to enrich the literature, and to influence the thought of the nation, than any man of the age'. But perhaps Coleridge had better speak for himself. Late in 1833 he acquired and annotated a copy of Heinrichs's *Apocalypsis Graece*, a two-volume work published in 1821, and in a marginal note he has this to say: 'I have too clearly before me the idea of a poet's genius to deem myself other than a very humble poet; but in the very possession of the idea, I know myself so far a poet as to feel assured that I can understand and interpret a poem in the spirit of poetry, and with the poet's spirit.' This humble estimate of himself as a poet is often expressed in his correspondence. In a late letter he ranked himself among the 'Dwarf Poets'.

Coleridge included his well-known *Epitaph* in a letter to Green of 28 October 1833: 'I send you the Epitaph, I rewrote last night, or rather re-*thought* (for I am now first to re-*write* it) on an Author not wholly unknown; but better known by the initials of his Name than by the Name itself.'

On a Tombstone

Stop, Christian Passer-by! Stop, Child of God!
And read with gentle heart. Beneath this sod
A Poet lies: or that which once was he.
O lift one thought in prayer for S. T. C.
That he, who many a year, with toil of breath
Found Death in Life, may here find Life in Death.
Mercy for Praise, *to be forgiven* for Fame
He ask'd, and hop'd thro' Christ. Do Thou the Same!

A few days later Coleridge sent Mrs. Aders another version of the lines, along with a request for a vignette which would illustrate his 'homely, plain, *church yard Christian* Verses'. He also drew a rough outline of an upright tombstone with his initials at the top—'P. S. —*I* like this Tomb stone very much.' In publishing the lines in his *Poetical Works* of 1834, Coleridge altered the word 'was' in the third line to 'seem'd'. Not the least of his virtues was humility.

There was in Coleridge an unquenchable intellectual curiosity which led him into every area of human knowledge. As he says of himself in *The Friend*:

Truth I pursued, as Fancy sketch'd the way,
And wiser men than I went worse astray.

Coleridge reveals his consciousness of his own mental habits—indeed, he was proud of them. 'Southey once said to me', he wrote, 'You are nosing every nettle along the Hedge, while the Greyhound (meaning himself, I presume) wants only to get sight of the Hare, & FLASH!—strait as a line!—he has it in his mouth!—Even so, I replied, might a Cannibal say to an Anatomist, whom he had watched dissecting a body. But the fact is—I do not care twopence for the *Hare*; but I value most highly the excellencies of scent, patience, discrimination, free Activity; and find a Hare in every Nettle, I make myself acquainted with.'

Not long before his death the late T. S. Eliot replied as follows to a suggestion made by an interviewer for the *Yorkshire Post* that Coleridge 'had failed as a religious person':

Coleridge certainly was a religious man, and has a very important place in the history of religious thinking in the 19th century. I believe some of his writings stimulated Cardinal Newman and Frederick Denison Maurice. But I am always in the process of revising my views of Coleridge in the light of further knowledge. . . . Coleridge was a man of infinite industry, far more industrious than I am myself. I certainly wouldn't accept the idea that Coleridge failed religiously.

Certainly the later letters show that among Coleridge's many intellectual interests religion played a pre-eminent role. From his young manhood there was in Coleridge a dominating need for an individual faith, and as he grew older that need was intensified. 'Within the last two years and more particularly within the last', he wrote to Daniel Stuart in 1826,

my mind without sustaining any revolution in faith or principles has yet undergone a *change*; I trust, a progression—and I am more practically persuaded, that toward the close of our Lives, if we have been at any time sincere in cultivating the Good within us, events & circumstances are more & more working towards the maturing of that Good, even when they are hardest to bear for the moment. I have not the slightest cause for even apprehending any tendency in my feelings to a servile & selfish religion of fear. . . . On the contrary, on all religious subjects I think & reason with a more cheerful sense of *freedom*—because I am secure of my faith in the main points—a personal God, a surviving principle of Life, & that I need & that I have a Redeemer—But in one point I have attained to a conviction which till of late I never had in any available form or degree—namely, the confidence in the efficacy of Prayer. I know by experience, that it is Light, Strength, and Comfort.

Coleridge probed deeply into religious and theological questions. He read and annotated work after work of the English divines. He studied the writings of biblical commentators, old and new, and kept abreast of the theological controversies of the day. He was conversant with the biblical criticism of the Germans and with the theological and mystical writings of Swedenborg. He examined the Books of Daniel and Revelation to deepen his own understanding and in an attempt to rescue Edward Irving from a too literal reading of Scripture and from a penchant for prophecy. He proposed a division of the New Testament 'into two parts—Apostolic and the earliest post-apostolic'. His study of the Bible never waned, and less than nine months before his death he wrote as follows to Green:

Would it, think you, justify the expence, to purchase . . . a *Quarto* Bible with the Apocrypha between the Old and New Testament—in sheets: and to have them half-bound in three or four Volumes interleaved ? . . . If I had such a Book, I certainly would begin the New Year . . . with the first of Genesis, and make a point of reading one or more chapters every night—so that I might hope at the end of the year to have left behind some 3 or 400 Chapters, corrected according to my best judgement, aided by the best recent German Versions—and on important points availing myself of Hurwitz's Aid as to Original Text.

Foremost among the innumerable projects conceived in Coleridge's teeming brain stands his never-completed *Opus Maximum* or *Magnum Opus*. Its genesis lies, as the early letters show, in the metaphysical and religious ideas which had been germinating and evolving in his mind since early manhood. Coleridge made his first public announcement of this work in *Felix Farley's Bristol Journal* in August 1814: 'I am about to put to the press a large volume on the LOGOS, or the communicative intelligence in nature and in man, together with, and as preliminary to, a Commentary on the Gospel of St. John.' A year later he inserted another and similar announcement in the chapters of the *Biographia Literaria* which were written and sent to the printers in 1815. In Chapter VIII, for example, he refers to 'a work, which I have many years been preparing, on the PRODUCTIVE LOGOS human and divine; with, and as the introduction to, a full commentary on the Gospel of St. John'. Finally, in *Aids to Reflection*, 1825, Coleridge made a third public announcement: 'The whole Scheme of the Christian Faith, including *all* the Articles of Belief common to the Greek and Latin, the Roman and the Protestant Church, with the threefold proof, that it is *ideally*, *morally*, and *historically* true, will be found exhibited and vindicated in a proportionally larger Work, the principal Labour of my Life since Manhood, and which I am now preparing for the Press under the title, Assertion of Religion, as necessarily *involving* Revelation; and of Christianity, as the only Revelation of permanent and universal validity.' He also announced his 'Logic' under the title 'Elements of Discourse', which, 'God permitting', would follow the *Aids*.

In a letter to Stuart of 1814 Coleridge entitled his work 'Christianity the one true Philosophy—or 5 Treatises on the Logos, or communicative Intelligence, Natural, Human, and Divine', and briefly described its contents. By 1815 the treatises had grown to six, and in October he again wrote to Stuart as follows: 'It's Title will be Logosophia, or on the Logos human & Divine, in six Treatises.—The first, a philosophic Compendium of the History of Philosophy from Pythagoras to the present Day. . . . The second— The science of connected reasoning (with the History of Logic). . . . The third, the Science of Premises, or transcendental Philosophy— . . . The fourth, a detailed Commentary on the Gospel of St. John: —to which the former is introductory. The object of both is to prove, that Christianity is true Philosophy, & of course that all true Philosophy is Christianity.—The fifth, on the Mystics & Pantheists.

Introduction

... The sixth, on the causes & consequences of Unitarianism.' The work 'will comprize two large Octavo Volumes, 600 pages each.'

In writing to John Sterling in 1833 Coleridge described his 'whole system' as he conceived it only nine months before his death:

> Many a fond dream have I amused myself with, of your residing near me or in the same house, and of preparing with your & Mr Green's assistance, my whole system for the Press, as far as it exists in writing, in any *systematic* form—that is beginning with the Propyleum, On the Power and Use of Words—comprizing Logic, as the Canons of *Conclusion*; as the criterion of Premises; and lastly, as the Discipline, and Evolution of Ideas—and then the Methodus et Epochae, or the Disquisition on God, Nature, and Man—the two first great Divisions of which, from the Ens super Ens to the FALL, or from God to Hades; and then from Chaos to the commencement of living Organization—containing the whole scheme of the Dynamic Philosophy, and the Deduction of the Powers & Forces —are complete—as is likewise a third, *composed* for the greater part by Mr Green, on the application of the Ideas, as the *Transcendents* of the Truths, Duties, Affections &c in the Human Mind.—If I could once publish these (but alas! even these could not be compressed in less than three Octavo Volumes), I should then have no objection to print my MSS Papers on positive Theology—from Adam to Abraham—to Moses—the Prophets—Christ—and Christendom.—But this is a Dream!

During the nineteen-year interval between his first public announcement in 1814 to his letter of 1833, Coleridge had much to say of his *Opus Maximum*. Indeed, the letters of his middle and later years provide an invaluable chronological record of his ideas, particularly those on philosophy, science, and theology. Sometimes he proposed a specific title, but more often his allusions are to 'my most important Work', 'my GREAT WORK', 'my greater Work', 'my Opus Magnum', 'my Opus Maximum'. The subject-matter, the arrangement of the materials, and the proposed '*Form*' differed from time to time, but the purpose, the harmonizing or reconciling of Coleridge's dynamic or constructive philosophy and his Christian faith, remained the same.[1]

In 1817 Coleridge first met Joseph Henry Green, who had spent three years in Germany as a schoolboy. Appointed demonstrator

[1] For a brief description of some of the surviving manuscripts of the *Opus Maximum* and the 'Logic', see Alice D. Snyder, *Coleridge on Logic and Learning*, 1929; and for a sympathetic discussion of Coleridge's philosophical writings, see J. H. Muirhead, *Coleridge as Philosopher*, 1930, and 'Metaphysician or Mystic?' in *Coleridge, Studies by Several Hands*, edited by Edmund Blunden and E. L. Griggs, 1934. See also Craig W. Miller, 'Coleridge's Concept of Nature', *Journal of the History of Ideas*, vol. xxv, No. 1, Jan.–Mar. 1964, pp. 77–96. More recent studies are: W. J. Bate, *Coleridge*, 1968; Thomas McFarland, *Coleridge and the Pantheist Tradition*, 1969; and G. N. G. Orsini, *Coleridge and German Idealism*, 1969.

of anatomy at St. Thomas's Hospital in 1813, Green received his diploma from the College of Surgeons two years later and set up a surgical practice in Lincoln's Inn Fields.[1] In April 1818 he and Coleridge were beginning a series of conversations on philosophy and its relationship to the 'Sciences on the one side and to Religion on the other'. In January 1819, Coleridge described Green as a man 'deeply studied in all the physiology and philosophy of the German Schools, and equally dissatisfied with them as myself; [he] writes down what I say—so that we have already compassed a good handsome Volume'. Coleridge had at last found a congenial young friend (Green was nineteen years his junior) whose philosophical bent made him an ideal associate and co-worker. During the years that followed the two men met regularly for '*philosophical* Intercommune'.

In November 1818 Coleridge questioned whether he would 'live long enough' to finish the *Opus*, to which all his 'past labors' were 'preparatory'. Again, in March 1820 he referred to his GREAT WORK, 'to which all my other writings (unless I except my poems, and these I can exclude in part only) are introductory and preparative'. In an earlier burst of enthusiasm he declared 'that a true System of Philosophy (= the Science of Life) is *best* taught in Poetry'. With the great system constantly hovering in Coleridge's mind, quite naturally his writings—the *Biographia Literaria*, the first twenty-two chapters of which were written in 1815, the *Theory of Life*, composed in 1816, the two *Lay Sermons* of 1816 and 1817, *The Friend*, 1809–1810, and particularly the revised 1818 edition with the addition of three essays on morals and religion and eight on method in the third volume—were all 'preparative' to his *Opus Maximum*.

In one of his letters Coleridge writes of his 'heretical Brat' as follows: 'I cherish, I must confess, a *pet* system, a bye blow of my own Philosophizing; but it is so unlike to all the opinions and modes of reasoning grounded on the atomic, Corpuscular and mechanic Philosophy, which is alone tolerated in the present day, and which since the time of Newton has been universally taken as synonimous with Philosophy itself—that I must content myself with caressing the heretical Brat in private—under the name of the Zoödynamic Method—or the Doctrine of *Life*.'

---

[1] Elected surgeon to St. Thomas's Hospital in 1820, four years later Green was appointed professor of anatomy at the College of Surgeons. In 1825 he became professor of anatomy at the Royal Academy, and in 1831 he was appointed to the chair of surgery in King's College, London. Characteristically, Coleridge took the greatest interest in his friend's professional career and did everything in his power to assist him.

By 1820 Coleridge had abandoned his plan of presenting his system in a series of treatises. Instead, he determined to prepare two works, an introductory 'Logic' and the 'Assertion of Religion as implying Revelation, & of Christianity as the only Revelation of universal Validity.' Although he devoted his energies to both works, neither was ever completed. Meanwhile, he turned to the *Aids to Reflection*, a 'small avant Courier' of his great work.

In January 1822 Coleridge proposed to John Murray a volume of selections from Archbishop Leighton with notes by himself. Murray declined the proposal, but in August 1823 Coleridge came to terms with Taylor and Hessey for the publication of a work then entitled *Aids to Reflection: or Beauties and Characteristics of Archbishop Leighton.* By February 1824, however, the volume 'in the course of printing' had become 'an original work almost', a 'little Pioneer' of his *Opus Maximum.* The work was published in May 1825 with the title, *Aids to Reflection in the Formation of a Manly Character on the several grounds of Prudence, Morality, and Religion: illustrated by Select Passages from our Elder Divines, especially from Archbishop Leighton.* Although ignored by the *Edinburgh* and by the *Quarterly,* of which Coleridge's nephew, John Taylor Coleridge, was then the editor, the *Aids* won its way among serious readers. A second edition was published in 1831. The *Aids* became one of the most influential and widely read of Coleridge's works.

On the eve of the publication of *Aids to Reflection,* Coleridge proposed to publish six supplementary disquisitions: '1. On Faith. 2. The Eucharist. 3. The philosophy of PRAYER: and the three kinds of Prayer, Public, Domestic, and Solitary. 4. On the prophetic character of the Old Testament: and on the Gift of Prophecy. 5. On the Church + Establishment, and Dissent—and the true character & danger of the Romish Church. 6. On the right and the superstitious use and estimation of the Sacred Scriptures: this last in a series of Letters.' Shortly afterwards he thought of adding a seventh disquisition 'on the Subject of Missions and Missionaries', and suggested to Hessey a quaint title for the series: 'The grey-headed Passenger: or Conversations on Ship-board during a voyage to the Mediterranean, supplemental of the AIDS TO Reflection by S. T. Coleridge.' No such volume ever appeared, but one of the proposed disquisitions, 'On the Church', eventually became, though augmented and adapted to a special occasion, a separate work, *On the Constitution of The Church and State, according to the Idea of Each; with Aids toward a Right Judgment on the Late Catholic Bill,* 1830. A second edition appeared in the same year. The value of this work lies in the ideas which Coleridge enunciated so brilliantly, particularly those concerning the functions of the 'clerisy' and of the clergy and the distinction between the National Church and the Christian Church.

Another of the disquisitions, 'On the right and the superstitious use and estimation of the Sacred Scriptures', was written in 1824. Originally intended to be a part of the *Aids*, it was omitted because of its length. It was published posthumously in 1840 with the title, *Confessions of an Inquiring Spirit*. In this work Coleridge attacked 'the servile superstition, which makes men *Bibliolaters*', but at the same time he set the Bible apart from all other religious and literary works and treated it with a spirit of reverence.

In a letter of May 1825 Coleridge indicated some of the abstruse theological topics to be reserved for his *Opus Maximum*.

In the 'Aids to Reflection' I have touched on the Mystery of the Trinity only in a *negative* way. That is, I have shewn the hollowness of the arguments by which it has been assailed—have demonstrated that the doctrine involves nothing contrary to Reason, and the nothingness & even absurdity of a Christianity without it. . . . But the positive establishment of the Doctrine as involved in the Idea, God—together with the *Origin* of EVIL, as distinguished from Original Sin (on which I *have* treated at large) and the Creation of the visible World—THESE as absolutely requiring the habit of abstraction, and *severe Thinking*, I have reserved for my larger Work.

In January 1826 Coleridge explained that 'the last twelve years [represented] the period of the intensest *conversion* of my mind and spirit' to 'my Opus Maximum containing the sum and system of my philosophy and Faith on reason & revelation, the life of Nature and the history of Man, of which the MSS *materials* are complete, and somewhat more than a third of the Work reduced to form, and in a *publishable* state'. He declared that no month would pass without some addition to the *Opus*. Coleridge pointed out, too, that the 'Logic' furnished 'the key' and contained 'the preliminaries' to all his other works. Somewhat amusingly, he also mentioned a 'complete volume' in which the 'main *Results*' of his *Opus Maximum* would be given 'in a dramatic and popular form', with the title, 'Travels in Body and Mind, or the Sceptic's Pilgrimage to the Temple of Truth'. It was to be 'ready for the Printer before the end of October next, so as either to appear at the same time with the . . . [Logic], or immediately after . . . [its] publication'.

In the following year Coleridge described himself 'as the author of a SYSTEM of Philosophy on Nature, History, Reason, Revelation; on the Eternal, and on the Generations of the Heaven and the Earth'. If he had obtained a sinecure, he would have been able, he said, 'to devote the scanty remainder of my breathing-time to the completion and bringing out of the two Works, on which I have laboured for thirty years past': the 'Logic' and 'my system of Philosophy and Faith, as the result of all my researches and reflections concerning God, Nature and Man—you will not wonder', he added, 'that I name it my OPUS MAXIMUM, the Harvesting of my Life's Labours'.

By 1828 illness, old age, and the magnitude of the task led to discouragement, and Coleridge looked to Green to publish the *'substance'* of his *Opus*. 'I have no wish to have my life prolonged', he declared to Green on 25 January 1828, 'but what is involved in the wish to complete the views, I have taken, of Life as beginning in separation from Nature and ending in Union with God, and to reduce to an *intelligible* if not artistical form the results of my religious, biblical and ecclesiastical Lucubrations'. Shortly afterwards he wrote in the same vein to another correspondent: 'Completely have I been for some time past swallowed up in the one anxiety of arranging and increasing my huge pile of Manuscripts, so that the *substance* at least of the results of my logical, physiological, philosophical, theological, biblical, and I hope I am entitled to add *religious* and *Christian* studies and meditations for the last 20 years of my life might be found in a state capable of being published by my dear Friend Mr Green, who has for ten years devoted the only vacant day of every week to the participation of my labors.'

In her work, *Coleridge on Logic and Learning*, 1929, the late Alice Snyder printed in part from one of Coleridge's autograph notebooks a detailed 'Synopsis' of the *Opus Maximum* as it was conceived in 1828:

May 24, 1828. It may be well to place on record the Synopsis of the Coleridgian (*Mem.* more euphonious it will be to name it the Ēstēsēān, or Esstĕcēan) Methodology, or Philosophy of Epochs and Methods, by S. T. C., R. A. R. S. L. &c. &c.

> Author of Tomes, whereof, tho' not in Dutch,
> The Public little knows, the Publisher too much.

or rather of its principal Divisions.

One paragraph of this document containing the initials of Joseph Henry Green merits inclusion here:

This Second Part comprizes the prior half of the Exposition of the Idea, first enunciated in the Estecëan Philosophy, that Life begins in detachment from Nature and ends in unition with God:—and as the First or Ideal Part concludes with the Fall of Angels . . . so the Second Part, which, I trust, will have an equal right to be named the J a h a g ë an, as the Estecëan System (J. H. G.—Jäaitchgëan too cacophonous . . .) concludes with the *Fall of Man*.

In preparing his Will in September 1829, Coleridge appointed Green his executor, 'as the Man most intimate with . . . [his] intellectual labors, purposes, and aspirations', and left to him 'upon Trust' his books and manuscripts, with the rights of publication. 'God knows!', he wrote to Green in 1832, 'it would be no pain to me, to foresee that my name should utterly cease—I have no desire for reputation—nay, no wish for *fame*—but I am truly thankful to God, that thro' you my labors of thought may be rendered not wholly unseminative.'

In July 1833 Coleridge took a transcript of the 'Logic' to Ramsgate, as he explained to Green, 'in the hope of rendering the Chapters already written a fit preparation for, & foundation of, the more important third Part—on the IDEAS, or the resolution of the Sense, the Understanding into the Reason, in the evolution of which I joyfully know that you have had at least an equal co-productiveness with myself'. Day followed day at Ramsgate, however, and instead of working on the 'Logic', he 'read thro' the four folios of Bingham's Antiquities of the Christian Church, [and] found a *continued* series of historical evidences of the truth of my Convictions'. After his return to Highgate, Coleridge sent Sterling a brief outline of his proposed *Opus* in the letter of 29 October 1833 quoted above. And on the last day of his life, as his daughter reported, 'he repeated to Mr Green his formula of the Trinity'.

After Coleridge's death in 1834 and that of his own father in the same year, Green came into a large fortune and was free to devote himself to the task of co-ordinating the many fragments of Coleridge's *Opus Maximum* into a unified system. He died in 1863 without completing his work for publication. In 1865 it was edited by John Simon and published under the title, *Spiritual Philosophy: founded on the Teaching of the late Samuel Taylor Coleridge*.

As a letter writer Coleridge reveals many of the characteristics of his conversation, both in manner and in subject-matter. Far from being masks to conceal his true identity, the letters present him as he appeared to his contemporaries. In writing to each of his correspondents he tried to attune himself to the interests and intellectual capacity of the person addressed, but his frank and open nature, his craving for sympathy and understanding, and his fundamental honesty led him to disclose the inner recesses of his being, to *un*mask himself. As his grandson once remarked, Coleridge 'wore his heart on his sleeve'.

The reader of these letters will miss, perhaps, the exuberance and spontaneity which characterize many of those written during Coleridge's earlier years. Yet here and there he will find the same irrepressible love of fun, the same kind of memorable epithets and striking description, the same awareness of the world without and the world within. The fatherless boy who 'saw nought lovely but the sky and stars', became the man who though dying made his way to the window of his attic room 'to look once more at the pretty Gardens and the glorious landscape'; the youth who listened to the 'delicious notes' of the 'merry Nightingale' at Stowey heard them again in 'Mr Robarts's Garden-grounds' more than two decades later; and the youthful 'library-cormorant' who had read 'almost every thing' devoted himself 'to a Life of unintermitted Reading, Thinking, Meditating and Observing'.

Not long before he settled at Nether Stowey, Coleridge remarked prophetically: 'The Light shall stream to a far distance from the taper in my cottage window.' Today that light shines brightly, and Coleridge is recognized as a poet of unsurpassed powers, a great literary critic—the late Herbert Read called him 'the greatest of them all'—and an important and influential political thinker, philosopher, and theologian. The letters of Coleridge, whether written in youth or old age, bring to the reader 'the infinity of . . . thoughts and feelings, . . . [the] hopes and fears, & joys, and pains, & desires, & presentiments' of an extraordinary man of genius.

II

The present volumes contain 609 letters written between January 1820 and July 1834. This total includes 8 letters which were added while the work was in the press: 3 letters (1232*a*, 1249*a*, and 1253*a*) written in 1820 and included in the chronological series in that year; and 5 letters (1320*a*, 1381*a*, 1453*a*, 1530*a*, and 1705*a*) written during the years 1822–31 and printed in Appendix B, Vol. VI. Of the 609 letters over half are now published for the first time; the text of 85 per cent. is drawn from manuscripts, 8 per cent. from transcripts, and 7 per cent. from printed sources.

Appendix B also contains 23 additional letters (identified by *a* or *b* after the letter number) which were written during the years 1795–1819 and received after Volumes I–IV were published; and 16 letters previously printed in Volumes I–VI from published sources or transcripts and now reprinted from the holographs.

The six volumes of this edition contain a total of 1,853 letters written by Samuel Taylor Coleridge between 1785 and 1834.

1219. *To Hyman Hurwitz*[1]

MS. British Museum. Hitherto unpublished.

4 Jany. 1820. —

Dear Sir

I am but now returned from Cheswick viâ Brompton, whither I was called off before I had time to give that attention to your letter, which it's contents required and were so fully capable of repaying. How entirely I assent to the justice of your complaints against the Anti-mosaic and anti-christian schism in the best half of all Religion, Love & charity, between Hebrew and Gentile, I need not inform you: nor how in this case as in almost all others I attribute 9 tenths of the responsible Blame to the stronger, the (in consequence of that advantage) more educated, and yet (o shame!) the oppressive and aggressive Party. Ah! strange & lamentable inconsistency! we despise an elder Brother because he is a Jew and yet demand of him virtues which we so *rarely* find among ourselves, that even in a Christian Country, & in a land governed & possessed by Christians, we consider them as proofs of an especial interference of the divine. Aid approaching to miraculous! I never read the Speech of Shylock (Merch. of Ven. Act 3, Scene I) without a glow of indignant Brotherly Love towards the persecuted race, the names of whose Forefathers we ourselves use as an attribute of our God, the Father of all Human Kind. In one breath we invoke the God of Abraham, Isaac, and Jacob, and in the next we utter the curse of contempt and hate against their lineal descendants whom our own Apostle declares 'beloved for the Fathers' sake[s]'[2] and that the promises are withheld for a time, 'that blindness *in part* is happened unto Israel', only in order that and 'until the fullness of the Gentiles be come in'[3]—when they shall again take their appointed place, their sworn and covenanted *Primacy*, the honors and privileges of Primogeniture, in the great Household of the true and only God!— At Malta, and at the time when the God of your Fathers vouchsafed to make me the poor instrument of preventing an intended Massacre of your (and my) unoffending Brethren, I read the eleventh Chapter of Paul to the Romans to the chief Criminal Judge, translating it literally into Italian. He begged my pardon with all the tricksy and slavish Shrugs and gesticulations of that idolatrous and fetisch-serving Crew; but was convinced that I had been reading out of some *heretical* Book & begged to hear no more

---

[1] Part of a letter to Mr Hurwitz probably. [Endorsement at top p. 5 of MS.]

[2] Romans xi. 28. [3] Ibid. xi. 25.

of such *'philosophical'* language. What recoiled from the petrified mud-rock of papistic Bigotry, fell back with deeper impression on myself: and as a Christian I put the question dictated by the Apostle—If the temporary *Chastisement* of the children of Abraham be the reconcilement of the whole World, what shall the again receiving of them be?—Surely, such a benefit to the whole *rational* & therein to the *whole,* Creation, as compared with our *present* Light and Warmth will be as Life from the Dead! If their *diminution* be the riches of the World, what will their *fullness* be?—The root (says Paul) remains holy—& if some of the branches be broken off, and thou, O Gentile, being a wild olive tree wert graffed in among them, and *with them* partakest of the root and fatness of the Olive Tree; boast not against the branches—but if thou (*art inclined* to) boast, (*remember, that*) thou bearest not the root, but the Root thee![1]—

You are not ignorant, with what Zeal I contend for the identity of the doctrines of the Old Testament and of our Gospel. Our church (would that I could say, our church men!) instructs us to believe in a coming of the Messiah, with a literal fulfilment of *all* the Messianic Prophecies, when the earthly Powers will be taken up into an identity with the Spiritual, and the Messiah appear in glory, as Conqueror and King of the World, having his throne on Mount Zion. And with this faith there is not one of the 13 Articles of your (Maimonidean) Creed, which a Christian is not bound to believe. Christ himself made War exclusively against the immoral & corrupt Comments which made the Law vain—declared expressly, that he taught nothing but what the Law had taught, and taught so plainly that he whose blindness of *heart* had been such as not to have been already convinced by Moses and the Prophets would receive no conviction tho' a *man should rise again from the dead*.[2] It is admitted by all rational and learned Divines, that the words, Heaven & Earth, throughout the N. T. (but especially in the writings of John & Matthew, the former of whom indeed expressly so interprets them in that sublime Drama, the Apocalypse) mean the Government (or Hierarchy) and the People—Now what could the most orthodox Jew under the circumstances of Jesus have said more in the spirit of wisdom & reverence than that even of such parts of the ceremonial Law, as had their object exclusively in a *People* forming a *Common-weal,* not one Jot should pass away till it pleased the Almighty to remove for a time by his own outstretched Arm the civil existence of that People—that no power less manifestly displayed, as divine Interference, than that which *gave* the Law, could be received as authority for it's *suspension*—that it ceased to be

[1] Romans xi. 15–18.   [2] Luke xvi. 31.

binding, only as far as, and only in those points in which, it had been
rendered *impracticable*—and that he, who even with good intentions
should presume to anticipate this time, on any pretence of spiritual
new lights, should be the least in the Kingdom of Heaven—i.e. was
to be held as in *effect*, even tho' not so by conscious purpose, an
enemy to the general *diffusion* of the Law as far as the *Law* given
to the Hebrews and in them to all mankind is distinguishable from
the *Statutes* enjoined on the Jewish *State*?—And what else do the
Rabbins, the Masters in Israel, say now? You know, that they say,
and that you practise, the very same—And with these exceptions,
and provided no direct mediatory power were ascribed, it is my confirmed Opinion, that were 'an Israelite, of the seed of Abraham' to
become a Christian, he would not the less remain bound by virtue of
his Lineage to perform every *jot* of your Law, as far as it is declared
or evidently implied, in the Books of Moses. Christianity in it's
purity (understand me as speaking *historically* only) is the developement & full growth of a Sect (I use the word in it's best & simplest
sense) the germs of which existed in the Jewish Church at least 250
years before the birth of our Lord.—As a Christian, I hold the doctrine to be the true sense of the Prophecies; but I confine myself to
opinions capable of *historical* proof; and yet earlier, if I am not
deceived, there were Doctors, especially among the Colonists in
Egypt, who had deduced from the Prophets a suffering and spiritual
Son of Man as preceding the full, final and glorious Appearance
of the Messiah. What wonder, that among those, who had long
and mournfully contemplated the extreme moral corruption and
the inveterate factions of the Jews (see Josephus), their incapability alike to submit to or successfully to resist the yoke of the
Romans—(N.B. not from defect of power, but of union, not from
any thing impracticable in the thing itself, but from the unfitness
in the temper of the People—see my Mss Note on the blank leaves
of Eichhorn, Vol. X.)—what wonder, I say, if among such men
such an interpretation found favor and made proselytes? Surely,
surely, my dear Sir! I may venture to say to *you*, that if an enlightened Jew, having studied calmly and comprehensively the
history of the World, as the course of divine Providence; having
traced the *means*, which God has undeniably employed in civil-
izing the human race, & the not less manifest paramouncy of Power
and Light delegated to the Inhabitants of Christendom; and among
them to those *most*, who have least polluted the Everlasting Law
revealed to the Patriarchs and thro' Moses by intermixture of idolatrous Superstition—; if such a man could (if it be in human nature,
that he could, wholly) remove from his feelings all the thousandfold recollections and associations of Wrong, Insult, and remorse-

less Savagery inflicted on his Brethren, and if with these he could emancipate himself from all the unhappy Prejudices that are the inevitable *re-action* in the hearts and opinions of the Sufferers;— *He*, I say, (however different my own belief may be) would be disposed *still* to consider the *main* difference between us, as a difference between Men of the *same* Religion tho' of different *Synagogues*; and that even now the true difference still exists in this:—viz. that *both* believing in, and expecting, a triumphant Messiah *yet to come*, the one party believes in this *only*; the other, that a suffering Messiah with a doctrine of Suffering and of the duties and affections contained therein & appropriate to the probationary & preparatory interval, was appointed to go before and has already appeared. In this view both are Christians, the one Followers of Moses, the other Followers of Moses and of Jesus.—Far be it from me to pretend that this is not a most important point of difference. —I regard my very life, as less vital to me than my faith as a follower of the suffering Messiah! But I *do* hold and will dare affirm, that great as it may be in itself, yet it is very far less, and a chasm far more capable of having a Bridge thrown across it, than the diversity between those, who calling themselves Christians reject the Old Testament (whether openly as the late Dr Geddes,[1] or virtually as the modern Unitarians), and Christians of my Stamp, who regard the Old and New Testament as the same Faith, *that* with, & *this* without, a national Costume—: or than the diversity between the Messianic Jews, who interpret literally the 12th Article of your Creed[2] and those, who, like Mendelsohn[3] & many of the educated Jews in Prussia, regard the whole doctrine of a Messiah as a vulgar misinterpretation of the prophetic Writings during the times of the Second Temple.

[1] Alexander Geddes (1737–1802), Scottish Roman Catholic theologian. In 1792 he published the first volume of *The Holy Bible, or the Books accounted Sacred by Jews and Christians, otherwise called the Books of the Old and New Covenants, faithfully translated from the corrected Text of the Original; with various Readings, explanatory Notes, and critical Remarks.* This publication aroused a storm of hostility by both Catholics and Protestants. The second volume appeared in 1797 but received no more favourable reception. Undeterred Geddes published in 1800 his *Critical Remarks on the Hebrew Scriptures* . . ., 'which presented . . . the then novel and startling views of Eichhorn and his school on the primitive history and early records of mankind'. Geddes 'absolutely denied the doctrine of the divine inspiration of the sacred writings'. See *D.N.B.* and *Encyclopaedia Britannica*, 1910–11, xi. 547.

[2] The twelfth of the Articles of Faith formulated by Maimonides reads: 'I firmly believe in the coming of the Messiah; and although He may tarry, I daily hope for His coming.' *The Jewish Encyclopedia*, 1916, ii. 151.

[3] As early as 1796 Coleridge commented briefly on Moses Mendelssohn (1729–86), Jewish philosopher. See Letter 164, i. 284 n. Coleridge's annotated copies of Mendelssohn's *Morgenstunden oder Vorlesungen über das Daseyn*

With such sentiments it is not possible that I should not highly approve of the substance of the Extract, with which you have favored me—and I can add that I think the whole as happily expressed as it is justly conceived.[1] I dare not doubt, that the completion and publication of such a work would be a public benefit— alike to Jews and Gentiles. Especially, if you would take the opportunity of impressing on your own Brethren the *duty* of availing themselves of that increased Light, the means, and of course therefore the moral necessity, of which God hath so greatly augmented in the present day. They should be reminded, that the glory and the contra-distinguishing character of the Old Testament collectively, contrasted with all the Books pretending to be revealed & not acknowleging the divine authority of your sacred Scriptures, is especially manifested in it's strong injunctions to seek after *Truth*. Not Veracity *only*, but likewise after *intellectual* Truth and *Knowlege*! Knowlege is not only extolled as the crown and honor of a man, but earnestly to endeavor after it's attainment is again and again enforced as one of our most sacred duties. Above all, to study the Scriptures themselves, with all the aids which ancient and modern Learning have prepared; and to regard all the great Book of natural science but as a Glass enabling them to take a deeper and more exact view of the Law which (as your Sages have profoundly said) was, before the World itself was.[2] Then addressing yourself to the Christians, place before *them* the fact of the Abyssinians, who were justified by a Christian Council for retaining Circumcision & various other parts of the Mosaic Law: because they *fancied* themselves descendants from Solomon, and a Colony from the Holy Land. That Germans, who have Homes and Birth-places but no Country, and who ambitiously disown even their own manly & thoughtful language for the heartless Noseage and mouthage of the Gaul—that *they* should exact a sacrifice from others which is none for themselves, is grievous but not surprizing. But that *Britons* should expect from an ancient family such a self-disherison at once from the more than regal honors of their ancestors, and from their own

---

Gottes. Erster Theil, 1790, and *Jerusalem oder über religiöse Macht und Judenthum,* 1791, bound in one volume, are in the British Museum. See Alice D. Snyder, 'Coleridge's Reading of Mendelssohn's "Morgenstunden" and "Jerusalem" ', *Journal of English and Germanic Philology,* Oct. 1929, pp. 503–17.

[1] This extract must have been from the manuscript of Hurwitz's forthcoming work, *Vindiciae Hebraicae.* See letter 1244.

[2] *Midrash Tehillim,* comment on Psalm xc. 3: 'Seven things, by two thousand years, preceded the creation of the world: the Torah [the Law], the throne of glory, the Garden of Eden, Gehenna, repentance, the sanctuary in heaven, and the name of the Messiah.' *The Midrash on Psalms,* trans. W. G. Braude, 2 vols., 1959, ii. 94.

reversionary Splendors—honors *confessedly* equal bestowed by God himself! and Hopes that have God's promise for their pledge, and the Christian's own peculiar scriptures for their warrant—this is strange indeed! most grievous is the unreflecting contempt which can alone explain it. Do Englishmen pride themselves on their *Nationality*? do they so wisely and earnestly contend that it is the Nest and Nurse not only of Patriotism and of all the Arts & Sciences but likewise of all the private Virtues, and all the domestic charities? Do they hold out to deserved Scorn that shallow exclusive Cosmopolitism, which in pretences to a Love of All precludes the effectual love of Any? Do they attach almost a religious Value to every remaining Antiquity that tends to bind them & the present Age with the Age of their Forefathers?—And blame the same virtues in *you*, who by their own admission have a thousandfold stronger Cause for the same? They believe you dispersed by God's especial Providence for the blessing of the whole Human Race—they believe that *one* great Object of your former Captivities was to spread among the Gentiles the aweful Truths committed to your especial Custody—and shall they aggravate the sorrows of those, who according to their own faith are Sufferers for *their* sakes—nay, deprive the Sufferers of the universal Comfort, *Hope*? Bid them *forget*, that the Chosen People of God were their Forefathers, and *despair*, that God will perform his Promises to them, as a Nation— Promises, the authenticity of the records of which is so solemnly attested by their own Apostle—nay, Promises, the fulfilment of which is to be an Object of their own prayers? You have talked (I speak in your person) much in late years of *converting* the Jews! Whether *any* arguments, that can be adduced by you, fit for good & wise men to offer, would avail, the writer leaves undebated; but he ventures to suggest, that there is one argument in your power of far greater promise and plausibility than any, he has hitherto met with—namely, let Christians, who profess in all things to imitate Jesus, convince us by *their* brotherly Loving-kindness to those of the same stock with the Founder of their Faith that *He* was our Friend: and permit us to avail ourselves of one of his Precepts, to judge of the *Tree* by it's *Fruits*.—Read our calamitous History from the year 900 P. C.[1] to 1600—nay, in Germany almost to the present Year—and ask yourselves, whether it is possible to evade one or other of two conclusions—Either that Christians are not Fruits

---

[1] An abbreviation for *Post Christum*. In his *Chronological and Historical Assistant to a Course of Lectures on the History of Philosophy, from Thales*, [1818], Coleridge uses both A. C. and P. C. A copy of this pamphlet is in the British Museum. It is reprinted in *The Philosophical Lectures of Samuel Taylor Coleridge*, ed. Kathleen Coburn, 1949, pp. 70–80.

of the Tree, of which they are the pretended Growth: or that the Tree itself was a Tree of Poison for *us*, who are yet persecuted because we will not gather ourselves under it's shade.—

Such is the language which a Descendant of the Patriarchs is entitled to use—and far more worthy & far more likely to be efficacious, than the attempt made by certain pseudo-philosophic Jews in France & Germany to conciliate the good opinion of Worldlings by *explaining away* their sacred Writings, and justifying their rejection of Christianity by the rejection of *all* revelation—as if they could find no ground for their denial that the Promises were fulfilled in Jesus but by joining with Heathens in denying, that any Promises were made—except in the clannish wishes of Enthusiasts expressed in the flighty language of dithyrambic Poets!—

It would be duplicity if I concluded without avowing my conviction, that too much of a something strictly analogous to the abuses, which Luther waged war against in the corrupt Romish Church, which all originated in the substitution of the doctrines of men for those of Revelation, and in having placed human Comments and hollow lifeless Traditions on a par (in practice if not in profession) with the Word of God, is to be complained of in *your* Church. Assuredly, the highest Ground on which a Jew can place himself, is the *Sufficiency* of the Law and the Prophets. I am aware of the difficulties that stand in the way of a Reform. But there is one way & that a way of Peace—. EDUCATE! And as an essential part of Education let *your* BIBLE be *studied* as well as READ. Common Sense, Good Taste, and the mere sense of *Contrast*, will gradually do the rest: and bring about, without strife of words, as much as is desirable; desired by you at least. To recommend this and to assist in removing all the outward & civil Obstacles to it's adoption, is the *only* form of Proselytism, to which I could subscribe, in order to bring about likewise whatever may be additionally prayed for by, dear Sir! your sincere Friend and not the less orthodoxly or fervently a *Christian*, because in so many and so fundamental points *your* Fellow-believer,

S. T. Coleridge.—

P.S. Concerning the Nature, person, and attributes of the Messiah I have been purposely silent: because I appear to myself to see in the fullness of evidence, that all convictions, at once sincere and enlightened, on this head suppose and require an accordance in the first principles and general complexion of the Believer's *philosophic* Code: and that in every age the speculative Philosophy—or what we now but too appropriately call the metaphysical *Opinions*—that happen to be predominant among the educated classes, ever *have* influenced, and must and will influence the Theology of that age. If

(7)

I needed confirmation, I should find it afforded abundantly and in it's most striking form in the writings of those Church of England Divines, who within the last hundred years have stept forward to defend the doctrines held in common by Romanists and the first Protestant Reformers, on the grounds and supposed truth of the mechanical philosophy. All those I mean, who have learnt the exclusive origination of the *omne scibile* in the Senses from Locke and the detail of the process from Hartley. *Defend*, did I say?

Permit me to imagine a case, which medical records have proved to be within the limits of possibility: viz. that a series of words could be so written, and the nerves of the Skin be so sensitive, as that two individuals, both of them blind and deaf, could have intelligible communion, each reading with his finger-ends what the other had placed before him, as if he were playing off a piece of Music on the keys of a Piano Forte. Suppose further, that one of them had been arguing against the asserted power of perceiving Objects at a distance as utterly irrational and consequently false, grounding his arguments on the assumption, that the Touch was the one and only sense. You will readily conceive the rabble of impossibilities and self-contradictions, which the triumphant Solitactian would detect in this mysterious Tenet, and it's accompaniments. That one and the same Object, and without undergoing any change, should be perceived at one time as angular, and at another time as round! Nay in one and the same moment, as flat and as projecting! With what exulting Irony would he repeat the old Riddle—

> What thing is that (tell me without delay)
> That's nothing of itself, yet every way
> As like a man as a thing like can be
> And yet so unlike as clear Contrary.
> For in one point it every way doth miss,
> The right side of it a Man's left side is.
> 'Tis lighter than a feather, and withal
> It fills no place, no room, it is so small!

If there are among your Brethren (and I cannot, I feel, congratulate your nation on an entire immunity from the general influenza) any pupils of French Philosophy and modern Materialism, and you should have observed one of these semi-demi-philosophists *crowing* over the Book *Jezirah*,[1] or *R. Abraham Bar Dior* in Sepher hakkabálah,[2] or similar Relics of the ancient Hebrew Wisdom; tho'

[1] The Book of Jezirah (Sepher Yezirah), a mystical book probably dating from the second century.

[2] Coleridge apparently refers to Abraham Ibn Daud, Jewish historiographer and philosopher, and author of *Sepher Hakabbalah* or the *Book of Tradition*, a chronicle down to the year 1161.

but once for twenty times, that I have heard the Hunts, Cobbetts, Carlisles[1] & Hones parodying our Creeds; you have a lively image of the triumph, with which the confidence in the impossibility of any solution, that could *stand touch*, would inflate the blind and deaf Unitarian, whom I have here imagined. Now then for his Antagonist, who under the same privation of sight and sound had yet '*on certain gentle considerations*' subscribed to the Articles of Vision, and now, as in duty bound, bestirs his hand in defence of the same: and too long intimate with classic Greek to remember the meaning of a word in the vulgar tongue entitles his Manual, perhaps, an *Apology* for Light and Vision.—Mark the Defence. *Favete digitis, Tangitores ingenui*—i.e. Gentlemen! keep your hands in your Gloves! Abeste, profani—i.e. Let the light-fingered Gentry confine their's to their own pockets!—Gentlemen! you now have fully apprehended my opponent's Arguments. Such indeed is his Learning, genius, and [MS. breaks off thus.]

1220. *To C. A. Tulk*[2]

Transcript Coleridge family. Hitherto unpublished.

[January 1820][3]

My dear Sir

I had been actually relieving my mind—as by changing the Muscles exerted we relieve the body in a Journey—by putting down

[1] Richard Carlile (1790–1843), freethinker. In 1817 he was imprisoned for 18 weeks for reprinting William Hone's parodies on the litany, the Athanasian creed, and the church catechism, but was released without trial when Hone was acquitted. (See Letter 1101.) In 1818 Carlile published the theological, political, and miscellaneous works of Paine, and by Oct. 1819 there were six indictments against him for the publication of *The Age of Reason* and other works of a similar character. In Nov. he was fined £1,500 and sentenced to three years' imprisonment. For further comments on Carlile and for Coleridge's lines, *The Bridge Street Committee*, see *Letters, Conversations and Rec.* 48–49, and *Poems*, ii. 982–3.

[2] Charles Augustus Tulk, a Swedenborgian whom Coleridge first met in 1817. Tulk never joined the New Jerusalem church founded in London in 1787 by a group of the followers of Swedenborg. Coleridge himself described Tulk as 'a Partizan and Admirer of the Honorable Emanuel Swedenborg; but of the genuine School, with the Revd J. Clowes, Rector of St John's, Manchester, who oppose strenuously all sectarian feeling and remain sincere and affectionate Members of the Established Church'. (Letter 1532.) In 1810 Tulk assisted in founding the London Society for publishing the works of Swedenborg. He also became connected with the Hawkstone Park meeting, which was projected by George Harrison in 1806 and fostered by John Clowes. Tulk translated *The Doctrine of the New Jerusalem respecting the Lord*, 1812, a copy of which he presented to Coleridge. He also translated *An Appendix to the*

Notes 2 and 3 continued overleaf

a few questions which I meant to have addressed to you concerning the peculiarizing Tenets of Swedenborg. When I receive your kind present I shall therefore destroy them, in order if occasion should remain, to reproduce them in a more definite & answerable form—after the perusal of the works—An *attentive* perusal I can promise, & if not an unprejudiced one, the fault will be neither in my will or my consciousness. Your kindness will make me waive the feeling of ceremony on any similar occasion—that indeed was not on your account, or that of your — I was about to let an epithet slip out of my heart, but I recollected that it is awkward to praise a Lady to her husband—or on Mrs Tulk's, but I did not know that you might not have a party already large enough.

As I am desirous to finish the paper to night and am a little fatigued from the letters I have been writing to some legal Friends, you will be so good as to excuse me for this Evening and to believe me with unfeigned respect & regard

your obliged   S. T. Coleridge

1221. *To Charles Mathews*

MS. Yale University Lib. Pub. The Life and Correspondence of Charles Mathews, the Elder, Comedian. By Mrs. Mathews, *ed. Edmund Yates, 1860, p. 247.*

[*Circa* 10 January 1820][1]

Extempore, on rising from my seat at the close of 'At Home', on Saturday night.

Treatise on the White Horse, 1824, a work to which Coleridge refers in his letter to Tulk of 26 Jan. 1824. With the Rev. Samuel Noble, Tulk revised several works of Swedenborg for publication, among them *The True Christian Religion*, 1819, a copy of which he sent to Coleridge. In 1841 he published in the *Monthly Magazine* Coleridge's marginalia appearing in copies of two of Swedenborg's works: *Œconomia regni animalis in transactiones divisa*, 1740–1, and *De Cultu et Amore Dei*, 1745 and 1791.

By bringing various works of Swedenborg to Coleridge's attention, Tulk stimulated his friend's interest in Swedenborgianism. Copies of nine of Swedenborg's works containing annotations by Coleridge have been identified. Several of these are mentioned in Coleridge's letters. See J. L. Haney, *A Bibliography of Samuel Taylor Coleridge*, 1903, pp. 130–1, and James Hyde, *A Bibliography of the Works of Emanuel Swedenborg*, 1906.

[3] In the present letter Coleridge refers to the 'peculiarizing Tenets' of Swedenborg and mentions the expected arrival of some of Swedenborg's works. By 20 Jan. 1820 he had received the two volumes of *The True Christian Religion*, and by 12 Apr. he posed a question concerning the 'Memorable Relations' in that work. It was, however, July before he commented at length on the tenets of Swedenborg. See Letters 1225, 1231, and 1243.

[1] The reference to Mathews's 'At Home', which took place on Saturday, 8 Jan. 1820, suggests an approximate date for this letter. See Letter 1222.

If in whatever decks this earthly Ball,
'Tis still great Mother Nature, *one in all*;
Hence Matthews! needs must be her genuine Son,
A Second Nature that acts *all in one*—

S. T. Coleridge

Dear Sir

I have been reducing a few thoughts [of] my own, excited by my Saturday Night's Feast, to so[me] sort of Shape in my own mind—and if I should find courage enough to transfer them to Paper for your perusal, my principal if not my sole object will be to rectify or to confirm my own judgement by bringing it into contact with the touch-stone of your Observation and Experience—I have seen enough of mankind to feel little apprehension of offending *you* by sincerity—for men are tolerant of blame in proportion as they are secure of admiration—even if I had, as is not the case, found any thing in your performance to be censured. But I am not equally confident that in some of my notions, as to the *order* of excellence in the different parts of the performance, considered independent of yourself and even exclusive (and permit me to say, without suspicion of flattery, that this excludes the *very* finest parts of the At Home) I might not offend others and even give you pain as their friend. I must therefore bargain, that as I shall submit what I write to no eye but your's, so you will consider the same in the light of a tête à tête conversation, having this particular advantage that you may listen to it just at your leisure or not at all.—Be assured that I shall have strangely perverted & misexpressed my own mind and feelings if you do not recognize in my remarks the unfeigned admiration & regard with which

I am, dear Sir, | Your obliged

S. T. Coleridge

My best respects to Mrs Matthews & to your [so]n.—

1222. *To J. H. Green*

Address: J. H. Green, Esqre | Surgeon | Lincoln's Inn Fields
MS. Pierpont Morgan Lib. Pub. with omis. Letters, *ii. 704.*
Postmark: Highgate, 15 January 1820.

14 Jany. 1820
HIGHGATE

My dear Green

Charles Lamb has just written to inform me that he and his Sister will pay me their *new year's* visit on Sunday next—& may perhaps bring a friend to see *me* tho' certainly not to dine—& hopes,

(11)

I may not be engaged.—I must therefore defer our *philosophical* Intercommune till the Sunday after; but if you have no more pleasant way of passing the ante-prandial, or still better, the day including prandial and post-prandial, I trust, that it will be no anti-philosophical expenditure of time—& I need not say, an addition to the pleasure of all this household. I should like too to arrange some plan of going with you to Covent Garden Th. to see Miss Wensley, the new Actress whose Father (a Merchant of Bristol, at whose house I had once been, but whom the Capricious Nymph of Trade has unhorsed from his seat) has called on me—a compound of the Oratorical, the Histrionic, and the Exquisite! all the dull colors in the Colour Shop at the Sign of the Bluecoat Boy would not suffice to neutralize the glare of his Colorit into any tolerably fair Likeness that would not be scouted as Caricature!—Gillman will give you a slight sketch of him.—Since I saw you, we have dined & spent the night (for it was near One when we broke up) at Matthews's & heard & saw his forthcoming *At Home*. There were present besides G. and myself, Mrs & young Matthews & Mr & Mrs Chisholm, James Smith, of Rej. Add. notoriety & the Author of (all the Trash of) M's Entertainment—for the good parts are his own: (What a pity that you dare not offer a word of friendly sensible Advice to such men, as M. but you may be certain that it will be useless to them & attributed to envy or some vile selfish Object in the adviser!)—Mr Dubois,[1] the Author of Vaurien, Old Nic, My Pocket Book, and a notable share of the theatrical Puffs & Slanders of the periodical Press; & lastly, Mr Thomas Hill, quondam Dry Sorter [Salter?] of Thames Street, whom I remember 25 years ago with exactly the same look, Person & Manners as now—Matthews calls him, the Immutable. He is a seemingly always good-natured fellow who knows nothing & about every thing, no person & about & all about every body—a compleat Parasite in the old sense of a Dinner-hunter at the tables of all who are or who entertain public men, Authors, Players, Fiddlers, Booksellers &c—for more than 30 years, indeed, he has hung at the Tail of Contemporary or Living Literature like a cylinder of Album Greek half-extruded from a costive Dog.—It was a pleasant evening, however.

Be so good as to remember the Drawing from the Alchemy Book.

Mrs Gillman desires her Love to Mrs Green; & we hope, that the twin Obstacles, Ague & the Boreal Weather, to our seeing her here will vanish at the same time. Mrs G. bids me tell her, that she grumbles at the Doctors, her Husband included; & is confident, that *her* Husband would have made a cure long ago. A faithful Wife is a common Blessing, I trust; but what a treasure, to have a

---

[1] Edward Dubois (1774–1850), wit and man of letters.

Wife *full of Faith!*—By the bye, I have lit on some (ὡς ἔμοιγε δοκεῖ, *analogous*) cases, in which the nauseating plan, even for a short time, appears to have had a wonderful effect in breaking the chain of a morbid tendency—and the almost infallible specific of Sea-sickness in curing an old Ague is surely a confirmation as far as it goes.—

Your's most affectionately,

S. T. Coleridge—

1223. *To James Gooden*[1]

Address: J. Gooden, Esqre | 46 | Wooburn Place | near | Russell Square.
MS. Dr. Williams's Lib. Pub. E. L. G. ii. 264.
Postmark: Highgate, 15 January 1820.

14 Jany 1814 [1820]—
Highgate—

Dear Sir

The matrimonial Goddess, & Boreas in conjunction have imposed so many *Labors* in expectation on our medical Hercules, & the latter Divinity growled so many threats to the poor Invalid, his unworthy Friend, your humble Servant, in addition to an accumulation of literary engagements to be fulfilled, that we are compelled to defer the pleasure of passing an Attic Evening with you, in pursuance of your kind invitation, to a more favorable conjunction of Planets.—Accept my thanks for the Rules of the Harmony. I perceive, that the members are chiefly Merchants; but yet it were to be wished, that such an enlargement of the Society could be brought about, as retaining all it's present purposes might add to them the groundwork of a Library of Northern Literature, and by bringing together the many Gentlemen who are attached to it be the means of eventually making both countries better acquainted with the valuable part of each other—especially, the English with the German: for our most sensible men look at the German Muses thro' a film of prejudice & utter misconception.

With regard to Philosophy, there are half a dozen things, good & bad that in this country are so nick-named, but in the only accurate sense of the term, there neither are, have been, or ever will be but two essentially different Schools of Philosophy: the Platonic, and

---

[1] James Gooden, whom Crabb Robinson in 1842 called 'an elderly gentleman, long an admirer of Wordsworth, and a good scholar'. *Diary, Reminiscences, and Correspondence of Henry Crabb Robinson*, ed. T. Sadler, 2 vols., 1872 (3rd edn.), ii. 232. Mrs. H. N. Coleridge printed all but the first sentence of the present letter in *Notes and Lectures upon Shakespeare*, 2 vols., 1849, ii. 273.

the Aristotelean. To the latter, but with a somewhat nearer approach to the Platonic, Emanuel Kant belonged; to the former Bacon and Leibnitz & in his riper and better years Berkley—And to this I profess myself an adherent—nihil novum, vel inauditum audemus: tho' as every man has a face of his own, without being more or less than a man, so is every true Philosopher an original, without ceasing to be an Inmate of Academus or of the Lyceum.— But as to caution, I will just tell you how I proceeded myself, 20 years & more ago when I first felt a curiosity about Kant, & was fully aware that to master his meaning, as a system, would be a work of great Labor & long Time—.[1] First, I asked myself, have I the Labor & the Time in my power? Secondly, if so & if it would be of adequate importance to me if true, by what means can I arrive at a rational presumption for or against?—I enquired after all the more popular writings of Kant—read them with delight.—I then read the Prefaces to several of his systematic works, as the Prolegomena &c—here too every part, I understood, & that was nearly the whole, was replete with sound & plain tho' bold and novel truths to me—& I followed Socrates's Adage respecting Heraclitus —all I understand is excellent; and I am bound to presume that the rest is at least worth the trouble of trying whether it be not equally so.[2]—In other words, until I understand a writer's Ignorance, I presume myself ignorant of his understanding. Permit me to refer you to a chapter on this subject in my Literary Life.[3]—Yet I by no means recommend to you an extension of your philosophic researches beyond Kant. In him is contained all that can be *learnt*— & as to the results, you have a firm faith in God, the responsible Will of Man, and Immortality—& Kant will demonstrate to you, that this Faith is acquiesced in, indeed, nay, confirmed by the Reason & Understanding, but grounded on Postulates authorized & substantiated solely by the *Moral* Being—These are likewise *mine*: & whether the *Ideas* are regulative only, as Aristotle & Kant teach, or constitutive & actual as Pythagoras & Plato, is of living Interest to the Philosopher by Profession alone. Both systems are

---

[1] In 1815, when Coleridge was composing the *Biographia Literaria*, he gave an enthusiastic account of his early study of Kant. Declaring that 'the writings of the illustrious sage of Königsberg . . ., more than any other work, at once invigorated and disciplined' his understanding, he added that he still read them 'with undiminished delight and increasing admiration' after 'fifteen years' familiarity'. (*Biog. Lit.* i. 99.) Letters 380 and 387 show that early in 1801 Coleridge had already begun a serious study of Kant.

[2] Diogenes Laërtius, *Lives of the Philosophers*, ii. 22.

[3] Coleridge was fond of this maxim. See *Biog. Lit.*, ch. xii; Letter 800; and *The Notebooks of Samuel Taylor Coleridge*, ed. Kathleen Coburn, vol. i, 1957, item 928/21.128/*f* 27.

equally true, if only the former abstain from denying *universally*
what is denied individually. He for whom Ideas are constitutive, will
in effect be a Platonist—and in those, for whom they are regulative
only, Platonism is but a hollow affectation.[1] Dryden *could* not have
been a Platonist—Shakespear, Milton, Dante, Michael Angelo, &
Rafael could not have been other than Platonists. Lord Bacon, who
never read Plato's works, taught pure Platonism in his *great* Work,
the Novum Organum, and abuses his divine Predecessor for fantastic nonsense, which he had been the first to explode.[2]—

Accept my best respects as, dear Sir, | Your's most sincerely,

S. T. Coleridge

1224. *To Thomas Allsop*[3]

Address: T. Allsop, Esqre
MS. New York Public Lib. Pub. with omis. Letters, Conversations and Rec. *13.*

[*Circa* 18 January 1820][4]

My dear Sir

You must have thought it strange, that I had taken no notice of
so kind a letter from you; but the truth is, I received the little
packet from Mr Williams, supposing it to contain the Cobbett only,
put it in my pocket for my reading at a leisure hour, & had not
opened it till the day before I last saw you. Within a few days I
hope to lay myself open to you, in an express letter—till when I can
only say, that the affectionate interest, you have taken in my well-

[1] Cf. *Table Talk*, 2 July 1830, *The Statesman's Manual*, 1816, Appendix (E),
p. xlvii, and *Literary Remains*, ii. 348, and iii. 33–34. See also J. H. Muirhead,
Coleridge as Philosopher, 1930.

[2] For Coleridge's discussion of Plato and Bacon see *The Friend*, 1818, iii.
169 n. and 193–216; and *S. T. Coleridge's Treatise on Method . . .*, ed. Alice D.
Snyder, 1934, pp. 37–51. As early as June 1803 Coleridge planned to show that
the 'Verulamian Logic' was 'bonâ fide' the same as the Platonic. See Letter 504,
and Alice D. Snyder, *Coleridge on Logic and Learning*, 1929, pp. 65–66.

[3] Allsop, a young business man in London, had attended Coleridge's lectures
in early 1818. By the following year he was on terms of intimacy with Coleridge,
and in Oct. 1819, after hearing of the bankruptcy of Coleridge's publisher, he
sent an unexpected gift of money. Crabb Robinson heard that it was £100.
See Letters 1104, 1155, 1205, and 1207, and *Robinson on Books and Their
Writers*, i. 315.

[4] The reference in the postscript to the visit of the Lambs to Highgate, a
visit which took place on Sunday, 16 Jan., establishes an approximate date for
this letter. See Letter 1222. The erroneous date of '20 March 1820' appearing in
the MS. of the present letter is in Allsop's handwriting.

It should be pointed out that Allsop inserted dates in the MSS. of certain
letters undated by Coleridge. Since these dates can easily be mistaken for
Coleridge's, each such interpolation in the MS. is explained in a footnote.

being, has been not only a comfort but a spur, when I needed both
—and was almost yielding at times to the apprehension, that I had
sacrificed all, that the World holds precious, without being able to
do any effective good in a higher & nobler kind. I have sent the 3
Volumes of the Friend, with my MSS corrections and additions.[1]
The largest, that toward the End of the last *philosophical* Essay in
the third Volume,[2] had a twofold Object, to guard my own character from the suspicion of pantheistic opinions, or Spinosism—(it *was*
written, tho' not so much at large, before the work was printed, &
omitted by wilfulness or such carelessness as does not fall far short
of it)—and next to impress, as far as I could, the conviction, that
true philosophy so far from having any tendency to unsettle the
principles of faith that may be & ought to be common to all men,
does itself actually require them as it's premises, nay, that it supposes them as it's ground.—I was highly gratified to hear, and from
such a man too as Mr J. H. Frere, that a man of rank and of a
highly cultivated mind, who had become reluctantly a Sceptic or
something more respecting the Christian Religion wholly in consequence of studying Leland,[3] Lardner, Watson, Paley & other
Defenders of the Gospel on the strength of the *external* Evidences—
not of Christianity but of the Miracles with which it's first Preaching was accompanied—and of having been taught to regard the
arguments & mode of proof adopted in the works above mentioned
as the only rational ones—had read the Friend with great attention,
and when he came to the passage in which I had explained the
nature of Miracles,[4] their necessary dependence on a credible Religion for their own credibility, &c dropt the Book (as he himself informed Mr Frere) and exclaimed—Thank God! I can still believe
in the Gospel: I can yet be a Christian.—The remark that a miracle
divested of all connection with a doctrine is identical with Witchcraft, which in all ages has been regarded with instinctive horror by
the human mind—and the reference to our Lord's own declarations
concerning Miracles, even his own stupendous Miracles—were
among the passages that particularly impressed his mind.

I should have sent a corrected Copy of the Sibylline Leaves; but
for a two-legged little *Accident's* having torn out two leaves at the
Beginning, & I will no longer delay this parcel, but will transcribe
at another time what I had written in them—& we hope, it will not
be long before you let us see you.—We must, I fear, give up the plan

---

¹ This copy of *The Friend* is in the Harvard College Library. The inscription
to Allsop is dated '1 Jany. 1820'. See C. C. Seronsy, 'Marginalia by Coleridge in
Three of His Published Works', *Studies in Philology*, July 1954, p. 473.
² Allsop printed this MS. note in *Letters, Conversations and Rec.* 15.
³ John Leland (1691–1766), divine.
⁴ See *The Friend*, 1818, iii. 102–6.

of Miss Wensley and her Rosalind till the Weather becomes a little
less hazardous. Mrs Gillman too, I am sorry to say, is but very
poorly—& Mr G. has his hands full of raising & distributing relief
for the Poor of the Hamlet. On the first day there [were] 750 Applicants to whom small sums were given.—It would be most un-
christian Moroseness not to feel delight in the unwearied Zeal, with
which every mode & direction of charity, is supported—and I hope,
that this is a sunshiny spot in our national character, & that this
Virtue will suspend the judgements that threaten the Land—But
it would on the other hand be wilful Blindness not to see that the
lower orders become more & more improvident in consequence—
more & more exchange the sentiments of Englishmen for the feelings of Lazaroni—.

Mrs Gillman transmits her kindest regards: as the *Good man*
would do, were he at home.

God bless you | &

S. T. Coleridge

P.S. Charles & Mary Lamb dined with us on Sunday—When I
next see you, that excellent Brother & Sister will supply me with
half an hour's interesting conversation. When you know the *whole*
of him, you will love him spite of all oddities & even faults—nay, I
had almost said, *for* them—at least, admire that under his visitations [they] were so few & of so little importance.—Thank God, his
Circumstances are comfortable—& so they ought: for he has been
in the India House since his 14th year.—

1225. *To C. A. Tulk*

Address: Charles Augustus Tulk, Esqre | Regent's Park
MS. Harvard College Lib. Hitherto unpublished.
Postmark: 22 January 1820.

20 Jany. 1820
Highgate

My dear Sir

Had some friendly Wizard given me a magic Camera Obscura
that had the quality of retaining sounds and even thoughts translated into visible letters and words, I should have proved a most
voluminous Correspondent of your's. But alas! on the contrary the
naked truth is, that I had so much to communicate, so many thoughts
intimately connected with the works and character of your illustrious tho' grossly misconceived Swede as collated both with the
results of my own meditations and the Cabbala of the Jewish church
as it existed centuries before the Birth of our Lord—that I had no

heart or hope to sit down to a work which the Time, that I dared consider as my own property, would not permit me to finish. Among many demonstrations, which I have educed, and (if I do not woe-fully deceive both myself and my fellow-enquirer, a man bred up in the very heart of the experimental and mechanico-material philo-sophy of the age) strictly warranting that name, I will mention that of the pre-existence of our Earth to the Solar System, and to it's existing relations as a part of that system; and likewise of a vege-table world anterior to the collection of Light, *as* solar Light, in the Focus of the vast Ellipse; and that in this must be sought & is to be found, the true difference of animal Life & Vegetable Growth, and the dependence of the former on Light and Gravitation, and the difference again of Gravitation both from the centripetal Power & from simple Attraction—and that I had arrived at this conclusion by necessary evolution from the First Principle of my Philosophy before I was aware of it's exact coincidence with the Mosaic Cosmogony.—

Heavily do I regret, that the cruel and imperious Commands of the daily To Day, conjointly with my ill-health and increasing slowness of composition from an increasing pain at incorrectness, make it almost a crime to devote a day together to any Work, either poetical, or in prose, which is suited to the powers, Heaven has entrusted to me, or by which I can hope to be permanently use-ful to mankind. Of three great Works I have all the materials in bonâ fide mss Existence, that require little more than transcription from the various slips & scraps & pocket-books and Book-margins (to be done unhappily by myself alone) and the putting them to-gether; and instead of this I am doomed to write or rather to at-tempt writing *popular* reading for Magazines. God knows my heart! that on this account alone I regret the res angusta—but that it is the serpent compressing & coercing in it's circular cordage of folds the Pinions of the struggling Eagle, no man could with more sin-cerity assume as his Motto—*Laeta* Paupertas. I should scarcely have uttered this useless strain of Querulity, but that I could not endure to *invent* an excuse for the necessity of deferring the perusal of the two Volumes,[1] which I owe to your kindness, till the time when I hope to avail myself of your friendly invitation to pass a week under your roof—when we can convey more to each other by word of mouth in 2 or 3 hours than by the pen in half a month.—

[1] Coleridge refers to Swedenborg's *The True Christian Religion; containing the Universal Theology of the New Church, which was foretold by the Lord, in Daniel, chap. vii. 13, 14; and in the Apocalypse, chap. xxi. 1, 2.* The fifth edition, 2 vols., 1819, was revised by the Rev. Samuel Noble and Tulk. Coleridge's annotated copy of this work is in the British Museum.

If I mistake not, one formula would comprize your philosophical faith & mine—namely, that the sensible World is but the evolution of the Truth, Love, and Life, or their opposites, in Man—and that in Nature Man beholds only (to use an Algebraic but close analogy) the integration of Products, the Differentials of which are in, and constitute, his own mind and soul—and consequently that all true science is contained in the Lore of Symbols & Correspondences.[1]— As soon as I can find time, I shall entreat your acceptance of a Copy of the Friend with numerous Mss corrections & additions— to one of the latter, at the conclusion of the Essays on Method, I shall solicit your particular attention—indeed I feel confident, that it will meet with an entire co-incidence on your part.

Mrs Gillman bids me not forget 'to remember me most affectionately to that angel woman of a wife of his—God bless him! for I do believe, he deserves her.'

Well, Ma'am! I have written it down.—'What? you have not been so foolish?—Now, pray, Coleridge! don't be so silly.'—

Alas, my dear & sisterly Friend! Wiser men have done foolisher things & better men far worse—and as it came from your heart, I owe it too great respect on account of it's Birth-place to beblot it [with i]nk and a foul Pen.

With every heart-felt wish for you and your's believe me, dear Sir, | with unfeigned respect and | regard | Your obliged
S. T. Coleridge

P.S. Mr Gillman desires his best respects.

1226. *To Hyman Hurwitz*

Address: Hyman Hurwitz, Esqre, | Highgate
MS. University of Pennsylvania Lib. Hitherto unpublished.

10 March, 1820—
Highgate—

My dear Sir

In order to obey one call of Friendship I was forced to defer another. The pleasant Duty yielded precedence to the more importunate claim of a worthy friend's affliction. This, I need not tell *you*, is the most imperious Form that Duty can assume: and the immediate case the sorest of afflictions—an exemplary but baffled Father's anguish over the hopeless—*almost* hopeless—baseness of a Son. Indeed I should not have retracted the expression of unmitigated Despair concerning the young man, who but a short season

[1] For further comments on symbols and correspondences see Letters 1370–1 and 1546.

past was with the greatest exertion of interest put once more on trial and reprieved from a public Disgrace, the menace and still more the occasion of which had, he well knew, distracted the best of Fathers, and covered his Mother and his kindred with darkness and shame not their own—but that I remembered the saying of Rabbi Hanania, the Son of Dosa[1]—A quocunque cessat Spiritus Humanus, ab eo cessat etiam *divinus*: et a quocunque non cessavit spiritus humanus, ab eo non cessat spiritus divinus.[2] O quamdiu verò, et cuicunque, datur adhuc humanam faciem retinere, apud quam nexu fatali moratur Dei Imago, haud licet Spiritum Θεανθρώπινον ab eo exulantem credere, vel sine reditu omnino decessum. (The last sentence I add myself, but as an evident Corollary of the wise master's Proposition.)—But I have done my best: sufficient to the day is the burthen thereof: and I return to the gratifying task of thanking you for so honorable (I will not affront my own feelings or your's by saying, *flattering*) a pledge of your regard and esteem. The Box shall be sacred, and as long as I live, perform the functions of a comforting angel while I am conscious of retaining the same however defective claim to the Sentiments and good opinion of which it is the Remembrancer—and if—which God forbid—I should turn renegade to the faith and the fruits of the Faith common to all the spiritual Sons of Abraham, whether children of the House, according to the Flesh, or adopted by the Father of Spirits who out of stones can raise up seed unto Abraham—then will it look me in the face as my Accuser. Nor will it want a voice: for my Conscience, the most fearful of the *Ōboth*,[3] the pre-eminent *Kosem Kesamim*,[4] will throw her voice into it, et vox ejus erit Beob (= sicut ἐγγαστριμύθον, sive Pythonis, sive Ventriloquentis) *Isaiah 29. 4*.[5]—

I only fear, as to the unpoetical part of the Contents, that your

[1] Coleridge refers to Rabbi Hanina (or Hananjah) ben Dosa; 'famous as a hasid and wonder worker, [he] belonged to the generation of those who saw the fall of Jerusalem'. *Pirkē Aboth, the Tractate 'Fathers', from the Mishnah, commonly called 'Sayings of the Fathers'*, ed. R. T. Herford, 1930, p. 76.

[2] See *Aboth*, iii. 13. 'Everyone with whom the spirit of mankind is pleased, the spirit of God is pleased with him; and everyone with whom the spirit of mankind is not pleased the spirit of God is not pleased with him.' Ibid. 77–78.

[3] Oboth is the plural of Ob, a Hebrew word meaning one who has a familiar spirit, a necromancer, a wizard, a ventriloquist. See Leviticus xx. 27: 'A man also or woman that hath a familiar spirit, or that is a wizard, shall surely be put to death.' See also *Table Talk*, 1 May 1823, and *Literary Remains*, iv. 54–55.

[4] Kosem Kesamim, literally a practitioner of witchcraft. See Deuteronomy xviii. 10–11.

[5] 'And thou shalt be brought down, *and* shalt speak out of the ground, and thy speech shall be low out of the dust, and thy voice shall be, as of one that hath a familiar spirit, out of the ground, and thy speech shall whisper out of the dust.'

delicacy and liberality tempted you into a venial aberration from the strict *matter of fact*—and that you had drawn upon the bank of *Hope*, and by the figure of Rhetoric, called Anticipation, substituted the Past for the *possible* Future, which perhaps your friendly Wishes might have varnished into the *Sub-probable*.[1] Be it as it may, I receive it without pain from *you*: because I could not *to you* pretend that my circumstances gave me a right to reject it, and because you know that no such object either has been or will be any motive, or excite any additional impulse, on any occasion in which my Pen, Influence, or Judgement can be at all serviceable or gratifying to you[2]—

As to the Persecutions of Bigots, I have all my life been exposed to them—and in for a penny, in for a pound. Nay, the latter is the better policy; for it is the Nature of these Cattle to hate in an inverse ratio to the magnitude of the Difference. You will find this point well stated (if the parental partialities of the Author do not delude me) in the Literary Life, Vol. I. p. 190—. As you have not the work, I will transcribe the two most important sentences. 'All my experience from my first entering into Life to the present hour confirms the warning maxim, that the Man, who opposes *in toto* the political or religious Zealots of his age, is safer from their obloquy than He who differs from them but in one or two points, or perhaps *in degree* only. By that transfer of the feelings of private life into the discussion of public questions, which is the *Queen Bee* in the Hive of Party Fanaticism, the Partizan has more sympathy with an intemperate *Opposite*, than with a moderate *Friend*.'

But least of all, will I shrink from maintaining principles, which are not only equally beneficial to both parties, but which are the indispensable *pre-condition* of the Cause being ever fairly tried. The Christian challenges the Jew to fair Combat—What? shall I not cry out—Aye! but your Crew have waylayed, stript, bruised and cut him—and before you can even ask him to appear in your *Tourney* Court, it is your sacred & urgent duty, as an honest man, to assist in healing his wounds, removing his soreness and stiffness, and to supply him or enable him to supply himself with the necessary Arms, common to both combatants—which in the present case are the habits and attainments formed & given by Education. Would you *gouge* a man, or at best continue to bind up his eyes—and then

[1] Coleridge apparently refers to the tribute to himself in Hurwitz's *Vindiciae Hebraicae*. See note to Letter 1501. For Coleridge's high estimate of the work see Letters 1244 and 1449.

[2] Coleridge had undoubtedly received a small sum of money from Hurwitz for assisting him with the *Vindiciae Hebraicae*. (See Letter 1244.) In 1825 Hurwitz paid Coleridge £12 for assistance with another work. See Coleridge's note to Letter 1448.

challenge him to a Trial with telescopes, in order to decide whose system of *Himmelslehre* is the true one?—God bless you, my dear Sir,

And your sincere Friend

S. T. Coleridge

1227. *To Frances Maria Kelly*[1]

Address: Miss Kelly | Henrietta Street | Covent Garden
MS. Professor R. C. Bald. Pub. E. L. G. ii. 266.
Postmark: Highgate, 28 March 1820.

Highgate
Tuesday Morning [28 March 1820]

Mr Coleridge feels and acknowleges Miss Kelly's kindness in the invitation which he has this moment received thro' his old and dear Friends, Charles and Mary Lamb—and assures Miss Kelly, that not He but his Health consents to his not availing himself of the opportunity. Were Mr C. but one tenth of the distance, he is so unwell and from many recent exertions and vexations so jaded, that his medical Friend would interpose his Veto—& yet were his Health only at it's ordinary or average *below par*, and instead of a party Mr C. could pass two or three hours at a Fire-side with a friend or two in Miss Kelly's Company, twice 5 miles would not scare him from the undertaking.

1228. *To Thomas Allsop*

Address: T. Allsop, Esqre | Messrs. Harding and Co | Pall Mall
MS. New York Public Lib. Pub. with omis. Letters, Conversations and Rec. 77.

Thursday Afternoon [30 March 1820][2]

My dear young Friend

The only impression left by you on my mind, of which I am aware, is an increased desire to see you again and at shorter intervals. Were you my son by nature, I could not hold you dearer or more earnestly desire to retain you the adopted of whatever within me will remain when the dross and alloy of infirmity shall have been purged away. I feel the most entire confidence, that no prosperous

---

[1] Fanny Kelly (1790–1882), the actress, was Mrs. Charles Mathews's half-sister.

[2] This date is established by Letter 1229, in which Coleridge refers specifically to the present letter and to Allsop's reply. The erroneous date of '10 Jany 1821' appearing in the MS. is in Allsop's handwriting.

change of my outward circumstances would add to *your* faith in the
sincerity of this assurance: still, however, the average of men being
what it is, and it being neither possible nor desirable to be fully
conscious in our understanding of the habits of thinking and
judging in the world around us, and yet to be wholly impassive and
unaffected by them in our feelings, it would endear, and give a new
value to, an honorable competence, that I should be able to evince
the true nature and degree of my esteem and attachment, beyond
the suspicion even of the sordid, and separate from all that is accidental and adventitious. But yet the gratitude, I feel to you, is so
genial a Warmth, and blends so undistinguishably with my affections, is so perfectly one of the family in the Household of Love,
that I would not be otherwise than obliged and indebted to you:
and God is my witness, that my wish for an easier and less embarrassed lot is *chiefly* (I think, I might have said, *exclusively*) grounded
in the deep conviction, that exposed to a less bleak aspect I should
bring forth flowers and fruits, both more abundant and more
worthy of the unexampled kindness of your *faith* in me.—Interpreting the '*wine*' and the 'ivy garland' as figures of poetry signi-
fying competence & the removal of the petty needs of the body that
plug up the pipes of the playing Fountain (and such, it is too well
known, was the intent and meaning of the hardly used Poet)—and
O! how often, when my heart has begun to swell from the genial
warmth of thought as our northern Lakes from the (so called)
bottom-winds when all above and around is Stillness and Sunshine—how often have I repeated in my own name the sweet
Stanza of Edmund Spenser—

> Thou kenst not, Percie, how the rhyme should rage
> O! if my temples were bedew'd with wine,
> And girt in garlands of wild ivy twine—
> How I could rear the Muse on stately stage
> And teach her tread aloft in buskin fine
> With queint Bellona in her equipage![1]

Read this as you would a note at the bottom of a page.

> But ah! Mecaenas is ywrapt in clay
> And great Augustus long ago is dead—[2]

this is a natural sigh, & natural too is the reflection that follows—

> And if that any buddes of Poesy
> Yet of the old stock gin to shoot again,
> 'Tis or *self*-lost the worldling's meed to gain,

[1] *The Shepheardes Calender, October,* 109–14.   [2] Ibid. 61–62.

(23)

And with the rest to breathe it's ribauldry:
Or as it sprung, it wither must again—
Tom Piper makes them better melody.[1]

but tho' natural, the complaint is not equally philosophical, were it
only on this account, that I know of no age in which the same has
not been advanced, & with the same grounds. Nay, I retract. There
never was a time, in which the *complaint* would be so little wise,
tho' perhaps none in which the *fact* is more *prominent*. Neither
Philosophy or Poetry ever did, nor as long as they are terms of comparative excellence & contradistinction, ever can be *popular*, nor
honored with the praise and favor of Contemporaries. But on the
other hand, there never was a time, in which either books, that were
held for excellent as poetic or philosophic, had so extensive and rapid
a sale, or men reputed Poets and Philosophers of a high rank were so
much *looked up to* in Society or so munificently, almost profusely,
rewarded.—Walter Scott's Poems & Novels (except only the two
wretched Abortions, Ivanhoe & the Bride of Ravensmuir[2] or whatever it's name be) supply both instance & solution of the *present*
conditions & components of popularity—viz—to amuse without
requiring any effort of thought, & without exciting any deep
emotion. The age seems *sore* from excess of stimulation, just as a
day or two after a thorough Debauch & long sustained Drinking-
match a man feels all over like a Bruise. Even to *admire* otherwise
than *on the whole* and where 'I admire' is but a synonyme for 'I
remember, I *liked* it very much *when I was reading it*', is too much
an effort, would be too disquieting an emotion! Compare Waverley,
Guy Mannering, &c with works that had an *immediate run* in the

---

[1] *The Shepheardes Calender, October*, 73–78. In Spenser lines 75–76 read:
Or it mens follies mote be forst to fayne,
And rolle with rest in rymes of ribaudrye.
[2] *Ivanhoe* and *The Bride of Lammermoor* were published in 1819.
In the light of Scott's unwarranted use of *Christabel* while the poem was still
in manuscript, Coleridge must have felt after reading *Ivanhoe* that no unpublished poem of his was safe from Scott's depredations, since the last three
lines of his *The Knight's Tomb*, a poem not published until 1834, were quoted in
ch. ix, p. 156 of that novel. Undoubtedly, too, the disparaging remark with
which Scott introduced the quotation—'To borrow lines from a contemporary
poet, who has written but too little'—reminded Coleridge of Scott's slighting
comment to Byron in 1815 concerning 'the want of inclination and exertion'
which prevented Coleridge from giving 'full scope' to his mind. In the present
letter Coleridge calls *Ivanhoe* a 'wretched Abortion', but makes no allusion to
the use of his unpublished poem. Four years later, however, he clearly revealed
his irritation in a note dated 20 Oct. 1824: 'The Lines [were] first *written down*
but very incorrectly by Sir W. Scott in one of his Novels—who had them from
J. H. Frere to whom I had repeated them as an experiment in metre.' See
Letters 845, 981, 1230, and 1413.

last generation—Tristram Shandy, Roderick Random, Sir Ch. Grandison, Clarissa Harlow, & Tom Jones (all which became popular as soon as published & therefore instances fairly in point) and you will be convinced, that the difference of Taste is real & not [any fancy or croaking of my own.][1]

But enough of these Generals. It was my purpose to open myself out to you in detail.—My health, I have reason to believe, is so intimately connected with the state of my Spirits, and these again so dependent on my thoughts, prospective and retrospective, that I should not doubt the being favored with a sufficiency for my noblest undertakings, had I the ease of heart requisite for the necessary abstraction of the Thoughts, and such a reprieve from the goading of the immediate exigencies as might make tranquillity possible. But alas! I know by experience (and this knowlege is not the less, because the regret is not unmixed with self-blame and the consciousness of want of exertion and fortitude) that my health will continue to decline, as long as the pain from reviewing the barrenness of the Past is great in an inverse proportion to any rational anticipations of the Future. As I now am, however, from 5 to 6 hours devoted to actual writing and composition in the day is the utmost, that my strength, not to speak of my nervous system, will permit: and the invasions on this portion of my time from applications, often of the most senseless kind, are such and so many, as to be almost as ludicrous even to myself as they are vexatious. In less than a week I have not seldom received half a dozen packets or parcels, of works printed or manuscript, urgently requesting my *candid judgement*, or my correcting hand—add to these Letters from Lords & Ladies urging me to write reviews & puffs of heaven-born Geniuses, whose whole merit consists in their being Ploughmen or Shoemakers—Ditto from Actors—Ditto, Intreaties—for money or recommendations to Publishers from Ushers out of place, &c &c —and to *me*, who have neither influence, interest, or money—and what is still more apropos, can neither bring myself to tell smooth falshoods or harsh truths, and in the struggle too often do both in the anxiety to do neither—. I have already the *written* materials and contents, requiring only to be put together, from the loose papers and numerous Common-place or Memorandum Books, & needing no other change whether of omission, addition, or correction, than the mere act of arranging & the opportunity of seeing the whole collectively, bring [*sic*] with them of course—the following Works. I. Characteristics of Shakespear's Dramatic Works, with a critical Review of each Play—together with a relative and comparative Critique on the kind and degree of the merits & demerits of

[1] MS. cut off; the words in brackets supplied from the printed text.

the Dramatic Works of Ben Jonson, Beaumont & Fletcher, and Massinger. The history of the English Drama, the accidental advantages, it afforded to Shakespear, without in the least detracting from the perfect originality, or proper creation of the Shakspearian Drama; the contra-distinction of the Latter from the Greek Drama, and it's still remaining *Uniqueness*, with the causes of this from the combined influences of Shakespear himself, as Man, Poet, Philosopher, and finally, by conjunction of all these, *Dramatic Poet*; and of the age, events, manners and state of the English Language. This work, with every art of compression, amounts to three Volumes Oct. of about 500 pages each.—II. Philosophical Analysis of the Genius and Works of Dante, Spenser, Milton, Cervantes, and Calderon—with similar but more compressed Criticisms of Chaucer, Ariosto, Donne, Rabelais, and others, during the predominance of the romantic Poesy.—In one large Volume.—These two works will, I flatter myself, form a complete Code of the Principles of Judgement & Feeling applied to Works of Taste—and not of *Poetry* only, but of *Poesy* in all it's forms, Painting, Statuary, Music &c.[1]—

III. The History of Philosophy, considered as a tendency of the Human Mind to exhibit the powers of the Human Reason—to discover by it's own strength the origin & laws of Man and the world, from Pythagoras to Locke & Condilliac—2 Volumes.[2]

[1] Although in his later letters Coleridge several times proposed to publish his 'lucubrations' on Shakespeare and other literary figures, and although he twice spoke of preparing an edition of Shakespeare, no such publications appeared during his lifetime. In 1836, however, H. N. Coleridge collected various fragmentary MS. lecture notes, marginalia, etc., and published them in *Literary Remains*, i and ii. Mrs. H. N. Coleridge subsequently reprinted this material, with some additions and with comments on her father's indebtedness to Schlegel and Schelling, in *Notes and Lectures upon Shakespeare and some of the Old Poets and Dramatists with other Literary Remains of S. T. Coleridge*, 2 vols., 1849. A new edition by Thomas Ashe, *Lectures and Notes on Shakspere and Other English Poets. By Samuel Taylor Coleridge*, 1883, included J. P. Collier's shorthand records of Coleridge's lectures (published 1856), as well as excerpts from Robinson's diary and various newspaper reports. *Coleridge's Shakespearean Criticism*, 2 vols., 1930, and *Coleridge's Miscellaneous Criticism*, 1936, both edited by T. M. Raysor in conformity with modern scholarship, greatly augment the materials previously made available and complete the task so admirably begun by the poet's nephew and daughter. A new edition, *Coleridge's Writings on Shakespeare*, imaginatively edited by Terence Hawkes, 1959, contains a brilliant analysis of Coleridge's Shakespearian criticism by Professor Alfred Harbage.

[2] Coleridge here refers to his proposed publication of his philosophical lectures of 1818–19. '*At a heavy expence*', J. H. Frere employed 'an eminent shorthand writer' to make a record of this course. (Letter 1177.) Later Frere gave the transcript of the shorthand notes to Green. In 1854 Green stated: 'These notes are wholly unfit for publication, as indeed may be inferred from the fact, communicated to me by Coleridge, that the person employed confessed after

IV. Letters on the Old and New Testament, and on the doctrines and principles held in common by the Fathers and Founders of the Reformation, addressed to a Candidate for Holy Orders—including advice on the plan and subjects of Preaching, proper to a Minister of the Established Church.[1]

To the completion of these four Works I have literally nothing more to do, than *to transcribe*; but, as I before hinted, from so many scraps & *sibylline* leaves, including Margins of Books & blank Pages, that unfortunately I must be my own Scribe—& not done by myself, they will be all but lost—or perhaps (as has been too often the case already) furnish feathers for the Caps of others—some for this purpose, and some to plume the arrows of detraction to be let fly against the luckless Bird, from whom they had been plucked or moulted!

In addition to these,—of my GREAT WORK,[2] to the preparation of which more than twenty years of my life have been devoted, and

---

the first lecture that he was unable to follow the lecturer in consequence of becoming perplexed and delayed by the novelty of thought and language, for which he was wholly unprepared by the ordinary exercise of his art.' (*Notes and Queries*, 10 June 1854, p. 544.) In 1949, however, Miss Coburn published the transcript of the shorthand notes, along with 'accessory manuscripts', as *The Philosophical Lectures of Samuel Taylor Coleridge.*

[1] Coleridge also mentions this proposed work in Letters 1229, 1236, and 1245. Both E. H. Coleridge and J. D. Campbell draw attention to the surviving manuscript of 'a commentary on the Gospels and some of the Epistles'. See *Letters*, ii. 632 n., and Campbell, *Life*, 247 n. and 279 n.

[2] With his projected *opus maximum*, Coleridge was much preoccupied to the end of his life. The title and the proposed contents varied from time to time. In 1814 he entitled it 'Christianity the one true Philosophy—or 5 Treatises on the Logos' (Letter 951); early in 1815 he spoke of it as 'a large theological Work on Revelation' (Letter 955 A, Appendix B); later in the same year he called it the 'LOGOSOPHIA: or on the LOGOS, divine and human, in six Treatises' (Letter 976); and in 1820 he referred to it as the 'Assertion of Religion' (Letters 1253-4).

As the years passed, Coleridge became less sanguine concerning the completion of his projected work. 'I have no wish to have my life prolonged', he wrote to Green in Jan. 1828, 'but what is involved in the wish to complete the views, I have taken, of Life as beginning in separation from Nature and ending in Union with God, and to reduce to an *intelligible* if not artistical form the results of my religious, biblical and ecclesiastical Lucubrations.' So, too, in the same year we find him declaring: 'Completely have I been for some time past swallowed up in the one anxiety of arranging and increasing my huge pile of Manuscripts, so that the *substance* at least of the results of my ... studies and meditations for the last 20 years of my life might be found in a state capable of being published by my dear Friend Mr Green, who has for ten years devoted the only vacant day of every week to the participation of my labors.' (Letters 1613-14.) Thus it was that when Coleridge came to make his Will in Sept. 1829 he named J. H. Green his literary executor.

For a description of the surviving manuscripts of the *opus maximum*, both

on which my hopes of extensive and permanent Utility, of Fame in the noblest* sense of the word, mainly rest—that, by which I might

> As now by thee, by all the Good be known,
> When this weak frame lies moulder'd in it's grave,
> Which self-surviving I might call my own,
> Which Folly can not mar, nor Hate deprave—
> The Incense of those Powers which risen in flame
> Might make me dear to Him from whom they came!

of this work, to which all my other writings (unless I except my poems, and these I can exclude in part only) are introductory and preparative; and the result of which (if the premises be, as I with the most tranquil assurance am convinced, they are—insubvertible, the deductions legitimate, and the conclusions commensurate & only commensurate with both) must finally be a revolution of all that has been called *Philosophy* or Metaphysics in England and France since the aera of the commencing predominance of the mechanical system at the Restoration of our second Charles, and with this the present fashionable Views not only of Religion, Morals and Politics but even of the modern Physics and Physiology—You will not blame the earnestness of my expressions or the high importance which I attach to this work: for how with less noble objects & less faith in their attainment could I stand acquitted of folly and abuse of Time, Talent, and Learning in a Labor of 3 fourths of my *intellectual* Life?—of this work something more than a Volume has been dictated by me, so as to exist fit for the Press, to my friend and enlightened Pupil, Mr Green—and more than as much again would have been evolved & delivered to paper, but that for the last six or 8 months I have been compelled to break off our weekly Meetings from the necessity of writing (alas! alas! of *attempting* to write) for purposes and on the subjects of the passing Day.—Of my poetic works I would fain finish the Christabel—Alas! for the proud times when I planned, when I had present to my mind the materials as well as the Scheme of the Hymns, entitled Spirit, Sun, Earth, Air, Water, Fire, and Man: and the Epic Poem on what still appears to me the one only fit subject remaining for an Epic Poem, Jerusalem besieged & destroyed by Titus.[1]—

those in Coleridge's autograph and those in Green's handwriting, and for the text of certain extracts from them, see Alice D. Snyder, *Coleridge on Logic and Learning*, 1929, pp. xi, 3–9, and 127–38; and J. H. Muirhead, *Coleridge as Philosopher*, 1930, especially pp. 266–72 and 277–84. See also Letter 1795.

* Turn to Milton's Lycidas, with Stanza—'Alas! what boots it with incessant care' to the end of that paragraph. The sweetest music does not fall sweeter on my ear, than this Stanza on both mind & ear as often as I repeat it aloud. [Note by S. T. C.]

[1] The first mention of these Hymns occurs in a notebook entry of 1796; by

And here comes, my dear Allsop!—here comes my sorrow and my
weakness, my grievance and my confession. Anxious to perform the
duties of the day arising out of the wants of the day, these wants
too presenting themselves in the most painful of all forms, that of
a debt owing to those who will not exact and yet need it's payment
—and the delay, the long (not live-long but *death*-long) BEHIND-
HAND of my accounts to Friends whose utmost care and frugality on
the one side and industry on the other, the wife's Management & the
Husband's assiduity, are put in requisition to make both ends meet,
I am at once forbidden to attempt and too perplext effectually to
pursue, the *accomplishment* of the works worthy of me, those I mean
above enumerated—even if, savagely as I have been injured by one
of the two influencive Reviews & with more effective enmity undermined by the utter silence or occasional detractive compliments of
the other,† I had the probable chance of disposing of them to the
Booksellers so as even to liquidate my mere *Boarding* accounts
during the time expended in the transcription, arrangement, and
Proof-correction—and yet on the other hand my Heart & Mind are
for ever recurring to them—Yes! my Conscience forces me to plead
guilty—I have only by fits and starts even prayed, I have not even
prevailed on myself to pray to God in sincerity and entireness, for
the fortitude that might enable me to resign myself to the abandonment of all my Life's best Hopes—to say boldly to myself—'Gifted
with powers confessedly above mediocrity, aided by an Education
of which no less from almost unexampled Hardships & Sufferings
than from manifold & peculiar advantages I have never yet found a
Parallel, I have devoted myself to a Life of unintermitted Reading,
Thinking, Meditating and Observing—I have not only sacrificed all
wor[l]dly prospects of wealth & advancement but have in my inmost
soul stood aloof even from temporary Reputation—in consequence
of these toils & this self-dedication I possess a calm & clear consciousness that in many & most important departments of Truth

July 1802 they had become a 'mere Dream'. In Oct. 1802 Coleridge told Tom
Wedgwood that since his twentieth year he had 'meditated an heroic poem
on the Siege of Jerusalem by Titus'; in a notebook entry of Nov. 1803 both
the Hymns and the Destruction of Jerusalem are listed among his projected
works; and in a letter of Sept. 1816 he wrote of 'concentring' his powers on them.
In 1832 and again in 1833 Coleridge spoke of the destruction of Jerusalem as
'the only subject now remaining for an epic poem'. See *The Notebooks of
Samuel Taylor Coleridge*, ed. Kathleen Coburn, vol. i, 1957, items 174/G.169/*f25*
and 1646/21.392/*f84*; J. L. Lowes, *The Road to Xanadu*, 1930, pp. 75–78;
Letters 449, 464, and 1031; and *Table Talk*, 28 Apr. 1832 and 4 Sept. 1833.

† Neither my Literary Life (2 Vol.) nor Sibylline Leaves (1 Vol.) nor Friend
(3 Vol.) nor Lay-Sermons, nor Zapolya, nor Christabel, have ever been noticed
by the Quarterly Review, of which Southey is yet the main support.—
[Note by S. T. C.]

& Beauty I have outstrode my Contemporaries, those at least of
highest name—that the number of my printed works bears witness
that I have not been idle, and the seldom acknowleged but yet
strictly *proveable* effects of my labors appropriated to the immediate
welfare of my Age, in the Morning Post before, and during the Peace
of Amiens, in the Courier afterwards, and in the series & various
subjects of my Lectures, at Bristol, and at the Royal, & Surry
Institutions; in Fetter Lane; in Willis's Rooms; at the Crown &
Anchor &c (add to which the unlimited freedom of my communications in colloquial life) may surely be allowed as evidence that I
have not been useless in my generation; but from circumstances the
main portion of my Harvest is still on the ground, ripe indeed and
only waiting, a few for the sickle, but a large part only for the
sheaving, and carting and housing—but from all this I must turn
away, must let them rot as they lie, & be as tho' they never had been:
for I must go to gather Blackberries, and Earth Nuts, or pick mush-
rooms & gild Oak-Apples for the Palates & Fancies of chance
Customers.—I must abrogate the name of Philosopher, and Poet,
and scribble as fast as I can & with as little thought as I can for
Blackwood's Magazine, or as I have been employed for the last
days, in writing MSS sermons for lazy Clergymen who stipulate that
the composition must not be *more* than respectable, for fear they
should be desired to publish the Visitation Sermon!'—This I have
not yet had courage to do—My soul sickens & my Heart sinks—&
thus oscillating between both I do neither—neither as it ought to be
done, or to any profitable end. If I were to detail only the various, I
might say, capricious interruptions that have prevented the finishing of this very scrawl, begun on the very day I received your last
kind letter with the Hare, you would need no other illustrations—
　　Now I see but one possible plan of rescuing my permanent
Utility. It is briefly this & plainly. For what we struggle with inwardly, we find at least easiest to *bolt out*—namely, that of engaging
from the circle of those who think respectfully & hope highly of my
powers & attainments a yearly sum, for three or four years,
adequate to my actual Support with such comforts and decencies
of appearance as my Health & Habits have made necessaries, so
that my mind may be unanxious as far as the Present Time is concerned—that thus I should stand both enabled and pledged to begin
with some one work of those above mentioned, and for two thirds
of my whole Time to devote myself to this *exclusively* till finished—
to take the chance of it's success by the best mode of publication
that would involve me in no risk—then to proceed with the next,
& so on till the works above mentioned as already in full material
existence should be reduced into *formal* and actual Being—while in

the remaining third of my Time I might go on, maturing & com-
pleating my great work, &—for if but easy in mind I have no doubt
either of the re-awakening power or of the kindling inclination, my
Christabel & what else the happier Hour might inspire—& without
inspiration a Barrel organ may be played right deftly; but

> All otherwise the state of *Poet* stands:
> For lordly Want is such a tyrant fell,
> That where he rules, all power he doth expel.
> The vaunted verse a vacant head demands,
> Ne wont with crabbed Care the Muses dwell:
> *Unwisely weaves, who takes two webs* IN HAND!¹

Now Mr Green has offered to contribute from 30 to 40£ yearly for
3 or 4 years; my young Friend & Pupil, the Son of one of my dearest
old friends,² 50£; and I think that from 10 to 20£ I could rely on
from another—the sum required would be about 250£—to be repaid, of course, should the disposal or sale & as far as the disposal
& sale of my writings produce the means.—

I have thus placed before you at large & wanderingly as well as
diffusely, the statement which I am inclined to send in a compressed
form to a few of those, of whose kind dispositions towards me I have
received assurances—& to their interest & influence I must leave it
—anxious, however, before I do this, to learn from you your very
very inmost feeling & judgement, as to the previous questions—Am
I entitled, have I earned *a right*, to do this? Can I do it without
Moral degradation? and lastly—Can it be done without loss of
character in the eyes of my acquaintance & of my friends' acquaintance who may become informed of the circumstances?—That if
attempted at all, it will be attempted in such a way and that such
persons only will be spoken to, as will not expose me to indelicate
rebuffs to be afterwards matter of Gossip, I know those, to whom I
shall intrust the statement, too well, to be much alarmed about.—

Pray let me either see or hear from You as soon as possible. For
indeed and indeed, it is no inconsiderable accession to the pleasure,
I anticipate from disembarrassment, that *you* would have to contemplate in a more gracious form & in a more ebullient play of the
inward Fountain, the mind & manners of,

My dear Allsop, | Your obliged & very affectionate Friend
S. T. Coleridge

¹ *The Shepheardes Calender, October,* 97–102. Line 98 reads:
For lordly love is such a Tyranne fell.

² This was Charles Stutfield, Jr. It was apparently through Poole that Coleridge became acquainted with the elder Stutfield, 'a Wine & Brandy Merchant'.
See Letters 288, 1270, 1290, and 1300.

1229. *To Thomas Allsop*

Address: T. Allsop, Esqre | 1 Blandford Place | Pall Mall
MS. New York Public Lib. Pub. with omis. Letters, Conversations and Rec. *24.*
Postmark: Highgate, 8 April 1820.

Saturday [8 April 1820]
Highgate—

My dear Friend

It is not the least advantage of Friendship, that by communicating our thoughts to another we render them distinct to themselves [ourselves?], and reduce the subjects of our sorrow and anxiety to their just magnitude for our own contemplation. As long as we inly brood over a misfortune (there being no divisions or separate circumscriptions in things of mind, no proper beginning nor ending to any Thought, on the one hand; and on the other, the confluence of our recollections being determined far more by sameness or similarity of the Feelings that had been produced by them than by any positive resemblance or connection between the things themselves that are thus recalled to our attention) we establish a center as it were or sort of nucleus in the reservoir of the soul, and toward this needle shoots after needle, cluster-points on cluster-points, from all parts of the contained Fluid and in all directions, till the mind with it's best faculties is locked up in one ungenial Frost. I cannot adequately express the state of confused feeling, in which I wrote my last letter: the letter itself, I doubt not, bore evidence of it's *nest* and mode of incubation, as certain Birds & Lizards drag along with them part of the egg-shells from which they had forced their way. Still one good end was answered—I had made a clearance so far as to have my Head in Light & my Eyes open: and your answer, every way worthy of you, has removed the rest.—

But before I enter on this subject, permit [me] to refer to some points of *comparative* indifference lest I should forget them altogether.—I occasioned you to misconceive me respecting Sir W. Scott[1]—My purpose was to bring proofs of the inergetic, or inenergetic state of the minds of men induced by the excess and unintermitted action of stimulating events and circumstances, revolutions, battles, Newspapers, Mobs, Sedition & Treason Trials, public Harangues, Meetings, Dinners, the necessity in every individual of ever increasing activity & anxiety in the improvement of Estate, Trade, &c in proportion to the decrease of the actual value of money, to the multiplication of competitors, and to the almost compulsory expedience of Expence & Prominence even as the means of obtaining or retaining competence;—the consequent craving after amuse-

[1] Scott received his baronetcy on 30 Mar. 1820.

ment as proper *relaxation*, as *rest* freed from the tedium of vacancy, and again after such knowlege & such acquirements as are ready coin, that will pass *at once*, unweighed and unassayed; & the un-exampled Facilities afforded for this end by Reviews, Magazines, &c &c—The Theatres, to which few go to see *a Play* but to see Master Betty, or Mr Kean, or some one Individual in some *one* Part; & the single Fact, that our Neighbor, Matthews, night after night has taken more, than both the regular Theatres conjointly, & when the best Comedies or whole Plays have been acted at each House and those by excellent Comedians; would have yielded a striking instance & illustration of my position.[1] But I chose an example in literature as more in point for the subject of my particular remarks, & because every Man of Genius, who is born for his age & capable of acting *immediately* and widely on that age, must of necessity *reflect* the age in the first instance, tho' as far as he is a man of Genius, he will doubtless be himself *reflected* by it reciprocally.—Now I selected Scott for the very reason, that I do hold him for a man of *very extra-ordinary* powers; & when I say, that I have read the far greater part of his Novels twice, & several three times, over with undiminished pleasure and interest; and that in my reprobation of the Bride of Lammar Muir (with exception, however, of the almost Shak-spearian old *Witch-wives* at the Funeral) and of the Ivanhoe, I meant to imply the grounds of my admiration of the others, and the *permanent* nature of the Interest, which they excite.[2] In a word, I am far from thinking, that Old Mortality or Guy Mannering would have been less admired in the age of Sterne, Fielding & Richardson, than they are in the present times; but only that Sterne &c would not have had the same *immediate* popularity in the present day as in their own less stimulated & therefore less languid Reading-World. Of W. Scott's *poems* I cannot speak so highly; still less of the Poetry in his Poems:[3] tho' even in these the Power of presenting the most numerous Figures & Figures with the most complex movements & under rapid succession in *true picturesque Unity*, attests true and peculiar Genius.—You cannot imagine, with how much pain I used,

---

[1] Cf. Coleridge's remark to Allsop: 'For one person who has remarked or praised a beautiful passage in Walter Scott's works, a hundred have said, "How many volumes he has written!" So of Mathews: it is not "How admirable such and such parts are!" but, "It is wonderful that one man can do *all this!*" ' *Letters, Conversations and Rec.* 54.

[2] For the Coleridge marginalia written in Scott's novels see *Coleridge's Miscellaneous Criticism*, ed. T. M. Raysor, 1936, pp. 321–38.

[3] Cf. Coleridge's comment quoted by Allsop: 'Not twenty lines of Scott's poetry will ever reach posterity; it has relation to nothing.' *Letters, Conversations and Rec.* 104. For Coleridge's criticism of *The Lady of the Lake* see Letter 808.

many years ago, to hear Wordsworth's contemptuous Assertions
respecting Scott—& if I mistake not, I have yet the fragments of
the rough Draught of a Letter written by me on this subject so long
back as my first Lectures at the Lond. Phil. Society, Fetter Lane,
and on the backs of the unused admission Tickets.[1]—One more
remark. My criticism was *confined* to the *one* point of the higher
degree of intellectual Activity implied in the reading and admiration of Fielding, Richardson & Sterne—in moral, or if that be too
high and inwardly a word, in *mannerly* manliness of Taste the
present age and it's writers have the decided advantage, and I sincerely trust that Walter Scott's readers would be as little disposed
to relish the stupid letchery of the courtship of Widow Wadham
[Wadman] as Scott himself would be capable of presenting it. Add,
that tho' I cannot pretend to have found in any of these Novels a
character that even approaches in Genius, in truth of conception
or boldness & freshness of execution, to Parson Adams, Blifil, Strap,
Lieutenant Bowling, Mr Shandy, Uncle Toby, & Trim, Lovelace;
and tho' Scott's *female* characters will not, even the very best, bear
a comparison with Miss Byron, Emily, Clementina in Sir C. Grandison; nor the comic ones with Tabitha Bramble, or with Betty (in
Mrs Bennett's Beggar-girl)—and tho' by the use of the Scotch Dia-
lect, by Ossianic Mock-Highland Motley Heroic, & by extracts from
the printed Sermons, Memoirs, &c of the Fanatic Preachers, there
is a good deal of *false Effect*, & Stage trick; still the number of
characters *so good* produced by one man & in so rapid a succession,
must ever remain an illustrious phaenomenon in Literature, after
all the subtractions for those borrowed from English & German
Sources, or compounded by blending two or three of the Old Drama
into one—ex. gr. the Caleb in the Bride of Lammarmuir.—Scott's
great merit, and at the same [time] his *felicity*, and the true solution
of the long-sustained *interest* that Novel after novel excited, lie in
the nature of the subject—not merely, or even chiefly, because the
struggle between the Stuarts & the Presbyterians & Sectaries is still
in lively memory, & the passions of the adherency to the former if
not the adherency itself, extant in our own Fathers' or Grand-
fathers' times; nor yet (tho' this is of great weight) because the
language, manners, &c introduced are sufficiently different from our
own for *poignancy* & yet sufficiently near & similar for sympathy;
nor yet because, for the same reason, the Author speaking, reflecting, & describing in his own person remains still (to adopt a painter's phrase) in sufficient *keeping* with his subject matter, while his
characters can both talk and feel interestingly to *us* as men without
recourse to *antiquarian* Interest, & nevertheless without moral

[1] See Letter 845.

anachronism (—in all which points the Ivanhoe is so wofully the contrary—for what Englishman cares for Saxon or Norman, both brutal Invaders, more than for Chinese & Cochin-chinese?)—yet great as all these causes are, the essential wisdom & happiness of the Subject consists in this: that the contest between the Loyalists & their opponents can never be *obsolete*, for it is the contest between the two great moving Principles of social Humanity—religious adherence to the Past and the Ancient, the Desire & the admiration of Permanence, on the one hand; and the Passion for increase of Knowlege, for Truth as the offspring of Reason, in short, the mighty Instincts of *Progression* and *Free-agency*, on the other. In all subjects of deep and lasting Interest you will detect a struggle between two opposites, two polar Forces, both of which are alike necessary to our human Well-being, & necessary each to the continued existence of the other—Well therefore may we contemplate with intense feelings those whirlwinds which are, for free-agents, the appointed means & only possible condition of that *equi-librium*, in which our moral Being subsists: while the disturbance of the same constitutes our sense of Life. Thus in the ancient Tragedy the lofty Struggle between irresistible Fate & unconquerable Free Will, which founds it's equilibrium in the Providence & the Future Retribution of Christianity—. If instead of a contest between Saxons & Normans, or the Fantees & Ashantees,[1] a mere contest of Indifferents! of minim Surges in a boiling Fish-kettle! Walter Scott had taken the struggle between the Men of Arts & the Men of arms in the time of Becket, & made us feel how much to claim our well-wishing there was in the cause & character of the Priestly & Papal Party no less than in those of Henry & his Knights, he would have opened a new mine—instead of translating into Leadenhall Street Minerva Library Sentences a cento of the most common incidents of the stately, self-congruous Romances of D'Urfé, Scudéri &c—. N.B. I have not read the Monastery; but I suspect that the Thought or Element of the Faery Work is from the German. I perceive from that passage in the Old Mortality where Morton is discovered by old Alice [Alison] in consequence of calling his Dog, Elphin, that W.S. has been reading Tiek's Phantasus[2] (a collection of Faery or Witch Tales) from which both the incident & name is [are] borrowed.—I forget whether I ever mentioned to you that some 18 months ago I had planned & half-collected, half-manufactured & invented a work, to be entitled: THE WEATHER-BOUND TRAVELLERS: or Histories, Lays, Legends, Incidents, Anecdotes and Remarks contributed during a

---

[1] Coleridge refers to the Fanti and Ashanti Negroes of West Africa.
[2] Ludwig Tieck, *Phantasus. Eine Sammlung von Mährchen, Erzählungen, Schauspielen und Novellen*, 3 vols., 1812–16.

detention in one of the Hebrides—recorded by their Secretary, Lory McHaroldson, Senachy in the Isle of ——. The *principle* of the work I had thus exprest in the first chapter—'Tho' not *fact*, must it needs be *false*? These things have a truth of their own, if we but knew how to look for it. There is a *humanity* (meaning by this word whatever contradistinguishes *man*)—there is a humanity common to all periods of Life, which each period from childhood to Age has it's own way of representing. Hence in whatever layed firm hold of us in early Life there lurks an interest and a charm for our maturest years;[1] but which *He* will never draw forth who content with mimicking the unessential tho' natural defects of thought and expression has not the skill to remove the *childish*, yet leave the *childlike* untouched. Let each of us then relate that which has left the deepest impression on his mind, at whatever period of his life he may have seen, heard or read it; but let him tell it in accordance with the present state of his Intellect and Feelings, even as he has, perhaps, (Alnaschar-like) acted it over again by the parlour Fireside of a rustic Inn, with the Fire & the Candle for his only Companions.'—On the hope of my Lectures answering, I had intended to have done this work out of hand, dedicating the most genial Hours to the completion of Christabel, in the belief that in the former I should be rekindling the feeling, and recalling the state of mind, suitable to the latter.—But the Hope was vain.—

In stating the names and probable size of my Works, I by no means meant any reference to the mode of their publication. I merely wished to communicate to you the amount of my labors.—In two moderate Volumes it was my intention to comprize all those more prominent and systematic parts of my lucubrations on Shakspeare as should be published (in the first instance, at least) in the form of Books—& having selected & arranged these to send the more particular illustrations, and analyses to some respectable Magazine.—In like manner, I proposed to include the philosophical critiques on Dante, Milton, Cervantes &c in a series of Letters entitled, The Reviewer in Exile: or Critic confined to an old Library—. Provided, the Truths (which are, I dare affirm, original & all tending to the same Principles & proving the endless fertility of true Principle, & the decision and power of growth which it communicates to all the faculties of the mind) are but in existence, & to be read by such as might wish to read—I have no vanity as to the mode—nay, should prefer that mode which most multiplied the

[1] Cf. Coleridge's translation of Schiller's *The Piccolomini*, II. iv. 116–18:
a deeper import
Lurks in the legend told my infant years
Than lies upon that truth, we live to learn.

chances—So too as to the order—For *many* reasons it has been my wish to commence with the theological Letters: one & not the least is the strong desire I have, to put you & Hartley & Derwent Coleridge in full possession of my whole Christian Creed, [with the grounds of reason][1] and Authority on which it rests; but especially to unfold the true 'glorious Liberty of the Gospel' by shewing the distinction between Doctrinal Faith & it's Sources, and Historical Belief, with their reciprocal action on each other; and thus on the one hand to do away the servile superstition, which makes men *Bibliolaters* & yet hides from them the proper excellencies, the one continued revelation, of the Bible-documents which they idolize, & on the other hand to expose in it's native Worthlessness the so-called evidences of Christianity first brought into *toleration* by Arminius, and into fashion by Grotius and the Socinian Divines. For as such I consider all those who preach & teach in the Spirit of Socinianism, tho' even in the outward form of a Defence of the 39 Articles.—

I have been interrupted by the arrival of my Sons, Hartley and Derwent, the latter of whom I had not seen for so dreary a time[2]— I promise myself great pleasure in introducing him to you—Hartley, I seem to remember, you have already met. Indeed, I am so desirous of this, that I will defer what I have to add that I may put this letter in the post, time enough for you to receive it this evening —saying only, that it was not my purpose to have had any further communication on the subject but with Mr Frere—& with *him* only as with a counsellor—. Let me see you as soon as you can, & as often. I shall be better able hereafter to talk with you than to write to you, on the contents of your last. Enough at present, that I trust that much less than the sacrifices, you are disposed to make but

[1] MS. cut off; the words in brackets supplied from the printed text.
[2] Coleridge had last seen Derwent in Mar. 1812. As early as July 1817, however, he had discussed with J. H. Frere the possibility of entering Derwent at Cambridge. Frere had offered 'all his interest'. In the following month Coleridge asked Mrs. Coleridge whether she could contrive to send Derwent to Highgate by October. On leaving school in 1817, however, Derwent pursued a different course. Acting on the advice of Southey and Wordsworth, but without consulting his father, he accepted a two-year appointment as private tutor in a Lancashire family. Because of his age—'he was but just turned of 17'— Mrs. Coleridge reluctantly agreed to this arrangement. She also questioned the prudence of sending him to the University at this time, probably for the same reason. Two years later, on 3 Oct. 1819, she 'had a letter from S.T.C. desiring to see Derwent *immediately*—with an intention of sending him off to Cambridge in November'. Derwent, however, could not relinquish his position in Lancashire on such short notice. Thus it was Apr. 1820 before he arrived at Highgate. Within a month he was admitted to St. John's College, Cambridge. True to his promise, Frere contributed financial assistance. See Letters 858, 1070, 1076, 1094, 1193, 1204, 1238, and 1286; *Minnow among Tritons*, ed. Stephen Potter, 1934, pp. 51 and 84; and *Letters of Hartley Coleridge*, 57.

which I could not see my way of duty at all clear in permitting, will suffice for the realizing of such wishes as Duty prescribes or authorizes in your

very affectionate & obliged Friend,

S. T. Coleridge

1230. *To Thomas Allsop*

Address: T. Allsop, Esqre | Blandford Place | Pall Mall
MS. New York Public Lib. Pub. with omis. Letters, Conversations and Rec. *21.*
Postmark: Highgate, 10 April 1820.

10 April, 1820. Highgate—

My dear Friend

May I venture to obtrude a business on you, which I cannot entrust to a messenger, much less to the Post?—Sackville Street, Piccadilly, is not, I hope, more than 15 or 20 minutes' walk from your House.—It is, to enquire if Mr Caldwell is *in town*: if he be, then to leave the Letter, & that is all. But if not, to learn whether he is at his Living, and to take down the direction, and transferring the same to the inclosed to drop it into the nearest General Post-Office Box.[1] It is of serious importance to Derwent that the Letter should reach Mr Caldwell, and with as little delay as possible: or, I need not say, I should not have taxed your time & kindness, merely to make a Letter Carrier of you.

On Saturday Evening I received a note from Matthews which I have inclosed. I took it very kind of him; but to obtrude myself on Walter Scott, nolentem volentem, and within a furlong of my own abode, as he knows (for Mr Frere told him my address) was a liberty, I had no right to take: and tho' it would have highly gratified me to have conversed with a Brother-bard, & to have renewed on the mental retina the image of perhaps the most extraordinary Man, assuredly the most extraordinary *Writer*, of his Age, yet I dared not purchase the gratification at so high a price, as that of risking the respect, which, I trust, has not hitherto been forfeited by,

my dear Allsop, | Your obliged & very affectionate | Friend

S. T. Coleridge.

P.S. Tho' I had not the least expectation, yet I could not suppress a sort of fluttering Hope, that my Letter might have reached you on Saturday Night, & that you might be disengaged & turn your Sunday walk Highgate-ward. You will be delighted with the affectionate attachment of the two Brothers to each other, the boyish high

[1] Mr Caldwell's address is No. 15, Sackville St, if my memory does not cheat me. [Note by S. T. C. written at top of page one of MS.]

(38)

spirits with manly independence of intellect, and in one word with
the simplicity which is their Nature, and the common *ground* on
which the differences of their minds and characters (for no two can
be more distinct) shoot & play. When I say, that nothing can exceed their fondness for their Father, I need not add, that they are
impatient to be introduced to *you*: and I can offer no better testimony of the rank you hold in my Bosom, my dear Allsop, than the
gladness with which I anticipate their becoming your *Friends* in the
noblest sense of the word. Would to Heaven, their dear Sister were
with us—the cup of paternal Joy would be full to the Brim! The
rapture, with which both Hartley & Derwent talk of her, quite
affects Mrs Gillman, who has always felt with a sort of lofty yet
refined enthusiasm respecting the relations of an only Sister to her
Brothers— . . .[1] Of all women, I ever knew, Mrs G. is the woman
who seems to have been framed by Nature for a Heroine in that rare
species of Love, which subsists in a tri-unity of the Heart, the Moral
sense, and the faculty corresponding to what Spurzheim calls the
organ of *Ideality*.[2] What in other women is *Refinement* exists in her
as by implication and a fortiori in a native *Fineness* of character.
She often presents to my mind the best parts of the Spanish Santa
Teresa Ladyhood of Nature.[3]—

VEXATION!—and Mrs Gillman has this moment burnt Mr Matthews's Note.—But I must not say any more about it: for Mrs G.
now sees that it was very unlucky—the purport, however, was this
—Dear Sir I have this moment received a note from Terry,[4] informing [me] that Sir W. Scott will do me the honor of calling on me
tomorrow morning (i.e. Sunday) at ½ M—Will you contrive to be
here at the same time?—Perhaps, the promise of having your company may induce Sir Walter to do me the honor of appointing a day,
on which he will dine with me before he returns to the North.—
Now as Scott had asked Terry on his first arrival in town for my
address, it is not *impossible* tho' not very probable, that Terry may
have said—'& you will meet with Coleridge at Matthews's'—tho' I
was not entitled to presume this.—The bottom of all this, my dear
Allsop! is neither more or less than as follows—I seem to feel that
I *ought* to feel more desire to see an extraordinary Man than I

[1] Two and three-fourths lines heavily inked out in MS.
[2] For Coleridge's comments on the phrenological theories of J. C. Spurzheim
(1776–1832), see Letter 1463 n.: *Aids to Reflection*, 1825, p. 147 n.; and *Table
Talk*, 24 June 1827 and 29 July 1830.
[3] A copy of *The Works of the Holy Mother St. Teresa of Jesus*, 1669–75,
containing annotations by Coleridge is in the Pierpont Morgan Library. Some
of the marginalia are published in *Literary Remains*, iv. 65–71.
[4] Daniel Terry (1780?–1829), actor and playwright.

really do feel—& I dread appearing to two or three persons (as the
Mr Freres, William Rose &c) as if I cherished any dislike to Scott
respecting the *Christabel*[1]—& generally speak[ing], an increasing
dislike to appear out of the common & natural mode of thinking &
acting—. All this is, I own, s[ad] weakness——but I am weary of
Dyspathy.—

1231. To C. A. Tulk

MS. formerly in the possession of the late Oliver R. Barrett. Hitherto unpublished.

Highgate
Wednesday Noon—[12 April 1820][2]

My dear Sir
  I cannot communicate any pleasant tidings respecting my Health
or Spirits: nor expect that I shall be able to do so till I have brought
my Son's affairs at least, if not my *individual* own, to a settlement.
A few days, however, will decide this. In the intervals of writing I
have won some hours from anxious thought in the more careful
reperusal of different parts of the two Volumes, particularly the
Memorable Transactions.[3] The only important question between
us may be thus stated: Is it required to believe, that the Agents,
Modes of Being, Thinking, and Feeling of the spiritual State are *in
themselves*, independently of the *perspective*, i.e. the mind *by* which,
& the state & point of view *from* which, they are contemplated,
such & wholly such as they appeared to Emanuel? Or is it enough
to believe, that they are such, as would according to the laws of
Spirit assume those forms and as it were translate themselves into
that visual & auditual Language to a Soul still connected with the
present Dispensation?—
  But of this, hereafter. I write now to solicit and intreat your &
Miss Julia's kind offices in favor of my truly excellent & enlightened
Neighbor, Mr Hurwitz—and I have sent the Book, which we so
earnestly wish to have presented to his Majesty.[4] Perhaps, if Miss

---

  [1] For details concerning Scott's knowledge and use of *Christabel* previous to
its publication, see Letters 632, 650, 708, 808, 845, 981, 1413, and 1448.
  [2] This and the preceding letter were written shortly after Derwent Coleridge
arrived at Highgate on 8 Apr., and at a time when Coleridge was arranging to
enter him at Cambridge. See Letters 1229–30 and 1238.
  [3] Coleridge apparently refers to the 'Memorable Relations' appearing in
Swedenborg's *The True Christian Religion*. See Letter 1225.
  [4] The present letter was sent to Tulk in an effort to place in the hands of
George IV a copy printed on white satin of *The Tears of a Grateful People, A
Hebrew Dirge & Hymn, Chaunted in the Great Synagogue, St. James's Place,
Aldgate, on the Day of the Funeral of His late most Sacred Majesty King George III*

Julia would shew it to her R. H. (that is, supposing she apprehended no impropriety in so doing) her Royal Highness might graciously suggest some channel, in which under the passport of Her Royal Highness's desire it might secure it's arrival at it's august destination.—A week or more having elapsed since the most respectful application was made (by letter) to Sir Benjamin Blomefield,[1] and no answer vouchsafed—this we must consider as res infecta—. In short, you will greatly oblige me by taking this into your own & submitting it to the Ladies' Consideration, and on your decision will depend, of course, your retaining of the Copy on the ground of Hope, or the returning of the same. I am, I confess, exceedingly desirous that so good and loyal a purpose should not be baffled by mere want of interest with any of the Stars, that shine near the Throne.

Present my most respectful and affectionate Regards to your dear Lady, my best remembrances to Miss De Soires, and my Love to John, Caroline, and Marmaduke, God bless him—and with the most heart-felt wishes & prayers for the Happiness, and Well-being of you and your's, believe me,
My dear Sir, | your very sincere & as obliged | so grateful Friend,
S. T. Coleridge

P.S. Should you not be at home, I have ordered the Messenger to wait for an hour or two—

P.S. I am sure, that the Ladies will admire the beauty of this Offering. I never saw a more elegant work in point of character & writing.

1232. *To Samuel Mence*[2]

MS. Mr. W. Hugh Peal. Hitherto unpublished.

Monday Evening.—[May 1820 ?][3]
My dear Sir
If nothing unforeseen step in between my lip & the promised cup, I shall not fail to avail myself of your kind invitation for Saturday.

of Blessed Memory. By Hyman Hurwitz, of Highgate. Translated into English Verse, by a Friend [S. T. Coleridge]. A second copy also printed on white satin and inscribed by Hurwitz, 'S. T. Coleridge, e dono Autoris, 15 March, 1820', is now in the British Museum. See T. J. Wise, *Two Lake Poets . . .*, 1927, p. 85. See also *Poems*, i. 436.

[1] Benjamin Bloomfield (1768–1846), private secretary to George IV.
[2] Samuel Mence (1781–1860), B.A., Trinity College, Oxford, 1802, B.D., 1814, and fellow until 1815, was appointed schoolmaster of Cholmeley's Free Grammar School at Highgate in 1816. In this capacity he served as the preacher in the school chapel. See headnote to Letter 1276.
[3] The paper on which this letter is written bears a watermark of 1820.

And seeing me writing, Mrs Gillman commissions me to give her &
Mr Gillman's acknowlegements to Mrs Mence & yourself, & that
they too will do themselves the pleasure of waiting on you. I am at
present . . . [Remainder of MS. missing.]

1232A. *To Unknown Correspondent*[1]

MS. formerly in the possession of the late T. S. Eliot. Hitherto unpublished.

[May 1820 ?]

My dear Madam
  Be so good as to let the Boy have the Undina[2] and the Huber on
the Ants,[3] if they are within *your* Reach—I lent both to HARTLEY
—the one being Mrs Gillman's & the other Mr Stanley's,[4] both of
whom have asked me more than once.—
  I was quite affected to see how unwell Miss B. looked—I am myself unusually unwell, with a recurrence of my stomach irritability
—Will Mr M. call in this evening & rubberize?—Truly
                                                         S. T. C.

1233. *To Thomas Boosey and Sons*

Address: Messrs. Boosey & Sons | Booksellers | Broad Street
MS. Yale University Lib. Pub. Yale University Library Gazette, *July 1947, p. 8.*
Postmark: 10 May 1820.

[10 May 1820]

Dear Sirs
  It is a duty I owe to truth and to myself that I should let you
know, that in diverting my time and labor from an original work,
on which I am now employed, (should this be the case) I have no
one earthly *motive*, and no other *impulse* but the pleasure, I should
have, in being of any real service to you, and the pain and reluctance I feel in refusing you any thing which I could, without
wronging myself and those connected with me, grant. Within the
last two months I have declined two offers, each from a different
person, to furnish critical materials on any work, I myself chose, at

  [1] This letter may have been intended for Mrs. Milne, a Highgate neighbour.
If so, the Miss B. mentioned in the letter would be Betsy Bullock, Mrs. Milne's
sister. It seems likely that Letter 1192 was addressed to Miss Bullock rather
than Charlotte Brent. See Letters 1030, 1178, 1202, 1257, and 1281. In Dec.
1818 Coleridge had asked the Milnes to lend him a copy of Shakespeare's *The
Tempest.* See Letter 1164.
  [2] F. H. K. de la Motte Fouqué's *Undine,* 1811, was first translated into
English by George Soane in 1818. See also Letter 1250.
  [3] Pierre Huber's work on ants was first translated into English in 1820.
See note to Letter 1260.
  [4] Evidently a Highgate neighbour. See Letters 1123 and 1192.

twenty guineas per sheet, the size &c that of the Edingburgh and
Quarterly Reviews. My reason for this was my dislike to writing *for*
any thing or any one, and the request of my best friends founded
on the conviction, that it is at once my interest and my duty to
bring into *publishable* form, one after the other, the entire works,
the component parts of which are already in my own papers, or
those of the Short-hand Writer.—

But there is another objection to the present proposal, to which
I dare not blind myself. If I have rightly understood you, you wish
to have no more *Leaves* of Letter-press, than Prints—allowing only
two or three additional for the introduction.[1] Now had this been
consequent on a Translation of the entire Faust under my Name,
with the substitutes for the passages morally or prudentially un-
translatable; I should in this case feel no impropriety in abridging the
tale and applying it to the illustration of the Plates.[2] But as it is, I

[1] Nothing came of the proposal to have Coleridge prepare a commentary for
an edition of Moritz Retzsch's illustrations to Goethe's *Faust*, but in 1820
Boosey and Sons published *Ret[z]sch's Series of Twenty-Six Outlines, illustrative
of Goethe's Tragedy of Faust, engraved from the originals by Henry Moses. And
an Analysis of the Tragedy.* When Goethe inquired who had prepared the
analysis, Boosey replied: 'The Author, or rather compiler of the Analysis, is a
German in humble circumstances, a man of no little ability, and possessing
a very considerable knowledge of the English language.' *Yale University
Library Gazette*, July 1947.

[2] That Coleridge was interested in Boosey's proposal is evidenced by the
following holograph in the Huntington Library. The MS. is inserted in a copy
of *The Life, Letters and Literary Remains of Edward Bulwer, Lord Lytton. By
his Son*, 2 vols., 1883, ii. 278.

My Advice & Scheme

S. T. Coleridge—
12 May 1820

1. A preliminary Essay, stating *briefly* the peculiar character of Goethe,
as man, philosopher, & poet; more at large, the specific character of his
Faust, including it's *purposes*, & the tone of mind presupposed in the Reader
as well as it's form of *Style*, Humor of Pathos, Imagery, &c. Then to explain
it's *Nationality* as a German Poem, with it's high merit on this very account
—it is, perhaps, the only properly *original* work of German Poesy, & with
the Louisa of Voss the most *national*—but from these very causes, especially
the state of mind in those, whom Goethe had a right to calculate on as his
readers, & the *inclosed* number of those Readers, often most unfit, & in large
portions uninteresting to the English Public.—

2. Exactly such an analysis of the Work from Scene to Scene, as we have
a delicious model of, in Gray's Anal. of the BIRDS of Aristophanes, in 2nd
Volume of Matthias's Edition of Gray's Works.

3. Interspersed *in* the analysis, beautiful or otherwise noticeable, yet
inoffensive, passages, translated in the manner & metre of the original: as
far as would be acceptable to the English Ear.

4. Each of the Scenes entire, exceptionable Lines excluded, on which
Retch's Plates are founded—translated poetically as . . . [MS. torn]

[S.] T. C.

scarce know how to ward off the notion, that I am connecting my name with a work in bad repute with the religious part of the Community without having space or opportunity to explain myself. What have the Purchasers of the PRINTS to do with the poetic or moral merits or demerits of the Poem? All, they want, is the *Story*: and *this*, any man of common sense who can write English & read German can do as well as I—Nor is that all. For such is my inveterate habit of doing as well as possibly *I* can whatever I do at all, that many other men could do it in half the time, & with less than half the tro[uble,] and perhaps having nothing in hand which this would interrupt would be amply repaid by a sum, it would be perfectly convenient to you to offer & yet a wrong to myself to accept.—

However this be, as I am quite certain that I have no trading feelings; that I never *have* derived & never shall derive any *advantage* from bargaining—so am I quite determined that I never will suffer any of it's contingent Mortifications or awkwardnesses. I never will subject myself to the chance of a refusal—or place myself under any other necessity but that of answering, Yes or No.— Without my name I should feel the objections & the difficulty greatly diminished, but to give *my name* to the mere Letter-press subservient to productions of an art not connected with my own pursuits—this, I more than fear, my Friends & Family will regard as a sort of Job-work, which they would not like to see *authored* by— your's sincerely,

S. T. Coleridge[1]—

1234. *To Mr. Chisholm*

Address: Mr Chisholme
MS. National Library of Scotland. Pub. Review of English Studies, *October 1934, p. 453.*

[May 1820][2]

Dear Sir
On Mrs Gillman's return from a call, I found that Mr G. had a party of Friends invited on Sunday next, and among them my Son

[1] On the fourth page of the MS. of Coleridge's letter there appears a rough draft of Boosey's reply, which is published in the *Yale University Library Gazette.*

[2] On 24 June Coleridge wrote that he had received invitations from the Chisholms 'twice in the course of the last month' and that on both occasions he 'was obliged to send an apology'. The present letter, which is written on paper watermarked 1820, was probably the first apology, Letter 1239 being the second.

and an Oxford Friend of his & Derwent's, & the latter (a Mr Burton,[1] Fellow of Exeter) for the express purpose of meeting *me*. Mrs Gillman will not leave Highgate till Tuesday.

I regret that the Day most at your own disposal, indeed the only one that 'a man of the law' can command (Sunday, I mean) should be the Day on which Mr & Mrs Gillman most expect to see their London Friends—the greater number indeed on that day only.

With our best Compliments to Mrs Chisholm & Miss Hall
your's, dear Sir, | with respect & regard
S. T. Coleridge

1235. *To J. H. Green*

Address: J. H. Green, Esqre | Surgeon | Lincoln's Inn Fields
MS. Pierpont Morgan Lib. Pub. with omis. Letters, *ii. 706.*
Postmark: Highgate, 25 May 1820.

[25 May 1820]

My dear Green

I was greatly affected in finding, how ill you had been: and long ere this should have let you know it, but that I have myself been in no usual degree unwell. I wish, I could with truth underline the words, *have been*: & in the hope of being able to do it was, that I delayed answering your Note. Unless a speedy change for the better takes place, I should culpably deceive myself if I did not interpret my present state as a *summons*. God's Will be done! I cannot pretend, that I have not received countless Warnings; and for my neglect and for the habits, and all the feebleness and wastings of the moral will, which unfit the soul for spiritual ascent, and must sink it, of moral necessity, lower and lower, if it be essentially imperishable, my only ray of Hope is *this*: that in my inmost heart, as far as my consciousness can sound it's depths, I plead nothing but my utter & sinful helplessness & worthlessness on one side, and the infinite Mercy and divine Humanity of our Creator and Redeemer crucified from the Beginning of the World, on the other! I use no comparatives nor indeed could I ever charitably interpret the penitential phrases (I am the vilest of Sinners, worse than the wickedest of my fellow-men &c.) otherwise than as Figures of speech, the whole purport of which is: in relation to God I appear to myself the same as the very worst man, if such there be, would appear to an earthly Tribunal. I mean no comparatives: for what have a man's

---

[1] Robert Burton, 'a man of the highest principles, and the most spotless life', had won a double first class at Oxford. 'He died young, after having commenced a successful career as a lawyer.' See *Poems by Hartley Coleridge*, ed. Derwent Coleridge, 2 vols., 1851 (2nd edn.), i, pp. lxviii–lxix.

permanent concerns to do with comparison? What avails it to a Bird shattered and irremediably disorganized in one wing, that another Bird is similarly conditioned in both wings? Or to a man in the last stage of ulcerated Lungs that his neighbor is Liver-rotten as well as consumptive? Both find their equation, the Birds as to Flight, the Men as to Life. In o o o's there is no comparison.

My nephew, the Revd. W. Hart Coleridge, came & stayed here from Monday afternoon to Tuesday Noon, in order to make Derwent's Acquaintance, & brought with him by accident Marsh's Divinity Lecture, No. 3rd.—on the authenticity and credibility of the Books collected in the New Testament.[1] As I could not sit with the party after Tea, I took the Pamphlet with me into my Bedroom, and gave it an attentive perusal. Knowing the Bishop's intimate acquaintance with the investigations of Eichhorn, Paulus, & their numerous scarcely less celebrated Scholars, & myself familiar with the works of the Göttingen Professor (Eichhorn) the Founder and Head of this daring School,[2] I saw, or seemed to see, more *management* in the Lecture, than proof of thorough conviction. I supplied, however, from my own reasonings enough of what appeared wanting or doubtful in the Bishop's to justify the conclusion—that the Gospel *History* beginning with the Baptism of John, and the Doctrines contained in the fourth Gospel, and in the Epistles, truly represent the assertions of the Apostles and the Faith of the Christian church during the first century; that there exists no tenable or even tolerable ground for doubting the *authenticity* of the Books ascribed to John the Evangelist, to Mark, to Luke, and to Paul; nor the *authority* of Matthew & the Author of the Epistle to the Hebrews; & lastly, that a man need only have common sense & a good heart to be assured, that these Apostles and Apostolic men wrote nothing but what they themselves *believed.*—And yet I have no hesitation in avowing, that many an argument derived from the nature of Man, nay, that many a strong tho' only *speculative* probability, pierces deeper, pushes more home, and clings more pressingly to my Mind than the whole sum of merely *external* evidence, the *fact* of Christianity itself alone excepted. Nay, I feel that the external evidence derives a great and lively accession of force, for my mind, from my previous speculative convictions or pre-

[1] Coleridge refers to Herbert Marsh (1757–1839), bishop of Llandaff, 1816, Peterborough, 1819. In 1820 Marsh published *The Authenticity of the New Testament.*

[2] Coleridge's annotated copies of the following works of J. G. Eichhorn are in the British Museum: *Einleitung ins Alte Testament*, 3 parts, 1787 (2nd edn.); *Einleitung in das Neue Testament*, 3 vols., 1804–14; *Einleitung in die apokryphischen Schriften des Alten Testaments*, 1795; and *Commentarius in Apocalypsin Joannis*, 2 vols., 1791.

sumptions; but that I cannot find that the latter are at all strengthened or made more or less probable to me by the former. Besides,
as to the external evidence I make up my mind *once for all*, and
merely *as* evidence think no more about it; but those facts or reflections thereon which tend to change belief into *in*sight, never lose
their effect, any more than the distinctive *sensations* of Disease,
compared with a mere *perceived* correspondence of Symptoms with
the Diagnostics of a medical Book.

I was led to this remark by reflecting on the aweful importance of
the physiological Question (so generally decided one way by the
late most popular writers on Insanity)—Does the efficient cause of
Disease and disordered Action, & collectively of Pain & Perishing,
lie entirely in the Organs? so that, namely, if you could suppose that,
my own proper Principle of Life being awhile suspended, some other
plastic Spirit should reconstruct my body & thoroughly repair the
defective organs, and then re-awakening the active principle in me
depart—that all pain and disease would be removed, and I should
stand in the same state as I stood in previous to all Sickness & to
the admission of any disturbing forces into my nature? Or on the
contrary would such a repaired Organismus be no fit Organ for my
Life, as if, for instance, a *worn* Lock with an equally worn key were
exchanged for a perfect Fac Simile of the same Lock, such as it was
when it was new, the Key might no longer fit the Lock?—The repaired
Organs *might* from intimate incorrespondence be the causes of Tor-
ture, and madness.—A system of Materialism, in which Organization stands first, whether composed by Nature or God, & Life &c
as it's *results*; (even as the Sound is the result of a Bell)—such a
system would, doubtless, remove great part of the terrors which the
Soul makes out of itself; but then it removes the Soul too, or rather
precludes it. And a supposition of co-existence, without any wech-
selwirkung, it is not in our power to adopt in good earnest; or if we
did, it would answer no purpose. For which of the two, Soul or
Body, am I to call '*I*'?—Again, a soul separate from the body, and
yet *entirely passive* to it, would be so like a Drum playing a Tattoo
on the Drummer, that one can not build any *hope* on it.—If then
the organization be, primarily, the *result*, & only by re-action a
cause, it would be well to consider what the cases are, in this life,
in which the restoration of the organization removes Disease—Is
the *organization* ever restored, except as continually reproduced—?
And are not the *majority* of instances cases of removal of mechanical
or chemical obstructions *from* the organization? And in the remaining number are they not cases into which the Soul never entered as a *conscious*, or rather as a moral *conscionable*, Agent?—The
regular re-production of Scars, Marks, &c; the increased suscepti-

bility of Disease in an Organ, after a perfect apparent restoration
to healthy structure & action; the insusceptibility in other cases,
as in the variolous; these & many others, are fruitful subjects—
and even imperfect as the Induction may & must be in our present
degree of knowlege, we might yet deduce that a Suicide under the
domination of disorderly Passions and erroneous Principles plays a
desperately hazardous game, and that the chance is, he may re-
house himself in a worse Hogshead with the nails and spikes driven
inward—or sinking below the organizing power be employed fruit-
lessly in a horrid *appetite* of re-skinning himself, after he had succeeded in *fleaing* his Life & leaving all it's sensibilities bare to the
incursive powers without even the cortex of a nerve to shield them
—Would it not follow too from these considerations, that a redemptive power must be necessary if immortality be true & Man be a disordered Being? And that no power can be redemptive which does
not at the same time act in the ground of the Life as one with the
ground, i.e. must act *in* my Will and not merely *on* my will; and yet
extrinsically, as an outward Power, i.e. as that which *outward*
Nature is to the Organization, viz. the causa correspondens et con-
ditio perpetua ab extra?—Under these views I cannot read the
VIth Chapter of St John without great emotion. The redeemer cannot be *merely* God—unless we adopt Pantheism, i.e. deny the existence of a God; & yet God he must be, for whatever is less than
God, may act *on*, but cannot act in, the Will of another—Christ
must become Man—but he cannot become *us*, except as far as we
become *him*—& this we cannot do but by *assimilation*: and assimilation is a *vital real* act, not a notional or merely intellective one.
There are phaenomena, which are phaenomena relatively to our
present 5 senses—& these Christ forbids us to understand as his
meaning, & collectively they are entitled the Flesh that perishes.
But does it follow, that there are no other Phaenomena? or that
these other media of manifestation might not stand to a spiritual
world & to our enduring Life in the same relation as our visible
Mass of Body stands to the World of the Senses & to the sensations
correspondent to, & excited by, the stimulants of that World?—
Lastly, would not the sum of the latter phaenomena (the spiritual)
be appropriately named, the Flesh and Blood of the divine Humanity? If Faith be a mere apperception, eine blosse *Wahr*nehmung:
this, I grant, is senseless. For it is evident, that the assimilation in
question is to be carried on by Faith. But if Faith be an energy, a
positive *Act*, and that too an *Act* of intensest power—why should
it necessarily differ in toto genere from any other *Act*, ex. gr. from
that of the animal Life in the stomach?—It will be found easier to
laugh or stare at the Question, than to prove it's irrationality.—

Enough for the present.—I had been told that Dr Leach[1] was a Lawrencian,[2] a materialist & I know not what—I met him at Mr

[1] William Elford Leach (1790–1836), naturalist.

[2] By 'Lawrencian' Coleridge refers to a disciple of William Lawrence (1783–1867). Lawrence had been engaged in a 'hot controversy' with John Abernethy (1764–1831). (See Letter 1186.) In 1814 Abernethy published *An Enquiry into the Probability and Rationality of Mr. Hunter's Theory of Life*. This interpretation of the writings of John Hunter was attacked by Lawrence in his first course of lectures delivered at the Royal College of Surgeons in 1815 and published as *An Introduction to Comparative Anatomy and Physiology* in the following year. For a brief summary of this controversy see Alice D. Snyder, *Coleridge on Logic and Learning*, 1929, pp. 16–25 and 31–32.

Coleridge not only followed this 'medico-philosophical' dispute with the greatest interest, but he was led to expound his own idea of life. In 1816 he tried to point out to Abernethy that as long as he 'clung' to certain points 'so long he would lay himself bare to the attacks of Lawrence, and the Materialists'. (Letter 1096.) By 10 Nov. 1816, as his letter to Gillman shows, Coleridge had 'written, or dictated' part of his 'Essay' on the *Theory of Life*. This treatise was probably completed soon afterwards. In his Introduction to the *Theory of Life* Coleridge writes: 'That the true idea of Life existed in the mind of John Hunter I do not entertain the least doubt.' Yet Hunter failed 'fully to unfold and arrange' his idea in clear conceptions, and in his writings 'the light' only 'occasionally flashes upon us'. In the *Theory of Life* Coleridge cites passages from Lawrence's lectures published in 1816 and states his objections to them. Of Abernethy he speaks more favourably: 'In Mr. Abernethy's Lecture on the Theory of Life, it is impossible not to see a presentiment of a great truth.' On the other hand, he points out that Abernethy had not brought the subject 'into full and open view'. In *The Friend*, 1818, iii. 179–80, Coleridge again introduces the name of Hunter: 'In his printed works, the one directing thought seems evermore to flit before him, twice or thrice only to have been seized, and after a momentary detention to have been again let go. . . . Yet notwithstanding the imperfection in the annunciation of the idea, how exhilarating have been the results! We dare appeal to ABERNETHY.' By the time he was reading proof for the third volume of *The Friend*, however, Coleridge had already read Abernethy's *Physiological Lectures* of 1817, and felt impelled to include the following note:

> Since the first delivery of this sheet, Mr. Abernethy has realized this anticipation, dictated solely by the writer's wishes, and at that time justified only by his general admiration of Mr. A.'s talents and principles; but composed without the least knowledge that he was then actually engaged in proving the assertion here hazarded, at large and in detail. See his eminent 'Physiological Lectures,' lately published in one volume octavo.

For Coleridge's preoccupation with the theory of life, see *The Philosophical Lectures of Samuel Taylor Coleridge*, ed. Kathleen Coburn, 1949, Lecture XII; and the two 'Monologues' Coleridge dictated to his philosophical class in 1822, published in *Fraser's Magazine*, Nov. and Dec. 1835. (Letter 1290.) See J. H. Muirhead, *Coleridge as Philosopher*, 1930, pp. 118–36; and Letters 1072, 1077, 1096, and 1186. See also Craig W. Miller, 'Coleridge's Concept of Nature', *Journal of the History of Ideas*, Jan.–Mar. 1964, pp. 77–96.

A manuscript of Coleridge's *Theory of Life*, not in his handwriting but containing corrections by him, remained among Gillman's papers. Eventually it came into the possession of James Gillman, Jr. The younger Gillman placed the manuscript at the disposal of a former schoolfellow, Seth B. Watson, who

Abernethie's, & with sincere delight I found him the very contrary in every respect. Except yourself, I have never met so enlarged or so bold a love of Truth in an English Physiologist. The few minutes of conversation, that I had the power of enjoying, have left a strong wish in my mind to see more of him.—

Give my kind love to Mrs Green. Mr and Mrs Gillman are anxious to see you—I assure you, they were very much affected by the account of your Health.—Young Allsop behaves more like a dutiful and anxious Son than an Acquaintance. He came up yesternight at 10 o'clock, & left the House at 8 this morning, in order to urge me to go to some Sea Bathing Place—if it was thought at all adviseable.—

Derwent goes on in every respect to my satisfaction & comfort.

Again & again | God bless you, | and your sincerely | Affectionate Friend,

S. T. Coleridge.

1236. *To Robert Southey*

MS. Pierpont Morgan Lib. Hitherto unpublished.

J. Gillman's, Esqre
Highgate.
Wednesday. [31 May 1820][1]

Dear Southey

I hope, that I shall have some opportunity of seeing you before your return to the North. I have four Books, the largest a thin octavo, which with a little Mss Commentary of my own, too large for the Post, I would request you to take for little Sara, if it be not too inconvenient.—

published it in 1848 under the title, *Hints towards the Formation of a more comprehensive Theory of Life. By S. T. Coleridge.* For an account of the circumstances concerning Watson's publication of the *Theory of Life* in 1848 and of the *Postscript* inserted in some copies, evidently the latest printed, which describes the work as the 'joint' production of Coleridge and Gillman, see E. L. Griggs, *Coleridge Fille*, 1940, pp. 162–5, and *Miscellanies, Aesthetic and Literary*, ed. T. Ashe, 1892, pp. 351–3. In 1890 E. H. Coleridge recorded in a note that a manuscript of the *Theory of Life* bears a watermark of 1815 and that the date of composition was probably the autumn of 1816. See Alice D. Snyder, 'Coleridgeana', *Review of English Studies*, Oct. 1928, pp. 433–4; and Wise, *Bibliography*, 164–5.

[1] The mention of such projected works as the *Weather-bound Travellers* and the 'theological and biblical Letters' clearly links this letter to Letters 1228–9 and 1235. The manner in which Coleridge speaks of his health, however, suggests a more specific date. To Green on 25 May he reported that he had been 'in no usual degree unwell'. A similar comment occurs in the present letter, which was written on a Wednesday, probably 31 May.

I have been for almost the whole time since I saw you unusually unwell in kind as well as degree. I have come round, however, within the last three days: tho' the awkward pain on my chest & some novel symptoms probably connected with the kidneys still remain.—

I have some reason for supposing that Mr Longman &c have no intention of ever reprinting my early Poems, or the Wallenstein. Should this be the fact, & they are of no use to them, tho' by reducing Wallenstein to one Play with some considerable additions of my own that would make the work a rifacciamento, they might be of considerable benefit to my Widow if not to myself, Longman & Rees might be induced to give up the right to me—if they were spoken to by any one who had an influence with me [them?].— If you see or feel any objection to mention it to them, obiter et in transitu—I do not wish, much less request it.—Otherwise, as the Sibylline Leaves are all sold, & neither the Zapolya nor the Christabel are on sale, I might perhaps dispose of an Edition of *all* my poetic Works.[1]—

I am at present engaged in a work of amusement, entitled the *Weather-bound Travellers*; but which I propose to publish without my name—for with the enmity of the Eding. & the altum silentium of the Quarterly Review & the prejudices respecting my supposed German Metaphysics (tho' Anti-german would be the more appropriate epithet) there is little chance of any work having a fair chance *with* my name.—As soon as I have finished this, I proceed (if God prolong my life) to the bringing into form my theological and biblical Letters, to a Candidate for Holy orders in the established church. The first two or three are on those parts of Faith & Preliminaries of Christian Belief which a man must seek and find in his own mind & spirit—the following on the import of Inspiration—then on the Books of the Old Testament, severally & collectively—then on the 3 first Gospels—on John's Gospel, Epistles, & Apocalypse—on the Epistles of Paul—lastly, on the Church of England as a church & *as* an Establishment.[2]—I am not aware, that any portion of the work will be less popular than any serious work on such a subject must be—My great Object is to strengthen as much as possible the

[1] It was Coleridge, not Southey, who approached Longman concerning *Wallenstein*. 'I had written to request', Coleridge wrote to Godwin on 28 Feb. 1823, 'and I actually obtained, Messrs. Longman & Co's permission to make what use I might wish of the Volume—and they kindly desired me to consider it as a manuscript, with the Copy-right of which I had not parted.' The edition of Coleridge's *Poetical Works, including the Dramas of Wallenstein, Remorse, and Zapolya*, did not appear until 1828.

[2] Coleridge emphasizes this distinction elsewhere and particularly in *The Church and State*, 1830. See also Alice D. Snyder, *Coleridge on Logic and Learning*, 1929, pp. 7–8, and Letters 1447, 1450, 1458, and 1480.

particular external Evidence, but yet to demonstrate it's necessary subordination to the internal and pre-existing evidence & to that of the fact of the existence and manifest *mundane* rank of Christianity itself.—

Derwent is well & going on well—& desires his best respects & duty.

May God bless you!

S. T. Coleridge

1237. *To Thomas Allsop*

Address: T. Allsop, Esqre | 2. Blandford Place | Pall Mall.
MS. The Wellcome Historical Medical Museum. Hitherto unpublished.

[Early June 1820][1]

My dearest Allsop

You will be pleased to hear that I am better: at least, that the more distressing and depressing symptoms of the perishing process are gone, and the rest reduced to the old Peace-establishment—my Omnium at par.

Our friend, Green, is canvassing hard for the vacancy made by his Cousin, Henry Cline's, Decease.[2] Could I abstract the personal affection, I owe to my fellow-student in the Lore of Life, yet after three years' intimate communion with his mind and such and so frequent opportunities of measuring his powers and attainments comparatively no less than positively, as scarcely occur in one case in a thousand, my knowlege of his superior claims and qualifications and of their especial & very unusual appropriateness for the situation, which he is now seeking, would make it my duty to exert my influence in his behalf—and I can truly say, that the sense of Green's Worth & Value has roused a pang of regret at the feebleness of this influence, which my own worldly Failures had never excited.—I send you a List of the Voters.[3] It is *possible*, that you or some one of your Connections, may know some of the Names. —It would argue an ungrateful feeling, to say another word to you. Were I as confident in your *power* as I am in your *will*, I should congratulate our Friend, as already Victor.[4]

[1] This letter, which Allsop endorsed '1820 no date', was written shortly after the premature death of Henry Cline, the younger, on 27 May 1820.

[2] In 1811 Henry Cline had succeeded his father, Henry Cline, the elder (1750–1827), as surgeon to St. Thomas's Hospital.

[3] This list is no longer with the MS.

[4] Green won the election and became surgeon to St. Thomas's Hospital in 1820, a post he retained until 1852. From 1818 he had shared with Astley Cooper the lectureship at St. Thomas's, first in anatomy and afterwards in surgery.

His Rivals are Titus Berry & Mr Tyrrel.[1] I wish, you had asked
me concerning their respective merits, a month ago!—See what insincerity leads to, and party spirit. Astley Cooper,[2] merely because
Tyrell was a Borough man, & a pupil, supported him against
Stanley[3] as Surgeon for the Eye Institution: and against-—I will not
say, his Conscience: for de mortuis nil nisi bonum, & I am not
sufficiently acquainted with Astley Cooper to decide, whether he
has one or no—but certainly against his better knowlege he pledged
himself for Tyrell in terms, which the known inexperience &
shallowness of the man made amount to downright impudence!—
not to speak of the injustice to *Stanley's* notorious superiority, and
his services & tho' so young a man his important additions both
scientific & practical, as Surgeon & as Anatomist, to the Profession
by which Astley Cooper has risen to Rank & Opulence.-—And now
both his Duty & his Inclination enlist him for my Friend, *Green*—
and a most important Influence he is & will be—But o! how lame
& *half*ish compared with what it might have been, if the praises
which he now so justly bestows on Green who has been constantly
under his eye as his own as well as Henry Cline's Substitute in the
duties of Surgeon & Surgical as well as anatomical Lecturer, had
not been prostituted in favor of Green's Opponent, whom he had
not *seen* since his pupilage but knew that he had been neither
studying nor practising! The names by which I have been long accustomed to designate the two competitors are, Goose *Berry*, and
Ophthalmia fatalis.—But all this is between you and
your affectionate | & obliged

S. T. Coleridge
P.S. If you move Highgateward tomorrow (as my wishes would
have you) come by the Stage—You cannot be too careful not to
risk being wet—& the weather is almost hysterical, more like Miss
April in the green sickness than Lady June newly married to Sir
Phoebus Summer.—

[1] Frederick Tyrrell (1793–1843) was appointed assistant surgeon to the
London Eye Infirmary in 1820.
[2] Astley Cooper (1768–1841) was first apprenticed in 1784 to his uncle at
Guy's Hospital but soon transferred to Henry Cline, the elder, at St. Thomas's
Hospital. In 1791 Cline made him joint lecturer with himself in anatomy and
surgery. Cooper continued to lecture at St. Thomas's until Jan. 1825. In 1800 he
succeeded his uncle as surgeon at Guy's Hospital. Later he established a
medical school there. (See Letter 1499.) A baronetcy was bestowed on him in
1821, and he was appointed surgeon to the king in 1828.
[3] Edward Stanley (1793–1862) served the latter part of his apprenticeship
under John Abernethy at St. Bartholomew's Hospital. In Jan. 1816 he was
elected assistant surgeon there, Abernethy having been advanced to full surgeon
in 1815. Stanley was appointed to lecture on anatomy at St. Bartholomew's in
1826 and became full surgeon in 1838. He held in succession the most important
offices at the Royal College of Surgeons, to which he was admitted in 1814.

1238. *To Richard Sharp*

[Addressed in another hand] Richd. Sharpe, Esqre | No 3. Mansion House
Place | London   Quarter before eight Wednesday—
MS. Historical Society of Pennsylvania. Pub. E. L. G. ii. 267.
Postmark: Highgate, 14 June 1820.

Highgate
Tuesday Night
13 June 1820

Dear Sir

My Son, Derwent Coleridge, came home, an evening or two ago,
much delighted with having met you in the street, and at the kindness with which you recognized him. Encouraged by this he has
twice called in Mansion House Street, the last time in company with
our common old and excellent Friend, Mr T. Poole, of Stowey; but
was not fortunate enough to find you at home. And this too has
encouraged *me* to solicit your good offices in his behalf, should the
Object, he is in pursuit of, chance to fall within the sphere of your
influence, directly or mediately. Derwent was entered, early in May
last, at St John's College, Cambridge, and will commence residence
(God permitting) next October.[1] There happens to be now vacant
a Cambridge Exhibition of 15£ a year in the gift of the Skinners'
Company, of which we heard but a few days ago.[2] Still however it
may not be too late: as he has an active Friend in Mr Nixon—tho'
the applications to be of any service must be made before Thursday.
I dare acquit my *judgement* of being warped by parental feelings,
when I affirm that he is a most amiable Youth and both in Talents
and Attainments one of no ordinary promise. I know no instance of
any one who has known him and not been interested in his Welfare.
I scarcely need say that with his narrow allowance this Exhibition
would be a very desirable [addition]. I have therefore taken the
Liberty of sending you the names of the Gentlemen who have
votes[3]—marking those whose good will we have [been] led to believe
of *especial* importance, tho' none can be other than important. If
any name be there, with whom you could with propriety be Derwent's Advocate, or should our present attempt be frustrated, if

[1] Derwent Coleridge was admitted to St. John's College, Cambridge, on
10 May 1820, came into residence on 7 Oct., and matriculated in the University
in the Michaelmas Term. Soon after his arrival he was elected to a Foundress
Scholarship in the College. (From information kindly supplied by Mr. F. P.
White, Librarian of St. John's College.)

[2] The Skinners' Company Court Book No. 20 shows that Derwent Coleridge's
petition, along with several others, was considered on 8 Dec. 1820 and that the
exhibition was conferred on James D. Glover of St. John's College, Cambridge.
(From information kindly supplied by Professor William F. Kahl.)

[3] The 25 names which appear in the MS. are not in Coleridge's handwriting.

any thing of the kind in the gift of any other Company offer itself hereafter, permit me to entreat your interest. I believe that I hazard little in saying that Mr Southey and Mr Wordsworth would feel themselves personally obliged by your exertion of it in Derwent's favor: and I confidently hope, that his Academic Career will be such as not to discredit his Patrons.

It is superfluous to add that I shall feel most sensibly this accession to the many kindnesses and services which have already obliged, dear Sir, your's with grateful respect and | regard

S. T. Coleridge

1239. *To Mr. Chisholm*

Address: Mr or Mrs Chisholm
MS. Editor. Hitherto unpublished.

Friday Night
16 June 1820.—

Dear Sir

I came down to explain myself in person, thinking it a better way of conveying a plain story than that of dead Ink. When your kind Invitation came, both Mr & Mrs Gillman were hesitating as to the power of availing themselves of it, in consequence of Mr Gillman's incessant pre-occupation from hour to hour, in this season of Measles—But I interfered, said that Derwent & myself should like to go; that if Mr Gillman should be detained at the dinner time, he cared nothing for a Set dinner & might come in afterwards—& this was no reason why Mrs Gillman should not come.—In consequence, Mrs G. walked down to you—So ends Chapter the first.—

Now Chapter the second must be retrospective History. Some month or six weeks ago, Mr J. H. Frere, our once ambassador in Spain, intimated to me that Lord Liverpool had expressed a wish to meet me, and that there were one or two other public men who (in consequence, no doubt, of Mr Frere's own partial expressions in my favor) had signified the same wish—and I engaged that whenever his Lordship should signify any particular day, I would not fail even to disengage myself, if engaged, by telling the plain story.—

Now Chapter the last & third is—that this morning I received a Note from Mr Frere, stating that Lord Liverpool reminding him of his promise had agreed to dine with him on Saturday, (tomorrow) & that Mr Canning & some other of the Magnates, Ministerial & Diplomatic, would be there at the same time—and within a few

Hours after the receipt of the Letter Mr Frere himself came, lest any accident should take place to prevent it.—

Now may I not confidently rely on your goodness to attribute my absence tomorrow to any cause rather than disrespect, or (motives of prudence, in my circumstances of prudential *Duty*, excepted) to any preference of the Society, I am seeming to prefer ? —Believe me, it is *but* seeming. For any personal gratification, I would ten times rather be sitting at your table.—

Now Mrs G. expecting that I should see you or Mrs Chisholm, & knowing the probability that Mr G. (who could not rest the sole of his foot till 8 o'clock this evening, & then only to eat a morsel & be *out* again) might not be able to come, & that she & Derwent might be but scanty Substitutes (which no one who knows *her* will allow, and Papa won't allow for *his* Son, Derwent) wished me to find out whether you would rather defer our visit—

With my best & sincerest respects to Mrs Chisholm do me the justice to consider me with high esteem & regard

Your obliged

S. T. Coleridge

1240. *To Thomas Monkhouse*[1]

Transcript Coleridge family. Hitherto unpublished.

Highgate

Saturday Morning. [24 June 1820][2]

Dear Sir

Twice in the course of the last month I had received an invitation to dine with Mr and Mrs Chisholm, our friends and neighbors, who have been particularly attentive and serviceable to Derwent Coleridge: and each time I was obliged to send an apology, the last time but a few hours before the dinner-hour and leave to my kind friends Mr and Mrs Gillman, to explain the particulars for me. Mrs Ch. had called, and asked me whether or no I was pre-engaged for Saturday: as her son, Mr Hall (the Etonian celebrated for having been *sent up* one and twenty times for his Compositions, 12 more than Mr Canning had been, and for sweeping away all the prizes at Cambridge) was to return from Paris, and (if I was not engaged)

[1] This letter was undoubtedly addressed to Thomas Monkhouse, Mrs. Wordsworth's cousin.

[2] In Letter 1239 Coleridge apologized to Chisholm for not keeping his engagement on Saturday, 17 June 1820. The present letter mentions this apology and shows that he had arranged to be with the Chisholms on the following Saturday, 24 June.

she wished to have a party of friends to dine with him. I accordingly engaged myself—and yesterday I received a note to remind me of my promise—

I have entered into this detail to let you understand, how little I yield to my inclinations in not joining Mr and Mrs W. and Dorothy at your table[1]—anxious as I am to see them—& obliged by your friendly invitation—

Yours, dear Sir, truly,

S. T. Coleridge

FOREWORD

to the Letters of 1820 concerning Hartley Coleridge's Loss of his Fellowship at Oriel College, Oxford

(Letters 1241–1257)

The following account, which includes the surviving papers concerning Hartley Coleridge's downfall at Oriel, presents the tragic circumstances in some detail, particularly as they relate to Coleridge. It will serve not only to clarify many of the statements in the letters which Coleridge wrote during the latter part of the year 1820, but also to reveal the extent of his activities in his son's behalf.

Wholly untutored in the ways of the world, Hartley Coleridge matriculated at Merton College on 6 May 1815. Awkward, little over five feet in height, and with black hair, thick eyebrows, and a beard 'which a Turk might envy', he was as unprepossessing in appearance as he was eccentric in manners. He was not only painfully conscious of his 'oddities', which in the past had subjected him to ridicule, but he regarded them as an unchangeable part of his nature and harboured a 'feeling or phantasy of an adverse destiny'. He was unusually endowed intellectually, his principles were thoroughly good, his nature open and lovable, but a deeply-ingrained habit of procrastination, an instinctive cowardice as to mental pain, 'an overweening confidence in his own talents', and a tendency to resist authority were ominous forewarnings of the future. At Merton, however, he won the approbation not only of his fellow undergraduates but of the college authorities as well. In the Michaelmas term of 1818 he successfully passed his examination, and early in 1819 he received his degree, being placed in the second class. Somewhat reluctantly he offered himself as a candidate for an Oriel fellowship, 'duty, vanity, and the fear of being shipped off to Brazil' leading him to make the trial. On 14 April 1819 he was elected probationary fellow of Oriel. As one of his examiners reported, he was successful 'against Candidates of powerful Talents and after an examination MOST HIGHLY to his Credit,

---

[1] The Wordsworths and Dorothy, who were in London at this time, left for the Continent on 10 July. See *Middle Years*, ii. 877.

(57)

as a Classic, a Logician, and a Theologian. In Logic, Moral Philosophy, and Theology his attainments were far beyond what his age authorized us to expect, and indeed generally where ever opportunity was given for the display of original Talent, and self-formed Views, his superiority was palpable'. (Letter 1193.) After 'the first flush of success', Hartley was 'seized with uneasy melancholy', a 'feeling' that he was 'among strangers', and a suspicion that his election arose in great measure from the failure of his 'county opponents' and the 'vague appearance of Talent', rather than from a 'hearty conviction' of his eligibility. Several of the Oriel fellows, too, felt misgivings. 'You probably stared', wrote John Keble to John Taylor Coleridge,

> I'm sure I did, when you found that we had really elected your illustrious cousin, but his examination was so superior that one could hardly make up his mind to reject him 'odditatis causâ'. I trust he is not yet too old to unlearn some of his manifold tricks, and he seems to have the first requisite for learning, a sense of his Imperfection. One thing especially I could wish him taught, i.e., to refrain from *abstract* questions in conversation. He sits silent and contented enough as long as indifferent matters and points of view are being debated, but a Proposition in A, as Arnold says, rouses him immediately.

As probationary fellow of Oriel, then the outstanding college at Oxford, Hartley was under the supervision of Edward Copleston, the provost, Richard Whately, the dean, and such resident fellows as John Keble, James Tyler, Edward Hawkins, and William James. In 1931 L. R. Phelps described the atmosphere in which Hartley found himself. Having been associated with Oriel since 1872, as student, fellow, and finally provost, and having known Edward Hawkins in the latter's old age, Phelps possessed an unusual knowledge of Oxford. His comments are particularly pertinent:

> It must be allowed at once that to be admitted to the society of the Fellows in the Oriel Common Room was a terrifying experience. Both Arnold and Keble found it uncongenial after the 'give and take' of the undergraduate society at Corpus Christi College. It was so for two reasons.
> 1. Oriel no doubt demanded a far higher standard of loyalty than other colleges. The Fellows were the picked men of the University and were encouraged by the Provost to set to other colleges a pattern in even the details of life. At a time e.g. when Common Rooms 'reeked' of port wine—the Oriel 'teapot' was a common source of chaff against its members. *Spartam nactus es, hanc orna* was, down to my time, made the motto of the Society. For pursuit of knowledge, for devotion to their pupils the Fellows of Oriel had a reputation which they were jealous in preserving.
> 2. The life of the Common Room and its conversation was of a critical type—insisting on clear definition of terms and logical sequence in argument. . . . Such a society is more likely to be a good training-ground for the wits, than a scene of cordial relations!

Now on both these grounds H. C. was chilled and repelled rather than encouraged and stimulated by the atmosphere in which he found himself. It stood in sharp contrast to the 'give and take', the genial discussions, the irresponsible statements, the camaraderie of undergraduate society at Merton, where he, no doubt, 'ruled the roost' intellectually.

On the other hand, the old Provost, Dr. Hawkins, was always careful to say that he much admired H. C.'s ability and good qualities, that he took him in hand and warned him, and did his very best to keep him in the straight path, but in vain. He was a born rebel against convention—and could not help showing it. . . .

At the time of his election as probationary fellow of Oriel, Hartley was informed of his duties and responsibilities, but he refused to adapt himself to the requirements of his position. He neglected the society of the Oriel common-room and continued to associate with his friends among the undergraduates, particularly those of Merton and Exeter. Thus when it was suddenly discovered by the Oriel authorities that he had been 'guilty of intemperance' as well, they resolved to deprive him of his fellowship.

The following 'Memorandum' explains the grounds for the resolution of the provost and resident fellows not to admit Hartley Coleridge to an 'actual Fellowship'.

A

Memorandum signed E. Copleston, Provost, and dated 15 June 1820

Mr. Whately the Dean having informed me that he had heard very disagreeable accounts lately of the conduct of Mr. Coleridge, Probationer Fellow, who has been keeping irregular hours, and had frequently come home late in a state of intoxication we agreed to assemble all the resident Fellows on the 30th of May and to confer upon this subject.

In the mean time accurate enquiries were made of the servants of the College and of his lodging-house—from whom it was learnt that the suspicions of the College were but too well founded—that he was often guilty of intemperance and came home in a state in which it was not safe to trust him with a candle.

His year of probation being nearly expired, it thus became a matter of serious consideration whether he ought to be admitted Actual Fellow; and upon a careful review of his whole conduct from the commencement of his probationary year, it was the unanimous opinion of myself and of all the resident Fellows that he was not fit to be received permanently into the Society.

I had had frequent occasions myself to advise and to expostulate with him about his conduct, which was not likely to recommend him to the favour and esteem of the College. I told him early in his probationary year, that he was not to regard himself as finally approved—that he was an entire stranger to us when he was elected—and that the year of probation was the means afforded us of discovering the worth of his character. I exhorted him to court the society of the Fellows and of the other Probationers, and in all respects to conform to the established habits and discipline of the College.

Notwithstanding this, his attendance at Chapel was very irregular, and all accounts agreed in representing him as not associating with the members of the Common Room, as is usual, but as giving his society to others, they knew not whom, and living differently from the rest of the College.

I had also had more than one occasion to reprimand him severely for inattention to the duty of 'Declaiming' [in hall] . . . .

For some time I had hoped that these irregularities, and his frequent absence from morning chapel were owing to a little eccentricity of character, unmixed with any immoral habits: but from the investigation lately instituted no doubt remained that intemperance was a principal cause of these delinquencies—that he was fond of society very different from that of his own Common Room, and by no means respectable.

Upon mature consideration of the case we were all of opinion that he was not fit to be admitted an Actual Fellow—and that had we known a tenth part of what his Probationary year had brought to light, he never would have been elected at all. It was thought also the best and kindest way to intimate to him this resolution of the resident Members of the Society, before the long vacation: which was accordingly done by the Dean—and was received by him with a very humble and contrite acknowledgment of its justice—although he supplicated to have his probation extended another year. He was however given to understand that such a measure could not be adopted; and that it was inconsistent with the very notion of *probation* —which was intended not to form and discipline a Junior Fellow, but to enable us to find out his real character.

As the preceding Memorandum shows, it was late in the probationary year before the Oriel authorities discovered that Hartley had been guilty of intemperance. This seemed to offer an explanation of all his delinquencies throughout the tenure of his fellowship. Although Copleston makes no mention of the fact, the dean and the resident fellows, John Keble in particular, tried to settle the matter in June by obtaining a resignation from Hartley. A serious controversy developed, and Hartley refused to accede to any such proposal. Thus the decision to deprive him of his fellowship—an unprecedented measure—had to be left until the October meeting of the provost and all the fellows, resident and non-resident. Since the loss of the fellowship would leave Hartley destitute, it was tentatively suggested that some pecuniary allowance from the college should be made. But that question, too, had to be delayed until October.

Hartley's own retrospective account of his experiences in pleading for an extension of the probationary year and of the controversy in which he became involved is contained in a letter written at Coleridge's request in September 1820.

Foreword to Letters 1241–1257

B

Hartley Coleridge to his father, September 1820

As you desire a full statement of all my transactions with Oriel College, and of the relation in which I stand to the Fellows, I will now give you all the particulars that my memory supplies of their and my own conduct, from which you may form a judgement, how far they have been justifi'd, in the severity to which they had recourse, or in their own language were driven; and of the provocation to terms like those employ'd by Keble in his letter to John. [See E.] I believe you will give me credit for concealing no part, even to spare your feelings much less my own. If there be any inaccuracy, due consideration should be had of the difficulty of recalling minute circumstances. ... I do not disguise my own feeling, that I have been wrong'd, illiberally, ungentlemanly treated, but I am a prejudiced judge— speaking of men I cannot pretend ever to have loved, though I highly esteemed and revered them—who have certainly done me almost as much harm as they could—do you judge whether that harm was injury. You know I was placed, by no choice of my own, in a College not famous for sobriety or regularity, without acquaintance with the world, without introductions, and after the first term, without any to guide or caution me. It is true, William Hart [Coleridge] had introduced me to Keble and Tyler, but it is also true, that neither of them thought proper to look after me, or give me either advice or warning, which, considering the friendship professed by the former for my family, might to one unacquainted with Oxford, seem rather extraordinary. At all events, I confess I felt it so; nothing was more to my wish, than to have had some one among the superiors of the University, interested for me, whose eye might have kept me clear of folly— and the consciousness of this, contributed in no small degree to the freedom, with which I afterwards gave my society to Undergraduates, which has been emphatically call'd '*keeping low company*'. It is needless to enter upon the History of what past at Merton: suffice it to say, that, as any who knew me will testify, I behaved as well as most would have done, and form'd no acquaintances but such as I should be proud to introduce to you. I don't deny that when at a party, I drank as others did, and this was sometimes too much, but I rather avoided than sought such company as induced drinking. In the latter part of my Undergraduateship, I kept chiefly with three men—all temperate, and one of them, as far as his choice carried him—a water-drinker. ... I had establish'd a good character in the College—I was highly respected by the Tutor—and I believe really beloved by many of the young men. From thence, I was elected, very contrary to my expectation, into Oriel, and past through my probationary year. Just at the end of this period, so that I had no time for recovering myself, I was summoned before the Provost, and inform'd, that my remaining Fellow, was extremely precarious—'as my conduct had, of late, been not only irregular, but grossly immoral'. I will confess, that I had,

within a short period, been at two [degree] passing parties—and I
can't say I came absolutely scot-free from either of them; feeling,
therefore, that in strict language, my conduct had been immoral, I
pleaded guilty—said I relied on the mercy of the College—whereby I
meant, not the mercy which is contrary to justice, but that which
takes a liberal and hopeful view of errors, which may be merely
accidental, and at [any] rate cannot be considered in a very heinous
light, as acts, tho' fearful in truth, if taken as symptoms of a habit.
Next day the whole was decided—the evidence, who or what, I know
not, were re-examined—in form their depositions—some of which
must have been wilfully false taken down—my exclusion resolved on
—and all this without any express communication to me. When I
found, however, how things were going, I immediately called on Keble,
and was inform'd of the result. He exprest great sorrow for the length
he had been obliged to consent to; and spoke in terms very vague, and
very severe, of my conduct—indeed his language might have [been]
addressed more properly to one who was hardly ever sober, than to
one who had been occasionally tipsy. I then formed a notion—that
the charges against me must have been exaggerated—but consciousness of a recent fault, my habitual respect for his character, the amaze-
ment into which I was thrown by my misfortune, united to prevent
my insisting, as I ought to have done, upon an explanation.

He advised me to resign my fellowship before the meeting of the
College in October—which might prevent 'disclosures'. . . . I sought
the advice of [Samuel] Rickards, my fellow-probationer. He appeared
deeply interested in my behalf, promised his best aid, counsell'd my
writing . . . letters [to the dean and resident fellows], and shew'd so
much apparent kindness, that I left him with tears of joy and affection. Next morning I set about the forementioned letters—which all
amounted to this—a confession that I had been careless in respect to
drinking, and deficient altogether in the gravity and circumspection
beseeming my order in the University. Habitual intemperance I
denied, but acknowledged that the suspicion required to be removed
by a particular carefulness in that respect. Throughout the whole I
was haunted with the fear of owning to less than the truth—of not representing myself in colours black enough. I measured my expressions
by the strictest standard, and as such I expected they would have
been taken. I had always understood that Oriel fellows made Xtian
perfection their rule and aim, and never suspected that they would
employ the overflowings of my contrition as a witness against me.
If a humble Christian, in his prayers, calls himself a miserable sinner
—shall this be made a handle to accuse him of murder, or theft?
The answers of Whately and Hawkins you have seen. [See c and D.]
I had little conversation with any of the fellows after that time. I saw
Whately twice; first, I exprest my hope, of getting into a school,
which he then highly approved of; but some time after—told me it
was but a precarious hope as 'I was a young man leaving the University in bad Odour' and advised my going to Canada—'on the ground

that damaged goods do best for the Colonies'. . . . I also conversed with James—who was very earnest, dwelling chiefly on my having taken too much wine with a *Stranger*, and afterwards invited him to dine with me. Now the fact was, that this Stranger was a Master of Arts of the College—with whom I consented (for I'm sure I should never have proposed it) to the introduction [of] another bottle. He certainly got drunk, and I, from weak compliance, not sottishness, drank more than I ought; but I was, at all events, sober enough to keep him out of mischief. This was the first offence. The two Parties occurr'd a good while after; at one of them I drank but little, coming in very late, but a few glasses, fast—and afterwards some beer—which made me giddy as I was not well. Drunk I was not, but probably appeared so on coming home. The other time I was certainly knockt up, for I had undertaken to pass the bottle about for a sick host, and was possess'd with the freak of playing the generous landlord at another's table—a very silly practical joke to be sure—and in my situation highly improper—but surely not enough to justify so damning a phrase as that whereby they have thought fit to designate it. I had a short interview with Tyler, who advanced me some money, and I believe the same day, I took leave of Keble. Then and then only, I attempted a defense—but he would not enter upon it. I told him the fellowship was out of the question, but I had a character to vindicate —he said (if I remember) it was only by amendment I could vindicate it. I spoke of the charges being exaggerated; he said—He hoped so, but added 'It's useless to deny the facts'. I stated that I did not intend to deny the fact of having been intoxicated more than once, but the habitual frequency of drunkenness. He replied—'You are availing yourself of vague terms—Frequency and Intoxication'; and then added—'I would not mind the intemperance, so much, if I could separate it from the praedilection for low company.' Whereby I understood him to mean: 'The preference of the Society of men below my own station in the University'—or at the utmost—the carelessly contracting acquaintance and even engagements as Tutor with men not famous for regularity of conduct—'above all, men of Colleges not liked by Oriel.' As I saw he was bent on not believing or hearing me, I bad him farewell. This was my last transaction till I dined with Dr. Copleston previously to my quitting Oxford. He spoke to me kindly—as to a young man, who had shewn himself unfit for his situation—as to an incautious man who needed warning—but still as to an unblemished character in the worldly acceptation of the word, whom the College had rejected partly as not being the sort of man they wanted—partly—as being more likely to do honour to another station. . . .

In the course of these interviews Hartley found that his explanations, expostulations, and promises of amendment had fallen on deaf ears. Nor were his letters of any avail. The replies of Hawkins and Whately have been preserved.

C

Edward Hawkins to Hartley Coleridge, 11 June 1820

... It is with the greatest pain ... that I express my conviction of the extreme improbability there is, after the disclosures which have been made to us, that the College should accede to your request of a further term of probation, if indeed such an indulgence were at all consistent with the spirit of our Foundation.

It may be some consolation to you to be assured that all the Fellows will continue to feel the most lively interest in your future welfare. ...

D

Richard Whately to Hartley Coleridge, June 1820

Your letter, painful as was the subject, gave me some pleasure still interested as I am in your welfare. ... There is no *punishment* contemplated, no *sentence*, no *condemnation*: the matter is not *judicial*, but purely *deliberative*: a man petitions to be allowed to place himself under our inspection for a year, that we may judge (not what he is likely to *become*, but) what he actually *was* at the time of election: at the end of that year we are called on to deliberate whether we were justified in that opinion of him with which we originally elected him: and if we decide in the negative, that does not imply that we judge him *incurably* bad, but that we think he has not shewn himself to be *already* such a man as ought to be admitted into the society. The probation in short is not designed to *make* a man what he ought to be, but to shew what he *is*. If the Statutes ... admit of our extending the term in any case, it is plainly in one where *from* a man's necessary absence, illness, or any other cause our minds are left in *doubt* (not as to his *future*, but) as to his present character. Now all that you promise is to become quite a *new man*; I am far from being without hope that it will be so: but even the fullest confidence of that, in all our minds could only relate to the *future*, and would not justify us in admitting into the society one whose *past* conduct had not proved him worthy of it. ... No formal decision of the College has taken place; but in Octr. we shall be called on to pronounce our opinion as to the period which has now expired; and it is hardly to be doubted that the non-residents will be guided by our observation. ... Do not therefore cherish any hopes ... but endeavour (as you profess your intention) to derive moral profit *from* what has befallen you: remember that your delinquencies are not merely academical but moral also: and consider that you are still under a more important probation at the termination of which there will be no profit in lamenting the past, no room to amend the future, and no hope of eluding the eye of an 'All-Seeing' Judge. ...

Deprived 'at once' of his 'fellowship' and his 'good name', threatened with exposure unless he resigned, and advised to quit the country Hartley was thrown into a state of 'confusion' and 'grief', with 'dim anticipations of future misery', and left Oxford, probably not long after mid-June. On 13 June he had dined with Southey, who received a D.C.L. degree from the University the next day. Hartley told his uncle nothing of his situation at Oriel but said he was soon going to Keswick.

In an undated letter addressed to John Taylor Coleridge and received by him on 19 June 1820, Keble gave an exaggerated account of Hartley's conduct at Oriel and made a devastating attack on his character. Keble, however, gave no hint of his own recent efforts to force Hartley to resign his fellowship.

E

John Keble to John Taylor Coleridge, c. 18 June 1820

... The fact is, My dear John, & I grieve to say it on your account as well as on his, that Hartley, as we have just discovered & ascertained upon unquestionable testimony, has been living in habits of such continued irregularity, & frequent sottishness, with all their degrading accompaniments of low company, neglect of college duties &c as to make it quite wrong & unfit for the college to admit him to his actual fellowship, or to retain him on the foundation any longer. After repeated warnings (for though I have but just known of the matter, it was known it seems to Whately & a few others long ago) he has still gone back again to his old courses: promising amendment ... but without any practical good effect. ... I am convinced that he is as utterly deficient (I will not say in good principles, but) in moral energy & self controul as he is wanting in conventional tact & good sense. ... I am *sure* we should not be doing our duty if we kept him. ... You know most of us too well ... to suspect us of coming to such a determination as this upon motives of personal dislike or pique at his oddities. ... As far as his manner in conversation goes, his oddities never were of a kind to disgust me. ... I was only amused by them. When he has been reading in Chapel or declaiming in Hall I have sometimes been annoyed by the thought of his being never likely to prove at all useful to the Society in any official character. ... He knows our purpose, himself, & has known it for this week past, & fully acquiesces in the justice of our decision—at the same time that he has in different ways attempted to get each of us, individually, to alter his own opinion. Some parts of his conduct in this kind of negotiation have ... (but never let it go farther) given me occasionally a kind of suspicion of his not being perfectly sincere. ... When he is to outward appearance most deeply impressed with a sense of what he has done, he has his wits most thoroughly about him & tries to take advantage of any palliation or anything else in the way of argument which may suggest itself. ... I am almost sure that as to the degradation to a lower rank in society he will not feel that at all, even if it should come upon him. I may just hint to you, I hope that it is not proposed to leave him at once destitute—but pray let this go no farther, as I do not know that I am justified in communicating it at

all, till the other part of the transaction is finally settled: & this cannot
be till the middle of October, at our statutable time of admission.—
Now had this better be communicated to Southey? & when? & by
whom? It struck me that it might be better for you to tell him as
much of this letter as you think proper before he leaves London, as
he might gradually prepare Mrs Coleridge for it & perhaps begin to
look out for some safer & better situation for the poor youth. Any
service that I can be of to him, short of giving him a good character
in the particular respects I have mentioned, would give me real
pleasure. . . .

Keble seems to have been unduly anxious to have Southey learn of
Hartley's situation at Oriel. Yet he had first met Southey at Oxford
while the latter was there on 13–15 June. Even then, as he explained to
John Taylor Coleridge, he had 'wished' to report the matter to Southey
but 'could not bear to embitter his visit'. On the other hand, Keble
utterly ignored Coleridge, as if Hartley had no father.

Keble's letter was the means of spreading abroad the news of Hartley's
misfortune in the worst possible form. On 19 June John Taylor Coleridge
sent it to Southey, who was then in London. On reading the letter
Southey said he had not the 'slightest suspicion' of Hartley's 'propen-
sities to sottishness, or to low company', but he immediately read it to
the Wordsworths, who were about to leave London for the Continent.
Writing from Geneva three months later, Mrs. Wordsworth commented
on the charge of 'sottishness' to her sister, Sara Hutchinson, at Rydal
Mount. Assuming that Hartley was with his father, she did not 'doubt'
that he was 'now in bad hands for a reformation to take place'. On his
return to Keswick early in July, Southey made known the contents of
Keble's letter to Mrs. Coleridge, who was soon sending 'letter after
letter' to Highgate. In August Sara Hutchinson wrote to Mrs. Wordsworth about the affair: 'Mrs Coleridge wants sadly to see me to talk
about her unfortunate Son—It appears that the Fellows have stretched
their power to the utmost—nothing can be proved against him but indiscretions—such as would not have stood in the way of any other
Probationer—but they wanted to be rid of him—Wm J[ackson, fellow
and later provost of Queen's College, Oxford,] was sure of it from the
very first and said if he had been guilty of any intemperance he must
have heard of it being Proctor—I am truly sorry for her—for what can
the poor helpless creature do for himself! She is very anxious that the
best of it shd be made to the Beaumonts—and it is to be feared they
will hear the very worst as John Coleridge's Letter [See F] was not
over delicate.' (The Letters of Mary Wordsworth, ed. Mary E. Burton,
1958, p. 66; and The Letters of Sara Hutchinson, ed. Kathleen Coburn,
1954, p. 189.)

Southey did not himself communicate with Coleridge. On 24 June,
however, he advised John Taylor Coleridge to disclose Hartley's situation to the Gillmans since 'anything which affects . . . [Coleridge] acts so
directly upon his bodily health'. Accordingly, John Taylor Coleridge
sent the following letter to Gillman on 29 June. Although the damaging

charges of 'sottishness' etc. against Hartley are drawn directly from Keble's letter, it is clear that another of the Oriel fellows had transmitted the report (false though it was) of Hartley's imprudent engagement to a girl at Oxford. This rumour about the love affair had also reached John Taylor Coleridge by 19 June. He immediately told Southey, who in turn spoke of it to the Wordsworths on the 20th. The same Oriel correspondent, and not Keble, was responsible, too, for the information that the college had no desire to make any 'unnecessary exposure'.

F

John Taylor Coleridge to James Gillman, 29 June 1820

Dear Sir

I am not aware whether my Uncle may have received from any other quarter the distressing news which this note will bring; but in case he should not, as it has been in some measure officially communicated to me, I think I can not help informing him of it, and for a great many reasons it seems advisable to do so through you rather than directly to him.

I find that the Provost and Fellows of Oriel have come to a resolution not to admit Hartley to his fellowship on the expiration of his probationary year. I never remember a similar determination being taken, and I am assured that they have come to it with the greatest reluctance and not till after repeated warnings, and repeated promises of amendment made by Hartley and broken. The charges against him are very painful ones to repeat; but for the purposes of admonition and reproof it is fit that my Uncle should be in possession of the whole case—they are 'sottishness, a love of low company, and general inattention to college rules.' Coupled with this I am informed from other sources, that he has contracted an attachment for a young person, the daughter I think of an architect; I hear her well spoken of individually, but any such engagement at his time of life and under the circumstances is to be deplored, and peculiarly so in his case if it is to be considered as connected with the alleged love of company beneath his own station.

Altogether it is a case of a most afflicting nature; what to advise in it I really do not know, or how to render him any effectual service. The college have no desire to make any unnecessary exposure, and if any situation could be procured for him which would give him a pretext of resigning before October, he might still keep his place in the world, and if he might be depended on for a steady amendment, all that he has now lost might be regained. I confess, however, I dread the perverse ingenuity of his mind in self-justification. . . . I am just starting for the Sessions and Circuit, . . . which will keep me out . . . to the end nearly of August. . . .

On 30 June, exactly a month after the provost and resident fellows of Oriel had resolved to exclude Hartley from the Society, Coleridge finally received the news in its most exaggerated and painful form. Since John

Taylor Coleridge's letter to Gillman contained only the bare details, Coleridge hurried Derwent off to Oxford to investigate. (See Letter 1241.) Hartley had already left there before his brother arrived, but from Hartley's friend, Robert Burton, a fellow of Exeter, Derwent learned something of what had occurred at Oriel during the preceding weeks and sent his father two letters, both of which Coleridge answered on 3–4 July. (Letter 1242.) Coleridge was distressed to hear that Hartley had 'bent his course to the North' instead of coming to Highgate. Soon, however, he was to wish that his son was 'bona fide on his road to Keswick', for Derwent's second letter brought further 'heart-wringing intelligence', probably concerning Whately's advice to Hartley to go to Canada. Thus Coleridge, whose letters show a penetrating and profound understanding of his son's character, so like his own in many respects, feared that Hartley was 'wandering on some wild scheme, in no dissimilar mood or chaos of tho[ughts and] feelings to that which possessed his unhappy father at an earlier age during the month that ended in the Army-freak—& that he [may] even be scheming to take passage from Liverpool to America'.

Hartley, however, had not gone to the North, certainly not to Keswick, and before mid-July, as Letter 1243 shows, both sons were with their father at Highgate. Coleridge had now gained a measure of composure, and after hearing Hartley's own account of the Oriel affair, he wrote to Tulk on 16 July that the afflicting news had been 'disarmed . . . of it's sharper and invenomed weapons'.

Realizing that the charge of sottishness emanating from Oriel would seriously injure Hartley's reputation and endanger his future utility, Coleridge determined to hold an interview with the provost prior to the October meeting of the assembled fellows. Meanwhile, he made every effort to get to the bottom of the affair. He consulted his friend, Samuel Mence, the minister of the school chapel at Highgate and formerly fellow of Trinity College, Oxford. Mence, who knew Hartley intimately and felt certain that the term 'sot' could not justifiably be applied to him, immediately wrote to William James, one of the resident fellows of Oriel. James's reply was posted from Worcester.

G

William James to Samuel Mence, 15 July 1820

. . . There has *not yet* been any meeting of *all* the Fellows of my College to consider Hartley Coleridge's case—therefore I should not say that any Resolution has yet been formally made by the Society— but when we meet in October, the question will, in the ordinary course of things, come before us, and there cannot be the smallest doubt but that the Resolution expressed in your letter will then be made— though the decision of the College may be considered as already fixed (for there is but one opinion amongst all with whom I have communicated on the subject) it may not be without use to observe the distinction I have made above—for what we have yet done, will not be *publicly known*, which must be the case, if he is formally rejected by the Society: this he may yet avoid, by not offering himself, where he must be sure that he will not be admitted. Repeated instances of intoxication, one at least of which seemed strongly to show a love of drinking (for his companion was till that day a stranger to him, a man of no talent, who had nothing particularly to recommend him except to one who could find it in getting drunk with him)—at other times keeping late hours, which with other circumstances afforded the strongest presumption that he had been drinking, though it was not then so evident—this too, in the year of his probation, and notwithstanding that he had been warned again and again of the consequences of irregularity, marks him as unfit to be admitted into a society established 'ad augendum Clerum'.

At the same time I trust that he is not a sot in the strong sense which you attach to that word. Habits exist in different degrees, are more or less completely formed—and I cannot consider one so young and I will add, so ready to receive advice, as 'irreclaimable'—but he has a great deficiency of that common sense, which would make the advice given really useful to him. Still, he is a young man of talent and there are many situations in which he might distinguish himself—I know, it has been suggested to him to go to Canada— . . . so great a change in the plan of his life, the design of residing abroad for a term of years would give to the world some reason for his apparently resigning his fellowship. . . .

In forwarding James's letter on 21 July, Mence warned Coleridge: 'In any use you may deem it expedient to make of the letter, I am sure you will recollect that it is a private communication . . . and to be shewn as such.'

In carrying forward his investigation, Coleridge now had in hand not only James's letter to Mence, but also John Taylor Coleridge's communication to Gillman and two letters which Hawkins and Whately had addressed to Hartley in June and which the latter brought with him to Highgate. It seems likely, too, that before long he had received the copy of Keble's letter to John Taylor Coleridge which survives among the papers relating to Hartley. In any case, by early July both he and Hartley knew its contents in detail from Mrs. Coleridge's letters. (See c–G.) In September he asked Hartley to put in writing a 'full statement' of all his 'transactions' with Oriel College and of the 'relation' in which he stood to the fellows. Hartley complied with his father's wishes by composing the letter quoted in B. He also sent a second letter, dated 2 October, in which he included a 'plain statement of *facts*' concerning his conduct at Oriel and cautioned his father not to attempt to defend him on 'untenable points'.

H

Hartley Coleridge to his father, 2 October 1820

. . . The account I have given you in that immeasurable scrawl [B] is the truth, and, as far as my recollections carry me, the whole truth;

but I am templed to say a few more words to you on the subject, that
you may not form a wrong judgement, either of the Fellows of Oriel
or of me. And first, allow me to express my conviction, that they
could not, under their circumstances, have confirmed my Election,
without injury to themselves. Of their system of government, it does
not behove me to speak: I could never reconcile myself to it, but I
acknowledge that discipline of all kinds is not so much to my taste,
as it ought to be. However you might be disposed to overlook the fact
of intemperance, once or twice committed by an inattentive young
man, under the excitement of company, yet you must reflect its effect
and example did not pass away as fast as the fumes of wine from my
brain. I might become sober and keep so, but I could not restore to
the College its spotless character: the spell was broken—it was seen,
and that too by the very persons, from whom it was most needful
to conceal it, that Oriel men were but as others. Nay had I been
suffered to remain among them, a very natural suspicion might have
arisen, that they tolerated in their own body, what they punish'd in
the young men committed to their care. . . . Consider this, as I know—
you can—impartially—put me, and all your knowledge of me, out of
the question, recollect that they could not know me as you do, and
state the Question as a pure case to be mooted, thus:

A. a young man, only known for some talent, some weak good
nature, and no little eccentricity, is removed from a society of lax
manners, to another society distinguish'd for the reverse. He is inform'd on his entering this new society, what is expected of him,
warn'd against such faults as have been supposed to attach to him,
and in fine, instructed that his permanent settlement in the same
society depends on his conduct during a year. Notwithstanding which,
he neglects much of what he knows is expected of him, does not take
pains to accommodate himself to their manners, is shy of their company, connects himself chiefly with his old comrades and others of
like character, and is heard to speak of the strictness of those who
have honour'd him by making him one of them, with ridicule: and
after a time it is discover'd that he has, at least more than once,
fallen into an absolute moral misdemeanour, which accounts fully
for a degree of indolence, irregularity, late hours, absence from stated
meetings, and neglect and slovenly performance of stated duties,
hitherto inexplicable. If to this be added, a hasty confession, and
apparent dislike of entering into particulars, you will not be surprized, if this Society reject the young man A. as an unfit person for
them, whom nothing but interest or vanity could have induced to
come among them. Now this, my dear Father, is a plain statement of
facts, which may prevent your committing yourself by defending me
on untenable points. I must further tell you, what in the other letter
I omitted, that of late I had been often seen with a man of no very
genteel appearance, and whose looks certainly indicated drinking.
The real truth was, this was a man of but moderate capacity, whom I
had seen made a butt of by others not so much better in head as they

were worse in heart. I knew that much was depending upon his getting thro' the University, and proffer'd my assistance, did my utmost, not without success, to make him read, and found much honesty and right feeling about him. I flattered myself I might be of service to him and certainly disregarded the impression my acquaintance with him might make on those who were but little inclined to impute any act of mine to the best motives. On the whole, you may easily perceive that I have been somewhat wilfully negligent of my own interest, and that, *entre nous*, I had a decided dispathy with the fellows. But yet all this, tho' it fully justifies their exclusion of me, is very far from even excusing the manner of it. Nothing I had done affected my character as a Gentleman; or made my credit worse than that of a Scout—nothing even palliated their undistinguishing avidity for reports against me. Above all, nothing that I can think of, can excuse their not making me we[ll] acquainted with the charges against me—their attempt to send me over the wide Ocean with a blasted character, to leave my name for a bie-word to my family—the one scabby sheep turn'd out of an immaculate flock—the sole jarring note in the concert of the Coleridges. . . .

In a letter to his brother, Hartley later wrote more freely of his superiors at Oriel: 'I thought most of them Bigots, ignorant deciders upon the conduct of others, conceited of their own dignity, and rather disposed to tyrannize. . . . I was induced . . . to vent my chagrin in certain impotent, but I dare say not forgotten threats, of great reformations to take place in the College and the University when my unripe fortunes came of age.'

Hartley was right in believing that his unguarded remarks had been noticed. Indeed, as late as 1851 James Spedding made the following comment: 'We have ourselves heard it confidently asserted by a very high and grave authority,—a man by no means given to think indulgently of intemperance, or suspiciously of dignities, and one whom the question must have deeply interested at the time,—that the charge of intemperance was in fact a pretext only, and that the real offence was of quite another kind, less venial perhaps in the eyes of college authorities, though not so easily reached by their statutes, and, in the eyes of the world, no offence at all,—namely, an indiscreet freedom of speech with regard to University reforms.' (*Reviews and Discussions*, 1879, p. 305.)

In a third letter to his father, Hartley wrote bitterly of the comment on his innocent love affair:

I think John Coleridge's letter [to Gillman] the unkindest stab of all. [See F.] The bare, unmitigated credit, he has given to every tittle . . . —Sot and all the rest—the unfeeling manner in which he alleges my acquaintance with the Harrises in proof of my love of low company; and his gratuitous assumption that I had enter[ed] into imprudent engagements—are instances of cold-heartednesses and prejudice I can sooner forgive than forget. Whatever I may have felt for Mary—and from you I wish not to conceal aught—I never expressed to her a thought beyond the most unimpassioned esteem.

Several months before the crisis at Oriel occurred, Hartley had written in the same vein to Derwent: 'M. is lovely and beloved as ever, tho' I am better reconciled to hopelessness than I was formerly. I know, at least I think, she does not care for me. I almost believe that she has no conception that I more than like her, and perhaps it is as well it should be so.'

As his letters of late September and early October 1820 show, Coleridge was preoccupied with his forthcoming interview with Copleston. On 30 September he expressed vexation that he had not yet received an answer from Oxford concerning Copleston's return, and he commanded Hartley to inform him of the exact date of the Oriel meeting. Uncertain as 'to the day', which he thought was 19 October, Hartley promised to write immediately. Subsequently, Coleridge himself heard from Oxford that Copleston was expected to arrive on Friday, the 13th. As a result of Mrs. Gillman's 'kind but unnecessary anxieties', Coleridge agreed to have Allsop accompany him to Oxford. They arrived there on 14 October, and the next morning Coleridge saw the provost.

Before going to Oxford, however, Coleridge wrote two letters, both of which he considered of the greatest importance. The first, Letter 1249 A, he composed for Hartley, whose own copy was laid 'before the Provost and Fellows officially assembled' on 17 October. Coleridge took this means of having Hartley himself deny Keble's charges of sottishness and an attachment to low company. This letter of 'self-defence' was designed in part to show the injurious effects of these charges on Hartley's present character and future utility. It concludes with a 'deliberate Protest' against charges 'calculated' to injure Hartley in addition to the loss of the fellowship, '& far more permanently, & to a far more aweful extent & degree'. On reading the letter, Keble noted that the very 'expressions' he had used in writing to John Taylor Coleridge were known to both Hartley and his father.

The second letter, 'a very long one' of which only fragments have come to light, Coleridge addressed in his own name to Copleston. (Letter 1250.) He planned to have it reach Oxford on 13 October, and thus give Copleston 'a day's preparation for the personal Interview'. Even from the surviving fragments, it is obvious that Coleridge was presenting not only a penetrating analysis of his son's character, but also a subtle refutation of the 'cruel charge' of habitual intemperance.

The long-awaited interview with Copleston was held at Oxford on Sunday morning, 15 October. That Coleridge may have had a specific proposal in mind is suggested by the following sentence from Derwent Coleridge's biographical memoir of his brother: 'It was indeed urged, that while his eccentricities unfitted . . . [Hartley] for collegiate duties, he might, under the very peculiar circumstances of the case, have been allowed to retain his fellowship on condition of non-residence.' There is no mention of this proposal in Coleridge's letters. If it was brought forward, Coleridge failed to persuade Copleston to retain Hartley on the foundation in any capacity.

Understandably, Keble's charge of 'sottishness' became a central topic of discussion. This is indicated by a brief account of the meeting published in 1882 by Thomas Mozley, who was elected fellow of Oriel in 1829: 'I am told that upon hearing of the College decision, either before or after the actual dismissal, the father came down to expostulate with Copleston, and got into a long argument with him. To the charge of disgraceful intoxication he replied that drunkenness was not necessarily intoxication. There were four kinds of intoxication, and it was possible for a man to be drunk neither disgracefully nor injuriously.' (*Reminiscences chiefly of Oriel College and the Oxford Movement*, 2 vols., 1882, ii. 411.)

'My father', Hartley later wrote, 'has been at Oxford, had an interview with Dr. Copleston, who talked in a very smooth strain, about my talents, acquirements, and dispositions, but continued to reiterate charges, which my father, and all my friends *believe*, and I *know*, to be false, as to *frequent* intemperance etc., etc. The Dr. also defended the secret, inquisitorial manner of investigating the conduct of Probationers, which puts it in the power of any Scout or Shoe-black . . . to ruin any man whose carelessness or occasional errors may dispose his superiors to receive ill impressions of him. . . . I never, before I left Oxford, had any idea of the extent of the charges against me. I suspected, nay, I knew them to be exaggerated, but little thought to what degree!'

Copleston was obviously deeply moved by Coleridge's impassioned defence of his son. Immediately after the meeting he sent Coleridge the following letter addressed to Cross Inn, Cornmarket, Oxford. Copleston admitted that 'exaggerated and even false reports' of the nature of Hartley's 'offences' had been circulated. He declared, too, that neither he nor 'any of the Fellows' believed Hartley to have been 'addicted to solitary drinking', which as Coleridge had observed, 'is commonly included under the imputation of "sottishness" '. Copleston also enclosed his Memorandum of 15 June 1820 (A) to explain 'the grounds of our proceeding'. Coleridge took this Memorandum with him to Highgate and had Hartley prepare a specific answer to it. (See J.)

I

Edward Copleston to Samuel Taylor Coleridge, 15 October 1820

Oriel College,

Sir

After the conversation of this morning it is almost needless for me to state how much I respect the feelings which you expressed during our interview and how anxious I am to lighten the load of this affliction which presses upon your mind, as far as I can consistently with the plain duties of my station. The enclosed *Memorandum* [A] which I made for my private use (and in case of my inability to attend the College Meeting at Michaelmas for the use of the College) explains so particularly the grounds of our proceeding, that it is not necessary to enter upon the painful task of describing your Son's case. But as it seems that exaggerated and even false reports have been spread of the nature of his offences, I declare most solemnly that I never heard the charge of licentious conduct with women laid against him, nor the slightest suspicion of that kind expressed.

I also say that although frequent intemperance during his probationary year was alledged, and the College were satisfied of the truth of the charge, yet it never occurred to my mind, nor do I believe that any of the Fellows entertained the opinion that he was addicted to solitary drinking, which as you justly observe, is commonly included under the imputation of 'sottishness.'

I will not lose this opportunity of declaring that in my opinion he possesses very amiable qualities, and that his abilities and attainments promise fair to place him in most respectable and useful stations, provided his conduct in future should be correct, and his choice of companions prudent. He will always have my best wishes, and my endeavours to serve him, wherever it can be done without a compromise of duty. . . .

P.S. Mr. Whately being absent I do not send a copy of his *Memorandum* which I read to you to-day, but I beg leave to remind you that he states that besides advising your Son frequently how to conduct himself so as to gain the approbation of the College, he repeatedly explained to him the precarious holding he had, and set before him the danger of ultimate rejection.

Coleridge returned to Highgate in a state of bitterness and frustration. 'Of this journey to Oxford', Allsop later wrote, 'I have a very painful recollection; perhaps the most painful recollection (one excepted) connected with the memory of Coleridge.' (*Letters, Conversations and Rec.* 68.)

On 17 October the fellows of Oriel held their formal meeting. It must have been a stormy one. Copleston gave a report of his interview with Coleridge and brought forward Hartley's copy of Letter 1249 A, which is addressed to the provost and fellows of Oriel, and Coleridge's Letter 1250. Commenting on these letters and on the report of Coleridge's conversation, Keble had this to say in writing to John Taylor Coleridge on 8 November: 'Poor Hartley, . . . I must own to you that the whole of what he wrote & his Father wrote & said in his defence rather seemed to me to make the matter worse. He seemed to be particularly annoyed at some expressions in my letter to you. I can only say that I cannot accuse myself of any intentional unkindness either in that or anything else— whatever I have said in a hurry.'

As a result of Keble's exaggerated charge of 'frequent sottishness', Hartley's elaborate protest and denial, and Coleridge's intervention, the Oriel men were led to examine the evidence concerning the frequency and the degree of Hartley's intemperance during the probationary year. On the preceding Sunday, 15 October, Copleston had admitted in a letter to Coleridge that 'exaggerated and even false reports' had been circulated. Furthermore, he had given Coleridge his Memorandum of 15 June, which showed that the testimony against Hartley had come from 'the servants of the College and of his lodging-house'. If Mozley is correct, however, one of the resident fellows had seen Hartley in a state of complete drunkenness. According to Mozley, James Tyler had 'closed his ears' to 'sad stories' about Hartley, but 'found at last the case was hopeless, and he either had a most wonderful vision, or he invented one, to cover his retreat from an untenable position. Perhaps the truth lies midway, and he had only caught a whiff of poor Hartley's own dreamy temperament. Midway on his ride home from a Sunday visit to his Northamptonshire parish, at a point of the road well known to Oriel men, suddenly road, hedgerow, trees, and cottages disappeared, and he found himself in Oriel Lane. A man lay in the gutter. It was ——.' (*Reminiscences*, i. 86–87.)

On the basis of the deliberations of the assembled group, Copleston was to tell Coleridge at their meeting in London on 20 October that Hartley had been three times 'picked up *dead drunk* in the Street'.

Formal action concerning Hartley's fellowship was taken on 17 October. 'Eodem Capitulo', the official Oriel record reads,

non accedente ad perpetuitatem Domus petendam Domino Coleridge, utpote cui nuper significatum esset eum non ita se gessisse per annum probationis (quamquam saepius de moribus melius conformandis a Praeposito et Decano admonitus fuisset) ut ab ipsis aut sociis Oxoniae commorantibus haberetur dignus qui in Societatem admitteretur, visum est eidem Capitulo locum Domini Coleridge in hoc Collegio vacare

ita testor

R. Whately, Decanus.

It was also agreed, though the Oriel record makes no mention of it, that £300 should be paid to Hartley from the funds of the college.

Copleston immediately hastened to London, and on 18 October he invited Coleridge to meet him on Friday, the 20th, 'for the purpose of a few minutes' conversation on the subject which he hinted to Mr. Coleridge at Oxford, namely some allowance from the College on his Son's leaving the University'. The interview in London was even more unsatisfactory than the one in Oxford. Coleridge presented the following protest which Hartley addressed to the provost and fellows of Oriel in answer to Copleston's Memorandum of 15 June (A).

J

Hartley Coleridge to the Provost and Fellows of Oriel College,
October 1820

Reverend Sirs

... I hold it my duty to signify to you, how far I plead guilty to the charges alleged against me—and in what sense I acquiesce in the justice of my exclusion. In the first place then, I would not be understood to interfere, in the slightest degree, with your right of judgement, much less to retract any confessions heretofore made, while I was ignorant of the nature and extent of the evidence on which you were proceeding. So far, therefore, as you deem certain instances of intemperance committed casually—without previous prospect of being so overtaken, and never amounting to a loss of self-command or recollection, together with omission of College duties, and neglect to cultivate the acquaintance and friendship of those into whose society I had been admitted; so far as these facts are the ground of your decision, I have nothing to object to it: it lies in your own bosoms; but that the instances of intemperance were frequent: that they were more than two or three—all arising from peculiar circumstances: that they were the cause of my irregularities or late hours, that I ever chose, or even tolerated companions, because of their love of drinking—that I kept low company, in any sense in which that term is understood in the world, or that I selected for companions any but Gentlemen—men of good principles, and in general of intellectual pursuits, I deny; at least, if ever I mistook the characters of my associates, it was my inexperience and no prepossession for what was objectionable. Permit me then to protest against the charges of *habitual* intemperance, irregularity as a *consequence* of such intemperance, and love of improper society. . . .

'The Provost', Hartley later wrote of this London meeting, 'received my *protest*',

praised it, continued his former affirmations against me, adding thereto, by way of descending from *generals* to *particulars*—that I had been 3 times picked up *dead drunk* in the Street, which, so help me God, *I never was in my life!* And, after all this, or rather along with it, repeated in the name of the College, an offer, which he made to my father in his own, while at Oxford, namely, that to prevent my feeling pecuniary embarrassment from my exclusion, I should accept from the College the Sum of £300 *and let the matters be hushed up*. . . . My father's answer to the proposal was in my name, and it expressed my feelings. 'If', said he, 'my Son be innocent of the heavier part of your charges, far be it from me to persuade him to compromise his honour: if, after all his denials to me, he is guilty—he may do as he pleases but *I* will not be the channel of conveying the money to him.'

Concerning this 'liberal proposal' Hartley also remarked: 'Among my friends, the Wordsworths, Mr. Frere, the Gillmans, etc., these have but one opinion with regard to the effect of accepting it, it would have tongue-tied me, it would have convinced the world that I was even such as they have named me. As to their promises of silence, of what use are they?'

More than ever convinced of the 'cruel and most calumnious persecution' of his son, Coleridge angrily denounced the Oriel authorities. In Letter 1253 A, which was addressed to the warden of Merton College and composed for Hartley, he referred to the 'Charges' on which the dismissal of his son was 'professedly grounded' and to 'the yet heavier private representations by which it's justification has been attended'; and he 'earnestly' entreated the warden's 'perusal of the accompanying documents'. In Letter 1254 Coleridge again revealed his bitterness in writing to Lockhart: 'It pleased God to afflict me most heavily by the unexpected & most cruel & unjust persecution of my eldest Son at

Oxford, just as I had supposed him settled in independence for a course of years at least & with the fairest prospects—I was stunned scarcely less by the suddenness of the Blow than by it's weight. I hurried here & there—went to Oxford—made every inquisition, & every attempt—& succeeded only in obtaining decisive proofs of what in fact I had never doubted nor possibly could doubt, that my Son had been most cruelly wronged & then calumniated in order to justify the agents—whom my Son has challenged in vain to produce their evidence.'

In December word reached Keswick of an appeal to the visitor of Oriel College, i.e. the king, acting through the lord chancellor. Coleridge's daughter mentioned the matter in a letter to Derwent of December 1820: 'My uncle [Southey] had a letter from John Coleridge. . . . He expresses himself kindly about Hartley & says there is a show of injustice in his expulsion [in] which my Uncle agrees, and thinks the King ought to be applied to.' On 19 December Southey also commented on the appeal: 'Copplestone I understand says that Hartley was more than once picked up dead drunk in the streets,—& this Hartley denies, & it is upon this specific point I suppose, that he rests his appeal. . . . It is very likely that he has been dealt with according to the rigour of the law, & that his manners may have contributed greatly to this. . . . How the matter will proceed I know not, but I rather think that an appeal to the Visitor is intended; if the charge of being picked up in the streets cannot be proved, the failure o fproof in that case is a complete acquittal on that point.' If Coleridge contemplated having Hartley make such an appeal, his letters do not mention it. Gillman probably persuaded Coleridge to abandon the plan. Further publicity would have been harmful to Hartley and Derwent, and further efforts injurious to Coleridge's health, which had already been seriously affected.

It remained for Coleridge to assist Hartley in exonerating himself in the estimation of those interested in his welfare. 'I shall write', Hartley said, 'to Sir G. B[eaumont] and my Uncle Edward, a true account of the case and of the whole proceeding; I shall send them a copy of my protest, and of all the papers in our possession necessary to the elucidation of the affair.' Undoubtedly Hartley also wrote to Poole. Coleridge made copies of many of the documents for Hartley, and he himself wrote the first draft of the letter to the warden of Merton. Although the Oriel authorities had paid little heed to Coleridge's pleas in behalf of his son, Hartley's friends and relations, nevertheless, were soon convinced of his 'comparative innocence'. Mrs. Coleridge told Poole that Copleston 'spoke of H's talents, acquirements & dispositions in terms of high commendation, but would not allow that he had been injured in regard to the *false charges* brought against him'. (*Minnow among Tritons*, ed. Stephen Potter, 1934, p. 86.) Poole, for his part, believed that 'the charges against Hartley Coleridge had been grievously multiplied and magnified', and 'even to the end of his life, the very name of Dr. Coplestone could never be heard by him with patience, or without some fierce word of denunciation of all the authorities of Oriel'. (Mrs. Henry Sandford, *Thomas Poole and His Friends*, 2 vols., 1888, ii. 261.)

'Mr. Mence, as well as my Father', Hartley wrote to Lady Beaumont in December 1820, 'strongly urges my returning to Oxford as the best mode of confuting the reflection thrown on my character, and thinks I may support myself by Private Pupils. I will be guided herein by good counsel, and circumstances—my task will be difficult, but my success will therefore be the more consolatory.' Hartley did not return to Oxford, however, nor did he follow in London the one course which would have discredited the verdict of his judges. Instead, his drinking became habitual. As Derwent says, 'the ruin of his fortunes served but to increase the weakness which had caused their overthrow'. Despondency and self-reproach overwhelmed him, and he found refuge in fatalism. 'But for self-condemnation', his father remarked, 'H. would never have tampered with Fatalism; and but for Fatalism he would never have had *such* cause to condemn himself.' For a time Hartley tried to pursue a literary career in London, a plan to which Coleridge gave assistance and encouragement, but his irresponsible conduct and growing intemperance during the next two years finally reduced his father to disillusionment and despair. By 1822 Coleridge was convinced that his 'bewildered Eldest born' must not live in London where temptation was ever at hand. Thus it was that late in that year Hartley returned to the Lake Country. There he remained until his death, to become the object of 'every one's sorrow and compassion'.

(The preceding account is based on MSS. and transcripts in the possession of the Coleridge family; *Letters of Hartley Coleridge*, 29–56, 61–62, and 300–23; and *Poems by Hartley Coleridge. With a Memoir of His Life*, ed. Derwent Coleridge, 2 vols., 1851, 2nd edn., i, pp. lxxx–xciv.)

1241. *To Thomas Allsop*

Address: T. Allsop, Esqre. | 1. Blandford Place | Pall Mall   To be forwarded to Clapham, should Mr A. have left town.
MS. New York Public Lib. Pub. with omis. Letters, Conversations and Rec. *40.*

On 30 June 1820, the day before the present letter was written, a communication from John Taylor Coleridge to Gillman brought in its 'most formidable shape' the news that Hartley Coleridge was to be deprived of his fellowship at Oriel College. The charges listed were 'sottishness, a love of low company, and general inattention to college rules'. To Coleridge the unjust charge of sottishness against his eldest born was almost unbearable. It marked the beginning of one of the four 'griping and grasping Sorrows' of his life. Derwent Coleridge, who was with his father at the time, later said: '[I] have never seen any human being, before or since, so deeply afflicted.'

In sending Gillman information purporting to be 'in some measure' official, John Taylor Coleridge gave only the barest details. He offered no explanation as to why he had been notified, and he failed to indicate whether Hartley himself had been apprised of his plight. See preceding 'Foreword', especially F.

Postmark: Highgate, 1 July 1820.

Highgate
31 [1] July 1820.—

My very dear Friend

Before I opened your Letter—or rather gave it to my best Sister and under God best Comforter[1] to open—a heavy, a very heavy Affliction came upon me, with all the aggravations of surprize—sudden as a Peal of Thunder from a cloudless Sky.— Derwent set off for Oxford yester afternoon—& till he returns, I can tell you only that Hartley has so conducted himself as to have given deep offence to the Master and Fellows of Oriel—& that there is the greatest possible danger that he will not be elected at the close of his probationary Year, i.e. in October next. He is neither charged with, nor suspected of, any criminal act, nor are any instances of intoxication urged against him—but irregularity & neglect of College Rules & Duties, Carelessness of Dress, low Company in contempt of the exprest warnings as well as wishes of the Master & Fellows, & *fondness for Wine*—the term by which the last Charge is expressed is the only one too mortifying for me to transcribe. I am convinced that this last is owing, *in great part*, to his habit almost constitutional (for it characterized his earliest Childhood) of eagerly *snatching* without knowing what he is doing, & whatever happens to be before him—bread, fruit, or Wine— pouring glass after glass, with a kind of St Vitus' nervousness— not exactly in the same way as my dear & excellent-hearted c. l., but similarly. Alas! both Mr and Mrs Gillman had spoken to him with all the earnestness of the fondest Parents—his cousins had warned him—& I (long ago) had written to him, conjuring him to reflect with what a poisoned dagger it would arm his Father's enemies—yea, and the Phantoms that half-counterfeiting, half-expounding the Conscience, would persecute his Father's Sleep.— My Conscience indeed bears me witness, that from the time I quitted Cambridge no human Being was more indifferent to the pleasures of the Table than myself, or less needed any stimulation to my spirits: and that by a most unhappy Quackery after having been almost bed-rid for six months with swoln knees & other distressing symptoms of disordered digestive Functions, & thro' that most pernicious form of Ignorance, medical half-knowlege, I

---

[1] The devotion of the Gillmans to Coleridge in his hour of trial is shown in Mrs. Gillman's letter to Allsop of Saturday morning, 1 July: 'He is as well as we can expect him to be. Yesterday he was convulsed with agony, tho' at first he was calm. In the evening he was tranquil, as he is today tho' of course remains deeply affected. His God & his Books are his refuge, & a sure help in time of trouble. He is now going to walk with me, and I think we shall succeed in diverting his mind from this sad subject, until he must of *necessity* go into it fully.' *Nineteenth-Century Studies* (Cornell), 70.

was *seduced* into the use of narcotics, not secretly but (such was my ignorance) openly & exultingly as one who had discovered & was never weary of recommending a grand Panacaea—& saw not the truth, till my *Body* had contracted a habit & a necessity[1]—and that even to the latest my responsibility is for cowardice & defect of fortitude; not for the least craving after gratification or pleasurable sensation of any sort, but for yielding to Pain, Terror, & haunting Bewilderment—but this I say to *Man* only, who knows only what has been yielded not what has been resisted. Before God, I have but one voice—Mercy! Mercy!—. Woe is me!—the Root of all Hartley's faults is Self-willedness—this was the Sin of his nature, & this has been fostered by culpable indulgence, at least, non-interference on my part, while in a different quarter, Contempt of the Self-*interest*, he saw, seduced him unconsciously into *Selfishness*. —Pray for me, my dear Allsop! that I may not pass such another night as the last. While I am awake & retain my reasoning powers, the pang is gnawing but I am—except for a fitful moment or two— tranquil—It is the howling Wilderness of Sleep that I dread.—

I am most reluctant thus to transplant the thorns from my own pillow to your's—but sooner or later you must know it—And how else could I explain to you the incapability, I am under, of answering your letter, of which I know no more than that it is so kind as that at another time it's contents would have inspired me with alarm & perplexity of mind, whether I have sufficient grounds of assurance that you are not wronging yourself?—But this would be superseded for the present (my late visitation & sorrow out of the question) by my anxiety respecting your Health.—Mr Gillman feels satisfied that there is nothing in your case symptomatic of aught more dangerous than irritable & at present disordered organs of digestion, requiring indeed great & systematic care but (with prudence, & *sensible* medical aid) by no means incompatible with longevity & comfortable Health on the whole. Would to God! that your uncle lived near Highgate, or that we were settled near Clapham—Most anxious am I (for I am sure, I do not *over*-rate Gillman's medical skill & sound medical good sense, & I have had every possible opportunity of satisfying myself on this head *comparatively* as well as positively from my intimate acquaintance with so many medical men, in the course of my life) I am most anxious, that you should not apply to any medical Practitioner at Clapham, till you have consulted some Physician recommended by Gillman & with whom our Friend might have some confidential

---

[1] For similar statements concerning the beginning of the opium habit see Coleridge's letter to Cottle of 26 Apr. 1814 (Letter 919); *Collected Letters of Coleridge*, Introduction to vol. iii, p. xxxii; and Gillman, *Life*, 246–8.

Conversation, either going with you or otherwise—so that you might have from some man of high medical character, as a Physician, a general Outline of the Treatment, Diet, &c, which would be a *guide* to a *judicious* Apothecary, should you have any occasion to apply while at Clapham, & a sort of inoffensive Moderator on the other supposition—in both an Index for yourself, to judge of him by.—The next earnest petition I make to you—for should I lose *you* from this world, I fear that religious Terrors would shake my strength of mind, & to how many are you, must you be, very dear— is that you would stay in the country as long as is *morally* practicable—Let nothing but *coercive* motives have weight with you— A month's tranquillity in pure Air (O that I could spend that month with you with no greater efforts of mental or bodily exercise than would exhilarate both body & mind) might save you many months' interrupted & half-effective Labor.—If any thoughts occur to you at Clapham, on which it would amuse or gratify you to have my notions—write to me, & I shall be served by having something to think & write about not connected with myself.—But at all events write—tho' but two lines—as often as you can, & as much as (but not a syllable more than) you ought—Need I say how unspeakably dear you are to your—you must not refuse me to say, *in-heart*-obliged

S. T. Coleridge

1242. *To Derwent Coleridge*

Address: Derwent Coleridge, Esqre | Exeter College | Oxford   To Mr Burton's care, who is respectfully requested to forward it to D. C. or send it after him, should he have left Oxford.
MS. Victoria University Lib. Pub. with omis. E. L. G. ii. 268.

The present letter was written immediately after Coleridge received a report from Derwent Coleridge, who had been sent to Oxford to investigate Hartley's affairs at Oriel. Hartley was missing when Derwent arrived, but he had previously confided in Robert Burton, a fellow of Exeter. Thus Derwent was able to send his father some of the details. The postscript to Coleridge's letter, dated 4 July, was written in response to a second communication from Derwent concerning Hartley. See preceding 'Foreword', p. 68.

Postmark: Highgate, 4 July 1820.

Monday
3 July 1820

My dear Derwent
    I were, methinks, to be pardoned if even on my own account I felt it an aggravation of my sore affliction, that your Brother without writing or any other mode of communication should have bent

his course to the North as tho' I were not his Father nor he himself
bound to Mr and Mrs Gillman by his own knowlege of the
affectionate & scarcely less than parental anxiety with which they
follow him thro' luck and unluck, good report and evil. Or am I to
suppose, that having taken his resolutions he found or fancied that
it would be less painful to him to imply by his absence than to tell
me by word of mouth, that my advice would be to no purpose and
my Wishes of the same stuff as my Tears? One thing at least is
certain: that had it been his object to make it known and felt, that
he considered me as having forfeited the interest and authority of
a Father per desuetudinem usûs, & as a Defaulter in the Duties,
which I owed his Youth, he could not have chosen a more intelligible (God knows! on his own account too afflictive to be mortifying)
way of realizing it.—Ignorant of all the *detail* of the case, of the
Persons, and their relative Bearings both on Hartley's present and
his prior situation, I do not permit myself to form any positive
Judgement on certain parts of your letter. But I conjecture, that
it will differ from your's & Mr Burton's: tho' neither of you will
have grounded his opinion less on mere worldly prudence, or on
self-interest in any lower sense than as it is the necessary Counterweight of self-indulgence. For O! my dear dear Boy! never forget,
that as there is a Self-willedness which drifts away from self-
interest to finish it's course in the sucking eddy-pool of Selfishness,
so there is a Self-interest which begins in Self-sacrifice, and ends in
God.—But deferring the whole question of your Brother's acquaintances & connections, I can only gather from your Letter the
ascertainment of what I had before supposed—that Hartley had
converted difference of manners, views and opinions into positive
dislike, and, I sadly fear, into settled enmity by his ungracious
style of repelling the requests and admonitions of the fellows of
Oriel—that then instead of fortifying himself against the hostility,
so excited, by more than common guardedness of conduct he
managed to put himself completely in their power by a succession
of trifling (many of them perhaps, unconscious) indiscretions,
irregularities & unpunctualities, which have been woven together
into a Web—with that cruellest sophism of Calumny, which destroying the actual distances & interspaces gives a false context &
interprets fault by fault—& that Hartley's mood of mind gives the
one only thing wanting to secure their triumph!—You have not
said, whether Dr Coplestone[1] is at Oxford or not? And if not,
where he is?—The names & present addresses of the Fellows of
Oriel you should likewise procure.—And then if your Brother have

---

[1] Edward Copleston (1776–1849) became provost of Oriel College in 1814,
bishop of Llandaff in 1827.

left Birmingham, or in disregard of my entreaties perseveres in going to Keswick, I expect you here with as little delay as possible.

My health is not worse—& during the day or as long as I am up, I am calm or at all events can manage what I feel—But—I cannot tell why—as soon as my head is on my pillow, my thoughts become their own masters, spite of every effort to go to sleep with indifferent trains of thinking & tho' I do not go to bed till I am downright weary of holding myself up & continue reading & trying to interest my intellect or my fancy in the subject to the last moment. Last night, however, I screamed out but once only in my sleep, & my stomach felt but in a very slight degree sore after I awoke— the exceeding order & wild *Swedenborghean* rationality of the Images in my Dreams,[1] whenever I have been in any great affliction, so that they haunt me for days—& the odd circumstance that these dreams are always accompanied with profuse weeping in my sleep toward morning, & probably not long before I wake—for my pillow is often quite wet: (for the screaming fits take place in the first sleep, & from dreams that are either frightful or mere imageless sensation of affright & leave no traces)—these are problems which I encourage myself in proposing & trying to solve, were it only to divert my attention from the occasion of them.—O surely if Hartley knew or believed that I love him & linger after him as I do & ever have done, he would have come to me.—

I never saw a man more thoroughly affected & occupied with a vexation, than Mr Gillman is at present—& never saw Love or Friendship shew itself in more fits & forms of Praise & Blame, Reproach & Defence.—

All send their kindest regards—& join with me in urging you to return (as soon as your further stay ceases to be necessary) to

my dear Derwent | Your afflicted & loving Father
S. T. Coleridge.

P.S.—If Hartley be at Birmingham, & you think, that your presence would enable you to persuade him to return hither with you, of course you will go there.—

I am vexed to find that the Post is gone.

---

[1] In one of his notebooks Coleridge reveals the extent of his suffering:
June 30th, 1820—Night. & 1 July, Morning strange & fearful Dreams, so distinct & conscience-like—after the σαδ νευσε φρομ Οριελ—The effort, I believing myself to have departed this life. O let me still pray to God!—God must still be here! & the prayer, soon after which I awoke.—How like the Hell of Swedenborg it appeared—how completely conceivable (some malignant, but all perfectly unbenignant, Spirits) did the different human Beings appear. *Nineteenth-Century Studies* (Cornell), 34.

A copy of Swedenborg's *De Coelo et ejus mirabilibus, et de Inferno, ex auditis et visis*, 1758, containing annotations by Coleridge is in the British Museum.

Tuesday Morning, 4 July—I have this moment received your heart-wringing intelligence.[1] I wish that I dared believe that Hartley is bonâ fide on his road to Keswick—but the same Dread struck at once on Mr G's mind & on mine—that he is wandering on some wild scheme, in no dissimilar mood or chaos of tho[ughts and] feelings to that which possessed his unhappy father at an earlier age during the month that ended in the Army-freak—& that he [may] even be scheming to take passage from Liverpool to America. Again I must say that the venom if not the sharpness of the Pang, which I am suffering, is on account of his own moral being, when I am forced to see that he seems to have had no more reference to *me* than as if no such person had been in existence. My very name appears not to have occurred to him!

If there were tolerable assurance of a Letter reaching him, I would by hook or crook get & send him a sum of money sufficient to prevent any additional bewilderment from immediate pecuniary distress—but if he should be at Keswick, this will not be immediately necessary—& if my fears be just, I must direct in the dark. And what if I write to Liverpool, to any of his or his Mother's friends, as the Cromptons, to look for him? this may be doing mischief & injure him by setting their heads at work on the, *what is it? what can it be?* For this reason among many others I intreat you to return hither without an hour's unnecessary delay—else it will be rumoured, that your Brother has run off, & that you are sent to seek after him. Unless therefore some strong probability of good rise up, contrary to all present probability, come back & let me have no answer to this letter but yourself. From what Charles Owen told me, I had augured nothing but evil of this Aubyn Connection[2]—but suffered myself to be quieted by Hartley's strong letter in vindication of his pupil, representing the cruel disadvantages under which he had grown up, his excellent

[1] Since Coleridge had learned from Derwent's first letter from Oxford that Hartley was believed to be at Birmingham and possibly on his way to Keswick, the 'heart-wringing intelligence' may have been a further report that he had been urged to go to Canada. (See 'Foreword', b.) A sentence from John Keble's letter to John Taylor Coleridge of June 1820 suggests that Hartley may have been asked to vacate his rooms in the college, probably by Keble himself: 'It [is] quite wrong & unfit for the college to admit him to his actual fellowship, or to retain him on the foundation any longer.' 'Foreword', e.

[2] Hartley's pupil, W. J. St. Aubyn, was a natural son of Sir John St. Aubyn (1758–1839). Despite Hartley's efforts, St. Aubyn failed his examination a second time and left the University at the end of the Michaelmas term in 1819. Hartley later said that his engagement with his pupil during this term left him little time for the Oriel Common Room. It was not until 1831 that he was able to collect from St. Aubyn the money due for tutoring. *Letters of Hartley Coleridge*, 23, 26–27, 62, 105, 129–30, and 319.

principles—that the root of his moral character was sound & vigorous—and the duty, that he (Hartley) felt, to persevere in assisting him to rescue himself.—Likewise, on the very first slight Hint, I ever received, from John Coleridge, which was but a week or so after Hartley's election as prob. fellow, & no more than that 'the men of Oriel meant to rally him out of his oddities',[1] & how advisable it was gradually to transfer his intimacies of mere acquaintanceship to his new College, I wrote to him tenderly requesting him to bear it with cheerful good humour, to manifest a disposition to check in himself what was confessedly not in harmony with the established forms & at least innocent assumptions of dignity & decorum in men, whose character as fellows of Oriel he had by his own act & choice so far identified with his own, that there must be more or less a re-action from the latter on the former, & therefore a rightful claim of interference on *their* part. But these are vain recollections.—What he should do now, is as evident as the hope, that he will do it, is (I fear) vain—He should put in execution what he *says* he can do, & I doubt not, truly says. He should state the whole affair in succession as it really was, in each point—distinguishing error from imprudence, and imprudence from admitted impropriety, bringing to it's just size what had been exaggerated, clearing up what had been misunderstood or misinterpreted, & admitting point by point whatever in his habits, conduct or demeanor appeared culpable to his own deliberate thoughts, & pledging himself to the requisite change, above all by assigning one sacrifice—that of wine or at least of never exceeding a third glass & never but at or after dinner—Add to this a solemn contract of honor entered into by himself, & by his Father, that on a proved breach of his engagement in any of these respects & the desire expressed by the Provost & Fellows in consequence, he will instantly resign his fellow-ship[2]—& then I might exert the influence of my friends with Dr C. & with each of the Fellows singly, to bring things about.—But all this he is precluding by gloomy resentment, or (as I would fain flatter myself with from one sentence of your last letter) from cowardice as to mental pain.—Oh! if he knew how much I feel *with* him as well as how much I suffer for him, he could not so forget that he has a most affectionate Friend as well as Father in

S. T. Coleridge

The first two pages written yesterday (Monday)—

---

[1] See 'Foreword', p. 58 ; and G. Battiscombe, *John Keble*, 1963, p. 57.

[2] It would appear that Derwent had reported to his father not only that Hartley had refused to resign his fellowship, but also that he could offer a defence of himself. See 'Foreword', B.

1243. *To C. A. Tulk*

Address: C. A. Tulk, Esqre. M. P. | Regent's Park.
MS. Swedenborg Society. Pub. New Church Magazine, *1897, p. 106.*
Postmark: Highgate, 17 July 1820.

Sunday—[16 July 1820]

Dear Sir

I have delayed the Messenger to the latest moment in the hope of such a relief from my bodily pain and oppression as might have enabled me to fulfil the engagement, I had made with you, which on more than one account would have been gratifying to myself.[1] But I find it withheld. Were it only for the uneasiness in which I should leave Mr and Mrs Gillman & my Sons, I am forbidden to attempt it. An incident of a very afflictive nature, and aggravated by it's suddenness and it's contrariety to what I had been led to expect even to the very moment of it's announcement, combined with those vehement hot days to overset me. Some time or other I will communicate the particulars to you. The Sum is, a disagreement between my eldest Son & his College. It came at first in a most formidable shape; but the following investigation has disarmed it of it's sharper and invenomed weapons—and my existing conviction is that more of what I must condemn might have been present without producing the same effect, if what I cannot wish otherwise had been absent. Give my words a Christian interpretation, & I may say that this occurrence has strengthened the sentiment, I have ever been, as it were, visited with—that there is a Nemesis awakened by the act of exulting or glorying in any thing mortal—and that to rejoice without tempering the joy with fear, is a species of Glorying, however natural the impulse, however desirable or estimable the occasion. We should treat Prosperity as the Lydian King, or whoever it was, with more prudence than justice or generosity treated his continuedly prosperous Friend— i.e. withdraw our love & confidence from it.—

Of the too limited time, which my Ill-health and the exigences of the To Day leave in my power, I have given the larger portion to the works of Swedenborg, particularly to the 'Univer. Theol. of the New Church'.[2]—I find very few & even those but *doubtful* instances, of tenets, in which I am conscious of any substantial difference of opinion with the enlightened Author; but many, in which fully coinciding with his statements of the main Christian truths & his

---

[1] Coleridge refers to his 'engagement' to spend a week with Tulk. See Letter 1225.

[2] *The True Christian Religion; containing the Universal Theology of the New Church.*

interpretation of the Scriptural Doctrine, I could nevertheless use & actually have been accustomed to use the words & terms, to which, & to those who so express themselves, he attaches and attributes notions very different, and which equally with himself I regard & should deprecate as more than erroneous—as *pernicious* errors. The probable explanation of this may be: that I, herein imitating Leibnitz, have been in the habit of considering what the meaning of the *words*, rightly & scripturally defined, *might* be; while Swedenborg, more gifted and more accustomed to distinguish the spirits of men, attended principally to the Meaning of the Users, the sense in which such words were in fact understood and employed by the majority of those who had adopted them for their *standard*, as the motto for their sectarian *Coat of Arms*, the heraldic scroll of their peculiar Guild.—Thus, in Swedenborg's definition of the term, Faith, I subscribe with my whole heart and spirit to his doctrine respecting Solifidianism, and I find a paragraph in one of my Memorandum Books, which I had written 15 or 16 years ago, in which I declared Faith in *this* sense, taken as meritorious or the source of merit, to be the Queen Bee in the Hive of theological Error.[1]—But I have been accustomed to give a far other definition of that Term—& have lately written a short essay or tract on the true nature of Faith,[2] the result of which is in perfect harmony with Swedenborg; & to it's completion it needs only what I am about to add, a collation of all the passages in the Old & New Testament in which the word occurs, with proof that the senses differ only as the same tree in different stages of it's growth & developement. So again with regard to the Tri-unity. As far as respects the *Christian* Dispensation, the first record of which is in my belief the first Chapter of Genesis, I hold the same conviction as is so admirably unfolded and enforced in the Univ. Theol.—& had long held it as the literal and only defensible sense of St John, i. 18, Θεὸν οὐδεὶς ἑώρακε πώποτε· ὁ μονογενὴς υἱός, ὁ ὢν εἰς τὸν κόλπον τοῦ πατρός, ἐκεῖνος ἐξηγήσατο.—But I do not see that this precludes the *philosophical* idea of an essential Trinity which God is: (i.e. *ess*ential as essentially *self-exist*ential) tho' I am ready to acknowlege, that the former alone is an article of Faith. The pseudo-athanasian Creed I reject as of no authority in the first place, as intemperate in the next, then as most inconveniently worded, and lastly as at once superfluous and defective—tautologically superfluous in the point of the co-equality, & dangerously defective in that of the subordination. Altogether I apply to it in increased

---

[1] See *The Notebooks of Samuel Taylor Coleridge*, ed. Kathleen Coburn, vol. ii, 1962, item 2434/17.8/*f 9*. The notebook entry is dated Thursday, 7 Feb. 1805.
[2] For Coleridge's 'Essay on Faith' see *Literary Remains*, iv. 425.

measure what Hilary says against Creeds in general, not sparing even the Nicene.—But yet I doubt, whether the authorized use of the term, person, was not posterior to the Council of Nice—& if I recollect aright, the words, οὐσία and ὑπόστασις, were, about that time, so little appropriated, that sometimes the οὐσία was used to signify that which was afterwards called πρόσωπον or person, and ὑπόστασις for [subsistence &][1] sometimes vice versâ. But I am pretty confident that this inappropriate term, Person (what indeed could be other than inappropriate to a subject absolutely unique?) was *at first* intended to convey the contrary to the crude εἴδωλον, into which it has since then been too often perverted. Assuredly, the etymon of the word, Persona, sive forma, per quam sonat aliquis (& you may be certain, I do not like the word the better for it's having been borrowed from the Greek Drama) suggests as the properest sense, that in and by which God manifests himself to us. —In the article of the Holy Ghost, which relies on the Baptismal Form for it's only plausible scripture-authority, I seem to detect clearly the *origin* of the common notions or rather notionless dicta of the Trinity in the confusion of the philosophical *Idea* of Deity with the Christian *Fact* of the incarnate Jehovah, God manifest in the Flesh.[2]

[1] MS. cut off. See *Literary Remains*, iii. 260–1.

[2] The following autograph fragment Coleridge may have intended to send to Tulk:

Swedenborg's sense of Redemption, the divinity of Christ, and the Trinity as contained in, and connected with, the Manifestation of the Divine Humanity, together with the doctrinal rejection of the Neo-calvinistic Doctrines of Soli-fidianism, vicarious payment, and imputed Righteousness —all these and others, not as the words are capable of being understood, but as they actually and really are understood by the immense majority of those who adopt and who oppose these tenets—I receive as a pure, perhaps the purest, form of the Gospel Truth.

The Creed falsely attributed to Athanasius, and even in point of congruity erroneously named Athanasian, I disregard as of no authority, and reject as imperfect, and if not necessarily erroneous yet conveying dangerous error by omission. But with regard to the Nicene Creed, I can agree to Swedenborg's denunciations of the same, only as far as the interpretations, that have (I admit) too generally been given and received, are in question, but not as to the sense, in which the words of this Creed may and ought to be interpreted.

I hold, that the religious and the philosophical world are alike indebted to Swedenborg for his not less perspicuous than profound enucleation of the distinction of the Divine ESSE and the Divine EXISTERE; but I hold likewise with the most tranquil conviction, that in this great and good man's own positions there lies involved the Truth of an *essential*, and (relatively to the Divine ΠΛΗΡΩΜΑ uncreate) existential Tri-unity, distinguishable from that Trinity, in which we are especially interested as *Christians*, and concerning which I am and long have been of the like, and, I believe, of the same mind with Emanuel Swedenborg. I am quietly conscious, that the Idea is vouch-

To all else, as for instance to the point on which Mr Arboyn
rendered his zeal more conspicuous than his own meaning perspicuous, & in honest truth somewhat at the expence of his discretion
and courtesy,[1] I can only say that I appropriate Mr Hartley's

safed to me; and that I form as distinct Conceptions (*Begriffe*) thereof, as of
any other *Idea*, strictly so called: ex. gr. of the Omnipresence, Eternity,
and Will; i.e. I clearly conceive the (in *material* or *sensible* Subjects & therefore for the mere understanding) *incompatible* Attributes, the contemplation
of the *identity* of which constitutes the *Idea*.

Scholium.

Suppose for a moment with me, that there were but one coloured Object
in the world given to the human eye, and let it be a vivid Rain-bow, or
whatever else might exhibit the prismatic colours. Suppose further, that
the vision of color existed *potentially* indeed in all, but *re et actu* only in very
Few. It is evident, that the names or terms, which these Few appropriated
to this unique Phenomenon, must, by virtue of it's uniqueness, have a
peculiar & as it were *technical* sense; that tho' every such term would
probably be borrowed from the Language of the Senses, on the ground of some
imperfect analogy, real or imagined—yet the term would convey it's true
meaning to those only who employed it as a *proper name*, or (quasi *algebraic*)
sign: while to others the analogy instead of aiding would mislead, and give
the same aberration from the truth, as the words, *high, low, sharp, brilliant*,
in the musical vocabulary would to a deaf man, who could read, but yet was
utterly unconscious of his deafness.—With no dissimilar view I acquiesce in
the use of the words begotten and proceeding, each as distinguished from
the other, and both as contra-distinguished from, created; and so too of the
term, *Person*, as the verbal exponent of Self-subsistence, in opposition to
Accident, Quality, Modification or Attribute, but neither including, nor
necessarily excluding, Self-origination. I am not partial to the word: I see
and lament the σκιοσωματισμός, the shadowy Idolism, which it does, and is
liable to, occasion; but any other mode of uttering the unutterable would, it
appears to me, fall under equal objections, and on the other hand I confess
myself apprehensive of a yet more perilous heresy in the opposite direction.
[MS. Coleridge family.] The Greek word in the last sentence is underlined
once in MS.

[1] James Arbouin (1742–1821) compiled *Select extracts from the Writings of
Emanuel Swedenborg*, 1801.
According to an article in the *New-Church Review*, Oct. 1909, p. 516, on
20 June 1825 at the sixteenth annual meeting of the Swedenborg Society,
'Mr. Tulk announced to its members that his friend Samuel Taylor Coleridge had
offered to write a history of the mind of Swedenborg if £200 should be given
him in remuneration. . . . The same proposition was presented by Mr. Tulk to
the London Coffee Meeting, but an action favorable to its acceptance was
successfully obstructed by Mr. Arbouin, an active New-Churchman, who had
"doubts of Mr. Coleridge's doctrinal fitness" '.
Arbouin's share in the matter is somewhat elaborated in an article in
Morning Light, 1883, p. 518:

Mr Arbouin having doubts of Mr Coleridge's doctrinal fitness, and knowing the gentleman with whom Mr Coleridge was stopping at Highgate, went
there just before the dinner hour, and was invited to stay dinner. After
dinner, he determined to satisfy his doubts by directly and openly asking

sentiments, Preface p. xv:[1] and *if* I differ from Mr Arboyn more or otherwise than as not approving his choice of expressions, I know no better way of explaining the nature and ground of my dissent than by reverentially applying the words of our Lord (John VI. 63) 'Doth this offend you? It is the *spirit* that quickeneth; the flesh profite[th] nothing. The words, that have been spoken to you (*and which I likewise receive, as far as they have yet come before me in the public Writings of the distinguished Person*) are *Spirit*, and they are truth.'—May I not add? 'But there are some who' seem to themselves to believe even beyond their brethren, yet 'believe not': for

> Mr C. his opinion of Swedenborg, when he received a guarded but unfavourable reply. This was conveyed to the Coffee Meeting, and put an end to the proposal to subscribe £200. Mr Tulk, no doubt mortified somewhat, asked Mr Coleridge for an explanation, when he said that, being, as he judged, rudely questioned before a mixed company, he was not prepared unreservedly to give his opinion, and so he replied accordingly. (J. B. Beer, *Coleridge the Visionary*, 1959, p. 41.)

Since Arbouin died in 1821, his discussion with Coleridge probably took place in June 1820. It would seem, moreover, that the present letter was a fuller 'explanation' to Tulk. See Letter 1276 for Coleridge's proposal concerning a 'moderate Octavo' volume on Swedenborg.

[1] Coleridge refers to a letter of Thomas Hartley (1709?–1784), friend and translator of Swedenborg. The letter is included in the preface to the 1819 edition of *The True Christian Religion*. The passage on p. xv reads:

> This highly gifted man's visions and communications with the spiritual world, in a frequent visible intercourse with angels, and other spirits, will be looked upon by many as an exceptionable part of his writings, owing to a general disbelief of these things, helped on by the weak arguments of some in a degree of reputation for their learning, in order to discredit the reality of such supernatural discoveries, urging, that since the publication of the Gospel they have ceased as useless: though it is most certain, that after the publication of the law they were frequent; and if any credit is to be given to the best human testimonies, they have been vouchsafed to some in every age of the Christian church. I verily believe with our author, that we have all of us communications with the spiritual worlds, by our connections with good or evil spirits, according to the fitness of disposition and choice that lead to such associations respectively, and that we receive influx from them: but few understand this, through want of visible supernatural representations, though the truth of the matter is provable from the Sacred Writings; and as to that portion of Scripture on which they mistakenly lay so much stress, viz. *If they hear not Moses and the prophets, neither will they be persuaded though one rose from the dead*, it is spoken of such as have hardened themselves in unbelief with respect to a future state, and therefore would bring themselves under still greater condemnation should they have the offer of such additional evidence as they would be sure to reject; whereas the same extraordinary vouchsafements to certain believers may be considered as their privilege, and of benefit to themselves or others; or, if dispensed to such as are weak in the faith, may serve for their confirmation in it: but of these matters we are seldom competent judges, as they are among the secrets of Divine wisdom.

the Letter hideth the spirit from them. As they read, so they believe—both with the eyes of the body: and when they hear of spirit, they think of *Spectre*. For such men it is either literal or metaphorical. There is no third. For to the *Symbolical* they have not arrived. But if there be *piety* at the Heart, this doubtless is ripening for them within the Husk: and 'thus the pious mystical, and the pious literal Christian may unite in the spirit of *Love*, and as different parts of the same temple, have their respective degrees of sanctity'. (Pref. p. viii.)

Make my affectionately respectful remembrances to Mrs Tulk, & with every kind and earnest wish for the welfare of all of your Household think me,

dear Sir, | most sincerely your obliged Friend
S. T. Coleridge

1244. *To John Murray*

Address: Mr Murray | Alberma[rle Street] By favor of Mr Hurwitz.
MS. Victoria University Lib. Pub. E. L. G. ii. 283.

[August 1820][1]

Dear Sir

The polite and—for so I felt it—the kind attention, with which you honoured a former note of introduction to you,[2] has tempted me to comply with a request of my friend & Neighbor, Mr Hurwitz; but to which, it must be confessed, I was myself accessory, tho' without intending any such effect, by what I had mentioned to him in a detail of my own literary mistakes and regrets. As however the consciously impressing false or exaggerated Notions of any thing or person is a something worse than mistake, & one in which I have, thank God! been more sinned against than sinning, I will proceed to the object of this letter.—

Mr Hurwitz is a man, concerning whom I have repeatedly conversed with Mr Frere, as in many respect[s] an extraordinary character. A Jew, not more by birth than by conviction, not merely honest & strictly conscientious, but even delicately and honorably so, liberal in all his principles & opinions & of all the religious men, I have known, perhaps most deserving the name of a *philosopher*, a sound Oriental Scholar, & a profound Hebraist—to which I am

---

[1] The reference to Hartley Coleridge's 'Essay on Metre' in the postscript to the present letter closely parallels Coleridge's remarks in the following letter and suggests that the two letters were written about the same time.

[2] See Letter 1201, in which Coleridge introduced Mariana Starke to John Murray.

bound to add (of course as the mere dictum of my own judgement) the most truly rational & grounded Philologist, with the most originality of insight into the universal principles, the philosophy, of Language—he who had been fortunate enough to discover by mere chance of neighborhood a man, of whom this could be affirmed with truth, must have [been] singularly lucky in his chance acquaintances, if he saw nothing extraordinary in such a character. For myself I should be thankful for the occurrence were it only that I have learnt what I before did not imagine, that a learned, unprejudiced, & yet strictly *orthodox* Jew may be much nearer in point of faith & religious principles to a learned & strictly orthodox Christian, of the Church of England, than many called Christians who hold a sincere Churchman & indeed every one who will not accept the hollow Shell of the history of Christianity for the Religion itself, in supreme contempt.—

Taking as his occasion & vehicle Mr Bellamy's various Attacks on our Bible & the European Versions in general (Attacks so well exposed in the Quarterly) but yet dressing this *Fish* only for the sake of the Sauce—as is the case with so many admirable Articles in your Review—Mr Hurwitz has written a vindication of the Established Version, and with it (and of yet greater importance) a defence of Revealed Religion itself as far as it has been attacked by Deists on the pretence of contradictory & immoral or absurd passages in the Old Testament.[1] I have myself gone thro' the whole, sentence by sentence, with the view of assisting the excellent Author in the removal of any errors or *ungraces* in the style & language—And I pledge myself, that there is not a sentence in the work, which might not have been written by the most orthodox Bishop on the Bench.—Mr H. wishes to prefix a long Letter of mine, stating & explaining my approbation of the work, & my reasons for attaching to it the value & interest which I really do—& if it were thought by any one authorized to form an opinion, that such a letter would be of any use to the work, I should comply with his wish with great pleasure.[2]

Now Mr Hurwitz is ambitious that you should publish the work. —He does not desire that you should run any risk—this he is ready to take on himself, any profit being . . .[3]

---

[1] Coleridge refers to Hurwitz's *Vindiciae Hebraicae; or, a Defence of the Hebrew Scriptures, as a Vehicle of Revealed Religion: occasioned by the recent strictures and innovations of Mr. J. Bellamy; and in Confutation of his attacks on all preceding translations, and on the Established Version in particular*, 1820. The work, which was published by F. C. and J. Rivington and Boosey & Sons, actually appeared in Feb. 1821. See *English Catalogue of Books*.

[2] No such letter was included in Hurwitz's work.

[3] A third of a page of the MS. cut off.

P.S. Is there any chance of seeing Mr F's [Ar]istophanics?[1]—My eldest Son & myself have b[een] labouring at an Essay on Metre, Metres, & [the] possibility of transferring, by compensation & equivalence of effect, the measures of the Greek Dramatists to the English Language—which we mean to offer to the Quarterly as a Candidate for a Review of Mr F's Imitations, from which our illustrations & examples are chiefly, indeed almost exclusively, taken—

1245. *To Thomas Allsop*

Address: Mr T. Allsop | Ireton Wood | Wirksworth | Derbyshire.
MS. New York Public Lib. Pub. with omis. Letters, Conversations and Rec. *54.*
Postmark: Highgate, 8 August 1820.

Tuesday Afternoon
July [8 August] 1820

My very dear Allsop

Neither Indolence nor Procrastination have had a place among the causes of my silence: least of all, either yourself or the subject of your letter or the purpose of answering it having been absent from my thoughts. You may with almost literal truth attribute it to want of Time from the number, quantity and quality of my engagements, the necessity of several journeys *to* and (still worse) *in* town being the largest Waster of Time and Spirits.—At length, I have settled Hartley for the next six or 8 weeks with Mr Montague, while he is writing an Essay on the principles of Taste in relation to Metre and Rhythm, containing, first, a new scheme of Prosody as applied to the choral and Lyrical Stanzas of the Greek Drama— & 2nd. the possibility of improving & enriching our English Versification by digging in the original *mines*—viz. the tunes of nature in impassioned conversation—both illustrated and exemplified from Mr Frere's Aristophanic Poems—. I have been working hard to bring together for him the notes &c, that I myself had taken down on this subject.—Derwent has been sadly out of health, & even now is far from well.—There are some persons—I have known several— who when they find themselves uncomfortable take up the pen & transfer as much discomfort as they can to their absent Friends. There are others—but I know only one of *this* sort—who as soon as they take up the Pen, instantly become *dolorous*, however smug,

[1] As his letters show, Coleridge had earlier read with enthusiasm J. H. Frere's translations of Aristophanes. These translations were not published until 1839–40. See Letters 1007, 1014–15, 1037, 1065, and 1148. See also 1245 and 1521.

snug, and cheerful the minute before & the minute after. Now just
such is Mrs Coleridge, God bless her!—& she has been writing
letter after letter to Derwent, about Hartley, & every discomfortable recollection & anticipation that she could conjure up—that she
has completely overset him.—*This must not be.*—Mr Gillman too
has been *out of sorts*—but at this present we are all better. I at
least am as well as I ever am, & my regular employment, in which
Mr Green is weekly my Amanuensis, the Work on the Books of the
O. and N. Testament, introduced by the Assumptions & Postulates required as the pre-conditions of a fair examination of Christianity as a scheme of Doctrines, Precepts, and Histories drawn or
at least deducible from these Books—. And now, in the *narrative*
line, I have only to add that Mrs Gillman desires to be affectionately
remembered to you, and bids me intreat you to stay *as long away* as
you possibly can, provided it be from *London* as well as from Highgate.—Would to Heaven! I were with you! In a few days you
should see that the spirit of the Mountaineer is not yet utterly
extinct in me.—Wordsworth has remarked (in the 'Brothers', I
believe)

> The thought of Death sits light upon the man
> That has been bred and dies among the Mountains.

But I fear, that this like some other few of W's *many* striking passages means less than it seems, or rather promises, to mean. Poets
(especially if philosophizers too) are apt to represent the effect
made on themselves as general—the Geese of Phoebus are all Swans,
& Wordsworth's Shepherds & Estatesmen all Wordsworths, even
(as in old Michael) in the *un*poetic traits of character. Whether mountains have any particular effect on the native inhabitants, by virtue
of being mountains exclusively, & what that effect is, would be a
difficult problem. If independent tribes, Mountainers are robbers of
the Lowlanders, from necessity; brave, active, & with all the usual
warlike good & bad qualities that result from habits of adventurous
Robbery. Add Clanship & the superstitions that are the surviving
Precipitate of an established Religion—both which are common to
the uncivilized Celtic tribes, in plain no less than in mountain—&
you have the Scottish Highlanders—. But where the inhabitants
exist as States or civilized parts of civilized states, they appear to
be in mind and character just what their condition & employments
would render them in level Plain the same as amid Alpine Heights.
At least, the influence acts indirectly only, as far as the mountains
are the causa causae, or occasion, of a *pastoral* life instead of an Agri-
cultural—thus combining a lax and common Property possessed by
a whole District with small hereditary Estates sacred to each, while

the properties in Sheep seem to partake of both characters. And truly to this circumstance, aided by the favorable action of a necessarily scanty population (for Man is an Oak that wants room, not a *Plantation* Tree) we must attribute whatever superiority the Mountaineers of Cumberland+Westmoreland & of the Swiss & Tyrolese Alps possess: as the shocking Contrast of the Welsh Mountaineers too clearly evinces.—But this subject I have discussed, & (if I do not flatter myself) satisfactorily in the Literary Life, & I will not conceal from *you*, that this inferred dependency of the human soul on accidents of Birth-place & Abode together with the vague misty, rather than mystic, Confusion of God with the World & the accompanying Nature-worship, of which the asserted dependence forms a part, is the Trait in Wordsworth's poetic Works that I most dislike, as unhealthful, & denounce as contagious: while the odd occasional introduction of the popular, almost the vulgar, Religion in his later publications (the popping in, as Hartley says, of the old man with a beard) suggests the painful suspicion of worldly prudence (at best a justification of *masking* truth (which in fact is a falsehood substituted for a truth withheld) on plea of Expediency) carried into *Religion*. At least, it conjures up to *my* fancy a sort of *Janus*-head of Spinoza and Dr Watts, or 'I and my Brother, the Dean'.—Permit me then, in the place of the two lines

> The thought of Death sits easy on the Man
> Who hath been bred & dies among the Mountains,

to say—

> The thought of Death sits easy on the Man,
> Whose earnest *Will* hath lived among the Deathless:

and I can perhaps build upon this foundation an answer to the question, which would deeply interest me by whomever put, and pained me only because it was put by *you*—i.e. because I feared, it might be the inspiration of Ill-health, & am jealous of any *Consenting* of that inward Will, which with some mysterious ferm-[entation][1] moves in the Bethesda-pool of our animal Life, to withdraw it's resis[tance.] For the Soul among it's other regalia has an energetic Veto against all underminin[gs of the] Constitution; & among [these] as not least insidious, I consider the thoughts & hauntings that tamper with the [love] of Life. Do not so! You *would* not, if I could transfer into you in all it's depth & liveliness the sense, what a Hope, Promise, Impulse You are to me in my present efforts to realize my past labors, and by building up the Temple, the shaped Stones, Beams, Pillars, yea, the graven Ornaments & the connecting Clamps of which have been piled up by me

[1] MS. torn by seal.

only in too great abundance, to enable you & my two—may I not say? *other* Sons to affirm—Vivit, quia non frustra vixit.—

In reading an extract in the German Encyclopaedia from Dobritzhoffer's most interesting account of the Abiponenses,[1] a savage Tribe in Paraguay, houseless yet in person, & morals the noblest of savage tribes—who when first known by Europeans amounted to 100,000 Warriors, yet had a tradition that they were but the relique of a far more numerous community, & who by wars with other savage tribes & by intestine feuds among themselves are now dwindled to a thousand (men, women & children do not exceed 5000)—it struck me with distinct remembrance, 1. that this is the History of *all* savage tribes, and 2ndly: that all tribes *are* savage that have not a positive Religion defecated from Witchcraft & an established Priesthood contra-distinguished from individual Conjurers. Nay, the Islands of the Pacific (the Polynesia, which sooner or later the swift and silent Masonry of the Coral Worms will compact into a rival Continent, a *fifth Quarter* of the World) blest with all the plenties of nature, & enjoying an immunity from all the ordinary dangers of savage life, were many of them utterly dispeopled since their first discovery, & wholly by their own feuds & vices—nay, that their Bread-fruit Tree & their delicious [and healthful climate had only made][2] the process of mutual destruction & self-destruction more hateful, more basely sensual.—This therefore I assume as an undoubted fact of History: and from this as a portion of the History of *men*, I draw a new (to my knowlege, at least, a new) series of proofs of several, I *might* say, of all the positions of *pre-eminent* importance & interest more than vital— a series which taken in harmonious Counterpart to a prior series drawn from *interior* history (the history of *Man*), the documents of which are to be found only in the archives of each Individual's own Consciousness, will form a complete *Whole*, a *system* of Evidence, consisting of two correspondent Worlds, as it were, correlative & mutually potenziating, yet each integral and self-subsistent— having the same correlation, as the Geometry and the Observations, or the Meta-Physics and the Physics, of Astronomy.—If I can thus demonstrate the truth of the doctrine of existence after the present life, it is not improbable that some rays of Light may fall on the question—what *state* of existence it may be reasonably supposed to be? At all events, we shall, I trust, be enabled to determine negatively, what it can *not* be *for any*, and *for whom* this or that, which

[1] Martin Dobrizhoffer, 1717–91, Jesuit missionary, published his *Historia de Abiponibus* in 1784. Sara Coleridge's translation of this work appeared in 1822.

[2] MS. cut off; the words in brackets supplied from the printed text.

does not appear universally precluded, is yet *for them* precluded—in plainer words—What *can not* be, universally speaking:—2. What *may* be. 3. What the differences may be, for different individuals, within the limits described in No. 2.—4. What scheme of embodied Representation of the future state (our *Reason* not forbidding the same) is recommended by the truest analogies? And 5. What scheme it is best for us [to combine with our belief of a]¹ Hereafter as most conducive to the growth & cultivation of our collective faculties in this life, or of each in the order of it's comparative worth, value, & permanence—. This I must defer to another letter. For [I cannot] let another Post pass by without your knowing[, my dear Allso]p, that we all are thinking of and loving you.

S. T. C.

1246. *To Hartley Coleridge*

MS. British Museum. Pub. with omis. Inquiring Spirit . . ., *ed. Kathleen Coburn, 1951, pp. 105, 143, and 203.*

[August 1820 ?]²

Yester morning, my dear Hartley! you appeared to agree with me on the truth of the first universal principle of the Polar Logic, as far as it is *Logic*, i.e. confined to the Objects of the Sense and the Understanding, or (what is the same) to the Finite, the Creaturely. You agreed with me, that *One* could not manifest itself or be wittingly distinguished as One, but by the co-existence of an *Other*: or that A could not be affirmed to be A but by the perception that it is *not* B; and that this again implies the perception that B *is* as well as A. We can become CONSCIOUS of *Being* only by means of *Existence*, tho' having thus become conscious thereof, we are in the same moment conscious, that Being must be prior (in thought) to Existence: as without seeing, we should never *know* (i.e. know ourselves to have known) that we had Eyes; but having learnt this, we know that Eyes must be anterior to the act of seeing. With equal

¹ MS. cut off; the words in brackets supplied from the printed text.
² This letter was probably written in 1820, after Coleridge 'settled' Hartley with the Montagus. (See Letter 1245.) Miss Coburn (pp. 421, 423, and 428) says that the manuscript bears a watermark of 1822, but Mr. T. C. Skeat, who examined the original (Egerton MS. 2801), writes: 'The first sheet of the letter (f. 126) has no watermark. The second sheet (f. 127) is torn across horizontally half-way down, and at some later date the loss has been made up with a different piece of paper, pasted on to bring the sheet out to its original size. The *added* piece has the watermark "Russell & Turner 1822". There is also a watermark on the upper (original) half of the sheet running vertically and reading: EMBR . . .
18 . . . .'

evidence we understand that Existence supposes *relation*—for it is, Sisto me *ad extra*, and thereby distinguished from Being. Well then. We know A by B: and B by A. We know, that between A and B there is, first, a something peculiar to each, *that*, namely, by which A is A and *not* B, and B is B and *not* A: and secondly, a something common to them, a one in both; namely, that which is expressed by the copula, *is*: and thirdly, that the latter, =Being, is in order of thought presupposed in the former. What is last in Reflection, is first in the *genesis*, or order of causation.

We proceed—(at a tortoise or pedicular Crawl, you will say—but believe me, dear Boy! there is no other way of attaining a clear and productive Insight, and that all impatience is an infallible Symptom that the Inquirer is not seeking *the* Truth for Truth's sake, but only *a* truth or something that may pass for such, in order to some alien *End*. And this may be right: the End may be justifiable. I may ask, what $9 \times 9 \div 4$ makes, in order to pay a Bill—or to understand the result of some statement given in proof of the accuracy of some deduction from a chemical experiment. I want the *fact* only, & it is indifferent to my purpose whether I get it from Archimedes or a Carpenter's Ruler. But then you must not affect to be studying *Arithmetic*: nor must an Egyptian who has no wish but to mark off his three Acres and a Half of Tillage Ground, after the overflow of the Nile, inveigh against Euclid for the lumbriciform (*wormy*) proserpence of his Elements of Geometry. There is no way of arriving at any sciential End but by finding it at every step. The End is in the Means: or the adequacy of each Mean is already it's end. Southey once said to me: You are nosing every nettle along the Hedge, while the Greyhound (meaning himself, I presume) wants only to get sight of the Hare, & FLASH!—strait as a line!—he has it in his mouth!—Even so, I replied, might a Cannibal say to an Anatomist, whom he had watched dissecting a body. But the fact is—I do not care twopence for the *Hare*; but I value most highly the excellencies of scent, patience, discrimination, free Activity; and find a Hare in every Nettle, I make myself acquainted with. I follow the Chamois-Hunters, and seem to set out with the same Object. But I am no Hunter of *that* Chamois Goat; but avail myself of the Chace in order to a nobler purpose—that of making a road across the Mountains, on which Common Sense may hereafter pass backward and forward, without desperate Leaps or Balloons that scar indeed but do not improve the chance of getting onward.—)

A blessing, I say, on the inventors of Notes! You have only to imagine the lines between the ( ) to be printed in smaller type at the bottom of the page—& the Writer may digress, like Harris, the

Historian,[1] from Dan to Barsheba & from Barsheba in hunt after the last Comet, without any breach of continuity.

Digress? or not digress? That's now no question.
Do it! Yet do it *not*! See Note* below.

Well! to proceed. What is affirmed of A is equally affirmed of B: and what is true of A relatively to B, is no less true of B relatively to C. In other words, Alterity leads to *Plurality*.—'Mora' is the term used by the Italian Philosophers, as when they define Beauty by Uno nel Più: but our 'The many' or 'Multeity' has this preference that it seems more naturally to include both *the more* and *the less*. Whether it be above the Unit in the progression of Integrals, or below it in the regression of Fractions

$$\begin{array}{c} 4 \\ 3 \\ 2 \\ \hline 1 \\ \hline \frac{1}{2} \\ \frac{1}{3} \\ \frac{1}{4} \end{array}$$

it is alike in both cases *the Many* as distinguished from One—tho' as One can never be *known* but as it is revealed in and by the Many, so neither can the Many be *known* (i.e. reflected on) but by it's relation to a *One*, and ultimately therefore, *Ones* being=Many, only by reference to THE ONE, which includes instead of excluding the Alter. The Aleph, say the Rabbinical Philologists, is no Letter; but that in and with which all Letters are or become. Even so, there is a higher than 1. or the 1. is an equivocal for two most disparate senses: in the nobler of which it is equivalent to the O positive, which is no *thing* because it is the ground and sufficient cause of *all* things, and no *number* because it is the Numerorum omnium Fons et Numerus.—N.B. No man can *be*, or can *understand*, a Philosopher, till he has acquired the power and the habit of attaching to words the *generic* sense purely and unmixed with the accidents of comparative *degrees*. It is this which constitutes the difference between the *proper* Nomenclature of Science and the inevitable language of ordinary life. The latter speaks only of *degrees*. With *quantity* and quality it is familiar; but knows nothing of *quiddity* but as a synonyme for worthless subtleties: and only grins wider and with more intense self-complacency when it hears the former speak of invisible *Light*, the *Heat* of Ice, &c. The *Uno* nel

[1] Probably Walter Harris (1686–1761), Irish historiographer.

Più of the philosophic Saint & Bishop of Geneva (Francesco Sales)[1] would be as senseless to a common Italian, as my 'Multeity in Unity' or 'The One in the Many'[2] could be to a Mr Wheatley of Oriel[3] or the *'cute* Isaacs of the Stock Exchange.—[MS. breaks off thus.]

1247. *To Thomas Allsop*

Address: T. Allsop, Esqre | 1 Blandford Place | Pall Mall.
MS. Harvard College Lib. Hitherto unpublished.
Postmark: Highgate, 22 September 1820.

Thursday Night
21 Septr 1820
Highgate—

My dear Allsop
    Derwent is at Mr Charles Lloyd's somewhere near Kensington—I have some semblance of a recollection, that it is at the Gravel Pits, but nothing that I can rely on.—C. Lamb can tell you, should any of your people be going into the City, & can take a note to him at the India House, between the Hours of 10 & 3.—You know, I suppose, that dear Miss Lamb is indisposed—& it is therefore not so certain, that Ch. Lamb will be at his own Lodgings in Russel St after the office Hours.—

    This change of the Weather has been on the whole a change for the better, for me—tho' I have not yet been able to bring the digestive process into any sort of regularity.—Mrs Gillman bids me convey her thanks to you for having executed her commission, & desires to be kindly remembered—

    Do not let any opportunity of our seeing you pass by when you have no other engagement or call, & believe me
        with unfeigned esteem | & most affectionate regard |

Your's ever,
S. T. Coleridge

[1] See Coleridge's note to the poem included in Letter 1666, and *Table Talk*, 27 Dec. 1831, and 1 Jan. and 23 June 1834.
[2] See *Biog. Lit.* i. 188 and ii. 230 fol.; *Letters, Conversations and Rec.* 106; *Hints towards the Formation of a more comprehensive Theory of Life. By S. T. Coleridge*, ed. Seth B. Watson, 1848, pp. 42 and 45; and Letter 956.
[3] Coleridge refers to Richard Whately (1787–1863), dean of Oriel and later archbishop of Dublin.

1248. *To Mrs. Mary Evans Todd*[1]

Transcript Coleridge family. Hitherto unpublished.

Highgate—
Tuesday 26th Septr. 1820.

Dear Mrs Todd

I inclose Lady C. L.'s[2] letter together with the Answer, which I have this morning received from Mrs Cootes.[3] I would I could accompany it with some 'compensating counterbalance'! But I have done my best—and at a time when I know not which way to turn, first in encountering perplexities & embarrassments that are pressing on me, partly on my own account, & yet more, or more urgently at least, on account of my sons—one of whom will leave me for Cambridge in a few days, while I am going to Oxford on be-half of the other—I had a note from Mrs Prickett, acquainting me with the terms of the house in Hornsey Lane—the rent 60£, the premium for the Lease 200£. They are considered here as very reasonable, the House being an excellent one. You blame me for not having written a plan. How can I, when you are yourself wholly undecided? Advertisements of any kind, merely to satisfy yourself whether you are likely to succeed, will but exhaust your interest, and convey an impression that you are trifling with the Applicants who answer them. A plan for a school will not answer for a scheme of a family Home for ladies, or for single gentlemen. I am incompetent to advise; but of this I am sure that what is begun in haste ends in disappointment. Were you fixed on a School and felt your-self adequate to the undertaking, the wisest way, as it appears to me, would be to settle on a house first, the rent of which should commence a month or so afterwards, so that you would announce the day on which you would be prepared to receive the Scholars & *then* to circulate the plan, and send the advertisements, i.e. the plan in its most abridged form. I said the *wisest* way, meaning of course to imply, *if* practicable. How very little the chance is of your procuring any sum from uninterested persons by subscription, for the purpose of enabling you to commence the attempt, any sum at all proportionate either to the object, or to your own toil & solicita-tion, you have had, I fear, more than sufficient grounds of presuming —But I feel that my own horizon is too thick with clouds for me to be a fair judge—and better be sanguine to no purpose, than

[1] In 1808 Coleridge first learned of the fate of 'the Mary Evans of 14 years ago'. See Letters 71, 76, 691, and 695.
[2] Probably Lady Caroline Lamb (1785–1828).
[3] The second wife of Thomas Coutts, banker and owner of Holly Lodge at Highgate.

despondent to no purpose: and if my present mood incline to the latter, I can most sincerely assure you that my own inability to befriend you, combined with the earnest wish that I could supersede the necessity of your applying to any other friend, has no small share in the depression of

My dear Mrs T. | Your faithful Friend

S. T. Coleridge

1249. *To Thomas Allsop*

Address: T. Allsop, Esqre | Blandford Place | Pall Mall.
MS. New York Public Lib. Pub. with omis. Letters, Conversations and Rec. *68.*
Postmark: Highgate, 30 September 1820.

Saturday [30 September 1820]

My dear Allsop

Doubtless, nothing could be more delightful to me, independent of Mrs Gillman's kind but unnecessary anxieties, than to go to Oxford with you—Nay, tho' it will be but a flight to & fro with a sojourn but of two days if so much, yet I should even ask it of you, if I were quite sure, absolutely sure, that none, the *least* point, of Prudence would be risked by you in so doing. But in the fear of this (for you will scarcely yourself be able to convince me that at such a time there is not something incurred or hazarded by your leaving business) I do say, that it does not appear to me that I could ask or receive it without some selfishness which would compleatly baffle itself.

I have not yet to my vexation received an answer from Oxford[1] respecting Dr Copplestone's return to Oriel—& I shall be too late for the Post if I do not leave off—

God bless you, | My ever dear friend &

S. T. Coleridge—

[1] No such letter has come to light, but on 2 Oct. Hartley wrote to his father: 'In obedience to the letter of your commands, I write immediately. . . . I cannot speak for certain to the day when the fellows will meet for confirmation, but think it may be about the 19th, but I will write to ascertain.' *Letters of Hartley Coleridge,* 41, and 'Foreword', p. 72.

1249A. *To the Provost and Fellows of Oriel College*

MS. Mr. A. H. B. Coleridge. Pub. Letters of Hartley Coleridge, *44.*

Coleridge composed the present letter for Hartley, whose own copy 'was delivered through the Provost to the assembled Fellows', resident and non-resident, at their formal meeting on 17 October 1820. For the effect on the assembled group of Hartley's communication, see Keble's comment, 'Foreword', pp. 72 and 74.

[October 1820]

To the Reverend the Provost and Fellows of Oriel College
Reverend Sirs

The regular time for the confirmation of the probationary Fellowships having arrived, and it having been announced both to myself and to my Father[1] that it is the determination of the Provost and Resident Fellows to negative the election in my instance; and it being in the highest degree probable that their suffrages together with the grounds and motives for the same will determine the suffrages of the Fellows non-resident; I take this mean of laying before the Provost and Fellows officially assembled the following declarations and avowals.—And first, I declare that I do not protest against the measure itself, severe in itself & heavy in reference to it's certain & probable effects as it is, & the more so from it's being almost an unprecedented measure.—On the contrary as far as the decision that during my probationary Year I have by sundry irregularities, omissions or careless performance of the duties imposed on me by my situation as probationary Fellow; by social preferences incongruous with the object which as a Competitor for a Fellowship of Oriel I had by my own act authorized the Provost & Fellows to expect that I should propose to myself, and therefore irreconcileable with my own virtual promise; and lastly, by single acts, if not of positive intoxication, yet of culpable intemperance; justified such doubts of my character as might conscientiously be deemed incompatible with an election implying in the minds of the electors a conviction of my fitness to become a member of their society and the belief that I should labor with them in the furtherance of the known Ends and aims of the Society—as far as the determination and the grounds assigned for the same, are thus stated, I repeat a formal avowal, that I admit the justice of the measure, and throw myself wholly on the mercy of the Provost and Fellows. But I beg leave to add, that by mercy I do not mean a mercy that is opposite to justice, but such as consistently therewith

---

[1] A reference to John Taylor Coleridge's letter to Gillman which was based in great measure on Keble's letter of June 1820. See preceding 'Foreword', E and F.

might be suggested either by circumstances of palliation in reference to the facts or by consideration of the severity of the punishment in reference to it's certain & to it's probable consequences on
my present and future plans and prospects.—

But statements having been made to my Father by such a channel & in such form as permits no doubt of their authenticity, or of
the full of the Belief of the Provost & resident Fellows in the truth
& accuracy of all and each of the charges contained in the same,
and as authorizes me in presuming that each had exerted an influence proportional to it's moral importance in leading to the determination, of which they are, collectively, the assigned grounds and
causes; and because by the ordinary course of things in similar cases
I hold myself warranted in apprehending, that the effects of these
statements, principally in consequence of sundry parts of the same
not contained in the preceding declaration and avowal, will without
& against the will of the Provost & Fellows extend far beyond their
purpose and intention, not merely to the injury of my character at
present, but to the endangerment of my future utility by depriving
me of the means of retrieving it, inasmuch as the charges in question would tend to prevent my obtaining the situations of trust,
which my acquirements & talents would otherwise entitle me to
look forward to;—for these reasons, and disclaiming all ref[er]ence
to any expressions used or communications made, by individuals
in their individual character, by letter or in conversation, I here,
secondly, protest against the charge of *frequent* acts of Intoxication,
if by the word frequent more than two or at the utmost three single
instances be meant; and declare that I am permitted by my conscience to admit the truth even of so many, only as far as by intoxication a culpable degree of Intemperance be understood, and not
if by intoxication a temporary deprivation of my mental & bodily
faculties, such as we commonly mean to express when we say that
a man is thoroughly *drunk*, i.e. either does not know what he is
doing or saying, or will be incapable of recollecting it on the return
of sobriety, or (recollecting the same, or having had it brought to
his recollection & knowlege) disclaims what he had said or done, as
said or done in the suspension of his judgement & moral will; or
finally, has lost or greatly impaired his powers of communicating
his meaning, and effectuating his purposes, ex. gr. staggering, or
stammering, or using one set of words when he meant another.

I solemnly declare that but for the recollection of *one* incident,
viz. that on my returning from a wine party given on the occasion
of a degree passing, the Servant desired me to take care of my
Candle, from which I inferred both at the time & again on the next
morning (for the words were my first thought on awaking) that I

must have had the appearance & marks of Intoxication, and felt (not without self-reproach & sincere grief) that I must have drunk too much, & beyond what any occasion could justify, above all in a man whose duty, moral and prudential, it was with peculiar solicitude to eschew all scandal, and every approach to an evil example —but for the recollection of this one incident & the rightful inference from the same, I solemnly declare that I could not without offending against my own conscience have pleaded guilty to more than the negative (though still, and with unfeigned penitence, I admit, the serious) offence of not having been sufficiently anxious & careful in the performance of the positive duty, that of making myself an example of the opposite virtue—of behaviour decorous and circumspect and of Temperance beyond suspicion.

Thirdly, I solemnly protest against the inference that my non-attendance at Morning Chapel was occasioned by the intemperance and the late hours of the preceding day; & moreover I protest against, and emphatically deny, the assertion that my late hours, when such did occur, were any way connected with Intemperance, as their cause, effect, or accompaniment.—And that either the testimony, on which the contrary has been believed, is false and slanderous; or that the conclusions grounded thereon have been erroneous and not sustainable by facts—and were it required or permitted, I am prepared to bring evidence in disproof of the charge, by positive proof of the contrary—viz. that to those late hours, whether more or less frequent, either Music, & the blameless pleasures of mixed society in respectable families, or literary discussion, were the sole inducements and temptations.

Lastly, respecting the company kept by me I have already admitted the charge as far as, but only as far as, the negative is in question—namely, that I did not cultivate the society, or the academic rank of society, which I had by an implied & virtual promise bound myself to cultivate, and which it might have been reasonably expected & rightly required of me to seek and prefer. But in no *moral* sense of the word dare I admit that the society, to which I did chiefly attach myself, can with truth be characterized by the words 'low company'—for it consisted of men, with whom I had formed a friendship during my Undergraduateship, all men of good morals & sound religious principles. And I intreat permission to add, that in the one, for me most unfortunate instance, of a private Pupil, my sole motive for prolonging my intimacy was [with ?] him was the hope of rescuing him from the effects of former bad influences, the belief that there was a basis of good in him, and a consequent reluctance to abandon him increased by my sense of his unfortunate circumstances, the very circumstances which should, on prudential grounds, and perhaps as a duty owing to my own credit, have made me discontinue the connection.[1]—

Having made these declarations, I submit myself to whatever measures the Provost & Fellows may determine on, entering no protest against the refusal to elect me, in and for itself, or as grounded on the charges enumerated and admitted by me in the first §§ of this appeal; but on the contrary, confessing and gratefully acknowleging the several distinct warnings and admonitions given me with paternal kindness by the Reverend the Provost, and with friendly earnestness by the Reverend the Dean—. If I protest at all against my exclusion from the Fellowship, I do so only as far as a belief in the truth of the Charges, here solemnly denied [by] me, may have influenced you to a more severe proceeding than you would have adopted had no such charges existed or been credited by you,—a point which none but yourselves can pretend to know, & concerning which no man has a right to question you—and therefore I do not protest against the measure at all—'I admit it's Justice & throw myself on your Mercy.'

But as a pressing act of the duty towards my afflicted Parents and at the dictate of my own conscience I enter the above deliberate Protest, *independently* of the fact or question of my non-election as Fellow of Oriel, against charges calculated to injure me in addition to my non-election, & far more permanently, & to a far more aweful extent & degree—and if in the pursuit of this end I have in any word or sentence transgressed the limits of mere self-defence, I disclaim the same—& subscribe [MS. breaks off thus.]

1250. *To Edward Copleston*

MS. Mr. A. H. B. Coleridge. Pub. with omis. Letters of Hartley Coleridge, *309–16.* These fragmentary drafts are all that have come to light of Coleridge's letter to Copleston, the provost of Oriel.

Before leaving for Oxford to confer with Copleston, Coleridge sent him this letter, 'a very long one', to give him 'a day's preparation for the personal Interview', which was held on Sunday morning, 15 October 1820. Copleston brought the letter and a report of his conference with Coleridge to the attention of the fellows of Oriel during their statutable meeting on 17 October. For further details see the preceding 'Foreword'.

Recalling that the Oriel fellows had determined 'but a week or so' after Hartley was elected probationary fellow to 'rally' him out of his 'oddities', Coleridge was convinced that the peculiarities of his son had aroused prejudice and antagonism at Oriel. Southey came to the same conclusion: 'It is very likely that his [Hartley's] peculiar manners, his love of paradox, and his uncomfortable propensity to disputation may have prejudiced the Fellows against

---

[1] Probably a reference to W. J. St. Aubyn. See Letter 1242.

him more than they are willing to acknowledge, and perhaps more than they are conscious of themselves.' (Southey to John Kenyon. See *The Oriel Record*, June 1938, p. 306.) Thus in the present letter Coleridge felt impelled to lay before Copleston the 'Habits and Dispositions' of his son and to point out that they had been characteristic of him since earliest childhood.

[*Circa* 11 October 1820][1]

[Fragment I]

Honoured Sir

Heavily afflicted as I am, and stunned scarcely less by the suddenness of the Blow than by it's weight, still if the purpose of this letter had been, in any degree or under any disguise, that of interference, whether to avert or to qualify your determination respecting my Son; or if it's expressions could be interpreted as complaint or remonstrance, it might perhaps have been *written* in the first turbulence of grief, could I have been unwise enough to write at all at such a moment—but (I dare promise myself) it would have exposed my weakness to no eye but my own. The well-grounded Respect, which I formed and had publickly avowed from the proofs of your Powers and Principles, before I could have anticipated that I or any of mine would stand in any relation to you, as the Provost of Oriel, which nothing since then has or can have diminished, tho' I should have reason to blush for my own nature if the *feeling* had not been at least enlivened by your friendly kindness to my eldest,[2] and your condescending and courteous [attentions?] to both my Sons, is of itself sufficient to secure you from any such impertinence. Dr Copleston will not condemn me of Arrogance, if I add that I have myself claims to respect (from my *efforts* at least and the Ends and Objects to which they have been directed) which I would not forfeit by consciously obtruding on any man the language of mendicance or irritability. I can indeed find nothing that leaves room for the one or could furnish a pretext for the other in any part either of your conduct, Sir! singly & personally, or in the resolution formed by the Provost and resident Fellows of Oriel collectively and functionally. But if against the writer's will and purpose any words should escape, *susceptible* of a different interpretation, it will,

[1] Writing to Allsop on 11 Oct. 1820 Coleridge says that the present letter 'will reach Dr Copplestone . . . on Friday Morning', i.e. 13 October.

[2] Writing to his father in Sept. 1820 Hartley described his last meeting with Copleston: 'I dined with Dr. Copleston previously to my quitting Oxford. He spoke to me kindly—as to a young man, who had shewn himself unfit for his situation—as to an incautious man who needed warning—but still as to an unblemished character in the worldly acceptation of the word, whom the College had rejected partly as not being the sort of man they wanted—partly— as being more likely to do honour to another station.' See preceding 'Foreword', B.

I trust, be precluded by this distinct avowal. But I am not in any serious degree apprehensive, that I shall give you offence. Would, there were no greater likelihood of my wearying out your patience. In this point only I must be the Beggar: and in intreating your *patient* perusal of this letter—tho' I shall endeavor to express myself as concisely as possible—I feel that I am asking not a little; yet when I assure you that the Hope of it's favorable reception acts as a relief to the wounded spirit of a Father, I dare promise myself that I shall not have asked in vain.—O Sir! it was an unwise and as we say in Devonshire, a *cruel* kindness on the part of my friends, that kept the true state of things concealed from my knowlege, to burst upon me at once and irrevocably [like a Squall from a Fog-bank in which the secure Mariner had been fancying images of shore and Coast-land, all calm and not a sail in reef.][1] How often since I first read the anecdote (Southey's Life of Wesley I. p. 39) Gravia passus sum; but whatever I am, my Hartley is Fellow of Oriel![2] It was & had so long been the prayer of my Heart to see my Sons in that profession, for which I was myself best fitted both by my studies and my inclinations, but from which I had been deterred in my 23rd year by insidious appeals to my unenlightened Conscience. I had so much reason to trust, that whatever doubts or difficulties might start for either in the course of their theological studies, he would have one man, and that man a Father 'who with similar powers and feelings no less acute had entertained the same scruples; had acted upon them; and who by after research, and in less than two years had discovered himself to have quarrelled with received opinions only to embrace errors, to have left the direction tracked out for him on the high road of honorable distinction only to deviate into a labyrinth, where when he had wandered, till his head was giddy, his best good fortune was finally to have found his way out again, too late for prudence though not too late for conscience or for truth!' Biogr. Liter. I. 232. But I am transgressing on your time, and taking a liberty for which I can plead no adequate motive.

[Fragment II]

—As the more serious articles of the Charge are grounded on

[1] Passage in brackets crossed out in MS.

[2] On learning of the election of his son, John Wesley, as fellow of Lincoln College, Samuel Wesley, then 'far advanced in the vale of years', wrote to him: 'What will be my own fate before the summer be over, God knows: *sed passi graviora.*—Wherever I am, my Jack is Fellow of Lincoln.' Robert Southey, *The Life of Wesley; and the Rise and Progress of Methodism*, 2 vols., 1925, i. 28–29. The first edition of Southey's work was published in two volumes in 1820.

presumptions;[1] and as Appearances and even admitted facts may excite, and be thought to warrant, a strong presumption against an Individual in the minds of those who are ignorant of his particular character, which would make no such impression and lead to no such inferences with those who had known the man intimately and understand his peculiarities; I have thought it right to lay before you what I myself know of Hartley Coleridge's Habits and Disposition, previous to his last Term at Oriel. To this, the sole Object of the present Letter, I propose to confine myself, without adverting—and as much as possible without alluding—to the recent Proceedings or the Provocations assigned for the same. And even here I have limited myself to such points of my Son's Character as are equally well known and will be as cordially attested by men of the first respectability in rank, intellect and moral worth, as by myself: among whom I beg leave to name particularly and to *refer* to, Sir George and Lady Beaumont, Mr Southey, and Mr Wordsworth, who have all known and have had very frequent—the two latter Gentlemen almost constant—opportunities of Observing my Son from his earliest childhood. And as few persons of his rank and age have been placed within a circle of equal eminence, so (let me be permitted to observe) scarcely any one perhaps [has] been more esteemed and beloved, than He with all his defects and eccentricities has been even from his infancy—had been at least, till his admission at Oriel.

[Fragment III]
Substance of a Letter addressed to the Reverend the Provost of Oriel by Mr S. T. Coleridge.

The more serious articles of the charge being grounded on Presumptions and Inferences; and as admitted facts may excite and appear to warrant a strong presumption against a man in the judgement of those who are ignorant or but imperfectly informed of his particular character, which would make no such impression on those, who know the man intimately, and understand his peculiarities—[and] would lead to no such inference but on the contrary admit of a satisfactory solution by causes indifferent or venial & sometimes even creditable to the man's feelings;—you will not, I trust, regard it as an impertinent or useless interference, if I lay before you what I myself know of Hartley Coleridge's Habits and

---

[1] Coleridge evidently alluded to a passage in William James's letter to Mence of 15 July: 'Repeated instances of intoxication . . . [and] at other times keeping late hours, which with other circumstances afforded the strongest presumption that he had been drinking, though it was not then so evident.' See 'Foreword', G.

Dispositions, (I might say, of his Nature) previously to his last term at Oriel. This is the sole Object of this letter, & to this I shall confine myself, without adverting and as much [as] possible without alluding to the recent proceedings or the causes assigned for them.—And even I shall limit my statement to those points of my Son's character which are equally as well known & will be as cordially attested by men of the first respectability in rank, intellect and moral worth, as by myself. Among many well-meriting this description I beg leave to name and to refer you to, Sir George and Lady Beaumont, Mr Southey & Mr Wordsworth, who have all known my Son from earliest childhood, and the two latter from his Birth.

The first point, which I must mention as it is the basis of all the rest, is the one that I have least hopes of communicating adequately and intelligibly—I mean, the infrequent recurrence, amounting almost to the habitual absence, of the idea of Self in his Thoughts. I am not speaking of any virtue opposed to Selfishness; but of Self as contra-distinguished from *another*.—A gentleman of high philosophical celebrity

[Fragment IV]

Copy of Letter to Dr Coppleston—

3rd Leaf

There has not been the least intercourse with respect to this subject between myself, & either Sir G. B., Mr Southey, Mr Wordsworth, or Mr Poole, but I could pledge my life, that each would at the first hearing of Hartley's artful ingenuity in putting the best construction on his errors, express with a livelier confidence their disbelief of the charge. From his earliest childhood he had an absence of any contra-distinguishing Self, any conscious 'I', that struck every one, the most unobserving, & which I never saw in the same *degree* in any other instance: & I have heard the same remark, and in far stronger terms, repeatedly from Mr Southey, Mr Wordsworth, Sir George & Lady Beaumont. It was either Mr Rogers or Sir W. Scott (I am not certain which) who made the Observation, that there was in this case no semblance produced by accident of language, or the more than usually prolonged habit of speaking in the third person, of himself & others indifferently, but a seemingly constitutional insensibility to the immediate impressions on the senses, & the necessity of having them generalized into *thoughts*, before they had an interest, or even a distinct place, in his Consciousness.—The remark was strictly just—& so much so, that this peculiarity not seldom made him appear deficient in affection & almost unimpressible—and never can I read De la Motte Fouqué's beautiful Faery Tale, founded on a tradition recorded in Luther's Table-Talk, of Undina,[1] the Water-Fay, before she had a Soul, beloved by all whether they would or no, & as indifferent to all, herself included, as a blossom whirling in a May-gale, without having Hartley recalled to me,[2] as he appeared from infancy to his boyhood—never, without reflecting on the prophecy, written by me long before I had either thought or prospect of settling in Cumberland, addressed to him then but a few months old in my Poem, Entitled, Frost at Midnight—

> Dear Babe! that slumber'st cradled by my side,
> Whose gentle Breathings heard in this deep Calm
> Fill up the interspersed vacancies
> And momentary intervals of Thought—
> My Babe so beautiful! it thrills my Heart
> With tender gladness thus to gaze on thee,
> And think, that thou shalt learn far other Lore
> And in far other scenes. For I was rear'd
> In the great city pent 'mid Cloisters dim,
> And saw nought lovely but the Sky & Stars,
> But thou, my Babe! *shalt wander like a Breeze*
> By Lakes & sandy Shores, beneath the Crags

[1] F. H. K. de la Motte Fouqué, *Undine, a Romance*, 1811. (See Letter 1232A.) 'Undine', Coleridge said, 'is a most exquisite work. It shows the general want of any sense for the fine and the subtle in the public taste, that this romance made no deep impression. Undine's character, before she receives a soul, is marvellously beautiful.' To this entry in *Table Talk*, 31 May 1830, H. N. Coleridge added the following note:

Mr. Coleridge's admiration of this little romance was unbounded. He read it several times in German, and once in the English translation, made in America, I believe; the latter he thought inadequately done. I think he must have read the English Undine, which I have, published in 1824, by E. Littell, Philadelphia. Mr. C. said there was something in Undine even beyond Scott, —that Scott's best characters and conceptions were *composed*; by which I understood him to mean that Baillie [*sic*] Nicol Jarvie, for example, was made up of old particulars, and received its individuality from the author's power of fusion, being in the result an admirable product, as Corinthian brass was said to be the conflux of the spoils of a city. But Undine, he said, was one and single in projection, and had presented to his imagination, what Scott had never done, an absolutely new idea.

G. Soane's English translation of 1818 was reprinted in Philadelphia in 1824. A second translation appeared in 1830. See V. Stockley, *German Literature as Known in England*, 1929, pp. 226–9.

According to *The Oxford Companion to English Literature* the story of Undine was suggested to Fouqué by a passage in Paracelsus. Undine, a sylph, receives a soul in consequence of her marriage.

[2] Cf. Coleridge's description in 1801 of Hartley, who 'whisks, whirls, and eddies, like a blossom in a May-breeze'. Letter 376.

> Of ancient Mountains, & beneath the Clouds
> That image in their bulk both Lakes, & Shores,
> And Mountain Crags.—

To what degree this was fulfilled, is pourtrayed not less faithfully as fact than exquisitely as verse in Mr Wordsworth's Lines, addressed to Hartley Coleridge, six years old—and I did not wonder to hear, that Robert Southey burst into audible weeping when a few days after the first unexamined Tidings from Oriel his Eye had happened to glance on the §§ of that Poem, beginning—

> I thought of Times when Pain might be thy guest,
> Lord of thy House & Hospitality!
> And Grief, uneasy Lover, never rest
> Save when she sate within the touch of thee.

To these men—& men of austerer morals & more enlightened minds where am I to find?—I appeal—whether the charge of 'perverse ingenuity',[1] '*artful* palliations' & the like[2] had not the effect of inspiring hope that the whole Charge would be found exaggerated, from the utter contrariety of these portions to the whole nature & habits of the accused?—Except the *very* few who from experience of their own feelings, and thus by a sort of recognition not only understand but can attest the existence of the same in another, & I will venture to say, that they only who have long & intimately known my Son can conceive to what a degree all *comparison* is absent from his mind in the Judgement which he passes on his own actions! how entirely he occupies the same relative Position as that in which Men like Herbert, Bish. Hall, Archbishop Leighton, present themselves in their confessions & words of humiliation. They were, confessedly, Men of clear & comprehensive intellects, Men intimately and extensively acquainted with the moral condition of the majority of mankind—For in the earlier periods of the Reformation the practice of *confession* was brought back indeed to it's pure & primitive state but in this state enforced rather than discouraged by the wisest & most pious Protestant Divines: and this was, I doubt not, one cause of their intenser influence on the hearts of their contemporaries—If their superlatives

[1] Based on Keble's derogatory statements concerning Hartley's insincerity, this charge appears in John Taylor Coleridge's letter to Gillman of 29 June 1820: 'I dread the perverse ingenuity of his mind in self-justification.' See 'Foreword', F.

[2] This charge was made in Keble's letter to John Taylor Coleridge of June 1820: 'When he is to outward appearance most deeply impressed with a sense of what he has done, he has his wits most thoroughly about him & tries to take advantage of any palliation.' See 'Foreword', E.

are to be interpreted, not as intended to express the relation in which they felt themselves standing in relation to the Alone Good, & to the absolute Command, Be perfect, even as your Father in Heaven is perfect! but as the result of a comparison of their own aims & actions with the average of men, who could acquit them of insincerity? Of Pharisaic Pride—of a Pharisaism that strove to unite the honors of humility and the gratification of Self-worship by chaunting it's own praises in a palpable irony, in which every word was sure to be rendered by one of the contrary meaning?—An hypocrisy of no very rare occurrence if I may dare judge from scenes to which I have myself been present, in the dialogues of complimentary Contradictions between those Professors, whom Lord Bacon excellently pre-designated as Schismatics in *Manners*, more effective in disunion than even the Dissentients in Doctrines or Ceremonies. But who will accuse, who will dare suspect, the men above named & their Compeers of so loathsome a Trick, of so piti-ful a Self-delusion?—Do I mean to identify my Son with these venerable men? You will not suspect me of the absurdity. But I do affirm, that the same measuring of act and deed by the abstract rule of Right, without adverting to the frequency of still wider deviations in others of the same age, & under like circumstances, & without seeking a palliative from the fact of *comparative* Inno-cence, as was the result of religious Discipline, & profound medi-tation in *them*, is in him *Nature*—for by what other word can I ex-press a quality or character prominent from earliest childhood? the germ of which disclosed itself even in earliest Infancy. When he was not a year old, my Friend & at that time my Neighbor, Mr Poole of Stowey now a justly distinguished Magistrate in the county of Somerset, used to remark, as a curiou**s** fact—that the little fellow never shewed any excitement at the *thing*, whatever it was, but afterwards, often when it had been removed, smiled or capered on the arm as at the *thought* of it.—There is another & perhaps more justifying reason for calling this peculiarity his *Nature*—for like all other natural qualities or tendencies, not the result of Reason, Religion, or moral Habits, it has been 'a twy-streaming Fount, Whence Good and Ill have flowed, Honey & Gall'.[1]—

And to this habit of being absent to the present, often indeed from the reverse extreme, and still oftener from eagerness of reasoning, & exclusive attention to mental acts or impressions, but not seldom from a mere absorption of the active powers, a seeming entire sus-pension of all distinct Consciousness—I intreat your attention with peculiar anxiety—For it is of the last importance to the just ap-preciation both of what he is & has been, and of what he is likely to

[1] Cf. *Religious Musings*, lines 204–5.

become, that it should be known that this habit so far from having been gradually contracted at School or at the university, & so far from growing on him, was strongest & most glaring from two years old to seven or eight. For the last four years, my Son has been with me twice yearly, from three weeks to two months each time, & for the last three years I have been each visit congratulated by the sincere and enlightened friends whose hospitable roof and regard he shared with me, & at the last time but one, when he accompanied his Brother, Derwent, hither, was most warmly congratulated by all his & my friends in this neighborhood on his manifest improvement in this point. The worthy Clergyman of this place, late Fellow & Tutor of Trinity, Oxford, expressed his satisfaction in words to this purpose & to the best of my recollection in these very words— 'Hartley will never be the man of the world, nor have the polish & conciliating manners, which Experience & good Company will ensure to his Brother, Derwent; but he has won so much mastery over himself since I first knew him, is so evidently trying & learning to accomodate himself to the customs & regulations of society, that tho' he will not be more loved by those who love him, he will however give no just cause of Dislike to those who do not.'—Let your heart plead in excuse for me, if I add his concluding words, that have since haunted my ear like a death-watch, in my own despite. —'But just or unjust, with such Talents, and such unsuspecting & unregarding Openness, requiring more than negative manners to counterbalance, Enemies he will be sure to have'; and it made me sigh when I heard him express his belief that he had not an Enemy in the World.—Indeed I cannot in truth and common justify [justice?] press this point too strongly.—When a little child, as soon as he [was] made to sit & had begun to take his food, he used to sink at once from a state of whirling activity into—it is painful to me even to recollect him—for he looked like a little statue of Ideotcy—and even up to the present year no one can have been intimate with him without having occasionally seen him, sometimes in abstraction, but of late more frequently in eagerness of conversation, eating fruit, or bread, or whatever else was before [him], utterly unconscious of what he was doing, or repeatedly filling his glass from the Water-bottle—for his friends were so well aware of this, that they either recalled his attention to what he was doing, or putting the Water by him silently, counted the times, in order to impress him afterwards with the unbecomingness & even danger of these fits of absence—. But as soon as this was used to give a colour to a darker charge, Hartley did not hesitate a moment; but gave up wine & every other liquor beyond table-beer as an ordinary practice, & even on what we call our company-days

days of rare occurrence, has strictly confined himself to one glass during Dinner, and a second after dinner—and this too at my recommendation, as I thought it at once bespoke more indifference to the pleasures of the table, and exercised more self-command than an entire rejection at all times, & was less calculated to attract notice. In this scheme he has not only persevere[d]; but in my inmost conscience I am convinced, that it never cost him a single effort. Let this fact be taken in combination with his Complexion, the condition of his digestive organs, his disposition to move after meals, &c: and I dare appeal to any medical Man, whether it does not afford more than a presumption against the cruel charge that he had formed a *habit* of intemperance.

1251. *To Thomas Allsop*

Address: T. Allsop, Esqre | Blandford Place | Pall Mall
MS. New York Public Lib. Pub. with omis. Letters, Conversations and Rec. *62.*
Postmark: Highgate, 11 October 1820.

[11 October 1820]

My dear Allsop

You will think it childish in me and more savouring of a jealous Boarding School Miss than a Friend and a Philosopher when I confess that the 'with the greatest respect Your obliged and obedient T A' gave me pain. But I did not return from Mr Cooper's, at whose house we all dined, till near midnight, & did not open the pacquet till this Morning, after getting out of bed: and this, you know, is the Hour in which the Cat-organ of an irritable Viscerage is substituted for the Brain as the Mind's instrument.

The Cobbett is assuredly a strong and battering production throughout, and in the best bad style of this political Rhinoceros, with his Coat-armour of dry and wet Mud and his one Horn of brutal strength on the Nose of Scorn and Hate—not to forget the fleaing *Rasp* of his Tongue! There is one article of his invective, however, from which I cannot withhold my vote of Consent: that I mean which respects Mr Brougham's hollow complimentary phrases to the Ministry & the House of Lords.—On expressing my regret that his poor hoaxed and hunted Client had been lured or terrified into the nets of the Revolutionists, & had taken the top-most Perch, as the flaring screaming *Maccaw* in the clamorous Aviary of Faction, Sheriff Williams, who dined with us, premising that his *Wishes* accorded with mine declared himself however fully and deeply convinced that without this alliance the Queen must have been overwhelmed, not wholly or even chiefly from the strength of the Party itself but because without the activity, enthusiasm, and combination peculiar to the Reformists her Case in all it's Detail & with all it's appendages would never have had that notoriety so beyond example universal, which (to translate Sheriff Williams into Poet Coleridge) with kettle-drum Réveillée had echoed thro' the Mine & the Coal-pit, which had lifted the Latch of every cottage, & thundered with no run-a-way Knock at Carleton Palace.[1]—I could only reply, that I had never yet seen, heard or read of any advantage in the long run, accruing to a good cause from an unholy alliance with evil passions and incongruous or alien purposes. It was ever heavy on my heart, that the People, alike high & low, do perish for lack of knowlege—that both Sheep & Shepherd, the Flocks & the Pastors, go astray among swamps and in desolate places for want of the TRUTH, the *whole* Truth, and nothing but the Truth; & that the sacred Motto, which I had adopted for my first political Publication (the Watchman) would be the aspiration of my Deathbed— THAT ALL MAY KNOW THE TRUTH; & THAT THE TRUTH MAY MAKE US FREE!—I observed further, that in bodies of men, not accidentally collected nor promiscuously, but such as our House of Lords, the usual effect of Terror was, first, self-justification as to the worst of their past violent & unconstitutional Measures, & next, a desperate Belief that their safety would be still more endangered by giving way than by plunging onward—& that if they must fall, they would

[1] The accession of George IV in Jan. 1820 brought to a crisis the long-standing dispute between the king and Queen Caroline, who had been living abroad for several years. Orders were now given that she be denied recognition as queen at any foreign court, and her name was formally omitted from the liturgy. Acting for the king, Baron Hutchinson met the queen at St. Omer early in June 1820 and proposed a settlement of £50,000 annually, on condition that she relinquish all English royal titles and remain abroad. She refused the offer, however, and despite a warning not to return to England, set off immediately. Ignoring the public clamour in her defence, George IV now determined to institute divorce proceedings, and on the basis of an investigation begun in 1818, charges of adultery were brought against her. On 5 July 1820 Liverpool introduced in the House of Lords a bill to deprive her of 'the Title, Prerogatives, Rights, Privileges, and Exemptions of Queen Consort', and to dissolve the marriage. Henry Brougham, who had long espoused her cause and whom she had appointed her attorney-general when she became queen, ably defended her on 3 and 4 Oct. By 10 Nov. the majority in favour of the bill had dropped to 9 on the third reading, and Liverpool abandoned the measure. Undoubtedly, the immense public sympathy on behalf of the queen was in part responsible for the decision of the ministry not to proceed with the bill in the House of Commons. The queen's supporters regarded the outcome as a triumphant victory.

As early as 1796 Coleridge had expressed sympathy for Caroline in his poem, *To an Unfortunate Princess*, subsequently published in the *Monthly Magazine* (Sept. 1796) under the title, *On a Late Connubial Rupture in High Life*. See Letter 134 and *Poems*, i. 152.

fall in that way in which they might take vengeance on the occasion of the Mischief. If the Proposition be Either —— or ——, and the latter blank is to be filled up by *A Civil War*: what shall we put for the former, to make our duty to submit to it deniable or even doubtful?—A Legislature, permitted by us to stand in the eye of the whole civilized World as the Representative of our Country, corruptly and ruthlessly pandaring to an Individual's Lust and Hate? —Open Hostility to Innocence, and the subversion of justice, a shameless Trampling under foot of the Laws of God and the Principles of the Constitution, *in* the name, & against the known will, of the Nation?—Well! if any thing, it must be this!—It is a decision, compared with which the sentence of the elder Brutus were a Grief, for which an onion might supply the tears—a dreadful decision! But be it so!—How much more then are we bound to be careful, that no conduct of our own, no assent nor countenance given by us to the violence of others, no want of courage & alertness in denouncing the same, should have the least tendency to bring about an act or event, dire enough to justify a Civil War for it's Preventive?—I produced, as you may suppose, but small effect—& yet your very note enforces the truth of my reply—for these very Answers of the Queen, conjointly with her *plebicolar* (or plebicolous) Clap-trapperies in the Live Puppet-shew of wicked Punch & his Wife that has come back again, and the Devil on all sides, make it impossible for me to ask you, as I should otherwise have done: What proof, proveably independent of the Calumny-Plot, have we of any want of delicacy in the Queen? What act or Form of Demeanour can be adduced on competent testimony, from which we are forced or entitled to infer innate Coarseness if not Grossness?—The dire disclosure of the extent & extremes to which Calumny may be carried, & perhaps the recent persecution of poor dear Hartley mixes it's workings, makes me credulous in incredulity: and I am almost prepared to reverse the proverb, & think that 'what every one says must be a Lie'—. They put a body up to the nostrils in the dunghill of reeking Slander, & then exclaim: There is no Smoke without some fire!—

It is my purpose, God willing! to leave this place on Friday, so as to take an afternoon Coach, if any such there be, or the Oxford Mail as the dernier resource—& so to be in Oxford by Saturday Morning,[1]

[1] 'Of this journey to Oxford', Allsop writes, 'I have a very painful recollection; perhaps the most painful recollection (one excepted) connected with the memory of Coleridge.' *Letters, Conversations and Rec.* 68.
On Saturday afternoon, 14 Oct. 1820, after his arrival at Oxford and the day before his conference with Copleston, Coleridge turned aside from his preoccupation with his son's affairs to read and annotate a copy of John Petvin's *Letters concerning Mind*, 1750. See *Notes, Theological, Political, and*

while my Letter,[1] which is unfortunately a very long one & I could not make [it] otherwise, will reach Dr Copplestone, if arrived, on Friday Morning—thus giving him a day's preparation for the personal Interview.—How long my absence from Highgate may be, I cannot of course predetermine—certainly not an hour beyond what Hartley's Interest requires.—

God bless you, my dear Allsop! | and your truly affectionate—
& if it did not look | like a *retort*, how truly might I not
add— | your obliged & grateful | Friend,

S. T. Coleridge.—

P.S. Sheriff Williams is apparently a worthy, & assuredly a very entertaining man. He gave us accounts, on his own evidence, of wonderful things, respecting Miss McEvoy and a Mr De Vains of Liverpool, so wonderful, as to threaten the stoppage even of my Bank of Faith.—

I have just heard from Derwent, who is well; but I have not had time to decypher his villainous Scrawl.

1252. *To Thomas Allsop*

Address: T. Allsop, Esqre | Blandford Place | Pall Mall
MS. New York Public Lib. Pub. with omis. Letters, Conversations and Rec. *69.*
Postmark: Highgate, 25 October 1820.

25 Octr 1820

My dearest Allsop

It will please you—tho' I scarcely know whether the pleasure is worth the Carriage—to know, that my own feelings and convictions were from the very commencement of this unhappy affair, viz. the terms proposed to the Queen by Lord Hutchinson[2]—in co-incidence with your present Suggestion, [and] that I actually began an Essay, and proposed a sort of *Diary*, i.e. Remarks Moral and political; according as the events, speeches, &c of each Day suggested them—& this in part in the hope of giving some advice & warning to the Queen herself—But Mr Gillman dissuaded me.—Again, about 5 weeks ago, I had written a Letter to Connor, the Editor of the Eclectic Review,[3] & ci-devant Bookseller, offering, and offering to *execute*, a scheme of publication—'The Queen's Case stated

Miscellaneous. By Samuel Taylor Coleridge, ed. Derwent Coleridge, 1853, pp. 262–4.
  [1] See preceding letter.
  [2] See note to Letter 1251.
  [3] Josiah Conder (1789–1855) became proprietor of the *Eclectic Review* in 1814.

morally—2. judicially. 3. & politically'—But again Mr G. earnestly persuaded me to suppress it—His reasons were—1. That my mind (in consequence of Hartley's affair &c) was not sufficiently tranquil to enable me to rely on my going thro' with the publication.—2. That it would probably involve me with certain of my Connections in high life, & be injurious to Hartley & Derwent, especially to the latter—with 3. the small chance of doing any good, people are so guided by their first notions—To tell you the Truth, Mr G's own Dislike to it was of more weight than all his 3 reasons—

However, we will talk of the Publication if *it be not too late*—and at all events I will compose the statement.—

I pray you, my dear Allsop! never, never make any apologies to me for doing that which cannot but add to the esteem & affection with which I am most

truly your *Friend*, fraternally & paternally,
S. T. Coleridge

We shall soon see you?—

Mrs G's kindest rememb[rances.]

1253. *To Thomas Allsop*

Address: T. Allsop, Esqre | Blandford Place | Pall Mall
MS. New York Public Lib. Pub. with omis. Letters, Conversations and Rec. 75.
Postmark: Highgate, 27 November 1820.

Highgate
Sunday Evening [26 November 1820]

My very dear Allsop

I have been more than usually unwell, with great depression of Spirits, loss of Appetite, frequent sickness, and a harrassing pain in my left knee—and at the same time anxious to preclude as much as I can the ill effects of poor Hartley's unhappy procrastination—indolence it is not: for he is busy enough in his own way, & rapidly bringing together materials for his future credit, as a man of letters & a poet; but shrinking from all things connected with painful associations, and of that morbid temperament, which I too well understand, that renders what would be motives for men in general, narcotics for him in exact proportion to their strength.—And this I could only do by taking on myself as much of the document writing as was contrivable.[1]—Besides this, I have latterly felt increasingly

---

[1] At Coleridge's insistence, Hartley sent explanatory letters, including copies of 'all the papers . . . necessary to the elucidation of the [Oriel] affair', to those who had provided financial assistance during his undergraduate years at Merton College—Lady Beaumont, Poole, and his Uncle Edward at Ottery. As

anxious to avail myself of every moment that ill-health left me, to
get forward with my Logic,[1] and with my 'Assertion of Religion'.—
Nay, foolish tho' it be, I cannot prevent my mind from being oppressed by the alarming state of public affairs, & as it appears to me,
the want of stable Principle even in the chiefs of the Party that
seem to feel aright—yet chirrup like Crickets, in warmth without
Light.

The consequence of all this is that I not only have deferred
writing to you, but have played the procrastinator with myself even
in giving due attention to your very interesting letters—For minor
things, your kindness & kind remembrances are so habitual, that
my acknowlegements you cannot but take for granted. Mr Gilman
has likewise been uncommonly out of health, but thank God! for
the last 3 days he has got round again, more rapidly than I expected.—Mrs Gillman—& this leads me to the particular object of
this Letter—expresses aloud and earnestly what I feel no less, her
uneasiness that 3 Sundays have passed & we have not had the comfort of seeing you. Do come up when you can, with justice to yourself & your other connections: for it is a *great* comfort to me—
Something, I trust, I shall have to shew you, a Note of Warning
from one who has been a true but unheard Prophet to my Countrymen, for 5 and 20 years.

May God bless you, | my dear Friend | &
S. T. Coleridge

1253A. *To the Warden of Merton College*[2]

MS. Mr. A. H. B. Coleridge. Pub. Letters of Hartley Coleridge, *320.*
    Coleridge composed the following first draft of an explanatory letter for his
son. For another incomplete rough draft of the letter in Hartley's handwriting
see *Letters of Hartley Coleridge*, 317–20. See also 'Foreword', pp. 76–77.

[December 1820]

. . . to put you in possession as fully as it [is] in my power to do, of
the relation in which I stand at present to my Electors, and in the

the present letter indicates, Coleridge himself did much of the 'document
writing'. He also wrote out for Hartley a rough draft of a letter addressed to
the warden of Merton. See next letter.

    [1] Coleridge made two attempts, both incomplete, to produce a work on
Logic. See Alice D. Snyder, *Coleridge on Logic and Learning*, 1929, and Letters
504 and 1324.

    [2] In a letter of explanation addressed to Lady Beaumont in Dec. 1820,
Hartley said: 'I have written to the Warden of Merton, a full account of the
whole transaction. As most of my evenings were spent with friends in that
College—he can vouch for some of my statements.' *Letters of Hartley Coleridge*,
54.

first place of all the facts connected with my own conduct that I am myself aware of, and can suppose in any degree calculated to influence their recent determination. These facts I shall communicate, without attempting to define the degree of comparative culpability which may be fairly attached to me in consequence, nakedly, and with one single exception without any comment. To extenuate my Conscience forbids, and I have been taught by a sore experience henceforward not to take on myself the business of condemnation, unless I wish to be a wilful accomplice in the misconceptions, to which, writing under the fear of appearing to extenuate, I might too probably furnish occasion by my own words.—I will then state in the same way the Charges, that have been *formally* alledged against me as the grounds of the hitherto unprecedented determination not to confirm my election—then those which, tho' not alledged or avowed by the Provost and Fellows of Oriel collectively, have yet been communicated to my Friends or Relations by the Provost or some one of the Fellows individually—and having solemnly and deliberately assured you of the falsehood (or gross exaggeration fully tantamount in it's effects to falsehood) of all and each of these Charges, except as far as they have been anticipated in my own statement, I will truly describe the nature and amount of the injury or at least detriment inflicted on me, not only or chiefly by the determination itself, or as the Loss of the Fellowship is alone considered; but likewise and in a far higher degree, by the measures necessarily consequent on the determination, by the Charges on which it is professedly grounded; and by the yet heavier private representations by which it's justification has been attention [attended?]—and then with perfect resignation submit it to your judgement, what proportion there has been between the demerit and the punishment, and what equity in depriving me at once of my fellow-ship and my good name on secret evidence which they refuse to name, & will not allow me to confront.—But there is one point on which I cannot too soon enter a *disclaimer*, by a distinct declaration, that I do not put my veracity against the veracity of the Provost and resident Fellows of Oriel; but my disavowals against the assertions of their *Informers*, whose evidence I solemnly assert to be false.

As to my conduct during my Terms at Merton, I trust that your Testimonials are a sufficient proof, that it was not sullied by any such glaring or frequent aberrations from Duty as to distinguish it to my disadvantage from the average conduct of Undergraduates. Compared with the men in general of the same age & under the same or similar Circumstances, I hope & dare assure myself that my errors and defaults were not such as to deprive me of the regard or exclude me from the good hopes of those who had the best means of knowing me, both among the superiors of my College & my equals.—At all events, this point must be supposed to have been inquired into by my Electors, as one necessary condition of my eligibility, previous to my Election. Otherwise instead of a benefit it would rather be an injury: inasmuch as the advantages derivable from the *confirmation* of the Fellowship would not bear a comparison even with the risk of such Evils as must needs follow a rejection. Who indeed with any sense of self-respect would from a pecuniary motive expose himself to a secret inquisition of all his past conduct in all it's minutiae to an indefinite period backward—perhaps even to his School-boy Days, but certainly comprizing all those years and circumstances, in which Faults & Errors, that imply no baseness, or deliberate perversion of principle, are usually considered as having their sufficient and appropriate punishment provided for them by the Discipline, the rules of which had been transgressed? We know, that among his sharpest grievances Job complained of those, who brought against him the follies of his Youth—. But how much stronger would the Objection be, if this inquisition was carried on by means of secret information? If the names of the informers were withheld from the accused, his intreaties to be confronted with them repelled, his pledges to prove the contrary as far as *a negative* can be proved set at naught, and his solemn assertions of *their* falsehood, tho' presumptively Servants & Dependents of his Inquisitors, and where Assertions were the only things in his power, to be treated as falsehoods of his own?—And if the *consequences* were, that he must begin life with a public Brand on his character, and by their denial of the usual credentials rendered necessary in order to preserve the consistency of his rejection not merely deprived of his immediate resources but precluded from the profession for which he had been educated?—May I not confidently appeal to you, honored Sir! whether the strongest probability of a Fellowship could be put by any honorable mind in competition with the chance of such evils: especially when he knows, that an unfavorable result would tend to compromise the names even of the revered Friends, to whose attestations in his favor he was indebted in part for his election in the first instance?—

You will not condemn these remarks as impertinent, if you find that they are no *comment*, no mere general Reasoning on my Case; but a necessary part of it's statement. On no hypothesis indeed, and to whatever period of my past life I suppose the inquisition to have extended, can I conceive how some of the charges alledged against me could be substantiated; but on this only can I imagine even a *pretext* for such accusations, or am able to acquit the unknown Informants of wilful Falsehood tho' I cannot acquit them of gross exaggeration and the strangest Misstatements.—

Be this however, as it may, my Statement as far as it refers to my own conduct & Actions, must be confined within the interval from my election as probationer of Oriel to the time when the unalterable determination of the Provost & Resident Fellows to exclude me from the Fellowship was formally communicated to me with the advice to resign before hand of my own accord, as the only means of preventing an *exposure*: that is, as I cannot but understand it, of going into life under *false colors*.—At that time indeed and for some weeks afterward, I neither comprehended the extent of the charge, nor even conjectured the nature of the most serious articles; but now that I have the whole before me, I can confidently appeal to any honest & conscientious man, whether, on the assumption of such charges having been satisfactorily proved, the *exposure* of the truth, or at least the abstaining from all participation in any attempt to conceal it, would not have been their duty.—

With these impressions, & under such heavy afflictions, which grievous as they are on my own account are tenfold more so on account of my Father, and Mother, and the kind Friends who have assisted them in procuring for me the advantages of a learned and Academic Education, I earnestly intreat your perusal of the accompanying documents: corresponding to the purposes expressed in the beginning of this letter; and to which at my Father's instance I have added an extract from a letter addressed by him to Dr Copplestone previous to his first interview with the Provost.—And permit me to assure you, which I do with heart-felt sincerity that it will be no slight alleviation of my misfortunes to know, that my errors have not been of such a nature as to deprive me wholly of that portion of esteem & regard, with which, reverend Sir, you had heretofore honored

> Your obliged and grateful | humble Servant,
> Hartley Coleridge.

1254. *To J. G. Lockhart*

MS. Huntington Lib. Pub. E. L. G. ii. 273.

The circumstances which occasioned the present letter began in the year 1819. In July Lockhart included a laudatory estimate of Coleridge's prose and poetry in *Peter's Letters to His Kinsfolk*, a work published under the pseudonym of Peter Morris; and in October a discriminating critique, 'Essays on the Lake School of Poetry. No. III.—*Coleridge*', appeared in *Blackwood's Magazine*. The article has been assigned to Lockhart. These tributes awakened a 'warmth of feeling' in Coleridge, and in November he addressed a letter to the 'Author of *Peter's Letters*'. In describing his treatment by '*Atticus*', he pointed directly to

Wordsworth. (See Letter 1212.) In 1820, however, Lockhart violated Coleridge's confidence by publishing this letter in the September number of *Blackwood's Magazine*—a reprehensible breach of faith. The letter was printed as a 'Letter to Peter Morris, M. D. on the Sorts and Uses of Literary Praise' and was introduced by a flippant communication to Christopher North:

Note from Dr Morris, enclosing a Letter from Mr Coleridge.

Rhayader, August 15th.
Dear North,
    I trust there is no impropriety in my sending to you for your Magazine ... a very characteristic letter of one whom I well know you agree with me in honouring among the highest. You will laugh, as I did, at some little mistakes into which our illustrious and excellent friend has fallen; above all, that highly absurd one about your humble servant's *personality*. On no account, however, omit one word of the letter, and I will be answerable to Coleridge for the making public thereof. . . .

Peter Morris.

In December 1820 John Scott, the editor of the *London Magazine* and the author of a series of articles denouncing *Blackwood's*, alluded scornfully to this '*unauthorized publication*' of Coleridge's '*private letter*'. He also pointed to Lockhart as the author of the infamous review of the *Biographia Literaria* in the October 1817 number of *Blackwood's Magazine*: 'After writing, as the first fruits of his Editorship, a most virulent and offensive libel against Mr. Coleridge, . . . he has found means to draw, for once, a private and civil letter from the object of these indecent aspersions; and this letter, contrary to the usage of gentlemen, he has published in his Magazine, without the writer's consent, and, as we have reason to know, *very much to the writer's displeasure*.' (*London Magazine*, December 1820, pp. 669 and 676.)

Scott did not consult Coleridge in thus bringing his name before the public, the assertion concerning Coleridge's '*displeasure*' being based on hearsay probably derived from Charles Lamb. On the other hand, the publication of Peter Morris's 'Note' to Christopher North clearly indicated that Coleridge's letter was a personal communication which had been printed 'without the writer's consent'. Lockhart, however, asked Coleridge for 'explanations'. The temperate way in which Coleridge replied suggests that he had become aware of the seriousness of the quarrel between Lockhart and John Scott, a quarrel which culminated in a duel and the untimely death of Scott in February 1821. Thenceforth Coleridge addressed his communications concerning *Blackwood's Magazine* to the publisher, William Blackwood. See Letter 1274.

[December 1820]
Dear Sir
    Be assured, that I will do my duty toward you, at whatever cost. The only wish, I dare encourage or express, is that the evil may not be made to extend *beyond* what is necessary for the accomplishment of the End in view: and *this* I am prepared to do in the face of all consequences, doubly painful and unfortunate as they are (even in the anticipation) in my peculiar state of Health. I feel indeed, that they have already commenced in the obligation, which the folly and malignity of I know not whom has *forced* you to impose on me—that of making explanations to you, which being personally

a stranger to me you may find it difficult not to suspect of affectation or lurking vanity—nay, as even arguing a thankless disposition. I am now mentally referring to the Fact, that from the time that the first friendly Article appeared in Blackwood's Magazine I have never opened a single number, not even that in which my Letter to you was published: and that Baldwin's Magazine[1] I never *saw*, till about a fortnight ago I *saw* indeed three or four numbers at Mr C. Lamb's, during one of my rare visits to town—& at Lamb's request read *his* Article on Christ's Hospital,[2] which (he told me) he had chiefly compiled from his recollections of what he had heard from me, as the set-off of a friendless Boy against his (Lamb's) former panegyrical account of the same Institution. I was about to read another of his Essays, on the South Sea House[3]—but the time for the Highgate Stage had come, & *excepting the above Article, and one paragraph* of a contribution signed W. H. (Hazlitt I suppose) in which I saw an abusive mention of my name in connection with Behmen and Swedenburg,[4] my eyes and ears are up to this moment innocent of the Work in toto.—As far as this Work is in point, I have no explanation to make. My sentiments on the nature of all intrusions into private Life, & of mere private *personalities* in all shapes I have given at large in the Friend, and yet more pointedly in the Literary Life, Vol. II. 118, 119, & 302. These you know; but you cannot know, my dear Sir! the peculiar depth of aversion, the actual detestation, which I *feel*, respecting malignity in this in it's fashionable form: nor how many causes accumulating thro' a long

---

[1] Coleridge's name for the *London Magazine*, of which Robert Baldwin, Cradock, and Joy were the original publishers. See Letter 1216.

[2] *Christ's Hospital Five and Thirty Years Ago* was published in the *London Magazine*, November 1820.

[3] See *London Magazine*, August 1820.

[4] In the *London Magazine* of December 1820, Hazlitt has this to say of Coleridge: 'Now would be the time for Mr. Coleridge to turn his talents to account, and write for the stage, when there is no topic to confine his pen, or, "constrain his genius by mastery".... Under the assumed head of the Drama, he might unfold the whole mysteries of Swedenborg, or ascend the third heaven of invention with Jacob Behmen: he might write a treatise on all the unknown sciences, and finish the Encyclopedia Metropolitana in a pocket form:—nay, he might bring to a satisfactory close his own dissertation on the difference between the Imagination and the Fancy, before, in all probability, another great actor appears, or another tragedy or comedy is written. He is the man of all others to swim on empty bladders in a sea, without shore or soundings: to drive an empty stage-coach without passengers or lading, and arrive behind his time; to write marginal notes without a text; to look into a millstone to foster the rising genius of the age; to "see merit in the chaos of its elements, and discern perfection in the great obscurity of nothing", as his most favourite author, Sir Thomas Brown, has it on another occasion.' See *The Complete Works of William Hazlitt*, ed. P. P. Howe, 21 vols., 1930-4, xviii, p. 369.

series of years, and acting perhaps on constitutional predisposition, have combined to make me shrink from all occasions that threaten to force my thoughts back on *myself* personally—as soon as any thing of the sort is on the point of being talked of, I feel uneasy till I have turned the conversation, or fairly slunk out of the room. The entire Loss of all the profits small as they were, from all my publications, added to the necessity of purchasing back the half copy-rights & the unsold Copies—& the thence pressing Sense of my unprovided state & immediate pecuniary perplexities, & the cruel prevention of being able to go on regularly with either of the great works, to the materials of which all lying before me 20 years had been mainly devoted—these alone, as far as *Self* was in question, and no disappointment connected with praise for it's own sake, made me complain inwardly of the silence of the Quarterly Review. —No one can lament more sorely than myself this morbid weakness, this mental cowardice. In an essay published by me, 23 Novr. 1809, that was lying open on the table as I began this Letter, I see the words—'as if he sought a refuge from his own Sensibility, he attached himself to the most abstruse researches, and seemed to derive an unmixed delight from such subjects only as exercised the strength & subtlety of his understanding without awakening the feelings of his heart.' But for *this* & embarrassed Circumstances I dare believe that I should have been a Poet—I am certain that but for the two conjointly I should have continued to write poems.—

Now shortly after the appearance of the truly friendly as well as complimentary Essay in Blackwood,[1] it pleased God to afflict me most heavily by the unexpected & most cruel & unjust persecution of my eldest Son at Oxford, just as I had supposed him settled in independence for a course of years at least & with the fairest prospects—I was stunned scarcely less by the suddenness of the Blow than by it's weight. I hurried here & there—went to Oxford— made every inquisition, & every attempt—& succeeded only in obtaining decisive proofs of what in fact I had never doubted nor possibly could doubt, that my Son had been most cruelly wronged & then calumniated in order to justify the agents—whom my Son has challenged in vain to produce their evidence. Even the time, I am now employing, had been destined to the pursual of this hopeless Business—. What made it particularly hard upon me, was that at this very time I had to bestir myself in order to contrive the means of placing my second son at Cambridge—& besides these other unfortunate circumstances befel me, as make-weights of vexation. My Health, bad before, has been most seriously affected—&

---

[1] 'Essays on the Lake School of Poetry. No. III.—*Coleridge*', *Blackwood's Magazine*, October 1819.

you will no longer wonder, that as often as possible I have hid myself in old books, & in the forwarding my 'Logic', and 'Assertion of
Religion as implying Revelation, & of Christianity as the only
Revelation of universal Validity'—or that I have not even looked
into a new book, and that the Publications of my intimate Friends
remain uncut on my shelves.—

I have sent to a Friend in town to borrow the Numbers of
Baldwin's Magazine hitherto published—& shall receive them this
evening or tomorrow—I will tell you all, I at present know or can
recollect—. Some weeks after the appearance of my Letter to you,
I heard that both my Sons had been vexed and distressed at the
circumstance, on the ground that so many persons would know that
it alluded in part to Wordsworth—that it would widen the breach or
rather convert a coolness[1] into a breach—but chiefly that it was so
distressing to them, & still more to their Mother & Sister at Keswick.—I was vexed myself at the circumstance, sorely vexed; but
only with myself. Not you—how could I? but myself I did blame inwardly for sending off a Letter in the first sketch, written in the
first warmth of feeling, & the *general* contents of which indeed I
remembered but not the particular sentences, or how far they enforced the interpretation that had been made, more or less strongly.
Shortly afterward, and while I was *shying* this new vexation
brought on by my own indiscretion, I recollect *some* Visitor, I think,
it must have been Lamb, but I cannot distinctly recollect, spoke of
it with strong expressions of regret, adding—You could never have
meant it for the Public Eye, I am sure—or to that purpose. Those
who know me know well my way when I am spoken to on a subject,
painful to me, and that I want to get rid of. I answered, or muttered
rather, impatiently—a foolish vexatious business—that there was
nothing in the Letter that my own feelings did not bear out and
justify—however, I was vexed at it & had not had heart to see what
I had written—& turned off the subject.—But as to telling any one
that it was a *confidential Letter* to a *Friend*—what nonsense a man
may chuse to *infer*, I cannot say—but that it should have been said
by me, or fairly inferable from my words, is out of the Question.
What, a Letter written to an imaginary Person, whose name I did
not know, nay, whom I rather supposed to be two Persons[2]—&
this too expressed in the Letter itself—! this a confidential Letter?

[1] Coleridge first wrote 'alienation' and then substituted 'a coolness'.
[2] Cf. Coleridge's remark to Allsop: 'Peter's Letters to his Kinsfolk seem to
have originated in a sort of familiar conversation between two clever men, who
have said, "Let us write a book that will sell; you write this, and I will write
that," and in a sort of laughing humour set to work. This was the way that
Southey and myself wrote many things together.' *Letters, Conversations and
Rec.* 51. See also the Greek inscription in the headnote to Letter 1214.

It is too absurd.—But as to my *authorizing* any person to affirm,
that it was written *in confidence*, in the sense that has been given to
the word—Merciful Heaven! had I had the most distant anticipation, the slightest suspicion, of either my name or your's being
brought forward to the Public on the circumstance, I should have
hastened to have first taken the whole on myself, and then to have
reproached the Friend, if a Friend as in the case of Charles Lamb,
with having even *intended* to make bad worse & bring me once more
before the Public Bar, as if for the mere wanton purpose of forcing
an open breach between me & Wordsworth's friends & family—.
But not feeling myself under any obligation to enter into any detail
that was painful to me, and not *suspecting* the least occasion for it,
I said just what was sufficient to put a stop to the conversation—&
this is one reason, why I conclude, that it was Lamb who spoke to
me—. We have loved each other from earliest manhood—& he has
a right on many accounts to be borne with by me, even in cases that
in any other friend I could not have borne without resentment—as
the keeping up any friendly connection with Hazlitt—his writing
in & for the same publication, by choice, & as if by some fatality
[MS. breaks off thus.]

1255. *To Thomas J. Pettigrew*

Address: T. Pettigrew, Esqre
MS. University of Texas Lib. Hitherto unpublished.

[December 1820][1]

Dear Sir

I should be a far stranger animal, than spite of the information
given me by the Writers in Baldwin's Magazine I have been as yet
induced to believe, if my wishes were not and had not been excited,
and my vanity gratified by the opportunities offered of meeting His

---

[1] This letter was written shortly after Letter 1254. In the preceding letter
Coleridge says he has sent to town to borrow the issues of the *London Magazine*
'hitherto published'; here he gives evidence of having read them, particularly
the December 1820 number. That issue contains three articles into which his
name is introduced. In 'The Mohock Magazine' John Scott speaks of Coleridge's 'displeasure' over the unauthorized publication of his private letter in
the September 1820 number of *Blackwood's Magazine* (see headnote to Letter
1254); in 'The Drama: No. XI', Hazlitt includes the 'abusive mention' of
Coleridge alluded to in Letter 1254; and in 'The Two Races of Men' Charles
Lamb refers to Coleridge as 'Comberbatch, matchless in his depredations'. In
1816 Lamb's 'wild Speeches' concerning Coleridge's borrowing but not returning
books had been a source of irritation. See Letter 1019. See also *Lamb Letters*,
ii. 284-6.

Royal Highness, the Duke of Sussex,[1] and sitting down with him at the same table. Indeed, such is my conviction of the Duke's Head, Heart, and conduct, that I should calumniate my own heart if I did not assert, that a far better and far nobler impulse, than that of Vanity, were not at work in my Bosom, in the strong Wish, I feel, to avail myself of your very kind invitation. And I intreat you to believe (in which you will do me but common Justice) that I both feel and appreciate your kind attentions both in this and in many other particulars, in their full worth. Of your friend, Mr Webb's Conversazioni, I have received from Mr Stanley such an account, that it is not in my nature to suppress the *desiderium*, the yearning, to be a participator of a feast so truly Attic and worthy of rational Beings.

But—ah that fatal Monosyllable! that canker-worm in the Flower-bed of Human Nature!—such is the peculiarity of my ill-health, that I dare not sleep away from my home—i.e. from those, who are accustomed to & prepared for, the sudden seizures, to which I am liable, & most liable after any excitement of animal spirits from genial Society. I am not ashamed to say, for there has been nothing shameful in the causes or occasions of it, that my circumstances will not allow me, rather will not enable me, to avail myself of any Vehicle, more at my will or less subjected to place & time than the Stage Coach—& that I am six miles from your House—and (for the Stage calls imperatively for your young friend) that I dare not promise any visit except *most* conditionally—

> I am obliged to | conclude | Your's most kindly
> S. T. Coleridge

1256. *To Charles Aders*[2]

MS. Cornell University Lib. Hitherto unpublished.

[December 1820 ?]

My dear Sir

Tho' it has been long since I have seen you, except for a few minutes, and my ill-health & consequent accumulation of unperformed Tasks have prevented me from seeking you out; yet I have

---

[1] Shortly before his death in Jan. 1820 the Duke of Kent recommended Pettigrew to his brother, the Duke of Sussex. Sussex appointed Pettigrew his surgeon and asked him to catalogue his extensive library.

[2] Charles Aders, a wealthy German merchant living in London, attended Coleridge's lectures of 1811–12. On 6 July 1820 he married Eliza Smith, the daughter of the painter and engraver John Raphael Smith. Aders owned a fine collection of paintings, including 'examples of the early Italian and, above all,

never, believe me, suffered myself to think of you as a lost Acquaintance or other than an absentee, to whose return I confidently looked forward. I shall be most happy to wait on you & Mrs Aders on any day, you may find most convenient, after new year's Day—& may probably have to avail myself of your kind offer of staying the Night.—Before that time, I dare not promise—first, because for the last month I, who am never other than unwell, from the time I awake till ten or past ten in the Morning, have been almost alarmingly so, from an unusual irritability of Stomach, and am now slowly mending, with strict management—2nd because of the few days, each with an interval, on which I dare go into Company, my most kind and invaluable Friends, Mr and Mrs Gillman have a claim to, for their immediate Circle, during the two next weeks—& lastly, the res angusta domûs (for tho' I have in the course of my life supported particular measures of all our Parties, especially of the present Ministry, I have never written a line *for* any party, and therefore have been patronized by none) compels me to *do something*—& I am very anxious to finish one of two or three Schoolbooks, which I believe Desiderata at present.—But of these and my other more properly called Literary Labors, we will talk when we meet—I am most indignant at the continued plagiarisms of Sir H. Davy from the Discoveries of Steffens and others—but this Country knows nothing of Germany but it's ungerman Kotzebues &c—

Your's, dear Sir, | truly

S. T. Coleridge

early Flemish and German schools', and their home in Euston Square was 'as much a picture-gallery as a house'. Among their friends were Wordsworth, Blake, Flaxman, John Linnell, the Lambs, and Crabb Robinson. In 1826 Coleridge addressed his lines, *The Two Founts*, to Mrs. Aders; Lamb in his poem, *To C. Aders, Esq. On his Collection of Paintings by the old German Masters*, called Aders the 'Friendliest of men' and spoke of the drawing-room as a 'Chapel' and an 'Oratory'. Aders purchased an estate at Godesberg on the Rhine, where Coleridge and Wordsworth visited Mrs. Aders in the summer of 1828. In 1836 a 'terrible reverse in trade' swept away Aders's fortune and the collection of paintings was sold and dispersed. See *Robinson on Books and Their Writers*, i. 56, 58, 256–7, 292, and 311; *The Correspondence of Henry Crabb Robinson with the Wordsworth Circle*, ed. Edith J. Morley, 2 vols., 1927, i. 190; Ellen C. Clayton, *English Female Artists*, 2 vols., 1876, i. 408; Alexander Gilchrist, *Life of William Blake*, ed. R. Todd, 1945, pp. 330–1; *The Works of Charles and Mary Lamb*, ed. E. V. Lucas, 7 vols., 1903–5, v. 85; and Letters 880, 1402, 1531, 1572, and 1629.

1257. *To H. F. Cary*

Address: The | Reverend H. F. Carey | Chiswick | near | London
MS. Pierpont Morgan Lib. Hitherto unpublished.
Postmark: Highgate, 1 January 1821.

31 Decembr 1820.
Sunday Evening
Highgate

My dear Sir

On Saturday I first received Mrs Cary's request, in which, how-ever, she forgot to mention the place at which and the name of the Vessel on board which Mr W. Carey was to embark—nor (which yet it would have been better than otherwise to have prefixed to my introduction of his name) his military Rank & the name of his Regi-ment. But the worst was, the difficulty from the intervention of Sunday to send the letter required before Monday—& the more so, on *this* account. Since Dr Middleton left Cambridge, at the close of *my* first term, I have seen him but once, & then only for a few minutes when he called on me some 12 or 14 years ago at the Courier office, & have never corresponded with him. I need not say, therefore, that to write a mere *Note* of Introduction besides being a liberty, I am not entitled to take, would be perhaps worse than of no service to your Son—& to finish the list of Items, I was under the necessity of going to Town, on a long engagement to a dinner party with Mr & Mrs Gillman, & Mr & Mrs Milne & Sister, which I could not break without giving offence both to the latter, and to our In-viters—from whence we did not return till ½ past 12.—I sat down, however, & have proceeded as far [as] I could (Sunday being the day, on which Mr Green attends me on my philosophical Lectures —his own Lectures at St Thomas's occupying him the other days of the week)—and I shall have finished such a letter, as warranting me in writing to the Bishop and enabling me to speak of *you* at large would, I hope, be or have a chance of being, serviceable to William if at least the Bishop has it in his power to be so. With this I mean to send a corrected Copy of my Friend and of the Lay Sermons—Of my Literary Life, in which I have mentioned his Lordship with high honor under the most unsuspicious Circumstance, namely the belief of his Death,[1] I have unfortunately no Copy—& the work is out of Print.—Now I have but one Comfort and one resource. The first is, the assurance given me by my Christian Neighbor of the Jewish Persuasion, that excellent Man & Scholar, Mr Hurwitz, that with this

---

[1] In chapter 1 of the *Biographia Literaria*, however, Coleridge added a footnote in which he explained that 'the report of Dr. Middleton's death on his voyage to India has been proved erroneous'.

wind or rather against this Wind no Ship can leave the River—and
the second, to have the Letter and accompanying small Pacquet left
at 'Mr Harding's, Public Notary, No. 7, Ball Alley, Lombard Street'
for William Carey, Esqre (the Honor, that his Mama will not let me
prefix, I must *af*fix)—N.B. My affectionate Respects to Mrs Carey,
happy Xtmas or, New Year's &c; & that when the weather becomes milder, I will furnish her ample opportunity & fit occasion
to repay me this Scolding in kind—However, I flatter myself that
your Son will still be able either to call at Mr Harding's (Mrs Gillman's Brother) or send for the thing.—

I have been very unwell—unusually in kind as well as degree—
my Son's ill-usage, like all other calamities, affecting my body when I
had supposed myself & mentally actually was, resigned and tranquil.
However, this sharp Weather has befriended me. All of our Household are tolerably well, except that James has a few Wheal-blotches
of Urticaria—& finds the invisible Nettle I fancy worse than even the
visible & tangible or twingible Birch—the Rash than the Rod. He
has got his Move into the sixth form, thank God! so that in case his
Health should make it requisite or highly desirable, he may now be
withdrawn for half a year without any injury to his Prospects—which
is a great Comfo[rt to] his dear Mother, no less than the Move its[elf
has] removed a great anxiety from both Parents. Litt[le] Henry, our
Pet, whose present name in vogue, is Fish of Finland, alias Loll of
Lapland, goes on very well, and is a most triumphant Slider, & in
blooming Health. He is very quick & retentive in his Learning—&
stands dodging in his declensions & Conjugations like a young
Priscian. But his raptures in this Frost—he came to request that
instead of Fish of Finland & Loll of Lapland, he might be called
Fish of Finland and Ice of Iceland.

Mrs Gillman, & all of us indeed, desire their kind Love to all.
Would I were even in a tolerable degree qualis eram:[1] & I assure
you, I should by hook or crook enjoy more of your Society. May God
bless you, my dear Sir! & your's with most affectionate Esteem

                                             S. T. Coleridge.

P.S. I shall have the pleasure of sending you a very sensible and
well-written Work of Mr Hurwitz's in defence of our established
Version. Hurwitz is a strictly orthodox Messianic Jew whose learning & sound judgement would qualify him to be the Luther of
Judaism, in recalling his Brethren from the Swamps of Talmudism
to the terra firma of the Holy Writ—Being asked, what his persuasion was, I replied—that he preferred the Hexameter alone to the
Elegiac of Faith—But O! how far nearer is an orthodox Jew to an
orthodox Protestant Christian, than the Socinian is.—

                    [1] Horace, *Odes*, iv. 1. 3.

1258. *To H. F. Cary*

Address: Revd Mr Carey | Chiswick
MS. Pierpont Morgan Lib. Hitherto unpublished.
Postmark: Highgate, 8 January 1821.

[8 January 1821]

My dear Sir

From the invalided state of my Messenger, the only one I could procure, and the absence of Mr Harding during the time that he could wait in Ball Alley, joined with his ill-luck in not being able to find out a Chiswick Carrier himself, I am left uncertain whether the Parcel sent from here on Wednesday last and inclosing the Books and Letter reached you in time for Mr William to have it. I need not say, that this has caused & causes me no little anxiety—I shall wish my corrections at the (*Printer's*) Devil, if the Delay occasioned by them & which with the search for a Messenger put off their final departure from our House till past One o/clock, should have *belated* the Letter & Books.—Pray, give me one Line just to say—Yea or No.—This uncouth rise of the Thermometer, 22 Degrees in scarcely more than the same number of Hours, with the dense Fog, a descendant of the Egyptian, and which I would fain conjure home again, with it's Cousin-germans, the Ghosts & such like Southeïo-Wesleyan burglarious Gentry, to the Red Sea,

(That the Fog we never might *see*	*punicè see*
And the Ghosts might cease to be *red*	do. read.

which couplet you should *have* recited to you, it being addressed to the mind's *Ear* exclusively) has with other things, ex. gr. two large dinner-parties within two days of each other, thrown me back into my *badly* way—Mr Gillman too is unwell, & both in stomach & nerves out of sorts—Mrs G. thank God & the two Boys pretty well. —Have you Lamb's Essays under the name of Elia? I have seen two that were extracted from Baldwin's Magazine, by the Times the one, & the other by the Morning Chronicle, which I think you would like very much. The last, that on the old Year,[1] I have some thought of answering; but alas! I have so many things to do, and such very pressing reasons for doing them, that I can do nothing!— I am, however, getting regularly on with my LOGIC—in 3 parts—1. The Canons (Syllogy) 2. the Criterions (Dialectic) 3. Organic or Heuristic (εὑριστικόν) with a sketch of the History of the science from Aristotle to Bacon, & a disciplinary Analysis of Condillac's ψευδο-Logic prefixed, & concluding with a Glossary of philosophical Terms arranged *methodically* in the order & connection of the

[1] Coleridge refers to Charles Lamb's 'New Year's Eve', which appeared in the *London Magazine*, Jan. 1821.

Thoughts; but with an Alphabetical Index—and every Sunday I devote with Mr Green, my Fellow-student & Amanuensis, to my (Anti-Paleyo-grotian) Assertion of Religion as necessarily implying Revelation, and of Xtianity as the only Revelation of universal validity.—Of the latter some thing more than a Volume is written.—

Mrs Gillman desires her best and kindest remembrances of Love to you & Mrs Carey—Believe me, I long to see you. And if I can but make a little way, if I can but push and pole myself off the shelvy Shores & sucking Sand-banks into smoothish Water, I will not be long in turning the helm & setting my sail for Chiswick.—God bless you, my dear & honored Sir

& your sincerely affectionate | Friend,
S. T. Coleridge.

P.S. If my fancy have not fascinated my sober Sense, I have thrown considerable Light over the first part of Genesis from Cap. I. to C. XI. v. 9—The first chapter, however, I exclude from what I now speak of—but I refer especially to the difficult contents of the 2nd and 3rd—and in these again more particularly to the supposed Post-Creation of the Woman, and to the immediate descendants of *the Man* (for it seems beyond all doubt, that neither Adam or Eve are *proper* Names in the original). I flatter myself too, that I have satisfactorily decyphered the import of Eden & the four River-heads into which the River that flowed out of Eden disparted itself. The more I study the Genesis of Moses, the more [prof]ound does my admiration of it become!—B[ut] Jehovah Elohim is undoubtedly, 'The self-exist[ent] *Strengths*'—Elohim being a plural derived from [the] Hebrew word for the Trunk of an Oak & used for the O[ak] itself—just as the *Robur* in the Latin—It is therefore strictly equivalent to the Scholastic 'Causa sui qui et Causa Causarum est', and finely contra-distinguishes the transcendent, and *positive* Unity of the God (Unity with Plenitude) from the sterile Unity of abstraction or the derivative and *negative* unity of the Creature or Anthropomorph Mono-idolism. A *is*: or $A = A + a$ b c d &c. as contrasted with a is—*not* b, *not* c, d, or $a = a - b, -c, -d$ &c—thus confuting the calumny of Gibbon & his Compeers, who describe the Jehovah of Moses, as a sullen solitary Jupiter, at jealous enmity with the Gods of other nations.

I was much pleased with my neighbor, Hurwitz's rendering of Leah's Dan—instead of *a Troop* cometh,[1] he translates it—Lo! a new *Bond* or Band (i.e. of my Husband's affection).

[1] Genesis xxx. 11.

1259. *To L. Neumegen*[1]

Address: Mr Neumagen
MS. Harvard College Lib. Hitherto unpublished. This letter is inserted in a copy
of John Walker's *A Dictionary of the English Language*, . . . 1775. The volume
contains manuscript notes by Coleridge.

[*Circa* 8 January 1821][2]

My dear Sir

From Verse 4, C. II. of Genesis to v. 24, C. III., and in this Portion only, the words Jehova Elohim occur (so Eichhorn informs me).
With the IVth Chapter the use of the word, Jehova, by itself,
begins: and with C. V. that of Elohim recommences.—From the
VIth to the IXth Chapter, both included, does the word, *God*, in our
version regularly and in all cases stand for Elohim in the original?
'The Lord' for Jehova? and *'the Lord God'* for Jehova Elohim?—I
do not possess a Hebrew Bible, nor a Pagninus—You would oblige
me, therefore, if you let one of your young Gentlemen (if you are
not at leisure) resolve the questions for me. Probably, Yes, or No—
may be sufficient—and if you would add the original word* rendered *'broken up'*, in C. VII. v. 11. and elsewhere in the Narrative
of the Deluge, you would additionally oblige me.—

Mem.—Is not the distinction of the Animals between 'clean and
unclean', as already existing before the Flood a problem of difficult
solution?—

Your's, dear Sir, | with unfeigned respect
S. T. Coleridge.

. . .[3] state of our Planet there might have been a *number* of Rings,
analogous to the two-fold Ring of Saturn—*belting* the Earth—.
The Hypothesis would at least help to explain the fact of a rain of
only 960 Hours covering the planet with waters five miles above
the Level of the Sea.—

[1] L. Neumegen, a friend and apparently the successor of Hyman Hurwitz as
master of the private academy for Jewish boys at Highgate. Hurwitz retired
from the school in 1821 or 1822. See Letters 1449 and 1603, and John H. Lloyd,
The History . . . of Highgate, 1888, p. 202.
[2] The references to the early chapters of Genesis, and particularly to the
words Jehovah Elohim, in this and in Letter 1258, suggest that the two letters
were written about the same time.
* together with the *radical*, and it's primary sense. [Note by S. T. C.]
[3] MS. torn; the beginning of this sentence is missing.

1260. *To C. A. Tulk*

Address: C. A. Tulk, Esqre. M.P. | Regency Park
MS. Pierpont Morgan Lib. Pub. Letters, *ii. 712.*
Postmark: Highgate, 12 February 1821.

[12 February 1821]

My dear Sir

'They say, Coleridge! that you are a Swedenborgian!'[1] Would to God! (I replied fervently) that *they* were *any thing*. I was writing a brief essay on the prospects of a country, where it has become the

---

[1] In his edition of Coleridge's *Lay Sermons*, 1852, Derwent Coleridge included the following note by his father in Appendix B (p. 70) of *The Statesman's Manual*: 'I have this morning read with high delight an admirable representation of what men in general think, and what ought to be thought, concerning the conscience in the translation of Swedenborg's Universal Theology of the New Church, II. pp. 361–370. 6 *January*, 1821.'

In Apr. 1827 Coleridge wrote as follows concerning Swedenborg in a marginal note in a copy of Samuel Noble's *An Appeal in behalf of the views of the Eternal World and State, and of the Doctrines of Truth and Life, held by the Body of Christians, who believe that a New Church is signified (in the Revelation, Chap. XXI.) by the New Jerusalem, including answers to objections, particularly those of G. Beaumont, in his work entitled, 'The Anti-Swedenborg'*, 1826:

I have often thought of writing a work to be entitled *Vindiciae Heterodoxae, sive celebrium virorum παραδογματιζόντων defensio*; that is, Vindication of Great Men unjustly branded; and at such times the names prominent to my mind's eye have been Giordano Bruno, Jacob Behmen, Benedict Spinoza, and Emanuel Swedenborg. Grant, that the origin of the Swedenborgian theology is a problem; yet on which ever of the three possible hypotheses— (possible I mean for gentlemen, scholars and Christians)—it may be solved— namely;—1. Swedenborg's own assertion and constant belief in the hypothesis of a supernatural illumination; or, 2. that the great and excellent man was led into this belief by becoming the subject of a very rare, but not (it is said) altogether unique, conjunction of the somniative faculty (by which the products of the understanding, that is to say, words, conceptions and the like, are rendered instantaneously into forms of sense) with the voluntary and other powers of the waking state; or, 3. the modest suggestion that the first and second may not be so incompatible as they appear—still it ought never to be forgotten that the merit and value of Swedenborg's system do only in a very secondary degree depend on any one of the three. For even though the first were adopted, the conviction and conversion of such a believer must, according to a fundamental principle of the New Church, have been wrought by an insight into the intrinsic truth and goodness of the doctrines, severally and collectively, and their entire consonance with the light of the written and of the eternal word, that is, with the Scriptures and with the sciential and the practical reason. Or say that the second hypothesis were preferred, and that by some hitherto unexplained affections of Swedenborg's brain and nervous system, he from the year 1743, thought and reasoned through the *medium* and instrumentality of a series of appropriate and symbolic visual and auditual images, spontaneously rising before him, and these so clear and so distinct, as at length to overpower perhaps his first suspicions of their subjective nature, and to become objective for him, that is, in his own belief

mind of the Nation to appreciate the evil of public acts and measures by their next consequences or immediate occasions, while the *principle* violated, or that *a* Principle is thereby violated, is either wholly dropt out of the consideration, or is introduced but as a Garnish or ornamental Common-place in the peroration of a Speech! The deep interest was present to my thoughts—of that distinction between the *Reason*, as the source of Principles, the true celestial influx and porta Dei in hominem internum, and the *Understanding*, with the clearness of the proof, by which this distinction is evinced—viz. that vital or zoo-organic Power, Instinct, and Understanding fall all three under the same definition *in genere*, and the very additions by which the definition is applied from the first to the second, and from the second to the third, are themselves expressive of degrees only and in *degree* only deniable of the preceding—(Ex. gr. 1. Reflect on the *selective* power exercised by the stomach of the Caterpillar on the undigested miscellany of food— the same power exercised by the Caterpillar on the outward Plants—& you will see the order of the conceptions.) 1. Vital power=the power, by which *means are adapted* to proximate ends. 2. Instinct, the power, *which adapts* means to proximate ends. 3. Understanding=the power which adapts means to proximate ends according *to varying circumstances*. May I not safely challenge any man to peruse Huber's Treatise on Ants, and yet deny their claim to be included in the last definition?[1]—But try to apply the same definition, with any extension of degree, to the Reason—the absurdity will flash upon the conviction. First, in Reason there is and can be no *degree*. Deus introit aut non introit.—Secondly, in Reason there are no *means* nor ends: Reason itself being one with the ultimate end, of which it is the manifestation. Thirdly, Reason has no concern with *things* (i.e. the impermanent flux of particulars) but with the permanent *Relations*; & is to be defined, even in it's lowest or theoretical attribute, as the Power which enables man to draw *necessary* and *universal* conclusions from particular facts or

of their kind and origin,—still the thoughts, the reasonings, the grounds, the deductions, the facts illustrative, or in proof, and the conclusions, remain the same; and the reader might derive the same benefit from them as from the sublime and impressive truths conveyed in the Vision of Mirza or the Tablet of Cebes. So much even from a very partial acquaintance with the works of Swedenborg, I can venture to assert; that as a moralist Swedenborg is above all praise; and that as a naturalist, psychologist, and theologian, he has strong and varied claims on the gratitude and admiration of the professional and philosophical student. (*Literary Remains*, iv. 422–4.) The copy of Noble's work containing annotations by Coleridge is in the British Museum.

[1] Pierre Huber's *Recherches sur les Moeurs des Fourmis Indigènes* appeared in 1810, an English translation, *The Natural History of Ants*, in 1820. Coleridge cites this work in *Aids to Reflection*, 1825, pp. 210–14.

forms—ex. gr. from any 3 cornered thing that the 2 sides of a
Triangle are & must be greater than the third.—From the Understanding to the Reason there is no continuous *ascent* possible, it is
a metabasis εἰς ἄλλο γένος, even as from the air to the Light. The
true essential peculiarity of the Human Understanding consists in
it's capability of being irradiated by the reason—in it's recipiency—
& even this is *given* to it by the presence of a higher power than
itself.[1] What then must be [the] fate of a nation that substitutes
Locke for Logic, and Paley for Morality, and one or the other for
Polity and Theology, according to the predominance of Whig or
Tory predilection?—Slavery: or a commotion is at hand!—But if
the Gentry and *Clerisy* (including all the learned & educated) do
this, then the nation does it—*or a commotion is at hand. Acephalum*
enim, aurâ quamvis et calore vitali potiatur, *morientem* rectius
dicimus quam quod vivit.—With these thoughts was I occupied
when I received your very kind and most acceptable present—&
the results I must defer to the next post.—With best regards to
Mrs Tulk

> believe me, in the brief interval, | Your obliged & grateful
>   S. T. Coleridge

1261. *To Mrs. George Frere*[2]

MS. Private possession. Pub. A Book for Bookmen, *by John Drinkwater, 1927,*
p. 253.

Monday
2 April [1821 ?]

My dear Madam
    I will not, no unforeseen insuperable Obstacle intervening, fail to
avail myself of your kind invitation on Friday next, 6 o'clock—.
I have too many delightful recollections, and too many grateful
emotions, connected with your friendly Fireside to need any additional inducement—tho' if it were not so, it would be a motive of
no ordinary force that I was likely to meet the man who beyond
all competition is entitled to the name of the greatest Benefactor of
the Race of all now living Individuals—viz. Dr Bell—
    With my best respects to Mr G. Frere and the young Ladies
believe me, my dear Madam, sincerely your obliged | Friend
                                                        S. T. Coleridge

----

[1] Compare this discussion with a marginal note written in a copy of *The
Statesman's Manual* presented to John Anster and bearing the date '*August,
1821*'. The volume is in the British Museum. For Coleridge's note see T. J. Wise,
Two Lake Poets . . ., 1927, p. 76. See also *Aids to Reflection*, 1825, pp. 208–42,
and note to Letter 1402.
    [2] This letter is endorsed 'To Mrs G. Frere'.

1262. *To Thomas Allsop*

Address: T. Allsop, Esqre | Blandford Place | Pall Mall   Favored by Mr Milne.
MS. New York Public Lib. Pub. with omis. Letters, Conversations and Rec. *102.*

Thursday Night
4 [3] May, 1821
Highgate.

My dear Allsop

Mr & Mrs Gillman's kind love to you—and we beg that the Good Lady's late remembering that (as often the very fullness & vividness of the purpose & intention to do a thing imposes on the mind a sort of counterfeit feeling of quiet, similar to the satisfaction which the having done it would produce) you had not been written to, will not prejudice the present attempt at 'better late than not at all'. We have a party *tomorrow*, in which, because we believed, it would interest you, you stood included in our thoughts, at six o'clock—In addition to a neighbor, and ourselves, and Mrs Gillman's most unmrsgillmanly Sister (but n.b. this is a secret to all who are both blind & deaf) there will be the Matthews (Mr & Mrs) *at home* Matthews, I mean—& Charles and Mary Lamb, who will stay the night, and we can get you your bed at the same place.

I hope, as it is so late a dinner-hour, there being a Stage too at 5 or about, that it will not interfere with the claims of the departed Day—and that we shall *have*, tho' we cannot *hold*, you. Mr Gillman is much better—indeed he stands on Terra firma again, & Mrs G. is *better*, tho' still paler & more weak than I like to see—Of myself, the best I can say is that in the belief of those well qualified to judge I am not *so* ill as I fancy myself to be—Be this as it may, I am always,

My dear Allsop, | with highest esteem & regard | Your affectionate Friend,

S. T. Coleridge

1263. *To Derwent Coleridge*

Address: Derwent Coleridge, Esqre | St John's College | Cambridge—   *Post Paid*
MS. Victoria University Lib. Pub. with omis. E. L. G. ii. 277.
Postmark: Highgate, 16 May 1821.

[16 May 1821]

My dear Derwent

I leave the two first sides of this sheet for your and my kind friend, Mr Gillman. We are quite satisfied that you both do and do without, to the utmost of your power—and God forbid but that by hook or crook you shall be enabled to make both ends meet, without incurring any Cambridge Debt—the very thought of which agitates me, who can never forget that the stupifying effect of my first Term Bill (including furniture &c &c, vaguely ordered by me, poor, friendless, & in all circumstantials most ignorant, Lad, tho' I had during the whole term not wittingly fallen into any expence, & for whom three or four Rush Chairs and a deal table would have looked as well as Mr Hope's or the King's Drawing Room) affected and infected my whole life following—and by pure terror and hauntings of mind brought about a cowardice as to mental pain, which has been the main source of all my real Misdoings & *Not*-doings, and the occasion of many and worse being attributed to me. For God knows! the dread of painful thoughts, of mental disruption, which sometimes furnished occasion for misrepresentation, and always prevented me from justifying myself, has been the most and most culpable of all the evil that would remain at the bottom of the brimming Cup of Slander when the downright falsehood was taken away.—I hope to make a little money within a month or six weeks: and if I can only prevent *my* debt to my more than disinterested Friends from accumulating, in the course of the present Year—& prevent *your* being in debt at all, I shall be tranquil, and hope for better times. Could I produce any work that should become popular, I might, I doubt not, sell the copy-right of an Edition of my Poems, Biography, &c that have been long out of print, for a sum that would go someway towards re-imbursing my best Friends, Mr and Mrs Gillman whose very virtues do at times throw me into a gloomy mood. How can it be otherwise when day after day I see them so generous, so high-hearted, & yet so industrious, self-denying, and economic—& know that they are at this moment out of pocket by me to between 3 and 400£—on a calculation of my bonâ fide prime cost & their extra advances?—I mention this for no other reason on earth, than because it is right that my children should know the facts.

And now one sentence respecting your Cambridge War-fare. A very high degree with it's consequents, a fellow-ship, a Tutorship, a late College Living, perhaps a Mastership, is doubtless a desirable thing; but it may, even were it [at] all a certainty, be bought too, far too dear—*culpably* too dear, if with the ruin of your Health—& *too* dear, if at the sacrifice of the *harmonious* developement of your intellectual powers. My highest Aspirations would be realized in your leaving the university with an honorable character, as a man, with a respectable Degree, or (should accidental Hindrances intervene) with the general conviction in the minds of your Contemporaries that you were entitled to it, and with *all* the several faculties of your mind, and all the acquirements subservient to their growth and application, cultivated in symmetry, and mastered in proportion to their inner comparative Worth and their outward utility in respect to society at large & your own worldly as well as moral Interests.—You may be a Tutor in a wealthy or noble Family —you may (& *I* fondly hope, will) be a Clergyman—a Man of Letters—a secretary to a public Man. What should a man, having your talents be and be master of, in all or either of these situations? In short, do you mean to find your World in the University, or to make use of the University as a stepping-stone to the World? This is the point on which you ought to make up your mind. Both are possible. But I hope to see you soon, & we will understand each other.

Your affectionate Father,

S. T. C.

I need not say, my dear Derwent! that if I had reason to suppose you inclined to scatter the stream of your Power and *Time* in a multiplicity of Channels, or to be dallying with the Desultories, which is the sad Case with Hartley, my advice would be as different as the source of my anxiety. But for *you*, I repeat it, the question is—and you alone must solve it for yourself—Which is or shall be your plan? The World *in* the University? Or the University *for* the World? Neither is *incompatible* with your moral and *trans*mundane interests. But which of the two is most suited to *you*, Health, Circumstances, Temper, Turn, Taste, and comparative Faculty (= facilitas fiendi et faciendi) included and considered? If you decide in favor of the latter, then I would fix on *Trinity*,[1] a fair Senior Optimacy, *systematic* and *exact* Study of the Greek Historians, Orators, and Dramatists, not neglecting the Roman, but studying them chiefly during and for the purpose of Latin Composition, prose & metre—(N.B. this latter as a sacrifice but not too dear a sacrifice to the attainment of a respectable *chance* for the classical Honors of your College & the University, including that of a Fellowship; but both only as a Lucro ponamus)[2]—and all your classical studies under the guidance and in the light of PHILOLOGY, in that original and noblest sense of the term, in which it *implies* & is the most *human*, practical, and fructifying Form, & (what is of no small moment in the present state of Society) the most popular *Disguise*, of Logic and Psychology—without which what is man?— (The last 5 words I wrote with the line 'Without black velvet Breeches what is man?' running in my head.)

[1] Although Derwent thought of transferring to Trinity College, Cambridge, he remained at St. John's. For his brother's advice on the subject see *Letters of Hartley Coleridge*, pp. 59–63.

[2] Horace, *Odes*, i. 9. 14 fol.

Would to God, my dearest Boy! that I had a Home of my own for you and your Friends—& that you might be the Inviter instead of the Invitee—alternately at least. It makes my heart ake, to know that I have not: tho' I have all and more than all, I fear, that my affectionate & more than generous Host & Hostess can supply, consistently with the performance of their own duties. Poor Hartley (who by himself is sure to find a welcome even* on Sundays, either at our house or Mr Milne's, or Dr Owen's, or Mr Sutton's or Mr Steele's) in shrinking from the momentary pain of telling the plain truth, a truth not dishonorable to him or me, has several times inflicted an agitating pain & confusion on me, by bringing up Mr Burton unexpectedly on Sundays, in the intention of dining here—& *twice* of late have we been *obliged* to make an excuse, from the incapability of finding room at our Table. And what right have I to obtrude a stranger, whom I respect indeed on your account & believe to be truly respectable, (& so do the Gillmans) but who is still a stranger, not personally interesting to them, & necessarily giving the conversation a general cast? Add to this: that during the hours before dinner I am engaged with Mr Green, or ought to be— and *fretting* either way—fearful of seeming disrespectful to Mr Burton, and yet seeing Mrs G. vexed & scarce knowing what to do. —This has given me pain, far beyond the particular occasion, as a symptom of an evil in H. that has been so unspeakably injurious to myself—for in the very first instance I spoke to him, explained the impropriety in detail—and my evident Suffering, which instantly affects my stomach & bowels, should have given a more than sufficient force to my intreaties. On the Sunday before last we, or rather Mrs G.—for it was not in my power or right, nor to tell you the truth even in my inclination *at the moment,* invited Mr B. and H. for the following (i.e. last) Sunday, as the only way of softening the awkward necessity of sending him away twice successively. And what was Hartley's excuse—that Mr B. had walked so far on the way with him, that he could not help asking him!—As if Mr B. could have been offended, had H. told him—I do not think, we can dine at Mr G.'s—indeed, we must say that we do not—but we can see my Father, have a Lunch of cold meat & pickle, & return—

H. has the noblest Subject that perhaps a Poet ever worked on— the Prometheus[1]—& I have written a small volume almost to him, containing all the materials & comments on the full import of this

* I say, '*even*': because Sunday is the only Day when the Gillmans are likely to see their London Friends & Relations, including those of mine (such as Allsop, the Lambs, &c) who can only come on Sundays. [Note by S. T. C.]

[1] Hartley's *Prometheus. A Fragment* was published posthumously in 1851. See *Poems by Hartley Coleridge,* ed. Derwent Coleridge, 2 vols., 1851 (2nd edn.), ii. 257–85. See also *Letters of Hartley Coleridge,* 29.

most pregnant and sublime Mythos and Philosopheme[1]—in short, the sum of all my Reading & reflection on this vast Wheel of the Mythology of the earliest & purest Heathenism, which makes it credible that (the names excepted) the Sybilline Poems contain far more of the *substance* of the genuine originals than it is the fashion to believe.—With his poetry I have had no concern, of course—but have simply brought together such Stuff, as the Poet must have sought for in Books, & therefore could not subtract an atom from his poetic Originality. I know, that in a work of this kind a man must wait for genial hours and cannot *sit* down to it mechanically. But I should be happy to see your Brother more totus in illo[2] —and [am] almost afraid, that as the Materials accumulate & the Plan becomes large and circular, his Passion has cooled. I do not want or wish to see a Volume of *Poems* either from him or you, in the *first* place. Let a man be known first, as capable of doing, and as having done, some one objective Whole, having a Beginning, Middle, and End—a Whole, in which the Thinker and the Man of Learning appears as the Base of the Poet—in which there is nothing about I, and I's strolling friend or mama or sweet heart (see Literary Life—II. p. 15. By the bye, your Friend will find my sympathy with him respecting the Farmers, in II. p. 40.) Then, if you please—Sonnets, Musings, Love-odes, &c. If they are good, they are delightful—but for the *first* introduction of a Poet I should greatly prefer the plan, that Mr Millman has adopted.[3]—Had it been possible for you to have spent the Long Vacation with me, here and at the Sea-side, I should have urged you to devote an hour or so daily to a Work on Metre & especially on the Prosody of the Greeks—. Such a work is an absolute Desideratum. I was much pleased with your remarks on Southey's Hex. (!!)[4]—Till we meet,

God bless you & your Father

S. T. C.

P.S. I find that Mr G. is writing to you on a separate sheet—I have therefore turned the back- into the fore-sides.

[1] As Derwent says, the 'profound and complex *philosopheme*' which Coleridge saw in the *Prometheus* of Aeschylus lay beyond Hartley's powers. Coleridge, however, utilized these 'materials & comments' in his essay, *On the Prometheus of Aeschylus*, which was delivered before the Royal Society of Literature on 18 May 1825. See *Poems by Hartley Coleridge*, ed. Derwent Coleridge, 2 vols., 1851 (2nd edn.), ii. 257; Chambers, *Life*, 309; and Letter 1463.

[2] Horace, *Satires*, i. 9. 2.

[3] After winning the Newdigate prize with an English poem on the 'Apollo Belvidere', Henry H. Milman (1791–1868) published *Fazio*, a poetic drama, in 1815, *Samor, the Lord of the Bright City*, an epic, in 1818, and *The Fall of Jerusalem*, a dramatic poem, in 1820.

[4] Southey's *A Vision of Judgment*, an apotheosis of George III in hexameters,

1264. *To Thomas Allsop*

Address: T. Allsop, Esqre | Blandford Place | Pall Mall
MS. Cornell University Lib. Pub. E. L. G. ii. 285.

Sunday afternoon, ½ past 4. [10 June 1821][1]
Highgate

My dear dear Allsop

So fully had I calculated on finding you at Highgate, when I left Grosvenor Square this morning at 12 o'clock, that tho' I rose from bed with the intention of calling at Blandford Place, yet having been detained an hour or more beyond my purpose in conversation with Sir George and Lady B., I did not think the mere *possibility* of your not having set off the evening before a sufficient Counterweight to the risk of missing the Kentish Town Stage which leaves Tottenham Court Road on Sundays at ½ past 12. Had I supposed even a *probable* chance of finding you at your rooms, I should have gladly availed myself of the opportunity of walking home with you, and if we were tired, of breaking the walk by a two shilling fare from the last Hackney Coach Stand—

On my arrival I found Mr & Mrs Gillman expecting you, & beginning to fear & be vexed—and Mrs G. apprehensive that you had misinterpreted her letter to you, and fretting herself that she had omitted to say expressly—(after the words—'C. dines on

---

was published in 1821. Hartley, too, had his opinion of Southey's poem: 'Have you seen Southey's Vision of Judgement! ! ! ! ! *O Tempora, O Mores*—And is it come to this? And our dear good mother gave me such a hint to praise in her last letter! ! ! I came off, I think, pretty well, saying that I did not think it the *best* of S.'s poems. Seriously speaking, our late lamented Monarch did not deserve such an insult to his memory. And who, but a converted Revolutionist, would ever have dream'd of spurring the wind-gall'd, glander'd, stagger'd, bott-begrown, spavin'd (Oh—for the Complete Farrier) broken-down gelding, that has turn'd blind with facing year after year the same round of Court Compliments—who, I say, but Southey himself would have forced the poor old beast into the Hexameter long trot; and so mounted as on another Rosinante, set off in search of adventures, in the world of spirits?' *Letters of Hartley Coleridge*, 65.

[1] In the postscript to the present letter Coleridge speaks of the forthcoming visit of Allsop's sister. In a letter to Allsop of 13 June 1821 Mrs. Gillman makes a similar comment: 'Let me know if you intend to bring your Sister for a night or two. I shall expect a longer visit after.' It seems likely, therefore, that Coleridge's letter and Mrs. Gillman's were written about the same time. Furthermore, Allsop replied to Mrs. Gillman 'by return of Post', as Coleridge requested, his letter arriving at Highgate on Wednesday, 13 June. See *Nineteenth-Century Studies* (Cornell), 71. Miss Allsop was staying at Highgate on 30 June 1821.

The erroneous date of '10 July 1821' appearing in the MS. is in Allsop's handwriting. In 1821 10 July fell on a Tuesday. Allsop did not date the extract from this letter printed in *Letters, Conversations and Rec.* 123.

Saturday at Sir G. B.'s')—*but he returns at latest in the first stage on Sunday Morning, & we shall expect you if you cannot come to night, yet tomorrow evening—at all events, that you will spend Sunday with us*—But I have told her—that this omission cannot have been the cause—for that the import of the words omitted was a Comment, which your knowlege of our united desire to see you at all times could not but have supplied—& that you would not allow yourself to fancy any rightful ground, cause, or occasion for not coming here but the Wish, the Duty, or the prudential propriety of going else-where, or staying at home—. When the Needle of your Thoughts begins to be magnetic, you may be certain that my *Pole* is at that moment *attracting* you by the spiritual magic of strong Wishing for your arrival—N.b. my *Pole* includes in this instance *both the Poles* of Mr and eke of Mrs Gillman, i.e. the Head and Heart.—

But seriously—I am a little anxious. So give me or my blest sisterly Friend a few lines by return of Post—just to let us know, that you are & have been well—& that nothing of a painful nature has deprived us of the expected pleasure—a pleasure which, believe me, stands a good many degrees above *Moderate* in the Cordi- or Hedonometer of,

my dear Allsop, | your's most *cordi*ally
S. T. Coleridge

P.S. My kindest regards to your Sister. I look forward with warmth of heart to the time, when she will commence her sojourn with us.—

1265. *To George Coleridge*

Address: Revd W. H. Coleridge | 15. Edwards Square | Kensington   For the Revd. George Coleridge
MS. Victoria University Lib. Pub. E. L. G. ii. 288.
Postmark: Highgate, 12 June 1821.

[11 June 1821]

My dear Brother

I will not attempt to conceal from you, that I felt the disap-pointment of not seeing you and my Sister most acutely. Not indeed your deferring the promised visit: for from the actual and still more from the threatening state of the Weather, tho' I could not help wishing to the very last, yet I did not fully *expect* to see you on Friday. But I did more than hope, that you would spare a few hours of your time of Sojourn for this purpose: and notwith-standing your letter can still scarcely persuade myself, that you have abandoned it determinately. Is it, that I grounded my anti-cipations too exclusively on my own feelings, in part on the

impressions, under which I left you, but far more on my inward certainty that from the hour, I quitted Cambridge, in no one instance,
no not even in a momentary thought, had I ever connected your
name or image, directly or remotely, with an alien or worldly view,
nor with any feelings but those of unalterable Love and (as was
natural from the relation in which I had stood to you from Boyhood
to the Dawn of Manhood) of almost filial Reverence. Thro' good
and evil Report & tho' knowing how unhappily on more than one
occasion I had been misinterpreted or misrepresented, I never had
a resentful thought,* never attributed to you conduct or purpose
unworthy of a good man; and the grief, which I never ceased to feel
at my apparent alienation from your affections, was confined to the
Alienation itself—and—for I am too deeply moved to attempt to
conceal any part of the truth—to the loss of *your* friendship, *your*
correspondence and occasional Society. From the undomesticating
influences of Christ's Hospital & perhaps my own intellectual pre-
cocity, I had learnt to love my Brother Luke, as an elder Brother,
and yourself as Father & Brother in one—beyond this I had for
a long time (and that too *the* time in which, if ever, our family
attachments take root) scarcely the opportunities—& when they
began, the striking difference of my character, much doubtless
consisting of faulty elements, but much likewise arising from
natural diversity and an education still more dissimilar, instead of
counteracting came in aid of the prejudices, that had been infused
—at all events, had found entrance—into my mind. But it is equally
true, that the affections, which I had formed, remained ineradi-
cably—and forgive me, if I confess that when I take the whole
retrospect of my Life, fixing my thoughts the most steadily on the
points that were or appeared to others most culpable, & making no
deductions on the score of exaggeration or misinformation, I find
it difficult to believe myself even suspected by any one, who had
ever known me, of professing a regard which I did not at the time
feel, or of proposing to myself an *end*, which I did not find in the
Means themselves or in their proper and natural Effects.

* Indeed, I cannot recall any one instance, in which by an act of my own
I could (I will not say, have *warranted*; but) have given rise to even a suspicion
in this point, with the single exception of my applying to you at the commencement of THE FRIEND to be one of four or five Patrons of the Work who were to
guarantee the Paper and Stamps of the first 20 numbers till the receipt of the
Subscriptions which were to be received by an Agent of their own appointment,
the number of Subscribers *then* exceeding 500. And this I did, as I fully
explained to you afterwards, with no other motive than that of shewing
Respect and affection—and suggested by the cordial approbation which you
had expressed of my plan & of the Objects to which I was devoting my efforts.
[Note by S. T. C.] See Letters 783 and 788.

When I learnt that you were near & wished to meet me, & while I was with you, as far as I thought of myself at all, I had but one wish—that you might see me as I was—in all that my own consciousness extended to. Fearful as the attribute of seeing into the Heart must be to every man not doting with Self-complacency, yet it seemed to me that I would gladly have had you possessed of such a power in my own particular instance—uncertain as to the general result but assured that in some points I should hereafter appear a very different if not a better man. Yet I could not bring myself to interrupt the delight of the first renewal of an intercommunion of minds by any personal concerns—personal tho' in no connection with circumstances or aught that is your's or mine rather than you and I.—But in such a state of mind & heart as that which I brought back with me from Kensington, how could I but look forward with anxious desire to a second meeting when I might have won from you your opinions, both as a Christian and an elder Brother, respecting myself, and the facts or assumptions on which they were grounded—might have rectified any mistakes, if such there should be, by laying before you proofs and documents of the real bearings—& above all, have attempted to shew you, that I earnestly wish to act in accordance with the prescripts of Duty, as soon as in reason and conscience I am made to perceive, that such they are when brought to the test of the Gospel or an impartial & dispassionate Judgement ? And if in thus disburthening my heart to you, I should be compelled to introduce any worldly incidents, as the bankruptcy and almost unexampled profligacy of my late Publishers, and events having similar results, I should do so wholly and exclusively for the purpose of shewing you, that this or that was not or had not been in my power—precluding, as far as the earnest expression of my inmost Intention could preclude, every object not connected with the attainment of your moral approbation, unless indeed it were the advantage of your advice.—

I have carefully re-perused, what I have above written, in order to satisfy myself whether in any point I have gone too far or have said more than a calm and more collected Recollection & Self-inquisition would justify. And in speaking of the causes why I felt the disappointment so acutely, and why I am so reluctant still to abandon the hope, I have certainly omitted one of minor consideration indeed comparatively with those, that have been stated ; but which cannot but have, nay which [ough]t to have, a proportionate influence on my feelings. For nearly five years I have lived in the hourly receipt of the most assiduous &—it is far too little to say—the most disinterested Kindness and friendship from Mr and Mrs Gillman—alike to me and to mine. To Mr Gillman I owe under

God all the health and means of being useful that I possess—to both of them the support derived as from their sympathy so from their daily example—and their affection shewn to me at the time, that I was defrauded of all that I had been laboring for for a course of years & even forced to raise money to purchase back the Half-Copy-rights and unsold Books, the number of the copies of which fraudulently printed exceeded in some works double, in others *quintuple* the number contracted for, was such as it was almost as impossible for me to have expected as it is, I trust, to be forgotten, or remembered without gratitude. Nor can I think without emotion of the generosity and parental kindness, they have exhibited towards my Sons—least of all, when I compare the whole with their worldly circumstances and strict tho' chearful habits of self-denial. But my Nephew, W. H. Coleridge, has been here often enough & long enough, not to have formed a right estimate of their characters & of their high respectability, in manners & connections as well as in more momentous points: & I must have grossly misunderstood him, if his experience as far as it has extended does not go on the same road with mine.—To other, in fact to the majority of the Neighboring Families of any rank or estimation I am indebted for the most respectful & friendly attentions—and even with some reference to *these*, tho' in a very much inferior degree, that sort of respectability which a known Visit from an elder Brother could not but add to a man hitherto valued as an Individual only, would have been prized by me, proceeding from *you*. But as a mark of respect shewn to Mr and Mrs Gillman on my account, it would have been a serious comfort, a relief to my best feelings.—

Derwent arrived here on Saturday Afternoon & brought with him the most satisfactory proof of the approbation of the Head Tutor of his College (Professor Calvert)[1]—He will take his chance of finding you at home this afternoon, previously to his dining with his Cousin, John.—

May God bless you, my dear Brother! I will offer no apology for this long epistle. A Letter, written with such motives and from such impulses as this has been, I can never regret the having written—however I should be pained were the one or the other to be misconceived—for most unfeignedly & unmixedly I am, with every kind & grateful recollection your affectionate Brother,

S. T. Coleridge.

P.S. My best Love & Respect to Mrs G. and my Nephew, George—

---

[1] Thomas Calvert (1775–1840), theologian, was Norrisian professor of divinity at St. John's College, Cambridge, from 1815 to 1824.

1266. *To Mrs. Basil Montagu*

Address: Mrs Montague | 25. Bedford Square
MS. British Museum. Pub. E. L. G. ii. 287.

Tuesday Afternoon [12 June 1821][1]
Highgate.

My dear Mrs Montagu

Mrs Gillman has this moment disclosed to me what had taken place during the time, I was at Kensington—and I cannot blame the tenderness, which hesitated to dash down at once the genial delightedness with which a most happy meeting with a most beloved & revered Brother (after an interval of 3 or 4 and twenty years, of something too like Alienation!) had filled me. I have at least won two days of Thoughts, that dared look forwards and I now seize the first *Stun*, if I may so say, and the calmness which results from it, to write to you so as to be secure of not writing what a Father, however cruelly a Son has mismanaged himself, ought not to write.—Towards yourself and Basil Montagu—I feel it almost like self-slander to imagine that there can be occasion to tell you— that I have no other thought or emotion but Esteem, Gratitude and Love. To the very utmost, that I could ask, you have done[2]— and what, I know, I ought not to ask, I neither will or can.—But with your permission I will take my chance of finding you at home tomorrow Noon, when I will state to you what *had* been my hopes and plans respecting Hartley—something as a Father I must do & that immediately, tho' what to do—I must not at this moment attempt to think—for it makes me feel just as I have felt in dreams

---

[1] The present letter was written on 12 June 1821, immediately after Mrs. Gillman informed Coleridge of the circumstances concerning Hartley, who had been staying with the Montagus in Bedford Square since August 1820. Twice during the early months of 1821 Hartley left for Highgate. Because he was ill when he arrived the second time, he remained under Gillman's care. On neither occasion, however, did he apprise the Montagus of his whereabouts, and in June they determined not to keep him in their home any longer. To spare Coleridge, Mrs. Gillman tried to prevail on them to change their decision by writing to Mrs. Montagu, but as her letter to Allsop of 13 June 1821 shows, they were adamant, and 'the remainder of Hartley's things were sent up on the Monday Night [11 June]'. Thus, despite the fact that Coleridge was wounded by his brother George not having kept his engagement at Highgate for Friday, 8 June, Mrs. Gillman 'was obliged to tell him about Hartley'. See *Nineteenth-Century Studies* (Cornell), 70–71, and Letter 1265.

[2] After having been excluded from the Montagus' home in June 1821, Hartley Coleridge resided with a boyhood friend, Robert Jameson, at No. 1, Gray's Inn Square, from which address he wrote to his brother on 27 Aug. Frequently, however, he disappeared, leaving no trace of his whereabouts and causing his distraught father great anxiety. See Letter 1300.

in which I have been trying to go somewhere in sore anxiety, and at every turn have found the passage blocked up—God knows! seeing him so ill & with his eyes in such a woeful condition, I took it for granted that he came with your and Mr Montague's cognizance —and after what had before past, and putting the claims even of common Courtesy to you aside, yet knowing so thoroughly my circumstances & how acutely I had suffered on the former occasion in body no less than mind, I so compleatly took it for granted that he would have instantly informed you of Mr Gillman's Opinion that it was expedient for him to stay for some days here under a course of medicine, that it never once occurred to me to put the question to him—the less so, perhaps, from my mind being occupied a good part of the time, first in preparing a brief scheme of the contents of my theological Work & it's plan & object in the hope, that I should have an opportunity of presenting it to the Bishop of London:[1] and then, with the heart-stirrings of having to meet my Brother George. —What advice you can give me, my dear Mrs Montagu! I am sure you will not withhold—at all events, in talking with you I shall see things in a less Mist than I shall while I continue to dream about them to myself—and at all events too I have a duty to perform, by assuring you personally how deeply I feel your and Basil Montague's friendship and kind efforts, & that with unmixed respect and unalterable Regard I remain, my dear Madam!

Your affectionately grateful Friend,
S. T. Coleridge

1267. *To Thomas Allsop*

[Addressed by Mrs. Gillman] Mr Allsop | Blandford Place | Pall Mall
MS. New York Public Lib. Pub. with omis. Letters, Conversations and Rec. *121.*
Postmark: Highgate, 23 June 1821.

Saturday before 4 o'clock[2]
[23 June 1821]

My dearest Allsop
I am just as much puzzled to find out what could have led you to apprehend that I had been offended, as you are & must be to guess the offence. Be assured, that nothing, bearing a nearer resemblance to Offence whether felt or perceived, than a Syllogism bears

---

[1] William Howley (1766–1848), bishop of London 1813, archbishop of Canterbury 1828.
[2] This is written in Coleridge's handwriting on the address sheet.

to the Colour of the Man in the Moon's Whiskers, has ever crossed my Brain—not even with that brisk diagonal Traverse, which Ghosts and Apparitions always choose to surprize us in. I have indeed observed or fancied that for some time past you have been anxious about something, have had some thing pressing on your mind—which I wished *out of you*—tho' not particularly *to have* it out of you.—I must explain myself. Say that X were my dearest Friend, to whom I would be as it were transparent—& have him so to me—in all respects that concerned our permanent Being, and likewise in all circumstantial accidents in which we could be of service to each other. Yet there are many things, that will press upon us, which are our *individualities*, which a man does not feel any tendency in himself to speak of to a man, however dear—that is—X does not think or wish to think of it when with Y, nor Y in his turn when with X—and yet still the great Law holds good— whatever vexes or oppresses ought if possible to be *out* of us—Now, I say, that I should exult if X had a female Friend, a Sister, an Aunt, or a Beloved to whom he could lay himself open—& never dream of any want of confidence in me on the part of X—tho' I should exult if the Confidante of X were *my* Friend too,[1] my Sister, or my Wife—But I shall write to you next week, about Derwent—

God bless you &
S. T. C.

[1] In commenting on this letter Allsop says that it 'relates to a domestic, not to say family perplexity, peculiarly and sacredly my own; one to which no counsel could apply, no consolation mitigate or assuage. Under the circumstances in which I was at that time placed, I could not, I felt it would be premature, to avail myself of the invitation contained in the above letter: and this will, to a great extent, explain much that is contained in the following letters. I had a still farther reason. The individual to whom allusion is made above [Mrs. Gillman], was at that time the *ne plus ultra* of my friend's love and fraternal admiration; yet with qualities of head and heart worthy of all acceptance, was partly (almost I had nearly said) on that very account disqualified in my innermost convictions, certainly according to the *judgment* of my then *feelings*, for the office indicated.' *Letters, Conversations and Rec.* 122–3. The letters which Coleridge addressed to Allsop in the second half of 1821 and during 1822 show not only that the latter was reticent concerning his matrimonial plans but also that he became offended with Mrs. Gillman.

1268. *To Unknown Correspondent* [1]

Transcript Cornell University Lib. Pub. Letters, Conversations and Rec. *171.*
Allsop drew his text from the transcript now at Cornell.

[June 1821 ?][2]

If there be any one subject, which it especially concerns a young
Woman to understand both in itself generally and in it's application
to her own particular habits and circumstances, IT IS THAT OF
MARRIAGE. And if there be any one subject of more perplexing
delicacy than any other to advise a young woman about, above all
for one of a different sex and of no [*sic*] marked inequality in respect
of age, however the attempt may seem authorized by Intimacy and
nearness of kindred—if there be one that at once attracts by it's
importance and repels by it's difficulty—IT IS THAT OF MARRIAGE.
To both sexes, indeed, it is a state of deep and aweful interest:
and to enter into it without proportionate Forethought is in both
alike an act of Folly and Self-degradation. But in a Woman, if she
have sense and sensibility enough to deserve the name, it is an act
tantamount to Suicide—For it is a state which, once entered into
fills the *whole* sphere of a Woman's Moral and personal Being, her
Enjoyments and her Duties, dismissing none, adding many and
modifying all. Even those Duties (if any such there be) which it may
seem to* leave behind, it does but *transfer.* Say rather, it re-imposes

---

[1] In printing the present letter Allsop inserted the heading, '*Letter to a
Young Lady*', and added 'S. T. C.' at the end. In the Cornell University Library
there is also a rough draft of a letter of Allsop's advising a 'Young Lady'
against making an 'ill-assorted' marriage. 'My dear Young Lady', the letter
begins, 'How you will receive this I know not, and the admonitions it contains
may be rejected rather because they did not emanate from your own mind, than
that they are suggested by a str[an]ger.' Allsop does not reveal his identity:
'This MUST be anonymous; your own happiness demands that it should be so;
too often the advice only would insure its rejection, as it would imply interference and more acute observation and insight. But offered as it is by one who
knows you, . . . by one who loves your virtues and not your person, you are
called upon to reflect.' It is possible that Coleridge's letter was written to
accompany Allsop's. Both letters may have been intended for Allsop's sister,
whom Coleridge called 'a favorite of mine'. Furthermore, it would seem that
Allsop planned also to send the 'Young Lady' his transcript of Letter 1169.
See note to Letter 1280.

[2] This letter may be the 'fragment' which Mrs. Gillman mentions in the
following note written on the verso of the address page of Coleridge's letter to
Allsop of Saturday, 23 June 1821: 'On Monday morning you shall have that
fragment—perhaps it may be finished, but Mr C will not let me take it now—
but done or not I may have it then. I shall be most happy to see you and your
Sister at our children's dinner if you will take a bit in that way—Do come.
Your affect. A. G. Mr C was prevented finishing his letter.'

* Too often, I fear, on the supposed Sanction of the *mistranslated* and still
worse *interpreted* Text, Genesis ii. 29. [24 ?] [Note by S. T. C.]

and re-consecrates them under yet dearer Names (tho' names more dear than those of Daughter and Sister it is not easy to imagine)— at all events with obligations additionally binding on her Conscience, because undertaken by an act of her own free will. A Woman—mark me: in using that term I still have before my mind the *idea* of Womanhood and suppose the Individual to possess it's characteristic Constituents—a Woman in a single state may be happy and may be miserable. But *most* happy, *most* miserable—these are epithets which, with rare exceptions, belong exclusively to a Wife. The tree of *full* Life, and that 'whose mortal Taste Brings death'[1] into the heart, these, my dear——, grow in the probationary Eden of Courtship alone. To the Many, of both sexes, I am well aware, this Eden of Matrimony is but a Kitchen-garden, a thing of Profit and Convenience, in an even temperature between *indifference* and *liking:* where the Beds bordered with *Thrift* reject all higher attractions than the homely charms of *Marrygold* and Penny-royal, or whatever else is good to boil in the Pot or to make the Pot boil. Or if there be aught of richer fragrance and more delicate Hues, it is put or suffered there not for the *Blossom* but for the Pod. But this, my dear——, is neither the Soil, climate or aspect in which *your* 'Heart's Ease' or your 'Herbs of Grace' would bloom or burgeon, To be happy in Marriage Life—nay (unless you marry with the prospect of sinking into a lower state of moral feeling and of gradually quenching in yourself all hope and all aspiration, that looks beyond animal comforts and the outside shews of worldly respectability) in order not to be miserable—*You* must have a *Soul*-mate as well as a *House*- or a *Yoke*-Mate! *You* must have a Husband whom before the Altar, making yourself at that moment distinctly conscious of the presence of the Almighty God to whom you appeal, you can safely—that is, according to your confident belief grounded on sufficient opportunities of observation, *conscientiously*, vow to love, *honor*, and *respect*. With what disgust would you not turn from a sordid—with what horror would you not recoil from a contagious or infectious garment offered to you? You would not suffer it to come near your *Skin*. And would you surrender your *Person*, would you blend your whole personality, as far as God has put it in your power to do so, all that you call 'I', soul, body and estate, with one, the contagion of whose Principles, the infection or sordidness of whose Habits and Conversation, you would have to guard against in behalf of your own soul; and the insidious influence of which on the tone and spirit of your thoughts, feelings, objects, and unconscious tendencies and manners would be as the Atmosphere in which you lived? Or were the Man's character merely

---

[1] *Paradise Lost*, i. 2–3.

negative in these respects, were he only incapable of under-standing the developement of your moral Being, including all those minor duties and objects of quiet pursuit and enjoyment which constitute the moral *Taste*—were he only indifferent to the Interest, you felt for his and your own Salvation, and for the conditions of your re-union in the World to come—still it would be a *benumbing* influence, and the Heart may be *starved* where it is neither stabbed nor poisoned. God said that it was not well for the human Being to be alone.[1] To be what *we* ought to be, we need Support, Help, Communion in good. What then if instead of a Help-mate, we take an Obstacle, a daily Counteraction? But the mere want of what God has rendered necessary or most desirable for us, is itself an Obstacle. Virtue sickens in the air of the Marshes, loaded with poisonous Effluvia: but even where the air is merely deficient in the due quantity of it's vital Element, and where there is too little tho' what there is may be faultless, human Virtue lives but a *panting* and anxious life.—For as to a young Woman's marrying in the hope of reforming the man's principles, you will join with me in smiling at the presumption or more probably the *pretext*; as if the Man was likely to appreciate as of very serious importance a danger which the Wife had not feared to risk on so slender a chance: or be persuaded by her to feel as hateful the very qualities which she had taken to her Bosom as a few weeds in a Nosegay that she might pick out at leisure.

Well! (you will perhaps reply) you would have convinced me, if I had not been convinced before, of the misery attendant on an unfit choice, and the criminal folly of a rash and careless one. But by what marks am I to distinguish the suitable from the unsuit-able? What are the criteria or at least the most promising Signs of a man likely to prove a good Husband to a good Wife, and as far as you can judge from your knowledge of my character, principles and temper, likely to find his happiness in me, and to make me happy and deserving to be so? For perfection can be expected on neither side.

Most true: and whilst the Defects are both in their *kind* and their degree within the bounds of that Imperfection which is com-mon to all in our present state, the best and wisest way that a Wife can adopt, is to regard even faulty trifles as serious faults in her-self, and yet to bear with the same or equivalent faults as trifles in her Husband. If the Fault is removable, well and good: if not, it is a Speck in a Diamond—set the Jewel in the marriage Ring with the speck downmost.—But it is one thing to choose for the companion of our Life a man troubled with occasional Head-aches or Indiges-

[1] Genesis ii. 18.

tions, and another to run into the arms of inveterate Gout, or consumption (even tho' the consequent Hectic should render the countenance still more winning and beautiful) or of Hemiplegia—that is of Palsy on one side. For as you will see, that I am speaking figuratively, and under the names of bodily complaints am really thinking, and meaning you to think, of moral and intellectual Defects and Diseases, I have hazarded the hard word, Hemiplegia: as I can conceive no more striking and appropriate Image or Symbol of an Individual with one Half of his Being, that is, his person, manners and circumstances, well and as it should be, while the other and inestimably more precious Half is but half-alive, blighted and insensate. Now for the prevention of the perilous mistake, into which a personal Prepossession is too apt to seduce the young and marriageable, and females more often, perhaps, than males from the very gentleness of their sex—the mistake of looking thro' the diminishing end of the Glass and confounding vices with foibles—I know no better way than by attempting to answer the questions, which I have supposed you to put, overleaf: viz. what are the marks &c, first generally, and secondly in particular application to yourself? In the latter I can of course only speak conjecturally, except as your outward circumstances and relative Duties are concerning: in all else you must be both Querist and Respondent. But the former, the knowledge of which will be no mean assistance to you in solving the latter for your own satisfaction, I think, I can answer distinctly and clearly. And with this therefore we will begin.

You would have reason to regard your sex affronted, if I supposed it necessary to warn any good woman against open Viciousness in a Lover, or avowed indifference to the great Principles of Moral Obligation, religious, social or domestic. By 'religious' I do not *here* mean matters of opinion or differences of Belief in points where good and wise men have agreed to differ. Religion (in my present use of the word) is but Morality in reference to all that is *permanent* and *imperishable*, God and our Souls, for instance: and Morality is Religion in it's application to Individuals, Circumstances, the various Relations and Spheres in which we *happen* to be placed—in short, to all that is contingent and transitory, and passes away leaving no abiding trace but the conscience of having or not having done our duty in each.

I would fain, if the experience of Life would permit me, think it no less superfluous to dissuade a Woman of common Foresight and Information from encouraging the addresses of one, however unobjectionable or even desirable in all other respects, who, she knew or had good reason to believe, was by acquired or hereditary constitution affected by those mournful complaints, which (it is well known) are ordinarily transmitted to the Offspring, to one or more or all! But alas! it often happens, that afflictions of this Nature are united with the highest Worth and the most winning attractions of Head, Heart, and Person: nay, that they often add to the native good Qualities of the Individual a tenderness, a sensibility, a quickness of perception and a vivacity of Principle, that cannot but conciliate an interest in behalf of the Possessor in the affections of a Woman, strong in proportion to the degree in which she is herself characterised by the same excellencies! Manly Virtues and Manly Sense with feminine manners without Effeminacy form such an assemblage, a Tout ensemble so delightful to the Womanly Heart, that it demands a hard, a cruel struggle to find in any ground of objection an effective Counter-poise, a *decisive* Negative. Yet the Struggle must be made, and must end in the decisive and, if possible, the preventive No: or all claims to Reason and Conscience and to that distinctive Seal and Impress of Divinity on Womanhood, the *Maternal* Soul, must be abandoned. The probable Misfortunes attendant on the early death of the Head of the Family are the least fearful of the consequences that may rationally and therefore *ought* morally to be expected from such a choice. The *Mother's* anguish, the *Father's* heart-wasting Self-reproach, the recollection of that Innocent lost, the sight of this Darling suffering, the Dread of the Future—in fine, the conversion of Heaven's Choicest Blessings into sources of anguish and subjects of Remorse—I have seen all this in more than one miserable, and *most* miserable because amiable and affectionate Couple, and have seen that the Sound Constitution of one Parent has not availed against the Taint on the other. Would to God the Picture I have here exhibited, were as imaginary in itself, as it's exhibition is unnecessary and the reality of improbable occurrence for *you*!—

Dismissing, therefore, as taken for granted or altogether inapplicable, all objections grounded on gross and palpable unfitness for a state of moral and personal Union and life-long Interdependence— and less than this is not Marriage whether the unfitness result from constitutional or from moral Defect or Derangement: and with these, and only not *quite* so bad, dismissing too the objections from want of competence, on both sides, in worldly means proportional to their former Rank and Habits—and yet what worse or more degradingly selfish (yea, the very Dregs and Sediment of Selfishness, after the more refined and *human* Portion of it, the sense of Self-interest, has been drawn off), what worse I repeat, can be said of the Beasts of the Field, without reflection, without forethought, of whom and for whose Offspring Nature has taken the responsibility upon herself? Putting all these aside, as too obvious to require argument or exposition, I will now pass to those marks which too frequently *are* overlooked, however obvious in themselves they may be; but which *ought* to be *looked for*, and *looked after*, by every Woman who has ever reflected on the words, 'my future Husband' with more than *girlish* feelings and Fancies. And if the *absence* of these *Marks* in an Individual *furnishes* a decisive reason for the rejection of his Addresses, there are others the *presence* of which forms a sufficient ground for hesitation. And I will begin with an instance.

When you hear a man making exceptions to any fundamental Law of Duty in favor of some particular pursuit or passion, and considering the dictates of *Honor* as neither more nor less than motives of selfish Prudence in respect of character—in other words, as conventional and ever changing regulations, the breach of which will, if detected, *black-ball* the Offender, and send him to Coventry in that particular Rank & Class of Society of which he was born or has become a member—when, instead of giving instantaneous and unconditional Obedience to the original Voice from within, a man substitutes for this, and listens after, the mere echo of the Voice from without, his knowledge, I mean, of what is commanded by *Fashion* and enforced by the foreseen consequences of non-compliance on his Worldly Reputation (this I myself heard a buckish Clergyman, a clerical Nimrod, at Salisbury avow, that he would *cheat his own Father in a Horse*)—then, I say, that to smile, or shew yourself *smiling-angry,* as if a Tap with your Fan was a sufficient punishment, and a—'For shame! you don't think so, I am sure' or 'You should not *say* so,' a sufficient reproof, would be an ominous symptom either of your own laxity of moral Principle, and deadness to true Honor and the unspeakable *Contemptibleness* of this gentlemanly Counterfeit of it, or of your abandonment to a blind passion kindled by superficial Advantages & Outside Agreeables, and blown and fuelled by that most base and yet frequent thought, 'one must not be over-nice, or a woman may say, No: till no one asks her to say, Yes.' And what does this amount to (with all the other pretty common-places, as What right have *I* to expect an Angel in the shape of a Man? &c &c) but the plain confession, 'I *want* to be married—the better the man, the luckier for me—I have made up my mind to be the Mistress of a Family—in short, I *want* to be married!'

Under this head you may safely place all the knowing Principles of action so often & so boastingly confessed by your clever fellows— 'I take care of *Number* One; hey, Neighbour! what say you?'— 'Each for himself, and God for us all: that's my Maxim.'—and likewise, as the very same essentially, tho' in a more dignified and seemly Form, the principle of determining whether a thing is right or wrong, by it's supposed Consequences.

There are men, who let their life pass away without a single effort to do good, either to Friend or Neighbour, to their Country or their Religion, on the strength of the Question: What *good* will it do? But woe to the Man who is incapable of feeling that the greatest possible good he can do for himself or for others, is to *do his duty* and to leave the consequences to God. But it will be answer'd: How can we ascertain that it is our duty but by weighing the probable *consequences*? Besides, no one can act without *Motives*: and all motives must at last have respect to the agent's own Self-interest—and that is the reason why Religion is so useful—because it carries on our Self-interest beyond the grave!

O my dear ——! so many worthy persons, who really tho' unconsciously, both act from, and are actuated by, far nobler impulses, are educated to talk in this language, that I dare not expose the folly, turpitude, immorality, and *irreligion* of this System, without premising the necessity of trying to discover, previous to your forming a fixt opinion respecting the true character of the Individual from whom *you* may have heard declarations of this kind, whether the sentiments proceed from the Tongue only, or at worst from a misinstructed Understanding, or are the native growth of his Heart.[1] [Transcript breaks off thus.]

1269. *To Thomas Phillips*

Address: T. Phillips, Esqre. | 8. George Street | Hanover Square.
MS. Huntington Lib. Hitherto unpublished. This MS. is inserted in a copy of Thomas Moore's *Letters and Journals of Lord Byron* . . ., 2 vols., 1830, ii. 450.

> Highgate
> 30 June 1821
> Saturday afternoon.

My dear Sir

I write as Mrs Gillman's reluctant Amanuensis to convey her best respects to you and Mrs Phillips, and her regrets that the arrival of a young Lady, the Sister of one of our most intimate Friends, on a Week's Visit obliges her to give up the high gratification, she has been looking forward to, from availing herself of your kind invitation for Monday with Mr Gillman and his and your troublesome *Patient*. Would to Heaven, that he could improve my

[1] In addition to the present letter, there are extant four other letters in which Coleridge offers advice to young persons contemplating marriage: Letters 1169, 1664–5, and 1723.

inner man (the animal part, I mean) as much as you will have improved the outer! Much, VERY much he *has* effected, or I should not be here to enjoy the honors of an Elevation into your Great Armchair. But it is not, I fear, within the power or scope of medical Skill to throw as much Life into my crusty Stomach and it's dependencies, as you have thrown into my *crumby* Face.

I am vexed, that this Visit, which has come a month later and a fortnight earlier than we had expected, will prevent Mrs G. from sharing the day with us, and could almost wish Miss Allsop, tho' a favorite of mine on her own account, a short sojourn in Paradise for some twelve hours or so—provided that some strong-backed Angel stood engaged to bring her back, in bodily statu quo, on Tuesday Morning.—First, for a selfish Reason—that so rarely leaving home, I enjoy fullest what I can afterwards recollect and talk of in common with those, who are as natural to me and (I am sure) quite as dear as a Brother and Sister, and from the *dependent* habits, incident to a sensitive mind in an ailing body, almost a part of myself. *Next* to what *You* possess and which has been denied to me by my wayward Stars, I have reason to be thankful to Providence for the Lot given in stead—which is equivalent to living with an affectionate Sister who had married one's most valued Friend.— And secondly, because Mrs G. had calculated on so much pleasure, or to use her own words—Mrs P. and Miss Turner are not Women, that one can meet every day.—

O!—permit me to mention to you, that it is not a trick or habit of mine to hold my handkerchief in my hand—but that I happened to do so, in consequence of the Walk and a faintness of Stomach having thro' [thrown?] my face & forehead into a perspiration.— My Snuff-box grasped in my left hand on my knee, and a book held down with my Thumb in it in the right, is my ordinary & unconscious way of sitting & talking.[1]—

Pray, make my best respects to Mrs Phillips and Miss Turner— and with hearty Wishes for you and yours, believe me, dear Sir,
Your obliged Friend,
S. T. Coleridge

[1] The Phillips portrait of Coleridge is reproduced in vol. iv. 912 of this edition of Coleridge's letters. In one of her notes written in a copy of Christopher Wordsworth's *Memoirs of William Wordsworth*, 2 vols., 1851, i. 309–10, Sara Coleridge refers to Phillips's two portraits of Coleridge: the original now in the possession of Lady Cave and the replica belonging to Sir John Murray:

Allston's portrait is the best that has been taken of my Father. That by Phillips has his social look, but very little of his intellect. It is a gentlemanly picture. The copy which Mr Murray has is inferior to the original at Salston House near Ottery. (*Sara Coleridge and Henry Reed*, ed. L. N. Broughton, 1937, p. 85.)

1270. *To Thomas Poole*

Address: Thomas Poole, Esqre | Nether Stowey   Favored by Mr Stutfield.
MS. British Museum. Pub. Letters, *ii. 753*.

[Endorsed July 1821][1]

My dear Poole

Mr Stutfield Junr has been so kind as to inform me of his Father's purposed Journey to Stowey and to give me this opportunity of writing—tho' in fact I have little *pleasant* to say except that I am advancing regularly and steadily toward the completion of my Opus Magnum on Revelation & Christianity, the Reservoir of my Reflections & Reading for 25 years past—and in health not painfully worse. I do not know, however, that I should have troubled you with a letter merely to convey this piece of information—but I have a great favor to request of you—this is—that supposing you to have still in your possession the two letters of the biography of my own childhood, which I wrote at Stowey for you,[2] and a Copy of the Letter from Germany containing the account of my Journey to the Harz, and my ascent of Mount Brocken &c[3]—you would have them transcribed & send me the Transcript, addressed to me, James Gillman's Esqre. Highgate, London.—

O that Riches would but make wings for me instead of for itself— and I would fly to the Sea Shore at Porlock & Lynemouth, making a good Halt at dear ever fondly remembered Stowey, of which, believe me, your image, and the feelings and associations connected therewith, constitute four fifths,

to, my dear Poole, | Your obliged and | affectionate Friend
                                                    S. T. Coleridge.

---

[1] Without assigning any reason E. H. Coleridge published this letter under the date of 1830. Poole, however, not only endorsed the manuscript, but in his catalogue of Coleridge's letters he dated this letter July 1821 and added a note: 'The letters were sent as desired'.

[2] Coleridge addressed five autobiographical letters to Poole. See Letters 174, 179, 208, 210, and 234.

[3] Three letters describe this expedition, the first two being addressed to Mrs. Coleridge, the third to Poole. (Letters 280–2.) Extracts from the first and second letters formed the narrative, 'Over the Brocken', which was published in *The Amulet*, 1829. The three letters were published in the *New Monthly Magazine*, Oct. 1835. See Letters 1596 and 1634.

1271. *To Robert W. Elliston*[1]

Pub. Times Literary Supplement, *21 September 1946, p. 456.*

The following extract appeared in an article, 'British Manuscripts in Russia', contributed by Mr. M. P. Alexeyev, who says that Coleridge's 'long and interesting letter' concerns 'the complicated relations that had arisen between the poet and the theatre when his plays *Remorse* and *Zapolya* were to be produced. The poet wrote asking the theatre to send him [Michael] Kelly's music to the incantation song in *Remorse*.'

Coleridge's holograph letter, which was formerly in the collection of Count G. Orloff, is now in one of the Russian libraries, but all efforts to obtain permission to publish it have proved abortive.

July 12, 1821

... Will you forgive me if I add that as a representative of the Drury Lane Theatre, though in no respect your own person and character, you owe me a little set off for the indignity, caprice and neglect shown by your predecessor to me with regard to *Zapolya*[2] ... but I have seen enough of you to be convinced that the theatre is now in better hands and has a worthier and more courteous high priest superintending the temple of dramatic muses. . . .

1272. *To Thomas De Quincey*

Address: T. De Quincey, Esqre | Mr Bothe's | 4 York Street | Covent Garden
MS. formerly in the possession of the late Miss Bairdsmith. Pub. E. L. G. ii. 293.
Postmark: Highgate, 9 August 1821.

Highgate
Wednesday Noon. [8 August 1821]

Believe me, I *intreat* you, my dear De Quincey! there was no need to remind me of a generous Act,[3] which during the long interval I have never ceased to think of, for the former and better half of the time with cordial satisfaction as of an obligation only less honorable to the Receiver than to you who had so nobly and in so truly delicate a manner conferred the same—but of late years with an unquiet and *aching* gratitude, which has often checked my enquiries after you from a pang of fear, a foreboding that I should hear of something that would make me feel my poverty as a *humiliation*—

---

[1] Robert W. Elliston, who in 1813 had played the part of Alvar in Coleridge's *Remorse*, was at this time the manager of Drury Lane.

[2] Coleridge obviously refers to Douglas J. W. Kinnaird, who with Byron and others was made a member of the sub-committee of Drury Lane in 1815. See Letters 1001, 1007, 1011, 1043, 1053, and 1213.

[3] Coleridge refers to the £300 presented to him by De Quincey in 1807. See Letters 658-9.

would turn an ever-recurring *Wish* of the Heart into an absolute *Want*, which not now for the first time I have anxiously looked about for some means of gratifying, and still baffled sink under a Regret that almost seems to border on Remorse. Few and transient have been the spots of Sunshine on my 'Way of Life', and these almost always on the distant land-scape; but whenever a brighter prospect has dawned on me, the recollections connected with your name took a foremost part in every scheme, that I proposed to myself.

I feel that I am lingering on the brink—and what to say, my dear Sir! I know not! Distressing—and in relation to you and the circumstances under which you have written to me—doubly distressing as the disclosure will be—nothing else is left me, but to lay before you the naked truth—the real state of my affairs. There are now in my drawer unanswered three menacing Letters for three several debts, amounting collectively to about 50£. Even to the House, from which you write, I am indebted four or five pounds, for books for Hartley when he was at Oxford, which I cannot think of without a sense of shame—which I have repeatedly been on the point of settling and the money snatched from me by some still more urgent necessity.—The fact is, that I came hither embarrassed—the successive Losses and increasing Distress of poor Morgan and his family while I was domesticated with them—and which being before my eyes, scarcely left me the power of asking myself concerning the Right or Wrong—absorbed and—but poor fellow! he is gone, and (I am persuaded) gone where his many excellent qualities, which never suffered any eclipse in his prosperous days, will greatly outweigh the one or two faulty acts done in the confused and feverish dream of Embarrassment—absorbed and anticipated my resources, even to the leaving of my own small debts unpaid.—Meantime, the Christabel, which I should never have consented to publish, a mere fragment as it was, but for his goading wants, the 80£ received for it from Murray going to make up the last sum, I was able to raise for him, fell almost dead-born from the Press[1]—and it became evident that a powerful and utterly unprovoked yet immitigable Party, at Edingburgh and elsewhere, had determined to rail or ridicule down every thing I should publish, and as much as possible (and with works so little popular as mine are & ever must be, it was to a very great extent not only possible but easy) to prevent their sale—and (which likewise they effected) to discourage *the Trade* from purchasing them.—Still, however, what by literary Job-work and what by Lecturing—tho' the latter sadly fell off, in consequence of my supposed political

[1] See Letters 1004 and 1448.

and religious apostacy, while the party in power gave me no support, nor did the Writers of the Quarterly Review condescend to notice my Works, except by one or two occasional and vague sentences—I made a shift to get thro' the first and tho' imperfectly the second year of my residence at Highgate. But now came the storm. I had Hartley's expences during his long vacations—as I have since had Derwent's—with other minor calls on their accounts—and last, the unparall[el]ed profligacy of my bankrupt Publishers, of which I will spare you the detail. Sufficient to inform you, that after printing double, and in one instance quadruple the number of Copies contracted for, for each Edition—and tho' the Bankruptcy took place within a *fortnight* after the Publication of the Friend in three Volumes[1]—still from the number sold in that fortnight, and from the sale of the Literary Life, the Sibylline Leaves, the two Lay-sermons and the Zapolya, a sum of 1200£ remained due to me —every farthing of which I lost—the ——, Curtis, a real partner but pretended Creditor of Fennor's, and who had carried on the Printing for the Concern, clapt a *lien* on 500 Copies of the Friend— of which the *Trade* Price was a guinea each—and which, tho' a proveable fraud, can only be removed by a Chancery suit—and after all, I was obliged to borrow 120£ in order to buy-up the Half-copy Rights of all my Works, which would have gone for trifles to Booksellers of no repute, and to prevent the unsold Copies from going for waste paper—perhaps, I had better have let them go— but I was in hope of better times, and that some more successful Work might occasion a call for them—till when I was advised to withdraw them from sale altogether.—Then came Hartley's cruel and most calumnious persecution and the loss of his fellow-ship— and for almost a year I have had him on my hands—& even this a less Loss than the necessity of writing and writing on this infamous business, and the effect on my health and spirits, which one with another incapacitated me from doing any thing for myself continuously—that would fetch money, I mean.—

I declare solemnly, that I must have wanted the necessities of Life, but for the almost unprecedented friendship of Mr and Mrs Gillman, under whose roof I live. Tho' the nominal sum, which I am engaged to contribute towards the expences of the House, is barely adequate to the first-cost of my actual maintenance—and tho' medicine, & medical attendance are not put down at all—yet so many sums have been paid by Mr G. on my account—that at this moment I stand indebted to him for 500£—of which, but a short time back, he struck off 120£, as incurred for Derwent and Hartley, as if

[1] *The Friend* was published before 19 Nov. 1818; the bankruptcy of Rest Fenner occurred in Mar. 1819. See Letters 1148, 1202, and 1204.

they had been his Visitors.—You will understand my feelings when
I add that Mr G. has only his professional income—& that with a
highly respectable practice indeed but from the nature & circumstances of the place, a practice of very limited extent—and that he
has himself two Sons and an Angel of a Wife.—So help me God! for
months past I have not [had] a shilling in my pocket—nor do I know
how or where to procure a guinea—. I am endeavoring to make up
a parcel for Blackwood's Magazine[1]—but even this has in part been
paid for—

Dear De Quincey! I conjure you to feel convinced that were it
in my power—let what would come the next week—to raise the
money, you should not have received this melancholy History as an
answer—Were you to see me at this moment, you would know with
what anguish & sickness of soul I subscribe myself your *obliged* &
grateful

S. T. Coleridge.

1273. *To Thomas Allsop*

Address: T. Allsop, Esq.
Pub. Letters, Conversations and Rec. *125.*

Sept. 15th, 1821.

My dear Friend,

I cannot rest until I have answered your last letter. I have
contemplated your character, affectionately indeed, but through a
clear medium. No film of passion, no glittering mist of outward
advantages, has arisen between the sight and the object: I had no
other prepossession than the esteem which my knowledge of your
sentiments and conduct could not but secure for you. I soon learnt
to esteem you; and in esteeming, became attached to you. I began
by loving the man on account of his conduct, but I ended in
valuing the actions chiefly as so many looks and attitudes of the
same person. '*Hast* thou any thing? Share it with me, and I will
pay thee an equivalent. *Art* thou any thing? O then we will
exchange souls.'

We can none of us, not the wisest of us, brood over any source of
affliction inwardly, keeping it back, and as it were pressing it in on
ourselves; but we must MAGNIFY it. We cannot see it clearly, much
less distinctly; and as the object enlarges beyond its real propor-
tions, so it becomes vivid; and the feelings that blend with it assume a proportionate undue intensity. So the one acts on the other,
and what at first was effect, in its turn becomes a cause; and when

[1] See Letter 1274.

at length we have taken heart, and given the whole thing, with all its several parts, the proper distance from our mind's eye, by confiding it to a true friend, we are ourselves surprised to find what a dwarf the giant shrinks into, as soon as it steps out of the mist into clear sunlight.

I am aware that these are truths of which you do not need to be informed; but they will not be the less impressive on this account in your judgment, knowing, as you must know, that nothing short of my deep and anxious convictions of their importance in all cases of hidden distress, and of their *unspeakable* importance in yours, could impel me to *seek* and *entreat* your *entire* confidence, to beg you, so fervently as I here am doing, to open out to me the cause of your anxiety, that I may offer you the best advice in my power,—advice that will not be the less dispassionate from its being dictated by zealous friendship, and blended with the truest love.

I fear that in any decision to which you may come in any matter affecting yourself alone, you may, from a culpable delicacy of honour, which, forbidden by wisdom and the universal experience of others, cannot but be in contradiction to the genuine dictates of duty, want fortitude to choose the lesser evil, at whatever cost to your immediate feelings, and to put that choice into immediate and peremptory act. But I must finish. I trust that the warmth and earnestness of my language are not warranted by the occasion; but they are barely proportionate to the present solicitude of,

Your faithful and affectionate friend,
S. T. Coleridge.

1274. *To William Blackwood*

Address: *Private* | Mr Blackwood | Bookseller | Edingburgh
MS. formerly in the possession of the late Arthur Pforzheimer. Pub. E. L. G. ii. 296. First published in *Blackwood's Magazine*, October 1821, p. 243.

Highgate
19 Septr
1821

Private[1]

My dear Sir

In the third letter (in the parcel,[2] on which I have written *Third Pin*) which you will permit me to address to yourself, I have

[1] To stress the fact that he did not want to have this letter published, Coleridge addressed it to Mr. Blackwood and marked it '*Private*'. Despite his precautions, however, the following mangled version appeared in the Oct. 1821 number of *Blackwood's Magazine*:

[*Notes 1 and 2 continued overleaf.*

assigned my reasons for particularly wishing all the inclosed to be published in the first instance.—Within ten days you will receive a second packet—consisting of 1. The ideal of a Magazine—2. the first article on the history and theory of Witchcraft &c. 3. The world without and the world within—a tale of Truth from Faery Land—Book I.[1]—4. The Life of Hölty, with specimens of his poems, translated into English Verse.—

I propose after these to condense the substance of my Lectures on Shakespear, Milton, Dante, and Cervantes—I owe this to myself and to my Auditors.—But in 'the Ideal of a Magazine' you will learn from my *private* notes the sorts of matter, with which I can furnish you.

LETTER FROM MR COLERIDGE.

DEAR SIR,—In the third letter (in the little parcel,) which I have headed with your name, you will find my reasons for wishing these five letters, and a sixth, which will follow in my next, on the plan and code of a Magazine, which should unite the *utile* and *dulce*, to appear in the first instance. My next will consist of very different articles, apparently ; namely, the First Book of my True History from Fairy Land, or the World Without, and the World Within. 2. The commencement of the Annals and Philosophy of Superstition ; for the completion of which I am waiting only for a very curious folio, in Mr **********'s possession. 3. The Life of Holty, a German poet, of true genius, who died in early manhood ; with specimens of his poems, translated, or freely imitated in English verse. It would have been more in the mode to have addressed myself to the Editor, but I could not give up this one opportunity of assuring you that I am, my dear Sir,

With every friendly wish, your obliged,
S. T. Coleridge.

Mr. Blackwood.

[2] The material in the parcel forwarded with the present letter was published in the Oct. 1821 issue of *Blackwood's Magazine* with the title, 'Selection from Mr Coleridge's Literary Correspondence with Friends, and Men of Letters'. Of this 'Correspondence' only 'Letter III', a second letter addressed '*To Mr Blackwood*', has been included here. See Letter 1275.

In *Aids to Reflection*, 1825, p. 171 n. Coleridge refers the reader to Letter II as follows :

See the '*Selection from Mr. Coleridge's Literary Correspondence*' in Blackwood's Ed. Magazine, for October 1821, Letter ii. p. 244–253, which, however, should any of my Readers take the trouble of consulting, he must be content with such parts as he finds intelligible at the first perusal. For from defects in the MS., and without any fault on the part of the Editor, too large a portion is so printed that the man must be equally bold and fortunate in his conjectural readings who can make out any meaning at all.

---

[1] See *Blackwood's Magazine*, Jan. 1822, where this contribution appeared under the title, 'Sundry Select Chapters from the Book of the *Two Worlds* Translated from the Original ESOTERIC into the Language of the *Border* Land : Comprizing the *Historie* and *Gests* of MAXILIAN . . . .' None of the other contributions mentioned in this and the following paragraph appeared in *Blackwood's*.

It is my intent to devote the next six weeks undividedly to the Magazine, should I remain convalescent & without any serious relapse, and in order to this be able to go to Ramsgate. But for this I must seek some assistance from you—. I venture to pledge myself, that no man on earth can accuse me of having received from him 5£ in advance, which was not liquidated by the promised work, or instantly returned—and I shall have deluded myself beyond all former experience, if the contents of my next parcel, which is all written & requires transcription only, do not leave a balance in my favor, should you comply with my request to advance me 50£.—

I shall hope for a speedy reply—till my next | believe me, | faithfully your's

S. T. Coleridge.

1275. *To William Blackwood*

Pub. Blackwood's Magazine, *October 1821, p. 253.*

To Mr Blackwood.

[*Circa* 19 September 1821]

Dear Sir,—Here have I been sitting, this whole long-lagging, *muzzy*, mizly morning, struggling without success against the insuperable disgust I feel to the task of explaining the abrupt chasm at the outset of our correspondence,[1] and disposed to let your verdict take its course, rather than suffer over again by detailing the causes of the stoppage; though sure by so doing to acquit *my will* of all share in the result. Instead of myself, and of *you*, my dear sir, in relation to myself, I have been thinking, first, of the Edinburgh Magazine; then of magazines generally and comparatively;—then of a magazine in the abstract;—and lastly, of the immense importance and yet strange neglect of that prime dictate of prudence and common sense—DISTINCT MEANS TO DISTINCT ENDS.—But here I must put in one proviso, not in any relation though to the aphorism itself, which is of universal validity, but relatively to my intended application of it. I must assume—I mean, that the individuals disposed to grant me free access and fair audience for my remarks, have *a conscience*—such a portion at least, as being eked out with superstition and sense of character, will suffice to prevent them from seeking to realize the *ultimate* end, (i.e. the maxim of profit) by base or disreputable means. This, therefore, may be left out of

---

[1] Coleridge's association with William Blackwood began in the year 1819. See Letters 1187, 1190, 1200, and 1216.

the present argument, an extensive sale being the common object of all publishers, of whatever kind the publications may be, morally considered. Nor do the means appropriate to this end differ. Be the work good or evil in its tendency, in both cases alike there is one question to be predetermined, viz. what class or classes of the reading world the work is intended for? I made the proviso, however, because I would not mislead any man even for an honest cause, and my experience will not allow me to promise an equal immediate circulation from a work addressed to the higher interests and blameless predilections of men, as from one constructed on the plan of flattering the envy and vanity of sciolism, and gratifying the cravings of vulgar curiosity. Such may be, and in some instances, I doubt not, has been, the result. But I dare not answer for it beforehand, even though both works should be equally well suited to their several purposes, which will not be thought a probable case, when it is considered, how much less talent, and of how much commoner a kind, is required in the latter.

On the other hand, however, I am persuaded that a sufficient success, and less liable to draw-backs from competition, would not fail to attend a work on the former plan, if the scheme and execution of the contents were as appropriate to the object, which the purchasers must be supposed to have in view, as the means adopted for its outward attraction and its general circulation were to the interest of its proprietors.

During a long literary life, I have been no inattentive observer of periodical publications; and I can remember no failure, in any work deserving success, that might not have been anticipated from some error or deficiency in the means, either in regard to the mode of circulating the work, (as for instance by the vain attempt to unite the characters of author, editor, and publisher,) or to the typographical appearance; or else from its want of suitableness to the class of readers, on whom, it should have been foreseen, the remunerating sale must principally depend. It would be misanthropy to suppose that the seekers after truth, information, and innocent amusement, are not sufficiently numerous to support a work, in which these attractions are prominent, without the dishonest aid of personality, literary faction, or treacherous invasions of the sacred recesses of private life, without slanders, which both reason and duty command us to *disbelieve* as well as abhor; for what but falsehood, or that half truth, which is falsehood in its most malignant form, can or ought to be expected from a self-convicted traitor and ingrate?

If these remarks are well founded, we may narrow the problem to the few following terms,—it being understood, that the work now in question, is a monthly publication, not devoted to any *one* branch of knowledge or literature, but a magazine of whatever may be supposed to interest readers in general, not excluding the discoveries, or even the speculations of science, that are generally intelligible and interesting, so that the portion devoted to any one subject or department, shall be kept proportionate to the number of readers for whom it may be supposed to have a *particular* interest. Here, however, we must not forget, that however few the actual dilettanti, or men of the fancy may be, yet, as long as the articles remain generally intelligible, (in *pugilism*, for instance,) Variety and Novelty communicate an attraction that interests all. Homo sum, nihil humani a me alienum. If to this we add the exclusion of theological controversy, which is endless, I shall have pretty accurately described the present EDINBURGH MAGAZINE, as to its characteristic plan and purposes; which may, I think, be comprised in three terms, as a Philosophical, Philological, and *Æsthetic

* I wish I could find a more familiar word than aesthetic, for works of taste and criticism. It is, however, in all respects better, and of more reputable origin, than belletristic. To be sure, there is *tasty*; but that has been long ago emasculated for all unworthy uses by milliners, tailors, and the androgynous correlatives of both, formerly called *its*, and now yclept dandies. As our language, therefore, contains no other *useable* adjective, to express that coincidence of form, feeling, and intellect, that something, which, confirming the inner and the outward senses, becomes a new sense in itself, to be tried by laws of its own, and acknowledging the laws of the understanding so far only as not to contradict them; that faculty which, when possessed in a high degree, the Greeks termed φιλοκαλία, but when spoken of generally, or in kind only, τὸ αἰσθητικόν; and for which even our substantive, Taste, is a—not inappropriate—but very inadequate metaphor; there is reason to hope, that the term *aesthetic*, will be brought into common use as soon as distinct thoughts and definite expressions shall once more become the requisite accomplishment of a gentleman. So it was in the energetic days, and in the starry court of our *English*-hearted Eliza; when trade, the nurse of freedom, was the enlivening counterpoise of agriculture, not its alien and usurping spirit; when commerce had all the enterprize, and more than the romance of war; when the precise yet pregnant terminology of the schools gave bone and muscle to the diction of poetry and eloquence, and received from them in return passion and harmony; but, above all, when from the self-evident truth, that what *in kind* constitutes the superiority of man to animal, the same *in degree* must constitute the superiority of men to each other, the practical inference was drawn, that every proof of these distinctive faculties being in a *tense* and *active* state, that even the sparks and crackling of mental electricity, in the sportive approaches and collisions of ordinary intercourse, (such as we have in the wit-combats of Benedict and Beatrice, of Mercutio, and in the dialogues assigned to courtiers and gentlemen, by all the dramatic writers of that reign,) are stronger indications of natural superiority, and, therefore, more becoming signs and accompaniments of *artificial* rank, than apathy, studied mediocrity, and the ostentation of wealth. When I think of the vigour and felicity of style characteristic of the age, from Edward VI. to the restoration of Charles, and observable in the

Miscellany. The word miscellany, however, must be taken as involving a predicate in itself, in addition to the three preceding epithets, comprehending, namely, all the ephemeral births of intellectual life, which add to the gaiety and variety of the work, without interfering with its express and regular objects.

Having thus a sufficiently definite notion of what your Magazine is, and is intended to be, I proposed to myself, as a problem, to find out, *in detail*, what the *means* would be to the most perfect attainment of this end. In other words, what the *scheme*, and of what nature, and in what order and proportion, the *contents* should be of a monthly publication; in order for it to verify the title of a Philosophical, Philological, and Æsthetic Miscellany and Magazine. The result of my lucubrations I hope to forward in my next, under the title of 'The Ideal of a Magazine'; and to mark those departments, in the filling up of which, I flatter myself with the prospect of being a fellow labourer. But since I began this scrawl, a friend reminded me of a letter I wrote him many years ago, on the improvement of the mind, by the habit of commencing our inquiries with the attempt to construct the most absolute or perfect form of the object desiderated, leaving its practicability, in the first instance, undetermined. An essay, in short, *de emendatione intellectûs per ideas*—the beneficial influence of which, on his mind, he spoke of with warmth. The main contents of the letter, the effect of which my friend appreciated so highly, were derived from conversation with a great man, now no more.[1] And as I have reason to regard that conversation as an epoch in the history of my own mind, I feel myself encouraged to hope that its publication may not prove useless to some of your numerous readers, to whom Nature has given the stream, and nothing is wanting but to be led into the right channel.[2] There is one other motive to which I must plead conscious, not only in the following, but in all of these, my *preliminary* contributions; viz. That by the reader's agreement with the principles, and sympathy with the general feelings, which they are meant to impress, the interest of my future contributions, and still more, their permanent effect, will be heightened; and most so in those, in which, as narrative and imaginative compositions, there is the least

letters and family memoirs of noble families—take, for instance, the Life of Colonel Hutchinson, written by his widow—I cannot suppress the wish—O that the *habits* of those days could return, even though they should bring pedantry and Euphuism in their train! [Note by S. T. C.]

[1] Thomas Wedgwood.

[2] This conversation is included in Letter IV of the 'Selection from Mr Coleridge's Literary Correspondence with Friends, and Men of Letters', where it is entitled 'Substance of a Dialogue, with a Commentary on the Same'. *Blackwood's Magazine*, Oct. 1821, p. 256.

shew of reflection, on my part, and the least necessity for it,—
though I flatter myself not the least opportunity on the part of my
readers.

It will be better too, if I mistake not, both for your purposes and
mine, to have it said hereafter, that he dragged slow and stiff-kneed
up the first hill, but sprang forward as soon as the road was full
before him, and *got in* fresh; than that he set off in grand style—
broke up midway, and came in broken-winded. *Finis coronat opus.*

Your's, &c.

S. T. Coleridge.

1276. *To C. A. Tulk*

Address: Charles Augustus Tulk, Esqre. M.P. | St John's Lodge | Regent's
Park.
MS. Pierpont Morgan Lib. Hitherto unpublished.

In the following letter Coleridge mentions 'the Governors of the Highgate
Chapel'—a reference to the governors of the Free Grammar School at Highgate
and to the chapel adjoining the school and belonging to it. The governors were
entrusted with the administration of the Highgate Charity, an endowment
founded for the support of the school. 'About the year 1564' Sir Roger Cholmeley
'did institute and erect' a free grammar school at Highgate. A royal grant
at that time being required for the endowment of a school, Queen Elizabeth,
by letters patent dated 29 January and 6 April 1565, 'ordained that there
should be a grammar school at *Highgate*, and constituted six persons a corpora-
tion, by the name of The Wardens and Governors of the Possessions, Revenues
and Goods of the Free Grammar School of Sir *Roger Cholmeley*, knight, in
Highgate'. By a deed poll dated 27 April 1565, Edmund Grindal, bishop of
London, 'granted, enfeoffed, and confirmed to Sir Roger Cholmeley and his
heirs, the chapel of Highgate and the premises thereto belonging, and two acres
of land adjoining the said chapel, to the intent that Sir Roger Cholmeley should
give and assure, as well the said chapel and premises as other manors, messuages,
tenements, &c. [in London] to the yearly value of 10*l.* 13*s.* 4*d.* to the wardens
and governors of the "Free Grammar School" . . . , to the use and behoof of the
said school for ever, for the better maintenance and support of the same'.
This grant was confirmed by the dean and chapter of St. Paul's on 16 May
1565, and by another deed poll dated 7 June in the same year, Cholmeley
transferred the grant to the wardens and governors of the school. Cholmeley
died in June 1565, and on 4 December 1571 the then governors of the Free
Grammar School set forth a table of rules designed to carry out his wishes.
The governors were to appoint 'an honest and learned schoolmaster, . . . [a]
Graduate of good, sober, and honest conversation, *and no light person*, who
shall teach and instruct young children as well in their A B C ["a black-letter
book, called *The A B C with the Catechisme*"] and other English books, and to
write, and also in their grammar as they shall grow ripe thereto'. The schoolmaster was to 'teach the number of forty scholars, and not above'. He was to
live on the school premises and his salary, which was to be paid quarterly, was
specified. He was also to '*say and read* openly, at the chapel at Highgate.

(171)

next adjoining to the said free school, the service now allowed and set forth by the Queen's Majesty', except on 'the *first Sunday of every month*'. On such Sundays the inhabitants of Highgate were 'to *resort to their several parish churches* to hear common prayers and sermons, and to receive the holy communion there', the school chapel 'being only a chapel of ease' for them. In the same instrument the governors with the assent of Bishop Sandys, then bishop of London, appointed Johnson, 'in Holy Orders', as the first schoolmaster.

A hermitage chapel, *sacellum*, or *cappella* in the gift of the bishop of London had existed on the site of the school chapel 'at least from the fourteenth century'. The last of the hermits to occupy the chapel before the suppression of the monasteries during the reign of Henry VIII was a William Forte, to whom it was granted, along with 'the messuage, garden, and orchard', by Bishop Stokesley in 1531. It was subsequently granted to Cholmeley in 1565 by Bishop Grindal, then bishop of London, but in 1577, on discovering that the chapel and premises 'had been deceitfully or erroneously withheld from the Crown, to which they were forfeit, either under the abolishing statutes of Henry VIII, or else under the statutes of Edward VI, against superstitious uses', Queen Elizabeth reclaimed them and granted them to John Farnham, a gentleman pensioner. In 1583, however, Farnham sold the chapel and land to the receiver-general of the school, who in turn 're-leased' them to the governors in the following year.

In 1575 a plan was drawn in connexion with the rebuilding of the school and chapel. A lithograph copy of this plan 'shows that the dimensions of the antient chapel were 50 feet long by 24 broad, no mean size for a hermit's oratory'. Between 1576 and 1578 the school and chapel were rebuilt. Enlargements and repairs of the chapel were made in 1616, 1628, 1719, and 1772, 'by subscription of the bishop, wardens, inhabitants, and others'. The various enlargements were obviously made for the purpose of accommodating the increasing population. When the chapel was enlarged in 1772, for instance, 'it was calculated to contain 700 persons'. From a school chapel which the inhabitants used as a convenient place of worship in Highgate, their parish churches, Hornsey and St. Pancras, being distant 'neere two miles', it gradually became a church serving the community. Indeed, early in the seventeenth century an area adjoining the chapel was consecrated as a burial ground, and many Highgate 'worthies', including governors of the school, were subsequently buried there.

As the chapel rose in importance, however, the school declined. Instead of providing a classical education according to the intent of the founder and as had formerly been the case, the school had come to offer merely 'reading and writing, and common arithmetic'. When the Revd. Samuel Mence was appointed schoolmaster in 1816, he found that 'for 12 or 14 years past' the instruction had been carried on by John Martin, who combined his duties as teacher with those of 'sexton and pew opener'. As his predecessor had done, Mence devoted his time and energy to preaching and ministering to the spiritual needs of his congregation and continued Martin as the teacher.

Over the years the revenues of the Highgate Charity greatly increased and in 1822 amounted to 'upwards of 1,000*l.* a year', the main source of income being derived from the two acres of pasture land granted to Cholmeley by Bishop Grindal. In administering the funds and in regarding their trust as a double one involving not only the support of the school but also the maintenance of a chapel of ease for the inhabitants of Highgate, the present governors were following a precedent established by earlier trustees. Furthermore, as a result of the increased revenues of the Charity, the school was now giving instruction to 140 boys 'under the Madras system'.

The 'Notice' to which Coleridge refers in the present letter was 'given out' by the governors of the Free Grammar School on 10 August 1821 and announced their intention to petition Parliament to bring in a Bill authorizing them to tear down the school chapel and erect a new one, the funds to be drawn from the Highgate Charity. To this plan the bishop of London gave his consent. Since the governors proposed to build a chapel commodious enough to seat 1,500 persons, it seems likely that they intended to raise part of the money by subscription. Meanwhile, the report of Henry Brougham which Coleridge asks to borrow had set forth the nature of the endowments belonging to the Highgate Charity and the manner in which the funds were being administered. On the basis of this information, a group of prominent and wealthy inhabitants of Highgate maintained that the governors' proposal to build a new chapel would involve a 'misuse' of the funds of the Charity. Thus arose the 'feuds' which Coleridge anticipated. In 1822 the governors' Bill was brought forward in Parliament but failed to pass. In that year, too, proceedings against the governors were initiated in the Court of Chancery at the instigation of those who opposed them. The controversy was not settled for several years. A decree issued in 1827 by Lord Eldon, the lord chancellor, led to the resuscitation of the decayed Grammar School; a further decree in 1829 by Lord Lyndhurst, then lord chancellor, effectively resolved the problem of the school chapel and the adjoining burial ground; and a parliamentary Act of 1830 not only gave the governors of the school the required authority for tearing down the old chapel but also authorized them to contribute funds from the Highgate Charity towards the cost of erecting a new parish church on another site in Highgate. See *Gentleman's Magazine*, April 1834, pp. 380–5; John H. Lloyd, *The History . . . of Highgate*, 1888, pp. 111–49; G. W. Thornbury and Edward Walford, *Old and New London*, 6 vols., 1872–8, v. 418–23; *The Times*, December 1823 and January 1824. Information has also been furnished by Mr. A. J. F. Doulton, the present headmaster of Highgate School.

As his letters show, Coleridge was an active supporter of the governors of the Free Grammar School, Lord Mansfield, William Belcher, Robert Isherwood, Richard Nixon, Thomas Hurst, and George Kinderley. In 1822 he wrote to members of the House of Commons asking their support of the Bill then being debated in Parliament, and he was equally outspoken in favour of the second parliamentary measure introduced on petition of the governors in 1830. He objected to the 'factious & vindictive attack on Mr Mence & the Trustees of the Highgate School', and he disagreed with Lord Eldon's interpretation of the words 'grammar schools': 'LORD ELDON's doctrine, that grammar schools, in the sense of the reign of Edward VI. and Queen Elizabeth, must necessarily mean schools for teaching Latin and Greek, is, I think, founded on an insufficient knowledge of the history and literature of the sixteenth century. Ben Jonson uses the term "grammar" without any reference to the learned languages.' *Table Talk*, 18 May 1830. As Coleridge said in 1830, he advocated the establishment at Highgate 'of a place of Worship with a regular Clergyman . . . and an effective School for the poor'. See Letters 1284, 1305, 1307–8, 1310–11, 1381, 1503, and 1690.

When the old school chapel was pulled down in 1833, the area was thrown into the adjacent burial ground. Here on the site where the chapel had formerly stood Coleridge was buried in 1834. See 'The Grave of Coleridge', Appendix A.

Postmark: Highgate, 22 September 1821.

To C. A. Tulk

Friday Afternoon. [21 September 1821]
Highgate.

My dear Sir

The state of my health, since your last kind visit till yesterday—
or to speak more correctly, the torpor of the intestinal canal, if that
be the worst and there be not, as I always dread and in the moment
of suffering am too apt to think, some stricture or thickening in
some of the folds—has been so depressive, that I have had no
heart to write to you, or to fix any time, relatively to your very
kind invitation. Generally, tho' with too many exceptions, I am
sufficiently easy during the latter half of the day—at least, under
any pleasurable excitement, as the meeting and conversing with a
friend, I should leave the impression of hypochondriasis rather than
of any determinable malady. This is owing in some part to the
circumstance that the constitutional fervor, which accompanies
the act of thinking and communicating my thoughts with me, is
frequently mistaken for animal Spirits. But the principal cause is,
that my complaint actually is local, and never affecting my head
and only seldom and slightly my Chest &c it disappears as soon as
the pressure is removed by the detrusion of the distending and
irritating substance into the lower viscus, even tho' there is no
bonâ fide elimination.—This spirit-wasting process, however,
begins with my first awaking, and for from 3 to 5 hours makes it
unpleasant to me to be seen by any one, and more than that to
be with those, whom I love and respect, and who yet are not used
to me. In addition to this, I could not ascertain till yesterday
whether I could procure the means of accompanying Mrs Gillman,
and her Sister, with the children to the Sea side—which I now
propose to do, Deo Volente, on tomorrow week. In the mean time,
however, I have so earnest and importunate a desire to enjoy a
portion of your society, and above all to converse with you on the
topics started in your letter—and on the expediency of a small
work, printed as a Companion to the two Volumes of the Universal
Theology,[1] and consisting of a methodical series of Swedenborg's
Positions, physiological and anthropological as well as theological;
—in one word, Swedenborg's system of Theanthropy,[2] reduced to
Theses as much as possible in his own words—with occasional
Scholia, and references to parallel positions in other philosophers,

---

[1] For Coleridge's earlier discussion of *The True Christian Religion; containing
the Universal Theology of the New Church* see Letter 1243.

[2] Coleridge first wrote Theanthroposophy and then altered the word to
Theanthropy. In Letter 1089 Coleridge speaks of Schelling's 'Theology and
Theanthroposophy'; in *Biog. Lit.,* ii. 217, he uses the terms 'PSILANTHROPISM
and THEANTHROPISM'. See also *Literary Remains,* i. 394.

especially those who have written since Swedenborg.—An introduction containing his Life, and an account of the contents of the Works written by him before his Mission, might be prefixed—and yet not extend the publication beyond a moderate Octavo.[1] I am so desirous of this that should you have any part of next week disengaged, I should be happy to come early on any one day, and return the evening afterwards—Any day will be equally convenient to me—that you & dear Mrs Tulk may fix. At all events, I shall prevent all engagements interfering with this, till I receive a line from you.[2]—

Mr Gillman presents his best respects to you, and ventures (under my encouragement) to ask of you the Loan of Mr Brougham's second Report on the Charities—containing the funds under trust of the Governors of the Highgate Chapel.[3] For owing to a self contradictory sort of Notice given out some weeks ago during the divine Service by the Governors, we are in danger of feuds in this Hamlet, which my worthy friend is anxious to do his utmost to prevent or at least to soften.

[1] In the manuscript, brackets enclose the passage beginning with the words 'and on the expediency' and concluding with 'a moderate Octavo'. Several words in this passage are underlined. The brackets and underscoring were probably added by Tulk.

[2] On the day after writing this letter to Tulk Coleridge inserted the following note in the front fly-leaf of a copy of Swedenborg's *Pars prima de cultu et amore Dei; ubi agitur de telluris ortu, paradiso, & vivario, tum de primogeniti seu Adami nativitate, infantia, & amore*, ab Eman. Swedenborg. Londini, MDCCXLV. *Pars secunda, de cultu et amore Dei; ubi agitur de conjugio primogeniti seu Adami, et inibi de anima, mente intellectuali, statu integritatis, & imagine Dei*. Ab. Eman. Swedenborg. Londini, MDCCXCI. The two parts are bound together and are now in the Harvard College Library.

Note (6) p. 4–5 would of itself suffice to mark Swedenborg as a man of philosophic *genius*, radicative and evolvent. Much of what is most valuable in the philosophic works of Schelling, Schubert, and Eschenmeyer is to be found anticipated in this supposed *Dementato*. O nos terque quaterque felices, si modo hujus seculo Doctis et Docentibus datum fuerit eandem insaniam insanire, dementiam scilicet celestem et *de mente* divina effluentem! S. T. C. Septr 22, 1821. Highgate. (From a transcript of the original kindly made by the late William A. Jackson, Librarian, Houghton Library, Harvard.)

This note is somewhat incorrectly printed in *Notes, Theological, Political, and Miscellaneous. By Samuel Taylor Coleridge*, ed. Derwent Coleridge, 1853, p. 110.

[3] Having obtained the appointment of a commission of inquiry on educational charities in 1818, in the following year Brougham instituted an investigation of charity abuses and extended its scope to the universities and to such schools as Eton, Winchester, and the Free Grammar School at Highgate. This and subsequent commissions continued their inquiries for many years, their reports being published between 1819 and 1840. Their findings led to the reformation of many cases of abuse or waste of endowments and eventually to the establishment of the Charity Commission in 1853.

With my most affectionate & most respectful remembrances to Mrs Tulk and your little ones, believe me, my dear Sir,
                              with high esteem & unfeigned regard your obliged
                                                                    S. T. Coleridge.

1277. *To Thomas Allsop*

Address: T. Allsop, Esqre | 1. Blandford Place | Pall Mall
MS. New York Public Lib. Pub. with omis. Letters, Conversations and Rec. *129.*
Postmark: Highgate, 25 September 1821.

                                                   24 Septr. 1821
                                                        Highgate
                              Inclosure safely received = 50£.—
My dearest Alsop
    I will begin with the beginning of your (to me most affecting) letter. Not exactly *Obligation*, my entirely beloved and relied-on friend! The soiling hand of the world has died and sunk into the sense and import of the term too inseparably for it to convey the kind and degree of what I feel towards you. On the one Scale—I love you so truly, that in the first glance as it were and *well-come* of this pledge of your anxious affection it delights me for the very act's sake. I think only of it and you—or rather both are one and the same, and I live in you as the Agent. Nor does the complacency suffer any abatement, but becomes more intense and lively. As a Mother would talk of the soothing attentions, the sacrifices and devotion of a Son, eager to supply every want and anticipate every wish—so I talk to myself concerning you: and I am proud of you, and proud to be the object of what cannot but appear lovely to my judgement, and which the hard contrast in so many heart-withering instances forced on me by the experience of my last 20 years compels me to feel and value with an additional glow. Lastly, it is a source of strength and comfort to know, that the labors and aspirations and sympathies of the genuine and invisible Humanity exist in a social world of their own, that it's attractions and assimilations are no platonic fable, no dancing flames or luminous bubbles on the magic cauldron of my Wishes; but that there are even in this unkind life spiritual parentages, and filiations of the soul.—Can there be a counter-poise to these ? Not a counter-poise—but as weights in the counter-scale, there will come, first, the Self-reproach, that spite of all the inauspicious obstacles, not in my power to remove without loss of self-respect, I have not done all I could and might have done to prevent my present state of dependence—but which in relation to you I should not feel as dependence in any sense of the

word that implies an inward hollowness from the absence of proper
strength, did not, secondly, the fear, the apprehension, intrude on
my mind—that even tho' the present inconvenience, or privations,
incurred by you should be overpayed by the satisfaction, yet it
may seriously interfere with and retard the attainment of independence for yourself. I have been very much worse, for the last two
months till within the last week, than I permitted my kind House-
mates to know, and for which the Sea-side promised little alleviation; but I am now able to hope, that my main alarm (that of a
thickening or stricture in some one of the intestinal folds) was
groundless—and that I may yet be capable of setting apart such a
portion of my *useable* time to my greater Work (in assertion of the
ideal truth & the *a priori* probability and a posteriori internal and
external evidence of the historic truth of the Christian Religion) as
to leave a sufficient portion for a not unprofitable series of articles
for pecuniary supply. I entertain some hope too, that my Logic,
which I could begin printing immediately if I could find a Publisher
willing to undertake it on equitable terms, might prove an exception to the general fate of my publications. It is a long Lane that
has no turning—and while my own heart bears witness to the
genial delight, you feel in assisting me, I know that you would have
a more satisfactory gladness in my not needing it.

And now a few, a very few, words on the latter portion of your
letter. You know, my dearest Allsop! how I acted myself—and that
my example cannot be urged in confirmation of my judgement.—I
certainly strive hard to divest my mind of every prejudice—to look
at the question sternly thro' the principle of Right, separated from
all mere expedience, nay, from the question of earthly happiness,
for *it's own* sake. But I cannot answer for myself, that the image
of any serious obstacle to your peace of heart, that the Thought of
your full developement of soul being put a stop to, of a secret worm
blighting your *utility* by cankering your happiness—I cannot be
sure, that this may not have made me *weigh* with a trembling and
unsteady hand—and less than half the presumption of error afforded
by the shrinking and recoil of your moral sense or even feeling,
would render it my duty and my impulse to bring my conclusion
anew to the ordeal of my Reason and Conscience.—But on your
side, my dear Friend! try with me to contemplate the question as a
problem in the *science* of Morals, in the first instance—and to recollect, that there are false or intrusive weights possible in the other
scale—that our very Virtues may become, or be transformed into
temptations to, or occasions of, *partial* judgement—that we may
judge partially *against* ourselves from the very fear, perhaps contempt, of the contrary—that Self may be moodily gratified by *Self-*

sacrifice, and that the Heart itself in it's perplexity may acquiesce for a time in the decision, as the more safe way—and lastly that the question can only be justly answered, when Self and Neighbor, as equi-distant   *?*   from the conscience[1] are blended in the common   term, *s⚠v a human Being*—that we are *commanded* to love our Selves as our Neighbor, in the Law that requires a Christian to love his Neighbor as himself.—

But indeed, I persuade myself that this dissonance is not real between us—and that it would not have seemed to exist, had I continued the subject into the possible particular cases—ex. gr. suppose a case, in which the misery and so far the moral incapacitation of both parties were certainly foreseen, as the immediate consequence—A morality of consequences I, you well know, reprobate—but to exclude the necessary *effect* of an action is to take away all meaning from the word, action—to strike Duty with blindness.—I repeat it, that I do not, cannot find it in myself to believe, that on any one case made out in all it's limbs, features, and circumstances, your heart and mine would prompt different Verdicts.—

But the thought of you personally and individually is at present too strong and stirring, to permit me to reason on any point.—If the Weather should be plausible, we propose to set off on Saturday—I do most earnestly wish, that you could accompany us—. A steam-vessel would give us 3 fourths of the whole day to tête à tête conversation.

God bless you | & your affectionate & | faithful Friend
S. T. Coleridge

1278. *To Thomas Cromwell*[2]

MS. Mr. W. Hugh Peal. Pub. Lippincott's Magazine, *December 1874, p. 767.*

Highgate
Sunday Evening
30 Septr 1821.

Dear Sir

My state of body, and mind and of circumstances in consequence of both, has almost disqualified me from passing a *reliable* judgement even on subjects, which I had familiarized to myself by study. Now the fit or unfit, the promising or discouraging, in a *theatrical*

---

[1] In the text Allsop interpolated 'or God' to explain the G in the drawing.

[2] Thomas Cromwell (1792–1870), author and dissenting minister, whom Coleridge mentions in writing to Allsop on 3 Dec. 1821.

view, I know as little of as an Infant. In my own play, to which you refer, I never ventured a single suggestion to the Managers or ever offered an objection.—Yet I have seen or heard enough of the present state of the Theatre to be convinced, that the faults & beauties, of which I have some perception, have little influence on the success of the piece. To destroy all sense of Metre is the avowed aim of Mr Kean, no less than his constant practice. All then, I can say of your Tragedy[1] that it would be of any use to say, is that I read it with more interest, felt myself carried on with the plot with a keener sympathy than I felt in the perusal of any one of the Tragedies that have been brought out in my recollection—and that I find nothing, in style, sentiment or imagery, that seems to me likely or calculated to contravene it's theatrical merit. Perhaps, 'I shall not be myself For many moments' is an exception—which it would be prudent to remove. Much, indeed, would depend on the actress—but it might be made ludicrous.

I am obliged to set about the to me exhausting task of packing up: as to morrow morning I leave this place for Ramsgate, my medical friend entertaining more hope of the beneficent effect of Sea air than I dare myself do. Sincerely wishing you the success, to which I believe your Drama entitles you, and regretting for your sake that my name & opinion will be more likely to weigh in the wrong scale and prejudice rather than prepossess, I am,

dear Sir, | very sincerely | your's
S. T. Coleridge

1279. *To Thomas Allsop*

Address: T. Allsop, Esqre. | Messrs. Harding and Co | Pall Mall   If Mr A. is not in town, to be forwarded to him.
MS. New York Public Lib. Pub. with omis. Letters, Conversations and Rec. *136.*
Postmark: 22 October 1821.   *Stamped*: Ramsgate.

Octr 20. 1821.

My Birth-day. 51—or as all my Collegiates
and Mrs Coleridge, swear—50.—

My dear Allsop

Not a day has past since we left Highgate, in which I have not been tracing you in Spirit up and down the Dells and Glens of Derbyshire, while my feet only have been in commune with the sandy beach here at Ramsgate—Once where I had stopt and stood stone-still for some minutes, Mrs Gillman's Call snatched me away

[1] Cromwell's tragedy, *The Druid*, 1832, was never acted. It is not clear whether this is the 'Tragedy' to which Coleridge refers.

from a spot opposite to a House, to the second floor Window of which I had been gazing, as if I had feared yet expected to see you passing to and fro by it. These, however, were Visions to which I had myself given the commencing act, fabrics of which the 'I wonder where Allsop is now' had layed the foundation-stone. But for the last three days your image, alone or lonely in an unconcerning crowd of human figures, has forced itself on my sleep in dreams of the rememberable kind, accompanied with the feeling of being afraid to go up to you—and now of letting you pass by me unnoticed, from want of courage to ask you, what was most on my mind—respecting the one awful to me because so awefully dear to you—(for there is a religion in all deep love, but the Love of a Mother is, at your age, the veil of softer Light between the Heart and the heavenly Father!)—Mrs G. likewise has been thinking of you in sleep and dreaming about you awake—and so, tho' I know not how to direct my letter, yet a letter—a few lines at least as a substitute—I am resolved to write.—I am sure, my dear Friend! that if aught can be a comfort to you in affliction, or an addition to your joy in an hour of Thanksgiving, it will be to know and to be reminded of your knowlege, that I feel as your own heart, in all that concerns you—and an elder Sister could not prize you more dearly, than Mrs G. does.—Next to this, I have to tell you, that the Sea Air and the Sea-plunges, and the leisure of mind with regular devotion of the Day-light to Exercise (for I write only after Tea) have been auspicious beyond my best hopes to my health, and spirits. And the change in my Looks is beyond the present reality—but may be veracious, as *prophecy*, tho' somewhat exaggerating as *history*. The same in all essentials holds good of Mrs Gillman—and I am most pleased that the improvement in her looks & strength has been gradual tho' rapid. First, she got rid in the course of 4 or 5 days of the *Positives* of the wrong sort—ex. gr. the black under her eyes, and the thinness of her cheeks—for some days she looked negatively well, only the eyes more than clearing—and now she is acquiring the Positives of the right kind, her eyes brightening, her face become plump, and a delicate yet cool and steady Color stealing upon her cheeks.—Mr Gillman, too, is uncommonly well since his *second* arrival here—the first week his arm, the absorbents of which had been perilously poisoned by opening a body, was a sad Draw-back, and prevented his Bathing.—In short, we are all better than we could have anticipated—and the better we are, the more I *long* and we all wish, you to be with us. If you *can* come, tho' but for a few days, I pray you come to us. In grief or gladness, we shall grieve less and (I need not say) be more glad, by seeing you, by having you with us.—I will not say, *write*—for I would a thousand times rather have you plump in on me, unannounced. But yet write, unless this be possible.—We have a noble House, with beds enough for half a dozen Allsops—if so many there were or could be —. The situation the *very best* in all Ramsgate—7. Wellington Crescent, East Cliff, Ramsgate—and we or rather Mrs G's voice & manners, procured it *shameful cheap* for the size & accomodations.—The steam-pacquet lands you, within sight of us—& Mr Watson,[1] who returned by it, speaks highly of it—

But I am called to dinner—So God bless you,

and receive all our Loves, | my very dear Allsop—

S. T. Coleridge

1280. *To Thomas Allsop*

Address: T. Allsop, Esqre | 1 Blandford Place | Pall Mall
MS. New York Public Lib. Pub. with omis. Letters, Conversations and Rec. *143.*
Postmark: 2 November 1821.   *Stamped*: Ramsgate.

[22 October 1821][2]

Antescript. The morning after our arrival a card with our Address and *all our several names* was delivered in at the Ramsgate Post office and *to* the Postmaster. And this morning, Monday, Octr. 22nd, I received your letter, dated 16th, which ought to have been delivered on Wednesday last—lying at the Post Office, while I was hour by hour fretting or dreaming about you—and you too must have been puzzled with mine, written on my birth day. A neglect of this kind may be forgiveable, but it is utterly inexcusable—a Blind-worm Sting that has sensibly quickened my circulation—and I have half a mind to write to Mr Freeling—: if my wrath does not subside with my Pulse, and I should have nothing better to do.

My dear Friend

First, let me utter the fervent, God be praised! for the glad tidings respecting your dear Mother—which would have given an abounding interest to a far less interesting Letter. May she be long preserved both to enjoy and to reward your love and piety!—And now I will try to answer the other contents of your letter, as satisfactorily, I *hope*, as I am sure, it will be sincerely and affectionately.

[1] John Watson was the son of Arthur Watson, a surgeon at Dalston, near Carlisle. In May 1822 Coleridge wrote to Southey that John Watson had been 'for the last 18 months a House-mate of mine, as a sort of temporary Partner of Mr Gillman's rather than as an ordinary Assistant'. Watson became one of Coleridge's devoted amanuenses. See W. T. Trimble, *The Trimbles & Cowens of Dalston Cumberland. Supplement to the First Edition*, 1937, p. 19, and Letters 1290, 1301, and 1324.
[2] This letter was begun on 22 Oct. 1821 and concluded on Thursday, 1 Nov.

—Conscious, how heedfully, how watchfully I cross-examined my-self whether or no my anxiety for your earthly happiness and free exercise of head and heart had not *warped* the attention, which it was my purpose to give whole and undivided to the one Question, What is the RIGHT ?—I can repeat (with as much confidence as the slippery and protean nature of all self-inquisition and the great a priori *likelihood* of my reason being tampered with by my affections, will sanction me in expressing) what I have already more than once said—viz. that I hold it incredible, at least, improbable to the ut-most extent, that you and I should decide differently in any one definite instance. Let a case be stated with all it's *particulars*, personal and circumstantial, with it's Antecedents and *involved* (N.b. not it's contingent or apprehended) Consequents—and my faith in the Voice within, whenever the Heart desiringly listens thereto, will not allow me to fear, that our verdict should be diverse. If this be true, as true it is, it follows—that we have attached a different import to the same terms in some *general* proposition—and that in attempting to generalize my convictions briefly and yet comprehensively, I have worded it either incorrectly or obscurely. On the other hand, your communications likewise, my dear friend! were indefinite—'taught Light to counterfeit a gloom':[1] and Love left in the Dusk of Twilight is apt to fear the worst, or rather to think of worse than it fears: and the momentary transformations of Posts and Bushes into Apparitions and Foot-pads must not be interpreted as symptoms of Brain-fever or depraved vision. In this I include dear Mrs G. as well as myself—but in her case it must be added, that from the very beginning she thought, felt and wrote under the strong and combined influence, first, of my Letter to Lawrence Wade,[2] and secondly, of the example supplied in my own instance, all the features of which were and long had been, vividly before her mind, and with an effect on her judgement, which the mere possibility, the very *assumption-for-argument's-sake* of their recurrence in the lot of one so highly hoped *of* and so affectionately hoped *for*, as yourself, could not but exaggerate—at least enough so to give a greater forceableness and a warmer colouring to her expressions than the Question in a connection of less immediate

---

[1] *Il Penseroso*, line 80.

[2] Coleridge refers to Letter 1169, in which his correspondent is addressed at the conclusion as 'my dear L——', i.e. Launcelot Wade. Recently a second and briefer copy of that letter in Allsop's handwriting has come to light. Across the top of the first page of his transcript Allsop wrote, '(for him read her & vice versa) T A'; and on the verso of the last page he added, 'Coleridge to a Lady about to marry a Man of thews & Sinews only'. Possibly Allsop intended to forward his copy of Coleridge's letter (1169) along with Letter 1268 to the young lady whom he was attempting to advise.

interest—above all, a greater generality, than she herself meant to
convey even at the time. The more so probably, as much both of
the opinions and of the language was naturally and almost unavoid-
ably adopted from my Letter before-mentioned and from my
conversation.

And now, my dearest Allsop! why should it be 'a *melancholy* reflection, that the three most affectionate, gentle and estimable
women in *your* world are the three, from whom you have learnt
almost to undervalue their sex'—in other words, those who in their
reasonings have supposed as possible, as not even improbable, arts
and (in more general terms) *unworthinesses* in the views and conduct
of females in the commencing and drawing on of marriage engagements, the frequency of which it is as impossible living open-eyed
not to have ascertained as it is with a heart awake to what women
ought to be and those of whom you speak substantially are? Why
should this, I say, be a melancholy reflection?—

(*Thursday, 1 Novr.* A fatality (to talk like a fool) seems to hang
over this Letter. I will not, however, defer the continuation for the
purpose of explaining it's suspension. Suffice, that Mr G. was here
till Monday—and partly, I could not deny him my society, during
the day, and in the evening he was exceedingly anxious to finish a
medical Paper, the matter of which he dictated & I wrote—And
Monday, & Tuesday were days (and thank God! the only days) of
Relapse in my Health.)

Why, dearest Friend! a melancholy reflection? Must not those
women, who have the highest sense of Womanhood, who know
what their sex may be, and who feel the rightfulness of their own
claims to be loved with honor and honored with love, have likewise
the keenest perception of the contrary? Understand a few foibles,
as incident to humanity; take as matters of course that need not
be mentioned because we know that in the least imperfect a glance
of the Womanish will shoot across the Womanly—and there are
Mirandas and Imogens, a Una, a Desdemona, out of Fairy Land—
rare, no doubt; yet less rare, than their Counterparts among men in
real life. Now can such a woman not be conscious, must she not feel,
how great the happiness is that a Woman is capable of communicating, say rather, of being, to a man of sense and sensibility, pure of
heart and capable of appreciating, cherishing, and repaying her
virtues? Can she feel this, and not shrink from the contemplation
of a contrary lot? Can she know this and not know what a sore
evil, fearful in heart-withering affliction in proportion to the capacity of be[ing] blessed, a weak, artful, and worthless Woman is—
perhaps, in her own experience, has been? And if she happened to
know a young man, know him as the good and only the good, know

each other—if he were precious to her, as a younger Brother to a
matron Sister—and so that she could not dwell on his principles,
dispositions, manners without the thought—If I had an only
Daughter, and she all, a Mother ever prayed for, one other prayer
should I offer—that freely chosen and chusing she should enable me
to call this man my Son!—would you not more than pardon even
an excess of anxiety, even an error of judgement, proceeding from
the disinterested dread of his taking a step, irrevocable, and if unhappy, miserable beyond all other misery—that of guilt alone
excepted?—Especially, if there were no known *particulars* to guide
her Judgement—if that Judgement were given, avowedly, on the
mere unbelieved possibility, on an unsupposed supposition, of the
worst? Of intentional deceit, for instance, as well as utter unfitness,
on the part of the woman? And if there were no breach of promise
on the man's part, in any sense that the strictest Moralists have
attached to the words 'a binding promise'—that is, where the one
party interprets the promise in the sense in which he or she did, at
the time of it's making, believe the other party to have meant it?—
    In Mrs Gillman I have always admired what indeed I have found
more or less an accompaniment of womanly excellence wherever
found, a high opinion of her own sex comparatively & a partiality
for female society. I know, that her strongest prejudices against
individual men have originated in their professed Disbelief of such
a thing as female friendship—or in some similar brutish forgetfulness that Woman is an immortal Soul—and as to all parts of the
male character, so chiefly and especially to the best, noblest, and
highest—to the germs and yearnings of Immortality in the Man.—I
have much to say on this—& shall now say it with comfort, because
I can think of it, as a pure Question of Thought—but I will not
keep this letter any longer. You will be delighted to see the improvement in Mrs G's Looks, and in my own. Her kindest regards
to you. God bless you, DEAR FRIEND! My next will be of myself and
my own concerns.

S. T. C.

1281. *To James Gillman*

Address: J. Gillman, Esqre | Surgeon | Highgate
MS. Harvard College Lib. Hitherto unpublished.

Wednesday Night
31 Octr. 1821
Portá Arietina.

My dear Friend
    As I had asked some half-score Sailors and Sailor-looking
Bodies, besides two or three Chit-chatters or extempore acquain-

tances at the head of the Pier, how the Wind and Tide were for the Eagle (having *previously* ascertained from Anne the answer)—for no reason on earth & for no other cause but that I was *missing* you all day—I had anticipated the tidings of your safe and early arrival under the protecting Pinions of the Eagle, and in company of your own Merry-thoughts, which, tho' not chickenish, were, I doubt not, picked and tender—tho' it be somewhat suspicious of the melon-colic, that you passed at once to a *Bar-too-low*—. Confound this spunging bo-peeping Pus atque Venenum Hanger-on on your arm! Deuce take such new-fangled Dead Folks! Time was when a body was harmless as soon as the Breath was out of it. I trust, however, that after *supper*ation it will *break-fast*, and take it's departure for good and all—P.P.C. or* P.D.A. tho' I do not mean that it should leave *it's card* on *your* Arm.—Now that last Pun, my dear fellow! is I admit, rather *obscure*—but if you will imagine a various reading in the margin, 'leave it scarr'd', all becomes clear as a Thames Fog, and so replete with Attic *Salt*, that you will conclude I have drank inspiration from *our Well* here.—

Spite of the *Pun*arhoea now on me, this lingering of the septic Venom in your absorbents vexes me—and will, I trust, for *you* be (if of no other, yet) of *preventive service*, at least.—

Mrs Gillman continues to thrive, and if she remain much longer a Sea-nymph in Amphitrite's Train, she will become as plump-cheeked as a Triton—i.e. comparatively with her looks before she left Highgate.—I wish, I could say only half as much of her Sister—but she is very poorly, annoyed with that painful involuntary Yawning, and is less able to walk for any length of time without bringing on pain, than when you were with us.—I was myself very unwell on Monday & Yesterday—but this morning I have cleared up again, and had such a Trio of Plunges into the very Heart, Liver, and Lights of three towering Billows this morning, the last of which fairly hurried me back, I might almost say, into the Machine—but actually, to the top-most step of the Ladder—so that I narrowly escaped a bruise—The wave set the Carpet afloat, and had I not instantly called out to Philpott, that his Pot was over-full, I should have had my outsides, alias, extra-cuticulars, alias, Cloathes, seized by the grim old *Surge-on* (happy Synonime for the Sea) without any to *redress* me, as if *Serges*† had a right as next of kin to run off with Superfines.—It was glorious! I watched each time from the top-step for a high Wave coming, and then with my utmost power of projection *shot* myself *off* into it, for all the world like a Congreve Rocket into a Whale. (N.B. It was certainly a Whale that

* Anglicè—Poor dear Jew!—gallicè, pour dire adieu—[Note by S. T. C.]
† *Surges*? [Note by S. T. C.]

swallowed Jonas: for how else could he have made so much *blubber*, such a blubbering Consarn of it, as we find he did?) The Weather still goes on, just as if it were made according to order—just often enough beclouded & *pretending to be going* to rain, to make a variety, & surprize us with the fine weather an hour after.—O I wish, you were here, and that we could all Ramsgatize till the midst of December!—

Remember me very kindly to Mr Watson.

I shall write immediately to Mr Wedgewood according to the Address—& eke to Ebony as soon as possible.

My Love to Mr and Mrs Milne, and to Miss Bullock—whose kindness and kind attentions to me from my earliest Abode at Highgate I should be ungrateful if I ever forgot—Remember me to Powell kindly—and my friendly respects to Mr & Mrs Mence, Mr & Miss Nixon, and to Miss Elizabeth Owen.—

Alas! alas!—the Eagle? Henceforward be it called the He-Gull: for it has gulled me out of my Snuff! I have gone to the Pier, and hailed—'Ho Hoy! the Eagle'—No Snuff to be heard of!—I called at the Office—Two little parcels *had* arrived—but neither for No. 7. W.C. East Cl[iff,] and the name of Coleridge, tho' repeated distinctly as S. T. Co le ridge, Esquire, seemed a sound, they had (O the barbarians!) never heard before!—And then in full cock-sureness of it's arrival I have been wasting the sixpenn'orth of vile ramsgate Plug-nostril, till it is now too late to replenish even if I could bring down my Nose's proud stomach to it. True as sad is the ancient Saying—Sine Baccho tremit Minerva[1]—i.e. Without 'bacco my nerves are all in a *tremmle*—I could write with Nose-tears instead of Ink; but that it would look so damned nasty. So I must conclude, your's, most affectionately, dear Snuff—(Gillman, I meant to write)

S. T. Coleridge

1282. *To T. Jones*

Address: T. Jones, Esqre
MS. New York Public Lib. (Arents Collections). Hitherto unpublished.

[31 October 1821][2]

Dear Sir

Friends' Commandments, tho' not comprized in the TEN, ought to be sacred—. You bade me knock at the door both of your Memory and your Snuff-Canister, for the replenishment of my

---

[1] Cf. Terence, *Eunuchus*, 732.

[2] This and the preceding letter both mention Coleridge's failure to receive a supply of snuff from Gillman and were probably written the same day.

Snuff-box. This, therefore, aided by the disappointment in receiving a paquet from Mr Gillman and by the abomination of the
Ramsgate Article, I hereby do—But, I pray you, do not measure
my modesty by the length & depth of the Box—Displace only one
third of it's present Contents, i.e. Air—and it will be enough.—But
I have no other Box, to send, except one infected by the ill-flavored
Rappee procured at Ramsgate.—I write in the Dark—
truly your obliged

S. T. Coleridge.

1283. *To Thomas Allsop*

Address: T. Allsop, Esqre | 1 Blandford Place | Pall Mall
MS. New York Public Lib. Pub. with omis. Letters, Conversations and Rec. *149.*
Postmark: Highgate, 17 November 1821.

Saturday Afternoon [17 November 1821]
Highgate

At length, my dear friend! we are safe and (I hope) sound at
Highgate. We would fain have returned as we went, by the Steam-
vessel; but gave it up for two reasons, the one that there was none
to go by, the other that Mr Gillman thought it hazardous from the
chance of November Fogs in the River. Likewise, my dear Allsop!
I have two especial reasons for wishing that it may be in your
power to dine with us tomorrow—first, it will give you so much real
pleasure to see my improved Looks and how *very well* Mrs Gillman
has come back. I need not tell you, that your Sister can not be
dearer to *you*—and you are no ordinary Brother—than Mrs G. is,
and ought to be, to me—and you will therefore readily understand
me when I say, that I look at the manifest and (as it was gradual)
I hope, permanent Change in her Countenance, Expression, and
Motion with a sort of *Pride* of Comfort.—Second (and in one respect the more urgent) my anxiety to consult you on the subject of
a proposal made to me in a Letter from Anster,[1] before I return an
answer which I must do speedily.—Should you (as my fear or
rather my common sense augurs) have been engaged, I will convey
the Letter to you by favor of Mr Milne on Monday Morning—&
endeavor at the same time to have concluded the half-reply, I am
still on debit to one of your letters and the whole reply to your

---

[1] John Anster (1793–1867) had invited Coleridge to deliver a course of
lectures in Dublin. (See next letter.) Anster entered Trinity College, Dublin, in
1810 and obtained a scholarship four years later. In 1819 he published a volume
of poems, and in the following year he contributed translations of parts of
Goethe's *Faust* to *Blackwood's Magazine* (June 1820, pp. 235–58), his complete
translation of the first part of that work appearing in 1835.

last—as far as is dictated by the wish to possess you with a permanent record of my thoughts.—But I must not lose the Post—which I shall do if I do not conclude. Mrs G. will herself thank your Sister for her kind present & accompanying note—My dearest Allsop! I can not help giving a relief to my feelings by assuring you how important a part your Love and Esteem constitute of the happiness, and thro' that (I will yet venture to hope) of the Utility, of your

affectionate Friend

S. T. Coleridge

P.S. All send their best regards—and the Absentees, as in nature bound, the most warmly—

1284. *To Thomas Allsop*

Address: T. Allsop, Esqre | 1. Blandford Place | Pall Mall
MS. New York Public Lib. Pub. with omis. Letters, Conversations and Rec. *161.*
Postmark: Highgate, 3 December 1821.

Monday Noon. [3 December 1821]

My dear Allsop

Ab Hydromaniâ Hydrophobia: from Water-lust comes Water-dread. But this is a violent metaphor, and disagreeable to boot. Suppose then by some caprice or colic of Nature an Aqueduct split on this side of the Slider or Sluice-gate, the two parts removed some 20 or 30 feet distance from [each] other, and the communication kept up only by a hollow Reed split lengthways, of just enough width and depth to lay one's finger or at the most one's fist in—the Likeness would be fantastic, to be sure; but still it would be no inapt likeness or emblem of the state of mind, in which I feel myself, as often as I have just received a letter from you and when after the first flush of interest and Rush of Thoughts stirred up by it I sit down or am about to sit down, in the intention of answering you. A poor fraction and finger-brea[d]th of the intended Reply fills up three fourths of my paper and time—and sinking under the impracticability of saying what seemed of use to say I substitute what there is no need of saying at all, the expression of my wishes, & of the Love, Regard and Affection in which they originate.—For the future, therefore, I am determined whenever I have any time, however short, to write whatever is first in mind—& tho' it should amount to but one side of the Sheet out of the four, to send it off 'in the self-same hour'.[1]

I do not know whether I was the most affected or delighted with your last letter—. It will endear Flower de luce Court to me, beyond

[1] Matthew viii. 13.

all other remembrances of my past efforts[1]—and the pain, the restless Aching, that comes instantly with the thought of giving out my soul and spirit where you can not be present, where I could not see your beloved Countenance glistening with the Genial *Spray* of the out-pouring—this in conjunction with your anxiety and that of Mr & Mrs Gillman concerning my health (an anxiety, which since I cannot remove it avails not that I myself do not entertain it) is the most efficient, I may say, imperious of the *retracting* influences as to the Dublin Scheme. The interruption of the Logic, and of the *Assertion* (the former Half and by far the most difficult, of which will have been completed at the next sitting—Sunday next) is the next weightier for which the Publication of the Shakespear Lectures would (in point of lucre-profit) alone be a compensation.—But the scheme is out of the Question.

And now I must break off—& defer my reasons for differing from you as to the merits of *Thomas* Cromwell (Oliver's, I have not seen)[2] till my next *scrap* of *time*—For I have to send you, first, our dear Friend's, my younger and your elder Sister's, kindest Love—& 2nd. her and all our disappointment in not seeing you yesterday, which not having heard from you to the contrary, she continued expecting to the last. 3rdly. in addition to seeing you as soon and as often as you can in the interval, must you dine with your *Uncle* on Christmas Day—or can you spend that day of retrospections, and onward-lookings, of Re-unions and Regrets, with *us*?

Basil Montague called on me yesterday—I could not [but] be pleased to hear from him, as well as from Mr Chisholm and two other several Visitors, the instantaneous expression of surprize at the apparent change in my health & the certain improvement of my Looks. One Lady said—Well! Mr C. really *is* very handsome—.

Highgate is in high feud with this factious stir against the Governors of the Chapel[3]—one of whom I was advising against a

---

[1] Allsop attended Coleridge's course of lectures of Jan.–Mar. 1818. See Letters 1095 and 1104.

[2] Thomas Cromwell published *Oliver Cromwell and his Times* in 1821; Oliver Cromwell published *Memoirs of the Protector, Oliver Cromwell, and of his sons, Richard and Henry*, in 1820.

[3] The announcement by the governors of Cholmeley's Free Grammar School at Highgate of their intention to seek parliamentary authority to tear down the school chapel and erect a new one from the revenues of the Charity which supported the school aroused bitter opposition from a group of wealthy inhabitants. A committee under the leadership of the Rev. H. B. Owen and with the support of Robert Sutton was appointed to investigate the administration of the funds of the Charity, to oppose the Bill in Parliament, and finally as relators to file information against the governors in the Court of Chancery. John H. Lloyd, *The History . . . of Highgate*, 1888, p. 146; *The Times* 2 Aug. 1822; and Letters 1276, 1305, 1307–8, and 1310–11.

reply addressed to the Inhabitants, as an *inconsistency*—But, Sir! we would not carry any thing to an extreme!—This is the darling watch-word of weak men when they sit down on the edges of two Stools—Press them to act on a fixed Principle, and they talk of extremes—as if there were or could be any way of avoiding them but by keeping close to a fixed Principle, which *is* a Principle only because it is the one medium between two extremes.

God bless you, my ever dear | Allsop! and your affectionately attached & | grateful Friend

S. T. Coleridge

P.S. Our friend, G. sees the factious nature and origin of the Proceedings against the Governors in some [so?] strong a light, and feels so indignantly that I am constantly afraid of his Honesty spurting out in the face of his Interest. If I had the craft of the Draftsman, I would paint G. in the character of Honesty levelling a Pistol (with 'TRUTH' on the Barrel) at Sutton in the character of Modern Reform, and myself as a Dutch* Mercury, with his *rod* in his hand hovering aloft and —— into the Touch-hole.—The Superscription might be, Pacification, a little finely pronounced in the first syllable.

The Books shall be returned tomorrow—as they might & ought to have been some 3 or 4 days ago. But both Servants have been alternately laid up with the Tooth & Face ach[e]—the Cook is now going & the new servant just come—& poor little Hen-Pen is sick in bed, with a fever or febricula—

1285. *To J. H. Green*

Address: J. H. Green, Esqre | Surgeon | Lincoln's Inn Fields.
MS. Pierpont Morgan Lib. Hitherto unpublished.
Postmark: Highgate, 8 December 1821.

Saturday [8 December 1821]

My dear Sir

I am so very much pressed for time in the performance of my engagement to Ebony, that I am compelled to defer the pleasure of meeting you till tomorrow Sen'night. I have just looked into Kleist's first play[1]—it seemed to me harsh and branny, and the freedom from sentimentality, for which our friend Tieck gives him so much credit, too evidently a matter of purpose, and fore-thought

---

* Mercury or Hermes, as the God of Lucre & prudential Interest, and Patron-god of Thieves, Tradesmen, Diplomatists, Pimps, Heralds, and Go-betweens—the soothing, pacifying God. [Note by S. T. C.]

[1] Heinrich von Kleist (1777–1811), *Die Familie Schroffenstein*, 1803.

—industrious omission not absence by nature and consequence of the some thing instead.—The encyclopaedia,[1] which did but float, sinks. Nothing can be more groundless in argument or contemptible in Spirit than the attack on the Natur-philosophen in Sprengel's Article, Arzney-kunde—and the attack on the Hamiltono-Abernethian Practice under the name of Gastricismus in the Article *Ausdünstung* is no whit better. I was indeed surprized to find, even in a Leipsig Undertaking, so gross a re-hashing of the Humoral— now atomisto-effluvial-Pathology. The relapse I anticipated; but I thought that the prevalence of dynamic views, with whatever errors they may have been blended by the followers of Reil and Herz,[2] would have secured a refinement in the *form*. So the *Athmen* is a poor *wildernessy* sort of a staggering kind of a thing.—The best are the mythological and palaeological Articles—and these are on too narrow an hypothesis. India—India—India—the Writer can see nothing but India, from Arctic to Antarctic, from Chile to China.—

With kindest respects to Mrs Green | believe me most truly your's

S. T. Coleridge

P.S. I met Dr Gooch the day before yesterday, & was really affected by his pale looks. He consulted me about studying Schelling, in consequence of having read my Biographia Literaria—& asked me whether *Robinson* was not the writer of the dissuasive Letter!!![3] It is so like him, I suppose.

1286. *To Derwent Coleridge*

Address: Derwent Coleridge, Esqre | St John's College | Cambridge
MS. Victoria University Lib. Pub. E. L. G. ii. 298.
Postmark: 12 January 1822.

11 Jany. 1822.

My dear Derwent

I sit with my pen only not touching the paper, and my head hanging over it; but *what* to write and with what purpose I write at all, I know not. What can I urge that would not be the mere

---

[1] Coleridge refers to the *Allgemeine Encyclopädie der Wissenschaften und Künste in alphabetischer Folge von genannten Schriftstellern bearbeitet*, ed. J. S. Ersch and J. G. Gruber, Leipzig, 1818 fol. Part VI, 1821, contains articles on 'Arzneikunde', by K. Sprengel, C. F. B. Augustin, and G. H. Ritter; 'Ausdünstung', by T. Schreger, G. H. Ritter, and J. F. Meckel; and 'Athmen', by Meckel and Schreger.

[2] J. C. Reil (1759–1813) and Marcus Herz (1747–1803), well-known medical nen.

[3] See *Biographia Literaria*, ch. xiii for the letter purporting to be 'from a 'riend' but actually written by Coleridge himself. See also Letter 1055.

repetition of counsels already urged with all the weight that my
earnest intreaties could add to them, so often both before you went
to Cambridge and since? What that would not be the echo of
echoes, which of late have *volleyed* round you in a circle—admonitions which Friends of all ages, of your own & even your Juniors
have given you—and I trust, that wisest and most faithful of all
Friends, your own Conscience? To study to the injury of your
health, and the undermining of your Constitution—was *this* required of you? You have long known both my judgment and my
wishes in this respect: that a Senior Wranglership with the first
Classical Medal as it's Appendage would be a poor compensation to
me and in *my* thoughts for shattered nerves and diseased digestive
organs. You cannot do without intermissions of Study, without recreation and such as society only can afford you—?—Be it so! But
is dissipation of mind and spirit the fit recreation of a Student?
Or not rather the fever fit, of which your Studies are like to be the
cold, feeble and languid Intermittents? 'I have known instances of
Drinkers and Whore-mongers', said Mr Montague to me a few
weeks [ago]; 'but in all my long experience of Cambridge never did
I see or hear of any one instance of a high Wrangler with or without
classical honors, who was a man of Pleasure, Dress, and Family
Visiting.' Even extra-collegiate Society, by preference & in a larger
proportion than that of his own college, and the flaring about with
distinguished Graduates &c; never yet made even if it left a man
friends in his own College—who are after all from obvious causes
the friends most likely to stick by us. But extra-academic Society,
Concerts, Balls—Dressing, and an hour and a half or two Hours not
seldom devoted to so respectable a purpose—O God!—even the
disappointment as to your success in the University, mortifying as
I feel it, arising from such causes and morally ominous, as it becomes
in your particular case & with the claims, that *you* must recognize
on your exertions, is not the worst. This accursed Coxcombry, like
Daeianira's gift, sends a ferment into the very Life-blood of a Young
man's Sense and Genius—and ends in a schirrus of the Heart.—I
know by experience what the social recreation is that does an undergraduate good. In my first Term, and from October till March, I
read hard, and systematically. I had no acquaintance, much less
suitable, (i.e.) studious, Companion in my own College. Six nights
out of seven, as soon as chapel was over, I went to Pembroke, to
Middleton's (the present B. of Calcutta) Rooms—opened the door
without speaking, made and poured out the Tea and placed his cup
beside his Book—went on with my Æschylus or Thucydides, as he
with his Mathematics, in silence till ½ past 9—then closed our books
at the same moment—the size and college Ale came in—& till 12

we had true Noctes atticae which I cannot to this hour think of
without a strong emotion—. With what delight did I not resume
my reading in my own Rooms at Jesus each following Morning.
Think you a Ball or a Concert or a Lady Party, or a Literary Club,
would have left me in the same state—and your studies mathematical? Were it possible even that it could be otherwise—yet your
character must suffer. If from Ill-health or any other cause, should
your (I quote Middleton's sweet Sonnet to me)

> young Ambition feel the wound
> Of blighted Hope and Laurels sought in vain—

what sort of *solution* will be the one current? He *trifled* away his
success!—Can you not controll your Love of appearance and
Showing off for two or three years? At the end of that time the
very qualities that indulged in the interval will stamp you a trifler
&, with such claims on you, far worse! would be construed into
merit by the major part of the world—as not too learned to be
agreeable &c &c—There was a passage in your letter to Mrs Chisholm which shocked & wounded me so much that I could not speak
of it to you at the time.—Mr J. H. Frere used these words to me—
That you are above the run of Readers, and cannot be remunerated
by the Press, increases not lessens the obligations of those who are
conscious of having been especially benefited by you. It is not in my
power to prove to you how much [I] feel this to [have] been my own
case—but I can spare a certain sum which is [at] your service, &
which I consider as your's—and then he asked me, whether the
enabling me to send you to College would be the most agreeable to
me—.[1] Wrangham and Caldwell were my old—the latter my oldest,
Friends.—Suppose that a Bookseller had given me 300£ for my
Lectures, instead of Mr Frere—would you think the sum more
earned by me? Mr Southey received an annuity from his old School-
fellow, Charles Wynne—which on Wynne's Marriage was com-
muted for a Pension—Had Southey used this for his Son's university education—would *Southey's* Son, think you, speak of himself
as a mere poor child of charity, a dependent on the I know not what
—and *contrast* his state with those, who are maintained by their
Fathers?—Had it been as true as it is false—should a Son have
placed his Father in so degrading a point of view—and this in a
letter to a vulgar tattling Woman?—But if such be your notions
respecting me & yourself (and how little you have been taught or
are in the habit of attributing to or connecting with me, as the
Source, I mourn to see, chiefly for your sake & because too
many others see & notice it)—if you are this mere Almsman, how

---

[1] For Frere's offer of support in 1817, see Letter 1070.

preposterous must your present conduct be ?—I was even hugging
myself with a letter from Prof. Calvert to Mr Caldwell—& wondered
that Mr Gillman read it with so blank a face. Worship too has twice
sent us a present[1]—without a single line—I suppose, because he
will not send ill-tidings.—But from different Quarters these ill-
tidings have flowed in on me in a head. Even Henry C. has written
to his Brother John 'in great grief and indignation' respecting
you—and as to your not writing to Mr Gillman (except as you make
use of him) or to me, especially since your examination[2]—'When
did you hear from your Son, (says Mr Wells to me) my Son stands
third on the List ?'—And Mr G. has been so kind to you! not only
striking of[f] the 50£ I was engaged to pay for your six months—
but at this very time undertaking a serious responsibility for you. O
Derwent! would to God you would so act as to permit you to
attribute all the kindness shewn you to your own account, with
some plausibility at least.—

I am not angry, Derwent!—but it is calamitous that you do not
know how anxiously & affectionately I am your *Father*—

S. T. Coleridge

P.S. I hear that you are Premier or Secretary of a Literary Club—
about old books.—If such things did not dissipate your time &
thoughts, they *dissipate* and perplex your *character*—They are well
enough for B.A.s & M.A.s—

1287. *To Derwent Coleridge*

Address: Derwent Coleridge, Esqre | St John's College | Cambridge
MS. Victoria University Lib. Hitherto unpublished.
Postmark: Highgate, 15 January 1822.

[15 January 1822]

My dear Derwent
Tho' my anxiety had spoken a yet stronger and more passionate
language, you would have your own ominous silence to blame for
it—aware too, as you must have been, with what deep interest I
had been waiting for the result of your examination—and that

[1] William Taylor Worship entered Jesus College, Cambridge, in 1818 and
received his B.A. in 1822. He was ordained to the diaconate in 1822, to the
priesthood in the following year.

[2] In June 1821 Derwent was 'Bracketed 4th in first class'; in December
'8th in first class'. In June 1822 he was '5th in first class'. In December of that
year, however, he was 'Inferior to those in the first class, but entitled to Prizes
if in the 1st class at the next examination'. He was 'not classed' in May 1823,
being 'absent from part of the Examination with leave'. (From information
kindly supplied by Mr. F. P. White, Librarian of St. John's College.)

young Wells would be at Highgate, and with him the one question-
stirring Fact, that he, whose powers natural or acquired I had been
led to suppose nothing above ordinary, stood third in a list, in which
your name was—he did not recollect, *where*. Add to this what you
were not or only partially aware. In consequence of a Letter from
your mother, in which she expressed herself with unjust and yet
in her state of information justifiable bitterness respecting my supposed indifference as to her and your sister, I felt myself bound to
acquaint her with the whole truth, and therein with the true
occasion of my so long delay in answering her main question which
I alone could answer—her other questions I having already given
the answers to, on Hartley's assurance that he was about to write
to Keswick and would include them in his letter—Of four Letter-
sheets so closely written, that one page would equal two of these,
the first two sides informed her in all points concerning myself, and
my own state of mind, body, circumstances and occupations—Of
the remainder three sheets gave a continued detail of Hartley's
goings- or rather ungoings-on, from my first interview with the
Provost of Oriel to his last week's determination (by the advice or
at least with the opinion of his Cousin John) to accept of the 300£—
a measure, the existence of any necessity for which is the melancholy side of the question[1]—Tho' I stated all in the least unfavor-

---

[1] Convinced that Hartley was innocent of the 'heavier part' of the charges
made by the fellows of Oriel, Coleridge had refused in October 1820 to become
the 'channel' of conveying to him the £300 offered by the College to prevent
'pecuniary inconvenience'. Hartley agreed with his father that to accept the
money would be a 'compromise of character' and an admission of 'the *degree*
of delinquency'. John Taylor Coleridge, however, felt otherwise, and as the
following extract from his journal of 1 December 1821 shows, he advised
Hartley to accept the £300:

> Poor Hartley Coleridge has been dining with me to-day—his condition
> seems a deplorable one—he said very unaffectedly that he by no means
> made it a practice regularly to dine, and always thought it a gain when he
> got a good dinner. He spoke with great good sense and right feeling about his
> unhappy dismissal from Oriel and said . . . that he had only refused to take
> the money offered him by the College because he thought it might look like
> an acknowledgement of the *whole* of the Charge. . . . If he took the money,
> which I rather persuaded him to do, he said he should wish to send it to his
> mother, and spoke of her in a very proper manner. (Transcript Coleridge
> family.)

As a result of this conversation, John Taylor Coleridge took the initiative and
wrote to John Keble, who replied on 30 January 1822:

> About poor Hartley's money Copleston desires me to say that some appli-
> cation should be made as it were officially—he said at first by Hartley him-
> self, or his father, but afterwards he said if you applied in his name as
> expressly authorised by him it would be sufficient. I suppose he means we
> ought to have a letter which might be produced at an audit and kept among

able light, and took occasion in different parts of the latter to keep Hartley's *good* points before her, & his freedom from all *active* bad, yet it was such a chain of strange almost Idiocies, Neglects, Provocations, and Promise-breach, that my own Hopes and Spirits sunk under the collective view—the more sorrowfully, that they are of a nature that does not enable me to love him less—& that I have to feel every time I see him, what a comfort and support his society and co-operation might be to me!—From this dreary subject I had turned to Cambridge as to a sunshiny spot—and was actually transcribing Prof. Calvert's Letter to Mr Caldwell—when the ill news flowed in, from the only reservoir as it were of my Hopes.

Secondly, my strongest terms were applied to the tendencies of a Disease, as proved by it's extreme stages,—and this generally, without adverting to the contingent counter-actions in this or that individual Case—not *to* you but for you, as at worst but a Patient under symptoms of the first stage of Infection. Taken, as I meant it, I cannot retract my assertion—that Dangling and Dandyism threaten a schirrus of the Heart, where this precious Dyad finds any heart to work on.—

And now for your letter. Of course, I am glad to be able to correct my fears as far as public Balls, Concerts, and Time-murder in Narcissism—glad, because your character will be less *noised* and publicly talked of, as a gay youth, likely to outshine Tom Moore as a Poet and pleasant Fellow—. *A Scholar* (said Sir H. Wootton)[1] *may easily be too much the Gentleman*—But after all deductions the result is all but the same. The old story of the Hairs & the Horse-tail.— Each *this* would have been a trifle, or venial, but for a *that*, and a *that*—You had ample time for deliberation—and in me you found rather a bridle than a spur to your academic Ambition—I did not goad you—You had my consent as soon as asked to your changing your scheme of study, your objects & your college—but when you after due reflection accepted Prof. Calvert's kind proposal, you were under a promise not to do as you have done—But for your *unseasonable* Controversial Conversation-Juntos who would or could have blamed your visits at the Freres?—But for your Literary

the College Papers, and as it need only be a request to have the money paid so and so without any kind of acknowledgement or allusion to past matters Hartley will probably have no objection to write or authorise you to write, tho' I confess I hardly see the necessity of it.

Subsequently the £300 was paid into John Taylor Coleridge's hands. In January 1823 Hartley asked that whatever remained of the money after his debts had been discharged should be paid to Mrs. Coleridge. See *Letters of Hartley Coleridge*, 36, 50, 54, and 76; *Minnow among Tritons*, ed. Stephen Potter, 1934, p. 86; and Letters 1289, 1314, and 1318.

[1] Sir Henry Wotton (1568–1639), diplomatist and poet.

Club—but this is past—Suffice that all, but plain dragging on with
the wheels in the old Ruts, are *prematurities*—February Buds and
Leafits, retarding the Shew of Spring and impoverishing Autumn—
That I charged you mainly with the *intempestivum* is proved by my
remark—Be a Student, a recluse, an *Autocrat* in good earnest for
the next two years & a half, and what are green Gooseberries & dry
Colic or wasting flux now will be a handsome *Desert* afterwards.—
For God's sake, my dear Boy! for mine, for your Mother's, for dear
little Sara's, do throw off these flappets and tag-points & appendages—Your business at present is to *learn,* to acquire, to *habituize*—
not to teach—to *be,* not not to *shew*—or rather to *become.*

God bless you! Write to your Moth[er] and assure her that your
past experience will not have been in vain.—

No one spoke to *me* about you except John Coleridge, & that in
consequence of what I spoke of having *heard* of—but it did alarm
me, that all were your equals in rank and age, and all spoke of
you highly in all respects that did not refer to your *university* Prospects.—

Do, do, give your poor Brother an example, instead of an excuse—
. . . nor did my letter deserve . . .[1]

1288. *To John Murray*

Address: Mr Murray | Bookseller | Albermarle St
MS. Sir John Murray. Pub. with omis. Letters, *ii. 717.*
Postmark: 19 January 1822.

Highgate
Jany. 18, 1822

Dear Sir

If not with the works, you are doubtless familiar with the name
of that '*wonderful man*' (for such, says Doddridge, I must deliberately call him) Archbishop Leighton.[2] It would not be easy to point
out another name, which the eminent of all parties, Catholic and

---

[1] Parts of the two concluding lines of MS. cut off.
[2] Philip Doddridge, D.D. (1702–51), nonconformist divine. In 1748 there
appeared a two-volume edition of *The Expository Works and other remains of
Archbishop Leighton. Some of which were never before printed. Revised by P.
Doddridge, D.D. With a Preface by the Doctor.* A copy of this edition formerly
owned by W. B. Elwyn of Queen's College, Oxford, contains annotations by
Coleridge. The note in the fly-leaf may be cited here:
Surely if ever work not in the sacred Canon might suggest a belief of inspiration,—of something more than human,—this it is. When Mr. Elwyn made
this assertion, I took it as the hyperbole of affection: but now I subscribe
to it seriously, and bless the hour that introduced me to the knowledge of the
evangelical, apostolical Archbishop Leighton.

(Pub. *Literary Remains,* iv. 156.) April 1814.

Elwyn's copy of Leighton has not come to light, but in 1838 it was in the

Protestant, Episcopal and Presbyterian, Whigs and Tories, have
been so unanimous in extolling. 'There is a spirit in Archbishop
Leighton, I never met with in any human writings; nor can I read
many lines in them without impressions which I could wish always
to retain'—observes a Dignitary of our Establishment and F.R.S.
eminent in his day both as a Philosopher and a Divine. In fact, it
would make no small addition to the size of the volume, if as was
the fashion in editing the Classics, we should collect the eulogies on
his writings passed by Bishops only and Church Divines, from Burnet[1] to Porteus.[2] That this confluence of favorable opinions is not
without good Cause, my own experience convinces me. For at a
time, when I had read but a small portion of the Archbishop's
principal Work, when I was altogether ignorant of it's celebrity,
much more of the peculiar character attributed to his writings (that
of making and leaving a deep impression on Readers of all classes)
I remember saying to Mr Southey—'that in the Apostolic Epistles
I heard the last Hour of Inspiration striking, and in Arch. Leighton's Commentary the lingering *Vibration* of the Sound.'[3] Perspicuous, I had almost said transparent, his style is *elegant* by the mere
compulsion of the Thoughts and Feelings, and in despite, as it were,
of the writer's wish to the contrary. Profound as his Conceptions
often are, and numerous as the passages are, where the most
athletic Thinker will find himself tracing a rich vein from the surface downward, and leave off with an unknown depth for to morrow's delving—yet there is this quality peculiar to Leighton—unless
we add Shakespear—that there is always a sense on the very surface, which the simplest may understand, if they have head and
heart to understand any thing. The same or nearly the same, excellence characterizes his Eloquence. Leighton had by nature a quick
and pregnant Fancy: and the august Objects of his habitual Con-

possession of a relative, Alfred Elwyn of Philadelphia. In that year Elwyn
sent a copy of Coleridge's annotations to Edward Moxon, who in turn transmitted them to H. N. Coleridge. They form in part the 'Notes on Leighton'
printed in *Literary Remains*, iv. 156–83. (From information kindly supplied
by Mr. John Beer.)

The note in the fly-leaf of Elwyn's copy of Leighton cited above and Letters
921–2, both of which are addressed to Cottle, show that Coleridge's enthusiasm
for the archbishop began as early as Apr. 1814.

[1] Gilbert Burnet (1643–1715), bishop of Salisbury and author of the *History
of His Own Time*, 2 vols., 1724–34. See also Letter 1350.

[2] Beilby Porteus (1731–1808), bishop of London.

[3] In one of his notebooks Coleridge made a similar comment:

Next to the inspired Scriptures,—yea, and as the vibration of that once
struck hour remaining on the air, stands Leighton's Commentary on the
first Epistle of Peter. *Literary Remains* (under the heading 'Omniana, 1809–
1816'), i. 346; reprinted, iv. 157.

templation, and their remoteness from the outward senses; his constant endeavour to see or to bring all things under some point of Unity; but above all, the rare and vital Union of Head and Heart, of Light and Love, in his own character;—all these working conjointly could not fail to form and nourish in him the higher power, and more akin to Reason—the power, I mean, of Imagination. And yet in his freest and most figurative passages there is a *subdued*ness, a self-checking Timidity, in his Colouring, a sobering silvery-grey Tone over all; and an experienced eye may easily see where and in how many instances Leighton has substituted neutral tints for a strong Light or a bold Relief—by this sacrifice, however, of particular effects giving an increased permanence to the impression of the Whole, and wonderfully facilitating it's soft and quiet *Illapse* into the very recesses of our Conviction, Leighton's happiest ornaments of style are made to appear as efforts on the part of the Author to express himself *less* ornamentally—more plainly.

Since the late alarm respecting Church Calvinism and Calvinistic Methodism (—a cry of Fire! Fire! in consequence of a red glare on one or two of the windows, from a bonfire of Straw and Stubble in the Church-yard, while the Dry Rot of virtual Socinianism is snugly at work in the Beams and Joists of the venerable Edifice—)[1] I have heard of certain gentle Doubts and Questions as to the Archbishop's *perfect* Orthodoxy—some small speck in the Diamond which had escaped the quick eye of all former Theological Jewellers from Bishop Burnet to the outrageously Anti-methodistic Warburton.[2] But on what grounds I cannot even conjecture—unless it be, that the Christianity which Leighton teaches contains the doctrines peculiar to the Gospel as well as the Truths common to it with the (so called) Light of Nature or Natural Religion—that he dissu[a]des students and the generality of Christians from all attempts at explaining the Mysteries of Faith by *notional* and metaphysical speculations, and rather by a heavenly life and temper to obtain a closer view of these Truths, the *full* Sight and Knowlege of which it is in Heaven only that we shall possess. He further advises them in speaking of these Truths to prefer scripture-language; but since something more than this had been made necessary by the restless spirit of Dispute, to take this '*something more*' in the precise terms of the Liturgy and Articles of the established Church.—Enthusiasm? Fanaticism?—Had I to recommend an Antidote, I declare on my Conscience that above all others it should be Leighton. And as to *Calvinism*, L's exposition of the scriptural sense of Election ought to have prevented the very [suspicion?].[3]

---

[1] Cf. Letter 1211.
[2] William Warburton (1698–1779), bishop of Gloucester.   [3] MS. torn.

You will long ago, I fear, have [been asking yourself,][1] To what
does all this tend?—Briefly then—I feel strongly persuaded—perhaps because I strongly wish it—that The Beauties of Archbishop
Leighton selected and methodized, with a (*better*) Life of the Author,
i.e. a biographical and critical Introduction or Preface, and Notes—
would make not only a useful but an interesting POCKET VOLUME—.[2]
'Beauties' in general are objectionable works—injurious to the
original Author, as disorganizing his productions—pulling to
pieces the well-wrought *Crown* of his glory to pick out the shining
stones—and injurious to the Reader, by indulging the taste for
unconnected & for that reason unretained single Thoughts—till it
fares with him as with the old Gentleman at Edingburgh, who eat
six *Kittiwakes* by way of *whetting* his appetite—whereas (said he) it
proved quite the contrary: I never sat down to a dinner with so
little!—But Leighton's principal Work—that which fills two
Volumes and a half of the 4—being a Commentary on St Peter's
Epistles, verse by verse, and varying of course, in subject, &c with
almost every paragraph, the Volume, I propose, would not only
bring together his finest passages, but these being afterwards arranged on a principle wholly independent of the accidental place of
each in the original Volumes, and guided by their relative bearings,
it would give a connection or at least a propriety of *sequency*, that
was before of necessity wanting.—It may be worth noticing, that
the Editions, both the one in Three, and the other in Four, Volumes
are most grievously misprinted & otherwise disfigured.[3]—Should
you be disposed to think this worthy your attention, I would even
send you the Proof *transcribed*, sheet by sheet, as it should be
printed, tho' doubtless, by sacrificing one Copy of Leighton's
Works, it might be effected by references to Volume, page, and line—
I having first carefully corrected the Copy.—Or should you think
another more likely to execute the plan better or that another name
would better promote it's sale—I should by no means resent the
preference—nor feel any mortification, for which the having
occasioned the existence of such a Work tastefully selected & judi-
ciously arranged would not be sufficient compensation for,

dear Sir, your obliged

S. T. Coleridge.

P.S. Might I request the favor of a single Line in answer?

[1] MS. torn.

[2] Although Murray showed an interest in Coleridge's proposal, he later
declined to publish the work. See Letters 1291 and 1339.

[3] The four-volume edition of Leighton mentioned here belonged to Gillman.
This was the 1819 reprint of the 'Middleton' edition of 1805. See Letter 1291.

1289. *To Thomas Allsop*[1]

Address: T. Allsop, Esqre | 1. Blandford Place | Pall Mall
MS. Bodleian Library. Pub. E. L. G. ii. 301.
Postmark: 19 January 1822.

Saturday [19 January 1822]

My dearest Friend

The Day, I was in town for the purpose of conversing with John Coleridge respecting Hartley and the 300£ (which I had refused to become the *Channel* of) from Oriel—it being too the day after my first acquaintance with the vexatious tidings of Derwent's failure and it's tenfold more vexatious Causes—I was pressing Hartley to rouse and revolutionize himself, were it but for my sake—as such a series of disappointments from both my children in addition to seeing him in pecuniary distresses which I could not relieve or in disgraceful dependence from which I could not rescue him, would infallibly bring me to the Grave. In the course of this earnest conversation, and while my feelings were thus moved, I said to him—in these or equivalent words—'Perhaps, I feel the pressure, as a heavier weight, at this moment—for it distracts my feelings when I would fain have given my whole heart and soul to one subject. For—of course, Hartley! you will take care not to repeat what I am about to say, for obvious reasons—I have this morning heard from Mrs Gillman—whose authority, however, rests on a hearsay—of an event, which must determine the future happiness of the Friend, who has been more than a Son to me. I have heard, that Allsop is just married.'—To no one else have I ever spoken on the subject— & I imagine that in writing to Derwent he may have supposed himself at liberty to deviate from the silence, I had imposed on him—. But even to Hartley, I should not have suffered it to overflow from me—had I not intended to write to you as soon as I returned if I found that Mrs G. had anticipated me. But on my return Mr Gillman strenuously dissuaded me, with arguments that derived their force in a very far greater proportion from his & Mrs G's requests & authority than from any satisfaction, they afforded to my feelings, or any efficacy in reconciling my silence to my dislike (that is a very tame word) to having a thought concerning you that was not as well known to you as to my own Soul.—I would not promise not to write—There was one motive and only one that weighed with my reason—viz. the assertion, which came from some of your young Women, was conjoined with another—that your Uncle had been & remained exceedingly offended, and that you yourself had never been observed in such apparent distress of mind—

[1] Allsop did not publish this letter, which refers to his marriage.

Now it did occur to me as possible, that you might have wished to let this state of things pass over & the matter be finally settled with your family, before you ventured on a new series of feelings—tho' God knows! let me only believe, that you love and are beloved, and all other considerations are light as straws in comparison—it is almost irreligious not to rely on Providence and the Life of Hope, that Love and Honor never fail to in-breathe, for the rest.—

So however I delayed—till you came to Highgate—. And then I think, nothing could have prevented me from telling you what we had heard but that Mrs G. called me out in a hurry—before I saw you—& said—'*Pray*, do not say a word of it to Mr A.—I have reasons for it'—and two hours afterwards, I asked Mrs G. if we had been *dreaming* with grave faces & open eyes for the last week or two?—

This, my dear friend! is the truth & the whole Truth, to the best of my Memory—the Name of the young Lady was Matthew—& that she was extremely handsome.—

I have not written; because till tomorning [this morning?] I could not get from Mr Gillman any positive opinion on the subject— On Sunday next you will come with the Lambs—& why not as you half promised, tomorrow likewise?—I will write by Monday.—

My dearest Allsop— | Words cannot express how dear you are | in all respects to your

S. T. Coleridge

1290. *To Thomas Allsop*

Address: T. Allsop, Esqre | 2. Albany Street | Regent's Park.
MS. New York Public Lib. Pub. with omis. Letters, Conversations and Rec. *165.*
Postmark: 25 January 1822.

[25 January 1822][1]

Dearest Allsop

My main reason for wishing that Mrs Gillman should have made her call on Mrs A.; or that Mrs A. would waive the ceremony, and taking the willingness for the act, and the praesens *in rus* (if Highgate deserves that name) for the future *in urbe*, would accompany you hither, on the earliest day convenient to you both; is that I cannot help feeling the old inkling to press you to spend your Sunday with me and yet feel a something like impropriety in so doing. Speaking confidentially, et inter nosmet, if it were prognosticable, that dear Charles would be half as delightful, as when we were last

[1] The MS. of this letter bears two postmarks, a London one, '7 o'clock 25 January 1822 Night', and a Highgate one, 'Evening 26 January 1822'. Since Coleridge speaks of the possibility of seeing Allsop on Sunday, he was probably writing on Friday, 25 Jan.

with him, and as pleasant relatively to the probable impressions on
a stranger to him as Mary always is—I should still ask you to fulfil
our first expectation. But as it is, I must be content to wish it—
and leave the rest to your knowlege of the circumstantial Pros and
Cons. Only remember, that what is dear to you, becomes dear to
me—and that whatever can in the least add to a happiness, in which
you are interested, is a Duty, which I cannot neglect without injury to my own.[1] One part of your letter gave me exceeding comfort
—that in which you spoke of the peculiar sentiment awakened or
inspired at *first sight*. This is an article of my philosophic Creed.

And now for my Pupil Scheme.[2] Need I say, that the Verdict of
your Judgement, after a sufficient Hearing, would determine me
to abandon a plan, of the expediency and probable result of which
I was less sceptical than I am of the present?—But first let me learn
from you whether you had before your mind, at the moment that
you formed your opinion, the circumstance of my being already

[1] At this point in the printed text Allsop made the following interpolation:
'*I am convinced that your happiness is in your own possession.*' This sentence is
taken from Letter 1296.

[2] On 25 Feb. 1822 the following announcement appeared in the *Courier*:

Mr. COLERIDGE proposes to devote a determinate portion of each week to
a small and select number of gentlemen, not younger than 19 or 20, for the
purpose of assisting them in the formation of their minds, and the regulation
of their studies. The plan, which is divided between direct instruction and
conversation, the place, and other particulars, may be learnt by personal
application to Mr. COLERIDGE, at Highgate. (Alice D. Snyder, *Coleridge on
Logic and Learning*, 1929, p. 71.)

A fuller description of this plan is given in Coleridge's letter to Stuart of
15 Mar. 1822.

Such a class did materialize. 'It was our fortune', writes the author of an
unsigned article in the Nov. 1835 issue of *Fraser's Magazine*,

to accompany a party of gentlemen to a private course on Logic, which he
[Coleridge] had undertaken to give them in common at set times; a task of
tuition on which the benevolent poet set no pecuniary price, but which no
honorable mind could suffer the performance of without rendering grateful
recompense. The occasion to which we are now referring bears date about the
year 1823; and it was Mr. Coleridge's wont then to dictate deliberately to his
pupils, whether from memory or immediate impulse, his sublime lessons,
permitting them to take his words down in writing. Sometimes he diverged,
always eloquently, from the dry theme of lecture into some branching topic,
having life in it, and a reference to life. Such is the history of the following
beautiful fragment, forming in itself a complete *Essay on Life*. It was
delivered as from the inspiration of the moment. . . . It was committed . . .
to paper, in the Poet's presence . . . [and] received the approbation of the
Master.

In a second article contributed to *Fraser's Magazine* in Dec. 1835, the same
writer explains that it was 'Mr. Coleridge's design to put his pupils in possession
of . . . a volume [on Logic] . . . taken down from his own lips', and prints 'an
Introductory Chapter' to that work.

in some sort engaged to *one* pupil already[1]—that with Mr Stutfield
and Mr Watson[2] I have already proceeded on two successive
Thursdays, and compleated the Introduction, and the first Chapter,[3]
amounting to somewhat more than a closely printed Octavo Sheet,
requiring no such revision as would require Transcription—and
that three or four more young men at the Table will make no addition, or rather no change. Mr Gillman thought my agreeing to receive Stutfield advisable—Mrs G. did not indeed influence me by
any express wish; but thought, that this was the most likely way
in which my Work would proceed with regularity & constancy
—in short, it was or seemed to be *a Bird in the hand*, that in conjunction with other reliable resources would remove my anxiety
with regard to the *increasing* any positive pressure on their finances,
of former years—so that if I could not lessen I should, however, prevent the deficit from growing—on all these grounds I did—perhaps,
I need not say—downright *engage* myself—but I certainly permitted Mr St. to make the Trial, in such a form that I scarcely know
whether I can in the spirit of the expectation, I excited, be the
first to cry *off*, he appearing fully satisfied and in good earnest.—
Now supposing this to be the state of the Case, how would my work
fare the better by dictating it to two Amanuenses instead of 5 or
6—if I could get so Many ? For the occasional explanations, and the
necessity of removing difficulties, and misapprehensions, are a real
advantage in a work, which I am peculiarly solicitous to have 'level
with the plainest capacities'.—To be sure, on the other hand, I
might go on three days in the week, instead of one—and let the work
outrun the lectures—but first, so I might on the plan of an increased
number of Auditors—& secondly, so many little obstacles start up,
when it is not *fore*known that on such a day I *must* do so & so—I
need not explain myself further—. You can understand the—'I
would not ask you; but it is only—and but that—& pray, don't
take any *time* about it'—&c &c—added to my own *startings* off.—
If I do not see you on Sunday, do not fail to write to me—for of
course I shall take no step till I am quite certain, that your judgement is *satisfied*, one way or other—for
I am with unwrinkled confidence & | inmost reclination | your
affectionate Friend   S. T. Coleridge
Kind Love from our Household—

[1] This was Charles Stutfield, Jr., whom Coleridge in writing to Allsop on
30 Mar. 1820 calls 'my young Friend & Pupil'.
[2] John Watson had been a member of the Gillman household for some time.
See Letters 1279 and 1301.
[3] For further comments on the *Logic*, which Coleridge had begun dictating
to Watson and Stutfield and which he considered almost ready for the press in
Dec. 1822, see Letters 1301 and 1324.

1291. *To John Murray*

Address: Mr Murray | Albermarle Street
MS. Sir John Murray. Pub. E. L. G. ii. 303.
Postmark: 26 January 1822.

Highgate—
[26 January 1822]

Dear Sir

Your suggestion entirely coincides with my purpose. I waited indeed only to know that you did not decline it primâ facie—to have proposed the same myself. There is a Copy of Leighton's Works here; but it is not my own—nor would it be proper for me to use it as such.[1] I will therefore embrace your offer of sending me your Copy—which I doubt not, I shall be able to send back with the passages marked, and with a sufficient numeration of the order in which I intend them to stand, and specimens of the Headings, to enable you to form a tolerably correct fore-judgement of the contents and appearance of the Volume.[2]—A few inaccuracies and slovenly combinations, I think, may be silently corrected where they chance to interfere with the effect of a passage otherwise eminently interesting—and I had some thoughts of adjoining, as a sort of appendix, some short biographical and critical notice of that every way interesting class of Writers, before and immediately following Thomas à Kempis, whose works and labors were the powerful and most effective Pioneers of the Reformation—with some short specimens from the very rare Works of J. Tauler which were with difficulty procured for me in Germany last year[3]—& which thoroughly bear out the high character, which I once heard Klopstock give of them—

I am almost sorry that my revered Friend, R. Southey, should

[1] Coleridge refers to Gillman's copy of Leighton, a reprint of the original edition issued under Middleton's name in 1805: *The Genuine Works of R. Leighton, D.D., Archbishop of Glasgow: with a Preface by Philip Doddridge, D.D. A New Edition, with Corrections and Additional Letters. To which is now prefixed, the Life of the Author, by the Rev. Erasmus Middleton*, 4 vols., 1819. Coleridge's annotations in this edition form in part the 'Notes on Leighton' printed in *Literary Remains*, iv. 156–83, but the volumes have not come to light.

[2] This copy of Leighton, a reprint of Jerment's edition of 1805–1808, is entitled: *The Whole Works of Robert Leighton, D.D., some time Bishop of Dunblane, and afterwards Archbishop of Glasgow. A New Edition, carefully corrected. To which is prefixed a Memoir of the Author, by George Jerment, D.D.*, 4 vols., 1820. This copy, which Murray sent to Coleridge 'for the purpose of selecting from it', is in the British Museum. It contains annotations by Coleridge and was used by him in the preparation of *Aids to Reflection*. When in 1823 Murray declined to publish the work on Leighton, he 'entreated' Coleridge's acceptance of the copy he had sent. See Letter 1339.

[3] See Letter 1063, in which Coleridge made inquiries concerning the works of Johann T. Tauler.

have suffered himself to enter into a *quarrel in print* with Lord
Byron. For what can he say that the World has not said even to
satiety long ago, & which probably his Lordship is not unwilling
that the World should say—? Besides, as long as Satan is universally admitted to be a Spirit of extra ordinary genius, and a
splendid character—so long will the epithet, Satanic, not stand in
the way of the admiration, and curiosity of the Public.[1]

I remain, | dear Sir, | respectfully | Your obliged

S. T. Coleridge

[1] The '*quarrel in print*' between Byron and Southey began with the publication of Cantos I and II of *Don Juan* in July 1819 but owed its origin to a false
report brought to Byron in the summer of the preceding year. According to
Byron's informant, Southey on his return from Switzerland in 1817 said that
Byron and Shelley were living 'in a league of Incest'. Byron was given to
understand, too, that '*Coleridge* went about repeating Southey's lie with
pleasure'. Accepting without question what he had been told—'my authority
was such as I had no reason to doubt'—Byron was convinced that Coleridge,
whom he had befriended and to whom he had made a gift of £100, had mali-
ciously repeated the ugly scandal. 'I can believe it', Byron wrote, 'for I had
done him what is called a favour. I can understand Coleridge's abusing me,
but how or why *Southey*—whom I had never obliged in any sort of way . . .—
should go about fibbing and calumniating is more than I readily comprehend.'
For his part, Coleridge must have been at a loss to understand why his former
benefactor had so venomously attacked him in *Don Juan*. Indeed, Coleridge
probably never knew that Byron believed him guilty of spreading calumny
abroad. Had the association between the two men been more intimate and of
longer duration, Byron would have known that ingratitude and a propensity
to scandalous gossip were equally alien to Coleridge's nature. If he accepted
Southey's '*direct and positive denial*' of the charge of having circulated calumnies
(*Courier*, 5 Jan. 1822), then, of course, Byron must have finally come to
realize that Coleridge was not the ingrate he had supposed him to be.

As his letter to Murray suggests, Coleridge had read Southey's letter to the
editor of the *Courier*, dated Keswick, 5 Jan. 1822, the latest in a series of diatribes
marking the quarrel between Southey and Byron. Earlier Coleridge had read
A Vision of Judgment (1821), in the Preface to which Southey launched an
attack on Byron and others, though he mentioned no names. Denouncing the
productions of what he insisted should 'properly be called the Satanic school',
Southey added that these works were 'especially characterised by a Satanic
spirit of pride and audacious impiety'. In his communication to the *Courier*
he was more outspoken. He not only renewed his attack on the '*Satanic
School*'—an appellation which he declared would 'stick'—but he now openly
called Byron 'its Coryphaeus' and 'Goliath'. Whereas Coleridge believed that
'the epithet, Satanic, [would] not stand in the way of the admiration, and
curiosity of the Public', Southey continued to use the term, and in replying to
certain charges appearing in Medwin's *Conversations of Lord Byron*, a work
published in 1824 not long after the poet's death, he addressed a second letter
to the editor of the *Courier*, dated 8 Dec. 1824, in order to lay before the public
'one sample more of the practices of the Satanic School'. See *The Works of
Lord Byron: Letters and Journals*, ed. R. E. Prothero, 6 vols., 1898–1901, iv.
271–2 and 474–95, and vi. 377–99; and *Keats–Shelley Journal*, Winter 1954,
pp. 27–38.

1292. *To Charles R. Leslie*

Address: C. R. Leslie, Esqre | 8. | Buckingham Place | Fitzroy Square
MS. Huntington Lib. Pub. E. L. G. ii. 305.

Feby. 1822
Highgate.—

My dear Sir

I have not the pleasure of knowing, or of being known to, Mr
...[1]—otherwise than as he will probably have seen my name in his
own Magazine, and as I have heard him spoken of distinguishingly,
as a spirited, intelligent and liberal Publisher. But I have both perused and re-perused the three Numbers (or Sections shall I call
them?) of the IDLE MAN,[2] and with exception of the Preface,
(which, I must confess, had one merit, that of occasioning a very
agreeable disappointment, and which on a re-print of these Essays

Southey's self-righteous tirades against Byron stand in sharp contrast to
Coleridge's single protest against a charge of drunkenness in Canto I of *Don
Juan*—a private letter to Byron of 4 Sept. 1819. Equally different are the
statements of the two men shortly after Byron's death. 'I am sorry Lord Byron
is dead', Southey wrote on 26 May 1824, 'because some harm will arise from
his death, and none was to be apprehended while he was living. . . . We shall
now hear his praises from all quarters. I dare say he will be held up as a martyr
to the cause of liberty. . . . I am sorry for his death therefore, because it comes in
aid of a pernicious reputation which was stinking in the snuff.' Coleridge was
more charitable. S. T. Porter, then a 'white-aproned youth of fifteen years of
age' apprenticed to T. H. Dunn, a chemist at Highgate, reported Coleridge's
conversation after Byron's funeral procession had passed through Highgate
on 12 July 1824: 'As I stood at our front-shop door, observing that small part
of the funeral procession which had ascended the hill from St. Pancras, Mr.
Coleridge who had been walking on the other side of the hearse, recognised me
and presently crossed over & poured forth for some time to me, certainly not
less than a quarter of an hour, a strain of marvellous eloquence on topics
suggested by the scene of the hour, or rather by what we felt to be the great
event of the day. . . . I recal distinctly the chief topics on which he spoke ; such
as Byron's unhappy youth; the extraordinary issue of it in his prodigious
works & his numerous & great public merits ; his great & special claims on his
countrymen's generous if discriminative appreciation ; the delightful fact that
even then, at that so early a period after his death, the funeral ceremonies
indicated strong public action, or re-action in his favour; & the certainty that
in the future, according to the noble wont of the English people, Byron's
literary merits would seem continually to rise, while his personal errors, if not
denied, or altogether forgotten, would be little noticed, & would be treated with
ever softening gentleness.' (E. L. Griggs, 'Samuel Taylor Coleridge and Opium',
Huntington Library Quarterly, Aug. 1954, pp. 371-2.) See also *The Life and
Correspondence of the late Robert Southey*, ed. C. C. Southey, 6 vols., 1849-50,
v. 178-9.

[1] The name is erased in the MS.
[2] Richard Henry Dana, the elder (1787-1879), edited *The Idle Man*, a
short-lived literary magazine published in New York, 1821-2. The first three
numbers are dated 1821.

in a collection of the whole may, and indeed should, be omitted, quite independently of it's comparative inferiority, supposing my opinion to be right) I read them with more than common satisfaction and interest. Assuredly, I cannot hesitate in giving it as my *Judgement* that a couple of Volumes of such Essays would be a valuable Addition to our Miscellaneous Literature, and maintain an honorable place on the same Shelves with the Lownger, Mirror, &c—and it is my *opinion*, that they would be received as such by the English Public. If I speak more diffidently on this point than on the former, the reason has no connection with the Essays themselves, which appear to me in all respects calculated to become popular; but is grounded on my own recluse habits and estrangement from the literary world of my contemporaries. That they have been admired by a man of such high and rare Genius, as Mr Allston, whether I contemplate him in the character of a Poet, a Painter, or a philosophic Analyst, would of itself afford a strong presumption that they will not lower the rank lately won for American Talent by the Author of the Sketch-book, and the History of New York.[1]

I wish, that I had more influence than according to my own belief I have—and I wish it, because in the present instance I could exert it *conscientiously*—i.e. in the full faith, that I was proposing what promised to be beneficial to the Publisher as well as to the Public—But be it's weight more or less, the Author of the Idle Man is entitled to the suffrage of, my dear Sir,

Your sincere friend

S. T. Coleridge

1293. *To Mrs. S. T. Coleridge*

Address: Mrs C[oleridge]
MS. Victoria University Lib. Pub. with omis. E. L. G. ii. 311. This fragment is all that remains of the original letter.
Postmark: Highgate, 9 February 1822.

[9 February 1822]

... SEVERE! my dear Sara? I could not help reading that caution of your's to Mrs Gillman, only to see the gravity of her smile. The truth is, that all my friends & they are all Hartley's, complain that I 'reverse the order of things' in my manners to both of them—by excess of attention to their feelings—and even Mrs Milne & her

[1] Washington Irving (1783–1859), author of *A History of New York, from the Beginning of the World to the End of the Dutch Dynasty*, by 'Diedrich Knickerbocker', first published in 2 vols., New York, 1809, and republished by Murray London, 1820; and *The Sketch Book of Geoffrey Crayon, Gent.*, first issued in 7 parts in New York, 1819–20, and republished by Murray, 2 vols., London 1820.

Sister who are *fond* of Hartley (I say, *fond*: for every one who knows him intimately, love[s] him) have several times reproached me—at least, kindly blamed me—for the extreme delicacy with which I speak to him of his follies, and my terror of giving him pain.—But this has not proceeded wholly or even principally from the pain, I suffer, in giving him pain—but from my knowlege of his nature— that if Hope and pleasurable Feelings are not *stimulants* for him, Uneasiness and Depression will be *Narcotics*. I never yet have used an angry word or spoken in an angry tone to either of them—tho' Derwent, in my last Letter without reason appropriated to himself the vehement epithet which I had attached to *Dandyism* in . . .

. . . tidings of me but what consisted in proofs of the respect entertained for me by all among whom I live, by their zeal in serving him, and by the attentions which they shew him?—But Excuses must not be scanned too narrowly.—His name is down in the Pocket-books of three men of great influence, two belonging to the Skinners', and one to the Fishmongers' Company—I do every thing in my power.—You again have misunderstood my letter—I have had no proof of Derwent's *Extravagance* from his Bills: tho' of course we began to fear, lest it might be so.—

I have not seen Hartley since I wrote to you, but once—and not a word of his *promised* Prometheus, to be finished in a fortnight!!— I am anxious to receive the Wanderings of Cain—. Derwent's Scrape consisted in very particular & blameable . . . of very respectable Family—which ended in having . . . Mother, a Mrs Chisholm— She is Sister of the . . . Eton & Cambridge. But for God's sake, do not . . .

H. was getting . . . not to interfere; but to let . . .

If Hartley reads *thro'* your letters, he pays you a . . .

. . . *very* dear to me—& a delig[ht] . . .

1294. *To Thomas Allsop*

Address: T. Allsop, Esqre | No. 2. Albany Street | Regent's Park   If Mr A. have left Albany St, to be taken to Blandford Place, Pall Mall.
MS. Cornell University Lib. Pub. Nineteenth-Century Studies (*Cornell*), 56.
Postmark: Highgate, 9 February 1822.

Saturday Afternoon, [9 February 1822]
My dearest Allsop

It is not '*my way*' to sit down to a Letter, with no other purpose than to make others uncomfortable by telling them how uncomfortable I am myself. But really I did so far over-rate my fortitude, that I must plead guilty to more pain from *missing* you for such a dreary Saturday-&-Sunday Recurrency, than I ought to have

suffered—or—for Self will manage to edge-*in* something, as a sort
of noun *adjective* in the excusative case—than I should have felt,
if I could have set up against it the assurance, that you were at ease
in mind, body and estate—and that no circumstances had arisen to
annoy you. Would to God that your feelings permitted, made it
possible for, you to unfold—not *yourself*: for that lies expanded before without a wrinkle—but your affairs & troubles, apprehensions
and expectations—even as I do or desire to do, to you. But do not,
I conjure you, do not mistake me!—I do not mean, or think, that
you love me less than I love you, or interpret it as the result of any
want of confidence in me, intellectual, moral, or prudential. I know,
that there are inward withholdings that are as the attendant
Daimon or Genius of an Individual, allotted to him together with
his personëity, and which will be listened to even tho' their utter-
ances should be at times but a nervous singing in the ear, were it
only from the remembrance that at other times & most often they
have been Voices of the Heart.—

I have blamed myself ever since for not going up when I called at
Albany Street—I am sure, I should have managed every thing with
Mrs A. & have had her by this time sitting at our fire-side here, as
an *In*quaintance—to use poor Hartley's phrase when he was not
four years old, and which with acquaintance and conquaintance
would go near to comprize all a man's social Wardrobe, above the
rank of mere Praetérfluents and Confluents.[1]—

With regard to Derwent, I never had any impression but what
is contained in the words—Non quòd malum, sed quòd intempestivum est—the suddenness of the disappointment, and the rush from
so many distinct quarters of the complaints & Statements, vexed
me; but I was & remain far more grieved by his excuses & tone of
Self-defence.

I am busily engaged—besides some letters to Keswick which I
have been obliged to write, in answer to a long list of Questions of
Mrs Coleridge who has a notable facility in misunderstanding the
plainest words. I expect her and my little Sara at the close of the
ensuing Spring for a month or six weeks. [How happy would it have
made me, if . . .][2] The Logic goes on briskly—& my greater work is
at least *accelerating* it's pace. Mr Gillman & Mr Green both liked the
Maxilian much—& it will improve.[3] But small interruptions in my
state of Health are not small.—

[1] See Letters 904 and 1467.

[2] The words in brackets are all that can be deciphered of a sentence heavily
inked out in the MS.

[3] Coleridge's 'Sundry Select Chapters . . . Comprizing the *Historie* and
Gests of MAXILIAN' appeared in the Jan. 1822 number of *Blackwood's Magazine*,
but there was no sequel.

When shall I see you?—When it can be with propriety, on that
very moment read that question as an intreaty of, my dear Friend,
Your with blended | fraternal & parental Regard & Love,
S. T. Coleridge

P.S. That Mrs G. sends her kindest remembrances, it scarce needs
a Post-script to say—nor how anxious she & Mr G. are to shew their
attachment to you by their respect & sense of Welcoming to your's.

1295. *To Thomas Allsop*

Address: T. Allsop, Esqre | Blandford Place | Pall Mall
MS. New York Public Lib. Hitherto unpublished.
Postmark: Highgate, 26 February 1822.

Tuesday Morning, ¼ after 11.—[26 February 1822]

This moment Mr Watson has delivered to me your letter which he
received last night, in the parlour while we were still round the Tea
Table.—He acted for the best; but it is most unfortunate that, as
Mr and Mrs G. went to rest before X, he had not availed himself of
the opportunity. I write this from anticipation—for I have not yet
done more than bolt the Nursery Door against sudden irruptions—
and by way of giving time to the little flutter to pass off, or as a
diversion of my attention from it, while it continues. Before I begin
the perusal (which, after locking up this *Ante*-script, I shall do
while walking in the lonely Lane behind Cootes's Garden) I have only
to say that Mrs G. is gone to town, or rather is already there—and
with the intention of calling at Blandford Place: and that neither
seeing, nor hearing from, you, and Mr Anster having been invited
to spend the week at Highgate, and anxious in discussing with me the
pros and *cons* of his taking Orders or continuing at the Temple,[1] some
prudential & circumstantial but most points of religious or rather
theological Scruples—and yet, even while most and with sincere
interest too engaged with him on the *Proscenium* of my Mind, thinking and asking and wishing of and about You behind the Curtin—
I rather promoted than discouraged Mrs G's purpose—my impulse,
perhaps, was anxiety respecting your health—in short, *a wanting*
to be in contact with you, mediately & by a conductor at least—but
my conscious motive arose out of the apprehension that Mrs A.,
now knowing that it is know[n] and understood to be known here,
might imagine it a slight, an indifference at least, if Mrs G. any
longer deferred waiting on her. And this I could not bear.—Dearest
Friend! if I have decided injudiciously, we will *share* the blame be-

[1] See Letter 1376.

tween us—you for not giving, I for needing, a more explicit hint—
And now for the Lane. Mr G. is just off from the Surgery Door.—
Mr Watson—an excellent young man—will henceforward know
how to manage it—and you may rely implicitly on my Organ of
Destructiveness as soon as I have thoroughly acquainted myself with
the contents of your's.—

Tuesday Afternoon, 2 o'clock.—

Most unlucky Delay!—I feel too unquietly to be capable of ascertaining my own thoughts—Enough however gleams thro' the
mist to make me see that they will be better communicated side by
side or vis à vis, than by the Post. Will Friday next suit you? Or
should you prefer this day week? To be sure, I might go on Saturday, spend the night in town, and return with Mr Green on the Sunday Morning.—Suppose it Saturday then—I mean, that you may
expect me on Saturday Afternoon, unless I hear to the contrary.—
Simply, a line to Mr Watson—with the *name* of the day, you would
prefer—thus a 'Be so good as to say, *Monday*' or whatever the day
may be—will be sufficient. Mr W. will understand it—

And now, my very dear Friend! I will add no more—than that
since the time, I left you, I had so far decyphered your feelings that
the performance of what I conceived a duty—a demonstration of
Respect to *you* in all your names and positions, an intelligible
Pledge that the Person, who was so highly respected as a single
Man, is equally respected as a Husband, and the *reflex* attentions
appropriate and due to him in that character willingly recognized—
was the most, I distinctly looked forward to, EXCEPT IN MY OWN
PERSON, *as unconnected with any other*.—Secondly, be assured that
whatever Rays passed from *me* to *you*ward passed *straight*, without
refraction thro' any second medium, without glancing aside—even
to an edge-breadth of a thought: and that I have had no proof of it's
having been otherwise with any other Mind or Set-of-feelings. Yet
I will not conceal from you that your Mode of viewing the Subject
has not come into my mind as an *utter* Stranger—tho' it corresponded but to a very dim & general impression, such as those Im-
presses are that are made by experiences of too little interest to be
particularized in the memory—

Till we meet—& at all times, God | bless you, my dear, very dear
Allsop! | And your faithful Friend

S. T. Coleridge

P.S. I have not written concerning your Health—considered
exclusively *body*-wise and in the immediate symptoms, your indisposition is, I am convinced, little more than Bile out [of] it's
Bounds—[a] Truant, which ten grains of Ipecacua[nha] with Camo-

mile Tea, followed, perhaps, by a sedati[ve, if][1] there should prove to be an undue degree of Irritability in the Stomach, would be adequate to reform *pro tempore*—But the cause is for *another sort of Doctor*—Only this—I am NOW quite convinced, that the Diploma is in your own possession, and unlike those, which the World bestows, includes at once the Right, the Skill, and the Medicine—in contempt too of 'compound Interest' which, however, shocked me even to a sick faintness as I read it.—

1296. *To Thomas Allsop*

Address: T. Allsop, Esqre | Blandford Place | Pall Mall
MS. Harvard College Lib. Pub. with omis. Letters, Conversations and Rec. *208*.
Allsop prints an extract from this letter as a conversation.

[Friday, 1 March 1822][2]

Friday.—The following has been long written—& waiting for a conclusion. But I have been for the last week & more *very* unwell—. This morning I have *begun* to convalesce.—God bless you and my kind Love to Mrs Allsop.—

My dearest Allsop

If I had not known by my own repeated experience, how when any thing has occurred, which there seems but one only way of explaining, that way will force itself upon the mind without and even against our will; and had I not likewise known, with what an altogether different feeling we, at the moment, regard an act or motive, while we attribute it to, or surmise it of, a dear friend from that, with which we should contemplate it in our own case, or on the supposition that we were ourselves on the point of doing the same;—had that *not* been which *was*, I *might* have been what I was *not*—hurt at your concluding me capable of such combined weakness and indelicacy as to have urged a visit after, nay, in consequence of, your full-hearted communication. But having given you this assurance, I *shall* be hurt if you should make any apology—as it would imply a *feeling* at least of a doubt as to the sincerity, the entire *self-transparency* with which I assure you that this part of your letter occasioned me *no* pain—*offence* is of course three semidiameters of the orbit of Common Sense on the other side of Possibility.

[1] MS. torn.
[2] This letter is the 'inclosed Détenu' mentioned in Letter 1297. Only the opening paragraph, which appears at the top of page one of the MS., was written on Friday morning, 1 Mar. 1822. The erroneous date of '12 Feby 1822' appearing in the MS. is in Allsop's handwriting.

But then, my beloved Friend! you must give the same advantage
to X and Y. On a retrospect of our correspondence you must ask
whether your own mode of proposing the problem, whether the
disposition of the Lights and Shades in your own broken Sketches,
did not render a similar *misapprehension* almost inevitable? And
the more so, when you take that word in it's peculiar application
to the point in question—when you reflection [reflect?], that at the
utmost it amounted only to a questionary *Fear*, to an *apprehension*,
lest—not to a *belief, that*. You murmured a charm, that was felt
thro' the whole sphere of our imagination: and not a single Spirit,
that could procure or forge testimonials of it's possibility, but
started up in it's turn, and asked, Is it *I*, that you want? You must
remember, how often I reminded you, that I was arguing not only
on a mere supposition, but on one (if I may hazard so strange a jar-
gon) suppositiously proposed, and for the express purpose of having
some mark on the wide target for the direction of the Arguments—
and *this* done, then to take, i.e. to suppose, another—& so on, till
the whole area seemed to have been exhausted—leaving it for you
to judge *which* of the imaginary Marks, if any, was nearest to the real
case & circumstance, as well as whether the shafts aimed thereat
had fairly *hit*. I said what I felt—viz. that I held it little less than
impossible, for you and me to have any essential difference of
Judgement, where an adequate Knowlege, on both sides, of the
particular Case in all it's individualities, and all the individual
circumstances, antecedent and concomitant, secured us from the
risk of misapplying the Principle, and of misunderstanding each
other's meaning.

And this leads me to a further point. I know right well what it is
to read a letter on a subject that had been before agitated, at a time
when the mind is at once full and restless. I was not surprized
therefore, that you had, or appeared to me to have, overlooked or
forgotten the passages in my letters & conversation—(and I cannot
but conclude from my knowlege of our friend's opinions in general,
that such there were in her's likewise) in which the case of exclusive
and reciprocal Attachment founded on, or where it had connected
itself with, that inward sense of *personal* fitness, of which no man
can judge for another, was put aside—as admitting but one answer—
or rather as permitting but one question, that of the *time*—and this
too in the words of Medea in Euripides. *'Tis done!* and now when
shall I do it?[1]—But you cannot have failed to notice the eagerness,
the exultation, the (this was, I think, the very word) the *unspeakable comfort*, with which I caught and welcomed the first definite
pledges of this, those that declared and those which implied that

[1] Cf. Euripides, *Medea*, 1064 and 1240–3.

this was the case. And was it without meaning, or hollow, that *after* my visit at Blandford Place and with one sentence in your (last but one) Letter in my thoughts, I wrote—'*Now* I am convinced, that your Happiness is in your own possession,' &c ?—Indeed, *indeed*, my dearest Friend! you must have misconceived Mrs G. The Notion, that Affections are of less importance than advantages—or that the latter dare even be weighed in the same scales—is less truly described as opposite to her opinion, than as alien from her very nature. And as to accomplishments, she thought—for she spoke to me at the time about it—that you were wrong in cherishing a positive dislike of an *indifferent* thing—that was neither good nor evil, ground of preference or rejection, in itself.—In reply, I observed among other remarks, that leaving all moral relations wholly out of view, such as vanity, or the disposition to underrate the solidities of the Soul male or female, &c &c—the question of accomplishments seemed to me to depend very much on the *individual* woman, almost in the way that Dress does—a l[ittle] more or a little less Dressiness—. Of two equally amiable and equally beloved Females one looks better in an evening, the other in a morning, Dress—It is just as it *suits*. And so with accomplishments— There are two women, to whom tho' in different ways I have been *deeply* attached in the course of my Life—The one had no so called *accomplishments*—and not only at the time when I had faith in the return, did I say—'and I love her all the better' but I am still convinced that such would be my feeling at the present moment of any such woman. Accomplishments would not *suit* her—Just as I should say to a Daughter, or might have said to the Lassy in question, had she been my wife—My dear! I like to see you with bracelets; but your hand and fingers are prettiest without any ornament— they don't suit *rings*. The other Lady on the contrary became them —they were indeed so natural *for* her that they never strike me *as* accomplishments—and to do her Justice, I must say that I am persuaded that the consciousness of them occupies as little room in her own thoughts.—But to imagine, that a sensible Woman like Mrs G. a duteous Wife, a solicitous Housewife, a fond and industrious Mother, and an anxious and full-hearted Friend should think, or feel, a young friend's Bride, less worthy of her or of anyone's regard, or a less suitable & susceptible object of a virtuous and sensible Man's abiding Love, for the absence of that modicum of French, Italian, & Piano-fortery which meets one now with such Jack a lanthorn ubiquity in every first and second story in every street, that the very want is really become a *presumptive* accomplishment, as the being free of Debt is a negative Stock—this, my dearest Allsop! is not *credible*—& be *most* confident, is as little true of Mrs G.

as of myself—. Mrs C. had no *accomplishments*—did you ever suspect from any thing, I ever said, that this lay in the way of my domestic Happiness—and She too had no accomplishments, to whom *the man* in the Poet sighed forth the

> Dear Maid! no Prattler at a mother's knee
> Was e'er so deeply prized as I prize *thee*—
> Why was I made for love, and love denied to me ?[1]—

1297. *To Thomas Allsop*

Address: T. Allsop, Esqre | Blandford Place | Pall Mall
[In another hand] favd by Mr Milne to be delivered Soon
MS. New York Public Lib. Pub. with omis. Letters, Conversations and Rec. *169.*

Friday Night [1 March 1822][2]
My dearest Allsop
    I have been much more than ordinarily unwell for more than a week past—my Sleeps worse than my Vigils, my Nights than my Days—'the Night's dismay sadden'd and stunn'd the intervening Day'.[3]—But last Night, shortly after I had layed my head on the pillow, I was visited with a pertinacious fit of Coughing, each cough ending in an expectoration or perhaps ex*guttur*ation, for nearly two hours. But whether that the effort threw me into, or the disordered action ended critically in, a gentle perspiration, or from the dephlegmatising so largely, I had not only a calmer Night, without roaming in my dreams thro' any of Swedenberg's Hells *modéré*; but arose this morning lighter and with a sense of *relief*.
    I scarcely know whether the inclosed Détenu[4] is worth inclosing or reading—I fancy that I send it because I can not write at any length that is even tolerably adequate to what I wish to say—and yet can not defer letting you know, how anxiously my thoughts follow you—and that I do most fervently pray that Dr Latham may prepare the way for a yet more efficient Physician, my dear Friend's own Mind.—Mrs Gillman returned very much pleased with all and every, save only your being too unwell to see her—evidently and in all the minutiae of evidence as a Mother or Aunt would have returned from a first introduction to a Son's or favorite Nephew's

[1] *The Blossoming of the Solitary Date-tree*, lines 76–78, *Poems*, i. 397.
[2] This letter was written on the Friday following Mrs. Gillman's visit to Mrs. Allsop on Tuesday, 26 Feb. 1822. See Letter 1295. The erroneous date of '4 March 1822' appearing in the MS. is in Allsop's handwriting.
[3] *The Pains of Sleep*, lines 33–34, *Poems*, i. 390.
[4] This was Letter 1296.

chosen Life-mate, and with the impression that it would be his own
fault, if she did not make him a happy home. I have see[n] two
instances, in which a young and almost domesticated Friend of
her's has married—and in both after a little while she has become
the Wife's Confidante and the Husband's thro' the wife. Indeed,
it is certainly one of Mrs Gillman's good qualities, her attachment
to the young and estimable of her own sex—and the fondness and
respect with which all the young Women of her acquaintance,
married and unmarried, at once look up and cling to her is a
pleasing proof of what I say. It is not on my own account, tho' it
would be insincere in me to deny that I should feel & find the loss
in the frequency of seeing you a grief and a privation—nor is it
chiefly on *your* account—but I do think, I am quite confident in
the belief, that not only all your apprehensions and imaginations
are groundless, and to be attributed in part to the state of your
health and the peculiarly depressing character of your indisposition
aggravated by the unavoidable cares and disquietudes of Business,
and by what cannot have been without it's effect on your spirits
(I am sure, it has had a very sensible influence on mine, and as far
as I can judge, unmingled with any reference to your worldly
interests)—I mean, your Uncle's Malignity—not only (I repeat)
are these surmises unfounded, but that you will be depriving Mrs
Allsop of a sincere friend, in whom she will not fail to find that sort
of support and comfort, which a Woman can receive only from a
Woman, and which a young married Woman receives most naturally from one much elder than herself, and yet [not] so old as to
interfere with the sympathies. If Mrs A. has still the least notion
that we are in love with *accomplished* folks at Highgate, I dare
promise that it would be the subject of a laugh between her and
Mrs G. before two months were past.—Add to[o] that spite of some
counter-weights or rather counter-*moods*, G's integrity, generosity
in all worldly concerns, his firmness where he has professed friendship, and his undoubted professional Skill and judgement render
him no every day character—and to you he is very much attached.

I shall make you smile—which I should have no objection to
do—by saying (what dear Mary Lamb indeed put in my head) that
I sometimes fancy that you do not think how I was bred up. As
Individual to Individual, from my childhood I do not remember
feeling myself either superior or inferior to any human Being, except by an act of my own will in cases of real or imagined moral or
intellectual Superiority. But in regard to worldly rank, from eight
years old to 19, I was habituated, nay, naturalized to look up to
men circumstanced and situated as you are, as my Superiors—a
large number of our Governors and almost *all* of those whom we

regarded as greater men still, and whom we saw most of, viz. our Committee Governor[s] were such—and as neither awake nor asleep have I any o[ther] feelings than what I had at Christ's Hospital, I distinctly remember that I felt a little flush of pride & consequence, just like what we used to feel at School when the Boys came running to us—Coleridge! here's your friends want you—they are quite *grand*, or—it is quite a *Lady*—when I first heard that you were a Partner in the House of Hyde and Scribe—and laughed at myself for it with that pleasurable sensation that, spite of my sufferings at that school, still accompanies any sudden re-awakening of our School-boy feelings and notions. And O! from 16 to 19 what hours of Paradise had Allen and I in escorting the Miss Evanses home on a Saturday, who were then at a Millaner's, whom we used to think, and who I believe really was, such a nice Lady— and we used to carry thither of a summer morning the pillage of the Flower Gardens within six miles of Town with Sonnet or Love- rhyme wrapped round the Nose-gay. To be feminine, kind, and *genteelly* (i.e. what I should now call, neatly) drest—these were the only accomplishments to which my Head, Heart, or Imagination had any polarity—and what I was then, I still am. Suffer Mrs A. to be loved in the first instance for *your* sake—& it will end in your being better loved for hers—or if *better* you cannot be, yet with an additional tie.—Your Children too will ere long be a new Reflex of the Rays of the Love, I bear you—and I owe it to Truth and Justice to say that both you and Mrs A. would have been much affected, had you heard Mrs G. who to this moment has not even a suspicion of what has passed between us, talking as she did with me last night tête à tête of the advantage it would be to your health as well as to the Mother and Child to be with us at Highgate—and laying out schemes for it, with such an unsuspecting Confidence, and guileless Taking-for-granted of Mrs Allsop's eventual attachment [to] her, an attachment as akin to daughterly as your's to me has been to filial. [God b]less you. I wish much to come in if I do not see you here—and if I knew [what] one day next week would be more con- venient than another, I wou[ld do so.]

Most affectionately,

S. T. C.—

1298. *To Daniel Stuart*

Address: D. Stuart, Esqre | 9. Upper Harley Street
MS. British Museum. Pub. Letters from the Lake Poets, *281.*
Postmark: Highgate, 15 March 1822.

Friday 15 March, 1822.
Highgate

My dear Sir

So very seldom as I go to town, it might seem almost a fatality that I should be not at home for so many successive Calls: for which and the kind purpose of which accept my sincere thanks. I had suspected previously to the receipt of your Note of inquiry, that the Advertisement sent to the Courier was not sufficiently clear as to my Object[1]—yet how to render it such without being more explicit, which from the heavy charge for all but very short Advertisements in the Times and M.C. I could not afford to do, and in fact had not the present means of doing, I did not know—and so e'en let it take its way, single and singly, like a solitary Wild-duck that has set out on its travels a week or more before the general Mustering.—I then thought of sending a full Outline of the Plan to the Edinburgh and London Magazines—but I begin to despond and on the strength of the Apostolic counsel 'whatever ye do, do it in faith' have done nothing.

The Scheme, however, has no analogy to Lectures—I will endeavor to explain it to you as briefly as possible—Personally, it can have no interest for, nor indeed *bearings* of any kind on, you. But it is possible, tho' perhaps not probable, that some one, within the Object and Conditions of the Plan, might occur to you, on whom your opinion or recommendation was likely to have some influence.

There have been three or four Young men (under five and twenty) who within the last five years have believed themselves and have been thought by their Acquaintance, to have derived benefit from their frequent opportunities of conversing, reading, and occasionally corresponding with me—this benefit consisting not merely nor even principally in the information received, but in the improvement and accelerated growth of their faculties, and in the formation, or at least in the grounding, strengthening, and *integration*, as it were, of their whole character. Under this persuasion at least a young man respectable in station and prospective circumstances expressed a strong wish—in fact, has importuned me to suffer him to be with me on any plan of instruction, I should myself think expedient, some one day in each Week—from Noon to 4 or 5 o'clock

---

[1] See note to Letter 1290 for the 'Advertisement' published in the *Courier* on 25 Feb. 1822.

—but as what he could afford would leave it doubtful whether it would compensate for the expenditure of my time & the interruption of my literary pursuits—(in plain English, whether I could not get more by employing the time in writing for the Magazines or the Booksellers)—it was suggested, that by making my intention publicly & generally known I might form a Class of five or six men, who are educating themselves for the Pulpit, the Bar, the Senate, or any of those walks of Life, in which the possession and the display of intellect are of especial importance.—That sort of *Knowlege* which is best calculated to re-appear as Power—all that a Gentleman ought to possess, and most of what it is most desirable that every gentleman should possess—the Root, and Trunk of the Tree, as the Antecedent common to all the different Branches—this conveniently systematized & divided—or to speak more particularly—the precise import of words—the ready command, and quickness in appropriation of words—the principles and laws of Language, as the Organ of Thinking, of appropriate Language, and the inherent forms of the Understanding, 1. as the Canon or formal Outline of all *conclusive reasoning*—2. as the Criterion for the detection of error in all the possible species of conscious or unconscious Sophistry—and lastly, the principles of Reason as the Organ of Discovery, whether in Man or in the science of Nature—with sufficient Psychology, to apply the whole to the Art of Persuasion—whether in writing or public speaking—not forgetting that the constant examples and illustrations that must or would be used in the teaching and enforcing of the above could not but of themselves comprize no mean bodily [body ?] of valuable particular information—or facts—

Such are the intended Subjects—the Mode was—from 12 to 2 or ½ past 2 I meant to *dictate*, each of my Auditors being his own & [my ama]nuensis—the remaining hour & a half t[o be spent in][1] conversation, questions, discussions &c—so as to enable me to form such opinions as would guide me in the private advice to each individually—as well as to all for the regulation of their studies, professional or otherwise.—The *whole* Course would be finished in 2 years ; but each half year contains some important branch, of high and independent Utility. Of course, I could receive no one not in *all* respects respectable—I must see & talk with him first—

The place might be either here or in London, Mr Green having most kindly offered me the use of the drawing Room in his Noble House in Lincoln's Inn Fields.—I should be highly gratified to hear your opinion of the scheme—& to talk with you about it, there not being a man on earth on whose sense and judgement I have so much reliance as I have on yours—But I fear, there is little chance.

[1] MS. torn.

—The Young men of the present Day are well satisfied with themselves as they are—. If you could drop me a single Line, what day
you were *likely* to turn your horse's head this way, without any
positive engagement, I would be certain to be at home and in the
house—

  With respects to Mrs S. believe | me, my dear Sir, | Your's very
  sincerely

                                        S. T. Coleridge

1299. *To Thomas Allsop*

Address: T. Allsop, Esqre | Blandford Place | Pall Mall
MS. New York Public Lib. Pub. with omis. Letters, Conversations and Rec. *180.*
Postmark: Highgate, 18 March 1822.

                           Saturday Morning. [16 March 1822]
                                        Highgate.

My dearest Friend
  Mr Watson is but now returned. I sate up till 12 last night,
Maria not knowing my motive and therefore not having informed
me that if Mr W. was not at home by 10, he was not to be expected.
Of course, I was anxious enough to hear how he had found you.
And vexed I am that it should have been or that you should have
thought it, expedient for you to return to Business and trust yourself in the Warehouse in such a tremulous period of convalescence.
Before you had regained strength enough to support the weight of
defensive armour, when the very Shield would turn traitor and
press down the arm that strove to protend it, to throw yourself
affrontively in the way of your three main enemies, Exposure, Exhaustion, and Anxiety. I intreat and conjure you by all the Rights,
which Love and Elderhood give me, do not repeat this risk on any
call less imperious than that of absolute *duty*. At such a moment,
when Recovery and Relapse make even scales, Expedience forfeits
it's name and quality. I allow of no plea short of Coercion, moral at
least. If I dared doubt the sufficiency of my Spell, I would set off for
Blandford Place and take turns with Mrs A. in watching you.—It is a
comfort, however, to hear that Mr Watson thinks you look not only
better than when he saw you before but more promisingly.

          Si tibi deficiant medici, medici tibi fiant
          Haec tria: Mens hilaris, Requies, Moderata Diaeta—
s the adage of the Schola Salernitana,[1] and his belief and judgement. Would to God, there were any Druggist's or Apothecary's
within the King's Dominions, where I could procure for you the

                  ─────────
                  [1] See Letters 409, 443, 550, and 817.

first ingredient of the Recipe, fresh and genuine. I would soon make up the prescription, have the credit of curing you and then make my fortune by advertising the nostrum under the name of Dr Samsartorius Carbonijugius's Panacea Salernitana Alsopiensis.— You will have thought, I fear, that I had forgotten my promise of sending you Charles Lamb's 'pistola porcina[1]—But it was not so—I should have sent it by the Post but that Mr Gillman had taken it into his custody—had gone out before I came down & did not return till after the Post. On Thursday Night I asked him for it— and he was to have left it out—but forgot it.—I have it now & shall inclose it—but he begs that you will return it as he has no one at hand to take a copy. I can make a Copy for you afterwards if you wish it: for I do not thinking [think?] that bending down your head, more than there's a necessity for, is good for you.—I am interrupted—'a poor Lad, very ragged, he says Mr Dowling[2] has sent him to you to shew you his poetry.'—Well! desire him to step up, Maria!—

Sunday Evening.

My very dear Friend—

As soon as Mr Green left me, Mrs Gillman delivered your letter to me.—I am not sorry therefore that the 'wild Irish Boy' made it too late to finish the above for that day's Post. His name, poor Lad! is Esmond Wilton—his Mother, I guess, was poetical. But he may be reserved for a side dish on our table of Chat when we meet.

In reply to your affectionate letter what can I say but that from all that you say, write or do I receive but two impressions—first, a full, cordial and unqualified assurance of your Love toward me, a genial unclouded faith in the entireness and stedfastness of your more than friendship, sustained and renewed by the consciousness of a responsive Attachment in myself, that blends the affections of Parent, Brother and Friend—

a Love of thee
That seems, yet cannot greater be[3]—

and secondly, impressions of Grief or Joy, according and in proportion to the information, I receive, or the inferences that I draw, respecting your Health, Ease of Heart and Mind, and all the Events, Incidents and Circumstances that affect or are calculated

---

[1] Charles Lamb's ' 'pistola porcina', to Coleridge of 9 Mar. 1822, 'probably led to the immediate composition of the *Elia* essay "A Dissertation [up]on Roast Pig", which was printed in the *London Magazine* for Sept. 1822'. *Lamb Letters*, ii. 317–18. See also *Letters, Conversations and Rec.* 114–15 and 183.

[2] Mr. Dowling, whose wife was Mrs. Kenney's sister, kept a school, presumably at Highgate. See Appendix B, Letter 1013 A.

[3] *The Happy Husband*, lines 23–24, *Poems*, i. 388.

to affect both or either. Only this in addition, whatever else may pass thro' your mind, never from any motive or with any view withhold from me your sorrows, your thoughts, or your feelings—what if they be momentary, winged Thoughts not native, that blowing weather has driven out of their course, & to which your Mind has allowed Thorough-flight, but neither nest, perch, or halting room? —Send them onward to pass thro' mine—and between us both we shall be better able to give a good account of them!—What if they are the offspring of low or perturbed Spirits, the changelings of Ill-health or Disquietude? So much the rather communicate them —when only on the white paper, they are already *out* of you—and when the Letter is gone, they will not stay long behind—the very anticipation of the Answer will have answered them, and superseded the need tho' not the wish of it's Arrival. And shall I not, think you, take them for what they are? With what comfort, with what security, could I receive or read your letters, or you mine, if we either of us had reason to believe, that whatever affliction had befallen, or Discomfort was harrassing or Anxiety was weighing on the Heart, the other would say no word of or about it under the plea of not transplanting thorns—or whatever other excuse a depressed fancy might invent, in order to transmute [a] friendly withholding into a self-sacrifi[ce] of tenderness?—If you had come to stay with me [while] I lay on a bed of pain, it would grieve you in[deed, if]¹ from an imagined duty of not grieving you I should suppress every moan—and not tell you, where my pain was—& whether it was greater or less.—*Grant* that I was rendered anxious, or heavy at heart, or keenly sorrowful by any tidings, you had communicated, respecting yourself! *Should* it not be so? *Ought* it not to be so? Will not the Joy be greater when the cloud is passed off— greater in *kind*, nobler, better—because I should feel, that it was my *right*? And is there not a Dignity and a hidden *Healing* in the Suffering itself—which is soothed in the wish, and tempered in the endeavor of removing, or lessening, or supporting it in the soul of a dear friend?—However trifling my vexations are, yet if they vex me, and I am writing to you, to you will I unbosom them, my dear Allsop—and my serious sorrows and hindrances still less will I keep back from you—General Truths, Discussions, Poems, Queries—all these are parts of my Nature—often uppermost—& when they are so, you have them—& I like well to write to, and to hear from, you on them—but these I might write to the Public—and with all proper Christian Respect for that gentleman I love your little finger better than his whole multitudinous Body.—I have scarcely left room for Mrs Gillman's message—1st. that her not calling arose

¹ MS. torn.

wholly from her fear lest your not expecting her should have fluttered or caused you to exert yourself—2. that her Health of late
taken in connection with her occupations and avocations may &,
she trusts, will plead in her *palliation*, but that this is not the first,
second or third time that she has reproached herself for not having
written to your Sister—which, however, she will no longer delay to
do.—Of this your Sister may be confident that no want, or change
or diminution of Mrs G.['s] Regard & kind recollections have had
any thing to do with her silence.

On Tuesday I fear that I cannot come—but soon I will if only to
arrange a longer sojourn with you—at all events, I will write.—
Give my Love to Mrs Allsop—& tell her, I will try to deserve her's.
—Ever and ever, God bless you, my dearest Friend!

S. T. Coleridge

1300. *To Thomas Allsop*

Address: T. Allsop, Esqre | Blandford Place | Pall Mall
MS. New York Public Lib. Pub. with omis. Letters, Conversations and Rec. *186.*
Postmark: Highgate, 18 April 1822.

Wednesday afternoon [17 April 1822]

My dearest Allsop

There was neither Self nor Unself in the flash or *jet* of pleasurable
sensation, with which I saw the old Tea-Canister
Top surmounting my name, but a mere unreflecting gladness, a sally of inward Welcoming,
on finding you near to me again. I am indebted
to it, however: for this and the dear and
affectionate Letter that sustained and substantiated it, like a Gleam
of Sunshine ushering in a genial South-West and setting all the
Birds a singing while the joy at the recall of the old dry *scathey* Vice-
roy of the discouraged Spring, the Tartar Laird from the North-
East, augments, yet loses itself in, the delight at the arrival of the
long wished for Successor to his native realm, gave a sudden spur
and kindly sting to my Spirits, the restorative effect of which I
felt on rising this morning, as soon after at least, as the pain, that
always greets me on awaking, and never fails to be my Valentine
for every day in the year, had taken it's leave.—

Before I proceed, I must convey to you Mrs Gillman's friendliest
remembrances, and that the anxiety respecting your health is the
one only painful or unpleasing thought connected with the recollection of you. I am sorry to say, that her own health has for
some time past been considerably below the average—and that this

has suffered an accessional *Minus* from a Blow on the left Temple
by running against the edge of a Shutter at Mr Grove's Shop, which
the wind had unfastened. It is still visible, with 'a green and yellow
Melancholy'[1] Bruising at Fairness—but what is far worse, it is
accompanied by a dull pain on the opposite temple and a slight
confusion in the head.—

Charles and Mary Lamb are to dine with us on Sunday next—
and Mr and Mrs Gillman both desire me to ask whether it would be
pleasant, and possible for you and Mrs Allsop to compleat the
party—and if so, whether Mrs Allsop will excuse the shortness of
the Invitation in the first place, and next whether she will be so
good as to let this pass for a more formal application—tho' I hope,
that she will regard as superfluous any re-assurance, how welcome
a Guest she will at all times be at their fire-side & social table—. I
wish very much, that you should come speedily—and so, foreseeing
no objection or obstacle but what may be looked at, according to
the *tact* of the moment, as of an opposite tendency as breaking any
little *surface*-feeling of *newness* on both sides, if any such feeling
there should be on either—and thinking, that it cannot too soon
have the coup de grâce given it—I wish, that it may be in your
power to come to us on Sunday. I will take care to be quite *free* to
enjoy your society from the moment of your arrival—and hope that
you will come in the Highgate Stage in order that Mrs A. may not
be too much tired for me to shew her some of our best Views and
walks–& perhaps, the Nightingales may do me the favor of commencing their ditties on or by that day—for I have daily expected
them. At all events, return me a Line by the next post.—

I had arranged to spend the Afternoon in Blandford Place on
Friday, should I find you at home & disengaged—and this was one
of my purposes in sitting down to write this letter—but while
writing it, I have received a Letter from Mr Stutfield, to apprize me
that particular business obliges him to request me to receive on
Friday instead of Thursday—his regular day.—But I will say no
more, till I hear from you as to Sunday—Since Holy Thursday,
when Mr Jameson[2] met Hartley & obtained a promise from him
that he would instantly write to his Mother and to me—and then
come up to Highgate—he has not been heard of.—Jameson has

---

[1] *Twelfth Night*, ii. iv. 116.

[2] Robert Jameson, a young barrister in London, had been one of Hartley's
boyhood friends at Ambleside. In 1825 he married Anna Brownell Murphy,
the authoress. Jameson and Gillman superintended the 1828 edition of Coleridge's *Poetical Works*. (See Letter 1580.) In 1829 Jameson went out to Domi-
nica as puisne judge. According to Oxford Univ. Press, Toronto, he was
appointed attorney-general of Upper Canada in 1833 and later vice-chancellor
of the Court of Equity, a post he held until his death in 1854.

walked about in all parts of the Town—called on every known
Acquaintance of Hartley's—left Letters for him at Taylor &
Hesse's—all in vain.[1]—The strangest Fears will at times flash
across me—his moody defences of the right of Suicide—his exces-
sive Cowardice of mental pain—&c &c—. But I put my trust in
God—. This is a case, in which Resignation is to be found only in
Prayer—and in this and in the humble Hope, that for the last seven
years at least I have done my best, I seek it.—

Need I say, what Thoughts rush into my mind when I read a
letter from you or think of [your] Love towards me.

God bless you!—Remember me very affectionately to Mrs
Allsop.

Once more, | God bless you, my dear dear Friend! &
S. T. Coleridge

P.S. *Missed the Post by 5 minutes.*

1301. To Robert Southey

MS. Boston Public Lib. Hitherto unpublished.

16 May 1822
Highgate.

Dear Southey

As I am not certain whether Mrs Coleridge will have left Cumberland on her visit Southward[2] before the arrival of Mr Watson, the
Bearer of this Letter, I have taken the liberty of addressing it to you,
for the purpose of procuring for my young friend the pleasure and
what he regards as the honor of being introduced to you. Half an
hour's conversation, or the drinking Tea once at Greta House,
would be the maximum of intrusion on your time, that he or I
would wish.—Had I been writing to Mrs Coleridge *I* should have
told her, that I was in the first instance prepossessed in favor of Mr
Watson by my imagination of his striking likeness to what you
were when I first saw you at Baliol. He has been for the last 18

[1] Taylor and Hessey were the publishers of the *London Magazine*, to which
Hartley Coleridge contributed both poetry and prose during the years 1821–3.
One of his essays, 'On the Poetical Use of the Heathen Mythology' (*London
Magazine*, Feb. 1822), pleased the Wordsworths 'very much'. Dorothy thought
the style 'wonderful for so young a man—so little of effort—& no affectation'.
The Correspondence of Henry Crabb Robinson with the Wordsworth Circle, ed.
Edith J. Morley, 2 vols., 1927, i. 115, and E. L. Griggs, *Hartley Coleridge: His
Life and Work*, 1929, p. 94 n.

[2] In February Coleridge had expected Mrs. Coleridge and Sara for a visit
'at the close of the ensuing Spring', but they did not leave Keswick until
6 Nov. 1822. They arrived at Highgate on 3 Jan. 1823. See *Minnow among
Tritons*, ed. Stephen Potter, 1934, p. 99, and Letters 1294 and 1324.

months a House-mate of mine, as a sort of temporary Partner of
Mr Gillman's rather than as an ordinary Assistant—and his remaining so long I have some reason to think owing in great measure
to the advantages, which he believes himself to receive from his
daily intercourse with me, and from the weekly attendance on my
Lectures on the principles of Reasoning, or Logic as a Canon, a
Criterion, and lastly an Organ of the mind.—Of his manners, morals
and gentlemanly demeanor I cannot easily speak too highly—and
when I add his unusual φιλαλήθεια, the solidity and single-minded-
ness of his pursuits both professional & for purposes of common
Interest, I can without apprehension venture to assure you, that
he is not unworthy of the introduction, I have given him.

I expect to have my introductory Work, on the art and Science of
Conclusive Discourse, or the Laws of Thinking & Inquiring, with
the rules of Acquiring, *testing*, arranging and applying Knowlege,
ready for the Press by August, with the History of Logic prefixed
and a Glossary of Philosophical Terms in the order of the Thoughts
but with an alphabetical Index, as the Appendix.—This done, I
shall attempt the publication of my (Anti-Grotian) Assertion of the
Christian Religion on the principle stated in a Note to my first Lay-
Sermon.—

Of Politics who dares now speak at all? It is enough to wonder.
Has the World got the *Staggers*?

Remember me affectionately to Mrs Southey and Mrs Lovell,
and to Edith—and believe me

with sincere regard and respect | Your obliged
S. T. Coleridge

1302. *To William Mudford*

Address: Wm. Mudford, Esqre | 19. Great Russell Street | Covent Garden
MS. Cornell University Lib. Hitherto unpublished.
Postmark: Highgate, 28 May 1822.

Tuesday Noon. [28 May 1822] Highgate
My dear Sir

I have but this moment received your note which I ought to have
had early enough this morning to have answered it by the 10 o/clock
Post—instead of the 4 o/clock P.M.—these being our only Post
Hours.—Nothing unforeseen and irresistible preventing, I will not
fail to wait on you, Saturday next, ½ past 5, in acceptance of your
kind invitation.

I am much of your correspondent, CRANMER's mind—tho' I flatter myself enough to suspect, on other and more statesman-like

Grounds. That the unqualified admission of the Romanists (for
'*Catholics*' is an impudent Assumption on one party and a most
mischievous concession on the other—*Words* (*they* say) are not
Things—No! I reply. Words are not *Things*; but they are *Spirits*
and *living Agents*[1] that are seldom misused without avenging themselves)—to political power will and cannot but lead to the Establishment of the Pontificial Hierarchy, I am fully convinced: and if
there were no other Alternative but this or the separation of
Ireland, I should not hesitate a moment in voting for the latter as
the less and more doubtful Calamity. Ad isthaec, qualiacunque
primo videantur aspectu, attendas quaeso, ut qui tibi forsan insanire videar, saltem quibus insaniam rationibus, cognoscas![2] At all
events, you will not, I trust, suspect me of any *religious* bigotry in
the matter, or that I should exclude any man from a seat in the
Cabinet for worshipping a Wafer, more than for worshipping the
M. of L. & even higher up. Qy. whether the Virgin Mary might not
be as an object of *private* devotion, without much loss, substituted
for the MSS. of C——? ?[3]

Your's, my dear Sir! sincerely
S. T. Coleridge.

1303. *To John Dawes*

MS. Mr. A. H. B. Coleridge. Pub. with omis. E. L. G. ii. 306. Only an incomplete rough draft of Coleridge's letter has survived.

From June 1821 when he left the Montagus for Highgate without telling
them of his whereabouts, Hartley Coleridge became increasingly a source of
vexation and despair to his father. Indeed, Hartley's procrastination, his pecuniary distress and 'disgraceful dependence', his fatalistic views and fits of
despondency, his 'moody defences of the right of Suicide', his frequent dis-
appearances, and undoubtedly a growing habit of intemperance convinced
Coleridge that above all else his son must be removed from the pitfalls of London
and placed in a situation where he would have regular employment. Thus it was
that Coleridge gratefully responded to the 'kind invitation' of the Rev. John
Dawes to have Hartley become an assistant in the school at Ambleside. He felt
honour bound, however, to express his 'inmost convictions' concerning
Hartley's peculiar temperament, and the present letter was torn 'piecemeal'
from his brain, 'a bit one day and another bit a day or two after'. It contains
not only an introspective defence of himself as a father, but also a remarkable
characterization of his son, even to the pathos of the conclusion: 'Of all the

---

[1] Cf. *Aids to Reflection*, 1825, Preface, xi: 'For if words are not THINGS, they
are LIVING POWERS.'

[2] This sentence from Bruno's *De Immenso et Innumerabilibus* is quoted in
Letters 718 and 722, in *The Friend*, 21 Sept. 1809, p. 87, and as a motto in the
title-page of *The Statesman's Manual*, 1816.

[3] It has been suggested that by 'M. of L.' Coleridge means 'Mother of the
Lord'; by 'MSS. of C——', 'Mass of Christ'.

Waifs, I ever knew, Hartley is the least likely and the least calculated to lead any human Being astray by his example.'

In making his arrangements with Dawes, Coleridge had to withstand bitter opposition from the households at Grasmere and Keswick. Southey was writing to John Taylor Coleridge of his and Wordsworth's unwillingness even to see Hartley, Wordsworth himself was corresponding directly with Gillman, and Mrs. Coleridge, whom Southey had warned that Hartley's coming to Keswick 'could not be', was sending frantic letters to Coleridge. Wordsworth's active interference in a matter so vital to Hartley's welfare was particularly galling to Coleridge and accounts for the indignant and denunciatory statements in his letters to Allsop. Yet this hostility in the North, disillusioning as it was for Coleridge, was far more unfortunate for Hartley. 'The going to Ambleside', he pathetically told his father, 'in the face of such unfavourable sentiments on the part of some, certainly weighed upon my heart', and he pleaded for a further trial in London. Suddenly in July 1822, during his brother's illness, he disappeared. Later he wrote of the period which followed: 'I must have had a hard heart and an indomitable spirit not to despair and die in that dark September.' Coleridge himself was 'almost broken-hearted' over his failure to effect anything for Hartley, and in early October he set off for Walmer, leaving behind him what he had 'no longer power to make better or worse'. In the end, however, Hartley was persuaded to leave London, probably through the good offices of Gillman, and by 19 November he was teaching in the school at Ambleside. 'I am now fixt', he reported to his brother several months later, 'in some-thing like a profession. . . . I have found more kindness both here and elsewhere than I have earn'd. I have been deliver'd, providentially deliver'd, when I was hopeless of delivering myself. . . . I receive kind and cheerful letters from father, and mother, and dear Sara. I am in no immediate pecuniary distress—I am free from embarrassment, and need not fear for my future independence. All these, and more than all these, are claims upon my gratitude.' See Letters 1266, 1287, 1289, 1293, 1300, 1304, 1310, 1312, 1314–15, and 1317–19; E. L. Griggs, *Hartley Coleridge: His Life and Work*, 1929, p. 97; and *Letters of Hartley Coleridge*, 75 and 78.

[Late May 1822][1]

. . . any presumptuous reliance even on efforts of indisputable propriety and duty. Too often the best result will be the consciousness of having done our best.) These are questions, my dear Sir! into which I shall not enter at present—. But I can not help questioning the *special* applicability of the remark or regret to myself or to either of my Sons—least of all, to Hartley. Giving no trouble to any one—to no one opposing himself—happy from his earliest infancy, 'a spirit of Joy dancing on an aspen Leaf'[2]—to what better can I appeal than to Mr Wordsworth's own beautiful lines addressed to H. C. six years old?—From the hour, he left the Nurse's Arm, Love followed him like his Shadow. All, all, among whom he lived, all who saw him themselves, were delighted with him—in nothing requisite for his age, was he backward—and what was my fault?

[1] On 30 May Coleridge informed Allsop that he had 'finished and sent off' his letter to Dawes.

[2] Coleridge thus described Hartley in 1801. See Letter 376.

That I did not, unadvised & without a hint from any one of my friends or acquaintances, interrupt his quiet untroublesome enjoyment by forcing him to *sit still*, and *inventing* occasions of trying his obedience—that I did not without and against all *present* reason, and at the certainty of appearing cruel, and arbitrary not only to the child but to all with whom he lived, interrupt his little comforts, and sting him into a will of resistance to my will, in order that I might *make* opportunities of crushing it?—Whether after all that has occurred, which surely it was no crime not to have fore-seen at a time when a Foreboding of a less sombre character was passionately retracted, as 'too [industrious] folly', as 'vain and causeless Melancholy'[1]—whether I should act thus, were it all to come over again, I am more than doubtful. Can I help remembering that so far from having fractious, disobedient or *indulged* children, I could count the times on the fingers of one hand, in which I had ever occasion to compel their obedience or punish their disobedience by a *blow* or a harsh sound? If I but lowered my voice, Hartley would say—Pray, don't speak low, Father!—and did or ceased to do as he was told.—Can I forget, how often, when I had expressed myself sorry to see such or such a child so indulged, and referred to the effects on it's Temper, I was told—that I could not expect that all children should be like mine?—At the ordinary time my Boys were sent to school, and found a Father under the name of a Master in You.[2] You, dear Sir! can best say, whether they were backward for their age, or gave proofs of having been neglected either in moral principles or in good dispositions—whether they were beyond boys in general undisciplined and disobedient. As soon as I was informed of Hartley's passionateness & misconduct towards his Brother, you will do me the justice to answer for me, whether I was not even more agitated and interested than in your opinion the case warranted—and whether I left any means untried to bring Hartley to a sense of his error.—A sad sad interval followed for me from the ill-fated hour, I left the North with Mr Montague, speedily as I

---

[1]   O too industrious folly!
    O vain and causeless melancholy!
    Nature will either end thee quite;
    Or, lengthening out thy season of delight,
    Preserve for thee, by individual right,
    A young lamb's heart among the full-grown flocks.

    (*To H. C. Six Years Old*, lines 19–24.)

[2] From 1808, when Hartley was placed in the school at Ambleside, Dawes had taken particular interest in his unusual pupil, and in 1810 he asked Coleridge for the 'honour' of instructing the boy 'without receiving any other remuneration than what arises from the pleasure of the performance'. (See Letters 713, 715, 807, and 856.)

supposed to return, and Hartley's first Vacation which he spent
with me at Calne—Whatever else has been said—how far truly,
and how far calumniously, I humbly leave it to my merciful God
and Redeemer to determine for me—it will not surely be said, that
the two Lads were left friendless, or under the protection of Friends
incompetent, or whom I dared believe myself permitted to apprehend
unwilling, to observe their goings-on, during their holidays or
holiday-tides—. Since the time of Hartley's first arrival at Calne to
the present day I am not conscious of having failed in any point of
duty, of admonition, persuasion, intreaty, warning, or even (tho'
ever reluctantly, I grant) of parental injunction—and of repeating
the same whenever it could be done without the almost certain consequence of baffling the end in view. I noticed, and with concern,
in Hartley and afterwards in Derwent a pugnacity in self-opinion,
which ever had been alien from my own character, the weakness of
which consisted in the opposite fault of facility, a readiness to
believe others my superiors and to surrender my own judgement to
their's—but in part, this appeared to me the fault of the[ir] ages,
and in part, I could not refuse an inward assent, tho' I mourned
over it in silence, to the complaint made by others—both at Calne
and at Highgate—of impressions made on their minds with regard
to myself, not more unjust in themselves than unfortunate for
them—. As far as the *opinions* & suppositions went, they indeed
speedily underwent a revolution, soon after they had been with me
& had compared them with those of the respectable Persons, who
had known me day & night uninterruptedly year after year—And
in Hartley, at least, the revolution was compleat. But the habit of
feeling remained—I appeal to God & to their own consciences and
to all good men who have observed my conduct towards them
whether I have aught to condemn myself for, except perhaps a too
delicate manner of applying to their affections and understandings
and moral sense—and by which, it is to be feared, I have in Hartley's case unwittingly fostered that cowardice as to mental pain
which forms the one of the two calamitous defects in his disposition.[1]
—For to whatever extent the 'indoles pervicax et reluctatrix'
betrayed itself during his sojourn at Calne, and afterwards on his
first arrival at Highgate, I have the testimony of our sensible and
exemplary Minister, the Revd. S. Mence, formerly Tutor at Exeter
[Trinity] College, and who took a lively interest in both my sons,
that it was less & less apparent at each successive visit, and but

[1] And this, my dear Sir! is the point which I had principally in view in this
etter—and I have to ask your indulgence for having been diverted from it by
the *smart* of the recollections, which the occasion of writing had conjured up.
[Sentence cancelled in MS.]

a few months before the unhappy fall-out at Oriel he had, in common with my excellent Friends, Mr and Mrs Gillman, warmly congratulated me on the striking improvement in Hartley's manners, above all in the points of Docility and Self-control.

But let it be, that I am rightly reproached for my negligence in withstanding and taming his Self-will—is this the main Root of the Evil? I could almost say—Would to God, it were! for then I should have more Hope. But alas! it is the absence of a Self, it is the want or torpor of Will, that is the mortal Sickness of Hartley's Being, and has been, for good & for evil, his character—his moral *Idiocy*—from his earliest Childhood—Yea, & hard it is for me to determine which is the worse, *morally* considered, I mean: the selfishness from the want or defect of a manly Self-love, or the selfishness that springs out of the excess of a worldly Self-interest. In the eye of a Christian and a Philosopher, it is difficult to say, which of the two appears the greater deformity, the relationless, unconjugated, and intransitive Verb Impersonal with neither Subject nor Object, neither governed or governing, or the narrow proud Egotism, with neither Thou or They except as it's Instruments or Involutes. *Prudentially*, however, and in regard to the supposed good and evil of this Life, the balance is woefully against the former, both because the Individuals so characterized are beyond comparison the smaller number, and because they are sure to meet with their bitterest enemies in the latter. Especially, if the poor dreamy Mortals chance to be amiable in other respects and to be distinguished by more than usual Talents and Acquirements. Now this, my dear Sir! is precisely the case with poor Hartley. He has neither the resentment, the ambition, nor the Self-love of a man—and for this very reason he is too often as selfish as a Beast—and as unwitting of his own selfishness. With this is connected his want of a salient point, a self-acting principle of Volition—and from this, again, arise his shrinking from, *his shurking*, whatever requires and demands the exertion of this inward power, his cowardice as to mental pain, and the procrastination consequent on these. His occasional Wilfulness results from his weakness of will aided indeed, now and then, by the sense of his intellectual superiority and by the sophistry which his ingenuity supplies and which is in fact the brief valiancy of Self-despondence.—

Such is the truth & the fact as to Hartley—a truth, I have neither extenuated nor sought to palliate. But equally true it is, that he is innocent, most kindly natured, exceedingly good-tempered, in the management & instruction of Children excels any young man, I ever knew; and before God I say it, he has not to my knowlege a single vicious inclination—tho' from absence & nervousness he needs to be guarded against filling his wine-glass too often—. But this temptation *at present* besets him only under the stimulus of society and eager conversation—just as was the case with his Grandfather, one of the most temperate men alive in his ordinary practice.—His Cousin, the Revd W. Hart Coleridge, assured me that nothing could be more correct, or manageable than Hartley was during the two or three weeks, that he lately passed under his eye—that what he wanted, & what was indispensable, was Kindness without too much Delicacy, Kindness without any regard to his immediate feelings of pain.—Whatever else is to be done or prevented, London he must not live in—the number of young men who will seek his company *to be amused,* his own want of pride, & the opportunity of living or imagining rather that he can live from hand to mouth by writing for Magazines &c—these are Ruin for him.—I have but one other remark to make—that of all the *Waifs,* I ever knew, Hartley is the least likely and the least calculated to lead any human Being astray by his example. He may exhibit a Warning—but assuredly he never will afford an inducement.—

I could not think of his proceeding to the North in acceptance of your kind invitation, without putting you in possession of my inmost convictions. In opening out my heart I may, I fear, have betrayed Symptoms of a wounded Spirit. But the errors of a wounded Spirit are what you, my dear Sir! will be least inclined to judge with harshness.

One assurance I dare give—namely, that at present my Son earnestly looks forward to the hope of making himself agreeable & that he would be most happy should it be in his power to become in any way aidant or serviceable. Under all events I must ever feel and profess myself,

my dear Sir, | with unfeigned respect & regard | Your obliged & grateful

S. T. Coleridge

1304. *To Thomas Allsop*

Address: T. Allsop, Esqre | Blandford Place | Pall Mall.
MS. New York Public Lib. Pub. with omis. Letters, Conversations and Rec. *192.*
Postmark: Highgate, 30 May 1822.

Thursday Afternoon [30 May 1822]
Highgate

My very dear Friend

On my arrival at Highgate after our last parting, I ought to have written. Not so much, however, (or rather, as a matter of *conscience,* not at all) respecting your & Mrs A's dining with us: for I had taken that as quite settled, and imagine that you misunderstood Mr

Gillman's words which were addressed exclusively to Charles & Mary
Lamb. But I ought to have written, were it only that I had fully
resolved to do so—and where I feel that I have not done what I
ought, and what you would have done, in my place, I will, as indeed TOO *safely* to make any merit of it I may do, leave the palliative and extenuating circumstances to your kindness to think of.—
This only let me say—that mournful as my experience of Messrs.
Southey & Wordsworth in my own immediate concerns had been,
of the latter especially, I was not prepared for their late behaviour
—or, to use Anster's words on the occasion, for 'so piteous a lower-
ing of human Nature' as the contents of Mr W's Letters to Mr G.
were calculated to produce. I have *at length*—for I really tore it out
of my brain, as it were, piecemeal—a bit one day and another bit a
day or two after—finished and sent off a letter of two $\frac{1}{4}$ *large* &
close-writting [written?] Sheets = 9 sides, equal to 12 of this size
paper, to Mr Dawes, Hartley's old friend & School-master at
Ambleside—which I will shew you the rough Copy of when we meet.[1]
—The exceeding Kindness & uncalculating instantaneous and decisive generous Friendship of the Gillmans—and the presence of *you* to
my Thoughts—prevent all approach to misanthropy in my feelings;
but for that reason render those feelings more acutely painful. If
I did not seem to myself to know, that Genius, like Reason tho' not
perhaps so entirely, is rather a Presence vouchsafed, like a guardian Spirit, to an Individual, which departs whenever the Evil Self
becomes decisively predominant—and not like Talents or the
Powers of the Understanding, a personal property—the contemplation of Wordsworth's late & present state of Head & Heart
would overwhelm me.—But I must not represent my neglect in
writing as worse than I myself hold it to be. For I feel that I could
not—nay, I know that dear Mrs Gillman would not have let me—
omit it, had we not known that you were so busily engaged. And I
am right glad likewise to hear that your Uncle has called.—

Now as to the Bill. That which will best suit you will be of most
comfort to me: and if I could be sure that the payment in November would not embarrass or in any way *push* you, I have little
doubt that we could get it discounted. As it is, Mr Gillman will not
let it pass out of his possession—will not, I mean, draw on you for
the amount mentioned at the assigned date, unless he wants it—
while as far as I am concerned, it will be the same as if I had put the
100£ in his hands—so that I *shall* have used it—. But if he does
want [it], he will first write to inform you. The 50£ Bill we will
restore to you the first time, we see you.[2]—You deprecate acknow-

[1] See preceding letter.
[2] Coleridge had received £50 from Allsop in Sept. 1821. See Letter 1277.

legements—and I *utter* none. On Saturday I am obliged to dine in town with Mr Mudford, the Editor of the Courier: and will contrive to see you, about One o'clock—when I will talk over all the rest. My kind love to Mrs Allsop—I look forward with an unexpected freshness of heart to my God-child—Mrs Gillman joins with me in all that is of kind and friendly Wishing & Remembrance—

God bless you, my dear Friend | and your affectionate

S. T. Coleridge

P.S. Charles & Mary Lamb and *Mr* (not Mrs) Green dine with us on Sunday next: and are to see Matthews' Dramatic Picture Gallery. Can you & Mrs Allsop join the party? Or if Mrs A's Health should make this hazardous or too great an exertion, can you come yourself?—I am sure, *she* will forgive me for putting the question—. At all events, be so good as to return Mrs Gillman an answer *tomorrow*, at least as soon as Mrs Allsop has received the Box, Mrs G. forgot to send to day.—

1305. *To Unknown Correspondent*

MS. Mr. W. Hugh Peal. Hitherto unpublished.

Lincoln's Inn
Tuesday afternoon
18 June 1822.

Dear Sir

Mr B. Montagu has almost given me courage enough to hope, that you will not be offended with me, as impertinent or obtrusive, in intreating, as a personal favor & honor to me, your support of the Bill,[1] described in the inclosed statement, tho' I have neither directly or indirectly the least personal interest in it's success—or indeed any interest but what a good man is bound to feel in a measure which he believes to be in the highest degree desirable for the orderliness, respectability, and (generally) the moral and social Wants of the Hamlet, in which he resides—and the opposition to which he KNOWS to have been factious in it's origin, and to be (to

[1] With the consent of the bishop of London, the governors of the Free Grammar School at Highgate petitioned Parliament on 4 Mar. 1822 for permission to bring in a Bill authorizing them 'to pull down their present Chapel, and to erect a new Chapel, and also for the purpose of giving the Master of the said school, who is also Minister of the said Chapel, the Cure of Souls in the said hamlet and its vicinity, and for constituting the same a consolidated Chapelry for ecclesiastical purposes'. A Bill in compliance with their wishes passed the House of Lords on 11 June 1822, and was sent to the House of Commons. There it met with bitter opposition. It was read for the first time on 12 June, but on the 20th the second reading was put off until 'this day six

use Lord Shaftesbury's[1] Words addressed to the Solicitor for the Opponents) 'beyond all his former experience frivolous in it's pretexts, and unprincipled in it's measures'. The Conduct of the Bishop of London has been most generous—and if Bills like these deserve the name of '*Bishops' Jobs*' would to heaven, Jobs Episcopal were of more frequent occurrence. The second Reading comes on tomorrow (Wednesday) Afternoon,[2] four o'clock—& I am so well aware of the probability of the inconveniency of your attendance at so early an hour and on an occasion of no public importance that I must attempt to excuse one request by another—that you will accept my assurance of the unfeigned Admiration & true Respect with which I am, dear Sir,

Your obliged Servt

S. T. Coleridge

1306. *To H. F. Cary*

Address: Revd. Mr Carey | Chiswick
MS. Pierpont Morgan Lib. Hitherto unpublished.
Postmark: ⟨19⟩ June ⟨1822.⟩

[19 June 1822][3]

My very dear Mr Carey

I was about to set off when lo! and behold! I find or rather Mrs Gillman has found *for* me, that the Invitation was for *last* Wednesday, *12*th of June.—But, my dear Friend! it was on last Wednesday Afternoon that I received your kind Letter.—I have no time to write more; but that I will very soon come over & enjoy a few days with you—

All our Loves to Mrs Carey—

God bless you and your's | with sincerest respect, regard and affection

S. T. Coleridge

months'. On 1 July 1822 the Bill was reintroduced and read for the first time. It was read a second time on 5 July, but had failed to reach a third reading when Parliament was prorogued on 6 Aug. 1822. See *Journals of the House of Lords*, lv, and *Journals of the House of Commons*, lxxvii. For details concerning a second parliamentary Bill in 1830 see notes to Letter 1690.

[1] Cropley Ashley Cooper, 6th Earl of Shaftesbury (1768–1851), succeeded to the earldom in 1811. At this time he was chairman of committees in the House of Lords.

[2] Actually Thursday afternoon, 20 June 1822. See Letters 1307–8.

[3] Although this letter is endorsed 'Mr Coleridge June 18th 1822', it was written, as the contents show, on Wednesday, 19 June.

(236)

1307. *To Unknown Correspondent*

MS. Wedgwood Museum. Hitherto unpublished.

Wednesday Night [19 June 1822][1]
Highgate

Dear Sir

A good man, I should think, could not but be glad to stand high in the respect and admiration of a Country, were it only that it enables him in obliging to make a man proud of having been obliged and justly more respectable in his own eyes in proportion as he feels delight and genial stirrings of heart in thinking highly and gratefully of a Superior. Yet I cannot suppress a sort of repugnance at the thought of again applying to your kindness, tho' I do not know how to refuse Mr Kinderley's and the other Governors' urgent request that I should ask your Support on tomorrow (Thursday) Afternoon. The Objection had been started in the House of Lords; but the Law Officers on being consulted had decided that it was not a Money Bill, as no money is asked in the Bill—it having been granted by Commissioners already authorized by the House to grant it.—Of the Gentlemen who oppose the measure, I have repeatedly inquired what their *Object* was; but from no one of them received an intelligible answer—except indeed that they thought it would be an advantage to the Hamlet to have a School like Harrow, or Winchester, instead of 150 ragged Pauper-Boys.[2]

Permit me to assure you of the very high sense which the Governors (with all of whom I have conversed, except Lord Mansfield) entertain of the value and import[ance] of your support, and of your kindness in having intended it—

With warm respect | I remain, dear Sir | Your obliged & grateful
S. T. Coleridge

[1] This letter is endorsed 1822.

[2] In his unfinished *Logic* Coleridge contrasts the Free Grammar School at Highgate with Christ's Hospital: 'The charters and other records of our oldest schools, both of those exclusively intended for the instruction of the more numerous class in and for their own rank (exempli gratia Sir Roger Cholmondely's School at Highgate, founded in Elizabeth's reign) and those of a mixed character, in which provisions were made for raising a certain number of the more promising scholars into a higher rank, and qualifying them for the learned professions (among which Christ's Hospital, never by me to be named without reverence, stands prominent) furnish striking proofs, how highly our great ancestors, the Fathers of our Church and the lights and pillars of Protestantism throughout the world, appreciated the advantages of learning, *in conjunction with common Arithmetic*, the A B C and the rudiments of Grammar, independent of any further progress in the learned languages and without the remotest view to the study of the books therein written, or to what we now call *Classical Scholarship*.' Alice D. Snyder, *Coleridge on Logic and Learning*, 1929, pp. 105–6.

1308. *To C. A. Tulk*

Address: C. A. Tulk, Esqre. M.P., | 19. Duke Street | [in another hand]
Westminster
MS. Mr. W. Hugh Peal. Hitherto unpublished.

> Highgate
> Wednesday Night
> 19 June 1822

My dear Sir

May I without impropriety take the liberty of intreating your attendance at the House, tomorrow afternoon (Thursday) 4 o'clock in support of our Highgate Bill? I have indeed no other interest in it's success than what a good man ought to feel in a measure which he believes requisite for the orderliness, respectability, and moral & social Wants of the Place, he lives in—and the opposition to which measure he *knows* to be frivolous in it's pretexts and un-principled in it's means—in short, groundless, objectless, and malignant—. But this is the very sort of Interest, as to which *you* are most certain to sympathize with,

My dear Sir, | with unfeigned and most | affectionate Esteem & Regard | Your obliged Friend

> S. T. Coleridge

P.S. My best remembrances to Mrs Tulk—and my Love to all her's and your's.

1309. *To Thomas Allsop*

Address: T. Allsop, Esqre | Blandford Place | Pall Mall
MS. New York Public Lib. Pub. with omis. Letters, Conversations and Rec. 195.
Postmark: Highgate, 29 June 1822.

> Saturday [29 June 1822]

My dear Friend

As fervent a Prayer, as glow-trembling a Joy, Thanks-giving that seeks to steady itself by Prayer and Prayer that dissolves into Thanks and Gladness, as ever eddied in, and streamed onward from, of Love and Friendship for Pain and Dread, for Travail of Body and Spirit, passed over, and a Mother smiling over the First-born at her Bosom—have sped toward you, from the moment I opened your Letter! For as if there had been a Light suffused along the paper at that part, 'birth of a Daughter after a very short labour' were the first words, I saw. Well-pleased? To be sure, you are. It was scarcely a week ago, that—during the only hour free from Visits, Visitors and Visitations that we have had to ourselves for I don't know how long—Mrs Gillman and I had settled the point: and after a strict, patient and impartial Poll of the Pros and Cons on both sides, a Girl it was to be—and a Girl was returned by a very large majority of Wishes. But as Wishes, like Strawberries, do not bear carriage well, or at least require to be poised on the *head*, I will send a scanty specimen of the Reasons, by way of Hansel.—Imprimis: a Girl takes five times as much spoiling to spoil her. Item: it is a great advantage both in respect of Temper, Manners, and the Quickening of the Faculties for a Boy to have a Sister or Sisters a year or two older than himself. But I devote this brief Scroll to Feeling—so no more of disquisition—except it be, to declare the entire co-incidence of my experience with your's as to the very rare Occurrence of strong and deep Feeling in conjunction with free power and vivacity in the expression of it. The most eminent Tragedians, Garrick for instance, are known to have had their emotions as much at command and almost as much on the surface, as the muscles of their Countenances—and the French, who are all actors, are proverbially heartless. Is it that it is a false and feverous state for the Center to live in the Circumference? The vital warmth seldom rises to the surface in the form of sensible Heat without becoming hectic and inimical to the Life within, the only source of real sensibility. Eloquence itself, I speak of it as habitual and *at call*, too often is, and is always like to engender, a species of Histrionism. In one of my juvenile poems, (On a Friend who died of a Frenzy-fever, p. 34.)[1] you will find, that I was jealous of this in myself—and that it is, as I trust, it is, otherwise, I attribute mainly to the following causes—A naturally at once searching and communicative disposition—the necessity of reconciling the restlessness of a[n] ever-working Fancy with an intense craving after a resting-place for my Thoughts in some *principle*, that was derived from Experience, but of which all other Knowleges should be but so many repetitions under various limitations, even as circles, squares, triangles, &c are but so many positions of space— and lastly, that my eloquence was most commonly excited by the desire of running away and hiding myself from my personal & inward feelings, and not for the expression of them, while doubtless this very effort of fleeing gave a passion & glow to my Thoughts and Language on subjects of a general nature, that they would not otherwise have had. I fled in a circle still overtaken by the Feelings, from which I was evermore fleeing, with my back turned toward them—but above all, my growing deepening conviction of transcendency of the moral to the intellectual, and the inexpressible

---

[1] In Letter 69 Coleridge quotes the *Lines on a Friend*. Lines 21–36 appear on p. 34 of the 1796 edition of Coleridge's *Poems*.

comfort and inward Strength which I experience myself to derive as often as I contemplate Truth realized into Being by a human Will—so that as I cannot love without esteem, neither can I esteem without loving. Hence I *love* but few—but those I love as my soul— for I feel that without them I should—not indeed cease to be kind, and effluent; but—by little and little become a soul-less fixed Star, receiving no rays nor influences into my being, a solitude, which I so tremble at that I cannot attribute it even to the Divine Nature.—

I will not fail to spend Sunday Sen'night with you: for that, I suppose, you meant.

*God*father or not—(have not Girls God-fathers?) the little Lady shall be to me a dear Daughter—and I will make her love me by loving her own Papa and Mama.—

It is with so much reluctan[ce] that I mingle any thing sad with this Le[tter] Gratulant, that were we not assured of his Amendment I should conceal for the present that poor Derwent has been confined to his Bed since Monday, when he came—with a high fever.

Mrs Gillman, you will know without words from me, joins in my joy & best wishes—Mr Gillman is unwell with a bowel-complaint—

God bless you or the Post will be gone—

								S. T. Coleridge

1310. *To C. A. Tulk*

Address: Charles Augustus Tulk, Esqre. M.P. | 19 Duke Street | [in another hand] Westminster
MS. Maine Historical Society. Hitherto unpublished.

								1 July 1822
								Highgate

My dear Sir

I should have returned your valuable Essay with the thoughts suggested by it's perusal, some days ago, but that in addition to my necessary avocations (*Brodt-wissenschaften,* as the Germans say) with Pupils, I have had to nurse my Second Son, Derwent, who came here last Monday week with a fever that attacked him on the preceding Saturday—so that next Saturday will be the 14th day— instantly took to his bed, and will, it is too probable, be confined to it till the Disease (a remittent, or 21 days fever) has run it's whole course. Unless it should degenerate into a low or typhoid character, Mr Gillman entertains no apprehensions of the Result—but his Brother happening unfortunately to be with us, and Derwent not

meaning to stay here more than 3 or 4 days, a small Bed room had
been hired, merely for his sleeping—and as he cannot bear to be
left alone, all the time, I can spare, is occupied in going backward
and forward & taking turns with Hartley in sitting by him.—I will,
however, devote to morrow evening in writing down the least un-
important of my small criticisms and transmit them with the MSS
before the end of the week.—

Permit me to intreat your attendance on Friday Afternoon, if
your convenience does not prevent, and your support, if (as I hope)
your judgement allow, of our Highgate Bill which is then to be read
the second time. Assuredly, the Governors & Trustees have not been
fortunate in their legal Advocates—or never could the Attorney
General have given his Fiat to the Chancery Suit[1]—which was

---

[1] The committee organized in 1821 by the opponents of the governors of the
Free Grammar School at Highgate not only offered strenuous opposition to the
parliamentary Bill of 1822 but also initiated a suit in the Court of Chancery.
(See Letters 1284, 1305, and 1307–8.) John H. Lloyd describes the legal action
as follows: 'At the time the [parliamentary] Bill was introduced, informations
exhibited by the Attorney-General, on the relation of the Rev. H. B. Owen,
B.D., against the Earl of Mansfield and others, the then Wardens and Governors of the Free School, in their individual capacity, and the Master of the
School, and also against the Wardens and Governors in their corporate capacity, were pending in the High Court of Chancery, whereby an administration
of the charity funds in accordance with a decree of the Court was sought to be
obtained.' *The History . . . of Highgate*, 1888, p. 146.

It was not until Dec. 1823 and Jan. 1824 that hearings were held under
Lord Eldon in the Court of Chancery. In the course of the testimony the
attorneys representing the relators and those retained by the governors argued
the case on the basis of the various sixteenth-century documents pertaining to
the Free Grammar School at Highgate and to the chapel attached to it. (See
headnote to Letter 1276.) In summarizing the case Lord Eldon, the lord
chancellor, 'found, by strict reference to the original deeds and the letters
patent of Elizabeth, that the grant was made absolutely for the maintenance
of a free grammar-school', and said that 'a grammar-school, according to all
decisions ever known in suits as to charitable trusts, meant a school for the
teaching of the Greek and Latin tongues'. Concerning the restoration of charitable trusts 'to the uses for which they were originally designed', Lord Eldon
went on to say: 'Whenever the object could be ascertained by reference to the
words of the original grant, . . . it would be the duty of the Court to restore the
charity to the condition in which it originally stood, and in which the founder
meant that it should stand, for the will of the founder was the only law by
which the Court could then proceed. Here was an intention most expressly
declared by Sir Roger Cholmondeley to found a free grammar-school for the
teaching and instruction of 40 boys, with a chapel, land and revenues assigned
for its support: here were the deeds of feoffment, the Queen's letters patent,
the Bishop of London's grant of the chapel, together with writings signed by
his successor, clearly affirming that grant; in all of which the grammar-school
was recited as the positive object of the trust; and in many of them the wording of
them expressly declared that the chapel, lands, and revenues were to be for the
benefit of the school, and the better education and teaching of the boys, "and

filed for the express purpose of *making* an objection to the Bill in
Parliament, and was never thought of till after the Bill had been
prepared & launched—

Present my respectfully affectionate remembrances to Mrs Tulk
and believe me,

my dear Sir, | with persistent esteem and | increasing Sympathy |
Your obliged Friend
S. T. Coleridge

1311. *To Horace Twiss*[1]

Address: H. Twiss Esq—[in another hand] M.P. | Serle St.
MS. Cornell University Lib. Hitherto unpublished.

Highgate
1 July 1822.

Dear Sir

If I am taking an improper freedom in thus obtruding on you, you
must halve the blame—and award the larger half to the impor-
tunity of our Chapel Governors and Trustees which has extorted
from me the promise that I would convey to you their grateful
sense of the support which you have given to their Bill and their
entreaties that you would continue it at the second Reading—i.e.

for no other purpose whatsoever".' Referring to the chapel attached to the
school, Lord Eldon was most explicit: 'There was nothing . . . upon which an
assumption could be grounded that the chapel was in the care of the bishop,
for the use and accommodation of the people of Highgate, in the sense of a
parish church or a chapel of ease. . . . Where was the obligation mentioned in
the instruments, which required either the bishops or the trustees to enlarge
the chapel as the population increased ? . . . If it were now binding on the trust
to find accommodation for 1,500 persons, it would be as binding on them by
and by to accommodate 3,000, and so on, until the means of supporting the
school, the only valid object of the trust, would be wholly swept away.' On the
other hand, the lord chancellor 'wished to be equally guarded in what he said with
respect to the rights of the bishop, and of the heir at law of the Cholmondeley
estates, both of which parties would have a right to be heard if it could be
successfully contended that the revenues of this charity might lawfully be
directed from the purpose designed by the founder to that of providing a chapel
large enough for the accommodation of all the inhabitants of Highgate'. Lord
Eldon was inclined to treat the governors with leniency: 'The perversion of the
charity, from a grammar-school headed by a "fit and learned person", to the
teaching of reading and writing by the sexton, . . . could not be attributed to
them, as it appeared from the evidence that from some change wrought heretofore in the public taste, the learning of Greek and Latin had been voluntarily
abandoned.' Concerning 'the best means of reinstating the charity as nearly as
possible, agreeably to the will of the founder', Lord Eldon said 'he might or
might not be called on to issue a decree'. (From *The Times*, 19 Jan. 1824.) It
was 1827 before a decree was forthcoming. See Letter 1690.

[1] Horace Twiss (1787–1849) was at this time a member of parliament for the
borough of Wootton Bassett in Wiltshire.

on Friday Afternoon. For myself, I can only say but can however most sincerely say, that I would not have joined in their request, if I were not convinced that with exception of the six or seven confederated Opponents the whole *House-holdery* of Highgate will thank you, & that with abundant reason.

Condescend to accept the assurance, | that I am, dear Sir, | with sincere respect | Your obliged Servt
S. T. Coleridge

1312. *To Hartley Coleridge*

MS. Pierpont Morgan Lib. Pub. with omis. Hartley Coleridge: His Life and Work, *by E. L. Griggs, 1929, p. 102.*

1 July 1822
Highgate—

My dear Hartley

You have tried—nay, that is scarcely true; but you have made the experiment of trying—to maintain yourself by writing for the Press—and the result—I do not know, what conclusion *you* have drawn from it—has been such, as makes *me* shrink, and sink away inwardly, from the thought of a second trial.[1] A domestic Tutorship seems out of all question: and even if by any sacrifice of my political free-agency I could—which I have no reason to believe, that I possess or could obtain interest enough to do—procure you any situation abroad—you would not like it or set about to suit yourself for it. What remains but something of the *School* kind? If you have thought of any thing else, let me know it. If not, and if you have resolved on availing yourself of whatever scheme or connection Mr Dawes shall point out to you—yet what must the result be if even under all the present *whelm* of circumstances you cannot accomodate your time or temper to the giving a couple of Lessons a day to one child,[2] or bear to be told of your irregularity, without

---

[1] 'The going to Ambleside', Hartley wrote to his father, 'in the face of such unfavourable sentiments on the part of some, certainly weighed upon my heart, and I felt a physical incapability of exerting the necessary authority, and preserving the necessary distance, among a set of boys, in whose number there must needs be found high spirits, and untractable natures. . . . In regard to my future plans, I shall not decide till I have heard from you. It is my wish to make another trial of my talents in London. I know I can make more than a livelihood, and I have hopes, more than hopes of my own steady perseverance in the right path, but I will not be obstinate. Only let me say, that what with my past failures, what with the unavoidable weakness of nerves, and defect of that sort of sternness, which is a necessary supplement to kindness and attention in a Paedagogue, I think schooling of all things, *possible*, the least eligible.' *Letters of Hartley Coleridge*, 75–76.

[2] Probably Henry, the Gillmans' younger son.

resenting it, as an insult ? And this, tho' you are aware that in this house every belatement produces confusion and increases a trouble already too great for Mrs Gillman's health and spirits—and tho', when you see how such a delicate frame both of body and mind goes on, working and toiling and keeping all parts of the house in order and respectable appearance, from seven in the morning to ten or eleven at night, and know how sadly of late we all are augmenting the difficulty and anxiety of making both ends meet, even an abrupt and angry Complaint or Reproof ought only to excite pain and both the inward feeling and the expression of Regret for having occasioned it.—What must my sufferings be when I see the growing alienation in Mr Gillman ? and know that I must stand mute, should he ever state the causes of it!—

Derwent, poor fellow! in his answer to Mrs Gillman's note, putting off the dinner party, complained that he was always the obliged party, without any means of returning the obligation. I need not reply—So must every young man be who has to *begin* the world, without fortune—For there is nothing, which either he or you could rationally wish, from which you would have been precluded by *my* circumstances (whatever they may be for myself and in other respects) or by your own—necessarily, or exclusive of what depended on your own wills.—Passing over the effect, which your being at Highgate must have in diminishing Mr and Mrs G.'s power of hospitality to Derwent, and of welcoming him during a portion of his long Vacation, and of shewing occasional attentions to a College Friend—yet I am scarcely more convinced of my own Being than I am that Mr Gillman would have made efforts and endured inconveniences beyond prudence, if Derwent from his first settlement at Cambridge had but done half of what Mr G. had a right to expect, and what Derwent could not be ignorant, would have been especially gratifying to *him*: above all, from a Son of mine. Had he *but once a month* (and once a fortnight ought to have been no Task exacted by Duty, but a duty made pleasurable by kind and genial recollections)—but had he once a month written such a letter, as he probably has written to the Hopwoods—now a rhyming epistle, or a description of his acquaintance—characters —jokes—criticisms—any thing which would have implied that his Father's best Friends, and his own most zealous & kind Hosts, had a place in his Heart and Memory—Mr G. would have struggled with contrivances for his reception, as long and as often as it would have been desirable or proper even on Derwent's own account.— But instead of this (it seems cruel to speak of it, while he is lying on a bed of sickness ; but it is *for* you and to *you* that I am now stating the truth) his whole conduct and the style of his Letters have been

that of a man *making use* of another—the one thing that of all
others could not but offend whatever was excellent . . .¹ in my
friend's character—Add too, that this process of alienation, that
commenced in the feelings, was carried on & deepened by his judgement and moral principles, when he believed himself to see that
shewing off, and shewy connections, were uppermost—and of late
by his most strange neglect of his old & faithful friend, Jameson.—
(If you know any *cause* of this (reason there can be none)—as any
little *miff* between them—for heaven's sake, make me or Mr or
Mrs G. acquainted with it: for it has sunk deep into their minds—
& Montague spoke of it with contemptuous reprobation.—)
Reflect—and then say—whether *my* Circumstances, tho' they
preclude or interfere with the power of remedying, have *caused*
any privations, that either you or your Brother have suffered—
Still, I am persuaded, that every thing necessary for your happiness
is in your power, if you are yourself in your power—I could not be
easy without making these remarks—& my spirits are too weak to
talk to you on the subject.—If any thing tries your temper here,
you ought to be glad of it, as an opportunity of disciplining it for
the severer Trials, which (if I can found anything on your Mother's
last letter & her conversation with Mr Watson² & of these it is
religion with me to say no more to *you* than that the Sum makes a
strong contrast with Mrs Gillman's Motives and Feelings respecting
you) you will meet with at Keswick, without the greatest caution
on your part. To Mr Dawes exclusively you must look and apply
yourself.—God bless you! While I live, I will do what I can—what
& whether I can, must in the main depend on yourself not on your
affectionate Father.³

S. T. Coleridge.

1313. *To S. Lutwidge*

Address: S. Lutwidge, Esqre. | Pembroke Place | Cambridge
MS. British Museum. Hitherto unpublished.
Postmark: 11 July 1822.

Highgate
Thursday Noon. [11 July 1822]

Dear Sir

My Son, Derwent Coleridge, is anxious that your friendly Letter
should be acknowleged, which it is not yet in his power to do with

¹ Several words inked out in MS.
² John Watson had visited Keswick in May. See Letter 1301.
³ Not long after reading his father's letter, Hartley disappeared. As Coleridge later wrote, his fourth 'griping and grasping' sorrow 'reached it's height
on the 19th day of Derwent's Fever by his Brother's desertion of him'. See
Letters 1314 and 1317.

his own hand—I have therefore offered myself as his Secretary at the bed-side to inform you, that his medical Friend, whose attentions are unwearied to him, expresses the fullest confidence that the Fever will quit him after the 21st day—which we calculate to be either Saturday or Sunday next—but does not expect that he will be able to sit up, or leave his Bed for more than a few minutes, before that period. We have reason to be thankful, that the course of the Fever has been marked by no malignant symptom—the secretions from the Skin and Bowels, tho' troublesome & for some days past requiring to be bridled, having prevented the irritation from falling on any important organ, as the Chest or Brain.— However, his Sufferings, poor Fellow, have been severe—and his present weakness distressing. All we have to do is to keep him as perfectly quiet, body and mind, as is possible.

Your very prudent suggestion respecting the State at Cambridge will be scrupulously complied with.—Not a word will escape us.

I am to convey Derwent's respectful remembrances to your family, and am, dear Sir, | respectfully | Your obedient Servt
                                                        S. T. Coleridge

P.S. As to Derwent's return, I cannot of course permit him even to speak about it at present—and have intreated him not to *think* about it; as little, at least, as he can.—As soon as his Strength returns, he will himself, doubtless, write.

1314. *To John Taylor Coleridge*

Address: John Coleridge, Esqre | Middle Temple
MS. British Museum. Hitherto unpublished.
Postmark: Highgate, 16 July 1822.

                                    Monday Night. [15 July 1822]
My dear Sir

You will oblige me by letting me know, by return of Post if possible, whether Hartley has called on you since Friday last. And if you should have any money on his account,[1] be so good as not to let him have any part of it till I have seen him and have had the opportunity of a few minutes' Conversation with you, as to the application of it if there be any.—Alas, Sir! I am almost broken-hearted.—It is now between four and five Weeks since Derwent left Cambridge, spent 8 or 9 days in London, and then came to me evidently ill—took to his bed with a remittent Fever, of which either Saturday or yesterday was the 21st day—. For the last week

---

[1] See Letter 1287 and note.

the Fever had continued abating, and Mr Gillman so late as Friday last considered him out of danger, as confidently as any Patient in the one & twenty day Fever can be so considered—But on that day and the next his spirits were fretted, we apprehend—and yesterday and to day the Fever has assumed an altered Type, and a tendency at least to a typhous character—just as I was fully expecting and anxiously waiting for his being able to quit his bed after a three weeks' confinement to it, in order to write to his Mother of what *had* happened!

There are, at present, no malignant symptoms; but it is in vain for me to hide from myself, that he is no longer out of danger—and what aggravates my affliction [is that] Mr Gillman has this day [forbidden?]¹ both Mrs Gillman and my[self] to sit by his bed-side. Nothing is wanting, however, tha[t] Skill, Tenderness and un-wearied Attention can supply—and what if he had been taken ill at Cambridge where a Typhus is raging!²—and no friend near him!

This is a sore visitation—and yet, I almost fear, it is not the sorest that hangs over, my dear Sir, . . .³

1315. *To Thomas Allsop*

Address: T. Allsop Esqre. | Blandford Place | Pall Mall
MS. Cornell University Lib. Hitherto unpublished.
Postmark: Highgate, 3 August 1822.

Saturday afternoon
4 [3] August 1822—

My dearest Allsop

I was sadly disappointed when Mr Watson came back without you: for tho' I preferred his telling you of all that happened, crash upon crash, to sending the account & detail in writing—it would yet have been a great comfort to have talked with you.—And since then I have been hoping, & Mrs Gillman almost expecting, to see, or hear from, you daily—and it has been quite out of my power to leave Highgate, or I should have done so, had it been only to

¹ MS. torn.
² On 6 Aug. 1822 Dorothy Wordsworth wrote to Edward Quillinan: 'Poor Derwent Coleridge has been at Death's door—6 weeks confined to his Bed in the Typhus fever—carried from Cambridge to Highgate, where, under the same roof with his Father and Brother, he was taken care of. His poor Mother and Sister remained at Keswick—suffering greatly in mind as you may suppose. . . . The same Fever has caused the Death of five young Men belonging to St John's College.' *Later Years*, i. 87.
³ I cut out the signature of my Uncle to this letter to affix it to a print of my Uncle, which I gave to Frank. [Note in MS. by John Taylor Coleridge dated 6 Dec. 1840.]

relieve my own anxiety about the little one and it's Mother. If we
do not see you tomorrow, Mrs G. I trust, will go to town and I will
try to accompany her.

Derwent is considered quite out of danger—and can sit up from
one to two hours in the course of the day—And we hear that
Mr Dawes is recovering, so that it will not be long, I trust, before
Hartley may set off to the North—much against the Wish of his
selfish *worretting* ever-complaining never-satisfied Mother. He
might go to perdition body and soul, the trouble, embarrassment
and anguish remaining on my shoulders, rather than be saved at
the risk of any occasional annoyance to her, or of Mr Wordsworth's
disapprobation—But hang her! she is not worth vexing about.—If
she had known all that I *now* know but did not know—say rather,
was fully satisfied of the contrary—till his last outburst—I should
not inwardly reproach her repugnance tho' I should have felt it
unmotherly. But this is not the case—it is grounded in pure
selfishness.—

Mrs G. told me, she had something to write or at least to transmit
in this note—but she is gone out with Mrs Kinderley & if I stay I
may miss the Post.—I fancy, it was something about Mrs Allsop's
& the Babe's being at Highgate.

My kindest Love to her. Need I repeat, how glad we shall *all* be
to see you *tri-unely* and as Mr Green comes now on Tuesdays, come
as early as you like, I shall be able to enjoy your society.—

Heaven bless you | and
S. T. Coleridge

1316. *To Thomas Allsop*

Address: T. Allsop Esqre | 2 Blandford Place | Pall Mall   Mrs A. will be so
good as to open this if Mr A. be not at home.
Transcript Mrs. R. L. Grigg. *Hitherto unpublished.*

Sept. 4, 1822

My dearest Allsop

I left Highgate unwell—indeed, I was (as they say) taken ill
during dinner yesterday, & had a wretched night—and I now feel
that it will be best for me to be at home as soon as possible. What
Derwent's Plans are, I know as much of as of the Votes of the
Govr. & Trustees of the Tancred Charities[1]—but the one (as I am
to see him again so soon) as well as the other may be put down if
not O then = O—. When a walk of a mile might have set me down

---

[1] Coleridge refers to a trust established by Christopher Tancred (1689–1754)
for twelve studentships.

at your side, you may be assured that the declining thereof is according to the reason but in no correspondence with the wish & inclination of my dear Allsop's most affectionately attached Friend

S. T. Coleridge

I saw Dr Davy,[1] who spoke like a wise & kind man. 'If I see *any* Chance, any rational ground of Hope, I will use my best efforts in Derwent's favor—and if not, you would not wish me to throw my vote away.' ! !

1317. *To Thomas Allsop*

Address: T. Allsop, Esqre. | Ireton Wood | Derby
[Readdressed in another hand] Mr. Allsop | Blandford Place | Pall Mall | London
MS. New York Public Lib. Pub. with omis. Letters, Conversations and Rec. *199.*
Postmark: Deal, 9 October 1822.

8 Octr 1822
Walmer—

My dearest Allsop
  You will readily forgive me for having broken off midway in an answer to your first and longer Letter; and for having destroyed what I had written: when I tell you, that the Terrors of that Saturday Night and of the two days succeeding, had left a disposition to a sudden *Confusion* in my head, accompanied with an odd but very distressing propensity to utter a faint shriek, followed by a feeling of heat that seemed to be somewhere *in* the Brain, and finally giving way to a numbness of my forehead & weight on and over my eyes—whenever any thing occurred that affected me or I had dwelt for any time on a subject that greatly interested my feelings & affections. In the course of my past Life I count four griping and grasping Sorrows, each of which seemed to have my very heart in it's hands, compressing or wringing—the first, when the Vision of a Happy Home sunk for ever, and it became impossible for me any longer even to *hope* for domestic happiness under the name of Husband—when I was doomed to know

That Names but seldom meet with Love,
And Love wants Courage without a Name![2]

  The second commenced on the night of my arrival (from Grasmere) in town with Mr & Mrs Montagu, when all the Superstructure raised by my idolatrous Fancy during an enthusiastic & self-

---

[1] Martin Davy (1763–1839) would have had, as master of Caius College, Cambridge, a voice in the awarding of the Tancred studentships.
[2] *Alice du Clos*, lines 111–12, *Poems*, i. 473.

sacrificing Friendship of 15 years, the fifteen bright and ripe Years, the strong summer of my Life, burst like a Bubble[1]—but the Grief did not vanish with it, nor the Love which was the Stuff & Vitality of the Grief, tho' they pined away up to the moment of Wordsworth's last total Transfiguration into Baseness, when with 1200£ a year, and just at the moment that the fraudulent Bankruptcy of Fennor & Curtis[2] had robbed me of every penny, I had been so many years working for, every penny I possessed in the world, & involved me in a debt of 150£ to boot, he first regretted that he was not able to pay a certain Bill of mine to *his* (Wordsworth's) wife's Brother himself—never wanted money so much in his life—&c—& an hour after attempted to extort from me a transfer to himself of all that I could call my own in the world, *my Books*, as the *condition* of his paying a Bill which in *equity* was as much, but in honor and gratitude was far more, *his* Debt than mine![3]

My third sorrow was in some sort included in the second[4]—what the former was to Friendship, the latter was to a yet more inward Bond—the former spread a wider gloom over the world around me, the latter left a darkness deeper within myself—the former is more akin to Indignation, & moody Scorn at my own folly in my weaker moments, and to contemplative Melancholy and Alienation from the Past in my ordinary state—the latter had more of Self in it's character; but of a Self emptied—a gourd of Jonas[5]—and is *this* it, under which I hoped to have prophesied?

My fourth commenced with the Tidings of *the Charge* against my first-born—remitted with the Belief & Confidence of the falsehood of the Charge—relapsed again—and again—and again—blended

---

[1] See Letters 809 (headnote), 866–9 and 888.

[2] Rest Fenner's bankruptcy occurred in Mar. 1819. See Letters 1202 and 1272.

[3] In Oct. 1809 John Hutchinson, Mrs. Wordsworth's brother, joined Poole and Sharp in advancing money to purchase paper and stamps for *The Friend* Hutchinson's share amounting to £53. 19s. 9d. It was arranged that George Ward, a London bookseller, should make repayment out of money collected from the subscribers to *The Friend*. When Ward discontinued accepting payments in Mar. 1810, he had on hand sufficient funds to reimburse Hutchinson but whether any part of the indebtedness was actually repaid is not clear See Letters 782–5, 789, and 798–9.

Mrs. Wordsworth's letter to Thomas Monkhouse of 12 Jan. 1819 shows that Coleridge was later asked to pay his debt to Hutchinson: 'We have not received the parcel from C. which you told us he meant to send! I fear he says nothing about paying his debt to John.' *The Letters of Mary Wordsworth*, ed. Mary E Burton, 1958, p. 50.

[4] The alienation from Wordsworth ended Coleridge's close association with Sara Hutchinson. Thereafter Coleridge saw her only infrequently.

[5] Jonah iv.

with the sad conviction that neither of my children thought of or felt toward me as a FATHER, or attributed any thing done for them to me—and lastly reached it's height on the 19th day of Derwent's Fever by his Brother's desertion of him, when it trembled in the scales whether he should live or die—& the Cause of this desertion first awakening the suspicion that I had been deliberately deceived & made an accomplice in deceiving others—

And yet in all these four Griefs my recollection, as often as they were recalled to my mind, turned not to *what* I suffered, but on what *account*—at worst, I never thought of the Sufferings apart from the Causes & Occasions of them—but the latter were ever uppermost—. It was reserved for the interval between six o'clock and 12 on THAT SATURDAY Evening to bring a Suffering which, do what I will, I cannot help thinking of & being *affrightened by*, as a terror of itself, a self-subsisting separate Something, detached from the Cause—and when I turn to the Cause, still the solemn Appeals to the Almighty for the falseness of the Charge at Oriel are far, far more terrible to me than the *Habit* charged on him—woeful, and ruinous, and all-*hollow*-making and *future*-dizzying as *that* is!—And then too, I cannot help hearing the sound of my Voice, at the moment when he took me by surprize, and asked for the money to pay a debt to & take leave of Mr Williams—promising to overtake me if possible before I had reached his Aunt Martha's, as I was to stop at Bothe's in York Street by the way—but at latest, before 5—'Nay, say before *Six. Be,* if you can, by *5*—but *say*, six—.' Then, when he had passed a few steps—Hartley!—Six! O my God! think of the *agony*, the *sore agony*, of every moment after six!—And tho' he was not three yards from me, I only saw the color of his Face thro' my Tears!—No more of this! I will finish this Scrawl after my return from the Beach.—

When I had left behind me what I had no longer power to make better or worse, and arrived at Walmer, I had soon reason to remember that I was not *at home*, or at Muddiford, or at Little Hampton, or at Ramsgate, but under the conjunct Signs of Virgo and the Crab, the one in the wane, the other in advance yet in excellent agreement with the former, by virtue of it's rare privilege of advancing backward. In sober prose, I verily believe that Mrs G., Masters James and Henry G. and Mr Myself should have found as genial a birth in a Nest-hillock of Termites or Bug-a-boos as with this single Ant consanguineous—(Observe, Miss Lucy![1] that have left *U* out!)—As soon therefore as dear Mr Gillman returned to us, you will not hold it either strange or unwise that in agreeing to accompany him to Dover, the Kingdom of France, West of Paris,

[1] Lucy Harding, Mrs. Gillman's sister.

Ramsgate, Dubton, [Dumpton Park?] Sandwich, and foreign parts
in general, I determined to give myself up wholly to each moment
as it came—with no anticipations, and with no recollection, save
as far as is involved in the wish every now and then that you had
been with me. And in this resolve, it was that I destroyed the Kit-
cat or Bust at least of the Letter, I had meant to have sent you.
But O! how often have I wished and do I wish, that Mrs Allsop and
Mrs Gillman could form a household in common at Ramsgate
next year—when one or the other of you (yourself or Mr Gillman)
might be there for the greater part of the Time.—

And now for your second Letter. What shall I say? When our
Griefs, and Fears and Agitations are strongly roused toward one
Object, we almost want some fresh memento to remind us that we
have other Loves, other Interests—. Forgive me if I tell you, that
your last letter did in something of this way make me feel afresh,
that there was that in my very Heart that called you Son as
well as Friend, and reminded me that a Father's Affection could
not exist exempt from a Father's Anxiety. I am fully aware, that
every syllable in the latter half of your Letter proceeded from the
strong two-fold desire at once to comfort and to conciliate—and that
I ought to regard your remarks, as the mere straining of the Soul
toward an End, felt and known to be pure & lovely—and proving
nothing but your *total* attention to that kind Thought.—And even
so I do regard them—. And yet I cannot read them without anxiety
—not indeed anxious Thoughts, but yet an anxious feeling.—
Sane or insane—a fearful thing it is when a Father could be comforted by an assurance of the latter—but I neither know nor *dare*
hear of any *mid* state—of no *vague* necessities dare I hear. Our own
wandering Thoughts may be suffered to become Tyrants over the
mind, of which they are the Offspring—and the most effective
Vice-roys or Substitutes of that dark & dim spiritual Personëity
whose whispers & fiery darts Holy Men have supposed them to be—
& that these may end in a loss or rather forfeiture of Free-agency,
I doubt not—But my dearest Allsop! I have both the Faith of
Reason, and the Voice of Conscience and the assurance of Scripture,
that 'resist the Evil one & he will flee from you.'[1] But for self-
condemnation H. would never have tampered with Fatalism; and
but for Fatalism he would never have had *such* cause to condemn
himself.—With truest Love,

Your S. T. C.

P.S. Mrs Gillman's affectionate remembrances to yourself and
Mrs A—in short, to You & your's—While I wrote the last words,
my Lips felt an appetite to kiss the Baby.

[1] James iv. 7.

1318. *To James Gillman*

MS. Pierpont Morgan Lib. Pub. with omis. Coleridge at Highgate, *by Lucy E. Watson, 1925, p. 86.*

[Early October 1822]

My dearest Friend

Walmer improves so much, every time I extend or vary my topographical researches, and experimental Ambulations (mono-syllabically, Walks: for amble-ations I leave to James and the Donky) that I am more and more in want of you. It seems to me the healthiest Spot, I ever sojourned on—the Clay here covering the calcareous Subsoil with a thin coat, and here mingled with the Lime, attracts the crude dankness from the sea-fogs, yet without retaining it on the one hand or chilling the air by sudden evaporation on the other. For what is not taken up by the plants, is carried off by filtration downward. The number of young Sylvages too, and of wooded and bushy Hollows and Bottoms, uneven as Quarries, and (duly magnified by and thro' the poetic Herschel of a *'picturesque eye'*) romantically sublime and really quite pretty, can not but contribute to purify and inspirit the air. The sea-breezes, I suspect, quicken the olfactory nerves: for I never remember to have caught the fragrance from the Birches and the aroma from the young Pines & arbor vitae Shrubs so perceptibly as from Lord Liverpool's Plantation on the side toward the Cliffs.—I am tolerably reconciled to the Salt-water Cradle-bath—and by Anne's advice I bathe two days and omit the third—and hitherto with increasing benefit during the whole *day*, from 8. A.M. to ½ past 10, P.M.—tho' my appetite at dinner, and for the animal part thereof, remains languid indeed in the —pole as the positive opposite of the +. I wish, I could speak as promisingly of my *Nights*; but my rest is far more restless, than it was at Highgate—and the Pain in my bowels, instead of having the good manners to wait till I awoke out of my second Sleep, commences it's dunning, like a bad conscience, as soon as my head is (bating a few inches for the doubled Pillow) level with my feet, and my body throughout the night is intolerant even of the upper Sheet, and on quarrelsome terms even with the Night-shirt—quoad the abdominal Region at least. Yet I am rather better than worse in the constipation line—& have abdicated Apples, & taken to my Milk in lieu of Bread and cheese and the hard Table-ale of this district, a beverage which can be harmless to the Iron-gutted alone. Nevertheless, I am disposed to flatter myself, that this is afflictive in the Sufferance rather than alarming as a symptom: for disturbed and even distressful as my Night-season is, I rise refreshed, and without the faintness, sickiness and phlegm-cough that were sure, more or less, to follow on my deeper Sleeps and Pain-furloughs at home—and I do not feel, or in a very diminished degree, the craving for Snuff at any time, or for Wine after dinner so that I trust, that I shall be able to bring myself back to the habit of three glasses as my maximum with more confidence than I dared entertain if any great effort of Self-conquest were necessary.—Hitherto, I have not attempted any Brain-work. On the contrary, I have tried to keep my mind as composed and vacant, as possible—excluding even day-dreams & attending to whatever is present to my Senses, and only as long as it is present—but I feel my head clearing up, & hope to wear it as unconsciously as I used to do—before poor —— forced his way into it from the heart upward. On Thursday, however, I propose to begin work in good earnest—my Logic, to wit.— And so much of I myself I.— I shrink, like a burnt Quill from the thought of disturbing you with any inquiries respecting Hartley, and would fain confine his name to my Prayers. But might I suggest (in the form of a Query at least) the propriety of calling in Pump Court on his Cousin, should you go to town—or if there were any chance of a letter reaching Hartley viâ Taylor and Hesse,[1] to remind him of his promise to his Brother, and the necessity of conveying an authority to Mr John Coleridge to give an order for the 30 or 40£, if he means to keep the promise? — . . . [Remainder of MS. missing.]

1319. *To James Gillman*

MS. Pierpont Morgan Lib. Pub. with omis. Letters, *ii. 721.*

28 Octr 1822
Ramsgate—

Dear Friend

Words, I know, are not wanted between you and me. But there are occasions so aweful, there may be instances and manifestations of friendship so affecting, and drawing up with them so long a train from behind, so many folds of Recollection, as they come onward on one's Mind, that it seems but a mere act of Justice to one's self, a debt we owe to the dignity of our moral Nature, to give them some record—a relief, which the Spirit of man asks and demands to contemplate in some outward Symbol what it is inwardly solemnizing.—I am still too much under the cloud of past Misgivings, too

---

[1] Taylor and Hessey had learned of Hartley's whereabouts in early Oct 'Hartley Coleridge', J. A. Hessey wrote to Taylor, 'is again safe in his friend Mr. Jameson's care, and is writing away very industriously.' Edmund Blunden *Keats's Publisher, a Memoir of John Taylor*, 1940, p. 140.

much of the Stun & Stupor from the r[ece]nt Peals and Thunder crash still remains, to permit me to anticipate, other than by wishes & prayers, [wha]t the effect of your unweariable Kindness may be on poor [Hartley's][1] Mind and Conduct.[2] I pray fervently, and I feel a chearful Trust, that I do not pray in vain, that on my own mind and spring of action it will be proved not to have been wasted. I do inwardly believe, that I shall yet do something to thank you, my dear Gillman, in the way in which you would wish to be thanked —by doing myself honor.—

Mrs Gillman has been determined by your Letter, and the heavenly weather & moral certainty of the continuance of *Bathing*-weather at least, to accept her Sister's Offer of coming in to Ramsgate, and to take a House for a fortnight certain at a guinea a week —in the Buildings next to Wellington Crescent, and having a certain modicum & segment of Sea-peep—. You remember the House—the end one with a Balcony at the Window, almost in a Line with the Duke of W. in wood, lignum vitae—like as Life.— I had thought of keeping my present bed-room, at 10S. 6D. a week—but on consulting Mrs Rogers, she did not think that this would satisfy the etiquette of the World—tho' the two Houses are on different cliffs—. And I felt so confident of the effect of the Bathing & Ramsgate Transparent Water—the San[ds,] the Pier &c—that as there was no alternati[ve] but of giving up the Bathing (for Mrs G. would not stay by herself, partly, if not chiefly because she feared, I might add more to your anxiety than your comfort in your Batchelor-state & with only Bessy of Beccles) or having Jane,[3] I voted for the latter—& will do my very best to keep her in good humor & good spirits.—

Dear Friend—and Brother of my Soul—God only knows! how truly and in the depth you are loved & prized by your affectionate | Friend

S. T. Coleridge

[1] This name is heavily inked out in MS.

[2] It seems likely that Gillman's 'unweariable Kindness' led Hartley finally o comply with his father's wishes. By 19 Nov. he was already at Ambleside. Hartley Coleridge is with Mr Dawes', Dorothy Wordsworth wrote to Edward Quillinan. 'He has not been long enough to have proved his skill and patience s a Teacher; but Mr D. says he is very steady. He is the oddest looking creature you ever saw—not taller than Mr de Quincey—with a beard as black as raven.' *Later Years*, i. 98.

[3] Jane Harding, Mrs. Gillman's sister.

1320. *To James Gillman*

Address: James Gillman, Esqre | Highgate | London
MS. Harvard College Lib. Hitherto unpublished.
Postmark: 11 November 1822.   *Stamped*: Ramsgate.

[10 November 1822]
My dear Friend

Up to this present Sunday we have had uninterrupted Bathing, the advantage of which will, I trust, extend beyond the immediate effects, which he who runs may read in our Looks, movements and upright carriage: tho' it would be want of openness in me to deny, that your not being with us and the consequent necessity of *the* Substitute for your presence have been for *me* (I speak of myself exclusively) and ever would be, a constant counter-acting influence. On the other hand, I am bound to say that since we have been here it has been merely a force *negative*—a *sensation* of dyspathy, which comes on at dinner time when I begin, not first to *wish for* but to want your society—. But it would be *selfish* to complain, because it is felt, if at all, in a very inferior degree by Mrs Gillman as is natural—and it would be unwise, for it will occasion me to leave the Ocean Strand, Cliff, Pier, and glistering Sails, grateful for what I have received yet glad that I have to announce our departure on Wednesday Morning next, by the Coach which has agreed to set us down by the Highgate Stage by or before Six o'clock. You or Mr Watson will be so good as to desire the Coachman to look out for us.

Tuesday is the last day of the Sovereign Steam from Ramsgate to London. As the Stage-proprietors have entered into an engagement with each other not to take less than 28 Shillings, for inside place, the difference (almost £2) was a temptation, on the side of the *Tempter*. But we scouted it. The Sovereign did not come in last night till past 9—the River Fog having prevented it from leaving the Tower-Stairs before One o'clock. The Harbour Man, indeed, assured or rather would fain have assured me, that at this season the River Fogs are early Risers—making their appearance about Four in the morning, and their good clearance shortly after Noontide—item, that the Wind (now Southish) is in our favor—&c &c. But we gave it—many words, indeed, for the amusement of pro and con Talk, in the lack of better Matter; but—not a single Serious Thought.

Mrs Gillman sends her Love to Mrs Steele—& begs her to attribute her silence to a disappointment in obtaining a Frank—

On Wednesday, as Mrs G. & I were on the Pier, whom should

see but Lord Liverpool & Mr Canning, with Lords Bentinck[1] &
Howard de Warden.[2] Lord L. did not recognize me—nor Mr
Canning—till I took of[f] my Hat (by Mrs G's desire as if to dry my
locks, I having just returned from the Machine)—he then looked at
me & I advanced & addressed him. He received me very cordially
—& called out—Liverpool! here is Mr Coleridge—and so I walked
arm in arm with them, down the Pier, thro' the Town, and up to the
Cliff, to see the Wellington Crescent &c—and they seemed pleased
to have me; but as the young Noblemen were behind, somehow or
other I felt as if I had stayed long enough, & said something about
my having left a Lady—which from their kind manner in taking
leave of me I was half vexed at—as I might, and I suspect ought to,
have accompanied them to the West Cliff & to their Barouche.—
On Friday the first Stone of the Pillar was laid—Lord L. came in
but not Mr C.—There was a public Dinner, Lord L. in the Chair—
as Lord L. retired, he stopt, as he passed, shook hands with me, and
said—he had not observed my being in the Room till above an
hour—when Sir W. Curtis[3] turned round to him—& Lord L. said—
You did know Mr Coleridge, Sir W?—on which Sir W. gave me
his hand—& they passed on.—The *meaning* seemed, an indirect
either censure or apology for my not having been placed at the
first Table—. Lord L. had before expressed his regret, that I
should have been at Walmer for a fortnight after his arrival
without [his] knowlege—as he should have been happy to have
welcomed me at Walmer Castle—all very pleasant in it's way,
because I knew it would please you & gratify Mrs Gillman—and
it may facilitate the introduction of my Work.

It is getting dark—or rather darker—for it has been the dreariest
day we have had—so I will now conclude—till we meet—
with God bless you | and your truly grateful | and affectionate
Friend

S. T. Coleridge

[1] W. G. F. C. Bentinck (1802–48), commonly known as Lord George Bentinck,
was at this time private secretary to his uncle, George Canning. In 1828 he was
appointed governor-general of India.
[2] Charles Augustus Ellis, Baron Howard de Walden (1799–1868), diplomatist,
was appointed under-secretary of state for foreign affairs by Canning in 1824.
[3] Sir William Curtis (1752–1829), at whose house in Ramsgate George IV
stayed in 1821.

1321. *To Mrs. Gillman*

MS. Pierpont Morgan Lib. Hitherto unpublished.

[December 1822 ?][1]

After the manner, in which you broke[2] away from me, I have striven in vain to force away my thoughts from the subject. It is but waste of time and an injurious retention of disturbing feelings to attempt it. I must draw the *swarm* out of the Hive and see them settle and cluster before I can remove them out of sight.

My dearest Friend! To few indeed, if to any, is it given to hit the golden *mean*, on any point of Judgement in which the Feelings are concerned—: and it is cruel to be angry with each other, because we are a hair-breadth above or below the exact line. Sometimes, a few general and preparatory remarks are of use in tranquillizing the mind, and thus fitting it for the examination of the particular object, as you wipe your eye-glass before you use it. It not seldom happens, that difference in opinion between two friends may arise from innocent differences in their several natures: and often from the difference of their education, past circumstances, and the incidents and accidents of their Life. Now to apply this to judgements respecting Servants and our inferior Dependents generally. I reflect, that formerly and in places remote from the Metropolis even in my childhood, the distinction of ranks was so felt as in a much less degree than at present to require a *distance* of manner for it's preservation. Servants were more in awe and yet more familiar. In old times Familiars meant Servants. In Scotland still the children of the best families *companion* with the servants from childhood upwards—However, at 8 years old I was taken away, to be for eleven years together a poor, friendless Blue-coat Boy—and many a meal, and delightful Bason of hot Tea and Bread and Butter have I been thankful for by a Kitchen-fire with a Schoolfellow, whose Father or mother or Aunt were in service:—tho' at the very time when Judge Buller's Lady gave me half-a-crown and bid me go down to the Butler's Room, I left the money (which, however, I detected to be a bad one) on the Table in the Passage, opened the Door and never went there afterwards. During the latter years I was now with rich, and now with poor—conversing as

---

[1] Coleridge's reference to a time 'no farther back' than Hartley's leaving his chambers indicates that the present letter belongs to 1822. It was undoubtedly written not long before 26 Dec., since on that date Coleridge speaks of the 'new servant', Dinah, probably a replacement for Maria, to whose dismissal he refers in the present letter. See Letters 1300, 1318, and 1323.

[2] Coleridge wrote 'broke' in the MS.; subsequently, someone altered the word to 'ran'.

an equal with all ranks indiscriminately.—Then came the Glow and Blaze of Democratic Notions—then the *critical eruption* of my six months' Light Dragoonery—and last, *Pantisocracy*, and perfect Equality on the banks of the Susquianna! !—And to all this add a certain laxness and facility of natural temper.—On the other hand, independent of Circumstance and education you, my dear friend! had a peculiar fineness of nature—and this by a gracious adjustment of events was matured into a genuine refinement in sentiment, manners, and address. Miss Dutton was ever before you like a *future Self*, a sort of magnifying Mirror, in gazing on which you became more gracious from the *selfless* complacency with which you contemplated and admired your own image already full-grown. Soon after this, in an opulent family in which you were treated as an elder Daughter, you undertook the charge of forming the minds and manners of three or four little girls destined for the higher ranks of society, and in a large house in which there was every convenience for preserving them from the influence of meaner manners and conversation. And this was at a time when the danger and ill-consequences of permitting Children to be in the company of servants was every where held up, as a first-rate Principle in education—and as all things will pass into extremes, in some instances left impressions not *quite* compatible with the dictates of Christianity. And even in minds and natures incapable of *such* result, as in your Sister Lucy's—nay, where as in your own case a more than ordinary tenderness and scrupulous considerateness & gentleness towards Servants were prominent & characteristic— still the tone and habit of feeling could not be altogether uninfluenced. You looked *on* them, as a Christian, and with Christian Benevolence; but at the same time looked *down* on them, with the alien-like feeling of a Gentle-woman, added to the inevitable inward with-drawing from the mere sense of diversity between them and your own *born* and innate character, all that which makes a *Lady* more than a *Gentle-woman*. Now when you compare your Life &c with mine, can you wonder that there should be some difference both in our notions and our feelings? For instance, of Powel's late conduct—I can readily believe that I think much too little: if you will allow me to imagine that you think a little too much—and unconsciously measure his distance from Maria without *at the same* moment measuring the immense moral and physical distance between yourself and him.—For the accident of sitting occasionally in the room, in which you are sitting, and his dining at the same table will not, I fear, lessen the latter distance, so as in any effectual degree to increase the former. The Attraction of inward Likeness is too strong to allow us to expect a better state of

Feeling even where we are entitled, nay *bound*, to demand from the individual that he shall abstain from all manifestation of the Contrary—and that he shall behave and conduct himself agreeably to his situation in your family, whatever he may inwardly feel.—

Will you forgive me if I confess that there seems to me to be one little inconsistence in your mode of thinking on this case? Far more delicately sensitive to, and more finely sentient of, the Right and Wrong, the Seemly and the Unbecoming, in all their shades than I ever knew any other Woman to be, it is quite impossible that you should not be very strongly acted upon by the contrast to yourself in females like Maria. And yet you appear to contemplate such and such particular results of this inferiority as every now and then come to your knowlege, tho' they are in reality only so many proofs and natural consequences of what you knew before hand, with almost the same disgust and aversion, and as uncomfortable feelings respecting the Individual, as if you had had a right to anticipate, and been in the habit of expecting, the contrary. Now I have more than once known, and often and often heard of, a young man severely and justly reproached and reprimanded for haunting the Kitchen, of talking over his own affairs & those of others with a Servant, but I never knew of the blame being layed chiefly or equally on the latter. It has been made part of the reproach—'I don't wonder, that she should be mightily flattered by a young gentleman's opening out his mind to her as if she were his equal—and having to sympathize with him and to pity him—especially when he took no improper liberties. But that *you* should seek such confidantes—at once degrading yourself and us, and turning a servant girl's head with vanity and idle discontented wishes'—&c &c—This is the sort of language which it has been common to use—. The fault was charged on the superior in rank for holding out a temptation which—as the inferior could not be expected to regard the talking with her as any thing in itself wicked: for no one, however humble her station, will think so meanly of herself as to believe that—an ignorant and vain Girl was not likely to persist in discouraging.

In short, the sum and substance of my judgement is that it may become your duty to remove Maria—that whenever (all things considered) it shall be proved desirable to discharge her, it will be easy to do so even as a matter of feeling, because (fault or no fault on her side) it will be evident even to herself, that you can not do otherwise—but if this alarm should have a salutary and lasting effect on Powel or on both, you will be more secure than with another perhaps who might, like Jane, under a very simple countenance disguise a worse passion than vanity.

Besides, when I think what you have gone thro' & had to bear from the time of H's leaving his Chambers (to go no farther back than that) I declare before God that I want words to express my admiration of your fortitude, and of that genial strength which the mere sense of Duty could not have supplied, had it not been fed by natural goodness—Yet your health has been heavily taxed— and I am afraid of any severity of Mr G. to P., just now, lest it should distress and flutter you—[MS. breaks off thus.]

1322. *To Charles Aders*

Address: Charles Aders, Esqre | Euston Square
MS. Lady Cave. Hitherto unpublished.

Christmas Day
1822.

My dear Sir

Seated tho' on Christmas Day with a Pupil discussing LOGIC, I have barely time to say that I arrived quite safe[1]—and neither thought nor suspected any thing amiss as indeed nothing there was except that the Hackney Coachman was something of a Rogue—& proportioned his terms to his discovery that the Family were in bed & that I was anxious to close the door—Pray, make my very best and kindest respects to Mrs Aders, and assure her from me that from 5 even to 1 o'clock were hours so happy either from enjoyment or the impressions left by it that I shall remember even

[1] On 21 Dec. 1822 Coleridge attended a party at the Aders's. Crabb Robinson's description of this occasion reveals Coleridge's attitude toward Wordsworth and Southey at this time, an attitude undoubtedly provoked by their active interference with the plan to remove Hartley from the temptations in London:

Dec. 21st. . . . The afternoon I spent at Aders's; a large party; splendid dinner prepared by a French cook and music in the evening. Coleridge was the *star* of the evening. He talked in his usual way, but as well and with more liberality and in seemingly better health than when I saw him last, some years ago. But he was somewhat less animated and brilliant and paradoxical. He had not seen Wordsworth's last works, and spoke less highly of his immediately preceding writings than he used and still does of his earlier works. He reproaches him with a vulgar attachment to orthodoxy in its literal sense. The latter end of *The Excursion*, he says, is distinguishable from the former, and *he* can ascertain from internal evidence the recent from the early compositions among his works. He reproaches Wordsworth with a disregard to the mechanism of his verse, and in general insinuates a decline of his faculties. Of Southey's politics he spoke also depreciatingly— he is intellectually a very dependent, but morally an independent man. In the judgment of Southey I concur altogether. Of Wordsworth I believe Coleridge judges under personal feelings of unkindness. The music was enjoyed by Coleridge, but I could have dispensed with it on account of Coleridge himself. (*Robinson on Books and Their Writers*, i. 288.)

Coachee the Rogue with a sort of kindness & pleasure for many a
year—that we shall all have great delight in seeing yourself or
Mrs Aders or any of the Household of Love, I can without a moment's hesitation add, altho' neither Mr or Mrs Gillman are at this
moment at home—A happy Christmas to you all—& remember
me particularly to your Sister and Miss [Kelly][1] whose face is a
Corelli[2] *Concerto* (the VIIIth), a silent Music—Your's with unfeigned regard & esteem

S. T. Coleridge—

1323. *To Mrs. Charles Aders*

Address: Mrs Charles Aders | Euston Square | New Road
MS. Cornell University Lib. Hitherto unpublished.
Postmark: 26 December 1822.

26 Decr. 1822

Dear Madam

O the plague of Servants! And the Egyptian Plague of *new*
Servants with old and leaky memories! Had our Maid and Jani-
tress, Dinah, not been a new servant, she would not only have
known without being told, that her Mistress and myself were
merely out for a short walk, and that from the time of our absence it
could not be many minutes before our Return; but she would have
received so many reproofs, remonstrances and injunctions (*anglice*,
scoldings) on this score, as would (I borrow the metaphor from the
great Locke who calls Memory the Storehouse of the mind) have
insured the Cock-loft or Lumber-garret of her Soul tho' it had been
treble-hazardous. And again, had she not had an old crazy bird-
cage with the door off and the bottom out by way of an Idea-
pantry, or Lock-up Drawer, or intellectual Card-rack, my special
instructions and 'vergessen sie nicht's on this very point, and
inspired in fact by a presentiment of Your Call, would never have
been delivered in at the one portal of her Skull to fly out at the
other.—So it was, however; and the Door had scarcely closed on
our return, when we discovered that your carriage had left it
scarcely ten minutes before! And to aggravate our disappointment,
Mrs Gillman *elicited* (as the *fine* style has it) by dint of a little cross-
examination, that you had not even been requested to alight &
stay a few moments. Instead of Mrs Harkort and Yourself we have
your Cards—prophets, I trust; but they are but the Prophets when
we might have had the Gospel. As it happened, I am rather glad

---

[1] This name is heavily inked out in MS.
[2] Arcangelo Corelli (1653–1713), Italian violin-player and composer.

that Miss [Kelly][1] was not with you—a proof of the wonderful
ingenuity of my optimism in the extraction of comfort.

I write now, first to return my own and Mrs Gillman's Acknowlegement to Mrs Harkort and yourself for your attention & friendly
intention—2. to express our regret—and lastly, our hopes that it
will have been a favor delayed only and not lost, and that with the
single exception of Saturday next,[2] when we shall all on different
errands be in town we know of no morning for the next 7 or 8 days
on which there is any chance of our not being at home, meaning
by morning the whole day.—

And now with an affectionate 'Happy, Happy, Happy, Happy,
Christmas' to Mr Aders, Mrs Harkort, your dear [Miss Ellen?][3] &
Yourself (there is one for each), permit me to subscribe myself
with sincerity,

dear Madam, | Your & Mr Aders' obliged | Friend
S. T. Coleridge

P.S. I have been writing in the Dark for the latter ten lines—and
cannot find the Wax.

1324. *To Thomas Allsop*

Address: T. Alsop, Esqre | Blandford Place | Pall Mall
MS. New York Public Lib. Pub. with omis. Letters, Conversations and Rec. *204*.
Postmark: Highgate, 27 December 1822.

26 Decr 1822

My very dear Friend

I might with strict truth assign the not only day after day but
hour after hour [employment], if not thro' the whole period of my
waking time yet thro' the whole of my writing power, as the cause
of my not having written to you with my own hand; but then I
ought to add, that it was enforced & kept up by the expectation of
seeing you. There were two ways of giving you pleasure & comfort
—would to God, I could have made the one *compossible* with the
other & done both—the first, the having finished the Logic, in all
it's three main Divisions, as the Canon, or that which prescribes
the rule and form of all *conclusion* or conclusive reasoning: 2. as the

---

[1] Heavily inked out in MS.
[2] Coleridge dined with John Taylor Coleridge on Saturday, 28 Dec. Henry
Nelson Coleridge, who had not seen his uncle since 1811, was also present and
made a brief record of Coleridge's conversation, a transcript of which is dated
29 December 1822. In his *Specimens of the Table Talk of the late Samuel Taylor
Coleridge*, 2 vols., 1835, excerpts from this conversation are printed under
the dates of 4 and 6 Jan. 1823.
[3] Heavily inked out in MS.

Criterion, or that which teaches to distinguish Truth from False-hood—containing all the possible sorts, forms, and sources of Error, and means of deceiving or being deceived—3. as the Organ, or positive instrument for discovering Truth—together with the general Introduction to the whole.—

The second was, to come to Town & pass a week with you & Mrs A.—The latter I could not have done & yet been able to send you the present good tidings, that with regard to the former we are in sight of Land—that Mr Stutfield will try to give 3 days in the week for the next fortnight, and that I have no doubt, notwithstanding Mrs Coleridge & little Sara's expected arrival on Friday next,[1] that by the end of January the whole work will not [only] have been finished—for that I expect will be the case, next Sunday Fortnight, but ready for the Press.—In reality, I have *now* little else but to transcribe—and even this would in part only be necessary, but that I must of course dictate the sentences to Mr Stutfield & Mr Watson, & shall therefore avail myself of the opportunity of occasional correction & improvement.[2]—When this is done, & can

[1] Since this letter was concluded on Friday, 27 Dec., and bears a Highgate evening postmark of that date, by 'Friday next' Coleridge refers to 3 Jan. 1823. Mrs. Coleridge and Sara were at Highgate on the latter date. See Letter 1325.

[2] There is extant in the British Museum a two-volume uncompleted manuscript of Coleridge's *Logic*. (Egerton 2825, 2826.) Miss Snyder, who gives an analysis of the two volumes, describes the manuscript as follows:

The copy, on paper watermarked variously 1823 and 1827, is in the writing of two different amanuenses or copyists and contains a table of contents and occasional corrections in Green's hand. . . . The treatise very evidently was not finished, as it breaks off before it has fulfilled what at various points it promises. The copy was not revised so as to be in fit shape for the printer. . . . There seems to be little question that the manuscript was in part at least dictated to members of the philosophical 'class' that Coleridge conducted [in 1822]. . . . Though the manuscript 'Logic' as it now exists gives evidence of being a second copy, rather than an original taken down directly from dictation, it is just such a work as might have been dictated. . . . In certain sections of the manuscript Coleridge deliberately addressed his readers as though they were present, and it is clear that he had in mind a group of students preparing themselves for such professions as . . . ['the Pulpit, the Bar, the Senate, or any of those walks of Life, in which the possession and the display of intellect are of especial importance'].

In 1854 J. H. Green insisted that he had exercised a 'sound discretion' in not publishing the two-volume unfinished *Logic*. Miss Snyder justifies Green's decision against publication and points out that 'the bulk of the second volume, and parts of the first, would have been condemned as plagiarized from Kant, and (by those who knew him) from Mendelssohn'. Except for the passages printed by her, the work remains unpublished. See *Coleridge on Logic and Learning*, 1929, pp. xi, 66–74, and 78–127, *Notes and Queries*, 10 June 1854, and Letters 1290, 1298, and 1301. See also J. H. Muirhead, *Coleridge as Philosopher*, 1930, pp. 267–8, and Campbell, *Life*, 251 n.

be offered as a *Whole* to Murray or other Publisher, I shall have the
Logical Exercises—or the Logic exemplified and applied in a
Critique on 1. Condillac, 2. Paley. 3. the French Chemistry &
Philosophy—with other miscellaneous matters, from the present
Fashions of the age, moral & political, ready to go to the Press
with, by the time the other is printed off—& this without inter-
rupting the greater Work on Religion, of which the first Half,
containing the Philosophy or *ideal* Truth, Possibility and a priori
Probability of the Articles of Christian Faith, was completed
Sunday last.—

My dear Fellow! let but these Works be once done, & my responsibility off my Conscience, and I have no doubt or dread of afterwards obtaining an honorable sufficiency, were it only by Schoolbooks & Compilations from my own Memorandum Volumes—
The publication of my Shakespear & other similar Lectures, sheet
per sheet in Blackwood, with the aid of Mr Frere's Short-hand
Copies—and those on the History of Philosophy[1] in one Volume
would nearly suffice.—

I pray you, therefore, put *me* out of the *Weights* in the Scales—
You will be ever of most important service to me by giving me as
much of your society, as you can—& by making me feel that I in
my turn am a Comfort to you—.

The Winter has, I cannot deny, set in somewhat suddenly—but
what then? It is but a *Season*—& common to you with thousands
—but that it has come unaccompanied with any ground of self-
reproach, on the score of extravagance, want of foresight, & the
like, is not quite so common—and where these aggravations do
not exist, Winter will but *brace* your nerves for the returning
Spring and Summer—.

I was unspeakably delighted to see Mrs Allsop look so *charmingly*
well—My affectionate regards to her, and a heart-uttered Happy,
Happy, Happy Christmas to You both, one for each & the third
'happy' for the little one, who (Mr Watson assures me) has now the
ground-work and necessary pre-condition of thriving, tho' it may
be some time before a notable change in the appearance may take
place, for the general Eye.—

I am commissioned by Mr & Mrs Gillman to ask you & urgently,

---

[1] The only known shorthand reports of Coleridge's lectures on Shakespeare
are those of the 1811–12 course made by John Payne Collier and J. Tomalin,
the latter on the initiative of Southey. See *Southey Letters*, ii. 247; *Coleridge's
Shakespearean Criticism*, ed. T. M. Raysor, 2 vols., 1930, ii. 24–25; and Letters
844 and 1228 and notes.

A shorthand report of Coleridge's lectures on the History of Philosophy
(1818–19) was made at the request of J. H. Frere. (See Letter 1177.) The
lectures were published in 1949. See note to Letter 1228.

whether you & Mrs A. will spend next Sunday Afternoon & Evening with us?— Pray, do if you can, for I shall not be easy till I
see you.

God bless you & your Friend

S. T. C.

27th. Decr. I have forgot to EXPRESS our thanks for the Turkey
& Ham[1]—

1325. *To Charles Aders*

Address: Charles Aders, Esqre
MS. Cornell University Lib. Hitherto unpublished.

Friday Night [3 January 1823][2]

My dear Sir
  It is a maxim with me, to make Life as continuous as possible,
by linking on the Present to the Past: and I believe that a large
portion of the ingratitude, inconstancy, frivolity, and restless
self-weariness so many examples of which obtrude themselves on
every man of observation and reflective habits, is attributable to
the *friable*, incohesive sort of existence that characterizes the mere
man of the World, a fractional Life made up of successive moments,
that neither blend nor modify each other—a life that is strictly
symbolized in the thread of Sand thro' the orifice of the Hour-glass,
in which the sequence of Grains only *counterfeits* a continuity, and
appears a *line* only because the interspaces between the Points are
too small to be sensible. Without Memory there can be no hope—
the Present is a phantom known only by it's pining, if it do not
breathe the vital air of the Future: and what is the Future, but the
Image of the Past projected on the mist of the Unknown, and seen
with a glory round it's head.[3] But where shall we find the Eternal,
which gives the Three in One, and makes all exist in each? It is
Love—Love that like Flame can pass successively, from this to
this, ever the same essentially and yet taking up into it's character
the nature of the Object in which it finds it's sustenance—! I of
course am a stranger to your dear now spiritual Mother; but as by
the beauty of a Daughter we may form an idea of the beauty (and
there *is* an almost *divine* Beauty) of Age that formed the shrine of
holy Love in the Parent, so by Mrs Aders' Countenance, Tones, and
Movements can I interpret what your Mother must have been—for

---

  [1] This sentence is written at the top of page one of the MS.
  [2] This letter was begun on Friday, 3 Jan. 1823, the day Mrs. Coleridge and
Sara arrived at Highgate. See preceding letter.
  [3] Cf. *Constancy to an Ideal Object*, line 30. See also Letter 1468.

no man can truly love diversely or *diverse* objects.—Mean is the
conjugal Love which does not partake of the *sisterly* and tend to
renew and re-animate the *filial.*—Need I say then, how unwilling
I am to return a negative to your more than kind invitation ?—
But my Daughter (a sweet and delightful Girl) is with me—&—Mrs
Coleridge.[1]—

Sunday Afternoon

My dear Sir

I have not time to detail the unforeseen causes that prevented
me from finishing and dispatching the above—I will therefore
finish by saying that I absolutely *yearn* to be with you—but that,
unless you can allow me to return a conditional answer—viz. that
I will if I can do it without giving offence to Mr and Mrs Gillman,
whom I had authorized to return a negative to an invitation of
Mr Sutton's of this place for the same evening, I must tho' most
reluctantly return a negative to your's—

A pupil is with me—& I cannot add more; but by the first post
tomorrow you shall receive a note from me at your Counting House
in the City—.

Believe me with | more than ordinary | esteem &
regard | Your's

S. T. Coleridge

1326. *To John Taylor Coleridge*

Address: John Coleridge, Esqre | 7 | Hadlow Street
MS. British Museum. Hitherto unpublished.

Sunday Night [9 February 1823][2]
Highgate—

My dear Sir

Believe me, (without any attempt seriously to explain what had
no meaning that could be called serious, in reference to any one)
that the words in my message to Mrs S. Coleridge had no bearing on
you or Mrs J. Coleridge at all—much less were they meant to convey
the slightest doubt as to my [being] kindly welcomed under your
roof. I never intentionally flattered any one, at any time of my

---

[1] On Sunday, 5 Jan., Henry Nelson Coleridge (1798–1843), the fifth son of
Coleridge's brother James, and John Taylor Coleridge came to Highgate,
where they met Mrs. Coleridge and Sara for the first time. Henry and Sara
were secretly betrothed before she and her mother left London for Ottery on
5 Mar. 'Sara and myself', Henry wrote in his diary on 21 Mar., 'are solemnly
engaged to each other.' E. L. Griggs, *Coleridge Fille*, 1940, p. 43.

[2] John Taylor Coleridge endorsed this letter '1823. Febry. 10th. S. T. C.
Highgate', the day it was received.

life—but experience, disappointment, and a wounded spirit, have certainly rendered me more chary of my good words—and when I assure you that I hold and have held, your head and heart and character in entire respect, in short, that I think of you with esteem & regard, you will but do me justice in believing that they are no every day phrases. I should not now have been tempted to this overflow, but that the Return of my Cough & the affection of my chest, puts it out of my power to dine with you tomorrow—.

Mr Mudford begs me to desire Mrs Coleridge to apply to him, (Wm Mudford, Esqre. 7. Charlotte St, Bloomsbury) should she & her friends wish for Orders for Covent Garden—. But I shall write to Mrs C. tomorrow[1]—

This Scrawl I hurry off by favor of Mr Jameson who will be so kind as to drop it at Hadlow St. With best regards to you & your's, I am, your affectionate Uncle

S. T. Coleridge

[1] After leaving Highgate at the end of January, Mrs. Coleridge and Sara paid a visit to John Taylor Coleridge and his wife in London. Everyone who met Sara, then twenty years of age, was struck by her beauty and intelligence. Modest and unassuming, she was, nevertheless, unusually gifted. In 1822 she had already published a translation from the Latin of Martin Dobrizhoffer, *An Account of the Abipones, an Equestrian People of Paraguay.* The work was issued in three volumes by John Murray. Coleridge later declared that his daughter's translation was 'unsurpassed for pure mother English by any thing I have read for a long time'. (See *Table Talk*, 4 Aug. 1832.)

On 8 Dec. 1822 Lady Beaumont had given her impressions of Sara in a letter written to Dorothy Wordsworth from Leicestershire:

Mrs Coleridge & Sarah called here on their way to Cambridge, after apprizing us of their intention, and spent 5 days. I never saw at her age such a delicate little sylph; so thoughtful, yet active in her motions, she would represent our ideas of Psyche or Ariel. Juliet would be too material. [MS. Dove Cottage. Transcript furnished through the kindness of the late Helen Darbishire.]

Even while Sara and her mother were staying with John Taylor Coleridge, Southey on 10 Feb. 1823 sent him a letter filled with devastating criticism of Coleridge, unkind comments on Hartley and Derwent, and the following passage concerning Sara:

If Lady Beaumont has formed any indiscreet scheme of showing off Sara, I am afraid Mrs C. would enter into it too readily, & set down any caution which might come from me, to a wrong motive. Most probably her warm manner of speaking has been interpreted more literally than it was meant. But I believe the Wordsworths are going to Coleorton, & they will prevent this kind of mischief.
[MS. Coleridge family.]

Not long afterwards the Wordsworths arrived at Coleorton, and certainly Sara did not see Lady Beaumont a second time before returning to Keswick.

1327. *To William Godwin*

Address: William Godwin, Esqre | 195 Strand | (opposite St Clement's Church)
MS. Pierpont Morgan Lib. Hitherto unpublished.
Postmark: 28 February 1823.

Highgate
Friday Afternoon—[28 February 1823]

My dear Godwin

I am much obliged to you for your kindness & am gratified by Lady Caroline Lamb's admiration of the Wallenstein—in the merits of which I must conclude myself to have some Share, since the celebrated German Poet & philosophic Critic, Ludovicus Tieck assured me that familiar as he was with the German play, he could never read my Wallenstein but as an Original—nor did he hesitate to declare that in *diction* and *metre* it was decidedly superior to Schiller's: and that it had the not ordinary good fortune of Mr Pitt's applause, in addition to Mr Canning's & Mr John H. Frere's. —As to Kean, it would be superfluous to say a word—a man, whose genial originality, whose unique and multiform energy in the evolution of Thought, Passion, and Character, in one word whose intense Genius in re-creating the creations of the World's first Genius, are granted—I had almost said—*conclaimed*—even by those whose Preconceptions of Tragedy are at variance with his—. It is odd enough, that some 12 months ago I meditated the attempt, difficult as I knew it must be to bring the quantum of at least *five* representable Plays into one—& the original an historical Drama, the movements of which are almost necessarily slow in order to be intelligible—I had written to request and I actually obtained, Messrs. Longman & Co's permission to make what use I might wish of the Volume—and they kindly desired me to consider it as a manuscript, with the Copy-right of which I had not parted.—I answer therefore that I will do my best—& present it to Mr Kean— but with very little expectation of the result unless he would kindly consent to regard my abridgement or *reduction* as a mere rough Copy, to be altered, abridged, added to, translocated &c under his advice & directions.[1]—

For the last 3 months or somewhat more, I have been an object of some Alarm to my dear good House-mates, in consequence of an obstinate Cough, with violent & difficult expectoration, soreness of

---

[1] Writing to George Ticknor on 16 July 1823, Southey remarks: 'Coleridge talks of bringing out his work upon Logic, of collecting his poems, and of adapting his translation of Wallenstein for the stage,—Kean having taken a fancy to exhibit himself in it.' *The Life and Correspondence of the late Robert Southey*, ed. C. C. Southey, 6 vols., 1849–50, v. 142.

the Chest & Pain in the Side—symptoms different in kind from those of my ordinary up and down, better and worse, Valetudin-arianism. This makes Mr Gillman so anxious about my being out at night, that I cannot follow my first impulse—that of acknowleging & availing myself of Lady C. Lamb's polite invitation, without consulting him—But as soon as I can settle this, I will write to her Ladyship—.

My best regards & kind remembrances to all of your fire-side, & believe me,

dear Godwin, | with affectionate esteem | Your poor, sick, and dejected | but very sincere Friend

S. T. Coleridge

1328. *To Sara Hutchinson*

MS. Mr. W. Hugh Peal. Hitherto unpublished.

[*Circa* 13 March 1823][1]

My dear Sara

I was much vexed and startled when on my return to the house I found that my *standing* Ticket had been lent & my sitting one locked up in Mr Gillman's Escrutoir—who is gone on a little Tour. I am glad however that I have been able to procure a substitute—and I believe a good Seat—It is but for *one*; but with management Mr Monkhouse will get in, I doubt not. As to a standing Room, if you are there by 10, there will be no doubt. I have just written on the other side what perhaps may in case of any scruple which I do not anticipate (for standing Room at least) with Mr Routh's Seat-Ticket, remove the obstacle—

May God bless you, | and your sincere and | faithful Friend

S. T. Coleridge.

[1] The ticket referred to in the present letter may have been for the 'Oratorio' mentioned by Sara Hutchinson in a letter written from the Monkhouses', 67 Gloucester Place, and postmarked 15 Mar. 1823: 'Last night Mr M. took me to the Oratorio where we both of us had a comfortable nap.' *The Letters of Sara Hutchinson*, ed. Kathleen Coburn, 1954, p. 248.

1329. *To Mrs. Charles Aders*

Address: Mrs Aders
MS. Indiana University Lib. Hitherto unpublished.

25 March 1823
Highgate

My dear Madam

It is an ill wind that blows no good. Grievously did I moan under the illness, that now supplies or rather precludes my apology, and which during the whole of my dear Girl's stay in town confined me to my chamber—Even while she & her Mother were at Highgate, I never had the power of going to town with them—& during the 5 weeks' interval between their leaving Highgate & returning for *one* day to take their parting Leave for Devon, I never saw them—. Mr Gillman was, for the first time, seriously alarmed on my account —my Cough almost making my nights sleepless, and both my Chest & Side affected, and with an aversion to food of all kinds—. I need not therefore do more than assure you that not only it had been my full intention to have introduced Mrs Coleridge & my sweet child to You & your dear [Girl][1] but that I repeatedly thought of it in my list of special disappointments.—I am, thank God! much better—tho' still very far from being as strong either in body or spirit as before the Attack.—

That Mr R. is Your's & Mr Aders' Friend had been enough; but besides this I should feel gratified by any opportunity in my power of proving my sense of Mr Rees' own Merits,[2] and of thanking him for the high & unusual delight, I received from him on that never-to-be-forgotten evening[3]—I know of no English Translation of the Poem—and in fact I have no distinct recollection of the Poem itself, having more than a year ago sent my only copy of Schiller's Poems with other German Books to my Daughter—& they are at Keswick.—But if Mr R. could give me *time*, unused as for so many many years I have been to versifying of any kind, and dried up as, I fear, my poetic Spring will be found by the *severities* of austere Metaphysics, I will *attempt* it for him—& as soon as I have procured the Volume.—

Remember me with cordial regard & esteem to Mr Aders—& with affection to your daughter—& believe me,

dear Madam, | with the same affectionate | respect & regard |

Your obliged
S. T. Coleridge

[1] This word is heavily inked out in MS.
[2] Crabb Robinson spells the name Reece. *On Books and Their Writers*, i. 293.
[3] 21 Dec. 1822. See Letter 1322.

1330. *To Thomas Allsop*

Pub. Letters, Conversations and Rec. *140.*

Allsop introduces this undated fragment with the following note: 'The enclosed extract of a letter written about this time [October 1821], I give for the sake of the conclusion.'

[April 1823 ?][1]

I am glad to learn that the dwellers at Rydal perceived an amendment in me. In self-management, in the power of keeping my eyes more, and my heart less open, in aversion to baseness, intrigue, in detestation of apostacy, to . . .*

. . . and *silent* or suggestive detraction it would be well for me if I were as I was at twenty-five. Amendment! improvement in outward appearance, in health and in manners, I owe to my friends here; who as they would not admit any improvement in innocence or blamelessness of life, so they would indignantly reject and repel any alteration for the worse.

1331. *To Derwent Coleridge*

Address: Derwent Coleridge, Esqre. | St John's College | Cambridge
MS. Mrs. E. F. Rawnsley. Hitherto unpublished.
Postmark: Highgate, 23 April 1823.

[23 April 1823]

My dearest Derwent

I am almost ashamed to take up such a Scrip of Paper for a Cambridge Destination—but infer from it that I do not regard it as a Letter which I promise you *very shortly* & you shall not have to pay the post for it—

I write now to beg you *forthwith* to send the requisite Certificates of your due residence &c to Mr Sutton—& at the same time your authority for paying the two half-yearly Exhibition-halves now

---

[1] Coleridge and Wordsworth had seen one another in 1820, but there is no evidence that they met again until 1823. On 4 Apr. Thomas Monkhouse gave a dinner at which Coleridge, Wordsworth, Moore, Rogers, and Lamb were present—'half the Poetry of England constellated and clustered in Gloster Place'. Crabb Robinson, Gillman, Mrs. Wordsworth, and Sara Hutchinson were also there. According to Lamb, Coleridge 'was in his finest vein of talk'. Robinson, too, says that Coleridge 'talked much and well. I have not for years seen him in such excellent health and spirits'. Again on 5 Apr. Coleridge and Wordsworth were guests at a 'musical party and supper' at the Aders's. The present letter may have been written not long after these two parties, and it may have been Lamb who informed Allsop that 'the dwellers at Rydal perceived an amendment' in Coleridge. See *Middle Years*, ii. 877; *Lamb Letters*, ii. 376–7; and *Robinson on Books and Their Writers*, i. 292–3.

* I have now no means of supplying this hiatus. [Note by Thomas Allsop.]

lying for you at the Company.[1] As you had Lady B's 30£, this 20£, I suppose, had better be paid in to Mr. Gillman for the settlement of the Tutor's Bills—

I *have* been very seriously indisposed with a tearing Cough, worse during the night, & soreness & oppression of the Chest—but am now considerably tho' not totally relieved—

Your Uncle & Aunt, Col. & Mrs James Coleridge with Fanny[2] are in Hadlow St. & I shall dine with them, Deo volente, on Saturday—

Our James & Fish have just got out of the Measles. We have had a sick house from Garrett to Cellar—

Mrs G. sends her kindest Love & Remembrances to you—and I will myself write, as soon as ever I can put the last hand to my *Elements of Discourse*—which is grown from a mere Pistolette into an adult Blunderbuss—without any pun on the *Canons* of Logic—

Again & again | My dearest Boy God | bless you & your most | affectionate Father

S. T. Coleridge

P.S. They say here, that I am Derwent-sick—Doubtless, I yearn to see you—. I have had great comfort in a letter from Hartley—& your dear Sister!—She *is* a darling.

1332. *To John Taylor Coleridge*

Address: John Coleridge, Esqre | 7. Hadlow Street | Tavistock Square
MS. Cornell University Lib. Hitherto unpublished.
Postmark: Highgate, 23 April 1823.

Wednesday Afternoon—[23 April 1823]

My dear Sir

God willing, I shall not fail to be in Hadlow St. at the time appointed—& congratulate you on the arrival of so dear & precious

---

[1] On 7 Nov. 1822 the Mercers' Company elected Derwent Coleridge to a Lady North Exhibition of £20 per annum 'from Lady-Day last, and during the pleasure of the Court, he bringing Certificates of his Residence at College, agreeably to the Rules of this Court'. The certificates, which were to be signed by the college authorities, certified that the exhibitioner had 'kept all the forms required by the Statutes of the University'. The 'two half-yearly Exhibition-halves' mentioned in the present letter were for £10 each, from Lady Day to Michaelmas 1822 and from Michaelmas of that year to Lady Day 1823. Derwent probably obtained the 'requisite Certificates' and gave the authority for paying these sums, as his father directed, but the loss of the cash books and ledgers in the fire which destroyed Mercers' Hall in 1941 makes it impossible to determine what sums were paid during his residence at St. John's College. (From information kindly furnished me by Mr. G. E. Logsdon, Clerk of the Mercers' Company.) See also Letters 1614–17.

[2] Frances Duke Coleridge (1796–1842), daughter of Colonel James Coleridge.

an Assortment—. Be pleased to make my affectionate respects to
my Brother & Sister—& most cordially to Fanny whom I seem to
love with a double love—direct & reflected from little Sara, to
whom she has been so altogether a Sister—God bless you, and your
dear Lady & the *fine* fellow | &

S. T. Coleridge

1333. *To Thomas Allsop*

Address: T. Allsop Esqre | 2. Blandford Place | Pall Mall
MS. Cornell University Lib. Hitherto unpublished.
Postmark: Highgate, 30 April 1823.

[30 April 1823]

My dearest Alsop

Can you give me a bed for tomorrow (Thursday) Night from
9 or 10 to 11—as I dine in Hadlow St. with my Brother Col.
Coleridge—& on Friday with Mr & Mrs Gillman at Mr Green's—
& am *now* about to set off for Mr Stutfield's ?—If you cannot, be so
good as to have a line dropt for me before six o'clock tomorrow
evening, at John Coleridge's Esqre. 7. Hadlow Street. If you can,
I shall be with you & there needs no answer—

God bless you | &
S. T. Coleridge—

1334. *To Mrs. Basil Montagu*

Address: Mrs Montague | 25 Bedford Square
MS. Harvard College Lib. Pub. Notes and Queries, *26 December 1931, p. 461.*
Postmark: Highgate, 3 June 1823.

Highgate
Tuesday 3 June 1823

My dear Madam

If Basil, you think, could without detriment make his from-Eve-
to-Morn-Sojourn at Bage's for 10 or 12 days, you might then have
(and for two months) apartments at Mrs Page's that combine all,
you wish for. She would put up two beds in a spacious Room that
commands the loveliest View beyond compare of our Highgate
scenery—with a neat Breakfast Parlour.—And your Landlady is
a most worthy motherly woman, the widow of a Professional Man
—in short, she is & deserves to be, very highly respected by all
classes—a plain simple-hearted Gentlewoman of the good old
School.

Mrs Gillman has made me write this note to the stoppage or as a
semi-colon at least, of my Breakfast, for one *cause* & *two* reasons—

the *Cause*, the impatience arising from her mind being stirring-full of the subject—the reasons, 1. in case, an opportunity should occur of sending this in the course of the Morning to Bedford Square or Lincoln's Inn—2. in case, Basil should be prevented from coming here this evening, that it might be ready for the last Post—

God bless you both &

S. T. Coleridge

1335. *To John Taylor Coleridge*

Address: John [Coleridge,] Esqre | [Pump] Court | [Tem]ple.
MS. British Museum. Hitherto unpublished.
Postmark: Highgate, 5 June 1823.

[5 June 1823]

My dear John

'The Elements of Discourse, with the Criteria of true and false Reasoning, as the ground-work and preparation for Public Speaking and Debate—addressed to the Students and Candidates for the Pulpit, the Bar, or Senate'[1]—this Product of how many Years' Labor is now in such a state that I am most anxious that it should be, not indeed read but, sufficiently looked over and into by some man of good sense and academic education, as to enable him to form a satisfactory general notion of the Plan, principal Contents, and Style of Execution.—Every point strictly metaphysical— ex. gr. the whole Doctrine of Ideas, sensu Platonico, as different from notions, conceptions, and whatever else the Understanding forms on the Data delivered by the Senses or acquired by reflection on it's own processes—in short, every point to which the Disciples of Locke would or could object, has been carefully excluded and reserved for a separate Work. It is (tho' I avoid the name in the Title-page) a Work of Logic for those purposes to which Lord Bacon in his Novum Organum very wisely confines the science of Logic—namely, *forensic* purposes, denying it's applicability, as a positive Organ, to all subjects, whether in natural, moral or religious Philosophy, in which the absolute Truth is sought for— while he admits not only it's great utility but asserts it's indispensability (as far as any discipline or ἄσκησις can be called indispensable) in all subjects of discussion or inquiry, in which the Truth relatively to the Sense and Understanding of *man* in all his social and civil Concerns and Functions is alone required or of pertinence.

---

[1] As Miss Snyder points out, the title of Coleridge's work on logic 'vacillated between the "Organum verè Organum," "The Power and Use of Words," "Elements of Discourse," and plain "Logic" '. *Coleridge on Logic and Learning*, 1929, p. 69.

—Still, however, the Work is not a Novel or a Memoir or a series of Observations and Descriptions, each intelligible and interesting in itself and deriving from it's connection or rather juxta-position no other aid or support, than the different precious stones in a well-set sprig of Jewellery.—It must be read for some purpose—and by one who is willing to take some trouble the reward of which is to be found in the greater satisfaction & facility with which he can fill the sphere and perform the tasks and duties of his profession—who will take trouble to save trouble.—But for such a Reader, I do flatter myself, that the 'Elements &c' will be found more interesting and informing than might be anticipated from a Work, the ostensible & main purpose of which is to be formative and disciplinary—προπαιδευτικόν.

Now, my dear John! I have two requests to make—but I make them on the condition that it will neither seriously inconvenience you in point of Time, Prudence, or Feeling, to grant them. The first is—that you would give me one whole Morning—or at least, some four Hours, at your rooms or house or (in case, you could dine with us here, & perhaps bring Mrs John & the children whom Mrs Gillman would be happy to see & do her best to entertain) at Highgate—in order to put yourself in possession of the Nature of the Work, and of the State in which it is, in point of fitness for the Press—2. that if you think sufficiently well of the Work (I include in 'well' both it's intrinsic value and the probability of such a sale as would authorize a Publisher to print an Edition) you would speak to Mr Murray on the Subject—If he could be induced likewise to publish my Poems—so long out of Print & lately called for —including my Remorse &c—& to take the remaining Copies of the Friend—in short, if he would be my Publisher[1]—tanto melius.—

Any time within the next 10 days, excepting only Tuesday, 10 June—when I dine with the Beaumonts—nor that either—for we do not dine till near 7.— . . .[2]

[1] It was not until 1828 that an edition of Coleridge's *Poetical Works*, including the dramas, was published by William Pickering. After Coleridge's death H. N. Coleridge edited the third edition of *The Friend*, 1837, the work also being published by Pickering.

[2] I cut out the signature to this letter to affix it to a print of my Uncle— S. T. C. the writer. [Note in MS. by John Taylor Coleridge, dated 6 Dec. 1840.]

1336. *To John Taylor Coleridge*

Address: John Coleridge, Esqre | 7. | Hadlow Street | Tavistock Square
MS. British Museum. Hitherto unpublished.
Postmark: 11 June 1823.

Tuesday Afternoon—. [10 June 1823]
My dear John

Your kind Reply was perfectly satisfactory: and I shall follow your advice to the letter. Had I been aware of § §. 2., the corporeal part of which I have sacrified to Vulcan while the spiritual remains consecrated to Harpocrates, the *business* half of my request would not have been made at all. And as it was, I must have expressed myself inaccurately and conveyed more and other than what I meant or intended. I was too sensible of the appearances and possible interpretations, to which our Relationship would give rise, to entertain even a wish, that you should positively *recommend* the work to Murray on the ground of your own opinion either of it's intrinsic merits or it's likelihoods of success. Had this been my object, I should not—I trust, I may say, that I *could* not—independently of any accessory indelicacy on the score of our near relationship, have expressly confined my request to your just looking into and running over the Work, as contra-distinguished from a reading of it. But more than the former I would not ask, for two reasons. First, because I should not think myself justified in proposing such a task to any friend who had not his time at his free disposal, and this too for many days successively—in short, where there was any thing better or more necessary to be attended to—Secondly, because I do look forward, and with an interest not the less deep from it's having but little of the *personal* and nothing of the *wordly* in it's composition, to your reading *this* Work hereafter, at your leisure hours; and still more *another*, the *pioneering* for which has been one great tho' not ostensible Object with me in undertaking & going thro' with the Present. But for the same reason I am anxious that this should be possible without any accidental or removable Obstacles or Draw-backs: and I am very much of Charles Lamb's mind, who never knows what a work is or what he shall think of it, till he sees it in Print, bound, cut and splashed.—Now my MSS is legible enough for the demands of the London Press—that is, it will occasion no more trouble to the Compositors than they are in the habit of submitting to. But what would be no Drawback to a man, who has only to look at word after word, and line after line, and who unconcerned with the sense and argument is not at all confused or bewildered by the crossings out, the side Slips to be substituted, the directory marks of trans-position, &c—all which are sad interruptions and annoyances to a Reader—even tho' it were a Novel or Pindaric Ode instead of an Elementary Treatise.—

In fact, the request, I made, was much less in relation to Murray than to yourself—in my then state of knowlege or supposition. No man on good terms with another & respected by him can be certain what degree of influence his mere mention of a thing might have—and I should be unwilling that you should take even this responsibility upon you, without having so far mastered the chapter of Contents, and the way in which the Book was written as to have satisfied yourself that it was not (from whatever cause) such as in your own opinion would be a dead loss to the Publisher. It might barely or scarcely return the expences of Publication; and yet from other considerations be worth the attention of a Man like Murray. Ex. gr. if it was likely to add to or support his respectability—But I should exceedingly regret that you should have your name men-tionable by Murray as the person, who had originated the proposal, tho' but *vehicularly*, of an unsold unselling Volume, in which you yourself on afterwards looking into it saw sufficient reasons for it's want of sale.—My utmost wish was—that some one for whose judgment M. had some respect should describe the nature and object of the work—and if he could conscientiously add—'I have merely looked over the Mss, so as to know the plan & principal Subjects treated of—and have read with somewhat more attention two or three Chapters, on different subjects, as specimens of the style & manner—and as far as I am entitled to form any opinion on so slight an examination, it appears to me a work of ability—and I think that a work of this *kind* is *wanted*—but whether there are people enough that *want* it—i.e. feel the want—I must leave to other judges—nor indeed would I have you rely on *my* opinion as to the former.'—

Under the present circumstances, however, I agree with you that it will be my best way to write to M. myself—and to offer to confer with any competent Person who possesses his Confidence, and who would explain to him the extent, &c.—

Derwent left me on Thursday Evening—having arrived here that morning—& left Town for Eton, I understand, on Sunday last.—He is in a very unsettled unhealthy [state] of mind—and I should be at a loss to say, [what] one advantage he has acquired by his University Campaigns—but more of this when we meet.

My love to all of your—the Weather is cold enough to say— fireside.—I heard from Mrs S. Coleridge a few days ago—They were to quit Bristol on this day. My dear Girl was not well—& I shall be glad to hear of her being a fixture again, at Keswick, for some time at least.—

Believe me | with cordial Regard and Esteem, | my dear John, |
Your affectionate Uncle
S. T. Coleridge

P.S. My Love to Henry—tell him, I shall be always delighted to see him when he can make a day's countrification—& pray, when you write to Ottery remember me most affectionately to Fanny who is worthy to be your Sister—She is indeed a delightful Creature—Mrs Gillman thinks her *very handsome*—of that I am no judge.—S. T. C.—

1337. *To Thomas Allsop*

MS. New York Public Lib. Pub. Letters, Conversations and Rec. *95.*

[Circa 12 June 1823][1]

My dearest Allsop

God bless you, and all who are dear & near to you; but as to your Pens, they seem to have been plucked from the *Devil's* Pinions, and slit and shaped by the blunt edge of the broad sprays of his Antlers. Of the Ink (i.e. *your* Ink-stand) it would be base to complain—I hate abusing folks in their *absence*—. Do you know, my dear friend! that having sundry little snug superstitions of my own, I shrewdly suspect, that some whimsical ware of this sort is connected with the state & garniture of your paper-staining Machinery. Is it so?—

Well! I have seen Murray—and he has been civil, I may say, kind in his manners—Is this *your* knock? Is it you on the Stairs?— No.

[1] This letter was written in June 1823, shortly after the 10th. On that date Coleridge informed his nephew that he would himself write to Murray. As a 'consequence of some conversation with Mr Tulk', however, Coleridge 'waited on' Murray and 'found him all courtesy'. In June, previous to this meeting, Tulk also consulted Murray concerning the publication of Coleridge's philosophical works, and he, too, met with a friendly reception. As the present letter suggests, Murray agreed to become Coleridge's publisher. This was the only time Coleridge was able to see Murray, although he twice came in from Highgate to consult him about the publication of the selections from Leighton. Indeed, on 7 July he complained that for three or four weeks he had been 'dancing attendance on a proud Bookseller . . . to little purpose'. See Letters 1335–6, 1338–9, 1344, and 1448.

The erroneous date of '1 June 1821' appearing in the MS. is in Allsop's handwriting. In publishing this letter Allsop dated it '*Blandford-place, March 1st,*1821'.

I explained my full purpose to him—namely, that he should take me & my Concerns, past & future, for Print & Re-printed, under his umbrageous Foliage—tho' the original Name of his great Predecessor in the Patronage of Genius, who gave the name of Augustan to all happy Epochs—Octavius would be more appropriate—and he promises [MS. breaks off thus.]

1338. *To Charlotte Brent*

Address: Miss Brent
MS. Pierpont Morgan Lib. Pub. Letters, *ii. 722.*

Monday Afternoon—7th July 1823

My dear Charlotte

I have been many times in town within the last 3 or 4 weeks; but with one exception when I was driven in and back by Mr Gillman to hear the present Idol of the World of Fashion, the Revd. Mr Irving, the super-Ciceronian, ultra-Demosthenic Pulpiteer of the Scotch Chapel in Cross Street, Hatton Garden,[1] I have been always at the West End of the Town—and mostly dancing attendance on a proud Bookseller, & I fear, to little purpose—weary enough of my existence, God knows! and yet not a tittle the more disposed to better it at the price of Apostasy or Suppression of the Truth.—If I could but once get off the two Works, on which I rely for the Proof that I have not lived in vain, and had these off my mind, I could then maintain myself well enough by writing for the purpose of what I got by it—but it is an anguish, I cannot look in the face, to abandon just as it is completed the work of such

---

[1] Edward Irving (1792–1834), Scottish church divine. After serving for a short time under Thomas Chalmers at St. John's, Glasgow, Irving accepted an invitation from the chapel in Hatton Garden and began his ministry in London in July 1822. As a result of his great popularity he began preaching in a new church in Regent Square in 1827. He met Coleridge in 1823, and for several years the two men were on terms of intimacy. By 1826, however, Coleridge had come strongly to disapprove of Irving's *'interpretations* of the Apocalypse and the Book of Daniel'. Subsequently, he objected to Irving's 'too adventurous speculations on the Persons of the Trinity and the Body of our Lord'. The publication of *The Orthodox and Catholic Doctrine of our Lord's Human Nature* in 1830 exposed Irving to charges of heresy, but the attempted prosecution failed because of his withdrawal from the jurisdiction of the London presbytery. In 1832 the trustees of the Regent Square Church removed him from the pulpit, but in the same year he and his adherents founded the 'Holy Catholic Apostolic Church'. Although Irving was now a dissenting minister, he retained his status as a clergyman in the Church of Scotland until 1833, when he was found guilty of heresy respecting the humanity of Christ. Later he was suspended by his own congregation in London. See Letters 1339–40, 1473–4, 1518, 1521, 1523, 1584, and 1692; and *The Church and State*, 180–3 n.

intense & long continued labor—& if I cannot make an agreement
with Murray, I must try Colbourn—& if with neither, owing to the
loud Calumny of the Edingburgh & the silent but more injurious
detraction of the Quarterly Review, I must try to get them published
by Subscription.—But of this, when we meet—I write at present
& to you as the less busy Sister—to beg, you will be so good as to
send me the Volume of Southey's Brazil,[1] which I am now in
particular want of, by the Highgate Stage, that sets off just below
Middle Row.—'Mr Coleridge, or J. Gillman, Esqre (*either will do*)
Highgate.'

My kind Love to Mary. I have little doubt that I shall see you in
the course of next week—

Do you think of taking Rooms out of the Smoke during this
summer, for any time?

    God bless you | my dear Charlotte | and your affectionate
              S. T. Coleridge—

1339. *To C. A. Tulk*

MS. The Carl H. Pforzheimer Library. Hitherto unpublished.

                  [July 1823][2]
My dear Sir

The several Friends whom I have had the opportunity of consulting since the (to me at least) delightful Afternoon and evening,
which I enjoyed in your and Mrs Tulk's society at Mr Hart's (that
fine Example of that interesting Species of THE GENTLEMAN, the
courteous and dignified English Merchant!) have express'd the
liveliest satisfaction at my resolve to publish the Elements of
Discourse & Criteria of True [Truth?] and Falsehood, and likewise the larger Work entitled, Assertion of Religion as *implying*
Revelation, and of Christianity as the only Revelation of universal
and permanent Validity, by Subscription. To write and circulate
the Prospectus will be my first business after this letter:—one
object of which is to confess to you, my dear Sir, that Mr Murray
completely puzzles me. For I am unwilling to adopt my excellent
Friend, Mr Gillman's Solution, which would unloose at once the

---

[1] A copy of Southey's *History of Brazil*, 3 vols., 1810–19, containing annotations by Coleridge is in the British Museum.

[2] The present letter was undoubtedly written about the same time in July
1823 as the one to Charlotte Brent of the 7th. Both letters refer to the abortive
efforts which Coleridge made to see Murray a second time after their conference
in June. See Letter 1337. It was 14 Aug. before Coleridge received from Brighton a reply to this letter to Tulk. See Letter 1344.

knot of my perplexity—namely, that Mr Murray wishes and is of
course determined to withdraw himself altogether from *any* connection with my literary Undertakings. I am not willing, I say, to
suppose this; and still less willing to act on the supposition without
some more decisive evidence—not that I shrink from the wound,
it might inflict on my pride, nor yet, as a prominent motive at
least, in reference to the Loss or positive Injury, I might sustain
from the Withdrawal of his friendly Aid and his Interest, highly as
I appreciate the value of both, and greatly as I should (and with
good reason too) regret the having been deprived of them—but
bacause without a convincing proof I dare not, and even with such
proof I could not without pain of heart, attribute to a man, I have
so much respected, and who has acted so liberally & shewn such
kindness and courtesy toward my Daughter, the Caprice and
Hardness of Feeling that so sudden and unprovoked a Retracta-
tion of Offers so recent would imply.—The case is this. On the Day,
I dined with you, I had called in Albermarle Street with the
Volumes of Archbishop Leighton's Works, with the several passages, I had considered as the characteristic Beauties of his Writings,
marked in the side Margins, and my own Notes in the blank space
at the top and bottom of the Page—and having waited an hour
or so & the young Gentleman in attendance informing [me] that
there was no chance of Mr Murray's coming for that day, I wrote a
few lines stating the proposed title, and scheme of the little Volume,
and intimated that I should call again on the Friday following at
two o'clock. I did so. But Mr Murray was not at home to me; but
had left a note, declining the publication on a ground, which he
knew as well when the Proposal was first made by me & to a certain
degree encouraged by him—namely, the existence of a Reprint of
Leighton's Works—and entreated my Acceptance of the Copy,
which he had sent me, for the purpose of selecting from it[1]—This,
however, is a mere Trifle—except as to my strong wish to have the
credit of Mr Murray's being the Publisher of whatever Works, I
put my name to, it was no disappointment.[2] But what *was* such,

---

[1] The Erasmus Middleton edition of Leighton was published in 1805 and
reprinted in 1818, 1819, and 1822. Gillman owned the 1819 reprint. The Jerment edition of 1805–8 was reprinted only in 1820. It was the 1820 reprint of
the Jerment edition which Murray sent to Coleridge in Jan. 1822. This edition,
annotated in preparation of *Aids to Reflection*, is in the British Museum. For
Coleridge's earlier correspondence with Murray concerning a work on Leighton
see Letters 1288 and 1291.

[2] On 8 Aug. 1823 Coleridge submitted his work on Leighton to Taylor and
Hessey, under the title, *Aids to Reflection*, and they promptly accepted it for
phblication. Shortly afterwards they also agreed to publish Coleridge's philoso-
puical works. See Letters 1343 and 1345.

was Mr Murray's entire silence respecting my Poems and my MSS Works—not even an allusion to his Conversation with you.[1] This, of course, was the main Object of my journey to Town—namely, to express my full conviction of the Wisdom of his advice, and both my acceptance & sincere acknowlegements of his very kind offers in rendering the undertaking as inexpensive as possible—by enabling me to have the Paper, and Printing &c at the Trade Price. (In fact, the connection with Mr Murray, as my Publisher, and not any money-bargain with him, was & ever had been uppermost in my mind—led thereto, perhaps, by my very great Love and Admiration of Mr John H. Frere, so that (childish as it may be) I could not help wishing to have the same name in my title-page as stands & is to stand in his—.) It was also of importance to me to have been advised by Mr Murray as to the Price, I was to set on the Work—& what number of Subscribers would justify me in putting the first Work (an Octavo of about 400 pages) to the Press. —Again—with regard to the Poems, I had meant to propose— that I in the first instance should give a Catalogue of all the Poems, on which I myself should wish to rest my character as a Poet—and that from this *my* Selection every poem should be further struck off, as to the omission of which any two men of Taste should coincide—and that perhaps I might be able to induce Mr Rogers or Sir Walter Scott, or (if the Time were no absolute precludement) Mr Frere,[2] on my part, with an honest and earnest intreaty to him (whoever he might be) to regard it as the truest service to me to put my feelings (real or imagined) wholly out of the Question— especially as the Question would be, not what were bad or meritless, but what were comparatively, and in their own kind, of *inferior* merit.[3]—

Now, my dear Sir! what would you advise me to do? Would it be in your power, and at the same time would it be not unpleasant

---

[1] It seems likely that Coleridge also mentioned the publication of his poems during his interview with Murray in June, especially since he had previously suggested the desirability of such an arrangement in a letter to his nephew of 5 June. (See also Letter 1337.) In a conference with Tulk, however, Murray set forth his conditions. He was willing to publish Coleridge's poems, provided that H. H. Milman supervise the edition, i.e. make the selection and such omissions and corrections as Milman deemed advisable. Murray's insolent proposal and Milman's presumption in acquiescing to it never ceased to rankle in Coleridge's mind. See Letters 1344, 1438, 1456, and 1742.

[2] J. H. Frere had been living in Malta since November 1820.

[3] Murray's plan to have Milman oversee the edition of the poems undoubtedly led Coleridge to consider making this proposal. By 14 Aug. 1823, however, Coleridge wrote more independently to Tulk: 'I am ready to present . . . the Poems by me selected. . . . If Mr Murray will take them as I send them, I shall be happy to make any arrangement, that shall be considered as equitable.'

to your feelings, to see Mr M. once more, and state to him my full coincidence with his judgement as to the Pub. by Subscription, and my grateful Acceptance of his kind offers as understood by you— and to ask him, with what number of Subscribers, or with what sum of money pledged or secured by competent persons, I might go to the Press with a Volume of 400 Pages or about ?—

In consequence of having been thus employed in town, and of being obliged on my return to meet Mr Irving at the Table of a Friend, I have not had the time to provide you with a specimen of the De Amore & Conjugio in Blank Verse[1]—which I will, however, do, by or before Tuesday next—. But on consulting my friends they are all decided, that the Point depends on whether it be or not an indispensable condition with the Bookseller, that the Translation should be published in the first instance with *my Name*—for they feel quite certain, that wholly independent as the work itself may be of any (so called & generally esteemed as) Sectarian peculiarities, yet the mere circumstance of it's being a work of Swedenborg's, would be ruinous to my present Efforts—as I have good reason to believe, that a large number of my Subscribers will be Clergymen and Residents of our Universities—and that at all events my name must be withheld till after my present Works have been published.—

Amid all these worldly & heartless anxieties I can with strictest truth assure you, that no hour of my waking Life has passed since we parted in which I have not been inwardly listening to earnest thoughts & prayers respecting the beloved Mother of your Darlings. I wish, I could adequately convey to you the strength of my Desire that Mrs Tulk should see & converse with Mr Gillman before you leave Town, as well as yourself. He will wait on you with great pleasure & a sincere friendly Interest on any day, you shall appoint by a Line addressed to him or to me—*I pray you*, do—& attribute this urgency & freedom to the affectionate Respect & Esteem of your obliged

S. T. C.

---

[1] Coleridge apparently refers to Swedenborg's *Delitiae sapientiae de Amore conjugiali; post quas sequuntur voluptates insaniae de Amore scortatorio*, 1768.

1340. To Edward Coleridge[1]

Transcript Coleridge family. *Pub. with omis.* Letters, *ii. 724.*

Highgate, 23 July 1823.

My dear Edward

From Carlisle to Keswick there are several routes possible and neither of these without some attraction. The choice, however, lies between two—which to prefer I find it hard to decide, & if, as on the whole I am disposed to do, I advise the former, it is not from thinking the other of inferior interest. On the contrary, if your *Laking* were comprized between Carlisle & Keswick, I should not hesitate to recommend the latter in preference—but because the first will bring you soonest to Keswick, where Mr Southey still is, having, as your Cousin Sara writes me, deferred his journey to town on account of his Book on 'the Church',[2] which has outgrown it's intended dimensions; and because the SORT of 'scenery' (to use that slang word best confined to the creaking Dauberies of the Theatre) on the latter route is what you will have abundant opportunities of seeing with the one leg of your compass fixed at Keswick.

First then you may go from Carlisle to Rose Castle—& spend an hour in seeing that & it's circumferency—and from thence to *Caldbeck*, it's Waterfalls & Faery Caldrons, with the Pulpit & Clerk's Desk Rocks over which the Cata- or rather Kitten-ract flings itself, and the Cavern to the right of the Fall, as you front it—and from Caldbeck to the foot of Bassenthwaite, when you are in the vale of Keswick & not many miles from Greta Hall.—The second Route is from Carlisle to Penrith (a route of little or no interest),

---

[1] Edward Coleridge (1800–83), youngest son of Colonel James Coleridge, was assistant master at Eton College from 1824 to 1850. He became a fellow of Eton in 1857. See Lord Coleridge, *The Story of a Devonshire House*, 1905, p. 83.

In a published note to the present letter E. H. Coleridge says that the *Confessions of an Inquiring Spirit* 'were originally addressed in the form of letters' to Edward Coleridge. The concluding sentence of Letter 1624—'Should you come up on Sunday . . . be so good as to bring with you the Letters on the true and false veneration of the Canonical Scriptures'—and the fact that Green contributed an Introduction to the second edition of the *Confessions*, 1849, led E. H. Coleridge, however, to 'infer' that the 'Seven Letters to a Friend' were addressed to Green. [MS. note by E. H. Coleridge.] Neither suggestion seems plausible. Coleridge forwarded the MS. of his work to Taylor and Hessey in 1824 for inclusion in *Aids to Reflection*, a year before his intimacy with Edward Coleridge began. Nor is there any reason why Green, who was a constant visitor at Highgate, should have been chosen as the addressee. It is more likely that Coleridge presented the *Confessions* in epistolary form to give an informal or familiar tone to the work. See Letters 1447, 1450, and 1480.

[2] Southey's *Book of the Church*, 2 vols., was published in 1824.

but from Penrith you would go to Lowther (Earl of Lonsdale's Seat & magnificent grounds), the village of Lowther, Hawes Water, & from Hawes Water you might pass over the mountains into Ullswater & when there you might go round the head of the Lake (i.e. Patterdale), and if on foot & strong enough & the weather was fine, pass over Helvellin & so get into the High Road between Grasmere & Keswick; or passing lower down on the Lake cross over by Graystock [Greystoke] or (if with a guide, or minute instructions) over the Fells so as to come out at or not far from Threlkeld, which is but 3 or 4 miles from Keswick. At least in good weather there is, I believe, a tolerably *equitible* (i.e. horse or pony-tolerating) Track. But at Patterdale you would receive the best direction. There is an Inn at Patterdale where you might sleep so as to make one day of it from Penrith to the Lake Head viâ Lowther & Hawes water; & thence to Keswick would take good part of a second. There is one consideration in favour of this Plan—that from Carlisle to Penrith or even to Lowther you might go by the coach, & I question whether you could reach Greta Hall by the Caldbeck Route in one day. When at Keswick, I would advise you to go to Wastdale thro' Borrodale, & if you could return by Crummock & thro' the vale of Newlands, the inverted arch of which (on the *a* ⌣ *b* points (A B) of which I once saw the two legs of a rich ⌣ Rainbow, so as to form with the Arch a perfect Circle) *faces* Greta Hall, you will have seen the very Pith & Marrow of the Lakes, & especially as your Route to Chester or Liverpool will take you that lovely road thro' Thirlmere, Grasmere, Rydale (where you will of course pay your respects to Mr Wordsworth), Ambleside & the striking half of Wyndermere—

God bless you! Pray take care of yourself, were it only that you know how fearful & anxious your Father & Fanny are respecting your Chest & Lungs in case of cold or over-exertion.

Derwent promised me a long letter. I will not say that I hope he is better employed, because where there is NO BELIEF there can be no *Hope*. I have heard both from Sara & from Mr Watson (a friend of mine who has just come from the North) a very comfortable account of Hartley.

Believe me, dear Edward, with every kind wish |
Your affectionate Uncle & sincere Friend
[S. T. Coleridge.]

P.S. Your quere respecting the Poem I can only answer by a *Nescio*. Irving (the Scotch Preacher so blackguarded in the John Bull of last Sunday), certainly the greatest *Orator*, I ever heard (N.B. I make & mean the same distinction between Oratory & Eloquence as between the Mouth+Windpipe & the Brain+Heart) is, however, a man of great simplicity, of overflowing affections and enthusiastically in earnest, & I have reason to believe, deeply regrets his conjunction of Southey with Byron—as far as the *men* (& not the Poems) are in question.[1]

The Remorse may be had at Pople's in Chancery Lane—The Christabel I do not know where if not at Baldwin's. The Wallenstein *only by chance*. I have not a single copy of either—nor (which *might* be of use to you) of the 2 vol. of the Literary Life—the second volume containing (I dare affirm) the true principles of judgement respecting Poetry, *Poem*, poetic & *poematic* Diction.—But like all my writings it has been remorselessly pillaged both by Reviewers & Magazinists.

1341. *To Charles Aders*

Address: C. Aders, Esqre | 25 Lawrence pourtney [Laurence Pountney] Lane | Cannon Street   by Mr Watson.
MS. Columbia University Lib. Pub. E. L. G. ii. 312.

Monday Morning
4 August 1823.

My dear Sir

The Gentleman (Mr Watson) who will present this to you, has been not only my friend and house-fellow for some years but has been as a Son to me in all the services and affections of a Son: and I on my part love him as such, and (I might almost say) esteem him more, because the duties, he has taken on him, are duties of Love, acts of free will and the election of unbiassed Reason.—To be with me for any continuance and in any bond of Sympathy, and not to feel attached to Germans, and to prize the intellectual Growth of Protestant Germany, is scarcely possible. You will not therefore find it strange, that my young friend['s] Compass-needle points and trembles in that direction. He intends to leave England in late Autumn, the last week in September: and he has made up his mind to pitch his tent at or near Berlin. His wish and mine are, to procure admission on moderate terms, proportioned to his not very ample means, into the House of some respectable Man, a Pastor or other *Gelehrte*, near Berlin as a temporary Member of the Family; and if possible within an English mile or two at the furthest, from Berlin rather than directly in the city. This, however, is no essential article, or indispensable Condition. Of his exemplary morals

---

[1] Coleridge refers to Irving's *For Judgment to Come, An Argument, in nine Parts*, 1823. According to the article in the *D.N.B.*, this work 'is in its origin almost incredibly silly, being a protest against the respective Visions of Judgment of Southey and Byron, which Irving thought equally profane'.

and manners, his regularity, and sanftes ruhiges Wesen, I need only say & on this I dare pledge my whole character for Sense and Sincerity, that [it] is impossible for him to reside six weeks, or half that time, as an inmate of a worthy, enlightened and German-hearted Family, without acquiring and securing their warm regard during his stay, and without being the Object of Regret and indelible remembrance after his departure.—He purposes to remain during the Winter Half Year Term, and to attend the medical, chirurgical and philosophical Lectures.—Unfortunately, Professor Solgar & another intimate Friend of my friend, Mr Green, are no more; but Mr G. will write to Professor Lichtenstein,[1] whose acquaintance he made in London. But on such acquaintanceships I dare not rest exclusively, where Mr Watson's Comfort is so deeply concerned.—Now my request to you, my dear Sir! is—first, to think of whom you happen to know at Berlin—& if you have any friend there, to write to him, to look out for a situation such as I have described—& to inform you, or (as you will be probably absent) to address the answer to me (S. T. Coleridge, Highgate, near London), what likelihood there is of my friend's wishes being realized.—Perhaps, you may know some Friend who has connections at Berlin, if you should not—whom you might induce to write to them. I forget the name of the Prussian Minister to whom you were so good as to introduce me. Will you favor me with his name by Mr Watson? And likewise with your judgement whether there would be any impropriety in your or in my giving Mr Watson a letter of introduction to him. But I hope, that Business may allow you to have ten or 15 minutes' conversation with my young friend—.

O that I could be your fellow-traveller up the Rhine—& a Sojourner at your Godesburgh!—But a *more rational* because not A PRIORI impracticable Wish is very, very busy at my heart—namely, that on your return we may be at Ramsgate or some other Sea-place on Albion's Coasts together!—Mrs Aders & Mrs Gillman are worthy of each other: and it is not in the power of Man to pay either a higher Compliment—You & Mr Gillman might so comfortably go down together by the Steam boat on the Saturdays—& I am convinced, that it would be a compleat Revalescence, I had almost said, reviviscence to Mrs A., Mrs G. and dear little E[llen].[2]

May God bless you, in your goings forth and in your returnings—for with *unfeigned* esteem & no every day Attachment

I am, my dear Sir, | Your obliged Friend
S. T. Coleridge

---

[1] M. H. K. Lichtenstein (1780–1857), African traveller. In 1811 he was appointed professor of zoology at Berlin.

[2] This name is inked out in MS.

1342. *To William Lorance Rogers*[1]

Address: To Laurence Rogers, Esqre.
MS. University of Texas Lib. Pub. Letters Hitherto Uncollected, *42.*

Coleridge's letter was originally inserted in an annotated copy of *The Statesman's Manual*, 1816, bearing the inscription, 'L. Rogers, Esqre. from the
Author'. This volume is now in the University of Texas Library.

8 August **1823**
Highgate

My dear Sir
This first Lay-sermon was addressed specially to Metaphysicians
and Theologians by Profession—and *es*pecially to the Ministers of
the established Church, too many of whom, I fear, treat the Articles
of their Faith as the Whale treated Jonah—swallow what they
cannot digest—but with this difference to their disadvantage, that
what they cannot digest, they are yet not permitted to *throw up.*
This Tract you will not find as interesting generally as the Second
Sermon; but yet the passages, marked below, will I think please
you for their own merits, and I dare flatter myself somewhat
beyond it for the sake of, my dear Sir,
Your & Mrs Rogers's sincere | and affectionate Friend
S. T. Coleridge

21, 22. 24–30. 36–39. 52. xvii–xxx of the Appendix.

1343. *To Taylor and Hessey*

Address: Messrs. Taylor and Hesse | Booksellers | Fleet Street
MS. Historical Society of Pennsylvania. Pub. E. L. G. ii. 314.

8 August 1823

Dear Sirs
I have the honor of agreeing with all the thinking Men, with
whom I have conversed, in their objection to 'Beauties' of this or
that writer, taken as a *general* Rule. In the greater number of cases,
these collections of striking and shewy passages without any connection given in lieu of that which had been destroyed is almost as
injurious to the Original, as the taking out of the Lights of a Titian
or a Correggio & presenting them apart from the Shades would
be, considered as a specimen of the Picture. And it is in fact no less
injurious to the Reader, and one of the most effective recipes for
depraving his Taste and weakening his memory.—But if, as in all

---

[1] William Lorance Rogers, a barrister of Lincoln's Inn and a London police
magistrate, married Georgiana Louisa Daniell, a sister of John Frederic
Daniell (1790–1845), physicist and later professor of chemistry in King's
College, London.

cases, there are any exceptions to this Rule, the Works of Archbishop Leighton form one of the strongest. I need not enlarge to
you on the high and peculiar Merits of Leighton—on his persuasive
and penetrating eloquence, or the fine Fancy and profound Reflection
which seem trying to hide themselves in the earnest simplicity and if
I may so express myself, in the cordiality and *conversing*ness of his
style and manner. The point, on which I mainly rest as to my present
purpose, is this: that from the nature and necessity of his principal
work, (A commentary on the 1 Epistle of St Peter, Text by Text)
the most important and valuable Lights of these precious Volumes
present themselves to the Reader in a far more *un-* or rather *dis-*
connected manner, than they would in the Work, I have in view: so
much so indeed, that I was first led to take it in hand from the observations of several, to whom I had strongly recommended the original
Volumes, that from the abrupt transitions from one subject to
other and wholly different, and the continual interruptions of the
thread of Interest as well as of Thought had prevented them, some
from continuing the perusal, and more from reading him with the
satisfaction, they would otherwise have received—.

Now the Volume, I have prepared, will be best described to you
by the proposed Title—

Aids to Reflection: or Beauties and Characteristics of Archbishop
Leighton, extracted from his various Writings, and arranged on a
principle of connection under the three Heads, of 1. Philosophical
and Miscellaneous. 2. Moral and Prudential. 3. Spiritual—with a
Life of Leighton & a critique on his writings and opinions—with
Notes throughout by the Editor.

I have marked out all the passages intended for Extraction in my
Copy of Leighton's Works—which, if you think the proposal worth
attending to in the first instance, I would leave with you—tho' you
are well aware, how much more favorable Impression the passages
would make, arranged and in sequence, with the necessary additions, or completions, & the occasional substitutions of a word or
phrase when the words in the original have acquired by association
& change of fashions a mean or ludicrous sense. Will you do me the
favor of letting me know your opinion either by my friend or by
a Line addressed to me at Highgate?[1]—In the mean time I remain,
dear Sirs, | with sincere respect | Your obliged Servt.

S. T. Coleridge

To
    Messrs. Taylor and Hesse

---

[1] The 'obliging communication' mentioned in Coleridge's letter to Taylor
and Hessey of 16 Aug. 1823 undoubtedly was an acceptance of *Aids to Reflection* for publication.

P.S. The volume, I should propose, would be a small pocket octavo (Fool's cap, I believe, they call the size, I mean) of about 300 pages: which, I can with truth aver, wi[ll] contain the greater portion of all in the 4 thick miserably misprinted Volumes that is peculiarly and characteristically Leighton's Mind and Genius— & give to nine Readers out of ten a much truer, livelier, and more retainable Idea than they would form from their own reading of the Works themselves, even on the assumption that their patience held out so far.

1344. *To C. A. Tulk*

Address: C. A. Tulk, Esqre. M.P. | 19. Duke Steet | Westminster
MS. Pierpont Morgan Lib. Pub. E. L. G. ii. 316.
Postmark: Highgate, 14 August 1823.

Thursday Afternoon [14 August 1823]
Highgate.

My dear Sir

Mr Gillman will wait on you tomorrow at half past One: and I propose to share with him the chance of finding you at home. I was in the act of sitting down to write to you, when your Note from Brighton reached me, this morning—. I feared that in my last I might have conveyed to you a notion of my being *anxious* as to a *favorable* decisive Answer from Mr Murray, beyond the truth. Anxious for a final Yes or No I undoubtedly am; but my Wish, that it should be the former, is not of that strength or earnestness, as to make me look forward to it's disappointment as to any serious misfortune. Habes quod arrogas, is an adage of especial application in the present age and in the existing state of literary reputation—but in addition to it's impolicy, it would be immoral and a paltry Sacrifice of Sincerity to the semblance of Meekness, to pass what I believed to be a false and wrongful sentence against myself by submitting my compositions, the offspring of intense thought, to the Judgement or perhaps the after-dinner mood of Men whom I know to be my inferiors in Learning, *comparative* strangers to the philosophic and genial principles of Criticism, & whose own Articles do not impress me with any respect for Critical Dogmas grounded on no principles, and resting wholly on in-dividual Tastes and Accidents of association.[1]—I am ready to present matter for two independent Volumes, as the whole of the

---

[1] In 1825 Coleridge made clear the terms under which Murray was willing to publish his poems: '[Murray] made a proposal that I had sufficient respect for my own Standing in the literary world to consider as impertinent—viz.

Productions to which I judge that my name as a Poet may be
confided—the one containing the Poems by me selected, the other,
containing the Remorse, the Zapolya (greatly altered, in the Plot
as well as in the Dialogue) and a free Imitation of a Tragedy of
Calderon's. If Mr Murray will take them as I send them, I shall be
happy to make any arrangement, that shall be considered as
equitable.—This is, however, in my mind, on which different as I
know it to be from Mr Murray's, I must, and ought to, act—and
the more so, as in him his counter-judgement rests wholly on a
pre-conception, which he has not given me even a *chance* of recti-
fying if erroneous, or of converting into a well-grounded Conviction
if otherwise. A single Hour would have sufficed for this purpose,
with any man of scholarly attainments.—However, this is gone
by: & on the whole I am glad that it is so.—There are now but
three Questions, tho' in their inseparability they are in effect *one*—
1. Satisfactory security for the Paper, Printing, &c of the Works
having been obtained, will Mr M. adhere to the kind Offer, communicated to me thro' your mediation—2. will he do for the Work,
when published, the same as he is in the habit of doing for Publications, in the circulation of which he has himself a direct and
immediate Interest—& 3. will he allow me to consider him for the
future as my Publisher, whether at my own risk or otherwise
depending (of course) on the character of the Works and his own
Anticipations of their saleableness—and with the proviso, that
nothing is offered by me to which he can object on political or
moral grounds?—It is of the most urgent importance that I
should know his decision, without delay; but yet I should scarcely
have held myself justified in throwing the mediatory task on *you*,
my dear Sir! if by his total silence & the whole tone and bearing of
his last *note*, and his evident Shunning of a personal Interview with
me, Mr Murray had not seemed to have been trifling with the respect due to you, as well as with *my* feelings:[1] & but that it *is* possible—not indeed probable; but *possible* it is, that Mr Murray had

An offer to purchase my Poems on condition that some friend of his whom I was
not to know, but who (I believe) was a third rate Poetaster by the name of the
Revd. Mr Millman, [was] to omit, what he pleased, and to make what corrections and additions, *he* might think desirable.' Letter 1456. See also Letter 1438.

Again in 1832 Coleridge spoke with contempt of Milman and Murray: 'I cannot yet persuade myself that it was consistent with either the modesty of a
much younger man, or with the delicacy of a gentleman & a Scholar to consent
and undertake, at the instance & under the auspices of an Anthropoïd, like
Murray . . ., to select, omit, correct, and by a few felicitous interpolations
improve and adapt my poetic Works . . . to the correct taste of the Age.' See
Letter 1742.

[1] It seems likely that when Coleridge and Tulk met next day, as proposed
in the opening sentence of the present letter, they agreed that Murray had

supposed his communication thro' you to have superseded the necessity of referring to the Circumstance in any other form, till he had ascertained whether or how far I had acceded, or whether I had received the communication.—

I rejoice to hear of Mrs Tulk's amendment. Never shall I have been more (I need not add, or more painfully) disappointed, if there be aught worse in that dear Lady's Case than Disorder as contra-distinguished from organic Disease—To quote a stanza of my own—

> O ye Hopes! that stir within her,
> Health comes with you from above!
> God is with her, God is in her—
> She cannot die, if Life be Love![1]

With unfeigned Esteem & inmost sympathy with all your Havings, Doings and Beings,

I remain, my dear Sir, | Your obliged
S. T. Coleridge

1345. *To Taylor and Hessey*

Address: Messrs. Taylor and Hessey | Fleet Street
MS. Mr. James M. Osborn. Hitherto unpublished.

Saturday afternoon
16 Aug. 1823.

Dear Sirs

I called to thank you for your obliging communication in answer to my note,[2] and your very *agreeable* Present[3]—Twenty times have I in the course of the last ten years felt and expressed the wish for such a work, as a Supplement to Withering.[4] It is delightfully executed—and in case of a Reprint, or perhaps independent of this, an appendix of the Trees and Shrubs, which tho' exotics, are of

trifled with them and abandoned further negotiation. See Letter 1448 for Coleridge's retrospective account of his relations with Murray from 1816 onwards.

[1] *On Revisiting the Sea-shore*, lines 21–24. *Poems*, i. 360.
[2] See Coleridge's letter to Taylor and Hessey of 8 Aug. 1823.
[3] A note in the MS. indicates that this gift was *Flora Domestica*. This work by Elizabeth Kent, Leigh Hunt's sister-in-law, was published by Taylor and Hessey in 1823, with the title, *Flora Domestica; or, The portable Flower-garden; with directions for the treatment of plants in pots, and illustrations from the works of the poets.*
[4] Coleridge refers to William Withering (1741–99), whose chief work, *A Botanical Arrangement of all the Vegetables naturally growing in Great Britain, according to the System of the celebrated Linnaeus*, 2 vols., was first published in 1776.

ordinary occurrence in our Gentlemen's Grounds, parks, [&c.,] treated on the same plan would be a valuable *Additament*, as old Hackett says. If I could write any thing that would be likely to further it's sale, I should consider it as a sort of duty of gratitude for the delight, I receive from Flowers the twelve months thro'.— The Leighton may be put to the Press *immediately* if you please —I wish only to learn from you, what number of pages you would consider as the advisable limit, and what proportion the Life and Critique should make. Would 50 pages for this latter be too much— ? Of course, it will be the elucidations from little known Writers of that age, and biographical sketches of the Men with whom Leighton was condemned to act, that will carry the Life to this extent— and it will therefore be no difficult, tho' from the beauty or curiosity of the quotations an unwilling, task to shorten it. But I should be much obliged to you, if you could procure for me the Loan of Archbishop Laud's Works, including his Diary or private Journal.[1] And (from Williams's or the Dissenters' Library?) the Zion's Plea of Leighton's Father, with the small Tract containing the Detail of his Sufferings and those of his Companions, Burton &c.[2]—I saw this latter once at Sir G. Beaumont's near Ashby de la Zouch—and a work of deeper interest I never read.—

There are two or three other things of more Moment to me at least, on which I should be glad to consult you—particularly, on two Works, one of which is finished and perfectly ready for the Press, and the other nearly so—works that have occupied the best hours of the last twenty years of my Life[3]—May I hope to find you, one or the other, at leisure on Monday next, about one o'clock ?— In the mean time I am,

dear Sirs, | with sincere respect | Your obliged
S. T. Coleridge.—

[1] The *Diary* of William Laud (1573–1645), archbishop of Canterbury, was first published, though in garbled form, by W. Prynne in 1644, previous to Laud's execution for treason. The *Diary* was published in full by Henry Wharton in 1695. See Letter 1350.

[2] Alexander Leighton (1568–1649), physician and divine, *An Appeal to the Parliament; or Sion's Plea against the Prelacie*, 1628 ; and *An Epitome . . . of the many and great Troubles that Dr. Leighton suffered in his body, estate, and family, for the space of twelve years and upwards*, 1646. Leighton and Henry Burton (1578–1648), puritan divine, suffered imprisonment and barbarous treatment.

[3] The two works were the *Elements of Discourse* and the *Assertion of Religion*. As subsequent letters indicate, Taylor and Hessey were to publish both works. See Letters 1369, 1376, 1442, 1448, and 1652. In *Aids to Reflection*, 1825, pp. 152, 174, and 196, Coleridge himself announced the forthcoming publication of these two works. The announcements remained unchanged in the second edition of *Aids*, 1831, pp. 148, 172, and 194.

1346. *To Unknown Correspondent*

MS. Mr. W. T. Trimble. Hitherto unpublished fragment.

[*Circa* 16 August 1823][1]

. . . Laud, Life, Diary—any thing about him or bearing on him.—

Any Tract containing the detail of the Punishment, Sufferings, Speeches &c of Leighton, Burton & others.—(Such a Tract there is)—

Archbishop Spottiswood's History[2]—& any History or historic Document of the Scottish Church from James I (inclusive) to the Revolution—

If not purchased, will be most carefully handled & returned within 10 days, by their obliged

S. T. Coleridge—

1347. *To Mrs. S. T. Coleridge*

MS. Mr. A. H. B. Coleridge. Hitherto unpublished fragment.

[August 1823][3]

. . . flocci-nauci-nihili-pilification of a Member of Parliament's Address, or a Recipe for forcing a stranger to pay for his Father's Letter, nolens volens—'O! (quoth good kind Mr Tulk) I guessed, it was *Mr Hartley*'—.

Few things I regret more than that I had not an opportunity of presenting Sara to *Mrs Tulk*—She is half an Angel—& alas! alas! her poor Husband, who is emphatically, a *Husband-lover*, fears that she will too soon be wholly such—But since her interview with Mr Gillman[4] . . .

Mr Tulk is and will for some time remain at *Brighton*—whither YOU (that is you & our dearest Girl) may direct your letters *under cover*, as usual, for *me*. I dared not ask any further privilege.—

Mrs Gillman is very poorly, I am sorry to say. God grant, we may be able to spend a few Weeks at the Sea-side—at least that she may be able to go— . . .

---

[1] This and the preceding letter contain similar references to Laud, Alexander Leighton, and Burton and were probably written about the same time.

[2] John Spottiswood (1565–1639). His *History of the Church and State of Scotland from the year of our Lord 203 to the end of the reign of King James VI, 1625*, was published posthumously in 1655.

[3] This letter was probably written in Aug. 1823, not long after both Coleridge and Gillman had called on Tulk. See Letter 1344.   [4] See Letter 1339.

1348. To James Gillman, Jr.

MS. Yale University Lib. Pub. with omis. Coleridge at Highgate, *by Lucy E. Watson, 1925, p. 130.*

[August 1823 ?][1]

My dear James

Your Mama derived great pleasure from your Aunt Lucy's Report of your orderly and accomodating conduct and behaviour, as likewise of your not having suffered any interruption from ill-health, during your Sojourn at Stonesfield. I may add that she would be *satisfied* as well as gratified, could she know, that your inward feelings and convictions were working in the same direction, and that you rated at it's right value, the opportunity given you of filling up the chasms, and *clamping* the loose stones in the foundations of your School-Learning. Your good sense cannot but admit that you have need of this: and I trust to your integrity for bringing your inclinations over to the same side.—I write to you at present, my dear young friend! not that I have any thing new to say; but in the belief, that having old opinions by you, and always at hand, should you read them in an easy and tranquil state of mind, and at a favorable moment, they may make a deeper impression than they were likely to make in the form of fugitive Talking. I shall confine myself to two points; but such that these once gained, all is gained—for every other good thing will follow, as the natural consequences. First—

What is true of all human Beings in respect to another World, may be said of Lads of your age in respect to the present Life. They are Caterpillars, with the future Butterfly not only inclosed, but already forming and unfolding within them. Great is the distance, on the scale of Creation, between the poor Reptile and a Youth like you. The Ladder, resembling that which Jacob saw in a dream (*Genesis, Chap. 28. Verse 12*) is of vast height: and the Reptile is almost on the lowest Round and the Youth but a few Rounds from the Top: of that Portion of the Ladder, I mean, which is within our View. But yet, my dear James, the most important, nay, the only *essential* and *permanent* Difference between You and your green-frock'd* Sister on the Cabbage-leaf, is this: that by the gift of Reason and Reflection, God has put it in *your* power and has left it to your own choice, *which* of the two you consider to be

---

[1] James Gillman, Jr., the 'Lad of 15 Years of age' mentioned in the present letter, was born on 8 Aug. 1808. See A. W. Gillman, *The Gillmans of Highgate,* 1895, p. 27.

* N.B. *This is the language of Holy Writ: 'He calleth the Worm his Sister.'* [Note by S. T. C.] See Job xvii. 14.

your true and proper Self, the Caterpillar, (that is, your present *boy*-nature) or the Butterfly (that is, the Man which is growing within you) behind the Mask (Larva) of the former. If a Lad of 15 Years of age is unhappy enough to regard the mere *Larva* as his true and only Self, if he thinks, feels and acts as if he was nothing else but the Caterpillar, and therefore with the Caterpillar only and with nothing else would concern himself: if he resolves neither to know or care about any Self but his present and immediate Havings, Likings, and Cravings, the consequence will, nay, *must* be, that he will not retain his Caterpillar Life and State of Being an hour the longer on this account, but will pass into a poor lame starveling lop-sided Butterfly, dragging and trailing his soiled and tatterdemal-lion Wings along the ground, which instead of being the means and organs of Elevation and Liberty, the Means of at once *rising* in the world and of becoming his own Master, are an additional Burthen and an object of mingled Scorn and Commiseration.—If on the other hand he considers his true Self to be the Butterfly, he will not on that account neglect the Caterpillar—on the contrary, he will carefully attend to it, only not (at all events, not *principally*) for *it's own* sake, but as the thing, out of which his true and precious Self is to burst into open View, as the *School*, within which the Eyes of this *true* Self are to be formed, it's wings to grow, and it's Powers and Instincts to be gradually matured and disciplined. It is true, this process cannot be carried on well or effectually without some-times crossing and contradicting the Caterpillar—that is, his present boyish Wants and Wishes, Likes and Dislikes.—But what then? I am no better (you should say to yourself) than the real Garden-caterpillar, I am *indeed* a Caterpillar, if I cannot or will not make the Crawler go *my* way and not his.—In short and to vary the simile, I would have you, my dear young Friend! consider the out-side and visible James of the present and the two or three following years, as the *Mule*, on which the inward and *Man* James is riding on a Life and Death Journey. If he flings and kicks and runs restive, you must spur and lash and *force* him on—or else the Mule will have disappeared, and have left an *Ass* in it's place.—

This is my first Advice. My second will take but few words.— If you would be happy and respectable, in whatever line of Life it may be your lot to move, you must begin in good earnest to *ground yourself*—to know, what you pretend to know, from the very foundations. In short, you must *begin at the beginning*. In what particular Branch of Knowlege, you commence this necessary measure, is comparatively a matter of indifference, provided you do commence it in *some thing*, and set to it with a *resolved* mind, and IN GOOD EARNEST. I have thought of the Science of Mechanics,

with such parts of Geometry, Trigonometry and Universal Arithmetic, as are requisite. Learn but *one* thing *fundamentally,* so as to
know what you know, and the habit will be formed which will at
length leaven all your other pursuits.[1]

God bless you, my dear James! Remember me respectfully and
affectionately to your kind & excellent Aunt. Do not forget to
express your acknowlegement to Mr Brown for the trouble, he has
taken in helping you onward in your studies—and do it like one who
has reflected on his words & feels what he says—and believe me
your sincere Friend

S. T. Coleridge

1349. *To John Gisborne*[2]

Address: —— Gisborne, Esqre | 33 | King Street West | Bryanstone Square
Or Mrs Gisborne
MS. Cornell University Lib. Hitherto unpublished.
Postmark: Highgate, 25 August 1823.

Highgate
24 August, 1823

Dear Sir

When I had last the pleasure of seeing you and your dear Lady
at Highgate—a pleasure linked to so many delightful and en-
nobling Recollections in my *Rome*-haunting Spirit; and to the
promised repetition of which my dear and incomparable House-
fellows scarcely less than myself have been looking forward not
without some impatience—Mrs Gisborne mentioned one particular
Drama of Calderon's and was so good as to say, she would bring it
with her when she next came.—I write in a blind hope of finding
you by this Note. Should I succeed, and you are still under the
truly English Constellation of *Aquarius* (should this Country ever
be reconciled to the old Mother Church, I should propose to substitute St Swithin for St George, as it's Guardian Saint) will you
permit me to remind you of your kind promise? and if Mrs Gis-

---

[1] For an earlier letter to James concerning his education see Appendix,
Letter 1180 A.

[2] John Gisborne and his wife Maria (1770–1836), friends of Shelley. In his
Letter to Maria Gisborne, 1820, Shelley described Coleridge as follows:

> You will see Coleridge—he who sits obscure
> In the exceeding lustre and the pure
> Intense irradiation of a mind,
> Which, with its own internal lightning blind,
> Flags wearily through darkness and despair—
> A cloud-encircled meteor of the air,
> A hooded eagle among blinking owls.—

borne will name any other favorites of her's in the Volumes of this *empyrean* Spaniard, and should it be in her power to let me have at the same time the Volume containing the Devotion of the Cross—it would at this moment be rendering me a very important Service: and I hope, I need not say that the Books shall be handled with religious Care and returned within a month or at whatever other date your Convenience or intended Movements may prescribe. Mendicants, you well know from the instance of the Friar Species, are capacious Leeches—or to come nearer home for a Metaphor, and to compleat the likeness by an *intestine* nuisance, they are tenacious Tape-worms, wonderfully gifted with the power of articulative Growth and of making one joint produce another. And I am about to give you a specimen, that literary Beggars form no exception to the Rule, by linking on another request—respecting the *Life* of Calderon, to wit. Do you possess any Spanish Biography, containing this article? Or is there a Life of any detail & particularity prefixed to his Works? Or could you refer me to any such Work?

But I must *break off* of my own accord: or you will send to the Apothecary for a quantum sufficit of Spirit of Turpentine or Pomegranate Root, to effect a riddance, for good and all, of the knotty *Beggagery* of,

my dear Sir, | with unfeigned respect and regard | Your and Mrs Gisborne's | obliged Friend

S. T. Coleridge

1350. *To J. A. Hessey*

Address: Mr Hessey | Messrs. Taylor and Hessey | Fleet Street
MS. Huntington Lib. Pub. with omis. Coleridge on the Seventeenth Century, *ed. Roberta Florence Brinkley, 1955, p. 247.*
Postmark: Highgate, 9 September 1823.

Highgate
Tuesday 9 Septr 1823—

My dear Sir

I find that my apology for the Life of Leighton—which I believe, whether from vanity or on good grounds to *deserve* as a yet more appropriate tho' less expedient Title that of—The first impartial and philosophical Account & Explanation of the Conflict between the Protestant Hierarchy (from Edward VI to the Revolution) and the Puritans of England with the Presbyterians in Scotland—which how especially it is the vital Center of the History of England might be presumed even from the unexampled interest felt by all ranks in the first Series of Sir Walter Scott's Novels—I find, I say (you must forgive my hasty *parentheses* in my letters, & I will take [care] that you shall find few to be forgiven in my future publications) that the Life &c will occupy a full half of the Volume—. I think it right to apprize you of this—that if you see any objection as to the saleability of the Book, it may be altered[1]—which however can only be done by retaining only the abstract of the main events of Leighton's Life which, however, I could give only as an Abstract from the Lives prefixed to the several Editions of his Works, not worthy to be called even an Apology for a Life—or such an apology as the fragments of a dry Caterpillar Skin could be for the Life of the Butterfly.[2]—

Now all my Materials are both ready, and arranged, save only a spot of terra incognita which I hope to colonize out of WOODROW's History of the Church[3]—to which, but of far less Likelihood, I may add the '*Bibliographia*[4] *Scoticana*'.[5]—But the former I *must* have looked thro' before I dare publish my Life—well aware of the immense importance of the Advice given me in the inclosed Note from that worthy & enlightened man, the Revd. Joseph Hughes, the Secretary of the Brit. & For. Bible Society. In my laborious Collation of Spottiswood, Heylin,[6] Prynne,[7] Wharton,[8] Burnet,[9] Hacket[10]

---

[1] Miss Brinkley erroneously reads 'allowed' for 'altered'.

[2] The 'apology for the Life of Leighton' was not included in *Aids to Reflection*. See Letter 1384.

[3] Robert Wodrow (1679–1734), ecclesiastical historian, *The History of the Sufferings of the Church of Scotland from the Restoration to the Revolution*, 2 vols., 1721–2.

[4] Here and elsewhere in this letter Coleridge wrote 'Bibliographia' for 'Biographia'.

[5] John Howie (1735–93), *Biographia Scoticana; or a brief historical account of the lives, characters, and memorable transactions of the most eminent Scots Worthies*, 1774. For Coleridge's annotations in a copy of the 1816 edition of this work see *Notes, Theological, Political, and Miscellaneous. By Samuel Taylor Coleridge*, ed. Derwent Coleridge, 1853, pp. 157–65.

[6] Peter Heylyn (1600–62), theologian and historian, *Cyprianus Anglicus: or, the History of the Life and Death, of . . . William [Laud] . . .*, 1668. A copy of the 1671 edition of this work with annotations by Coleridge is now in the British Museum. For Coleridge's annotations see T. J. Wise, *Two Lake Poets . . .*, 1927, pp. 123–6.

[7] William Prynne (1600–69), puritan pamphleteer, *A Breviate of the Life of William Laud, Arch-bishop of Canterbury: extracted . . . out of his owne Diary . . .*, 1644; *Hidden Workes of Darkenes brought to publike light, or, a necessary introduction to the history of the Archbishop of Canterburie's Triall*, 1645; and *Canterburie's Doome . . .*, 1646.

[8] *The History of the Troubles and Tryal of . . . William Laud . . . Wrote by Himself during his Imprisonment in the Tower. To which is prefixed The Diary of his own Life . . .*, ed. Henry Wharton, 1695.

Notes 9 and 10 continued opposite

&c I have had reason to congratulate myself on the having submitted to the Task.—Now Woodrow's Work (in two Volumes
Folio) is, Mr Irving assures me, a common book in Scotland—and
he was surprized at his disappointment in not being able to procure
it for me from any of his Scottish Acquaintance and Church-
members in London—Neither is it or the Bibliographia Scoticana,
in Sion College or in Dr Williams's Library in Red Cross Street—.
I should be much obliged to you to have it enquired whether it is
in the London Institution Library—. I trust that it will, at all
events, be in the British Museum, & have this morning written to
Sir H. Davy to be admitted, as a Reader there—. If not, my last
resource must be to procure it by Mr Irving's means from Scotland.
—But should it be in any of the London Catalogues, and could be
purchased for any tolerable price (for instance, not exceeding five
guineas) I would gladly have the sum put to my Account—if the
Loan of it for a fortnight could not be obtained—and so too (but
with less anxiety) the Book entitled, Bibliographia Scoticana.—

I shall not go to the Sea side till I have the whole of the 'Aids to
Reflection' ready for the Printer—& my Sojourn at the Sea-side I
shall give to Calderon's Devotion of the Cross. Mrs Gisborne, an
excellent Spanish Scholar, together with her Husband passed the
whole of yesterday with me—in reading Calderon—and highly
amused I was.—Some time or other, when I have acquired a power
of reading Spanish, even idiomatic Spanish, rapidly (which by Mr
& Mrs Gisborne's aid I shall soon do, God permitting) I will make
a Volume, either at once, or for the London Mag. (a set of which I
mean, please God! to *earn* from you: for I have not even *seen*

---

⁹ Gilbert Burnet (1643–1715), bishop of Salisbury and historian, *The History
of the Reformation of the Church of England*, 3 parts, 1679–1715. For Coleridge's
annotations in a copy of the 1730 (Dublin) edition of this work see *Notes,
Theological, Political, and Miscellaneous. By Samuel Taylor Coleridge*, ed.
Derwent Coleridge, 1853, pp. 62–72. One of the notes is dated 'S. T. Coleridge,
28th December, 1823'. In *Aids to Reflection*, 1825, p. 180, Coleridge included a
quotation from this work. A copy of Burnet's *The Life of William Bedell*,
1692, with Coleridge's annotations is in the Stanford University Library. For
these annotations see *Literary Remains*, iv. 71–76.

¹⁰ John Hacket (1592–1670), bishop of Coventry and Lichfield, *Scrinia
Reserata: A Memorial offer'd to the Great Deservings of John Williams, D.D.*,
1693. A copy of this work with annotations by Coleridge is in the British
Museum. For these annotations see *Literary Remains*, iii. 183–202, and T. J.
Wise, *Two Lake Poets . . .*, 1927, pp. 130–2. A copy of Hacket's *A Century of
Sermons*, to which is prefixed a Life of Hacket by Thomas Plume, 1675, with
Coleridge's annotations is in the British Museum. For the annotations see
Literary Remains, iii. 171–83, and T. J. Wise, op. cit., 129–30. In *Aids to
Reflection*, 1825, pp. 146–7 and 156–7 n., Coleridge included extracts from this
work.

above 4 or 5 Numbers—) in Mr Carey's manner—i.e. Anecdote, History, Biography, abstracts, and Translations or Imitations of beautiful or whimsical passages from two lines to a hundred—. I have been trying to persuade that dear Man to give you (no man in the Kingdom can do it as he would) a Volume or two of Italian Scraps, from Dante downwards—what a delicious Book it would be—a Lounge-book for a literary Elysium, to open upon where you like. Such Books are sure to please every body.—

A friend brought me, on Sunday last, a Selection from Leighton by a Mr Wilson, printed at Oxford[1]—. I was amused, first, by the *Cut* of Leighton's Face which is a *Cacophysiognomical Improvement* (in the Methodist use of that word) on the Cut before Dr Jarment's Edition, which draws from Dr J. the extatic exclamation—*Quantae pietatis Imago!*[2] & which, one might have almost sworn, had been tak[en] from the Method. or Evang. Magazine, as the very own Face, Look, and Trim of some shoemaker, shortly after his *Call* that cost nothing & his Licence to set up as the Reverend Mr that cost one Shilling—2. by the circumstance that *no one passage* had been selected by us both.—

May I ask the favor of you & Mr Taylor to send me Neuman's Spanish Dictionary—or if it can be had cheaper, any old Spanish & Italian, Spanish & Latin, or Spanish and German, Dictionary— and to put it to my account.

Believe me, with sincere respect, my dear Sir, | Your obliged
S. T. Coleridge

Mr Gillman's Erasmus Middleton's Edition of Leighton's Works is just come home from the Binder's—& I see that the Portrait to this (tho' all three are evidently copies from the same Picture or Engraving) is really a Face that might have resembled Leighton's —Dr Jarment's is a Libel, and Mr Wilson's, were it not so irresistibly laughable, might almost be prosecuted for Petty Blasphemy.

[1] According to the *English Catalogue of Books*, W. Wilson published in 1824 a *new* edition of *Selections from the Works of Archbishop Leighton, to which is prefixed a brief sketch of his life.*
[2] Cf. Virgil, *Aeneid*, vi. 405.

1351. *To C. A. Tulk*

Transcript Coleridge family. Hitherto unpublished.

Sunday Night [5 October 1823][1]

My dear Sir

Whether my idle prejudice against French Books prevented the little work from leaving any impression on my memory I cannot say, but so it is, that after a fatiguing hunt in every corner I had given it up in despair when lo! I found it *under* my hand—and that I must have turned it over repeatedly during my search. I have some others which I beg leave to retain till I have transcribed some passages from them—which I will do before my return from Ramsgate, for which place we set off tomorrow morning Six o'clock— I have perused Mr Hormby's Poem with great interest and have taken the liberty of adding some *Pencil* marks of several passages that I especially admired, and of a few easily removeable faults ὡς ἔμοιγε δοκεῖ. They all arise either from the dire necessity of rhyme compelling a change & choice of Metaphors which the Judgment and imagination would not have of themselves suggested or from inattention to the *quantity* of words which must be consulted no less than the *accent* in order to harmonious verse.

All here desire their kind and respectful remembrances to you & yours—& sympathize with me in fervent wishes that no change will take place in dear Mrs Tulk's convalescence—I am so sorely fatigued with packing up my Books & Papers that I must abruptly subscribe myself, dear Sir,

yours with most unfeigned | respect & regard
S. T. Coleridge

1352. *To Unknown Correspondent*

MS. Mr. W. T. Trimble. Pub. The Trimbles & Cowens of Dalston, Cumberland. Supplement to the First Edition, *by W. T. Trimble, 1937, p. 16.*

8 Octr 1823
Highgate

I, the undersigned, and as one not unknown to the Men of Letters of Germany, among others to Professor Von Schlegel now in this country, testify that Mr John Watson, the Bearer, is a Gentleman who deservedly possesses the regard and respect of his numerous

[1] Coleridge did not leave Highgate on Monday, 6 Oct., as planned, but on Saturday the 11th. See *The Letters of Sara Hutchinson*, ed. Kathleen Coburn, 1954, p. 264.

and respectable friends, and that his intended Residence in Berlin
has been determined by motives calculated to ensure him the respect of all men of Science, and a pledge of the high estimation in
which the Professors and Schools of Physiology and Medicine
under the protection of his Prussian Majesty are held in this
country—

S. T. Coleridge

1353. *To J. H. Bohte*

Address: Mr Bohte | York Street   from Mr Coleridge favored by Mr Watson.
MS. Cornell University Lib. Hitherto unpublished.

9 Octr 1823
Highgate

My dear Sir
    The Bearer, Mr John Watson, is a very dear and particular
Friend of mine—and when I say that, permit me to flatter myself
with the belief, that you will take for granted that he is entitled to
the kind services of all worthy men. He is indeed in all respects a
most amiable and estimable Man—Having finished his medical
Studies both at Edinburgh and at the London Hospitals, he has
determined on making himself acquainted with the Medical Philosophy and Physiology of your famous German Professors, and with
the German Language & Literature generally—and in order to this
is now on the point of setting off for Berlin, in which city he intends
to reside for 7 or 8 Months.—Now the object of this introduction is
to request, that you will be so good as to give him any information
in your power respecting his Journey from Hamburgh to Berlin—
what the expences on an economical plan may and ought to be—
the sort of money, & the way of exchanging &c—. In short, whatever hints or instructions you can give him, will be as gratefully
felt and acknowleged by me as if they were personal favors to myself—And be assured, that if in any way literary or otherwise you
imagine that I can be of service to you, you will confer a gratification on me by proposing it. For as I feel cordially towards *all* my
Cousins-*german*, so permit me to assure you that in no every-day
sense of the words I am,
my dear Sir, | with sincere respect | and regard | Your
obliged Servt

S. T. Coleridge

1354. *To Sara Hutchinson*

MS. Folger Shakespeare Lib. Hitherto unpublished.

Saturday Morning—[18 October 1823]

My dear Sara[1]

I shall have *great* pleasure in dining & spending the evening with
yourself and Mrs Monkhouse, which will not be the less for the
opportunity of meeting so warm an admirer & sincere a friend of
Wordsworth, as Mr Q.[2]—For the rest, we will talk when we meet.—

I am sorry, & *was* vexed yester Evening, to find that the only
person who takes in the London[3] to Mr Burgess's knowlege & from
whom he might have procured it, left Ramsgate last week—and
Mr B. believes that it does not find a place in any of our Ramsgate
Librarian's Parcels—

May God bless you & your ever faithful Friend
S. T. Coleridge.

1355. *To J. A. Hessey*

Address: Mr Hessey
MS. Professor Earl Daniels. Hitherto unpublished.

[Early November 1823]

Dear Sir

Having an opportunity of trusting them to a young friend on
whom I can rely for delivering them to your own hand, I have sent
the more important MSS, in the first instance—while the books,
corrected proofs, and all that belongs to the Work, the Essay on the
Life, Character, & Times of Leighton not included, will be forwarded
per Coach on Thursday Night—unless an old Highgate Neighbor
should decide on returning to Town by the Saturday Morning's
Steam-vessel, which I shall know before Thursday—

[1] After the salutation someone erroneously added '(his daughter)' to the
MS. Sara Hutchinson and Mrs. Thomas Monkhouse were staying at Ramsgate
in 1823, and Coleridge called on them on Monday, 13 Oct. The dinner party
referred to in the present letter took place on the 18th. See *The Letters of Sara
Hutchinson*, ed. Kathleen Coburn, 1954, pp. 262–7.

[2] Edward Quillinan (1791–1851), poet, married Wordsworth's daughter
in 1841.

[3] Coleridge had mentioned Charles Lamb's 'Letter of Elia to Robert
Southey', which appeared in the Oct. 1823 issue of the *London Magazine*. In a
review of M. Grégoire's *Histoire de la Théophilantropie*, entitled 'Progress of
Infidelity' (*Quarterly Review*, Jan. 1823), Southey had remarked of Lamb's
Elia, then just published in book form, that it wanted a 'sounder religious
feeling'. Lamb rightly objected to the insinuation that his 'little volume' was a
'vehicle for heresy or infidelity'. *The Works of Charles and Mary Lamb*, ed.
E. V. Lucas, 7 vols., 1903–5, i. 226 and 476.

You will then see the causes of my silence & in part at least, the
rewards of the Delay—. I am rapidly *convalescing* from a very
distressful indisposition affecting my head & eyes from indiscreet
overbathing at my first arrival—but my young Friend is hurry-
ing—.

S. T. Coleridge

1356. *To J. A. Hessey*

Address: Mr Hessey
MS. New York Public Lib. Pub. E. L. G. ii. 331.

[6 November 1823][1]

Dear Sir

You will see by the accompanying that I have been busily and
anxiously employed since I last saw you—. As soon as I saw the Proof,
I was struck with the apprehension of the disorderly and hetero-
geneous appearance which the Selections intermixed with my own
comments &c would have—I had not calculated aright on the relative quantity of the one and the other—and the more I reflected, the
more desirable it appeared to me to carry on the promise of the Title
Page (*Aids* to reflection) systematically throughout the work—But
little did I anticipate the time and trouble, that this *rifacciamento*
would cost me—Mrs Gillman could inform you, that with the exception of a few days of Illness I have been at work on this Volume &
the Essay on the times of Leighton & the causes of the Schism in
Protestantism, every day of my absence, from Breakfast to Dinner
and from Tea to Bed time—merely allowing myself two hours for
Bathing and Exercise—

On the return of the next proofs, the conclusion of the last Division
(Spiritual & Philosophical) will accompany them—And the historical & biographical Essay will be ready—I suspect, it will stand in
strange *Contrast* of Opinion with Southey's *Church*, which will come
out about the same time—!

I leave it to your better Judgement; but it strikes me, that by
printing the Aphorisms *numerically* with interspace, as I have
written them—thus—

Aphorism I

Then the title or heading of it, if any: and then the passage itself,
would be so very much the best way, as to make it worth while—

---

[1] This letter was probably written on Thursday, 6 Nov. 1823. In the post
of that day Coleridge first learned that he was to leave Ramsgate for Highgate
on the following Monday. (See next letter). In the present letter Coleridge tells
Hessey that he will call on him on Tuesday morning, i.e. 11 Nov.

and instead of the (Leighton, Vol. I. p. —) at the *end*, simply to have
an L. either thus

Aphorism V. L.[1]

or before the first word of the aphorism, on the same line with it.

L. A reflecting mind &c—

and when it is not Leighton's, to put either E. (Editor's) or nothing.—
  In those Aphorisms in which part only is Leighton's, they might
be marked L. E.
  But I shall call on you, please God, on Tuesday Morning—

Your obliged

S. T. Coleridge[2]—

If it were feared, that there is too much matter—all the extracts
from 1. 2 of p. 52, viz. Aphorisms, 12, 13, 14, 15, might be omitted.[3]—

1357. *To Edward Quillinan*

Address: Edward Quillinan, Esqre. | Lee Priory | near | Wingham | Kent.
MS. Dove Cottage. Hitherto unpublished.
Stamped: Ramsgate.

8 Waterloo Plains, Ramsgate.
Friday afternoon.

7 Novr 1823.

Dear Sir
  A serious indisposition, which at every recurrence I connect (hypo-
chondriacally, I hope; but) involuntarily with something more than
disorder in the *functions* of the Homo *intestinalis*, has been the cause
of, & will be, I doubt not, my Apology for, the Delay in acknowleging your very kind Invitation. There was, however, an accessary
reason at work. I had till within the last two or three days not given

---

  [1] In *Aids to Reflection*, 1825, the aphorisms, as Coleridge suggested, are
printed '*numerically* with interspace', but instead of 'L.' the name 'LEIGHTON'
appears in the headings. Those aphorisms by Coleridge are headed 'EDITOR',
those by both authors 'conjointly', 'L. & ED.' In the second edition of the *Aids*
(1831) the authorship of the aphorisms, whether by Coleridge himself, or by
Leighton or another of the 'elder divines', is not indicated in the headings.
  [2] The following notation appears in the address sheet. It was probably
writen by Hessey.

APHORISM I.   (LEIGHTON)

– – – – – – – – – – – – – – –

– – – – – – – – – – (Vol 4. P. 32)

APHORISM II   (ED.)

  [3] These aphorisms, all of which are from Leighton, appear on pp. 45–48 of the
Aids, 1825. They were omitted from the second edition, 1831.

(307)

up the hope that either Mr Gillman or Mr Nixon, the Father of Mrs
Gillman's fair Friend and Companion would come down and spend
the whole or greater part of the last week here—in which case I
should gladly and at once have availed myself of your kindness. The
Post of yesterday not only extinguished this prospect, but summoned
the Ladies home—and as of course I cannot leave them, we leave
this place on Monday Morning, by Coach or the Steam-Vessel, as
Wind & Weather may advise.—Permit me to use your own words—
for with the utmost *integrity* of Meaning I can assure you that I feel
this Miss of what I had longed for as a *mortifying* Disappointment—
and if after my return I can bring my Print-and-press Concerns
under the requisite arrangement, and you should happen to be fixed
at Lee Priory, a little before, or after, or during Christmas Holidays,
it would be an unusual Holiday Gratification to step into the Canterbury Stage & be your Visitor for the better half of a Week—. My
address is simply, Highgate, near London—whither should choice
[or] chance lead you, you will be cordially welcomed by my dear &
excellent Friends, Mr and Mrs Gillman, and most cordially by, dear
Sir, your's with unfeigned

Respect and | Regard
S. T. Coleridge

1358. *To Dr. Williamson*

Address: Dr Williamson, M.D. | Leeds
MS. The Carl H. Pforzheimer Library. Hitherto unpublished.
Postmark: 12 November 1823.

Highgate
10 [11] Novr 1823.[1]

Dear Sir

This answer goes by the *first* Post after my *first* Perusal of your last
Favor, and my *first* knowlege of it's existence or that of the preceding.
My Friend, Mr Gillman, who had been requested by me to open all
letters for me the writing not being that of known correspondents,
had only glanced over them sufficiently to be able to inform me, that
one contained a very kind proffer from Mr Watt[s], and that the
other was from yourself[2]—. They were forwarded to my Publisher,
to be inclosed with a proof sheet for Ramsgate—in what way lost, I
have yet to make out—for I will not suffer a single Post's voluntary

---

[1] This letter was written in reply to a communication which Coleridge found
on his return to Highgate 'yesternight', i.e. 10 Nov. 1823, and should be dated,
therefore, the 11th. See Letter 1364.

[2] As the next letter shows, Coleridge had been invited to lecture at the
Literary and Philosophical Society at Leeds.

Delay in my acknowlegement of that which I found on my return to Highgate, yesternight. For the last five weeks I have been a Roamer rather than a Sojourner at the sea side—in the hopes of gathering enough Strength and Health to serve me, with good and careful Husbanding, for my Winter Stock—tho' I should grieve to see a Friend in that state of poverty as to both, which *I* have long been forced to consider as comparative Wealth.—But I am trespassing on your time instead of answering your letter.

First, let me assure you, that I feel both honored and gratified by your proposal—and next, that in no one instance in my Life, either in respect of Copy-right or other Honorarium from Booksellers, or in respect of different proposals for series of Lectures from the Managers of Institutions—(the Royal Institution and the Surry alone I ever, in fact, did lecture at—& so many years ago, that I forget the date)[1] could I ever bring myself to state a price. I never even attempted it. My attachment to Sir H. (then Mr) Davy, who had shortly before commenced his March of Glory as the Chemical Lecturer, a Glory not brighter or filling a larger space to my mind now that I look back on it, than it did at Bristol, in his 20th year, when I had to look forward to it.[2]—I can with truth say, that I lectured for *Pride*; but it was the Pride of being a fellow-lecturer with the Father and Founder of philosophic Alchemy, the Man who *born* a Poet first converted Poetry into Science and *realized* what few men possessed Genius enough to *fancy*.—The wish to gratify Mr Saumarez & a few other friends, from whom I had received great kindness, determined me likewise in my Lecturing at the Surry Institution a few years afterwards—By the latter I neither gained or lost—in the former the Honorarium did not nearly cover my necessary expences to and from Keswick, and during my stay in London.—

After as much reflection on your flattering proposal as the Time has allowed, I know not therefore what better or franker Reply I can make than this—At this present time I am employed, day after day, as many hours each day as my Health & Strength render *possible*, as *successive* exertion—and when I make a rude calculation of the Loss, I must submit to by diverting my labor to another channel (for such is my nature, that I can do but one thing at a time—& what I do at all, I give my whole head and heart to)—and add to this the expences of Travelling &c—laying aside (what in truth does not & would not influence me, one way or the other) all thought of any pecuniary *accession*—I have no wish to *get*, and my circumstances (or to tell the plain truth, *Honesty* to others) will not justify me in *losing*—and *suspending* all consideration of Health, and all that Doubt & Anxiety of my Success in Public Speaking, to which I have

[1] The lectures of 1808 and 1812–13. [2] Sentence incomplete in MS.

been so long disused—the Result is, that the sum, that would leave me on my return to Highgate in the same state *financially*, as I should have been, had I remained at home, is more than I have the vanity to believe that any pleasure or instruction, in my power to communicate, would be *worth*—either by a series of Lectures or even by conversation, by which I have in the course of my Life atchieved ten fold more than by all my public Efforts, from the Press or the Lecture-Desk.—

On re-perusing what I have thus rudely put down (for it is so painful & distressing to me to speak of myself in any relation to my *individual* self or private circumstances, that I feel, as if I were intellectually *stam[mering]*[1] and suffer the awkwardness, tho' not the apprehensions, of [a] guilty Witness at a cross-examination) I find it necessary to *explain*—. If I had conveyed to you the notion, that my literary Labors *during any six weeks* (unless I had been employed on a Drama or a Poem, and had been (which I have not the least right to *calculate on*) eminently successful) would be worth 150£, I should have egregiously deceived you and flattered myself. But taking *the* particular time from now to January, and the character of the works on which I am engaged, the *trade*-value of which will be seriously diminished if they are not brought out about Christmas; and that, of course, the interruption will act on the value of several months' preceding Labor; I might have said this, and said less than the Truth—and tho' I should suppose 3 courses of six Lectures each, it is altogether improbable that any Audiences, I could have at *Leeds*, would come near to such a sum, much less to defray my expences, in addition.

A few words more. I mean this letter only for your perusal & Mr Watts'—& I trust that you will interpret it as I mean it—namely, as a proof, 1. that my inclinations are strongly in favor of my acceptance of the Proposal—and secondly, that I not only hold myself obliged by it, but that I write under impressions of sincere *Respect*. For as nothing less would have authorized me, either in prudence or moral dignity, to have been thus communicative, so nothing less than the belief, that I was writing to those who had that within which would understand me, would have tempted me—But after so long a Delay, tho' without fault on my part, something more than a mere Acknowlegement & Declining of the Proposal seemed requisite: and I would rather hazard an *indiscretion*, than go counter to any honest impulse of my Nature.—Should choice or chance bring you in the neighborhood of Highgate, you will find a cordial welcome from, dear Sir,

your obliged

S. T. Coleridge

[1] MS. torn.

1359. *To Alaric A. Watts*[1]

Address: Alaric Watts, Esqre | Leeds
MS. Cornell University Lib. Pub. E. L. G. ii. 319.
Postmark: Highgate, 3 December 1823.

[3 December 1823]

Dear Sir

A very severe Cold caught by me, as the Irishman caught the Tartar, in changing houses[2] and moving from small and warm to comparatively large and *not* draftless rooms, *struck* in (as the wise women say) on my chest and bowels, and till it struck out again in the shape of an adhesive mask or muzzle, or rather the most unsightly fragments and patches of one, it so confused my head and depressed my spirits that I was both morally and intellectually unfit to return such an answer to your letter as such a letter deserved and demanded—not to speak of the indisposition to the mechanical act of writing produced by the heaviness in my eyes and the dead weight that seemed Drawing down my eye-lids.—Under such circumstances I could not venture to decide for myself without consulting two or three of my friends, above all my Publisher, in order to determine whether I could undertake the proposed expedition to the North without a breach of my positive engagements to him—. This statement, however, I give, almost exclusively in explanation and excuse of my Silence, or Delay in Writing. For as to the expedition itself, I could not disguise from myself, that but for the great kindness of your and Dr Williamson's Letters, and my very strong wish to pass a few weeks under your Roof, (*very* strong, I say, since I received & in good part have perused your volume of Poems)[3] [nothing] could have induced a moment's hesitation—or have prevented me from instantly clearing away the misinterpretation into which I had, most unintentionally or rather contrary to my intention, led you, thro' mere anxiety *not* to be misinterpreted. I intended my letter as a full and final *Declining* of the flattering proposal of the Literary and Philosophical Society at Leeds. But writing in a hurry (*against* Time & the Post) & writing about my own concerns were, as from experience I well knew, sadly against my expressing myself clearly,

---

[1] Alaric A. Watts (1797–1864) was at this time editor of the *Leeds Intelligencer*.

[2] During Coleridge's absence at Ramsgate, Gillman moved from Moreton House to No. 3 The Grove, Highgate. Coleridge chose an attic room as his 'Bed and Book-room'. In Letter 1376 he describes the view from his window. A lithograph of the attic room as it appeared not long after Coleridge's death is reproduced in Letter 1568.

[3] *Poetical Sketches*, 1823. Coleridge annotated this volume. See *Coleridge*, ed. E. Blunden and E. L. Griggs, 1934, p. 118.

and saying enough yet not too much. I sate down to write under the
influence of an anxiety to remove from your mind any suspicions
which the non-receipt of any answer to your letter for so long a time
could not but have excited—by assuring you of the truth—namely,
that I received the proposal with lively feelings of Respect to the
Society, of Regard to Dr W. and yourself—that I considered the
proposal as a compliment, but the personal kindness, that pervaded
the communication of it, as calling for feelings of a deeper order. The
best pledge, I thought, that I could give of the latter was full confidence. In one instance only had the Lecture-scheme repayed me in
any proportion to the time & effort—and even this did not amount
to a third of what I lost by the publication of the Friend on stamped
Sheets for Subscribers, who forgot (and have long forgotten) to pay
their subscriptions—and this Course especially mortified my Relations (i.e. my Brothers & Nephews) and was regretted by some
Friends, whose Judgement had greater weight with me than I ever
yet allowed to Feelings originating in the Pride of this World.—
With this result in my mind I was led to explain to you, how it was,
that in full manhood I became a *Lecturer*—and at the same time
hinted the *no* pleasant feelings associated in my mind with Lecturing,
and some of the occasions of them—and the addition & confirmation,
they received, from the peculiar circumstances of my Health, and
of my present engagements.—My Health indeed, and the fact that
for now eight years I have not above four times ventured to sleep
away from my home (that is, under the same Roof, wherever it be,
and within call of, the more than my best Friends, of whose family I
[am] a member) with the motives for this—*this*, my dear Sir! is what
I should have assigned as my strongest determining reason, had I
been conversing with you instead of *writing*—For not to say, that I
had not time to give the detail necessary to prevent the chance of not
being rightly understood, there are feelings which the sight and
voice of a respected Person will soon remove but which are oppressive
in the *fixture* of a written communication—Hence I but hinted this
—and ended by stating the Truth, that in my present occupations
there was no remuneration which I could specify without injustice
to myself, that would not expose me to the charge of folly and
vanity with regard to the Society—

I wrote in a hurry—and on hastily glancing over the paragraph
was seized with the apprehension, that I might easily be interpreted
as passing myself off for a second Scott, Byron, or Moore—the ridiculous contrariety of which to the fact forced from me a sardonic
laugh at the moment—. I set about explaining it away—mentioning
a sum hypothetically for the exclusive purpose of making it *clearer*—
in short, I *put a case*, as the Lawyers phrase it, merely as illustration.

And thus in the anxiety to remedy one possible mistake unluckily led you into another & a real one—

Your Letter came & the Volume—& for a short time staggered me—*not* indeed the advantages stated but the wishes, it excited— Illness confined me to my Room—. Mr Gillman, both as my dearest Friend and as the medical Adviser & Superintendent, to whom I owe, under God, my Life & power of being useful, decisively negatived the undertaking in both characters—And with this opinion the two other Friends whom I consulted, co-incided.—I must therefore repeat what I before supposed myself to have conveyed, my sense of the honor, and my regret at the necessity of declining it—To other parts of your letter & respecting the Poems I will write in a few days—. Your's cordially

S. T. Coleridge

P.S. Your Letter is just arrived—I shall miss the Post if I stop even to read it—but I will write tomorrow, if necessary—at all events in a day or two—

1360. *To William Worship*

Pub. Coleridge at Highgate, *by Lucy E. Watson, 1925, p. 51.*

[December 1823 ?]

Our new home is and looks comely, and of an imposing respectability ; the views from the garden-side are substitutes for Cumberland especially from the attic in which I and my books are now installed ; Mr. Gillman has shewn much taste in smart-smoothing and re-creating the garden a gloomy wilderness of shrubs.

1361. *To Thomas Allsop*

Address: Thomas Allsop Esqre | 2. Blandford Place | Pall Mall
MS. New York Public Lib. Pub. with omis. Letters, Conversations and Rec. *207.*
Postmark: 11 December 1823.

Grove, Highgate.
10 Decr 1823

My dear Allsop

I shall be alone on Sunday next, the whole day : and need I add, that I shall be happy to spend it with you ? Besides, Mr and Mrs Gillman are growing uneasy at your long absence.

Had I written as many letters, as I have composed to you, the Two-penny Post Man would have been unusually familiar with

your Knocker—But first, ignorant of the circumstances I had
after all no better than generalities to offer, or advice on suppositions and imagined conditions. 2ndly. I have been very unwell,
and am still unusually oppressed, probably (so at least Mr G. thinks)
from an obstinate Cold—for a week or more it broke out in my
face, like the patches and fragments of an adhesive *Muzzle* of
dirty Plaister of Paris, & the pain in my limbs & *miserableness* in
my Bowels were much relieved—but since the disappearance of
these unsightly Strangers I have been with but short intermission
annoyed with the noise as of a distant Forge-hammer incessantly
sounding, so that for some time I actually supposed it to be an
outward sound.—To me who never before *knew* by any sensation
that I had a head on my Shoulders, this you may suppose is
extremely harrassing to the spirits & distractive of my attention.
Thirdly, Mrs Gillman in stepping from my Attic slipt on the first
step of a steep Flight of nine high stairs, precip[it]ated herself &
fell head foremost on the 5th Stair, turned head over heels, & when
at the piercing Scream I rushed out, I found her on her back on the
Landing Place, her head at the wall, her feet & legs on the two last
Stairs—Even now the Image & the Terror of the Image blends with
the recollection of the Past a strange expectancy, a fearful sense as
of a something still to come—& breaks in, & makes stoppages as it
were, in my Thanks to God for her providential Escape. For an
Escape we all must think it, tho' the small bone of her Right Arm
was broken & her Wrist sprained.—No fever supervened—and her
nerves are nearly restored to their former tranquillity. In short,
she is doing as well as can be.—She went without a Light—tho'
(O the vanity of Prophecies, the truth of which can be established
only by the proof of their uselessness) two nights before I had
expostulated with her on this account even with some acerbity,
having previously more than once remonstrated against it on
stairs not familiar, & without carpeting.—

As I shall *rely* on your spending Sunday here & some hours with
me alone, I shall defer to that time all but my kindest regards to
Mrs A.—and the superfluous Assurance that I am evermore, my
dearest Allsop,

your most constant, attached, and | affectionate Friend
S. T. Coleridge

P.S. You will be delighted with my new Room.

1362. *To Thomas Allsop*

Address: T. Allsop, Esqre | 2 Blandford Place | Pall Mall
MS. New York Public Lib. Pub. Letters, Conversations and Rec. *209.*
Postmark: Highgate, 24 December 1823.

[24 December 1823][1]

My dearest Allsop

I forgot to ask you, & so did Mr & Mrs G. whether you could dine with us on Christmas Day—or on New Year's Day—or on both!— If you can, need I say, that I shall be glad—

My noisy forge hammer is still busy, quick, thick & fervent—.

With kindest regards to Mrs A.—your ever faithful |
& affectionate
S. T. Coleridge

1363. *To Mrs. Thomas Allsop*

Address: Mrs Allsop | 2 Blandford Place | Pall Mall
MS. New York Public Lib. Pub. with omis. Letters, Conversations and Rec. *210.*
Postmark: Highgate, 26 December 1823.

Highgate
26 Decr 1823

My dear Mrs Allsop

Indeed, indeed, you have sadly misunderstood my last hurried note.[2] So over and over again has Mr Allsop been assured that every invitation to him included you—so often has he been asked, why does not Mrs Allsop come? &c that in a few lines scrawled in the Dark, with a distracting quick, thick and noisy Beating, as of a distant Forge-hammer, in my head, and lastly written, not so much under any expectation of seeing him (in fact, for *Christmas* Day I had none) as from a nervous jealousy of any customary mark of respect & affection being omitted, the ceremony of EXPRESSING your name did not occur to me.—But the blame, whatever it be, lies wholly and exclusively on *me*. For on asking *Mr* Gillman whether an Invitation had been sent to Blandford Place, he replied by asking me, if I had not spoken &c—and on my saying, it was now too late, he still desired me to write, his words being—'for tho' A. must know how glad we always are &c, yet still as far as it is a mark of Respect, it is his due'. Accordingly, I wrote. But after the Letter had been sent to the Post, on going to Mrs Gillman's

---

[1] The date of 'Decr 24' appearing in the MS. is in Allsop's handwriting.

[2] Mrs. Allsop opened Letter 1362 and replied that Allsop was spending Christmas with his parents but that if he had been at home 'this was a season of *family* re-unions'. *Letters, Conversations and Rec.* 209.

Room to learn, how she was, & saying that I had just scrawled a note in the dark, in order not to miss the Post, *she* expressed her disapprobation, as nearly as I can remember in these words— 'I do not think a mere ceremony any mark of respect to intimate Friends—How in such weather as this, and short days, can it be supposed that Mrs Allsop can either leave the Children or take them? But to expect Mr A. to dine away from home at this time is what I would not even appear to do—for I should think it very wrong, if he did.'—I was vexed & could only reply—'This comes of doing things of a hurry! However A. knows me too well to attribute to me any other feeling or purpose than the real one.'— I give you my word and honor, my dear Madam! that to the *best* of my *recollection* these were Mrs Gillman's very words; but I am quite CERTAIN, that they contain the same Substance—And for this reason, knowing how sorely it would vex and fret on her spirits, that you had been offended, and (if the Letter of itself without any interpretation derived from the character & known sentiments & feelings of the writer were to decide it) *justly* offended, I have not shewn her your Note, nor mentioned the circumstance to her—For this sad accident has pulled her down sadly—coming too in conjunction with the distressful state of my Health & Spirits. For such are the symptoms at present, that tho' I would myself have run any hazard to have spent tomorrow with Mr Southey; his Daughter & my own Sara's Friend & Twin-sister; and with Miss Wordsworth, my God-daughter; at Mr Monkhouse's in Gloster Place; yet Mr Gillman has not only dissuaded me strongly as a Friend and peremptorily forbidden my leaving home as my Medical Adviser but he has himself written to Mr M. to inform him of his reasons &c.—

I trust, therefore, that finding Mrs G. *more* than *blameless*, and that in *me* the Blame was in the *judgement* not in the *intention*, you will think no more of it—but do me the *justice* to believe, that any intentions or feelings, of which I have been conscious, have ever been of a kind most contrary to any form of disrespect, omissive or commissive—to which let me add that *I* should be doing what Mr Allsop (I am sure) would *not* do *if having* shewn you *consciously* any *dis*respect I continued to subscribe myself *his* Friend, not to speak of any profession of being what in very truth I am,

my dear Mrs Allsop, | sincerely and affectionately *Your's*,
S. T. Coleridge

1364. *To Mrs. Charles Aders*

Address: Mrs Aders | 11. Euston Square
MS. Mr. W. Hugh Peal. Hitherto unpublished.
Postmark: Highgate, 30 December 1823.

Grove, Highgate—
30th Decr. 1823—

My dear Madam

If Paradoxes were in fashion, I might commence by telling you, that with great regret I am, perforce, Mrs Gillman's most willing Amanuensis. Last Thursday was three weeks—N.b. we returned from Ramsgate to Highgate, 10 Novr., and drove to the new House in the Grove—well, tomorrow will be a month, that Mrs Gillman all alive and stirring in the unpacking, re-arranging, and all the long et ceteras consequent on changing Houses, came one evening, between 8 and 9, into my Attic where I was writing, with some printed loose Sheets in her hand to ask if any of those were the *Proofs*, I had missed, and on my replying in the negative disappeared so suddenly that I had not time to attend her to the door with a Light, even tho' I had not (as in fact, I had) taken for granted, that she had come from, & was going back to, the Room next mine, where I supposed that she had left Preda, our House Maid, and a Light. For only two nights before I had remonstrated with Mrs G. in a tone of almost angry earnestness against her running up and down the steep and not yet familiar flights of Stairs, each so much higher than those in the old house, without Lamp or Candle. 'Some shocking accident or other will come of it, I am certain!'—Alas! the vanity of these Prophecies, which must be proved *useless* in order to be proved *true*. So it was. My eyes were not yet withdrawn from the Door, when I heard a piercing Scream and rushing out with the Light found Mrs Gillman on her back on the landing place at the foot of the first flight of Stairs (consisting of 9 high Stairs), her head touching the wall and her feet and legs on the two last stairs—: crying out, Don't be frightened! I am not hurt! Her foot had slipt on the first stair-edge, uncarpeted & smooth as polished Steel—She had plunged head-foremost, fell on her head on the edge of the 5th Stair, turned round and head over heels and thus glided down—. Mr Gillman was happily at home, and was by her side, while I was yet raising her. We carried her to her Room—and the Result of the Examination was, that her Right Arm was broken, the Wrist sprained, and the fingers likewise. But neither the Head, or Neck, or Back were at all injured.— No Fever supervened—nor has she been obliged to keep her Bed. Nevertheless the Pain and the Burthen and the fretting Thought of being disabled at so busy a time have pulled her down sadly. The Splints will, I trust, be removed in a few days; but it will be some weeks yet before she can drop the Sling, and still longer before she will have any free use of the hand.—Afflicting as the reality is, we must still consider it as an *Escape*, as a most providential Escape. But the Image and the Terror of the Image, is so before my eyes and upon my Spirit, that the recollection of what has happened seems confusedly blended with a strange and fearful *Expecting* as of a something yet to come—half-realizing what might have happened, what was so near happening. My Soul hangs trembling still on the *edge* of the Peril.—

I grieve that I cannot balance this information by any thing more cheerful respecting myself—. For the last 5 weeks I have been almost confined to the House—so much so that Mr Gillman strongly dissuaded me, as a friend, and as my Medical Superintendent peremptorily prohibited me, from availing myself of the only opportunity, I was likely to have, of spending a few hours with Mr Southey, with his Daughter, my own Sara's friend from Infancy and twin-Sister, together with Dora Wordsworth, my God-daughter, and Miss Sara Hutchinson, the dearest of many dear Housemates in happier Days—by dining at Mr Monkhouse's, 67. Gloster Place.—The most distressing of my symptoms is an almost incessant Sound in my head, loudest in my left ear, as of a Forge-Hammer at a small distance—and which on the least flurry or even excitement, or after writing for more than 5 minutes at a time, becomes so quick, thick, heavy and importunate as to be distractive of all Attention, except to it's own Larum.—As it's Accompaniments, however, are chiefly in the visceral System, & there is no head-ache, and the weight on my eye-lids, and the pain and difficulty in the tryals to awake thoroughly at my first awaking in the morning, are much diminished, no *present* danger is apprehended—and this with the whole of my indisposition is attributed to the conjoint operation of a violent cold, derangement in the digestive functions, and over-exertion of mind—

Mr Gillman, thank God! is better, and has been for some months, than I ever knew him—the blessed effects of limiting his food to 12 Ounces in the 24 Hours, and a very small portion of Fluid.—

You cannot imagine, my dear Madam! how passionately I do wish, that you were under Mr Gillman's Care—and how often Mrs Gillman exclaims—'If we could have Mrs Aders & Miss [Kelly][1] here but for a week or fortnight!'—And this, we all hope, will be the case when the weather gets milder & the days longer—. It has been the chance of my life, that I have counted an unusually large

[1] This name is heavily inked out in MS. here and in the last paragraph.

number of medical men (several of them Men of great celebrity & eminence) among my friends, at least my intimate acquaintances. But I have not the least scruple in declaring, after the opportunity of eight years' Condomes[tica]tion, that I never knew a medical man into whose hands I could so confidently place my Life and Health as Mr Gillman's—and this (I could easily convince you) arises from no *blind* partiality, or exaggeration of his Talents & Acquirements *generally*, tho' they are all highly respectable; but that I see weekly such instances of MEDICAL Tact; such a freedom from pedantry and the influences of the *names* of Diseases; so thorough and so familiar a knowlege of what is known in the medical World shaped and vivified by personal Experience; but above all, that quickness of sound good sense in the application of the right means to the particular case in each particular patient, as I never witnessed in the same perfection in any other medical Man.—

Mrs Gillman expects me to say every thing that is kind, respectful, and sympathizing—and so as best to express her unfeigned Esteem & Regard—She desires her best Love to Miss [Kelly]—and to be remembered to Mr Aders—. In short, she has an Amen at her heart to all, that I feel and mean in subscribing myself, dear Madam!

Your's and Mr Aders's sincere Friend
S. T. Coleridge

1365. *To J. A. Hessey*

Address: Mr Hessy
MS. Harvard College Lib. Hitherto unpublished.

[December 1823]

Dear Sir

I should be more miserable than I dare think of if this sad interruption had been owing to any indolence on my part, or any inconstancy of pursuit, or to defect or deficiency in my Will in any way.—But indeed I can scarcely describe to you, in what a state I have been, originating *perhaps* in a severe Cold which seized me within a few days after my arrival at our new and *large* House here—. For a little while I was relieved by a most unsightly eruption on my face—but this disappearing, the whole train of my bowel complaints & Stomach-sickness returned in an aggravated degree—These, however, I could have fought up against, so far that I was able to do something—but at this time my nerves received a shock from a fearful Accident—Mrs Gillman had stept into my *Attic* one evening while I was writing, to enquire whether a printed Proof-Sheet was the one which had been mislayed— My Eye had scarcely turned from the Door closing after her when

I heard a piercing Shriek, and rushing out found Mrs G. on her
back on the Landing-place at the foot of a steep and high Flight of
Stairs, from the very first of which she had precipitated, fell on her
head on the sixth or seventh Stair, & then turned round & over—
That neither her neck, or Back were injured, was scarcely now
conceivable—Her Right Arm was broken & the Wrist & Fingers
sprained & I fear injured—. I suppose, that the fright & dreadful
sickness, I felt, had something to do with what followed—viz. a
loud and continued Noise in my Ear as of a Forge Hammer at some
distance, & which for a whole day I actually took for an outward
Sound—. This has but few and short intervals; but after sitting
above ten minutes or so writing, the noise becomes so distractive
of all attention, and the Strokes so strong and hurried, that I am
obliged to start up & either walk or sit *stretching* myself upright—
And the attempt to look out or compare any thing in the mechanical part of the work (for instance, the finding out the places in
Mr G's Edition of Leighton, corresponding to those in my own) has
a worse effect than writing itself—. I must therefore intreat you to
go on with the printing—. With the inclosed (and the *numbers*,
& names of the Pages, &c for the remainder of the Spiritual
Aphorisms, which you will have on Monday, there being nothing
more to be composed) you will have matter enough for some three
weeks at least—. And tho' it grieves me that I cannot send you the
biographical Essay, being really unable to put the different *Parts*
together—yet I feel the necessity of making a full stop for a *week* &
without attempting as I have day after day been doing, to effect
what is not in my power—. Let the worst come, the materials of
the Essay are all in existence, & if Medicine, Starving, and doing
nothing do not bring me round in the course of six or eight days, I
will get Mr Carey or some other literary Friend to put them together for me—You may rely in the mean time for the Proofs being
corrected & returned without an hour's further delay—

                         Your obliged

                                   S. T. Coleridge—

1366. *To J. A. Hessey*

Address: Mr Hessey
*MS. Montana State University Lib., the H. W. Whicker Collection. Hitherto
unpublished.*

                         Grove, Highgate—
                         Thursday Afternoon. [January 1824?]
Dear Sir
    I have no other way of accounting for the detention of the in-
closed Sheet, but that it having been drawn off on fine Paper, I had

been led to suppose that the whole Number had been drawn off—the more readily, that with the exception of the omission of the word, raises, in p. 144, there was nothing that absolutely required further correction. The few corrections made by me in the proof were intended for my own copy, ex. gr. p. 135—and tho' the insertion would improve the §§ ph., I am by no means desirous to have it done, if it cannot be done without displacing the type or other trouble.—The stop after the Vocative Case, Lucili! (Ita dico, Lucili! SACER instead of Ita dico: Lucilî SACER)[1] is of more importance.—By the bye, of the Sheets printed off I possess B.C.D.E.F.G.I.—but not H. 97–112.—

But in the sheet M.—p. 161 of the former proof, and p. 163 of the proof inclosed, there must have been some oversight, whether mine or the printer's I know not, and therefore hold myself bound to suppose the former. A Slip was written by me, to be inserted, instead of the bewildering long and entangled Sentence—& I *feel positive* that I put it into the Proof & sent it off. But as experience has long ago taught me not to confound the *feeling* of POSITIVE- NESS with the *sense* of *certainty*, but rather to consider the former as a strong presumption that there is no ground for the latter, but that my fancy, in some odd way blending with a *sensation* of Memory, has been playing me a trick—therefore, tho' I can no where find the said Slip among my Scraps, I conclude that it is a blunder of my own making. I found the beginning of a first Copy of the Slip, which I have completed so as to make sense, and this I have inclosed—in case, the true Simon Sly should not turn up at the Printer's.

And yet when I look over the proof as it now is, omitting only 1. 10, I become doubtful whether my meaning is not rendered suffi- ciently clear.—You will greatly oblige me, my dear Sir! if you will compare the two—and if *you* think the superior clearness of the Slip inclosed will make it worth while to unsettle the type, you will, of course, have it substituted. But if not, I shall be content with the present, omitting the 10th line, and put the — after 'Consequences'—

respectfully | your obliged

S. T. Coleridge

[1] *Aids to Reflection*, 1825, p. 142 (signature K).

1367. *To Mrs. J. H. Green*

Address: Mrs J. Green | 18 Lincoln's Inn Fields
MS. Cornell University Lib. Hitherto unpublished.
Postmark: 9 January 1824.

Grove, Highgate
Wednesday Night [7] Jany. 1824.

Dear Madam

Mrs Gillman requests me to become her Amanuensis: which I should do with much greater pleasure, if there had been neither Rhyme nor Reason for it. But alas! many weeks, I fear, must yet pass by, before her Wrist and Fingers will be brought to give evidence of their Pen-womanhood, in spite of the Support, which the Arm is already qualified to afford. Towards Evening the Parts are especially painful and wearisome, and Mrs G. is a good deal pull'd down. Still however, neither her Health, Strength or Spirits have given way nearly to the extent, that might with good reason have been apprehended—and I am myself still the worst Invalid of the Family. But for my business!—which is to convey Mrs Gillman's best Love to you, and her acknowlegements and thanks for the Birds &c, with all cordial Christmas—and New-Year Wishes to you and to Mr Green, and for all that are near and dear to you.

Your good husband has almost spoilt me, I find—for a long time past the Sundays have seemed like Saturdays or Washing-days. They come with unwashed faces and in their *day*-before's Neckcloth & Beard.—The Forge-hammer in my head is, however, not in such full or constant play as it has been. Tho' not silenced for good and all, the intermissions are longer (to day I have heard it but once & only for about half an hour—and then not so loud or thick) so that I hope, that it will disappear altogether as soon as the Weather and my Tasks will permit me to take exercise and do nothing for a few days but walk longish Walks without a book in my Hand.—

If Mrs Green senr be with you, be so good as to make my best and most respectful remembrances to her, and believe me

with most sincere esteem and | cordial Regard,
dear Madam, | Your obliged Friend
S. T. Coleridge

1368. *To J. A. Hessey*

Address: Mr Hessey
MS. Mrs. J. L. Staufer. Pub. Modern Language Notes, *May 1929, p. 302.*

Wednesday Noon [January 1824 ?]
Dear Sir

God be praised! I have here inclosed the last of the manifoldly and intricately altered and augmented Proofs—and I venture to assure you, that the Copy you will receive the day after tomorrow will be a fair specimen of all that will follow—and that there shall be no further delays on my part—except only what I cannot help, that I take more than twice the time in correcting a proof, and in fact in every mode and appurtenance of Composition, than Writers in general—partly, no doubt, from the state of my health, but in part likewise from the distressing activity and if I may use such a phrase, the excessive *productivity* of my mind.—

respectfully | and truly your | obliged
S. T. Coleridge

1369. *To J. A. Hessey*

Address: Mr Hessey
MS. Wisbech Museum and Literary Institute. Hitherto unpublished.

Monday afternoon—[19 January 1824][1]
Dear Sir

I feel a more than selfish gratification in being able to announce to you, that during the last week my Health had made such progress that yesterday, for the first time, I was able to venture out—& walked to my friend, Mr Charles Lamb's, concerning whose illness I had suffered much anxiety, and returned by the stage, without finding myself the worse for it—I think, therefore, that I can now promise you a *straight going on*—without delays.[2] I shall send off every other day the remaining *copy*—& am ready for the *Proofs*, as soon as they are ready.—

In the next work (the Elements of Discourse) I must make a bargain with the Printers or Compositors, that the Initial Letters

---

[1] Writing to Bernard Barton on 23 Jan. 1824 Lamb speaks of having been ill for 'many weeks'. This is undoubtedly the illness which had caused Coleridge anxiety and to which he refers in the present letter. Coleridge's visit to Lamb of 'yesterday', therefore, probably took place on Sunday, 18 Jan. See *Lamb Letters*, ii. 415.

[2] Lamb's comment to Barton of 23 Jan. 1824 concerning the *Aids* was probably based on information which Coleridge supplied during his recent visit to Islington: 'Coleridge's book is good part printed, but sticks a little for

shall be printed as in the MS.[1]—When Adjectives are used substantively, as the Beautiful, the Good; or Substantives are used that in other places are participles, as the Being, a capital is necessary. In the present work it is not of so much importance—& I shall make no corrections that are not absolutely required in order to perspicuity.—

The inclosed III and IV Aphorism, with a Vth, consisting of a beautiful passage from a Sermon of Hooker's,[2] the transcript of which I have mislaid—& am afraid of losing the Post if I stay to look it up—is the whole additional matter—the rest are Leighton's or my own—& the *numbers*, pages, &c—will be sent off as soon as I can get thro' with the collation—the Edition, I have, being differently paged from that at the Printer's—I am obliged to conclude abruptly—

Your obliged

S. T. Coleridge

1370. *To C. A. Tulk*

Address: Charles Augustus Tulk, Esqre. M.P. | 19 | Duke Street | Westminster
MS. Pierpont Morgan Lib. Hitherto unpublished.
Postmark: Highgate, 26 January 1824.

Grove, Highgate
Monday—[26 January 1824]

My dear Sir

The appendix to the white Horse[3] painfully renewed the strong and ever baffled Yearning that has so long possessed and so often taken possession of my mind, to write to you a part at least of the many thoughts that crowd on me in the perusal of Swedenborg's Writings—The following hasty note may serve as a very slight specimen—the beginning of which I must transcribe as I unluckily began it on the second side of a Leaf in my Mem. Book—

Swedenb. App. de Equo albo.[4]—

more copy. It bears an unsaleable Title, Extracts from Bishop Leighton, but I am confident there will be plenty of good notes in it, more of Bishop Coleridge than Leighton, I hope, for what is Leighton?' *Lamb Letters*, ii. 416.

[1] In *Aids to Reflection*, 1825, p. 196 (signature O), Coleridge announced that 'God permitting', the *Elements of Discourse* would follow his *Aids*.

[2] The passage from Hooker's sermon, 'Of the Nature of Pride', appears in *Aids to Reflection*, 1825, pp. 188–9 (signature N), where it is numbered Aphorism VI.

[3] Coleridge refers to Tulk's translation of Swedenborg's *An Appendix to the Treatise on the White Horse*, 1824.

[4] A copy of Swedenborg's treatise, *De Equo Albo, de quo in Apocalypsi, cap: xix. Et dein de Verbo et ejus sensu spirituali seu interno, ex Arcanis coelestibus*, 1758, containing annotations by Coleridge is in the British Museum.

But surely the *Doctrine* of Sym[bols] or Correspondences should first be proved or at least exhibited as a Science. It's *Principles* should be stated and established: then it's *Canons* deduced: then it's *Classes* (Ordinates, Co-ordinates, and Subordinates) unfolded & contabulated.—Lastly, in consonance with the Principles, Canons, and Generic Characters, the Symbols hitherto determined. —*Then*, if by the application of these to the Sacred Writings a worthy and coherent sense should be successively and (as it were) *articulately* evolved, this would be, no doubt[1] at once Exemplification, Confirmation, and Test. Otherwise, and if the Bible be taken in the outset as instances in proof, and proof by accumulation of instances, and more than a bare probability is to result, the words of the Bible ought to be shown incapable of any other sense—or at least incapable of any sense not dependent on the existence of the symbolic Sense. Thus a human Soul may be supposed to exist, as an integral Being: without the co-presence of a Body. But an organized and living Body may indeed co-exist with a Soul (a Literal with a Symbolic Sense) but neither have begun to exist, nor continue to exist, without a Soul.—But that the direct and verbal Sense of the Sacred Pages is such a Body; soulless, if the Sense afforded by the Science of Correspondences be not accepted as the Soul—few, I suspect, will be induced to believe who has [have] not previously and on other grounds convinced himself [themselves] of the truth and reality of the Science in itself.

An intercepted Letter in unknown characters or words, or in unintelligible combinations of known characters or words, if rendered into coherent and probable sense by a Cypher, will be a sufficient Proof of that Cypher even tho' it should have been formed by tentative processes from the Letter itself, but of course not so strong a proof, as if the Cypher had been previously formed from other Letters intercepted from the same Channel—. But to take a Page of ordinary import$=a$, and turn it into another page of import$=\beta$, by asserting of each word that it stands for some other (ex. gr. for Horse read Doctrine)—this, however admirable the import$=\beta$, and tho' incomparably more interesting than the import$=a$, would strike every sober mind as arbitrary, and even whimsically so. I infer, therefore, that the Disciples of Emanuel Swedenborg should join in constructing or causing to be constructed an Accidence, and a Grammar (i.e. the Syntax and the Prosody) of Correspondences—with a Vocabulary, as a Ground work and plat-form of a future (not Lexicon but) Logicon. For the Νούμενον, that which is to be *understood*, that which contemplated

[1] The text from this point to the postscript is drawn from two small pages cut out of one of Coleridge's notebooks and sent with this letter to Tulk.

Objectively, and as one with the φαινόμενον, is the true Numen; and which taken subjectively, and distinctly, is the *Nomen,* or Noun, and Nominator—the Noumenon, I say, is the Logos, the WORD. The Phaenomenon, or visual and literal Apprehension, is ῥῆμα[1]— a fluxion.[2]

P.S. Of the Writers who should be consulted previously to the Understanding Mr Hartley's scheme I would suggest Achmetes, Artemidorus, and the Oneirocritici generally—(I *believe,* they have been edited, the Greek at least, collectively)[3]—then the incomparable Mystics before the Scholastic AEra, viz. Hugo and Ricardus de Sancto Victore, and after or toward the close of that AEra, as Joan. Gerson—to which tho' not mystics professedly, should be added that delightful Book of the Spaniard, Raymund de Sabunde, & above all, the Lullian Logical and Mnemonical Treatises of Giordano Bruno—Campanella should be looked into—. Of Flavel I know nothing—Fludd I found indigestible—but both the Helmonts should be remembered—. I write hastily & without any Books to consult that could assist me.—

[1] Underlined once in MS. The Greek word for fluxion is ῥεῦμα.

[2] The second page cut from Coleridge's notebook also contains the following notes:

William Occam, of the County of Surry, became Provincial of the Minorites, 1322—in 1328 silenced and compelled to find an asylum in France by the papal Anathema of Pope John XXII—his speech to the Emperor 1330— Tu me defendas gladio, ego te defendam calamo.—His Master, D. Scotus & himself the greatest minds of the Schoolmen—proof that Realism pursued to its whole Extent melts into Nominalism. Indeed, Occam appears himself to have considered his great Master as not differing from himself in essentials— Of all the Titles conferred on the several eminent Schoolmen that of *Venerabilis Inceptor* applied to Occam pleased me most—

Compositio entis et non-entis—of Campanella & many before him—with the same confusion, viz. the non-ens being now the mere logical negation, $3+1+0=4$, just as Cold considered as not heat, and now as a real some*what* tho' no *thing*—as cold = the contractive Power. Qy. What these men & Anaxagoras Inf. et Finitum were striving after, might it not be expressed by *relative* and *irrelative* Being, ens in se vel in alio, per se vel per aliud, et ens compositum sui et alius, limites per se et per aliud ?—The πρωτοψεῦδος, as I have elsewhere & often remarked, is the application of Dichotomy to the Conception, Reality—instead of the Trichotomy

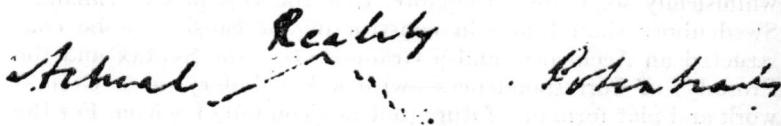

[3] *Artemidori Daldiani & Achmetis Sereimi f. Oneirocritica.* [With a Latin version of Artemidorus, by J. Cornarius: and of Ahmad, by J. Leunclavius.] *Astrampsychi & Nicephori versus etiam oneirocritici.* Lutetiae, 1603.

I avail myself of your kind permission to inclose a letter for franking—not for myself indeed but what is the same to me & I well know equivalent to you, for Mr Gillman[1]—.

Poor Mrs Gillman's Health is sadly undermined by this accident —and I fear that it will be more months than six or eight before she will have any use of her arm & hand—The fracture of course is already quite removed—but her *Wrist* and *Hand,* and the dull wearying Pain—

Remember me with cordial most respectful regards to dear Mrs Tulk—who, be assured, lives often in my heart of Prayer.—

I am under great affliction of mind from the diseased state of mind in relation to his moral & religious System of *Thinking* (N.b. —not of Action, thank God!) in which I find my second Son— O what a Place of Poisons that University of Cambridge is— Atheism is quite the *Ton* among the Mathematical Geniuses, Root and Branch Infidelity!—And 'the arrow flieth in Darkness.'[2]—

Your obliged Friend
S. T. Coleridge

1371. *To C. A. Tulk*

Address: C. A. Tulk, Esqre. M.P. | Duke Street | Westminster
MS. Pierpont Morgan Lib. Hitherto unpublished.
Postmark: Highgate, 14 February 1824.

13 Feby. 1824

My dear Sir

I again avail myself of your kind permission in entreating you to frank the inclosed to

Mrs Coleridge Keswick Cumberland.

O dear Sir! out of your own house I dare believe that there is not a Spirit that follows you with a keener sympathy in your present sore anxiety than mine does!

As soon as my Proofs are out of hand, the *introductory* Essay to the Science of Correspondences shall be corrected & sent to you. I say *introductory* because in the exposition of Noumena ⚹ Phaenomena (⚹ is my notation for '*in antithesis to*') as a Principle of Logic it is shewn, that in the very mechanism and [con]stitutional forms of the Understanding the mind is framed and predispo[sed] for the Science. All real science is *mythological*—κόσμος ἱερότατός ἐστι [*sic*] Μῦθος.—

Your obliged & sincere | Friend
S. T. Coleridge

[1] The Address is *on* a *Slip* half *in* the Letter. [Note by S. T. C. written at top of page one of MS.]   [2] Psalm xci. 5.

1372. *To Mrs. S. T. Coleridge*

Addressed and franked: London February Fourteen 1824 | Mrs Coleridge |
Keswick | Cumberland   Cha: Aug: Tulk
MS. Pierpont Morgan Lib. Hitherto unpublished fragment.
Postmark: 14 February 1824.

[13 February 1824]

. . . I cannot find the British Critic; but I will endeavor to procure
[it.] In the changing of House, I was at Ramsgate—& you may
imagine in what confusion the Books are—

I am exceedingly anxious to have that pacquet entitled Literae
Sacerrimae, containing Lamb's & other Letters—. But there are
likewise some Books, I particularly want—and therefore—unless
you should have an opportunity by some trusty person who will
not be as long on the Road as Mr Carne with dearest Sara's nice
letter, I must wait & will write again about it.—I think that
Gassendi's works are among my books—at least some part of them
—Desire Sara to see whether the *Syntagma Philosophicum* is the
name of the work in the Gassendi Volumes that I have—.¹ Likewise, I want Fracastorii opera²—but I will write on this again,
when I can think of some method. . . .

1373. *To J. H. Green*

Address: J. H. Green, Esqre. | Surgeon | Lincoln's Inn Fields
MS. Pierpont Morgan Lib. Pub. with omis. Letters, ii. 726.
Postmark: Highgate, 16 February 1824.

Grove Highgate—Monday Afternoon
15 [16] Feby. 1824.

I mentioned to you, I believe, Basil Montagu's kind endeavors
to have an associateship of the Royal Society of Literature (a
yearly 100£ versus a yearly Essay) conferred on me.³ I knew nothing
of the particulars till this morning, or rather till within this hour,
when I received a list of names (Electors) from Mrs Montagu, with
advice to write to such and such & such—while he, and he, and he
had promised—'*for us*'—in short, a regular Canvas, or rather Sack-
cloth with the ashes on it, pulled out of the Dust hole & moistened
with Cabbage-water and other culinary Excretions of the same
kidney—Of course, I *jibbed* and with proper (if not equa; yet)
mulanimity returned for answer—that what a man's friends did

---

¹ P. Gassendi's *Works* were published in 6 vols. in 1658 and again in 1727.
In both editions the *Syntagma philosophicum* occupies the first two volumes.
² The complete works of Girolamo Fracastoro were published in 1555.
³ See Letter 1382.

sub rosâ, and what one friend might say to another in favor of an Individual, was one thing—what a man did in his own name & person, was another—and that I would not, *could* not, *solicit* a single vote. I should think it an affrontive interference with a decision, in which there ought to be neither ground or motive, but the Elector's own judgement & conscience—and all for what?—It is hard if in the same time as I could produce an Essay of the sort required I could not get the same sum by compiling a School-book.—

However, I fear that having allowed my name at Montagu's instance to be proposed, which it was by a Mr Jordan, (N.b. neither the one sub cubile, nor that in Palestine; but the Jordan of Michael's Grove, Brompton, No. 1.)[1] I cannot now withdraw my name without appearing to *trifle* with my Friends, & without hurting Montagu—so I must submit to the probability of being black-balled as the penalty of having given my assent before I had ascertained the conditions. So I have decided to let the thing take it's own course—but as Montagu wishes to have Mr Chantrey's Vote *for us*, if you see and *feel* no objection (an Objectiuncula will be quite sufficient) you will perhaps write him a Line to state the circumstance—It comes on on Thursday next—. One of the Electors' names is Cattermole ! ! ![2] I wonder what twi-bestialism that Fellow committed in his pre-existent state to bring down such a name upon him!

I look forward with a *feel* of regeneration to the Sundays.—
My best and most affectionate respects to Mrs J. Green—& to your dear & excellent Mother if she be with you—
    and till we meet, may God bless you | and your obliged & sincere
        Friend
                                                    S. T. Coleridge

1374. *To George Skinner*[3]

Transcript Coleridge family. Hitherto unpublished.

                                                    Grove Highgate
                                                    17 Feby 1824
Dear Sir
    I take the liberty of troubling you with a few questions in behalf of a Friend & Neighbor of ours, Mr Johnson of Muswell Hill, a man

---

[1] William Jerdan (1782–1869) helped to found the Royal Society of Literature.
[2] Richard Cattermole (1795?–1858), miscellaneous writer, was secretary of the Royal Society of Literature from 1823 to 1852.
[3] The Rev. George Skinner, fellow of Jesus College, Cambridge, 1818–42.

highly respectable both in what is and in what ought to be re-
pected—id est—he is a worthy man and a man of property. One of
his sons, now about 18 I believe, he means to send to Cambridge
as his immediate destination, the Medical profession being the
ultimate. Mr Johnson and the young Gentleman himself are fully
impressed with the substantial as well as inherent advantages of a
liberal and academic education & this in an English & National
University to a Physician who is to start *as* an M.D.[1] Now I have
strongly recommended and the parents as decisively wish a small
College, and of small colleges I need not add that I advised our
beloved Jesus College—which I never think of without an Esto
perpetua! uttered with as filial a fervor as ever shot a prayer sky-
wards. —What I request is a few lines of information, first whether
you see any objection to his being entered at Jesus—2. whether if
entered he can have rooms in the College or whether you are so full
that he must lodge in the Town ? 3. If the latter be the case whether
any of the other small Colleges are differently circumstanced, &
what you would recommend (I scarcely know why; but I have
rather a prejudice against Sidney, Magdalene, and Catharine Hall)?
And lastly whether for a young man who looks forward to no
Collegiate *after* emoluments and is to begin life as a physician,
you would yourself advise any other College in preference to Jesus,
independently of the accidents of Room ?

I should have been glad had time & opportunity permitted to
have had some confidential conversation with you respecting the
state of my son Derwent's mind & opinions. From all I could bring
out of himself, he had picked up second hand from Mr Austin thro'
young Macauley[2] a set of captious Questions & objections startling
only to those for whom they are new, and new only to those who
had read so little on the subject as to have no claim, but that of
their own vanity & presumption, to express any Opinion at all. I
found him unable to define (I speak not of exhaustive or constitutive definition, which the Mathematician alone can be asked to
give) or to tell me precisely what he meant & what he did not mean
by any one philosophical term he made use of; but soon found that
he had got hold of the *fag-end* of every argument that had come
within his reach. In short, Vanity was so manifestly at the bottom
of the whole, that I was more mortified by the shallowness than

[1] Frederick Johnston (not Johnson), the son of William Johnston of Muswell
Hill, was admitted pensioner to Jesus College, Cambridge, on 1 Apr. 1824. He
received an M.B. degree in 1829.

[2] Charles Austin (1799–1874), who attended Jesus College, Cambridge, and
Thomas Babington Macaulay (1800–59), who attended Trinity College, Cambridge, were among Derwent Coleridge's undergraduate friends.

frightened by the profligacy and wickedness of his Creed; if only that same vanity (aided as it is unhappily in his instance by a sterile fluency, a sort of sand torrent—no unusual occurrence in a desert soil, that looks and sounds exceedingly like water to strangers and at the proper distance) will but permit him to hold his tongue.

As to the great question itself—I have only this to say, that the man who can have *no assurance* of a God that does not rest on an apodictic proof, even tho' it should be susceptible of strictest demonstration that such a proof is incompatible with the nature of the truth to be proved and equally incompatible with all the purposes of this truth relatively to the human Being—such a man I say is not in a state to be reasoned with on any subject. If like Mr Austin he further denies the *fact* of a law of conscience or any obligation directly resulting therefrom I should be puzzled what to answer. I could not without a contradiction address him as a moral Being—or else I should admonish him that as an honest man he ought to *advertize* it as a Cavete omnes! scelus sum—and being an honest man myself, I ought not to advise him by way of prudence and for his own sake to keep his naturam monstrosam to himself, lest I should help him on with a *Wrap-rascal* and furnish him with a Mask.[1]—

Excuse this obtrusion on your attention and demand on your time—& believe me with respect and regard

dear Sir | Yours truly
S. T. Coleridge

1375. *To Basil Montagu*

Address: Basil Montague, Esqre
MS. Cornell University Lib. Hitherto unpublished.

[February 1824?]

My dear Montague

Never any thing happened more unluckily—Yesterday Mr Stutfield came & took my whole morning, so that I could not get off my proof, my Publisher raving—To day an oriental Traveller with Letter from the North &c &c whom Mr Gillman had detained—so that I can but merely put down a few *names*[2]—God bless you &
S. T. Coleridge.

[1] See *Aids to Reflection*, 1825, p. 178 n. (signature N).
[2] The following names, etc. appear on the verso of the address page:

Plato—throughout, as an *Askesis* or Discipline of Invention—
Aristotle's Categories must be so considered; but as a Book, who will read

P.S. Besides, the word, Invention, is so general that unless I had seen the work & knew your purpose, I could not do any thing to the purpose—.

1376. To John Anster[1]

MS. University of Texas Lib. Hitherto unpublished.

Grove, Highgate
18 Feby. 1824—4 o'clock afternoon.

My very dear Anster

As I will not after so long an interval send an apology for a Letter instead of one, I must seize what half hours I can, to begin and to continue what I cannot on the same day complete. I have been indeed VERY unwell, and during a long time with symptoms of a distressing and incapacitating kind—a constant noise as of a fulling Mill or Forge in my Ear, which for a man who till then had never felt or (except when shaving) been conscious of having a Head on his Shoulders, was sufficiently alarming: and which as often as I bent my head in the act of writing, became perfectly bewildering. *Indolent* has at least 3 senses, 1. freedom from pain, which I have long been a stranger to, and of late the Pain has acquired a locality, viz. in inguine sinistro, and across the umbilical region: 2. idle or at least unenergizing, which I wish it were oftener in my power to be, than it is, or at all events less systematically: 3. a cowardice & putting off of the *Hoc age* quod *nunc* agendum est, to which I plead guilty.—Lastly, incidents and accidents, directly or indirectly affecting me or my circumstances, have like pale-faced Messengers with the two-fold object, ill-news and their own safety, followed one another in thick succession. But be assured that neither of the three causes, nor any thing short of the Dunning of the Bookseller and the exhausted Patience of the Printer with the accumulating expence of

the Organon?—Besides, the Parts appertaining to Invention have been superseded by Kant—
Raymond de Sabunde
Lully (Raymond)
Campanella. Cardan.
* Giordano Bruno—particularly, his De Umbris Idearum, Logici Venatrix Veritatis, in short, his *Mnemonic* Tracts generally.
Leibnitz—
** Kant's Examen of the pure Reason, and of the Judicial Power.
But after all, Kant & Bacon supersede, I am convinced all the rest—except perhaps Giordano Bruno's Work.
[1] This letter was franked by C. A. Tulk to John Anster, Esqre—5 Walworth Place, Dublin. See next letter.

keeping the Press in suspense (the consequences of having been thrown so far behind hand partly by the above-mentioned causes, and partly by the work growing and new-forming itself under my hand)[1] would have prevented you from receiving an immediate

[1] In the Advertisement or '*Pre*-preface' to *Aids to Reflection*, 1825, Coleridge commented on his 'original plan' and pointed to its alteration during the progress of his work:

In the introductory portion there occur several passages, which the Reader will be puzzled to decypher, without some information respecting the original design of the Volume, and the Changes it has undergone during its immature and embryonic state. On this account only, I think myself bound to make it known, that the Work was proposed and begun as a mere Selection from the Writings of Archbishop Leighton, under the usual title of The Beauties of Archbishop Leighton, with a few notes and a biographical preface by the Selector. Hence the term, *Editor*, subscribed to the notes, and prefixed alone or conjointly to the Aphorisms, accordingly as the Passage was written entirely by myself, or only modified and (*avowedly*) interpolated. I continued the use of the word on the plea of uniformity: though like most other deviations from propriety of language, it would probably have been a wiser choice to have omitted or exchanged it. The various Reflections, however, that pressed on me while I was considering the motives for selecting this or that passage; the desire of enforcing, and as it were integrating, the truths contained in the Original Author, by adding those which the words suggested or recalled to my own mind; the conversation with men of eminence in the Literary and Religious Circles, occasioned by the Objects which I had in view; and lastly, the increasing disproportion of the Commentary to the Text, and the too marked difference in the frame, character, and colors of the two styles; soon induced me to recognize and adopt a revolution in my plan and object, which had in fact actually taken place without my intention, and almost unawares. It would indeed be more correct to say, that the present Volume owed its accidental origin to the intention of compiling one of a different description, than to speak of it as the same Work. It is not a change in the child, but a changeling.

Still, however, the selections from Leighton, which will be found in the prudential and moral Sections of this Work, and which I could retain consistently with its present form and matter, will both from the intrinsic excellence and from the characteristic beauty of the passages, suffice to answer two prominent purposes of the original plan; that of placing in a clear light the principle, which pervades all Leighton's Writings—his sublime View, I mean, of Religion and Morality as the means of reforming the human Soul in the Divine Image (*Idea*); and that of exciting an interest in the Works, and an affectionate reverence for the name and memory, of this severely tried and truly primitive Churchman.

To the last section of the *Aids*, 'Aphorisms on that which is indeed Spiritual Religion' (p. 150), Coleridge prefixed the following comment:

In the selection of the Extracts that form the remainder of this Volume and of the Comments affixed, the Editor had the following Objects principally in view. First, to exhibit the true and scriptural meaning and intent of several Articles of Faith, that are rightly classed among the Mysteries and peculiar Doctrines of Christianity. Secondly, to show the perfect rationality of these Doctrines, and their freedom from all just Objection when examined by their proper Organ, the Reason and Conscience

Answer to your welcome letter. For You are to me, and have a place in my heart, as a Son: and if the Accident of Nature had made you so, I could not love you otherwise or yearn after you with more anxiety. Indeed, I owe it as an act of Justice to Mr and Mrs Gillman, that you are a Fixture at our Fire-side, irremoveable beyond the power of Absence or Distance: nor is any Name of Interest mentioned, but your's is sure to occur to one or the other of us—and the Answer commonly is—Dear Fellow! I was just thinking of him.—After this need I say, how great a comfort to me is the knowlege of your recovered health, and how fervent my prayers for it's continuance? I rejoice too, that you are girding yourself in decided earnest for a Profession, and the Law seems to be clearly that to which Providence by the allotment of your circumstances (cuncta quotquot stant *circum*) has called you.[1] And I know you too well to have any apprehensions that the Law should make you forget the Gospel. Theology and all the Questions and Answers that have their birthplace in the abstract Understanding, you may think as little about as you like: except for a Clergyman and for him too chiefly in a large Town, they are at best but respectable Amusements. But I know by experience, that there are sorrows & infirmities for which Religion is the only Antidote—by strong and unwillingly received Experience I know too, that Religion is the only Blessing in this world, on which an entire reliance that needs fear no disappointment can be placed, and that the Commandment which enjoins us to love our neighbour as ourself, but *God above* all, is like all other duties, enjoined in Love and Mercy to ourselves.

And now for *all about* your friends. First, Mr Gillman. Some 8 or 9 months ago, he found himself inconvenienced by his size, and took and strictly kept the resolution of confining himself to 12 ounces of solid food, with a very scanty portion of Fluid & no wine, in the 24 Hours. The scheme has worked like a miracle—strength, activity, elasticity of spirits, the power of bearing fatigue, & of early rising have been the more than Hesperidean Fruits—and in person he has become almost a young man.—I am sure, you would start at first seeing him. My friend, Mr Green, burst into a long and hearty Laugh, and stared as if he was saying—'Zounds! what a succession

of Man. Lastly, to exhibit from the Works of Leighton . . . an instructive and affecting picture of the contemplations, reflections, conflicts, consolations and monitory experiences of a philosophic and richly-gifted mind, amply stored with all the knowledge that Books and long intercourse with men of the most discordant characters can give, under the convictions, impressions, and habits of a Spiritual Religion.

[1] In Easter term 1824 Anster was called to the Irish bar, and in the following year he took the degree of doctor of laws. From 1850 until his death in 1867 he was regius professor of civil law in the University of Dublin.

of Skins you must have sloughed!'—Would to God, I could give
you as cheering an account of Mrs Gillman. We were at Ramsgate
for a month at the close of last Autumn, leaving Highgate on the
same morning that dear Mr Watson took leave [of] us for Germany,
where I trust he now is & well at Berlin—for to our surprize, les-
sened indeed by our knowlege of his Letterophobia, we have not
yet heard from him. During our stay at Ramsgate Mr Gillman
executed the operose part of changing Houses: and we returned to
the center house in the Grove, next door to Mr Nixon's—a large &
handsome Mansion, and the View from the window of the Attic,
which I have chosen as my Bed and Book-room, commands a view
over Southampton Farm, Kenn Wood, & Hampstead not surpassed
within a hundred miles of London.—A few weeks after our return,
one Thursday Night about 9 o'clock Mrs G. came into my room
with some papers in her hand to know whether a Paper, I had
mislayed, was among them—I had scarce answered, No! before she
was gone; and my eye was still on the door, when I heard a fearful
Scream and rushing out found her on her back with her head to the
wall at the bottom of the Landing of the first flight of Stairs—a
steep flight of very high stairs, 9 in number. Her foot had slipped
on the first step; she had plunged forward and fell head-long, almost
perpendicular on the edge of the 5th or 6th Stair, then turned round
and over, & was propelled head-foremost to where she was lying.
Mr Gillman was fortunately at home, and already by her side as I
was raising her—. It was little less than miraculous that neither
her head, or Neck, or Back were injured; but the Right arm
was broken, halfway between the Elbow & Wrist, and her
Wrist, Hand & Fingers fearfully sprained. The Bone has long been
cemented; but it will be many months yet, I fear, before she will
have any *use* of it, from the obstinacy that characterises all serious
Sprains. Meanwhile, I grieve to say that tho' it is impossible that
any human Being should bear up against it with more fortitude, or
allow himself to fret less about it, yet the constant dull and not unfrequent severe pain, the necessity of hot fomentations & the fatigue
and awkwardness of supporting the arm in a sling, have considerably affected her general health.—I am strongly enjoined by
her to say every thing that is most kind and affectionate to you,
and to assure you that she thinks of you with the most lively and
cordial Regard. Neither can you well have a sincerer friend than
Mr Gillman.—

Hartley takes little Pupils at Ambleside, and is healthy, happy,
industrious and universally beloved.[1]—Derwent passed thro' High-

---

[1] Dorothy Wordsworth was equally enthusiastic. 'My nephew William', she
wrote in Oct. 1824, 'attends Hartley Coleridge, who has now fourteen Scholars

gate on his way to Plymouth, having accepted of the third Master's Place at a Public School recently instituted. He is well in body, and even improved in person; but alas! he has compleatly idled away his three years in talking and vanity, acquired no real knowlege of any kind but (of course, I write confidentially to you as to a Son) has come back an avowed Atheist, with an atheism of the grossest and most immoral description. I found however that he had been converted by young Austin & Macauley to this brutish Anti-Faith, & was so incapable of defining any one term, he made use of, and the arguments were so silly & so vaguely apprehended by him, that clearly perceiving that Vanity, aided by a sterile fluency which Girls and the Literaturi [*sic*] of the Talking Clubs take for Genius and Eloquence, is at the bottom of it, I was more mortified by the shallowness than frightened by the wickedness & profligacy of his Creed: if only the same Vanity will but permit him to hold his tongue.—Still his Failure at Cambridge, having merely taken an οἱ πολλοί Degree,[1] & his Presumption, cannot but have been a heavy affliction to me. On the other hand my Daughter, who with her Mother spent some weeks at our House on their journey to my Brothers, is a good & lovely Girl & every thing (save that her Health is delicate) that the fondest & most ambitious Parent could pray for. The young men, & some of their elders, talk in raptures of her Beauty. She is exceedingly industrious, has gained 130£ by a translation of the History of the Abipones in two volumes from the Latin of a German Jesuit, and is now compiling a Biography of the Chevalier Bayard.[2]—

As to my own works, a little volume will soon appear under the title of *Aids to Reflection*,[3] which was at first intended only for a Selection of Passages from Leighton's Works but in the course of printing has become an original work almost. How can I send you a copy with less expence than it's price if ordered at Dublin? Tho' it is written for minds of a lower class than your's, being intended for serious young men of ordinary education who are sincerely

—a flourishing concern for an Ambleside schoolmaster!—and he is steady and regular.' *Later Years*, i. 157.

[1] i.e. a poll or pass degree. Derwent Coleridge resided at Cambridge until the close of the Michaelmas term of 1823 and was admitted to the B.A. degree on 24 Jan. 1824.

[2] Sara Coleridge's *Account of the Abipones* was published in 1822 in three not two volumes; her *The right joyous and pleasant History of the feats, gests and prowesses of the Chevalier Bayard, the good Knight without fear and without reproach. By the Loyal Servant* [Translated from the French of J. de Mailles], 2 vols., appeared in 1825.

[3] Despite Coleridge's statement, *Aids to Reflection* did not appear until May 1825. See note to Letter 1384 for Coleridge's attempts to find an appropriate title for his work.

searching after moral and religious Truth but are perplexed by the common prejudice, that Faith in the peculiar Tenets of Christianity demands a Sacrifice of the Reason and is at enmity with Common-Sense—yet you will, I flatter myself, read some parts with interest, particularly the establishment of the distinct nature of Prudence, as referable to the Sensations, Senses & Understanding; Morality, as [referable] to the Conscience and the Affections; and Spiritual Religion, as grounded in the Reason and Will, (the Supernatural in Man) and comprehending Morality.[1]—As soon as this little Pioneer is out of hand, I go to the Press with the Elements of Discourse, or the Criteria of true & false Reasoning—and meantime shall devote myself to the completion of my great work, on the Philosophy of Religion—and in which my whole mind will be systematically unfolded.—The advertising of the Wanderings of Cain was a mistake[2]—I have written a few verses lately, which I will transcribe for you in my next.—They talk of conferring on me an associateship of the new Royal Society of Literature—100£ a year versus a yearly Essay. But it is urged, that it may lead to something better. I am in a puzzle about it—But it is one o'clock—& I must say, God bless you, my dear Anster! & your affectionate &

paternally attached Friend,
S. T. Coleridge.

[1] In the Preface to *Aids to Reflection*, 1825, Coleridge pointed out that it was a *'didactic'* work designed *'especially* . . . for the studious Young at the close of their education . . . yet more particularly . . . [for] Students intended for the Ministry'. Coleridge also listed the 'Objects of the present volume . . . arranged in the order of their comparative importance': '1. To direct the Reader's attention to the value of the Science of Words. . . . 2. To establish the *distinct* characters of Prudence, Morality, and Religion. . . . 3. To substantiate and set forth at large the momentous distinction between REASON and Understanding. . . . 4. To exhibit a full and consistent Scheme of the Christian Dispensation, and more largely of all the *peculiar* doctrines of the Christian Faith; and to answer all the Objections to the same, that do not originate in a corrupt Will rather than an erring Judgement. . . . There are indeed Mysteries, in evidence of which no reasons can be *brought*. But it has been my endeavour to show, that the true solution of this problem is, that these Mysteries *are* Reason, Reason in its highest form of Self-affirmation.'

[2] According to Edmund Blunden, in May 1824 Taylor and Hessey announced the forthcoming publication of not only 'THE WANDERINGS OF CAIN' but also of the 'ELEMENTS OF DISCOURSE'. (*Keats's Publisher, a Memoir of John Taylor*, 1936, p. 154 n.) Coleridge's comment to Anster, however, indicates that an advertisement of *Cain* had appeared by Feb. 1824. For the lines from *The Wanderings of Cain* as published in *Aids to Reflection*, 1825, p. 383, see Letter 1454.

1377. *To C. A. Tulk*

Address: C. A. Tulk Esqre. M.P. | Duke St | Westminster.
Transcript Coleridge family. Hitherto unpublished.

Feb. 19. 1824

My dear Sir

  I am really beginning to be ashamed of the frequency with which I have of late availed myself of your kindness. But I have a particular reason for wishing the inclosed to *go free;* yet cannot effect this with delicacy except by a Frank. The address is

  John Anster, Esqre—5 Walworth Place, Dublin.

Mr Gillman, I understand, will take the earliest day possible to call on you—and we hope that he will bring us back a confirmation of the hopes & trusts with which he cheered us on his return from you last time.—I am working night & day for the Press, and with answering an unusual influx of Letters, which must be answered & some of them at *length.* My name, I find, has been proposed as an Associate of the Royal Society of Literature; it is a 100£ a year versus a Yearly Essay. Mrs Gillman begs to be remembered with anxious good wishes and affectionate respect to Mrs Tulk—. May God long preserve her as his choicest & most precious earthly, and I doubt not, heavenly gift to you & your's is the heart-felt **Prayer** of,

my dear Sir, | Your obliged Friend
S. T. Coleridge

1378. *To the Secretary of the London Institution*

MS. Cornell University Lib. Hitherto unpublished.

Grove, Highgate. 19 Feby. 1824.

Sir

  Your Letter of this morning occasioned the discovery of your former Letter, which by the oversight of a new servant had been placed among the accumulated Letters and Notes of the Friend, in whose family I reside, during a short absence on professional duties. The Managing Committee of the L. I. will therefore, I trust, be so good as to consider the present as an *immediate* Reply to a Proposal, which in itself I receive as a Compliment, and to which the character of the senders alone would have secured respectful attention.

  Were I resident in London, and at a moderate distance from the Institution; and if my Health were such as allowed me to rely on my ability to perform the engagement with the requisite regularity;

I should not hesitate in intimating my disposition to comply with
the Wish of the Committee by soliciting further information, respecting the particulars. But situated, as I am, five miles or more from
the Spot, and in a Hamlet, the last stage for which leaves Town at
an early Hour, the Time employed in the Going and Returning, and
the Expenditure in the Hire of a Glass Coach in Highgate (which
what it is I know by experience) would of themselves render any
terms, that the Committee could be justified in offering or I without
a presumption bordering on coarseness could propose, much less
desirable than they might very reasonably be considered by a
Literary Man resident in the metropolis, or than they probably
would be by myself under other circumstances. But when to this I
add, that such is and for a long time has been the state of my
Health, that for the last six or eight months it has prevented me
from accepting a single invitation from my oldest Friends or nearest
Neighbors, and that I have never once spent an evening abroad—
and this not more in consequence of my own convictions and feelings
than in obedience to the positive injunctions of my Friend and
Medical Adviser—and further that my literary Engagements are
already to the utmost extent of the power and time, that my
Ill-health allows me to call my own; the Committee of the London
Institution will, I doubt not, do me the justice to believe, that in
declining the proposal I am best consulting the Respect which I both
owe and feel to the Gentlemen from whom it proceeded.

And I intreat you, Sir! to accept the assurance of the personal
Regard & Esteem of your obliged humble | Servant,
S. T. Coleridge.

1379. *To George Skinner*

Transcript Coleridge family. Hitherto unpublished.

Grove Highgate
Tuesday Afternoon
Feb. 24. 1824

My dear Sir
Accept my thanks for your kind Letter, the handsome language
of which I should be sorry not to have been gratified by, coming
from a Man of whose sincerity my own heart is my assurance—and
Jesus College and 'the Combination Room' at Jesus were more than
mere garnish to the dish. I have had a series of interruptions inflicted on me this morning, and am under promise to send off this
Letter by the Post, or I should (as I had intended to do) indulge myself in carrying on the very just and interesting remarks in your letter

on young converts to Infidelity, and adjoining what with less experience of Youth and Human Nature I should perhaps fancy an infallible Prophylactic (Common Sense and honesty of Character being presumed), could I but prevail on the Patient not to eject; but to make the due allowance and requisite Corrections for his *Vanity*, for the pleasurable excitement attending the communication of a *new* argument, and lastly for the power of his faith in the solar Genius of some *surprising* Man of the year above him, and rising full-orbed in the academic Horizon, & one of whose parhelia or Mock Suns it might be his ambition to appear. But I must defer this to a future opportunity, and I hope shortly to send to you a small avant Courier of my larger work entitled 'Aids to Reflection',[1] the principal object of which is to open out the Road by the removal of Prejudices as far at least as to throw some sprinkling of Doubt on the secure *Taking for granted*, that the tenets of the Christian Faith asserted in the Articles & Homilies of our National Church are in contradiction to the common sense of Mankind. But I must now hasten to the business of this scrawl. Will you be so good (I ought to be & am ashamed of needing to ask the question) as to inform me, what & whether any form be required for entering Mr Frederic Johnson's name as Pensioner on the Books of Jesus, for October next—what testimonials, what sum of money, and when & where it is to be or may be paid—whether to be sent to yourself or to your Banker in Town, and on receiving your Answer the whole shall be done forthwith? I remember, that I *went* an examination by Dr Layard in London; but this, I imagine, was in connection with the Rustat Scholarship. His register (Birth I mean & Christening) must be sent I suppose.—He was educated at Charter House & I have every reason to believe a worthy & well-disposed youth and not under par as a Scholar (Pace doctoris Latini Parrii[2] si dicere liceat).

I have received a comfortable Letter from Derwent, so far at least that he is determined to lay aside all his imagined convictions & consider them as tho' they never had been, & employ his leisure hours seriously in the systematic Acquirement of the preparatory and passionless Knowledges. Heretical as it will sound from & to a Cambridge Man, yet I confidently anticipate a convert in you to my Creed respecting the importance of Logic as the one of the two Organa of Philosophy and physical Science—Mathematics taken as the other and the imperfection of either without the other. Shall I take a step further and plunge over head and ears? Yes! to you I

---

[1] The remainder of this sentence appears almost verbatim in *Aids to Reflection*, 1825, p. 110, lines 12–18.

[2] A reference to Samuel Parr (1747–1825).

will whisper my belief, that hitherto neither Logic nor dialectic has been presented to the English Reader or even to the University Students otherwise than in a dress at once tattered and repulsive, and that on the strength of this belief I devoted so many laborious months, I might say Years to my 'Elements of Discourse'. A recent perusal of Aristotle's Analytics & Topics with a superficial looking thro' his Metaphysics convinces me likewise, that we have not even a philosophic statement either of the value or the defects of his logical Works or of what parts possessed only a temporary and accidental Value and what possess a permanent worth.

Believe me, my dear Sir, | with sincere regard & esteem |
Your obliged
S. T. Coleridge

P.S. Do I mistake in addressing you the *Revd.*?

1380. *To Unknown Correspondent*

MS. Mr. W. Hugh Peal. Hitherto unpublished.

Sat. Noon—[6 March 1824][1]

My dear Madam

I am (as we Devon Folk say) *very kindly obliged* to you for your kindness—but *this* Debate & in the Times I have seen & read.—The Debate I alluded to is the Attack on the Lord Chancellor in last Tuesday's Paper in which out of 250 members that were in the House *110* voted for something like bringing the Chancellor to the Bar of the House—for Breach of Privilege, and in no obscure times [terms] calling Mr Abercrombie a Liar[2]—

With unfeigned | respect &c
S. T. Coleridge

[1] Since the debate to which Coleridge alludes took place in the House of Commons on Monday, 1 Mar. 1824, this letter was written on Saturday, 6 Mar.

[2] On 24 Feb. 1824 the following motion was introduced in the House of Commons by John Williams: 'That a Committee be appointed to inquire into the Delays and Expenses in the Court of Chancery, and the causes thereof'. James Abercromby, later Lord Dunfermline, spoke against the motion, since such a committee 'would, in all probability' be named by the lord chancellor. In the course of his remarks Abercromby 'discussed the lord chancellor's practice in admitting new evidence in appeals against decisions made on motions'. At the conclusion of the debate Williams's motion was withdrawn. On 28 Feb., Lord Eldon, lord chancellor, who was misled by an inaccurate newspaper report of Abercromby's remarks, publicly denounced as 'utter falsehood' the charge that he had heard 'appeals and re-hearings . . . on new evidence, and thereby brought discredit on some part of the Court'. Abercromby thereupon laid the matter before the House of Commons on 1 Mar. and

1381. *To Thomas H. Dunn*

Pub. Canadian Magazine, *June 1909, p. 103.*

Thomas Henry Dunn, from whom Coleridge surreptitiously obtained supplies of opium, kept a chemist's shop at Highgate until late 1829, when he moved to Tottenham Court Road. A description of Coleridge's relations with Dunn from 1824 to 1829 is contained in an interesting autobiographical document prepared in old age by Seymour Teulon Porter, who was apprenticed to Dunn during that period. See E. L. Griggs, 'Samuel Taylor Coleridge and Opium', *Huntington Library Quarterly*, August 1954, pp. 365–78.

Of the eleven letters to Dunn which have survived, six came into the possession of one of Dunn's daughters whose husband became a clergyman near Toronto, Canada, four into the possession of another daughter who settled in Australia.

[10 March 1824][1]

Dear Sir,—

I do not doubt that within a few days my settlement with my publishers will enable me to settle with you. In the meantime be so good as to accept the enclosed, in addition to the account, as fairly your dues. The Day I left Highgate for Ramsgate a letter arrived [which] contained a draft for the sum, £26; but it was accompanied with a request in relation to a late unfortunate Public Measure, and Controversy or Feud in this District, which (had the compliance been less repugnant to my own private and disinterested conviction) I could not but resent as compromising my independence.[2] Meantime, for motives of great literary and not trifling pecuniary magnitude, I was under the necessity of changing at a heavy present loss, the whole . . . of the work I was engaged on, and of re-writing the whole. I mention these circumstances to you in confidence in justice to myself. For be assured, that few things have given me so much pain as this Delay has done. A few months' hard work will enable me hereafter to be beforehand with you rather than behind.

With true respect, | Your obliged,
S. T. C.

P.S.—I entreat you, be careful not to have any note delivered to me unless I am alone and passing your door.

---

declared that a breach of privilege had occurred. The House, however, did not uphold him. The vote was 102 in favour, 151 against. Subsequently Lord Eldon tendered an apology. See T. C. Hansard, *The Parliamentary Debates*, 1824, x. 372–437 and 571–623.

[1] This letter is endorsed 'March 10th' and the reference to the 'changing' and 're-writing' of *Aids to Reflection* clearly indicates that it was written in 1824. See Letters 1356, 1376, and 1383–4.

[2] Before he left for Ramsgate on 11 Oct. 1823 Coleridge had been asked to write something by one of the group of inhabitants of Highgate opposed to the governors of the Free Grammar School. See Letter 1310.

1382. *To Richard Cattermole*

Address: To the Reverend | Richard Cattermole, | Secretary of the Royal |
Society of Literature, | &c &c—
MS. Huntington Lib. Pub. E. L. G. ii. 322.

Grove, Highgate.
16 March 1824

Reverend Sir

I received your announcement of the Distinction and Honor successively conferred on me by the Council of the Royal Society of
Literature with those inward acknowlegements, which not to have
felt would argue me altogether unworthy of the Boon.[1] And let me
[be] allowed to add that my satisfaction was rendered more perfect,
and my sense of the favor enlivened, by my previous unqualified
approbation of the Objects of the Society, and the reverential gratitude, I had felt toward it's Royal Patron, merely as a Literary Man,
and prior to any hope or anticipation of a personal interest in my
Sovereign's Munificence. Finally, had there been aught wanting to
compleat my gratification, I should have found it supplied by the
circumstance, that the only Conditions required were such as every
honest Man must regard as a debt long before incurred, and the
Prohibitions extended to no point of principle or conduct, that was
not already precluded for a Scholar, an Englishman and a Christian by his own reason and Conscience.

Ignorant of the way in which a more formal notification of my
grateful Acceptance of the Honor of a Royal Associateship should
be conveyed, and uncertain whether it is usual and regular to have
a more distinct and explicit Acknowlegement layed before the
Council, than the present Letter can be considered, I must press on
your kindness for the requisite information: and likewise at what
date from the Election of an Associate the ESSAY should be delivered. I observe too in the printed papers, which I owe to your kind
attention, that every associate is required to state the particular

---

[1] Coleridge was one of ten Royal Associates elected by the Royal Society
of Literature, the others being the Rev. Edward Davies, the Rev. John
Jamieson, the Rev. T. R. Malthus, T. J. Mathias, James Millingen, Sir William
Ouseley, William Roscoe, the Rev. H. J. Todd, and Sharon Turner. As Royal
Patron, George IV provided the Society with an annual grant of 1100 guineas
from the King's Privy Purse. The sum of 100 guineas was used each year by the
Society to purchase two gold medals for presentation to distinguished British
and Foreign literati. Out of the King's grant, too, each Royal Associate received 100 guineas annually, with the obligation of reading a yearly essay.
Coleridge was formally presented to the Society on 6 May 1824. (See Letter
1395.) For the 'Substance' of his 'Address to the . . . Royal Society of Literature
on . . . [his] election and introduction, as a Royal Associate', see Letter 1711
and note.

department of Letters, to which (relatively at least to the Society) he would be understood as being especially attached. For myself I have chosen a double branch, but with a common stem: namely,

1. The reciprocal oppositions and conjunctions of Philosophy, Religion, and Poetry (the heroic and dramatic especially, the former comprizing both the homeric and hesiodic species, and the latter including the lyric) in the Gentile World, and in early Greece more particularly.—To which, as an Offset, I add—the differences between the Popular, the Sacerdotal and the—if I may hazard the word—*Mysterial*, Religion of civilized Paganism.[1]

2. The influences of the Institutions and Theology of the Latin Church on Philosophy, Language, Science and the Liberal Arts from the VIIth to the XIVth Century.

In whatever point I am informal or deficient, I presume on your goodness to set me right: and shall receive every correction, your superior judgement and information shall suggest, as an additional ground and motive for the high respect, with which I am,

Reverend Sir, | Your obliged humble Servant
S. T. Coleridge

1383. *To J. A. Hessey*

Address: For Mr Hessey
MS. Harvard College Lib. Hitherto unpublished.

[March 1824]

Dear Sir

In the last Proof sent to Fleet Street I omitted to insert the word '*not*' on the last page, & I believe, nearly the last period. I mean to say, that even Taylor's meaning is not clear. Be so good as to insert the words 'not quite' before 'clear'.[2] You would oblige me likewise by hinting the number of pages, which it is desirable this Work should consist of.[3] The title, of course, must be altered for one more truly characteristic of the Work in it's present state—Something to this purpose perhaps—

Aids to Reflection in the formation of fixed Principles, prudential, Moral and religious, illustrated by extracts from Leighton—& other eminent Divines.[4]

But of this in a future letter.

S. T. C.—

[1] See Letter 1442 and notes.
[2] See *Aids to Reflection*, 1825, p. 256 (signature R): 'In the passage before us, Taylor's *meaning* is not quite clear.' On pp. 251–6, at the beginning of his discussion of original sin, Coleridge introduces an aphorism taken from Jeremy Taylor, 'the ablest and most formidable Antagonist of this Doctrine'.
[3] When published in 1825, *Aids to Reflection* amounted to xvi+404 pages.
[4] See next letter.

1384. *To George Skinner*

Transcript Coleridge family. Hitherto unpublished.

Grove Highgate
22 March 1824

Dear Sir
 As soon as I myself can procure a Copy of the 'Aids to Reflection' it shall be forwarded to you; but from prudential motives I
have resolved on not publishing at present the biographical Essay,
or impartial view of the Causes and consequences of the Schism
between the Protestants in Great Britain, tho' I should do myself
injustice if I neglected to add that the Prudence is public as well
as private, and has the dislike of even appearing to cast a weight
into the Dissenter scale for one source; and from the great over-
balance of the original writing I have changed the Title to Aids to
Reflection &c, illustrated by Aphorisms & select passages extracted
from our Elder Divines, and chiefly from Archbishop Leighton[1]—
But if I do not stop, I shall lose the Post.
 I take the liberty of enclosing Mr Johnson's Testimonials according to your direction, with the request that you will give them to
Mr Calvert and inform him that the £15 caution money has been

---

[1] In Jan. 1822 Coleridge proposed to Murray a book to be entitled 'The
Beauties of Archbishop Leighton selected and methodized, with a (*better*) Life
of the Author, i.e. a biographical and critical Introduction or Preface, and
Notes'. In offering the work to Taylor and Hessey in Aug. 1823, he said it
would be 'best described' by the proposed title, 'Aids to Reflection: or Beauties
and Characteristics of Archbishop Leighton, extracted from his various
Writings, and arranged on a principle of connection under the three Heads, of
1. Philosophical and Miscellaneous. 2. Moral and Prudential. 3. Spiritual—
with a Life of Leighton & a critique on his writings and opinions—with Notes
throughout by the Editor'. In Sept. 1823 Coleridge suggested a 'more appropriate tho' less expedient Title' for his 'apology' for the Life of Leighton—
'The first impartial and philosophical Account & Explanation of the Conflict
between the Protestant Hierarchy (from Edward VI to the Revolution) and
the Puritans of England with the Presbyterians in Scotland'. In Nov. 1823,
when he already had some of the proofs in hand, he realized that he had not
'calculated aright' on the disproportion of his own writing and reported that he
had been 'busily and anxiously' employed in preparing a '*rifacciamento*' of the
work in order to 'carry on the promise of the Title Page (*Aids* to reflection)
systematically'. By Feb. 1824 the *Aids* had become, 'in the course of printing
an original work almost'. By March he had determined 'from prudential
motives' to omit the 'biographical Essay, or impartial view', and 'from the great
over-balance of the original writing' he again altered the title for one 'more truly
characteristic of the Work in it's present state'. When the volume appeared in
1825, it bore the title, *Aids to Reflection in the Formation of a Manly Character
on the several grounds of Prudence, Morality, and Religion: illustrated by select
passages from our elder Divines, especially from Archbishop Leighton.*

paid in as desired at Messrs Currie & Co on account of the Cambridge Bank for the use of the Revd T. Calvert.

I remain, my dear Sir, | with Esteem & regard | Your's truly

S. T. Coleridge

1385. *To Thomas and Mrs. Allsop*

Address: Mr *or* Mrs Allsop | 2. Blandford Place | Pall Mall *From Mr Coleridge.*
MS. New York Public Lib. Pub. with omis. Letters, Conversations and Rec. *212.*
 In late March 1824 Coleridge left Highgate and stayed with the Allsops for 'about ten days'. On 7 April Mrs. Gillman, who was away at Chelsea, sent Coleridge the following conciliatory note:

 I was in hopes I should hear from our kind friend Mr A how you were this morning, but I have not. I cannot tell you how I reproach myself, for now I begin to fear your leaving us may have arisen from my cool behavior yet indeed I feel for you as *formerly,* and know not how to bear up against the fear even of losing you. If you have been in despair take courage, a *little* time, patience, and *prudence* will yet set all to rights, and we may once more all three be happy. Gillman thinks you want to leave us. Pray come to me here if you do not judge wrong. Mr G wd not disapprove it I am sure. Only convince him that you love him and will not be so inconsiderate again, and all will yet be well. I will learn a lesson and not suffer my own impatience at your faults for so I call them to put me so much out. Do pray let Mr A write if you cannot. Tell me all about your health, your feelings &c. I scarcely know how to appear tranquil and wish like you I could abstract myself from my *heartfelt* pain even for a short time. I shall call on you as I return home but it will be before twelve, Tuesday, Wednesday, or Thursday. I do reproach myself bitterly, but as yet have said little to Mr G—for as far as he is concerned you have been sadly in fault, and it is best perhaps to let just anger pass by a little. He is likewise much hurt about your Book not being out, and this appears reasonable. But still I do believe that things may yet be settled—if you don't come could Mr A come any time in the evening to me here. My ignorance & suspense are very painful. G loves you so much, I am sure if things are well arranged matters may be adjusted. And I feel confident that the happiness perhaps well doing of all *three* is concerned, so do not let us two suffer pride or temper to interfere in such a serious affair where there exists so much love. I should not write this but that I am persuaded of your attachment being unaltered. If you write to H[essey?] send it me first, if by a messenger. But I wish above all things to see you. Yours as ever

A. G——

(Nineteenth-Century Studies (Cornell), *67.)*

 Writing to Green, Coleridge says that 'Mr Gillman fetched me home in a Coach on Wednesday Night', 7 April. (See letter 1386.) The difficulties seem to have been in part with Mrs. Gillman. See Letter 1394 and especially Letter 1430, in which Coleridge complains of being 'fidget-watched' by Mrs. Gillman.

8 April 1824
Grove, Highgate—

My dear Allsop

 You, I know, will have approved of my instant compliance with Mr Gillman's proposal of returning with him—and I know too, that

both Mrs Allsop and yourself will think it superfluous in me to tell
you what you must be sure I cannot but feel. I trust, that when
I next return from you, I shall have—not to thank you less—but
with less painful recollections of the trouble and anxiety, I have
occasioned you.

In the agitation of leaving Mrs Allsop, I forgot to take with me
the Translations of Virgil.[1] I shall be in a sad scrape if I do not get
them soon & safe—& yet how to accomplish this, I know not. For
I dare not trust them to the Stage or to the Carrier. Mr Jameson
did not come up last night: and Mr G. is sadly anxious lest he should
have been too ill to come. Were he coming, this would be an opportunity. Could I—that is, dared I wait till Sunday, I might make it
one way of inducing you to spend the day with us.—Upon the
whole, I had better spend a couple of shillings than increase my
anxieties: so I will send Riley with this Note.

I never saw Mr Gillman look so unwell—it made me quite
hysterical this morning when I met him in the Gig.—He has behaved with great kindness to me.—

I am better—and had a tolerable Night.

I have written to Mrs G.—

My grandfatherly love & kisses to the Fairy Prattler, and the
meek boy. I did heave a long-drawn Wish this morning, as the Sun
& the air too, were so genial, that the latter had been in the good
woman's Arms at Highgate, well wrapped up. A fortnight would do
wonders for the dear little fellow—You and Mrs Allsop may rely on
it, that I would see him every day during his being here—if there
were only one hour in which it did not rain vehemently.—

God bless you & your obliged & most affectionately attached |
Friend

S. T. Coleridge—

Dear Mrs Allsop—There are three Rolls of Paper, Mr W's translation of the 1. 2. and 3rd Books of Virgil, two in letter-paper, one
in a little writing book, in the Drawer under the side board, in your
dining Parlour—Be so good as to put them up & give them to the
Bearer, should Mr A. not be at home.[2]—

[1] Coleridge dined at the Monkhouses' in Gloucester Place on Saturday,
3 Apr. 1824, at which time it seems likely that Wordsworth gave him the trans-
lation of the first three books of the *Aeneid* for examination and criticism. See
Later Years, i. 139, and Letter 1389. For Wordsworth's translation of the
Aeneid see *The Poetical Works of William Wordsworth*, ed. E. de Selincourt and
Helen Darbishire, 5 vols., 1940-9, iv. 286-357.

[2] Coleridge's note to Mrs Allsop is written at the top of page one of the MS.

1386. *To J. H. Green*

Address: J. H. Green, Esqre | 22. Lincoln's Inn Fields
MS. Pierpont Morgan Lib. Hitherto unpublished.

Friday, ½ past 12=Saturday.—9=10 April, 1824.—

My dear Friend

I have been more than very unwell: and for two days & nights suspected dysentery. Mr Gillman fetched me home in a Coach on Wednesday Night: and by a few successive aperient doses, not of my own prescription, I am reascending *to par*. It is not therefore on my own account that I am anxious—for both anxious and alarmed I am—but for Mr Gillman. You may perhaps have heard that 8 or 9 years ago he had a near risk of losing his Arm, or his life, or both by a cut, while opening a body, and the absorption of dead-flesh Poison. About two years ago he had another accident of the same sort—and a long, tedious and painful time he had of it, one ill-faced bad conditioned Boil after another breaking out on his Arm. A man of his Age and Constitution & with a family ought to leave the Dead to open as well as bury the Dead—God knows, how earnestly & almost cryingly I have conjured him to take an Oath not to be using his knife on any dead flesh, but that which the Butcher had pre-dissected for him.—Three weeks ago, however, I have learnt that he assisted in opening a man who had dropt down dead, and (as it afterwards appeared) with a dropsy of the Pericardium—and no doubt Mr G. either absorbed a new portion of Virus, or in some way awoke the former into renewed activity. A number of ugly Boils are pushing out their cursed knobs on his arm—& he looks so ill, that yesterday, meeting him full and suddenly it made me almost hysterical. To day he most imprudently, I think, whatever the business might be, went to Town, & walked good part of the way— and all this evening he has had pains all over him, distressing sensations in his head, and since he has been in bed, two distinct shivering fits.—Mean time, poor Mrs Gillman is at Chelsea, whither Mr Gillman sent her, she was so ill & getting worse—and there is no one in the house, that has the least influence over him but myself —and I cannot persuade him to let me send for some Physician. For of old he is a notoriously intractable Patient and does and omits to do himself what he would be outrageous with another for. —Not that I wonder at his reluctance to lie by—for this is the saddest part of the medical profession, especially in a general Practitioner & peculiarly so in Highgate where the 3 other medical men are typified in the Copper-plate of Esculapius in Tooke's Pantheon[1]

---

[1] Andrew Tooke's *The Pantheon* was first published in 1698.

—1. a snake, a very Cobra! 2. a Stick, and 3. an old woman. Comparatively at least, there is no flattery in saying that Gillman completes the Group, as the Demi-god. ('Ιατρὸς φιλόσοφος ἡμίθεος)—I do not know what your engagements are, or whether what I am wishing is either practicable in itself or proper for me to ask—But Gillman is very much attached to you, and has for a long time past had an increasing high opinion of you—and if I cannot induce him tomorrow morning to send for Dr Farr,[1] it would yet be a great comfort to him to see you after your Lecture—& if it were possible to bring Dr Lister (if I recollect, that is the name of the Physician of whose judgement you think so favorably) or any other Physician with whom you are intimate & who happened to be at leisure to accompany you, either without any pretext but that I had desired you, or under the pretext of introducing him to me as you were passing by, it would be relieving me from a very distressful state of anxiety.—I know how many engagements you are likely to have that may put it out of your power to come in the course of tomorrow—& yet on Sunday I am uncommonly solicitous to pass the day with you alone.—But why do I say more? or why have I said so much? Your own kind feelings will make you do what you can without breach of other duties.—I shall keep this letter open till the morning—and if I add nothing, you will infer that Mr Gillman is either worse or not better. At this moment, he has all the signs of an approaching Fever.

Give a troublesome but not unthankful Guest's affectionate respects to Mrs J. Green, and if she be with you to your sincerely respected Mother: and believe me with constant regard and unmingled Esteem

your obliged
S. T. Coleridge.—

Qy. Is the VIth the last vol. of the Biology? Has Trevir[a]n[u]s published the work promised in this work—on comparative *Encephalology* (n. b. not *his* word)?[2] By the bye, the Editor of the Eding. Medical Review, last number, wonders why Dr J. Davy[3] should lengthen out a long word by putting *to* after ma, in Pneuma*to*thorax—instead of Pneuma-thorax!! What is real, must be possible.

---

[1] John R. Farre (1775–1862), physician and one of the founders of the Royal London Ophthalmic Hospital. Gillman recommended Dr. Farre to Wordsworth in 1820. See *Middle Years*, ii. 877.

[2] G. R. Treviranus (1776–1837), German naturalist. His *Biologie, oder Philosophie der lebenden Natur für Naturforscher und Aerzte*, 6 vols., appeared 1802–22. Coleridge met his brother, L. C. Treviranus, the botanist, in London. See *Table Talk*, 30 Apr. 1830, note.

[3] John Davy, M.D. (1790–1868), physiologist and anatomist, was the younger brother of Humphry Davy.

Ergo, such a remark is possible—for a Scotch M.D. but for no
other Breather under the cope of Heaven. Indeed, a Doctor of some
sort it must be to have called air in the chest by that jewel
of a word, Pneumatothorax, i.e. a *chest of* air! tho' Pneuma, I
believe, when it does not mean Breath (πνεῦμα βίου) means *Wind*
not air. Good night.—

P.S. Saturday Morning—but not yet in bed. A loud Peal of the
Night-bell and in rushed poor Mr Pownal (a Solicitor who lives on
the *Bank*, about half way up the Hill from Holloway) mad with
fright, his child *dying*—I ran down, suspecting the truth—the child
was dead—no breath, pulse, or swallow—& the lungs collapsed.
At 8 o'clock this evening the child (a very fine Infant) was put to
bed, in perfect health—The assistant, Douglas, tried to open a
vein; but the veins were collapsed—& [he] had before found by
breathing down the wind-pipe & inflating the lungs, that they had
collapsed.—The Mother was like a Tyger-cat—abusing every body
round her—I should not have thought it in my nature to have
witnessed a mother's distress with so little sympathy. Had she been
a quiet woman, and had I been strongly impressed with the belief
that it was a case of Water-stroke, or Neurolepsia hydrencephalia,
I should have tried—at least, I felt a vehement impulse to try Zoo-
magnetism, i.e. to try my hand at a resurrection. I felt or fancied a
power in me to concenter my will that I never felt or fancied before.
—However, I saved Gillman a most hazardous journey: for he was
in a commencing perspiration when the Bell rang—. I have just left
him—his Pulse is above a 100; but this may be excitement. He is
wild about going down tomorrow morning, to induce Pownal to
have the child opened—& says, he would give 20 guineas that you
could come up after your Lecture.—At all events, I shall send off
little John Anderson with this Letter—tho' I hope to find G. so much
better, as to supersede *my* request. Assuredly, the Question so
cavalierly treated by the Physicians of your Society is as rational as
it is important—& a priori, I should declare it utterly improbable,
that any action not brought on by a specific Poison, & having it's seat
and origin in a subordinate & merely instrumental System clearly
deriving it's life from the nervous system should produce an inflammation adequate to a mortal effusion in an hour or two. In short, that
the dissolution of a structure into a fluid almost elementary should
be producible by inflammation only, is a mere and a vulgar
Assertion; but that a very slight inflammation accompanying the
stimulus of death might produce effusion, as the sequel, is congruous
both with Reason & the most decisive Facts. Nay, an active
inflammation, had it been possible, might save the child—& could
the case be pre-determined, I would give the strongest cordials.—

1387. *To J. H. Green*

Address: J. H. Green, Esqre | 22. Lincoln's Inn Fields
MS. Pierpont Morgan Lib. Hitherto unpublished.

Saturday Noon
10 April 1823

My dear Friend

Mr Gillman['s] fever-symptoms are abated—and tho' his arm is fearfully inflamed & painful, and I am anxiously desirous that you should see it, yet as I take for granted that you will come tomorrow, I send the inclosed for no wiser reason, than that I had written it, and as Mrs Cram says to Master Chock-full—It is a pity, it should be wasted.—Only if it should win me your coming an hour or so earlier, I have be-inked many a lusty Sheet minori lucro.— Utinam totam et integram Prelectionem τῷ τῆς τυπώσεως problemati dare potuisses. Facilius et gratius esset, quam vel umbram vel superficiem meramque speciem rei uno vel duobus §§phis projicere—Tam est magnifica et pregnans Involutio! Ideam dico quae evolvenda est. Prelectionem dixi? Imo, Librum potius, καὶ μέγα[1] βιβλίον. Ego quidem (hoc velim scias, Vir amicissime) penitus despero, me unquam physicas τῆς Γενέσεως partes (scilicet, primum Pentateuchi Capitulum) exacturum fore. Me totum metaphysicae, ethicae, historicae et theologicae interpretationibus systematicῶς[2] conficiendis devoturus sum, si vel haec perficere permissum fuerit! For all else, si qua in vineto meo digna carpi crescunt, they grow on the other side of the hedge & overhang the private pathway, qui hortos nostros dividit.—The fruits will improve by being grafted on a congener.—I have not the slightest doubt, that such a Work ab Homine usque ad Polypum, a Diabolo ad Febrim Croceam, would inaugurate you at once as the IATROS PHILOSOP[H]os of the Age—& all your labors, & acquisitions, & habits of thinking hitherto, fit you for this work, and have been all disciplinary to this—all sterling money layed out in the purchase of secure Reversions.—

If there are any later works of Treviranus in your possession, I should like to see them. Tr. is a striking instance of a mind rendered staggering and dizzy by agglomeration of *Facts*—. His Judgement is in a state of congestion—

God bless you &

S. T. Coleridge

P.S. As early as possible tomorrow!—

---

[1] This word underlined once in MS.
[2] The Greek letters ῶς underlined once in MS.

1388. *To C. A. Tulk*

Address: C. A. Tulk, Esqre. M.P. | 17. Duke Street | Westminster
MS. Pierpont Morgan Lib. Hitherto unpublished.
Postmark: 10 April 1824.

[10 April 1824]

My dear Sir

I can truly say, that never before in my life have I thought so much or looked forward from day to day with so much hope & fear to the Weather as I have done for the last four months in reference to Mrs Tulk. Heaven knows! there were other & those strong motives for the anxiety—and Mrs Gillman's slow & vibratory progress weighed & weighs heavily upon my feelings—but the more instant & urgent Desireableness of genial Breeze & Sunshine for Mrs Tulk made her Image the representative and exponent of all others.—Since your last I was for three or four days in the feverish excitement of some almost necessary Visitings & Dinner-parties occasioned by Mr Wordsworth's & his Family being in town—& my career was cut short by an attack of Dysentery, with accompaniments [of] Brain & Stomach from which may my worst Enemies be preserved. [On] Wednesday Night dear Mr Gillman (who is himself very unwell, with a new *insurgency* in his dissection-poisoned Arm) brought me home in a Coach—& I am now recovering apace.— Yesterday I crawled out—& a remarkably genial *Flush* of Air coming on my Face, I actually for the indivisible moment—I cannot describe how, or even express it conceivably—I imagined myself *You*—& found myself saying, Come, come, my dear!—what I was about to add, I know not—but no doubt, some promise or other of Spring come at last.—I wish, I had but [a] month to be with you any where—or that we might meet at the sea side—for I have much to talk of.— The experiment, you mention, is a familiar acquaintance of mine—it was first announced by Wolfart some 8 or ten years ago in his Asclepion or Annals of Magnetism.[1] Mr G. & myself, & half a dozen others tried it without success—but the fact is certain, & hitherto has been explained into an Electrical Influence, from the dryness of the Fingers & the friction of the Glass. At the same time, a Berlin Physician discovered a power in himself to fling long sparks from his Fingers by pure force of his Will—& after vehement efforts mastered the power sufficiently to do it before Doubters & Scoffers—

---

[1] K. C. Wolfart published the journal, Ἀσκληπιειον, *allgemeines medicinisch-chirurgisches Zeitblatt*, 1811–12, later continued as *Jahrbücher für Lebensmagnetismus, oder neues Asklepieion*, 1818–23. See also Letters 1057 and 1065. In a note in *Table Talk*, 30 Apr. 1830, H. N. Coleridge quotes a long passage on animal magnetism which Coleridge wrote in a copy of Southey's *Life of Wesley*, 2 vols., 1820.

the very phaenomenon, which the early Christians considered as a daemoniacal miracle in the case of some Emperor—I forget the particulars—

Most faithfully your obliged
S. T. Coleridge

P.S. I again trouble you with the inclosed—the Address, Mrs Coleridge, Keswick, Cumberland.—My dear child has a distressing inflammation of the Tarsal Glands: & I dare not trust to a country Doctor the necessary Remedies—.

1389. *To William Wordsworth*

Pub. Letters, *ii. 733.*

Monday Night, [12 April 1824][1]

Dear Wordsworth,—Three whole days the going through the first book cost me, though only to find fault. But I cannot find fault, in pen and ink, without thinking over and over again, and without some sort of an attempt to suggest the alteration; and, in so doing, how soon an hour is gone! so many half seconds up to half minutes are lost in leaning back in one's chair, and looking up, in the bodily act of contracting the muscles of the brow and forehead, and unconsciously attending to the sensation. Had I the MS. with me for five or six months, so as to amuse myself off and on, without any solicitude as to a given day, and, could I be persuaded that if as well done as the nature of the thing (viz., *a translation of Virgil*, in English) renders possible, it would not raise but simply sustain your well-merited fame for pure diction, where what is not idiom is never other than logically correct, I doubt not that the irregularities[2] could be removed. But I am haunted by the apprehension that I am not feeling or thinking in the same spirit with you, at one time, and at another *too much* in the spirit of your writings. Since Milton, I know of no poet with so many *felicities* and unforgettable lines and stanzas as you. And to read, therefore, page after page without a single *brilliant* note, depresses me, and I grow peevish with you for having wasted your time on a work *so* much below you, that you cannot *stoop* and *take*. Finally, my conviction is, that you

---

[1] This letter, in which Coleridge expresses his opinion concerning Wordsworth's translation of the first three books of the *Aeneid*, was probably written on the Monday after his return to Highgate on Wednesday, 7 Apr. (See Letter 1385.) E. H. Coleridge dates the letter 'Monday Night,? 1824? 1829'. *Letters*, ii. 733.

[2] In printing the present letter Christopher Wordsworth, *Memoirs of William Wordsworth*, 2 vols., 1851, ii. 74, reads 'inequalities' for 'irregularities'.

undertake an *impossibility*,[1] and that there is no medium between a prose version and one on the avowed principle of *compensation*[2] in the widest sense, that is, manner, genius, total effect.[3] I confine my-self to *Virgil* when I say this.

I must now set to work with *all* my powers and thoughts to my Leighton, and then to my logic, and then to my *opus maximum*! if indeed it shall please God to spare me so long, which I have had too many warnings of late (more than my nearest friends know of) not to doubt. My kind love to Dorothy.

S. T. Coleridge.

1390. *To Thomas Allsop*

Address: T. Allsop, Esqre. | 2. Blandford Place | Pall Mall
MS. New York Public Lib. Pub. with omis. Letters, Conversations and Rec. *214.*
Postmark: Highgate, 14 April 1824.

Tuesday Night.—[13 April 1824]

My dear Allsop

Mr Gillman had an excellent night last night, slept sound and perspired copiously and rose every way better, and indeed quite revived. The Carbuncles on his arm have likewise put on a more promising appearance: and have (he says) nothing to do but to heal. For he had the fortitude to exforcipate all the impoisoned cellular Substance from the six or eight abscesses, or gimlet-holes, of the main Carbuncle, the Captain Robert *Boyle* of the ghastly Crew: and he expects no further trouble from the rest, one excepted: and from that nothing to compare with it's precursors. He is drinking Tea at Miss Somers's. You say—One and *all*. N.B. Neither Miss H. or my-self have given a hint to Mrs G., how unwell Mr G. has been—& he was anxious that she should not know it.—But as you do not mention her name, probably you have not seen her since Sunday.

I called this Morning at Mrs Constable's, induced by the very fine tho' unwarm day to hope, I might find the little boy there—& I was rather disappointed to see her return without him. But doubt-

---

[1] 'A literal translation of an ancient poet in verse, and particularly in rhyme, is *impossible*.' Wordsworth to Lord Lonsdale, 23 Nov. 1824. *Later Years*, i. 161.

[2] 'I became convinced that a spirited translation can scarcely be accom-plished in the English language without admitting a principle of compensation.' Wordsworth to the editors of the *Philological Museum*, 1832. See *The Poetical Works of William Wordsworth*, ed. E. de Selincourt and Helen Darbishire, 5 vols., 1940–9, iv. 470.

[3] The editors of *The Poetical Works* suggest that Coleridge's 'verdict' on the translation of Virgil 'may have influenced W. against going farther'. Op. cit. iv. 470.

less, every day we are entitled to expect a change of the present to a more genial wind.

I am sorry to learn from Miss H. that her Sister intends to leave Chelsea on Saturday. Unless the Damps from the River affect her arm, or there be some other motive tantamount to this, I can not but think that change of place and perfect Repose must prove restorative to her.—And here all goes on quite smoothly: & Miss H. says, she can very well manage matters with the new Sempstry-maid that is to come on Tuesday next.

I am myself at my ordinary average of health, and beat off the blue Devils, with the Ghosts of defunct Hopes chasing the Jack-a-lanthorns of foolish Expectation, as well as I can—in the which, believe me, I derive no small help from the faith that in *your* Affection and Sincerity I have at least one entire Counterpart of the Thoughts and Feelings, with which I am evermore and most sincerely,

my dear Allsop, | your affectionate Friend
S. T. Coleridge

My kindest love & remembrance to Mrs Allsop—& assure her that if the meek little one does not crow and clap his wings in a week or so, from Thursday, it shall not be for want of being looked after.

1391. *To Charles Aders*

MS. Central Library, Auckland, New Zealand. Hitherto unpublished.

[April 1824][1]

My dear Sir

Mr Gillman's Health is such as to render it almost impossible for him to venture—& were he better, yet his expected Patients would make it unsafe—. I am therefore commissioned to say, & really meant to have said it but that I cannot bear to keep your young man waiting, every thing kind & thankful, &c for Mr and Mrs G.—But if you and dear Mrs Aders will accept the fragment, me—and I should not be too ill to leave my room I will do my best to find my way to you. May God bless you & your affectionate | Friend

S. T. Coleridge

[1] This letter was probably written in Apr. 1824, before Gillman had recovered from the infection in his arm and soon after Mrs. Gillman's return from Chelsea on Saturday, 17 Apr. See Letter 1390.

1392. *To John Taylor Coleridge*

Address: Jo[hn Co]leridge, Esqre | Harlow street | Tavistock Square
MS. British Museum. Hitherto unpublished.
Postmark: Highgate, 19 April 1824.

Grove, Highgate.
19 April 1824.—

My dear Nephew

The pleasure, which my nomination as an R A of R S L appears
to have given my friends, has in good measure reconciled me to a
preferment, which I owe in a two-fold sense to Basil Montague—
first, to his zeal in conciliating the Council, and secondly to the
effect on myself, by depriving me of all heart to withstand it. My
inability to inflict pain where so much kindness was displayed, by
persevering in the refusal overcame the inward dislike to the thing
—not, Heaven knows! from any disapprobation of the Objects of
the Society, or of the Principles required of it's Members—for nothing is prohibited that an English Gentleman, a Scholar and a
Christian does not find already precluded by his own Reason &
Conscience—but it was Saul's Armour—and the yearly Essay (for
I cannot compose without an effort after the best & completest) is a
serious set off against the yearly £100.—Believe me, my dear John!
that I should be right joyous in my self-gratulation, had it given
me the 20th part of the Delight, which the news in your letter did.
I am not ashamed to say, that I was *weeping* glad. It has taken out
all the *sting* from your anxiety—Every year, I am confident, will
make your professional income less and less inadequate to your
present expences & desires—and the Future is in Sunshine. I do not
know whether it be that Gladness brings Hope with it; but I never
before felt such a cheering faith, that a change will soon take place
in Mrs John Coleridge's Constitution, and that she will be as great
a comfort to you in this as she is dear & precious to you in every
other respect.—

All the circumstances of my life and all the good and all the faulty
ingredients of my character, have unhappily joined in nipping or
diverting the growth of the affections of consanguinity—and it has
certainly additionally endeared you and your Sister Fanny to me,
that with regard to both I first felt in the full force that those
affections had been only suppressed & driven to the root, not killed
or alienated.—I have been so very unwell for the last two or three
months, as to be incapable of working with any satisfaction or
success—& the consequent accumulation of business has added to
the depression of my spirits, both Mr and Mrs Gillman too having
been sadly out of Health—But still the calores poetici begin to

manifest their chest-expanding power—& if this fine weather continue, I hope to send Fanny an Epithalamion.[1]—About an hour
after the receipt of your letter, I read Spencer's delightful Ode,
which needs only the omission of something less than a third to be
the most perfect Lyric Poem in our language, aloud to myself—and
whoever had seen me, as I applied different passages in my mind
to Fanny & placed her before my eyes, would assuredly have
voted me mad—.

I wrote soon after my receipt of a Note from the Bishop of Barbadoes[2] to Mrs S. Coleridge to send up immediately the birth-dates
of Hartley, Derwent & Sara, with the names of her own Father &
Mother—tho' it went sorely against the *Coleridgean* Grain to be
accessary in having the plusquam-plebeian & malnominable name
FRICKER intruded on my Nephew's Heraldry—and I am very uneasy, that I have received no answer—tho' to confess the truth,
William's Letter impressed the suspicion, that he would be quite
as well pleased if the answer should not arrive till after the Patent
had been filled up—However, if no answer come tomorrow, I shall
write to Sara, who is going to Dublin this Spring. On account of
that vexatious affection of her tarsal Glands, which if not overcome
by the improvement of her general health or *blown up* by local
remedies will—not indeed (except by making her fret) injure her
eyes; but yet—end in a deformity by thickening the eye-lids, I
should have been glad that she should have passed four or five
months with me—for the only known effective remedies are of
such a nature, that I could consent to their application only where
she could be under the constant inspection of a medical man of
abilities & of *specific* practice & experience, who would himself apply
them two or three times a day.—In the country this is impossible—
indeed, I should be at a loss where I could find the same combination
of knowlege, skill and friendship as in Mr Gillman. I communicated
his and Mrs Gillman's friendly Invitation; explained the grounds
of it at large—& left it to Sara's own judgement to determine.

Remember me affectionately to Mrs J. Coleridge—& with love &
kisses to the dear little ones, I | remain . . .[3]

Yesterday was the eighth Anniversary of my Domestication at
Highgate!

[1] Frances Duke Coleridge married John Patteson on 22 Apr. 1824.
[2] In 1824 William Hart Coleridge (1789–1849) was consecrated bishop of
Barbados and the Leeward Islands.
[3] I cut out the signature to affix to my Uncle's Print in my study. [Note in
MS. by John Taylor Coleridge.]

1393. *To George Skinner*

Address: Revd. George Skinner
MS. Cornell University Lib. Hitherto unpublished.

Grove, Highgate.
Monday Evening
26 April 1820 [1824]

My dear Sir

Mr Gillman much regretted his absence at the time of your call—
& both Mr & Mrs G. blamed me for not having pressed you to stay
[to] dinner.—I forgot, in talking of Universals, to ask you respecting
our young Jesuita futurus, Mr Frederic Johnston—whether he will
have rooms in College on his arrival in October? The money &c has
been payed into the Bankers' hands &c.—I should not, after the
assurance of your letter, have thought it necessary—or rather Mr
Gillman would not have thought it necessary to remind me to ask
this question—had it not been for Mr Johnston Senr.'s Delay (from
ill health, I believe) of 3 or 4 weeks in which interval others might
perhaps have been entered & so acquired a prior right.—Be so kind
as to give me the remaining portion of the Ink in your pen, for one
line—when you are writing otherwise—

& believe me, my dear Sir, | With unfeigned regard | & esteem
your obliged

S. T. Coleridge

1394. *To Thomas Allsop*

Address: Thomas Allsop, Esqre. | Messrs. Harding & Co | 92 | Pall Mall
MS. New York Public Lib. Pub. with omis. Letters, Conversations and Rec. *214.*
Postmark: Highgate, 28 April 1824.

27 April 1824
Grove, Highgate.

My dearest Allsop

I direct this note to the *House*, or *Firm* should I say? because I
should not think myself justified in exciting in Mrs A. an alarm, for
which I have no more valid grounds than my own apprehensions
and unlearned conjectures. And yet having these bodings I cannot
feel quite easy in withholding them from you. On Saturday, the
morning Mrs A. was here, I was on the high hope, the little boy
looking so much clearer and livelier than on the Thursday. (The
Friday from the unintermitting rain and raw weather, and being
under the action of a couple of Calomel Pills, I did not stir out the
whole day.) But the weather since then being on the whole genial,

and the Baby shewing no mark of progress, but rather the reverse—
& it seeming to me each returning day to require a stronger effort
to rouse it's attention, and the relapse to a dullness which, it is
evident, the upright posture alone prevented from being a doze,
becoming more immediate, I cannot repel the boding that there is
either some mesenteric Affection, which sometimes exists in infants
without betraying itself by any notable change in the ingestion or
the egesta, yet producing on the brain an effect similar to that which
flatulence or confined Gas pressing on the nerves of the Stomach
will do: or else that it is a case of chronic (slow) hydrencephalus.—
Against this fear I have to say, first, that I have not been able to
detect any insensibility to light in the pupils of it's eyes; and that
the little Innocent has no convulsive twitches, and neither starts or
screams, in it's sleep. For the first, I had no opportunity (the Sun
being clouded) of making a decisive experiment, & requested Mrs
Constable to try it with a candle, as soon as it was taken up after
dark—& tho' the presence of the symptom is an infallible evidence
of the presence of Effusion, or some equivalent cause of pressure,
it's absence is no sure proof of the absence of the disease, tho' it is a
presumption in favor of the *degree*.—The freedom from perturba-
tion in sleep, however, is altogether a favorable circumstance, and
allows a hope that the continued heaviness & immediate relapse
into slumber on being placed horizontally, may be the effect of
weakness. But then the poor little fellow habitually keeps it's hand
to it's head: and there is a sensible heat, and throbbing at the
temples.—On the whole, you should be *prepared* for the possible
event: and Mrs Constable is naturally very anxious on this point,
not merely lest any neglect should be suspected on her part but likewise from an anticipation of the Mother's Agitation, should she at
any time come up just to witness the Baby's last Struggles, or to
find no more what she was expecting to see in incipient recovery.

Do not misunderstand me, my dearest friend! nor let this note
alarm you beyond what the facts require. I have seen no decisive
marks, no positive change for the worse, no measurable *retro*gression.
I have of course repeatedly spoken to Mr Gillman; but he says, it is
impossible to form any conclusive opinion. There is no proof, that
it may not be weakness, at present and hitherto; but neither dare he
determine, what the continuance of the weakness may not produce.
Nothing can be warrantably attempted, in this uncertainty, but
mild alteratives; watchful attention to the Infant's Motions, & to
keep them regular; with as cordial nourishment as can be given
without endangering heat or inflammatory action.

I do not think, that I have been able to remain undisturbed for an
hour together for the last three days—such a tumble in of Persons

with requests or claims on me has there been—House-hunting &c.

Mrs Gillman is much better—& all goes on with much kindness & kind attentions, which in part I attribute, perhaps erroneously, to some conversation on the subject between you & her—I am content, well knowing that the genial glow of Friendship once deadened can never be rekindled.

> Idly we supplicate the Powers above—
> There is no Resurrection for a Love
> That uneclips'd, unthwarted, wanes away
> In the chill'd heart by inward Self-decay.[1]
> Poor mimic of the Past! the Love is o'er,
> That must *resolve* to do what did itself of yore.[2]

God bless you & your ever affectionate

S. T. Coleridge

P.S. To our great surprize & delight Mr Anster came in on us this afternoon—& in perfect health & good Spirits.—

1395. *To John Taylor Coleridge*

Address: John Coleridge, Esqre. | 2 Pump Court | Temple
MS. British Museum. Hitherto unpublished.
Postmark: Highgate, 4 May 1824.

3 May [1824], Monday Night.

My dear Nephew

I write merely to acknowlege the Draft for 30£, which came acceptably, as I was under the necessity of ordering a new suit of Clothes in order to my appearance at the Royal Society of Literature on the 6th of this Month—and I should have been compelled to increase the Debt to my kind Friend, to settle the Taylor's Bill for two Suits, of elder date—& more than two suits on a Taylor's Books, especially for a man who has but 3 suits in two years, is not to be done salvâ famâ.—And yet if Mrs C. has suffered Sara to

---

[1] A variation of these four lines was first published in 1852 as *L'Envoy* to *Love's Apparition and Evanishment*. (See *The Poems of Samuel Taylor Coleridge*, ed. Derwent and Sara Coleridge, p. 374.) J. D. Campbell pointed out that *L'Envoy* was not added until 1852 and doubted whether 'these four lines had originally any connection with the poem'. (*Poetical Works*, 209 and 644.) E. H. Coleridge, however, printed from MS. a 'first draft' of *Love's Apparition and Evanishment* which begins with the four lines quoted in the letter to Allsop. (*Poems*, i. 488 and ii. 1087.)

[2] In 1893 these six lines were published by J. D. Campbell from a manuscript dated 24 Apr. 1824. See *Poetical Works*, 644.

advance the money, it shall be replaced at all hazards—& whatever
I do to obtain it—for I fear, that the Exhibitions[1] will not be procured without note of residence. But as soon as my Clothes come
home, I shall wait on Mr Sutton & get him to see what must &
what can be done.[2]—

Saving to Mrs Gillman, I had kept my wishes & opinions respecting the circumstance to which you allude, religiously to myself—
but about a month ago, Wordsworth, who greatly esteems you,
questioned me on the subject—& I confessed to him that it had
made me very uneasy, & assigned all my reasons, especially the
prudential, against it.[3] As they appeared to him to be strong &
sound, & I thought it possible that low spirits & self-underrating
had some share in the decision, I sate down & wrote a long letter
to you—but as I was hesitating from the consciousness, that I was
not in possession of the facts or of the motives, I was told by Mr
Gillman who had heard it from Montagu, & on the next day by
Mr Lockhart, Sir W. Scott's Son in law, who did me the honor of
calling on me,[4] that it was all settled—which co-inciding with some
words that fell from Henry when he was here last (I wish, he would
come oftener), I threw my letter into the fire.—But on the receipt
of your Note of good Tidings I felt certain of what I am most
HEARTILY rejoiced to hear—yea, *relieved & comforted*!

The late fit of genial weather, which the three days past have interrupted, produced so marked an effect on Mrs Gillman's Health

[1] Derwent Coleridge not only held an exhibition from the Mercers' Company
(see Letter 1331), but on 14 May 1823 the Court of Assistants of the Goldsmiths'
Company nominated him and two other Cambridge students to exhibitions of
£20 each 'which they are severally to hold and enjoy as from Christmas last
for the term of five years, provided they shall so long reside and be of good
conduct'. Derwent is not mentioned again in the Court Minutes of the Company and 'the education records for that period have not survived'. (From
information kindly supplied by Miss Susan M. Hove, Librarian, Goldsmiths'
Company.)

[2] When Derwent left Cambridge after taking his degree in Jan. 1824, the
residence restriction imposed by the Goldsmiths' Company made him ineligible
to receive further proceeds of this exhibition. Later in this year and again in
1825 Coleridge made 'baffled Efforts' to obtain for Derwent the proceeds of the
exhibitions from both the Goldsmiths' and the Mercers' Companies. See Letters
1412, 1416–17, 1441, and 1503. Payments by the Mercers' Company were made
in 1828–9. See Letters 1614–17.

[3] Coleridge evidently refers to the editorship of the *Quarterly Review*, a
position held by John Taylor Coleridge from Dec. 1824 to Nov. 1825. See E. H.
Coleridge, *Life & Correspondence of John Duke Lord Coleridge, Lord Chief
Justice of England*, 2 vols., 1904, i. 20.

[4] 'I have seen a host of lions', Lockhart wrote after this visit, 'among others,
Hook, Canning, . . . and Coleridge. The last well worth all the rest, and 500
more such into the bargain.' Mrs. Gordon, *'Christopher North', a Memoir of
John Wilson*, 2 vols., 1862, ii. 70.

& on mine, that it encourages me to hope that it's return will bring Mrs J. Coleridge *up* again. May God bless you!

S. T. C.

1396. *To Thomas H. Dunn*

Facsimile Canadian Magazine, *June 1909, p. 103.*

[May 1824 ?][1]

I have this morning received a long desired Letter which enables me to state this day week for the settlement—It would remove an unpleasant weight from my mind, if I could with propriety explain to you why with a hundred pound of my own in the house I yet could not, without imprudent exposures, settle a 25£ Account.— *Destroy this instantly.*

1397. *To Henry Taylor*[2]

Address: Henry Taylor, Esqre. | [in another hand] Chapel Street | Grosvenor Square.
MS. Bodleian Library. Pub. Guests and Memories, *by Una Taylor, 1924, p. 58.*
Postmark: Highgate, 19 May 1824.

Grove, Highgate
Tuesday Evening [18 May 1824]

Dear Sir

I have some half dozen times, and if I say a score, I shoot not far beyond the mark, [been] on the point of writing to you. I cannot tell why; but so it is, that the mistake occasioned by Mrs Gillman's forgetting that what it was impossible that you should understand it was scarcely possible that you should not misunderstand (videlicet, that on Thursdays we drank Tea at our ordinary dinner hour, on Mr Irvine's [Irving's] and Basil Montague's account) has recurred to me with a frequency and an annoyance, strangely disproportionate to the occasion. Of one thing I am certain, that I did not pay you so ill a compliment as to imagine that you would not think an evening passed with so interesting and highly gifted [a] Man as Irvine, and so acute and effective a Reasoner as my excellent

---

[1] The reference to £100 in the house suggests that this letter was written shortly after Coleridge became a Royal Associate of the Royal Society of Literature on 6 May 1824. See Letters 1382 and 1395.

[2] Henry Taylor (1800–86), author of *Philip Van Artevelde*. In 1824 he was appointed to a clerkship in the colonial office. In 1869 he was made K.C.M.G.

Friend Montague a sufficient compensation for a bad dinner, or rather for a bad apology for a dinner. But it sometimes happens that against our will a painful sensation, that takes one by surprize, hooks itself in, like the microscopic hairs of the Caterpillar, that are said to occasion the Urticaria—& the pain, I myself suffered, from the thought of the Oversight striking you as virtual disrespect, i.e. the want of that respect which should have prevented it, made it easier for me to fancy this possible.—I console myself, however, with the hope, that a suspicion so particularly contrary to the truth, both in my own feelings & in those of my friends, Mr & Mrs Gillman, will have passed thro' no head but my own—& perhaps I ought rather to apologize for so *lengthy* a preface to the inclosed Card, which Mrs G. desires me to inclose—and if you are fond of dancing I can promise you more than one handsome Partner; & tho' I regret that we cannot offer you a bed in our house, yet I can (if you wish it) secure you a comfortable & well-aired one, a few stone-throws distant.—

I am, | dear Sir, with much esteem | your's truly
S. T. Coleridge

1398. *To Robert Jameson*

Address: R. Jameson, Esqre. | at the Chambers of | B. Montague, Esqre. Lincoln's Inn
MS. Mr. Walter T. Spencer. Hitherto unpublished.
Postmark: Highgate, 20 May 1824.

Grove, Highgate, alias,
Ædes Nemorosae apud
Port' Altam,
but the Postman will understand the former best.
19 May 1824

My dear Jameson
Need I say, that I have been and am very anxious respecting your health? Mrs Gillman has sent up the inclosed, she having forgot your address, to me who never heard it mentioned. I must therefore direct to Mr Montague's Chambers: whom we have long been expecting to see.

God bless you | and
S. T. Coleridge

1399. *To J. H. Green*

Address: J. H. Green, Esqre | 22 | Lincoln's Inn Fields
MS. Pierpont Morgan Lib. Pub. with omis. Letters, *ii. 728.*
Postmark: Highgate, 20 May 1824.

Ædes Nemorosae, apud
Port' Altam.
19 May 1824.

Mr S. T. Coleridge, F R S L, R A, H M P S B, &c &c has the
honor of avowing the high gratification, he will receive, should any
Answer from him be thought to oblige Lincoln's Inn Fields. When
he reflects indeed on their many and cogent claims on his admiration and gratitude, what a FUND of LITERATURE they contain, what
a Royal Society, what royal Associates—not to speak of those as
yet in the egg of Futurity, the unhatched Decemvirate and Spes
altera Phoebi![1] what a royal College, where Philosophy and Eloquence unite to display their fresh and vernal Green! what a conjunction of the Fine Arts with the Sciences, Law and Physique,
Glossurgery and Chirurgery! when he remembers the memorable
fact, that if the Titanic Roc should take up the Great Pyramid in
his Beak, and drop the same with due skill, the L. I. F. would fit as
Cup to Ball, Bone to Bone—tho' if S. T. C. might dare advise so
great and rare a Bird, the precious Transport should be let fall
point downwards, and thus prevent the adulteration of their intellectual Splendors with 'the Light of common Day', while a Duplicate of the Elysium below might be reared on it's ample base, in
mid air—(ah! if a Duplicate of No. 22 could be found!)—when
S. T. C. ponders on these proud merits, what is there he would not
do to 'oblige Lincoln's Inn Fields'? In vain does Gillman talk of a
Stop being put thereto! Between *oblige* and Lincoln's Inn Fields
Continuity alone can intervene for the Heart's Eye of their obliged
and counter-obliging

S. T. Coleridge.

who with his friends Mr and Mrs G. will &c. on June 3rd.—

[1] Cf. Ovid, *Fasti*, iii. 625.

1400. *To Henry Taylor*

Address: Henry Taylor, Esqre | 4. King's Street | St James's
MS. Bodleian Library. Hitherto unpublished.
Postmark: Highgate, 25 May 1824.

Grove, Highgate
Wednesday [Tuesday]—[25 May 1824]

Dear Sir

Since Mr Irvine's residence in Essex, we have lost the pleasure of his & (from what cause I know not) of Basil Montague's Thursday Visits—which formed my only motive for [having] mentioned that day in preference to any other. I so very rarely leave the House for more than a Walk, and from my return from my after-breakfast Walk to our Dinner-hour (5) so irremissibly task-worked, that all *days* are alike to me—and one evening as little likely not to be at home as at another. And from 6 o'clock I always am *at home* to my friends, when I am *in the house* at all. The exceptions at least are rare—and yet it unfortunately happens, that in consequence of the preparations and the consequents of the House-warming on the 1 of June, the upside down, to wit, of Carpets, Furniture, &c in order to the compression of 150 *accepters* of the invitation Cards; and of an old pre-engagement to a similar party at my dear friend, Mr Green's, of Lincoln's Fields on the 3rd—the two days, you mention, no body in or out of the House will be at home.—From after that time, any evening, you are at leisure, Shall I say the Thursday after?—But really the chances of my being out are so trifling, that whenever you feel disposed for a walk Highgateward, you may pretty safely rely on finding me any time after 5, and I need not add happy to see you. The 1 Shilling Kentish Town Stages take you half way up the hill—within a furlong or so of our house—

With sincere respect | dear Sir | your's truly
S. T. Coleridge

1401. *To Mrs. Charles Aders*

Address: Mrs Aders
MS. Mr. W. Hugh Peal. Hitherto unpublished.

1 June [1824][1]
Grove, Highgate

My dear Madam

We *are* sorry—very sorry for the *effect*, and very *very* sorry for the cause: I trust, however, that if this weather continues, the air,

---

[1] The present letter was enclosed in Letter 1402.

which is not yet *un*chilled, will become genial, and [Ellen's][1] best restorative. Pray, give my kindest love to her.—I had promised myself the pleasure of introducing my highly and justly valued Friend, Mr Green, of Lincoln's Inn Fields to you, with his pretty & amiable Wife. I have long wished that he & Mr Aders should know each other—for Mr Green like myself is half German—& in the best sense, *all* German.—I was likewise about to solicit your permission to bring Mr Green some morning next week that might not be inconvenient to you to see the Pictures, I having inflamed Mr G. with a vehement desire—But I fear, that this must now be deferred—. Again and again be assured that all of this Household unite in the same regard and esteem with which I

am, dear Madam, | your sincere Friend
S. T. Coleridge.—

P.S. Your note has doubled Mrs Gillman's wish for your and [Ellen's] sojourning a while with her at Highgate, & you will not blame her & will I trust, in some measure rely on me, for our confidence in Mr Gillman's skill & medical wisdom.—

1402. To Mrs. Charles Aders

Address: Mrs Aders | 11 | Euston Square
MS. Mr. Robert H. Taylor. Pub. E. L. G. ii. 323.
Postmark: Highgate, 2 June 1824.

1 June 1824.

My dear Madam

While I was *gallop-scrawling* the inclosed Note,[2] your little Messenger not having, I suppose, understood me, was off—before I could have thought it practicable for him to have taken any refreshment—and the marks of our little Joseph (who from the disproportion of his size to his age I am in the habit of calling Infra du, i.e. infra duodecimo, tho' he is nearer 15) on the said Note, impressed by his living *port-folios*, commonly called Hands, renders it scarcely fit to be sent at all—. I mean to say, that Joseph ran after your little lad, but returned without having overtaken him.

I am resolved to tell Miss [Kelly],[3] as soon as ever the Rose makes it[s] appearance on her cheeks, that she deserves to have a gray-haired Poet's Kiss inflicted on her for the Gloom, her sad naughty Sore throat has thrown over our anticipations. 'Bless me', cried

___

[1] This name is inked out in MS. here and in the postscript.
[2] See preceding letter.
[3] In this paragraph 'Kelly', 'Ellen', and 'child' are inked out in MS.

Mrs Gillman before she had read half down the first side of your
letter, 'I would rather have received a score "Declensions" than
this, let them have come from whom they might. I wish, that she
and dear Mrs Aders had been here.'—What? said I—do you suppose that the *sight* of Mr Gillman would have cured E[llen]'s Illness
in it's pre-existent state?—'I don't know but it might—and the
Walks in the South hampton Gardens, & our being all so glad to have
them with us—and there *is* something in change of Air.'—Be
assured, dear Madam! that if there be any medical efficacy in fervent & affectionate Wishing, your dear [child] will not long remain
on a sick bed. Mr Green, of whom I spoke in the inclosed, is the
Nephew of Mr Cline, and one of the Surgeons at St Thomas's
Hospital, and who has lately distinguished himself so greatly by
his Lectures on Animated Nature & the Laws of Life, Instinct, &c
at the College of Surgeons.[1] He is an incomparable German Scholar,
in addition to his other powers and attainments—above all, he is
among the very best men, I know. But probably you may have
heard Mr Robinson (that Pine-apple of a *Crab*, as Charles Lamb
says) speak of him.—I feel confident, that if any cause should make
it inconvenient that I should call with him during the next week,
you will not hesitate a moment in saying so—. If not, we shall not
however intrude on you for more than half an hour—and
you will perhaps favor me with a line, stating what day & what
hour would be least inconvenient. Mr Green has heard from a
German Correspondent of the superiority of Mr Aders's Collection
to those in Bavaria, and of the beauties of the Estate which Mr A.
has purchased from the Elector of Cologne.—

[1] J. H. Green became professor of anatomy at the Royal College of Surgeons
in 1824 and delivered 'four annual courses of twelve lectures on comparative
anatomy'.
 At the conclusion of his disquisition on Understanding and Reason in *Aids
to Reflection*, 1825, p. 234, Coleridge remarks: 'Since the preceding pages were
composed, . . . I heard with a delight and an interest, that I might without
hyperbole call medicinal, that the contra-distinction of Understanding from
Reason, for which during twenty years I have been contending, . . . has been
lately adopted and sanctioned by the present distinguished Professor of Anatomy, in the Course of Lectures given by him at the Royal College of Surgeons,
on the Zoological part of Natural History; and, if I am rightly informed, in one
of the eloquent and impressive introductory Discourses . . . explaining the
Nature of Instinct.' Coleridge included in the *Aids* (pp. 235–40) Green's
'Exposition' as it had been reported to him.
 In an Appendix to his 'Vital Dynamics', 1840, Green published his 'On
Instinct', with a prefatory comment: 'The following remarks on the import of
instinct are those to which Coleridge refers in the "Aids to Reflection" . . . and
whatever merit they possess must have been derived from his instructive conversation.' Green's essay on instinct was also published as Appendix B in the
fifth edition of *Aids to Reflection*, 1843, ii. 328–34.

Be pleased to make my best respects, together with Mr & Mrs Gillman's to Mr Aders—& believe me, dear Madam,

respectfully & warmly your | obliged Friend
S. T. Coleridge—

1403. *To Mrs. Charles Aders*

Address: Mrs Aders | 11. Euston Square
MS. Harvard College Lib. Pub. E. L. G. ii. 325.
Postmark: Highgate, 3 June 1824.

3 June 1824.

My dear Madam

Mrs Gillman sends her love & requests that you will allow her to expect you and [dear Ellen][1] on Wednesday next, June 9th.—I know, *you* need no additional inducement; but yet I *should* like you very much to be here one of the Evenings which Basil Montagu and Mr Irving spend with us—Whether the friendly Sympathies and Collisions between Mr I. and myself act as exciting causes, I cannot say; but I am not the only person who thinks Mr Irving more delightful still at these times than even in the pulpit.—Now we fully expect him on Thursday, 10 June—.

I shall be most happy to accompany my friends, Mr & Mrs Green—& nothing but some necessity moral or physical shall prevent me—I must, however, have expressed myself obscurely as to the time—. To Night is their Great Ball[2]—which, I daresay, will not break up till after Tomorrow's Dawn—& Mrs Green, I suspect, will scarcely be fit for any excursion for the next day or two—You know what there is to do after a hundred and fifty people have been in a house—I am equally surprized and delighted to see Mrs Gillman bear up so well, amid such an ocean of Glasses, Jelly Cups, Ice Saucers, & Lord knows what to be packed up & off.—I must therefore defer our visit till I have seen Mr Green & heard from you. At all events, I will trouble you with a note after I have seen them: and I hope, that Mr & Mrs Green may be induced to spend Thursday Evening with us—as I know, that Mr Green is very desirous to meet Mr Irving at one of our 'Attic nights'—We shall remain in strong hopes of a Note from you—'We will be with you by Wednesday Noon.'—

[1] Words in brackets inked out in MS.
[2] 'At nine (much too early)', Crabb Robinson wrote in his diary for 3 June 1824, 'I went to a dance and rout at Mr. Green's (Lincoln's Inn Fields), where I stayed till three. A large party. Luckily for me Coleridge was there, and I was as acceptable to him as a listener as he to me as a talker.' *Robinson on Books and Their Writers*, i. 307.

I write in a great hurry—& in consequence of an impudent
Demand from a worthless Clergyman, in some flurry of thought—
but with cordial respects to dear Mr Aders believe me, my dear
Madam,

your's with affectionate Esteem
S. T. Coleridge

1404. *To Basil Montagu*

MS. Mr. W. Hugh Peal. Hitherto unpublished.

Grove Highgate
Tuesday, June 8 [1824]

My dear Friend

We shall be *so* disappointed if you & Mr Irving do not come on
Thursday next. Pray, do give Mr I. a brief word of Impulse, in a
special Note. If I knew his address, I would do it myself.—How
glad we shall be if Mrs M. should come with you & likewise Anne—
not merely because we are always glad to see them but because it
will be the best proof of their being what we all are anxious that
they should be.—

God bless you | &

S. T. Coleridge

1405. *To Henry Taylor*

MS. Bodleian Library. Pub. with omis. Guests and Memories, *by Una Taylor,
1924, p. 60.*

Grove, Highgate
Tuesday Noon, 8 June 1824

Dear Sir

On Thursday Evening (10 June) Mr Irving with Mr Basil
Montagu and two or three 'female Intelligences' will, we expect,
light up the hours from 5 to 10, in our Drawing-Room: and Mr and
Mrs Gillman would feel gratified if your leisure permitted and
'mood of mind' inclined you to join the Group. We dine at 4 o'clock:
and if you will take your meal with us, you will indeed find only a
family dinner but yet *a* dinner, and not only $\dot{\eta}\delta\grave{\upsilon}\nu^{1}$ $o\hat{\imath}\nu o\nu$, $\dot{\eta}\delta\upsilon\tau\acute{\epsilon}\rho\alpha\varsigma$ $\tau\epsilon$
$\mu o\acute{\upsilon}\sigma\alpha\varsigma$; but may pass judgement on a batch which my friend has
received into his Binn under the name of Falernian, with some
tolerable Port as an Alternative.—You will meet likewise, I hope,
my Friend, Mr Green, of Lincoln's Inn Field, whose Lectures on
Life, Form, and Instinct introductory to his Course on Comparative

---

[1] Underlined once in MS.

Physiology, at the Royal College of Surgeons, have deservedly
attracted so much attention. He is a remarkably well-informed
Man—and as good as he is tall, being six feet 3 inches high.—Will
you favor me with a line by return of Post?[1]

and believe me, with respect and regard, | Your's truly
S. T. Coleridge

1406. To J. H. Green

Address: J. H. Green, Esqre | 22 Lincoln's Inn Fields
MS. Pierpont Morgan Lib. Hitherto unpublished.
Postmark: Highgate, 28 June 1824.

[28 June 1824]

My dear Friend
When you come next, be so good as bring with you any work
that contains a succession of the Figures of the animated, I mean,
animal World—Oken's Plates would do[2]—. You do not possess, I
believe, any work (if indeed such a work exists) containing figures
of the different Families of the Vegetable World.—When you come
in your carriage, do not forget the Volume of the Encyclopaedia—.
Would you have supposed it an easy matter to *out-Boehmenize* J.
Boehmen? Steffens however has overcome the difficulty—in his
grave—theory? no—matter of fact *Biography* of Water.[3] During
the, or rather constituting the, Moon Epoch of this *now* and this
here Planet, the Earth and Air were bedevil'd by a spirit of Self-
lust and reciprocal Hate—Each stood in sullen Japanese Incluse-
ness, a realized Alien-Act, on the stale maxim of keeping one's self
to one's self—the Earth would have no sort of intercourse with the
air, nor the air with the Earth—. Take a long string and twist the
middle of it in a noose round the top of a Post, so that the two
equal lengths should be extensible in opposite directions, and sup-

---

[1] Crabb Robinson gives a description of this 'Attic' night of Thursday,
10 June 1824. He and Charles Lamb 'walked to Highgate self-invited'. There
they found 'a large party: Mr. and Mrs. Green, the Aders, Irving, Collins, R. A.,
a Mr. Taylor, a young man of talents in the Colonial Office, Basil Montagu, a
Mr. Chance, and one or two others'. As the *advocatus diaboli* Taylor 'affirmed
that those evidences which the Christian thinks he finds in his internal convictions the Mahometan also thinks he has'. Lamb, Robinson noted, asked
Taylor 'whether he came in a turban or a hat'. *Robinson on Books and Their
Writers*, i. 307–8.

[2] Coleridge refers to Lorenz Oken (1779–1851), German naturalist. See note
to Letter 1438.

[3] Coleridge apparently refers to H. Steffens's *Beyträge zur innern Naturgeschichte der Erde.* Erster Theil, 1801. A copy of this work with Coleridge's
annotations is in the British Museum.

pose a bird tied to each End, at the time that the two ends of the string were side by side at the bottom of the Post—and suppose them seized with sudden fright and antipathy, and to take wing, fleeing & flying in opposite directions, till they were stopped by the common Noose—& there to remain tugging.

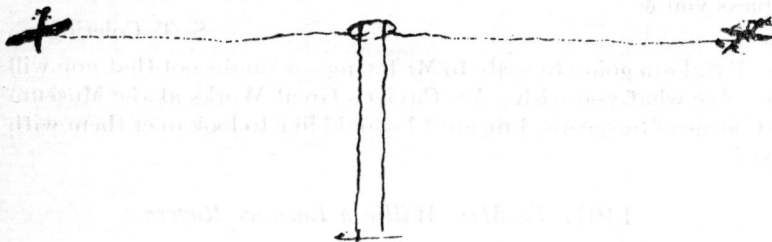

(I have not made out the feet or feathers of the two birds, so that you will not be able to determine the *order* or Genus to which they belong, from this Drawing.)

Now so were Earth & Air; Noose and Post representing the Magnetismus—

At length, the Redeemer (either Jesus Christ or the Holy Ghost) passed an electrical twitch of Conscience thro' the cord or perhaps Wire—& they *repented*. '*And Water* is *the Repentance* of Earth & Air'!!!!—

Now I should have thought that the very contrary would have been the effect, and that it was the way to prevent *any water from being made*—For what says the ancient oracle?—The more you cry, the less you'll *ΠΙΣΣ*.

But is it not *grievous* that such a man as Henry Stevens should play the fool in this way, the maudlin drivelling Fool!—The best part of the Volume is the Statement of the Deluge Question, especially of the Alluvial and Diluvial Animals, in connection with the Problem of the Polar Climate: and here Steffens is quite himself again. It is done with equal clearness and eloquence—alas! it occupies but a few Pages.

I have been thinking a great deal on the subject of our yesterday's confab.—& I am more and more satisfied of the great importance & pregnancy of the distinction between the reines *logisches* Anschauen, which I would call the Meditative Intuition—which is an identity, as it were, of Abstract and Concrete—ex. gr. the successive evolution of the Lever, and of the wondrous Properties of the Circle, the Cycloid &c from the simple reines Anschauen of a line circumvolving, while fixed at one end—and the pure contemplative Anschauen of Ideas, Types, which admit of no semblance

of Abstraction—which are *generic* in Thought because they are the
counterparts of the *Genetic* in Nature, but are the very *individuities*
of all individuals. Now of the former I say—So it *must be*!—They are
apodictic, i.e. truth *because* the contrary is absurd; but of the latter,
I only say, I only wish or *need* to say, So it *is*—because it *is*.—God
bless you &

S. T. Coleridge

P.S. I am going to write to Mr Irving—& doubt not that you will
receive what you wish—Are Cuvier's Great Works at the Museum
(College of Surgeons, I mean)? I should like to look over them with
you—

1407. *To Mrs. William Lorance Rogers*

Address: Mrs Rogers
MS. University of London King's College. Pub. E. L. G. ii. 327.

[Endorsed July 1824]

Dear Madam
        As the Representative or Substitute of Mrs Gillman's Absentee
Hand, I am to say that we are not elsewhere engaged, on Saturday
Afternoon. To add that we shall be glad to see you & Ellen, would
be quite superfluous. 'I wonder, whether Miss Johnson would like
to come with you.'—N.B. This is a quotation from myself.
        I was caught in & drenched by the Rain, Hail & Thunder Storm
this morning while reading with great pleasure the Review on your
Brother's Work[1] in the R. I. Journal. But indeed it was not possible
that such a Book could be without it's fame. And yet I do feel the
conviction that I should be able to convince Mr Daniel that his
Coalescence with the Grenville Penn[2] Party and the Pressing of
Moses & the Bible into the Service of Geological Theory is inconsistent with his own judicious Remark—and that every attempt of
this kind has ended hitherto, & from obvious causes must end in the
triumph of Infidels. If there be one sure Conclusion respecting the
Bible, it is this—that it not only uniformly speaks the language of
the Senses, but adopts the inferences which the Childhood of the
Race drew from the appearances presented by the Senses. The Bible
must be interpreted by it's known *objects* and *Ends*; & these were
the moral and spiritual Education of the Human Race.—These
ends secured, the truths of Science follow of their own accord—.

[1] John Frederic Daniell's *Meteorological Essays* were published in 1823.
[2] Granville Penn's *A comparative Estimate of the Mineral and Mosaical
Geologies*, 1822, 'was received with some approval in religious circles, but was
severely censured elsewhere as an unscientific attempt to treat the book of
Genesis as a manual of geology'. *D.N.B.*

With my affectionate Respects to Mr Rogers, & Love to Ellen,
Willy, Lady Ann, Eyelashina & Mrs Dante, I remain,
dear Madam, | with no every day | regard | your obliged Friend
S. T. Coleridge

1408. *To Thomas H. Dunn*

Facsimile Canadian Magazine, *June 1909, p. 101.*

21 Septr. 1824

Dear Sir

It has mortified me that in consequence of the prolonged stay of
a Friend at Paris I have been obliged to disappoint you, and must
still defer it for a few days. I do not doubt, however, that by or
before this day week I shall be able to settle it—independent of
my friend's return—tho' certain circumstances render me reluctant
to make use of other resources, which I can indeed at any moment
command but not so easily keep sacred to my own knowlege.

S.T.C.—

1409. *To Thomas H. Dunn*

Facsimile Canadian Magazine, *June 1909, p. 102.*

[Autumn 1824?]

Dear Sir

If it be in your possession, could you favor me with an oz of the
Liquor Morphii, equal in strength to Laudanum or in lieu of this
half a scruple of the Acetate Morphii[1]—

S.T.C.

[1] S. T. Porter, an apprentice in Dunn's shop at Highgate from 1824 to 1829,
says he was accustomed to fill Coleridge's 'laudanum-bottle every five or six
days', and goes on to 'state the amount of laudanum which . . . Mr. Coleridge
found to be essential to life & usefulness. . . . It was more than an ordinary
wine-glass-ful a day; the bottle which he brought for it being "a twelve ounce
pint", . . . five days being the average time for which this sufficed; & "a wine-
glass-ful" being fairly equal to two ounces & a half. . . . His payments for the
drug were much more irregular than his calls for supply. . . . The ordinary retail
price of good laudanum . . . was eight pence an ounce; but Dunn had undertaken to supply Mr. Coleridge for five pence, that is, to fill his bottle for five
shillings.' E. L. Griggs, 'Samuel Taylor Coleridge and Opium', *Huntington
Library Quarterly*, Aug. 1954, pp. 372 and 374.

1410. *To Thomas H. Dunn*

Facsimile Canadian Magazine, *June 1909, p. 102.*

Wednesday Noon. [Autumn 1824?]

Dear Sir

I am setting off for town, which I was prevented from doing yesterday by a Cold and the Weather. I leave this note in case I should return too late to call at your House this evening—

S.T.C.

1411. *To James Gillman*

Address: J. Gillman, Esqre | Highgate
MS. Mr. Henry Hofheimer. Hitherto unpublished.
Postmark: 7 October 1824. *Stamped*: Ramsgate.

[6 October 1824]

My dearest Friend

I arrived safe at Ramsgate ¼ after 5, with no other disagreement than that occasioned by the roll and sway of the Vessel when the machinery was stopped opposite to Broadstairs to disemboat half of our scanty Crew, Mr Burton being one who had been my Shadow during the Day.—For some 15 or 20 minutes I was disordered, a thick perspiration bursting from all parts of my Body, from Crown to Sole.—Mr Chance & Mr Burton called this morning in the Carriage—& stayed an hour & a half. Mr & Mrs C. had called on Mrs Gillman on Sunday last, when she was at Church—. And Mr C. this morning invited the Contents of No. I. Waterloo Plains, to meet the Joneses at dinner on Saturday.—I found the Ladies & Henry waiting for the arrival of the R. S. on the Pier—Mrs G. but poorly. They had had, it seems, a perilous as well as retarded Voyage—being twice in danger, and once in imminent or eminent or both sorts of, danger from a couple of drunken Ships, the one of which having staggered and plunged against the other, then thought proper to thrust it's Nose (alias, Bow-sprit) across the Steam-Vessel—but by the alacrity of the Sailors the Nose was torn off before it came against the Main Mast of the Steam Vessel—. A clear account—if it require a comment to render it intelligible, you understand these matters & will supply one for yourself. Relata refero.—But the oldest Seaman on board declared, he had never &c &c—as usual on all such occasions.—

There was a mistake about the Umbrellas—as I suspected—One only was taken, excepting Windsor's own. I called on Sir Thomas

& Lady Grey, who asked after you—And this, I believe, is all the News—except that I witnessed on board the Vessel a most laughable & long continued dispute between a violent Anti-Abernethian, whose Wife he had be-bruted, and a violent rustical Abernethian, who had taken up his Wife after having paid a mint of money to five different Doctors, in his Vicinity, a set of damned pick-pocket Ignoramuses &c &c—while Mr A. *would* cure her to a certainty, had already had some '*blue*-colored pills' made up for her, & ordered her to get a *book* & to read only *one page*—& that would do for her—. 'Aye! he is a queer body—but he's the Man—& he tould me myself as he before said to my wife, that our Doctors know all nothing about the matter'—&c &c—Now is not this most ignominious Quackery on the part of Master Abernethie? Could Dr Cameron, the Piss-Prophet, surpass it?—& this goes on, day after day!!—

I cannot help regretting that I had not another week with you—within which time the Essay might have been fit for the Press, with the exception of the concluding new Chapter on the source and seat of the Disease, & the physiology & pathology of specific Poisons, of vital origin & elaboration.[1]—

I strongly suspect, that some time ago I put some Mss of my own, in that little Box or box-like thing with a Shutter atop, that pulls backward & forward—& in which Watson's Copy of the Logic is contained. It lies in the Cup-board nearest the Window, beside the Wash-hand Stand, in my Bed-room where my Pocket-books mainly are.—The papers, I mean, are in *my* hand-writing—*not* Mr Green's MSS which lie under the long black Port-folio.—It is a wooden Box, that I mean, and the Shutter runs in a groove on each side.—Should there be any such, pray, be so good as to put them up in a Parcel, & have them booked by the Ramsgate Coach that sets off, I believe, from Grace-Church St & arrives at the Union Office on the Quay here—or by any other quick convenience—as soon as you can—. I will write as soon as I have finished the Ballad,[2] I promised you to finish—which, if no unforeseen change for the worse take place, will be in a few days. [I have now no doubt, that my complaint is an irritable Bladder—but that the kidneys are likewise impaired. Indeed, I should not wonder if there should be found an ... stone adhering to the upper part of the Bladder, from the pain across that whole region with ... & weakness. My pain is almost agony ...—& ... in proportion to the length of time ...][3] I have lain in the stupor of Sleep, and to the length & degree of the

[1] See Letters 1412 and 1416.
[2] Possibly the lines entitled *The Knight's Tomb*. See Letter 1413.
[3] Passage in brackets inked out in MS. Several words are indecipherable.

Pain, I suffer, can scarcely be an indifferent Symptom—. I have more than suspected Diabetes, ever since I first read Dr Prout's Work[1]—or rather, I should say, have recognized it.—Well!—My most earnest prayer is, that I may never be coward enough to shorten the path to the Church-yard from dread of the Brakes & Thorns—

God bless you &

S. T. Coleridge—

Pray remember Mrs Gillman to the maids.

1412. *To James Gillman*

Address: James Gillman, Esqre | Highgate
MS. Pierpont Morgan Lib. Hitherto unpublished.
Postmark: 18 October 1824. *Stamped*: Ramsgate.

Friday Night [15 October 1824]

My dear Friend

Your welcome Letter, in or with Miss Nixon's parcel received by us this day noon, quickened our pulse, as you may suppose. Where a strong interest is felt, the clearest and most distinct Anticipation does not weaken the effect of the thing itself, or perceptibly subtract even from the vividness or flurry of one's feelings. Foreseeing is Forestalling only where Curiosity is the sole or paramount Impulse. Let a Mother expect a long absent Son as confidently as she may, and with as good reason by Letter & Message for that confidence, there will be a shock of suddenness on his arrival, not differing *in kind* from what would be felt on a Ticket's coming up a 10,000£ Prize. It is the homage, which the Heart of Man pays to the Powers of chance and change! It's inmost acknowlegement of the drifting Clouds of Uncertainty, thro' which the Moon of our desires toils out into the blue interspace of possession. I had been drawing out to Mrs Gillman Mr Sutton's Scheme of action—namely, to do every thing by his own weight, but in order to have it seen and felt that he was every thing, to call up a shew of opposition and difficulty—a bustle of Canvas, a display of impartiality, a magistratical *duplexity* of character, R. Sutton, Esqre, the confidential Trustee and Publicist of a rich and munificent Company, and Mr Sutton, the kind and patronizing Neighbour, on whose single vote *with whatever small weight that* might carry, you might rely. Feeling the full delicacy and responsibility of the Trust placed in him, he could not interfere with the free-agency of his Brother Wardens—to

---

[1] Coleridge evidently refers to William Prout's *Inquiry into . . . Gravel, Calculus, and other Diseases of the Urinary Organs*, 1821.

(376)

canvas in his own person would be an inconsistency, a resumption in effect of a power which he had previously declined—but if the individual members of his Family exerted their influence, he could have no objection[1]—&c &c—.

Such having been my prenotions of the matter, I need not tell you, that you have acted throughout well and wisely, with prudence and yet with dignity—To say what would be *effective*, you had only to say what was true. I rely exclusively on *you*; and it is in that reliance, that I now go to solicit the votes of others. For what I shall always consider as owing to you, I am willing to owe to you in the way, you yourself point, and which is most agreeable to your sense of propriety, and to the respect due both to the Members of the Court and to the office itself: since the Credit of success rises with the keenness of the Competition.—

All, I was afraid of, was—how far you would stand your feelings, and innate aversion to all round-abouts and indirect courses. Herein if in any thing, I have the advantage of you. I begin like our Father Adam by giving every Beast it's right name—and pre-determining what I may and what I ought not to expect from the particular Animal, I have to deal with, I square my advances accordingly. In other words, I endeavor to *make the best of him*—the best for myself, but likewise the best of *him*, and therefore the best *for* him— seeing, I cannot re-create or re-cast him.—We shall have a wishful day of it, next Thursday. I don't think, I should feel half as anxious, were I at Highgate. The very distance seems to give a feeling of uncertainty. I need not ask you to write immediately, tho' but a single Line or Word.—

I dined yesterday (my last dinner visit) at Sir Thomas Grey's, with rather a pleasant party—a Sir Charles Devò or Duveau,[2] who seems to have taken a mighty liking to me—Our Ladies noticed him from his likeness to Hartley—Major Gardner, Captn & Mrs Dundas, R.N., Mr Moneypenny, and an Odd Fish from the Red Sea, an Oriental Traveller whose name I could not catch.—We have had three beautiful days; but this evening the Rain has returned— My head, which has annoyed me sorely from a sort of apoplectic weight upon it, is considerably relieved since by aid of some tepid water I threw up a spoonful of light-yellow Bile from my stomach, followed by a discharge of wind. I bathed to day & yesterday.—Mrs Gillman goes on well—but it seems to me, that there is a defect of Bile.—

---

[1] For further comments concerning Gillman's 'competition with a worthless medical Man', a Mr. Snow, and loss of the election 'by intrigue and treachery', see Letters 1414–16, 1418, 1437, and 1446.

[2] Sir Charles Des Voeux (1779–1858).

Henry Coleridge is going out with his Cousin, the Bishop, to Barbadoes—for the benefit of his health. I will write to Derwent forthwith.[1]—Our Henry takes to his Greek—& will return, I expect, thoroughly grounded in the Greek Grammar.

I daily think of the Hydrophobia—and I most earnestly hope, that you will not give up the design. Many reasons have occurred to my mind in favor of a new hypothesis—viz. that the Nerves act on the Brain or the central Power but that the Brain does not act *on* the Nerves—in other words, that the Nerves are alive to the relatively lifeless (excitants ab extra, Light, Odors, &c &c) but lifeless and alien to the Life a centro—and on this account the fit *Conductors* of the Power, the activity or efficient Action of which first commences on the irritable system, and *appears* only in the irritability. Sensibility *as* sensibility is always *subjective* & antiphaenomenal—it becomes *objective* in the act of instinctive motion, when it is no longer Sensibility. Again—Sensibility is not an active power—but a *source* of active power—and it's *negative* Condition. How I apply this to Poisons, you will see hereafter if I live to return.—

God bless you!—This Letter is scarcely worth the postage—but Paw and Pen are the only Substitutes for Tongue & Talk.—
Your ever affectionate

S. T. Coleridge.

P.S. Anne could not help qualifying the pleasurable part of the interest excited by your letter by the regret, that we were not at home to help you—and likewise by her retrospective anxiety for the addition to your cares & troubles by Mr Rowlandson's sudden & alarming attack. She cannot bear to think, that you should have had the whole weight and conflux of the To Do and To Suffer on your Heart and Hands, without help and without any one at home to talk and feel with, to see you off, to be on the watch during your absence, and to expect and receive you on your return.—Need I say, that I have had the same feelings? tho' there is this shade of difference between the characters of your Friend and your Wife, that she is more haunted by the Past, especially by Regrets where she seems to herself to have been out of the way when there was a Duty of Business or Feeling to be performed—while I am more prone to project my thoughts & anxieties into the Future.

Eliza N. & Miss Bradley's best love.—Pray, do you think that the taking 4 or 5 grains of Blue Pill every other night for a week or ten days would be incompatible with Mrs G's bathing on the alternate days—? 'There *is*,' she says, 'a defective secretion of Bile, by unequivocal proofs.'—The Weather cold and fine. Sunday Noon.

---

[1] Coleridge was writing to Derwent concerning the exhibitions from the Mercers' and the Goldsmiths' Companies.

1413. *To Unknown Correspondent*

MS. Cornell University Lib. Hitherto unpublished.

The novel to which Coleridge refers in the present letter was *Ivanhoe*, 1820 (issued December 1819). In *Ivanhoe* (ch. ix, p. 156) Scott quoted, or rather misquoted, the last three lines of Coleridge's unpublished poem, *The Knight's Tomb*, with the following comment:

> To borrow lines from a contemporary poet, who has
> written but too little—
>
> > The knights are dust,
> > And their good swords are rust,
> > Their souls are with the saints, we trust.

As his letter to Allsop of 30 March 1820 shows, Coleridge had read *Ivanhoe* by that date and had characterized it as a wretched abortion.

A second manuscript of *The Knight's Tomb* is extant. To it Coleridge prefixed a note in which he expressed his irritation at Scott in terms similar to those in the present letter:

> Mem. The lines, which Mr J. H. Frere, I surmise, must have repeated from memory to Sir W. Scott (for I had never committed them to paper) and which Sir Walter has in part cited in one of his Novels, were the first stanza of an intended Ballad—& should have been printed thus—
>
> > The knightly Sword, a Ballad.

In his *Life of Coleridge*, 1838, p. 277, Gillman also explains how Scott became acquainted with *The Knight's Tomb*, but he does not give Frere's name:

> The lines were composed as an experiment for a metre, and repeated by him [Coleridge] to a mutual friend—this gentleman the following day dined in company with Sir Walter Scott, and spoke of his visit to Highgate, repeating Coleridge's lines to Scott, and observing at the same time, that they might be acceptable to the author of Waverley.

Scott, indeed, was so pleased with *The Knight's Tomb* that he again quoted the last three lines in *Castle Dangerous*, 1832 (issued November 1831).

In 1824 Thomas Medwin published his *Conversations of Lord Byron*, and on reading the work Scott was mortified to find that his unacknowledged indebtedness to Coleridge had been laid before the public. Bluntly Byron had remarked to Medwin:

> 'Christabel' was the origin of all Scott's metrical tales. . . . It was written in 1795, and had a pretty general circulation in the literary world, though it was not published till 1816, and then probably in consequence of my advice. One day, when I was with Walter Scott (now many years ago), he repeated the whole of 'Christabel'. (pp. 261–2.)

> I hope Walter Scott did not write the review on 'Christabel'; for he certainly, in common with many of us, is indebted to Coleridge. But for him, perhaps, 'The Lay of the Last Minstrel' would never have been thought of. The line
>
> > 'Jesu Maria shield thee well!'
>
> is word for word from 'Christabel.' (p. 309. The infamous review alluded to appeared in the *Edinburgh Review*, September 1816.)

Byron's comments undoubtedly goaded Scott into making a belated public statement of his obligations to Coleridge. Thus in the 1830 edition of his *Poetical Works*, Scott added a Preface to *The Lay of the Last Minstrel* in which he acknowledged his indebtedness to *Christabel*. He explained the circumstances whereby he had heard Stoddart recite *Christabel*, then still in manuscript, and had found the 'singularly irregular structure of the stanzas . . . exactly suited to such an extravaganza' as he had meditated. 'It was in Christabel', he added, 'that I first found it used in serious poetry, and it is to Mr Coleridge that I am bound to make the acknowledgment due from the pupil to his master.' Scott, however, went on to comment on Coleridge's caprice and indolence:

> I observe that Lord Byron, in noticing my obligations to Mr Coleridge, which I have been always most ready to acknowledge, expressed, or was understood to express, a hope, that I did not write an unfriendly review on Mr Coleridge's productions. On this subject I have only to say, that I do not even know the review which is alluded to; and were I ever to take the unbecoming freedom of censuring a man of Mr Coleridge's extraordinary talents, it would be on account of the caprice and indolence with which he has thrown from him, as if in mere wantonness, those unfinished scraps of poetry, which, like the Torso of antiquity, defy the skill of his poetical brethren to complete them. The charming fragments which the author abandons to their fate, are surely too valuable to be treated like the proofs of careless engravers, the sweepings of whose studios often make the fortune of some painstaking collector.

Scott again meted out qualified praise of Coleridge in a footnote included in the reissue of *The Abbot*, 1832 (*Waverley Novels*, 48 vol. edn., xx. 237). After giving an account of the popular belief that evil spirits 'cannot enter an inhabited house unless invited, nay, dragged over the threshold', he turned to *Christabel*:

> But the most picturesque use of this popular belief occurs in Coleridge's beautiful and tantalizing fragment of Christabel. Has not our own imaginative poet cause to fear that future ages will desire to summon him from his place of rest, as Milton longed
>
> > 'To call him up, who left half told
> > The story of Cambuscan bold?'
>
> The verses I refer to are when Christabel conducts into her father's castle a mysterious and malevolent being, under the guise of a distressed female stranger. [Here follow lines 123–44 of *Christabel*.]

In the reissue of *Ivanhoe*, 1832 (*Waverley Novels*, xvi. 124), Scott added an explanatory note to the quotation from *The Knight's Tomb*. Again the praise is grudgingly bestowed:

> These lines are part of an unpublished poem by Coleridge, whose Muse so often tantalizes with fragments which indicate her powers, while the manner in which she flings them from her betrays her caprice, yet whose unfinished sketches display more talent than the laboured masterpieces of others.

Scott, who was putting his literary house in order, did not live to superintend the republication of *Castle Dangerous*, 1834, but to the three lines quoted from *The Knight's Tomb* in that work, J. G. Lockhart, the editor, added a footnote in which he printed all of the poem, with the following introductory comment: 'The author has somewhat altered part of a beautiful unpublished fragment of Coleridge'. (*Waverley Novels*, xlvii. 451.) Lockhart's text differs markedly from that in the present letter. *The Knight's Tomb* was first published by Coleridge himself in his *Poetical Works*, 1834.

20 Octr. 1824

Here follow the Lines first *written down* but very incorrectly by

Sir W. Scott in one of his Novels—who had them from J. H. Frere to whom I had repeated them as an experiment in metre that had passed thro' my brain—Suppose it the first Stanza of a Ballad.—

> Where is the Grave of Sir Arthur O'Relhan?
> Where may the Grave of that gōŏd mān bĕ?
> By the side of a Spring, on the breast of Helvellan,
> Under the Twigs of a Yŏ͞ung Bĭrch Tree!
> Thĕ Oāk thăt ĭn / sŭmmĕr wăs / swēĕt tŏ hēar
> Ănd rūstlĕd ĭt's / lēaves ĭn thĕ / Fāll ŏ'¹ thĕ Yēar,
> And whistled / and roar'd in / the Winter, / alone—
> Is gone! And the Birch in it's stead is grown.
> The Knight's Bones are Dust:
> And his Good Sword Rust:
> His Soul is with the Saints, I trust.²

1414. *To James Gillman*

Address: J. Gillm[an]
MS. Pierpont Morgan Lib. Hitherto unpublished.

Friday Noon. 22 Octr 1824

My dearest Friend

If I wished to be with you during this and the preceding week, I have been wishing it ten times more since the last two hours—so much so, that I could not have withstood the impulse that took possession of me at the first sentence of your Letter, to set off immediately, but for the apprehension of distressing you, and then the doubt, how my sudden return might be interpreted. And after all, it would not be what I want—namely, to have been with you at the very moment—tho' God knows! what other comfort I could have been or use but that of turning off your mind in part from your own vexation to my sufferings.—It would be foolish—and irritating not comforting—to pretend that I do not see & feel the *cut* and the *bruise*—or that I overlook the consequences, at least the possible results which for the moment force themselves on us as consequences. If I held them as trifles, I should be too ignorant of the world and the particular Circumstances, to be capable of sympathizing with you, or competent to advise or comfort—and I should myself be worse than a trifler, if at this moment I could attempt to pass them off as trifles on you, or make you regard them in a

¹ of [Cancelled word in line above.]
² On the verso of the MS. lines 12–26 of *Youth and Age* are copied in another hand.

different light from what they appear to my own judgement. The very *name* of the Man contains the whole Case, the symptons and the sequels: and if I endeavored to extenuate, the aversion to utter the name, the *hate* that supervenes or the disgust, I have always felt, would convict me of a virtual Lie. When it was mentioned a few minutes ago, I started as if I had been bit by an adder.—Yet one comfort there *is*—and to me it is—I already feel that it is—a great comfort. You have in no respect been wanting to yourself— You have neglected nothing, in nothing have you deceived yourself! And even tho' you had pre-apprehended the result, as a not improbable Contingency, yet unless you had been almost sure of it's realization, I do not see how you could have acted otherwise, than you have done. The antipathy, that from the first notice of a card to be left announcing a vacancy was at work in me—the antipathy to a competition with that man would have left me inexcusable in my own eyes, if I had by advice or assent influenced you to concern yourself with it without having done my utmost to ascertain the ground, on which you were to stand. It is true, indeed, that I ought to have known that the person of all others most likely to delude and over-reach himself, is a vain man, whose vanity puts on the form of pride, and who wants to support a double-character, at once the hero in Plot and Under-plot—But it would be almost arrogant to blame either myself or you for not conjecturing that he was ignorant of a Canvas of many months having already gone on, or that his ruling passion would have suffered him to excite and expressly sanction an entire Reliance on his Interest and Influence, had he had reason even to doubt the result. On any ordinary principle of calculation, the very desire to have a competition must under such circumstances was [be?] a proof and pledge of his Security as to having the final determination in his hands, and waiting only for the Grasp.—And that he should re-confirm and like a man throwing off all ceremonious disguise more strongly confirm this belief, in the heat & mid conflict of the Canvas—this is an instance of sincere self-deception, which you cannot reproach yourself for not having anticipated.—I am persuaded, I have a strong presentiment, that some good will come out of all this.—Whatever you do (pardon, dearest Friend! this superfluous anxiety) do not suffer a syllable of anger or reproach to escape you respecting Mr S.—*not to any one or any where.* He cannot but feel that you have a strong claim upon him, for all future exertions of all kinds—and he may have it in his power to make abundant compensation for the evil if not for the mortification of this unlucky Blunder of his—. He is now your full Friend—& the bonds, which the Chapel Devilry had loosened, are knit anew—

I must hurry.—Poor dear Mrs Tulk![1]—This too will grieve you. —Should I be any comfort to you—if I came for 10 days or a fortnight? It would be a delight to me—& nothing but the fear of vexing or displeasing you prevents me from coming instead of writing—. If you thought, it would—do, do, say so by return of Post.—. . .[2]

Mrs G. is silent, but sorely cut at heart—tho' she says, it is only her head—

1415. *To James Gillman*

Address: J. Gillman, Esqre | Grove | Highgate
MS. Harvard College Lib. Hitherto unpublished.
Postmark: 25 October 1824. *Stamped*: Ramsgate.

Sunday afternoon—[24 October 1824]
My dearest Friend

I was glad of your letter: and sensible what your feelings could not but be, I was even glad of the contents—so far at least, that it would have increased my uneasiness, had a single sentence been omitted or qualified. It is not in my power not to wish, not to *long*, to be with you; but your injunction is decisive. It gives me, however, an additional claim on your continuing to unbosom yourself to me—not only to *think*, but to *feel*, aloud, just as the pulse beats at the instant moment, without looking back on what you had written. I expect from you, because I *know* that I *deserve*, that you should see in me at least a Friend, who acknowleges, and with the single *impossible* exception of a base act ever will acknowlege no other difference between you and himself, your interests and his, but that in the latter the sense of duty will be more faithfully and effectively backed by inclination, than his self-experience allows him to pledge himself for in the former. A Wife excepted, I hardly know whether the best of us is entitled to expect more than one friend in *this* sense of the word. In *this* sense at least I am right well content to call you alone my Friend: for I regard Mrs Gillman as a part of you in all serious concerns, or (to state my feelings as nearly as I can) just as if she had been my confidential Sister and her being so had been one strong motive for your choice of her as a Wife.—But yet I should utter a falsehood in effect, if I did not avow my conviction, that you have *many* sincere Friends, each according to his character and the extent and quality of his Nature.

[1] Mrs. Tulk, *née* Susannah Hart, died in Oct. 1824.
[2] About a fourth of page 3 cut out of MS., thus mutilating the address on the verso.

And you ought to remember, that generosity, and a frankness and
fervor in any cause or person, you are attached to or think highly
of, and (so to say) an entireness of Being in the object pursued, are
your constitutional good qualities—and what is characteristic of
one, cannot rationally be looked for generally. I apply the same
rule to myself. I do not pretend to be ignorant (tho' for many
many years of my life I was so) that there are points in *my* character that *distinguish* me, for good as well as e contra—and my
deepest mortifications have part originated in, part resulted from
my unconsciousness of this; and many a shaft has fallen blunted
and hurtless since I have become aware of it, and prepared my
feelings accordingly.—

I have two Franks here—one for tomorrow, the other for Tuesday's Post—and yet I cannot withstand the restlessness of my
mind, to write to you by to night's. For in thinking over my last
letter (and having besides to support Mrs Gillman, on whose mind
& I am sorry to say body this affair has taken more serious hold
than I had seen on any former occasion—n.b. not from your letter,
which she has not seen—) I am persuaded, I feel certain, that my
vexation had presented the matter thro' a mist—In all matters that
are yet to come, and where any opinion or advice may possibly be
of some use, I dare rely on myself for perfect unqualified singleness
& minute sincerity—but sometimes a weakness, a fear of giving
useless pain, a yearning to support and enliven, tempts me—in
retrospective matters—to express myself not indeed otherwise than
I feel at the moment but in less well-weighed phrases than a strict
comparison with the dictates of my judgement would have sanctioned. And yet in re-considering my letter I can find but one
phrase that I could now alter—namely—for 'well and wisely' it
would have been a more faithful representation of my total Judgement had I said 'not unwisely'.—Two days before I had written
that first letter, Eliza Nixon seeing me thoughtful, said—'But you
have no fears, have you?' I answer—It is impossible, Eliza! to
wish any thing so much as I do this, without fearing—especially,
where as in the present case the wish itself is two thirds made up of
a fear—but besides this, I am superstitious wherever there is any
change in a plan as originally formed. I did not need the entreaty
that followed not to say any thing that could depress or dishearten
—but even at this moment I do not feel that if I had been at Highgate I could or should have urged you to do otherwise than you
did—and still, notwithstanding what you have said, I cling to the
opinion that more good & of a more abiding nature will come of
this than inconvenience—and again I conjure you, taking S. as he
is—without any false colors, but likewise without stripping him

of all good points—not to stand on a semblance of irritation with him. I am anxious on this account, chiefly, for your own dignity of character.—You cannot know, that he is not wounded & grieved—to keep aloof from him, will wound his pride & vanity—whereas by acting, as if you were fellow sufferers, by displaying a sort of taking for granted that he is vexed on your account—will call forth whatever is human & of a better nature in his feelings—& will, you may rely on it, give you a sense of inward elevation, as well as a calm & manly appearance—completely precluding and disappointing any little malicious triumph, that little Wretches would be on the watch for.—O God! that I were with you! For I see how awkwardly & inappropriately I express myself.—But I will write again. Do you write or not, just as your feelings dictate—.

God bless you &

S. T. Coleridge—

P.S. Mrs Abud would be obliged to you to let the Servant at their house know that they will be at home tomorrow evening, by Tea time—& that Tea is to be got ready.—They have been very civil & friendly.—

1416. *To James Gillman*

MS. Private possession. Hitherto unpublished.

[25 October 1824][1]

My dear Gillman

This, I propose, shall be the last letter in which I will hazard annoying you by repetitions of a painful text, with fresh comments. Yester evening, between dinner and tea, finding myself sickish & with a confused sense of *weight* all over me, and attributing it to the bowel torpor which any vexation is sure to produce, I took three grains of Calomel.—The medicine procured me a night of sound sleep, and by the quantum of solid and not particularly offensive matter it eliminated, and by the general Relief that has followed, gave proof that I had not judged amiss. This morning therefore, my head being clear (for what is to be an organ of Sense must not be a Subject of Sensation) I set myself the task of looking steadily and distinctly at this occurrence, and of separating it into all it's several constituent ingredients—. These I divided into two Heads—Accompaniments; and Consequences, certain or probable: and

---

[1] In Letter 1415 Coleridge says he has two franks—'one for tomorrow, the other for Tuesday's Post', i.e., 25 and 26 Oct. 1824. The present letter and the one following would seem to be those referred to.

under the former I placed our *feelings*—those that neither you or I could avoid having, & which there is no other way of dealing with than by giving them free *thoroughfare*—i.e. opening the front door, but not closing the back-door. Let them stay without struggle or contradiction as long as they *will* stay; but do not *detain* them. And we must not forget, that they are their own Glass-Blowers— both Breath and Vessel: and that the size of the latter depends mainly on the heat and vehemence of the former—. As these there- fore are not proper subjects of reasoning, too variable in themselves to have either measure or scales *objectively*, I will only ask you to run over in your mind the names and characters of those, who (you have every reason to believe, nay, ground to know) regard and respect you—and on not one of whom the late accident can be imagined to have the slightest influence, beyond that of sympathy, and indignant contempt towards the fit objects of contempt.— Even in Individuals, whom neither you or I would place among the lowest on this List, I have seen unequivocal proofs of a right feeling in this respect. I assure you, that both Jones and Wm. Abud spoke to me on this subject with a warmth that surprized me—Each of them separately and severally expressed their grief that they had not known of it—and had not had an opportunity of exert- ing themselves, as they believe, they could have done with con- siderable effect—. And what is more—both of them without a single leading hint from me interpreted the thing exactly as I do—and as it ought to be—and even Jones, whose recent *thickness* with S. makes him speak tenderly of his 'undoubted friendly intentions', yet with regard to the Highgate Opinion & Gossip says, that the Shaft only *grazes* you, but hits and fixes on Sutton. None but those who were your known enemies before, & whose malice is it's own detection, can be blind to the evident fact, that under the circumstances it was impossible that you should succeed. Had S. to the surprize of the World *broke*, and you had lost a hundred pound by his failure, the triumph of your Antagonist would not be more absurd than in the present case.—Be assured, my dear Friend! that tho' Knaves & Hypocrites, Snows & Delafosses, fraternize by instinct; yet a worthless fellow, who is insolent and ignorant to boot, cannot but have enemies both with good and bad men, the former of whom for your own sake, and the latter on the score of Snow's undeserved success and anticipated *Swell*, will have a new inkling to think & talk highly of you—where the contrast is so pat and palpable. The re-publication or rather the publication of the re-written 'Essay on the Bite of the Mad dog, and the Virus of rabid animals generally'[1]

[1] Gillman's essay, *On the Bite of a Rabid Animal*, was published in 1812. It is dedicated to Anthony Carlisle and contains an appendix written by him. See

will do you more service than ten times the disservice of this Election can weigh down.—I see, I have already passed into the Head
of CONSEQUENCES—And here there is one striking point—which I
put by supposing that you had been a Physician, and aiming at
town practice—Then indeed the failure must have been appreciated by the advantages that would or might have followed on the
success. But in your case, even tho' you should suppose (which
would, however, be a most extravagant supposition) that every one
of the Electors, who was prevailed on either by Snow's Canvassers
or his own jealousy of *S.* to vote for Snow, would in case of illness
in his family call him in—yet how many, I pray, are so situated or
domiciled as to make it a contingency worth looking at to a General
Practitioner settled at *Highgate*?—It is at Highgate & in it's
vicinity that your character is to work—aided by what you have
& Snow has not, the known esteem & friendship of the ablest & the
most rising men in London.—One thing only you have to guard
against, for which the Malignants will be anxiously expecting—the
appearance of a coolness, a woundedness in your manners towards
Mr S.—For God's sake, do not give them this their only tangible &
more than momentary, material for exultation. Indeed, indeed, you
ought not to expect from a proud man stung and mortified a conduct which would suppose the direct contrary character. I cannot
tell you, how much I have this at heart. Had I been at home (and
it was no idle presentiment, that made me for the first time so
reluctant to set off for Ramsgate) I could myself have done the
needful during the first unconquerable ebullition of your nature.
Not that I suspect, that you will say any thing. Your own dignity
of character, nay, the faulty part of your character, a disposition to
keep your strongest feelings when they are painful ones, to yourself,
are my sufficient securities for that—But I would fain have more.
From your own letter I could shew you that you should in look,
tone, and visit [visage?] demean yourself as to a man who had
certainly calculated on the power of serving you, & received a
mortifying *trip-up* in the experiment. And spite of the result of this
unforeseen intrigue can you imagine that [Sutton's][1] influence is
gone, or seriously weakened?—I do not believe it—

The moment, I hear from Derwent, I shall write to S. myself;[2]
but I shall inclose my letter in a frank to you, which you will seal &

Letter 1412, in which Coleridge urges Gillman not to give up the 'design' of the
'Hydrophobia'. See also Letter 1411.

[1] MS. torn.

[2] As Coleridge had mentioned to John Taylor Coleridge on 3 May 1824, he
was seeking Sutton's assistance in obtaining for Derwent the proceeds of the
exhibitions from the Mercers' and the Goldsmiths' Companies.

send or not, as your *then* judgement & feelings determine. Good
will come out of this, I am certain, in the long run—aye, & before it
has run long—. I am perplexed by solicitations to dine with the
men of Title—to meet the Dutchess of Leinster &c—offers to have
only a *very* small party &c—Sir Charles Des Voeux is a good-
natured Irish Baronet, of high connections & large estates in both
countries. Sir Alexander Johnston[1] you will probably become acquainted with & will like.—

Mrs Gillman is but very poorly—yet I hope, better than yesterday.—God bless you—I shall probably write a few lines tomorrow,
with some notes to be sent by you—.

God bless you again & again | &
S. T. Coleridge—

1417. *To James Gillman*

Address: J. Gillman, Esqre
MS. Pierpont Morgan Lib. Hitherto unpublished.

[26 October 1824]

My dear Friend

A night of clamorous Rain, blustering Wind, and yet hot and
heavy Air, occasioned me a distressful night rudely compacted of
ten or a dozen several Sleeps, each with it's own Swedenbergian
Devilry: of which the most amusing is the Fancy's Apery of Reason,
and self-conceit in her cleverness to *prove* that it *is* a Dream—with
her speculations on the Nature of the Figures, nay, her grave
experiments by putting questions for that very purpose to some one
of them & receiving the Answer, with the grave puzzle that follows
whether the Thought in the said Answer was or was not, or might
not have been, a Thought of her own—all to determine pro or con
on the subjectivity of the Dream-Objects—and then (as last night)
her acuteness in detecting the objectivity of the Subject, i.e. of that
which had the feeling 'me' given to it, & which yet is clearly (thinks
she) no true 'I'—for it hath a *form* for me, just as the other Figures
have, & partakes of the common Objectivity—. But yet (some
gripe perhaps taking place) this may be the nature of the Soul in
Hades, or the Self-world detached from God—or that stormy

[1] Sir Alexander Johnston (1775–1849), reorganizer of the government of
Ceylon. In 1805 he was made chief justice of Ceylon, and in 1811 he was
knighted by the prince regent. In the latter year he became president of the
council of Ceylon and in 1817 acted as admiralty judge. When Johnston returned
to England in 1819, Lord Grey declared in the House of Lords that his 'conduct
in the island of Ceylon alone had immortalised his name'. In 1823 Johnston was
instrumental in founding the Royal Asiatic Society; in 1832 he was made a
privy-councillor. *D.N.B.*

foamy Water between strange sludgy rocks may be the appearance that the Urine passing by a stone in the Bladder may appear to the Soul that sees them within, or from the under side of the Things, of which Calculus and Urine are the Outside Phaenomena[1] —&c &c—Well this night with the overpowering White Glare of the Sun; and then a Letter of request to transcribe my version of Know'st thou the Land[2] from Sir A. Johnston—then a Call from him, on a question I had put to him tête à tête respecting his personal knowlege of Professor Baron Schlegel (*our* Sch.) to whom he had entrusted & con-domiciled his Son—& lastly, Henry's Lesson—have all combined to frustrate my expectation of sending sundries by this frank, over and above a letter to you—. I have barely time to answer your letter of this morning in the way that is uppermost—videlicet—a hearty wish that as you cannot come to me, I were with you. I am not however altogether sorry that I cannot answer it at length as without the drawbacks aforementioned I should have done; because, exclusive of all temporary mood of mind, I was exceedingly interested with the contents, and want to bring into some coherent, at least intelligible, shape the result of my own observations, reflections, and deliberate convictions respecting the traits of character, you appropriate to yourself. For if I do not grossly delude myself, I have the Key of Exposition, which by fairly explaining your feelings & notions respecting yourself will go far in determining how much you are right in & wherein you tax yourself wrongly—. So far I see plainly, that your having been from Boyhood compelled to struggle for yourself with the Hopes & Fears, both of Life and of your own striving Nature, while your faculties were left to develope themselves by their own heat, unaided & untempered by the warmth ab extra of a setting and hatching Sympathy. Had we, each of us, known the other from 12 to 15 years earlier, we should both of us have been *entirer* men— and (I speak it with solemn conviction of it's truth) I should have been even more benefited than you—for my evil is in *habit*, supervening on a constitutional weakness, hidden beneath a vivid Varnish of extra-ordinary *Power*—the maximum of Power with the minimum of Strength,[3] being my invoice—while your's is in a hypochondria that subjects your imagination to your animal spirits,

---

[1] Cf. *Literary Remains*, iii. 355–6.

[2] See *Poems*, i. 311, and note to Letter 1691.

[3] Cf. Coleridge's letter to Davy of 25 Mar. 1804: 'There *is* a something, an essential something wanting in me. I feel it, I *know*, it—tho' what it is, I can but guess. I have read somewhere that in the tropical climates there are Annuals [as lofty] and of as ample girth as forest trees. So by a very dim likeness, I seem to myself to distinguish power from strength & to have only the power.' See also Letter 1617.

under this special aggravation—that you are not permitted, &
from your early youth never have been enabled, to withdraw yourself in thought or act from real life for any continuity of time, and
that this real life has forced upon you, & ever forces on you,
specimens of folly, imbecillity, and selfishness—your best harbour
from which was for too long a time your own vivid perception of
their being such—while there was no one individual, no *man* at
least, to whom you could revert as a part of yourself, as a *holden*
and appropriated Stay, whom you could consider as absolutely on the
other & better side of Humanity. If you had but one whole year,
that you could use as your own, it would throw a light even now
on all your views—. Even I, in one respect, have been the occasion
of your wrongly mistrusting yourself—I will only give one instance—.
You compare yourself with regard to power of abstraction, and
intellectual construction with me, whose most remarkable quality
it is, and in whom it has been nourished even to disease and mis-
growth, by domestic disappointment and by constitutional Indolence, Cowardice of Pain, & the accidental sad Consequents—and
then unjustly put yourself down at Zero.—

But I must close—. We shall be on the look out for dear James,
who will be trebly welcome to me, *now*— There is a native integrity
in him, to which I have at all times reverted. I doubt not, that he
will prove a Blessing to you—and that even his intellectual Attainments will not in the end be less profitable or efficient, for having
grown slowly and with seeming reluctance out of the rock of Duty,
instead of the garden mould of Liking & the manure of Emula-
tion.—

Now for *Dr French*[1]—*I never before heard the name*—the only
Fellow, I know, is Mr Skinner, the Classical Tutor. Of course, to
him only I can write[2]—whence the mistake, I know not—.

All send their love—Miss Bradley, I believe, is going to Walmer
for a few days, and should I induce Mrs G. to let Henry stay there
for a week, he will not be worse—& it will be all the better for
James, to whom I shall then be able to give more of my time &
society, during his sojourn. Miller has disappointed us in the
Front-House—or rather Mrs G. in her good nature has allowed him
so to do, his present Tenant wishing to continue a week longer, & he
not liking to put him *out*—as if the House had been his own, after

[1] William French (1786–1849), D.D., became master of Jesus College in
1820. French took a distinguished part in the translations of the Proverbs
(1831) and the Psalms (1842) made by himself and George Skinner.
[2] Coleridge asked Skinner, fellow of Jesus College, Cambridge, to find out
whether the authorities of St. John's College would be willing to sign a certificate as required by the Goldsmiths' and the Mercers' Companies. See note to
Letter 1441 for Skinner's reply.

he had let it to Mrs G.—or that Mr Spottiswood's unwillingness to go in the Steam boat with a Hooping-Cough Family would have hindered him from taking the House, we are now in.—But poor Mrs G. was not in spirits to press the matter.—God bless you!— You will hear from me in a day or two.—

Your ever affectionate

S. T. Coleridge—

1418. *To James Gillman*

Address: James Gillman, Esqre | Grove | Highgate | London
MS. Cornell University Lib. Pub. with omis. Letters, *ii. 729.*
Postmark: 3 November 1824. *Stamped*: Ramsgate.

2 Novr 1824
Ramsgate.

My dear Friend

That so much longer an interval has passed between this and my last letter, you will not, I am sure, attribute to any correspondent interval of oblivion. I do not indeed think, that any two hours of any one day, taken at 16, have elapsed, in which You, past or future, or myself in connection with you, were not for a longer or shorter space my uppermost thought. But the two days following James's safe arrival by the Coach I was so depressively unwell, so unremittingly restless from bowel-ache and tenesmus, and so exhausted by a tearing cough and thick blue expectoration from some thing irritating my stomach (an acid of some sort) and by two of those bad nights, that make me moan out, O for a Sleep for Sleep itself to rest in—that I was quite disqualified for writing—. And since then, I have been waiting for the Murrays to take a parcel with them, who were to have gone on Monday morning—. But again not hearing from them, & remembering your injunction not to mind postage, I have resolved that no more time shall pass— and should have written to day, even tho' Mrs Gillman had not been dreaming about you last night, and about some letter &c.— Upon my seriousness, I do declare that I cannot make out certain dream-devils or damned Souls that play pranks with me, whenever by the operation of a cathartic Pill or from the want of one, a ci devant Dinner in it's feculent metempsychosis is struggling in the mid fold of the lower intestines. I cannot comprehend, how any thoughts, the offspring or product of my own Reflection, Conscience, or Fancy could be translated into such images, and Agents and actions—and am half tempted (n.b. between sleeping and waking) to regard with some favor Swedenburgh's assertion, that certain foul Spirits of the lowest order are attracted by the precious

(391)

Ex-viands, whose conversations the Soul half-appropriates to itself, and which they contrive to whisper into the Sensorium. The Honorable Emanuel has repeatedly caught them in the fact, in that part of the Spiritual World corresponding to the Guts in the World of Bodies, and driven them away.[1]—I do not pass this Gospel; but upon my honor, it is no bad Apocrypha. I am at present in my best sort and state of health; bathed yesterday, and again this morning in spite of the rain and in so deep a Bath, that having thrown myself forward from the first step of the machine Ladder & only taken two strokes after my re-emersion, I had at least ten strokes to take before I got into my depth again—so that it is no false alarm when those who cannot swim are warned that a person may be drowned a very few yards from the machine.—I returned to *fetch out* our Ladies to see the huge lengthy Columbus, with the two Steam Vessels, before & behind—the former to tow, and the latter —to God knows what. By aid of a good glass we saw it '*quite stink*', as the poor Woman said—the people on board &c. It is 310 feet long, and 50 wide—& looks exactly like a *Brobdignag Punt*. The spots ⟨ · · · · ⟩ pourtray it's four Masts.—And on our return we had (from Mrs Jones) the Morning Herald with Fauntleroy's Trial[2]— which (if he be not a treble-damned Liar) completely bears out my assertion, that nothing short of a miracle could acquit the Partners of *virtual* accompliceship—this on my old principle, that the Absence of what ought to have been present is all but equivalent to the Presence of what ought to have been absent. Qui non prohibet quod prohibere potest et debet, *facit*.—Glad I am to tell you, that notwithstanding the weather being so very much against all walking & exercise, damp, mizzly, comfortless, Mrs Gillman is manifestly improved in looks and in strength. She *begins* to look *plumper* in Neck and Cheeks—. Henry too looks & on the whole goes on, remarkably well.—Dear James was very poorly when he arrived, with lax and disordered bowels; which he attributes with good reason to his long fasting on the Doctor's Day & then taking a bason of Pea Soup—. He is now pretty well—& with Lieutenant Hill, who has married a very nice young woman & is stationed at Pegwell Bay, & other agrémen[t]s, he enjoys himself exceedingly.— Miss Harding is very much out of health, with some tumours in the Abdomen—. Mrs G. asked my advice about going—& I advised her by all means to accompany the Boys & Miss Bradley, as [s]he had

---

[1] For other comments on Swedenborg's *De Coelo . . . et Inferno* see Letters 1242 and 1550.

[2] Henry Fauntleroy (1785–1824), banker, was found guilty of forgery on 2 Nov. 1824 and was executed on the 30th. Coleridge introduces an account of 'the late Mr. Fauntleroy' in *Aids to Reflection*, 1825, pp. 324–5 (signature Y).

prevented Jane from coming to Ramsgate—& she b[eing k]nown
to be so near, her not going with James & Hen[ry] would, indeed
could not but be interpreted both by Jane and the Brandrams, as an
intentional Slight—which, I was assured, in her state of Health &
Spirits you would not wish Mrs G. to hazard. Accordingly she went,
& returned next day by one o'clock.—Jane, it seems, had exerted
herself with the Styans, &c; and from their information confirms
the existence of a long-planned *secret* intrigue, & conspiracy, to take
the first opportunity of humbling Mr Sutton—If you had been an
Angel, they would have sacrificed you to it. They did not *see* you—
you were a mere & perfect transparency between them & Sutton,
the Bull's Eye of their Target.—

Sir Alexander Johnston has payed me great attention—There
is a Lady Johnston, not unlike Miss Sara Hutchinson in face and
mouth, only that she is a taller . . .[1] of high rank & title. Sir A. himself is a fine gentlemanly man, young-looking for his age, & with
exception of one not easily describable motion of his head that
makes him look as if he had been accustomed to have a *pen* behind
his ear, a sort of *'Torney's Clerk*-look, he might remind you of J.
Hookham Frere. He is a sensible well-informed man—*specious* in
no bad sense of the word—but (I guess) not much depth. In all
probability, you will see him. We have talked a good deal together
about you & me, & me & you in consequence of *occasion* given.—
Sir A. is one of the Leading men in *our* Royal Society of Literature
—& beyond doubt, a man of *influence* in town.—I am apt to forget
superfluities; but a Voice from above asks—if I have said, that we
begin to be anxious to hear from you—. But probably before you
can sit down to answer this, you will have received another & I
flatter myself, more amusing, at least pleasure-giving, Scripture
from me. (N.B. Coleridge's Scriptures—a new title?) . . .

1419. *To James Gillman*

Address: James Gillman, Esqre | Highgate | London
MS. Mr. W. Hugh Peal. Pub. with omis. Coleridge at Highgate, *by Lucy E.
Watson, 1925, p. 104.*
Postmark: 13 November 1824. *Stamped*: Ramsgate.

Thursday [11 November 1824]
29. Wellington Crescent

My dear Friend

As Sir Alexander Johnston who leaves Ramsgate on Saturday
Morning, will take a pacquet for me, I should have delayed this

---

[1] Two or three lines of MS. cut off at this point, thus destroying the conclusion and signature on the verso of the page.

letter but that Mrs Gillman begins to be anxious at the no-knocks or barren knocks of the Post man, and lest you should wonder at not hearing from us.—The best thing, however, that I have to communicate—& what better could I have ? is the manifest and the more sure, I trust, because slow progression in Mrs Gillman's Health. I am convinced that if circumstances rendered it feasible, if any change of circumstances should hereafter enable you to arrange it so as that she could stay long enough for the Basin to be once refilled, she would begin on a new lease of Life. For the first month or 5 weeks it was not easy to distinguish between the temporary and superficial effects of change of air, and Sea-bathing, and a true addition to her strength—Nay, I was at times fearful, that the less desirable interpretation was the more probable one—These doubts are now fully removed. She can sit up much longer—indeed, between rising and bed time she does not need above an hour's resting on the Sopha, and even during this time that weight on her eye-lids, impatience of Light, and sleepiness from debility are greatly diminished—and her own feelings correspond to the improvement in her looks. The progress is indeed barley-corn by barley-corn, but it is steady.—As to Miss Bradley, she is almost in robust health. Eliza has a little sore-throat—a slight inflammation in the Glands, I believe. I have advised her to discontinue Bathing, to which indeed in her case I was never friendly—thinking it superfluous, at the best. James looks well—and is in good spirits. I have not felt myself justified in returning an affirmative to his Mother's question —whether it would be advisable to prolong his stay here after the beginning of next week. For I dare not disguise from myself, that without the immediate Stimulus of his School Duties he cannot bring himself to sit down to any thing—and the habit even of innocent dissipation is not innocuous.—Henry goes on well—he complain[ed] of his head this morning, & was evidently unwell—but a dose of salts appears to have set him right again. I flatter myself, he will return so thoroughly grounded in his Greek-grammar, and in regular parsing, as that it will require culpable neglect on the part of his instructor to hazard his losing it again. I have found much less difficulty in making him understand the true meaning and intent of the Tenses and their two-fold relation to the Act and to the Time of the Act, than I had or indeed could have anticipated.

For myself, all I can say is that I have with advantage omitted Bathing for some days. Sir Thomas Grey had twice advised me so to do—he regarded the refreshment and tone that followed Bathing as delusive, and that it was more than counterbalanced by the tendency to increased action in the chest and bronchia or what he called, a state of passive inflammation—meaning I suppose, nascent.

Certainly, I have not expectorated nearly so much since I have contented myself with the Air-bath of the Cliff, Sands, and Pier.—

I met the Trotters, (Mrs Coutts Trotter & Daughter) Antrobus, Des Voeuxes, Mrs Macginnis at Sir A. Johnston's last night—a musical & musico-poetical Party. It is some part of my time to answer Sir A. Johnston's notes & letters to me—of which I receive one a day on an average—I will send you a specimen by James. One compliment he payed me, and with manifest emotion which I really felt—'Sir, I have never in the course of my life received so much and so valuable information from any man as from you. It is not this however that I shall most remember you by; but that every time, I have left you, I have felt myself a better man.' I record this to you at Mrs Gillman's especial request.—

We have shifted to the Corner House of the Colonnade, No. 29—that end of Wellington Crescent, next to Albion Place.—When the Wind is South, or South West, and strong, it requires a strong man to shut the Door again when opened, & the House is taken by storm—likewise, the chimneys smoke *on* occasions—. Nathless, it is roomier, pleasanter, & above all, better bedded. Mrs G. has it for a guinea a week—and to the sorrow of my ears it has a pianoforte in it, which James takes great delight in strumming—not to speak of the after-dinner dancing, to which the Currant wine in the glass & bottle dances in sympathy, in the room below—where I am sitting.—But they are happy, God bless them!—

I have had a laugh at Mrs Gillman, on account of a Cask of strong-Beer from DOVER which she took in & paid the Carriage for, *because* it was directed to, Mrs *Gilbart*, Waterloo Plains—(no *number* mentioned) and Mrs Gilbart was so like Mrs GILLMAN—and Mrs Gillman *had* lived at No 1. Waterloo Plains—And here the Barrel remains—& perhaps may travel to Highgate, as a Godsend: tho' I have written to the Man at Dover.

Here comes one of Sir Alexander's Orientalists, i.e. Footman with an ALBUM and a petitionary Note from the young Ladies to honor it with a few lines in my own hand-writing, as a remembrance &c &c. Now this is one of the Grievances under the Sun which King Solomon did not foresee—If the first syllable (videlicet the sum total of these precious MSS) were applied to the last, it would be an approach to a Christian Purpose—since Cleanliness is next to Godliness— . . .[1]

---

[1] A third of page 3 of the MS. cut off.

1420. *To James Gillman*

Address: James Gillman, Esqre | Grove | Highgate | near | London
MS. Pierpont Morgan Lib. Pub. with omis. Coleridge at Highgate, *by Lucy E.*
Watson, 1925, p. 106.
Postmark: 24 November 1824. *Stamped*: Ramsgate.

23 Novr 1824
Wellington Crescent
Ramsgate

My dearest Friend

I could not procure a frank on Sunday, Sir Charles Des Voeux
and Family being out; and Mr Macginnis[1] (M.P.) I believe, with
them. Not that this would have prevented my writing, had I had
any thing to communicate, beyond meteorological Grumps and
Grumblings. The Weather has indeed been unusually perverse, now
moody and now passionate, for the last fortnight—but I console
myself with the reflection, that tho' *positively* bad, it is *comparatively* good, not only from the absence of mud, dirt, and withered
leaves, but from the new lengthy Colonnade, and the life and stir
in the harbour. The gales have been tremendous—at this moment
the Waves at the mouth of the Pier look like a surf-cliff, and it is
fearful to watch the Skiffs, how they are tossed and twisted & what
hair-breadth escapes several of them have from being dashed
against the pier-head. At day-break this morning a West Indian
was descried that had struck on Goodwin Sands—and long before
this time must have gone to pieces. Had she been made of Iron, she
could not have stood out. The Breakers were distinctly visible from
our window; and with a glass had the appearance of a very high
& bold Coast. No Boat could possibly approach to her: and if the
Crew are saved, it will be little short of a miracle.—I shall speak
well of the Ramsgate Masons—for last week to cure the intolerable
Smoking, in parlour, kitchen and drawing-room, Mr Miller had the
chimnies raised two feet and a half—. The Night but one after, it
blew great guns the whole night—and last night up to the present
moment the South West Wind has let Bedlam loose on the air.
To move only the length from the second pillar from our house
[and] back again required the utmost effort of my strength. A
torrent of water would scarcely have pressed with a more *compact*
force.—The inner harbour is almost a solid mass of shipping—and
Captn Martin is hoarse, nay, his very speaking Trumpet has got a
sore-throat, in his efforts to keep the French and Dutch Skiffs &c
from running foul against the Pier & each other—. For the moment
there is any danger, or aught to be done instantly, the french

[1] R. Magennis.

fellows stand and look at each other, like Petrifactions of the last gesticulation, they happened to have been making. Every time, I go to the window—about once every ten minutes—I cannot help vexing myself that you are not here—You would enjoy the scene so keenly, and I by the *rebound.*—Thank God! we are all well, i.e. each in his or her own line & measure: and Mrs G. continues to gather strength, tho' the impossibility of taking exercise in the open Air or of *remaining* out of doors is unfavorable to all our *complexions.* She has not, however, fallen back at all: only she distresses herself about not hearing from you—the more so, that we do not know, how your spirits are—or what to write, except about ourselves.—

I shall come back, a free man: as far as books and publishers are concerned—and please God, I will starve, rather than send a sheet to the press or make any promise of so doing, till the whole Work, thoroughly revised and corrected, is sent along with it.—

The Joneses are more than civil, they are really friendly—and they are all very fond of James—whose picture Mr Clover has taken, and I think it a *likeness* & that he has given one of James's best expressions of countenance & yet a characteristic one.—The only fault I have to find with Mr Jones, and which is not peculiar to *him*, is the importunately repeated invitations to dinner parties.—There was a very pleasant Music-party there yester-evening: and I could not get off the dining with him to day to meet Sir Thomas & Lady Grey, but by promising to come early in the evening. Sir Charles Des Voeux & Family are very civil likewise—& [he] sends us the Courier every day, the precious John Bull weekly, & whatever else of this kind he receives. He told me, he hoped, he had made more than an *acquaintance* in me—& both he & Lady D. V. made me promise to visit them in Harley Street. Sir Charles has a Sister married to one of Earl Grey's Brothers. Lady Johnstone (Sir Charles informs me) is of the Argyle Family, the Daughter of Lord Frederic Campbel[l].[1] I thought, there was something high and haughty in her mien and manner—to me, however, she became *gracious*; and toward the last, *very* gracious.

Miss Trotter (Sir Coutts Trotter's Daughter), who is here with the Antrobuses, has been just *driven in* by the storm-wind, with a Miss Huxley (a very pretty Rose and Lily Doll)—i.e. *to* our door & by my active gallantry harboured in our drawing-room—[She] informs us from Sir Charles Des Voeux that the Crew of the West Indian have been saved by the matchless courage & skill of the Deal Men—. While we were standing at the Drawing-Room Window, 10 minutes ago, a Skiff w[as] dashed against the back of the

---

[1] Lady Johnston was the daughter of Lord William Campbell, son of the fourth Duke of Argyll.

Pier, her Rudder unseated and disabled—& the poor skiff will, I
fear, never reach Broad stairs—Ha! a storm of Rain! & all the
folks running up the East Cliff & by the Sea Wall—I suppose, it is
driven ashore—this *moment* another Ship dashed against the Pier.—
½ One P.M.—I must *push off*, & hear the Pier News—& perhaps,
I may get a frank at the same time.—

Alas! Sir Charles's information was incorrect. The Crew of the
West India man (500 Ton) perished.—The Vessel has run ashore a
little below Lord Keith's Gothic Castle—. Of the two Vessels that
were dashed against the Pier-head & whirled round, the men have
been saved by the Cranes—but the vessels hopeless. Just as I went
out, I met Sir Charles, & we saw the Vessel—we both thought it
safe—when the jib sail gave way or was let loose & swung from the
light-house side of the Mouth, the Vessel was whirled to the other
side just like a Hat snatched off from one's head by an eddy-gust—.
Within 3 minutes came another and much larger Vessel—O how it
was tossed & tormented, dipping, reeling, mounting, diving—
seemingly nearer to the Pier than the former—one aweful *second*—
and the shout—*It is safe!*—O that you were here!—Mr Macginnis
unluckily left Ramsgate this morning, but I will send the letter,
nevertheless.

Mrs G. bids me say—that we are to go on Tuesday, 30 Novr by
the Telegraph, which reaches the Saracen's Head, Snow Hill (or
Skinner St) about 5 o'clock in the evening—& wishes that you
would send *Hales' Stage*, or a Stage from Hales's, to meet us there
& take us home.—

A *Pelt* of Rain, ½ past 2; a slight abatement, I think, in the Storm.
I do like that Sir Charles hugely. He is so like Hartley. Nothing can
be plainer & less *ornate* than his manners; and yet see him by the
side of Mr Antrobus—you could not avoid supposing the latter to
be his *Butler*. God bless you! do write a Line or two to Mrs G.—

S. T. Coleridge—

40 m. after 3. I have this moment returned from the Pier—
crash on crash! the accursed narrowness of that Harbour mouth—
one small vessel crashing bow-sprit, and then flung out midway the
mouth—A large ship at the same moment just missed the harbour.
—I had not nerve to stay—She instantly grounded with her bow-
sprit towards the Pier—amid the roar & fury of the Billows—I got
home with a deadly *sickness* at my stomach. I see them now, however, getting the poor sailors from the bow-sprit, with the crane-
basket—. All with life will be saved, I trust; but the Ship will be
in pieces on the waves.—God grant! that the storm may abate before the *Dark* comes: for it will be double-darkness from the thickness of the air.—

1421. *To James Gillman*

Address: James Gillman, Esqre | Grove | Highgate | Middlesex
MS. Cornell University Lib. Pub. with omis. Coleridge at Highgate, *by Lucy E. Watson, 1925, p. 109.*
Postmark: 29 November 1824. *Stamped*: Ramsgate.

[26 November 1824]
My dearest Friend

Often, even to a common-place frequency, have the World with-out and the World within been compared to the deceitful Sea—now a Host of Bedlamite Furies, billow-mounted, the Marauders of Death and Ruin!—and now a group of wooing Mermaids, 'Come unto these Yellow Sands; And here join hands!'[1] Tempè! Tempèr! Tempèst! Before my last Scrawl had reached you, the Superlative had sunk into the Comparative, and for about sixteen hours seemed to fret and fume that it could not keep up it's rage and rampancy—it was a tired Scold's *Temper.* Saevities nolenter desaeviens. To day it is a watry Elysium! a vale of Tempè reflected in a blue Mirror!—And here begins the *not*-common-place part of my Simile. Alas! that stately Wreck looks ten times more forlorn, and melancholy—*strikes* and seems to *feel*, a sadder, sicker dejec-tion, as it circumscribes the Sunshine with it's scarcely heaving Shadow, than when the waves were breaking thro' it and over it and the poor Mariners clinging to, and hiding their faces on, the Bow-sprit feared to catch at the Ropes that were thrown to them, lest the Blast should tear them off and fling them on the billows.—And such is the Mood, that will at times and for a while take pos-session of us, in the disconsolate Silence that follows any malicious freak of fortune. We cannot help fancying that we see the same hand, that had beat us down, at a distance, with protended finger pointing at us.—But here it is, my dear Friend! that Philosophy will tap at our door, to ask how we do—leaves her card, and will call again. And if we can bring ourselves to give orders that we are at home, at the next call; here, & in this mood, it is, that she can do us 'yeoman's service'. By winning us to give *utterance*, an *outer* being, or at least an outward *position*, to our thoughts, fears and fancies, she makes them *objects seen*, and no longer mere Vizards and Metamorphoses of the *Subject* see*ing*—. However we may po! and psha! against it, yet when they are once out of the Mist of *Subjectivity* (like the old and young Brobdingnaggers with the Brobdingnag Beasts that emerging at once from the strait-ruled Cloud on the upper third of Skiddaw disappeared into a Shepherd

---

[1] *The Tempest*, I. ii. 376-7.

(399)

& Shepherd lad with Dog and Sheep) we cannot but use our comparing faculty—We can't help seeing, that what we had taken for causes were for the greater part the *effects* in ourselves: not the tiny black speck of a *thorn*, which we find between the Tweezers, but the swelling &c of the irritated nerve. From the hour of the arrival of your last, I have felt impatient of the stay here: and had not our departure been definitely arranged, the Telegraph secured &c, your letter would not only have settled but accelerated it. My dear Gillman! I stand pledged to you, as my Brother, as *the* Friend, to whom firm and devoted attachment is a *duty*, by an act of my own Will, my reason consenting—and no longer a mere impulse of the heart. Not a day has passed, during which I have been half an hour alone with Mrs Gillman, in which you and the incidents after we left you have not been passed on to, as to a subject often perceived by each to be occupying the other's thoughts when it could not be talked of—and the sole and whole reason of my not carrying it on, instead of writing of Ramsgate matters, was the fear of re-awakening distressful trains of feeling which I was not present to partake of or dissipate. Many and many times it has been a question put— Should I, do you think, or should I not, write what I have been saying? or let the subject drop till I return?—Mrs G. had written a long letter to you, but could not satisfy herself with it—When she read it over, sometimes she feared that what she had written was too much for your present state of mind—& more often, the words did not seem to convey what they were meant to do, or give a true reflection of her own state of feeling—so that she at last burnt it, under the fear that her letter might interfere with any comfort, that mine might give. I have only to add, that the Postman being ill, from some blunder of the novice, his Substitute, your letter was not delivered till the day after.—Indeed what can I, so shortly I trust to be once more by the same fire-side with you, say more to the purpose than to assure you of the confidence, with which I hope and look forward to the being a greater comfort and support to you than I have ever been hitherto—& that the time is coming, when we shall pursue the voyage of Life in company, and abreast, with a fair wind and bellying sails?—GOD BLESS YOU!—and enable me to make you feel as well as confess, that the impressions, you make on me, are a far truer & more faithful Looking-glass than your own Imagination, subject as it is to condense the occasional vapors of your constitutional Idiosyncracy into moist dimness on it's surface—and especially when it has been be*craped* by some unlucky accident.—I have faith that God never meant you or me to want the necessary comforts of our mortal life, while our own efforts are not wanting—such efforts, I mean, as we have it in our power to

exert. And what else is necessary for our happiness while we continue to love and comfort each other? There is no fear that your
Boys will not be provided for, if they are not grossly suicidal of
their own well-being: and what more can the richest Father promise himself? The Boys too, taking the whole of their characters,
are better and of fairer hope than most of those, I meet with, and
if inferior to *him* or *him* in *this* or *that*, the points in which they are
equal or superior, are the most important—good principles and
honorable sentiments and strong domestic attachments.—

I forget whether I told you that the name of the Wreck is
Cornelia from Batavia to Amsterdam, laden with Coffee & Spices;
and ensured at Lloyd's & elsewhere up to 80,000£, valued 100,000£.
She takes 18 feet water; and the water over the sand-bank across
the mouth of the Harbour was not at that period of the tide more
than 14. The Consequence was, that she struck, unshipped her
rudder, the Sailors became bewildered, & the Ship (the head being
in comparatively still water; and the body and stern in the strong
tide and current that runs diagonally toward the back of the Pier)
was whirled round & grounded—. All the Masts are now gone—and
I suppose that by this time to morrow not a plank will remain. The
Bow-sprit that lay across the Pier wall has driven in ten of those
huge granite Blocks and made a tremendous Gap in the Wall—
Heaps of Coffee are lying about, swoln as large as Beans by the
salt water—and (I suppose) good for nothing. The old adage
Audi alteram partem was most amusingly exemplified to me this
morning by Mr Philpot, (the Bathing-machinist) who in a strain of
eloquence & with an animation of Tone & Gesture which I never
could have supposed him capable of, set forth to me the delights &
great advantages of a *good Wreck*—which he *euphoniously* entitled
'*a diffusion* of Property'—and again—'a providential *multiplication*
of Properties' (meaning, I suppose, of Proprietors or Appropriators)
—'For, Sir! there is a Providence in all these things—It is a loss to
the Underwriters, I don't deny that—but it is a *great thing* for the
Poor Folks and for our town of Ramsgate'—. ON MY HONOR, these
were *his very* words: I could not mistake—for he repeated 'DIFFU-
SION', & '*multiplication*' half a dozen times as if proud of their
fineness. 'What is dispersed, Sir! isn't always *lost*, you know!'—
and then Mr Philpot proceeded to illustrate & exemplify his theory
in a detail of small & great facts and findings, his own & his
neighbours—that will long, I trust, people my memory for fire-
side uses. It particularly amused me to observe the very comprehensive List of Articles, he deemed too trifling to be trusted to the
Salvage remuneration—Telescopes, Spies-glass, Barrels of Brandy
and Wine—when there was no sharp ones at the Preventive Bar-

rack on the Beach, &c—. I am not ashamed to say, that it had the
effect on my mind of an excellent Farce after a deep Tragedy—the
one entitled, The Ship-wreck, a Tragedy—the other, the Wreckers,
an *Entertainment*.

Again, God bless you & grant us a happy meeting!—Mr Jones*
thinks, that the Telegraph will be at the Saracen's Head about† six
o'clock.

S. T. Coleridge

Mr Pattison at the Telegraph office tells us, that if the roads are
tolerable, the Telegraph will be at the Bricklayers' Arms, a little
after 3: and that the Highgate Coach ought to be at the Saracen's
Head, at half past 4, on Tuesday Aftern. or $\frac{1}{4}$ before 5.

P.S. Friday Night.—This afternoon we had an influx of Callers,
and these too of the genus, Remora, or Sucking Fish. Amongst
them, Mrs Austin, the Ramsgate Banker's wife, who called on me
in order to be introduced to Mrs G. & in the press of Talk, it escaped
me that there was no post on Saturday—& it was 5 o'clock, before
we were alone—& I was faint—& after dinner unfit to finish the
letter, had there been time.

1422. *To Unknown Correspondent*

Pub. The Gillmans of Highgate, *by A. W. Gillman, 1895, p. 20 B.*

[December?] 1824.[1]

What seems to me wanting in our fashionable vocal music is
Eloquence. As oratory is Passion in the service of Reason, so should
vocal music be Passion connective in the service of Passion—
Pr[a]ecipitandus est liber spiritus.[2] If there were as much Spirit and
Liberty, as Feeling and Sweetness in her singing, Mrs. Gillman would
excel to my judgment all the singers I have ever heard. Oratory—
Passion in the service of Reasoning fusing the Links of connection,
so as to soften away the Angles, and fill up the interspaces without
destroying the distinctness. Vocal Music—Connection in the service
of Passion, giving it at once order and Progression.

S. T. C.

* *mistakenly* [Note by S. T. C.]
† But Mr Pattison says, $\frac{1}{2}$ past 4, at the latest: if the Roads are tolerable.
[Note by S. T. C.]
[1] A. W. Gillman dates this fragment 1824, says it is an extract from one of
Coleridge's letters, but gives no clue concerning the correspondent.
[2] Petronius Arbiter, *Satyricon*, 118. See *Biog. Lit.* ii. 11.

1423. *To H. F. Cary*

Pub. Letters, *ii. 731.*

Highgate, Monday, December 14 [13], 1824.

My dear Friend,—The gentleman, Mr. Gabriel Rossetti,[1] whose letter to you I enclose, is a friend of my friend, Mr. J. H. Frere, with whom he lived in habits of intimacy at Malta and Naples. He seems to me what from Mr. Frere's high opinion of him I should have confidently anticipated, a gentleman, a scholar, and a man of talents. The nature of his request you will learn from the letter, namely, a perusal of his Manuscript on the spirit of Dante and the mechanism and interpretation of the 'Divina Commedia',[2] of which he believes himself to have the filum Ariadneum in his hand, and a frank opinion of the merits of his labours. My dear friend! I know by experience *what* is asked in this twofold request, and that the weight increases in proportion to the kindness and sensibility and the shrinking from the infliction of pain of the person on whom it is enjoined. The name of Mr. John Hookham Frere would alone have sufficed to make *me* undertake this office, had the request been directed to myself. It would have been my duty. But I would not, knowing your temper and habits and avocations, have sought to engage you, or even have put you to the discomfort of excusing yourself had I not been strongly impressed by Mr. Rossetti's manners and conversation with the belief that the interests of literature are concerned, and that Mr. Rossetti has a claim on all the services which the sons of the Muses, and more particularly the cultivators of ancient Italian Literature, and most particularly Dante's 'English Duplicate and Re-incarnation' can render him. If your health and other duties allow your accession to this request (for the recommendation of the work to the booksellers is quite a secondary consideration, of minor importance in Mr. Rossetti's estimation, and I have, besides, explained to him how very limited *our* influence is), you will be so good as to let me hear from you, and where and when Mr. Rossetti might wait on you. He will be happy to attend you at Chiswick. He *understands* English, and, he speaking

[1] Gabriele Rossetti (1783–1854), father of Christina and Dante Gabriel Rossetti, had been forced to flee from Naples for his share in the insurrectionary movements. After a brief residence in Malta, he came to England in 1824. He was appointed professor of Italian in King's College, London, in 1831. He is best remembered as a commentator on Dante.

[2] *La Divina Commedia . . . con comento analitico di Gabriele Rossetti,* 2 vols., 1826–7. Later Rossetti presented Coleridge with a copy of his *Sullo Spirito Antipapale che produsse la riforma,* 1832. E. H. Coleridge notes that Rossetti also gave Coleridge 'some of his verses in MS.' *Letters,* ii. 731 n.

Italian and I our own language, we had no difficulty in keeping up an animated conversation.

Make mine and all our cordial remembrances to Mrs. Cary, and believe me, dear friend, with perfect esteem and most affectionate regard, yours,

S. T. Coleridge.

P.S. Both Mrs. G. and myself have returned much benefited by our sea-sojourn. Mr. Rossetti has, I find, an additional merit in good men's thoughts. He is a poet who has been driven into exile for the high morale of his writings. For even general sentiments breathing the spirit of nobler times are treasons in the present Neapolitan and Holy Alliance Codes! Wretches!! I dare even *pray* against them, even with Davidian bitterness. Do not forget to let me have an answer to this, if possible, by next day's post.

1424. *To Samuel Mence*

Address: Revd. S. Mence
MS. Bristol Central Lib. Pub. E. L. G. ii. 333.

Saturday [8 January 1825][1]
My dear Sir

Miss Bradley, whom you met yesterday, is the Daughter of a very dear Friend of Mr and Mrs Gillman's, and in fact little less than a Father in the love and veneration of the Latter. Of course to Miss B. as the sole Relic of her departed Friend, she feels the duties of a Sister. When in addition to this I say, that Miss B. is liable by any unsettling forces, bodily or circumstantial, to get into 'a *low* way', commencing with extreme nervousness & disposition to *eddy* round and round any past event or act that had distressed or perplexed her, and (if not cut short) passing into temporary Melancholia, I have told you all.—

Now at present there are symptoms that give us reason to apprehend a coming-on of this Complaint—and for a week past her thoughts have been running on some supposed omission or other, of which she fears to have been guilty, in her preparation for the last Sacrament, she received. My dear Sir! I cannot help thinking, that Jer. Taylor and other great & good men who wrote the practical treatises, 'Way to the Altar' &c &c—commonly in the hands of Church-members, were not sufficiently on their guard against the effects, many passages in these books, (not to say the

[1] This letter was written on Saturday, 8 Jan., since by the 12th Coleridge had received a reply from Mence.

Spirit of some of them) are calculated to produce on nervous females under the mental irritation of Debility.—However, Miss B. has been importuning Mrs Gillman to consent to her consulting *you*. She conceives that she ought not to suffer her mind to be quieted by any thing, I might say as I am not a Minister &c. But from you it possibly might be of medicinal effect to be told, what a sad perversion of the Eucharist it is to turn a means of grace, and comfort, an act of confidence in the promises and all-sufficient Death of the Redeemer into a thorn-brake of Scruples and a Snare for the Conscience—that if there was any thing to be done or to be done otherwise, her duty is to do it for the future—and that brooding on the past, and fretting and perplexing herself about what cannot be recalled, is the way to consume the very strength of mind and purpose, requisite for the due performance of what she has to do—shews a great ignorance of the true meaning of Christian Repentance, and argues a distrust in the Saviour's assurances—

I take the liberty of throwing out these hints, from the apprehension that the triflingness or mistaken nature of the Lady's Scruples might (judging unfairly, perhaps, of you by what happened to myself) *put you out*.—As far as there is any thing more than what may be best attributed to the state of bodily health in these Scruples and Hauntings, I have most often found, that there is an *irresolution* at the bottom, a clinging at the *core* of the Heart to a somewhat, which they can neither resolve to eject or retain— and that such persons are sure to do the thing which, when done, they then set about repenting OF. Rarely, I fear, do they repent *from* it.—

With great regard & respect, | my dear Sir | Your's truly
S. T. Coleridge

1425. *To Samuel Mence*

Address: Revd. S. Mence
MS. Bristol Central Lib. Pub. E. L. G. ii. 334.

12 Jany. 1825.

My dear Sir

Your expectations and mine stand at the same low degree above Zero on the Elpidometer. Now and then, however, there occurs a temporary re-agency of Thought on Organic Action, even in cases that most evidently originate in the disorder of the latter. Still I would not have imposed a task of so little hope, had I not known that even to have administered an Anodyne to a worthy and simple-hearted tho' weak Sister in the Faith, or even the indirect palliative of preventing the broodings and hauntings which the refusal would super-induce on her existing melancholies, will be considered by you as a warrant for the time spent. In cases like these the *Doctor* and the Parson must consent to *prescribe* each other—for alas! after a few aperients, and a little dieting the former has generally arrived at his ne plus ultra.

I am aware of few subjects more calculated to awake a deep [and] at once practical and speculative interest in a philosophic mind than the analogies between organic (I might say, organific) Life and Will. The Facts both of Physiology and Pathology lead to one and the same conclusion—viz. that in some way or other the Will is the obscure *Radical* of the Vital Power.—My dear Sir! am I under the inebriation of Self-conceit? I trust, not.—Yet there are not half a dozen men in the world of my acquaintance, to whom I should dare utter the sentiment, which I now confess to *you*—that there are *Libraries* of Works from infra-duodecimos to Ultra-folios on the two great Moments of the Christian Faith, ORIGINAL Sin (i.e. Sin, as the *Source* of sinful actions) and Redemption; that the *Ground*, and this the *Superstructure*, of Christianity.[1]—And yet (it is my persuasion that) only not every thing is yet to be said! In the article of Redemption, Metaphors have been obtruded as the Reality: and in all the Mysteries subordinate to Redemption, Realities have been *exinanized* into Metaphors.[2] Luther indeed was a mighty Wrestler: and the very *Halt* on the Thigh[3] bears witness of the Manfulness of his Struggles. But Luther had no Elisha to succeed him.—

Believe me | with sincere respect | and regard, my dear Sir, | Your's truly

S. T. Coleridge

P.S. Mrs Gillman, I find, has arranged the time &c with you.—However, I am vain enough to fancy, that you would vote for my not throwing this Note into the fire.

1426. *To Charles Aders*

MS. *Cornell University Lib. Hitherto unpublished.*

Grove, Highgate
16 Jany. 1825

My dear Sir

So stiff-necked are we in looking over our shoulder at the bunch on our own back, that I was really half-sullen, half-angry at neither

---

[1] Cf. *Aids to Reflection*, 1825, p. 301.	[2] Ibid., p. 294.
[3] Genesis xxxii. 24–32.

hearing *of* you nor *from* you for so long a time, nor how or where Mrs Aders is, and how Miss [Kelly][1]—till I recollected, that you had exactly the same *cause* and perhaps better *reason*, to complain of *me.*—But from the evening of our return from Ramsgate, I have been so busy, so unwell and so depressed that I have not payed a single visit to town: or I should certainly have called either at Euston Square or at Compting House, were it only to learn the particulars of your dear Wife's state of Health.

I write now, however, to ask a question, which if I had reflected but for half a moment, and had called to mind, as I ought to have done, the press and manifoldness of your business, and how completely such a commission was out of *your* way, I should not have had the occasion to ask.—I allude to two German Works, DE WETTE's Lehr-buch der historischen kritischen Einleitung in das alte Testament, Berlin, 1823, and J. L. HUG's Einleitung in die Schriften des Neuen Testament[s], Tübingen, 1821. Do not, I beseech you, my dear Sir! imagine, that I am reminding you of a Promise, or (as we say) *refreshing* your memory. It is neither my Wish nor my Object: and least of all my Feeling. My whole and sole motive for thus recalling it to you is that my friend, Mr Green, is shortly about to order a chest of Books from Germany: and if you have not sent for the Works above-named, I would avail myself of the opportunity. You will really give me pain, if you say a word or think a thought more about them, beyond the Yea or Nay.

But now I am in the way of it, there is one promise of your's that I will venture to claim—that is, the loan of the second Volume of Steffens' Caricaturen[2]—or rather of both, & I will speedily return both at the same time. And yet another promise I must entreat you to make, to your own mind at least—namely, that till I have ceased to deserve your regard, you will allow me to subscribe myself, my dear Sir! your & Mrs Aders's very sincere and affectionate FRIEND,

S. T. Coleridge.

Give my kind love to Miss [Kelly]: and tell her, that spite of absence and dreary Weather she buds and blossoms in the Greenhouse of my fairest Recollections. Mr Gillman is pretty well—and Mrs Gillman returned from our Sea-sojourn better enough to excite and warrant an anxious wish on my part, that circumstances would permit and enable her to remain at Ramsgate or Hastings in a prolonged enjoyment of the mild sea air, the restorative Sea-bath, and the still *more* restorative and *more* needful FAR NIENTE, i.e. des Nichtsthuns, for six or eight months.

[1] This name is inked out in the MS. both here and in the postscript.

[2] A copy of H. Steffens's *Caricaturen des Heiligsten*, 2 vols., 1819–21, containing Coleridge's annotations is in the British Museum.

1427. *To John Flaxman*[1]

Pub. Collection of Alfred Morrison, *1895, ii. 263.*

Grove, Highgate, 24 January, 1825.

Dear Sir,—

I will attempt no other apology for this intrusion or of that of which *this* is meant to apprize you, than by stating my motive and the occasion. I am preparing an Essay on the connection of Statuary and Sculpture with Religion, the Origin of Statuary as a Fine Art, that is, as a form or species of Poesy—(which I distinguish from Poetry, as the Genus from one of the Species). This origination or new birth is beyond controversy the result of the Grecian Mind. I then proceed to the re-action of Sculpture after its escape from the Caves and Temples of Egyptian and Indo-Egyptian hieroglyphical Idolatry into Greece on the religious conceptions and imaginations of Men and in what way it joined with Philosophy and the Mysteries in preparing the Graeco-Roman World for Christianity and that great article of the *Divine* HUMANITY and its mediative Offices. Lastly, on the true essence of the Ideal, and its intimate connection with the Symbolic.[2] Now, my dear Sir! I trust, you think too well of me to suspect that I am capable of Flattery. If I were sufficiently sunk in self-estimation to endure the thought of such a degradation of my own moral Being, I am not so callously vulgar as to offer such an affront to your Feelings. What therefore I can affirm with entire sincerity, I venture to communicate with perfect simplicity—namely, in all that respects ideal Beauty, and all the Intuitions, Expressions, Affections and States of Being, that belong or are akin to the Beautiful (& the Beautiful is always *elevated*—even in the face of a sleeping Infant—Alas! that almost one half of the world mistake the *pretty*, and almost the remaining half the *agreeable*, for the Beautiful!) I consider you as the *First*— not only of our contemporaries; but of all modern Sculptors. You must not wonder, therefore, if before I go on with my Essay, I should wish both to kindle and embody my Thoughts by the contemplation of such works as you may happen to have in your Laboratory; and at the same time to obtain from you or your dear Sister and Daughter[3] a list of your chief works, that are accessible in or near London—and you would greatly oblige me by mentioning

[1] John Flaxman (1755–1826), sculptor.

[2] Coleridge was gathering materials for his lecture of 18 May 1825 at the Royal Society of Literature. See Letters 1442 and 1463.

[3] Flaxman had no children. Mary Ann Flaxman (1768–1833), artist, his half-sister, and Maria Denman (born 1779), Mrs. Flaxman's half-sister, were members of the Flaxman household.

any two or three to which you would wish to have my attention especially directed.[1]

A kind and most respectable neighbour, Mr. Chance, is going to your end of the town to-morrow with Mrs. Chance and another lady in their carriage, and I have availed myself of their kind offer to take me with them. Mrs. Chance, from the sweetness of her manners and look, by the unfeigned gentleness and humility of her character, uninjured by opulence, reminds me (tho' but by a faint reflex) of that dear lady, the sweet, rich light from whose eyes I shall never more behold till I meet her in heaven.[2] Oh, dear sir! doubtless a sharper, more crushing pang than I felt at her loss, but not a deeper or more enduring grief than I felt and shall feel, can our friend himself or Mr. Hart, have suffered. But I dare not trust myself with this subject.

Should you not be at home, or should business call you out to-morrow from 12 to 2 or 3, will you intercede for me with Miss Flaxman, so that I may be permitted to introduce Mr. and Mrs. Chance to your Laboratorium. O, that I may find the Michael there![3]

Present my best and most cordial respects to the ladies. I have just heard a very good account of Mrs. Aders from Mr. Aders, who expects her return to Euston Square. I remain, dear and honoured Sir, with entire respect and affectionate regard, your's most truly.

[S. T. Coleridge.]

1428. *To Thomas Allsop*

Transcript Mrs. R. L. Grigg. Pub. E.L.G. ii. 263.

[Early February 1825][4]

My dear Friend

It was eleven o'clock this morning, when Mrs Gillman brought up your letter—and as soon as I had shaved and shifted, which from a distressful night and increased pain in a wrong place altho'

[1] The text of this paragraph (except the opening sentence) is drawn from an excerpt from the MS. recently printed in a bookseller's catalogue. This text is obviously closer to the original than that in the *Collection of Alfred Morrison.*

[2] A reference to Mrs. Tulk (Susannah Hart), who died in Oct. 1824. In 1810 Flaxman and Tulk had assisted in founding the London Society for publishing Swedenborg's works.

[3] Flaxman completed and exhibited his 'Michael and Satan' in 1821.

[4] This and the next letter, a 'note of introduction' to Davy, were written in early February and were delivered by messenger the same day. A second, 'more particular letter' to Davy has not come to light, but on 11 Feb. Davy wrote to Poole that he had heard from Coleridge. See John A. Paris, *The Life of Sir Humphry Davy*, 2 vols., 1831, ii. 285.

in recto I could not accomplish till 12, I walked out to con over the
letter best calculated to effect your wish—so that I was unfortunately out when your messenger arrived.—I now in- or rather *con-*
close a letter to Sir Humphrey Davy, so worded that if it should be
necessary to deliver it *to day*, it will, I hope, serve the purpose—but
yet I should be glad if your schemes allow of deferring it's presentation till the time mentioned in your first letter, in order that Sir H.
Davy may have received the more particular letter which I shall
write to him as soon as Riley is dispatched, to go by our afternoon
($\frac{1}{4}$ before 5) Post—by way of preparing him for the note of introduction—God bless you, my dearest Friend—I will yearn & even
pray for your success, especially if you will henceforward never
begin a letter to me with My dear *Sir*—for I am in very truth your
loving & I trust

beloved Friend

S. T. Coleridge

I have not the honor of any such acquaintance with Dr Woolaston,[1]
having only occasionally met him at dinner parties, as to be privi-
leged to write him introductive letters or any letters—but I will
try forthwith to think of some common friend of mine & the
Doctor's—You will inclose my letter to Davy in the coverture &
seal it.

1429. To Humphry Davy

MS. Mr. W. Hugh Peal. Pub. Nineteenth-Century Studies (*Cornell*), 60.

Grove, Highgate
[Early February 1825]

Dear Sir Humphry
    Will you permit an old Friend, who (as you are well aware) knew
six and twenty years ago in faith and foresight what all the civilized World now knows by the fact, to ground for the first time a
claim on you on the score of youthful intimacy and never intermitted honor and admiration? The Gentleman, who will present
this letter to you, is a very near and dear friend of mine, of whose
head, heart, and character I have the best possible reasons to think
with unqualified approbation—his Name, T. Allsop, of the House
of Harding, Allsop and Co. He delivers it, however, as the Organ
and Representative of a Company formed and forming for the
purpose of mining in Derbyshire. To the best of my knowlege and
judgement it's prospects are grounded on sound data, furnished by

---

[1] William Hyde Wollaston (1766–1828), physiologist, chemist, and physicist.

(410)

a long and intimate knowlege of the local facts. Of one thing I am assured—that the expectations of the Gentlemen concerned in it are wholly derived from their confidence in the ultimate success of the undertaking, and in no degree from the hope of getting rid of the Shares at a premium previous to it's commencement.—What the proposal or request, which Mr Allsop may have to submit or prefer to you, he will himself explain. My office and object are to solicit for him access to you and an attentive hearing.—I scarcely know a favor, that I could ask of you with greater earnestness, or should be more disposed to regard as a proof that you recollect not without kindness,

dear Sir Humphry | your sincere Admirer and | obliged Friend
S. T. Coleridge

1430. *To Thomas Allsop*

Address: T. Allsop, Esqre. | 2. Blandford Place | Pall Mall
MS. New York Public Lib. Pub. with omis. Letters, Conversations and Rec. *217.*
Allsop's text consists of excerpts taken not only from the present letter but also from Letters 1435 and 1436. The letter is printed under date of 20 March 1825.
Postmark: Highgate, 11 February 1825.

Thursday Night. [10 February 1825]
My dearest Allsop

I should have answered your last by return of Post, but for three causes—first, that I had Proofs to correct and a passage of great nicety to add, neither of which could be deferred without injustice to the Publishers and the breach of a definite promise on my part. Second, that I was almost incapacitated from thinking of and doing any thing as it ought to be done by poor Mrs G's restless and *inter-rogatory* anxieties, which in the first instance put the whole working Hive of my Thoughts in a Whirl and a Buz, and then, when I see her care-worn countenance & reflect on the state of her health (and it is difficult to say which of the two, ill-health or habitual anxiety, is more cause and more effect) a sharp fit of the Heart-ach follows. There is no medium. Either the unworthy notice-exciting *Un-noticing* and feverish Mock-indifference of a Quarrel: or to be fidget-watched and 'are you going on ?—what are you doing now ? is this for the Book ?' &c &c, precisely as if I were Henry at his Lesson. O heavens! how often do I think of Charles & Mary Lamb's Bodement after their first visit at the *Grove*, the purport of which, tho' not exactly the words, was—that they had never known a valued family change their old dwelling for a grander House and finer

Chattels without leaving the better part of themselves and their Happiness behind. But enough of this odious subject. I ought to be ashamed of myself for troubling you with it. You have enough frets and frictions of your own—and so I proceed to the third cause, which is that—(how far imputable to the mood of mind I was in, I cannot say) I did not understand your letter.—My very dear Friend! when a scheme already set on foot is confided to me, I think it mere wantonness to throw cold water on the hopes of a friend, when it is only by the spirit and activity that grow out of hope that the scheme can succeed, or be brought into a chance of succeeding. I know too by my own experience respecting THE FRIEND and more than one other Plan during my intimacy with Wordsworth, what mischief a *chill* of this kind is capable of effecting. In the present case likewise, I was too ignorant of the City-World, too bare of Data whereon to form an opinion, whether it was a promising or unpromising, an advisable or *dis*advisable thing for *You*. I could only raise hopes and fears on the common ground of a strong Wish. The next evening or next but one after your first distinct Mention of it I had to fight up against the latter, and expressed my apprehensions to our friend, Jameson, in the shape of questions: and finding that he thought it a thing of promise, and feasible, I took heart. Still however I was only competent to think of the Scheme on it's *abstract* merits—viz. 1 *Mine*-working—2 in Derbyshire—3 on the assurance of given facts & documents—4 by a joint-stock Company—5 in the present state and circumstance of the Kingdom. What may be truly stated and argued in favor of such a plan, as deserving the countenance of the Public and as likely to be profitable to the Share-holders? What are the Objections, that may or will be started? What the arguments that will probably be urged against it? In what way may the one be obviated, the other answered?—Of course, when with you I felt that I had the functions of an Advocate to perform; but when I threw off my Barrister Wig and Gown, still I thought and now continue to think that the arguments in favor of the Scheme greatly pre-ponderated, and that the Objections to it and the arguments against it were all answerable—and that the answers returned by us in the Prospectus were solid and satisfactory. I am still firm in the opinion, that the Reasons, that have been, & others that might be, urged in defence and in support of Joint-stock Companies, in respect both of Right and of Policy, under existing circumstances, are sufficient to dispel all the quirks, phantoms and law-superstitions of the Chancellor and Lord Chief Justice, as the scent of the Morning Breeze scatters Ghosts and Goblins.—I am no less firm in the conviction, that Companies are peculiarly desirable & requisite for *Mineral* Researches;

and *most & especially* so for Mining in *Derbyshire.*—And here I am
at the end of my Tether. Of the right mode of going about to form
a Company, and who are the right persons, as well as the persons
who can make the attempt *with safety to themselves*, &c; and
whether *you* are included in the latter; of all these momentous
points I am Ignorance itself.

At the present juncture, however, I cannot persuade myself that
any Article, however well written, *payed for to be put* in the Times,
which with most (I understand) of the other influencive Papers has
joined the *No Bubble!* cry, and would perhaps head the Article with
Advertisement, or something tantamount—I cannot, I say, persuade
myself that any Article sent by an Individual and so published
is likely to be of much service, tho' I think, that either a Paper or a
short Pamphlet written under the sanction of a Meeting of Directors
& other respectable Share-holders—or even the Reports of Speeches
made at a Public Meeting would be of essential service. In fact, I
see no other Step that suits the emergence, but to call on any two
or three Men of any *Name* that you or Mr O. happen to know, and
to see whether a meeting might not be arranged, more or less public
as should be thought advisable. In this case I would gladly draw up
for you a string of Resolutions, comprizing the most weighty, and
generally intelligible grounds in pre-confutation of Lord Eldon's
Bill & Preamble. What else you can do for the present, I do not see
—or what I can do except (it being past One) wish you good night
& go to bed—God bless you &

S. T. C.—

1431. *To J. A. Hessey*

Address: Messrs. Taylor and Hessey | Fleet Street   For Mr Hessey
MS. Harvard College Lib. Hitherto unpublished.
Postmark: Highgate, 17 February 1825.

Wednesday Evening. [16 February 1825] Grove, Highgate.

I am sorry that any mistake of mine should have occasioned any
delay; but I took the inclosed for a clear printed-off Sheet—tho' I
now see that there is one word misplaced and which the Corrector
has marked *Tr.*

I am very anxious for some Proofs. The remaining Copy is ready
—and whenever wanted, will be sent by return of Post.

S. T. Coleridge

1432. *To Thomas H. Dunn*

Pub. Advertiser, *Adelaide, South Australia, 28 July 1934.*

16th Feb., 1825.

My dear Sir—

I must interest your patience for another ten days. The last
sheet of my work is now going to the Press—and be assured that
for every week since Autumn I will consider the sum as out at
interest.

S. T. C.

1433. *To Unknown Correspondent*

MS. New York Public Lib. Pub. with omis. Poems, *ii. 1110.* The text of this
letter is taken from a draft which Coleridge wrote in a notebook now in the
Berg Collection.

21 Feby. 1825.—

My dear Friend

I have often amused myself with the thought of a self-conscious
Looking-glass, and the various metaphorical applications of such a
fancy—and this morning it struck across the Eolian Harp of my
Brain that there was something pleasing and emblematic (of what
I did not distinctly make out) in two such Looking-glasses fronting,
each seeing the other in itself, and itself in the other.—Have you
ever noticed the Vault or snug little Apartment which the Spider
spins and weaves for itself, by spiral threads round and round, and
sometimes with strait lines, so that it's Lurking-parlour or With-
drawing-room is an oblong square? This too connected itself in my
mind with the melancholy truth, that as we grow older, the World
(alas! how often it happens, that the less we love it, the more we
care for it; the less reason we have to value it's Shews, the more
anxious are we about them!—alas! how often do we become more
and more loveless, as Love, which can outlive all change save a
change with regard to itself, and all loss save the loss of it's *Reflex*,
is more needed to sooth us & alone is able so to do!)

What was I saying?—O—I was adverting to the fact, that as we
advance in years, the World, that *spidery* Witch, spins it's threads
narrower and narrower, still closing in on us, till at last it shuts us
up within four walls, walls of flues and films, windowless—and well
if there be sky-lights, and a small opening left for the Light from
above. I do not know that I have any thing to add, except perhaps
to remind you, that *pheer* or *phere* for *Mate, Companion, Counterpart,* is a word frequently used by Spencer, G. Herbert, and the

Poets generally, who wrote before the Restoration (1660)—before I say, that this premature warm and sunny day, antedating Spring, called forth the following

Strain in the manner of G. HERBERT—: which might be entitled, THE ALONE MOST DEAR: a Complaint of Jacob to Rachel as in the tenth year of his Service he saw in her or *fancied* that he saw Symptoms of Alienation. [N.B. The Thoughts and Images being *modernized*, and turned into *English.*—][1]

All Nature seems at work. Slugs[2] leave their lair;
The Bees are stirring; Birds are on the wing;[3]
And WINTER slumb'ring in the open air
Wears on his smiling face a dream of Spring.
And[4] I, the while, the sole unbusy Thing,
Nor honey make, nor pair, nor build, nor sing.

Yet well I ken the banks, where* Amaranths blow,
Have traced the fount whence streams of Nectar flow.
Bloom, O ye Amaranths! bloom for whom ye may—
For me ye bloom not! Glide, rich Streams! away!
With unmoist Lip and wreathless Brow I stroll:[5]
And would you learn the Spells, that drowse my Soul?
WORK without Hope draws nectar in a sieve;
And HOPE without an Object cannot live.[6]

I speak in figures, inward thoughts and woes
Interpreting by Shapes and outward Shews.
Call the World Spider: and at fancy's touch[7]
Thought becomes image and I see it such.

[1] Passage in brackets crossed out in MS.
[2] Snails [Cancelled word in line above.]
[3] Compare the last stanza of George Herbert's *Praise.* [Note by E. H. Coleridge, *Poems*, i. 447.] The stanza reads:

> O raise me then! Poore Bees, that work all day.
> > Sting my delay,
> > Who have a work, as well as they,
> > And much, much more.

See *The Temple*, 1633, p. 53.
[4] But [Cancelled word in line above.]
* *literally* rendered is Flower Fadeless, or never-fading—from the Greek a *not* and marainō, to wither. [Note by S. T. C.]
[5] Coleridge did not cancel this line but wrote above it,
> ? *Lips unbrighten'd, wreathless B.*—
He published the line as 'With lips unbrightened, wreathless brow, I stroll'.
[6] These 14 lines, with slight variations, were first published in *The Bijou* for 1828 under the title, *Work without Hope. Lines composed on a day in February.* See *Poems*, i. 447.
[7] This and the next seven lines are on another page of the notebook. Coleridge indicated by cross reference marks that he intended them to be inserted here.

With viscous masonry of films and threads[1]
Tough as the Nets in Indian Forests found
It blends the Waller's & the Weaver's trade[s]
And soon the tent-like Hangings touch the ground—
A dusky Chamber that excludes the Day[2]—
But cease the prelude & resume the lay.[3]

Where daily nearer me (with magic Ties,[4]
Line over line & thick'ning as they rise)
The World her spidery threads on all sides spun,
Side answ'ring Side with narrow interspace,
My Faith (say, I: I and my Faith are one)
Hung, as a Mirror there! And face to face
(For nothing else there was, between or near)
One Sister Mirror hid the dreary Wall.
But *That* is broke! And with that bright Compeer[5]
I lost my Object and my inmost All—
Faith *in* the Faith of THE ALONE MOST DEAR!

JACOB HODIERNUS.

Ah! me!!

[1] The first version of this and the following lines reads:

> Skill'd in light masonry of films and threads
> It joins the Waller's and the Weaver's trades.
> And see a twilight tent inclose me round
> A dusky cell!—but hush! for all too long
> I linger in the precincts

[2] Coleridge first wrote 'A chamber'd Cell!—But I digress too long,'. He altered this line to read 'A chamber'd Cell!—Hush, Muse! thou lookedst too long,'. Both versions are cancelled in the MS.

[3] Cease the preamble, & begin the [Cancelled words in line above.] Instead of the word 'Cease' Coleridge first wrote and then cancelled the word 'And'.

[4] Coleridge first wrote:

> 'What time, and where (wove close with magic Ties,'.

Neither version of the line is cancelled in the MS.

[5] This and the eight preceding lines are written on a slip of paper which Coleridge affixed by sealing wax to the page in the notebook. The slip has now been removed by the authorities at the New York Public Library.

The eight lines which Coleridge originally wrote in his notebook and then covered with the slip of paper read as follows. (I am indebted to Mr. David V. Erdman for the text.)

> 1 Where rising still, still nar[row]ing [?] as they rose;
> 2 And *walling-in* an ever-narrowing Space,
> 3 The WORLD her spidery lines in arches spun,
> 4 My FAITH—(say, I: I and My Faith are one!)
> 5 Hung as a Mirror there: and face to face
> 6 (For not a thing between us did appear)
> 7 One Sister Mirror hid the dreary Wall.

1434. To Thomas Allsop

Transcript Mrs. R. L. Grigg. *Pub. with omis.* Letters, Conversations and Rec. 227
Postmark: 5 March 1825.

Grove, Highgate
Saturday. [5 March 1825]

My dear Allsop

You well know, that in this house you can need no apology but for thinking it necessary to make any apology. This indeed *does* give us pain: for it seems to imply, that you have not that confidence in our repeated Assurances of the pleasure we have in seeing you at all times, which we are inwardly certain that they deserve.

In like manner, with regard to myself individually. You say— 'if you *retain* the interest, you felt etc.'—as if, my dear Allsop! I could feel any interest in schemes of this sort beyond that excited by my knowledge that *you* had a *serious* interest in this undertaking; or as if that interest were one that I was likely to *throw* off, or one which there was any chance of my *not* retaining.—I am sure, you did not mean this; but I would fain have you not even speak or write below that line of friendship & mutual implicit reliance, on which you & I stand. We are in the World & obliged to chafe & chaffer with it; but we are not *of* the World—nor will we use it's idioms or adopt it's *brogue*.

I write now to inform you, that Mr Chance, our wealthy & opulent Neighbor (one of the two largest Glass-Manufacturers & Merchants in the South of England) having read your Prospectuses has sent to me for Shares—i.e. to be informed, when & to whom he

8 But *That* is broke!—and with that only* pheere
*Mate, Counterpart.

In the preceding lines, 1, 2, 3, 6, and 8, the following changes appear in the MS.:
Line 1: 'still narrowing' is altered to 'and deep'ning'; then 'and' is changed to 'still'; finally, the line is cancelled and the following couplet substituted:
What time & where, wove close with magic ties
Line over line, & thick'ning as they rise.
Line 2 is cancelled in the MS. and 'A walled Chamber with a straiten'd space' substituted. Coleridge altered 'Chamber' to 'Room'; he then substituted the line:
Side answ'ring Side with narrow in[ters]pace.
Line 3: 'lines in arches' is altered first to 'threads on ca', then to 'threads about me', and finally to 'threads on all sides'. Coleridge also indicated in the MS. that this line as corrected—'The WORLD her spidery threads on all sides spun'—was to precede line 2 as amended: 'Side answ'ring Side' etc.
Line 6: above this line Coleridge wrote,
'nothing else there was, between or near'.
Neither version is cancelled.
Line 8: above the words 'only pheere' Coleridge wrote '? bright Compeer'.

is to address the Request—I shall be glad to find the time come, when your or your friends' clerks may call out like Rothschild's— Hand down a hundred *Regrets* hither!—(i.e. Lithographic Epistles in the negative to the Swarm of Applicants.) I wish, I were more in the way of exciting applications, & 'making a favor' of granting them—& doubt not, that it would be really such. At least (to use your own words) I *hope* so—

God bless you & your most | affectionate Friend
S. T. Coleridge

1435. *To Thomas Allsop*

Address: T. Allsop, Esqre. | 3. Clement's Lane
MS. New York Public Lib. Pub. with omis. Letters, Conversations and Rec. *218.*
Postmark: Highgate, 10 March 1825.

Thursday Afternoon—[10 March 1825]
My dearest Allsop

Is there any definite service or any chance of any definite service, great or small, that I can do or promote or expedite by coming to town?—If there be, for friendship's sake, let me have a Line— or if you will, a monosyllable—YES—& mention the time. I would take the chance & have set off without the question; but that I have so many irons in the fire at this present moment—1. my preface. 2. My Essay—3. a work prepared for the Press by my Hebrew Friend[1]—in which I am greatly interested, morally and *crumenically*, tho' not like the Modern Descendants of Heber, one of a 'crumenimulga Natio'[2]—i.e. a purse-milking Set—and 4—Revisal &c for a friend only less near than yourself in the regard and affection

of, my dear Allsop, | Your ever faithful
S. T. Coleridge

1436. *To Thomas Allsop*

Address: T. Allsop, Esqre | 3 Clement's Lane
MS. New York Public Lib. Pub. with omis. Letters, Conversations and Rec. *218.*
Postmark: Highgate, 12 March 1825.

Sat. Morn. 8 o'clock. [12 March 1825]
My dear Allsop

I have this moment received your Note. Mr Chance spoke to me on Thursday Night; & I take for granted, has written to you. My

[1] Hyman Hurwitz's *Hebrew Tales.* See Letter 1446.
[2] See Letter 591 and n.

opinion is: that he is and will be a valuable Man, not only generally to the *Concern*; but *especially* to that which alone concerns *me*, *your* Comfort and Happiness. He is a vain man, but of the very kindest & best sort—Prosperous in all his concerns, and with peace in his own conscience & family, I regard such vainness but as the overflow of humanity—I do not like him the better *for* it; but I should not like him the better *without* it. Meantime, he is active, shrewd, a thorough man of Business—SANGUINE, I should think, both by constitution and by habitual Success—but *you* are fitful, i.e. alternately sanguine and timid—and an embarrassing timidity, or rather an inward perplexity which and it's causes I thoroughly understand but need not unravel, sometimes diminishes your use of your powers.—Now at such moments, and under any sudden emergency, I think that Mr Chance, not so deeply interested in interest and yet (such is his nature) with equal liveliness in feeling, would be a comfort & support to you—to ask, to talk with, &c &c— If you think the same, I would manage that You & Mr Chance should *so* understand each other.—I shall miss the Post if I do more than add that whatever really serves *you*, will—and on his death-pillow quite as much as in his present Garrett,

delight your sincerely affectionate | Friend
S. T. Coleridge

1437. *To C. A. Tulk*

Address: C. A. Tulk, Esqre. M.P. | 19 Duke Street | Westminster
MS. Mrs. Valerie W. Lucas. Hitherto unpublished.
Postmark: Highgate, 16 March 1825.

Tuesday 15 March 1825
Grove, Highgate

My very dear Sir

You do me justice in believing that I can not have forgotten you and with great justice you complain of me tho' your complaints are but faint echoes of the Reproaches, that have long sounded in my own bosom. If I said, that not a day has past since the hour of the tidings of desolation, in which I have not thought of you, and often (O how often!) with intense sympathy, I should affirm less than the truth. Would that I had followed my first feeling. For full three days after I had read unawares the sad record in Burgess's Library at Ramsgate, with exception of the first hour when I was so stunned as to feel a strange almost ideotic wonder at Mrs Gillman's strong Weeping, I remained not merely in a tranquil but in an elevated state of mind and spirit—and in that state I wrote a long Letter to you, and had

begun another to Mr Hart. On the fourth day, as I was sitting alone
at my breakfast, I felt a sudden sensation of heat and fullness about
my eyes as I was bending to take up a paper-knife that I had let fall
—and instantly I had the most distinct ocular spectrum of the now
blessed One exactly as I once saw her in your Carriage in Pall Mall,
when she raised her eye-lid & streamed forth that soft yet rich
light from her eyes as she returned my greeting—and of which I
had so often spoken afterwards.—Instantly, a total change of my
feelings took place—I became hysterically affected—and for days
after I continued, sometimes involuntarily, at other times with a
sort of wilful self-infliction, presenting you, and the dear children
in every affecting attitude to my imagination—and in this mood
the Letter, I had written, appeared to me unnatural, a mixture of
intellectual and spiritual Self-exaltation, and an ante-dating of the
calmness and resignation that should have followed the payment of
the debt which the heart of flesh owes to the Sorrower in the freshness of his Anguish—And in this distemperature both of body and
mind I destroyed the Letters—.

   I could now tell you a weary tale of the vexatious and distressful
accidents and incidents that in long succession have followed each
other from our departure from Ramsgate almost to the present
hour. At one time there were six persons confined to their beds in
the House, Mr Gillman being one—Mr G. had, during my absence,
been cheated into a competition with a worthless medical Man, his
bitter enemy, by false promises—& lost the election by intrigue
and treachery.—The effect on his spirits, his whole tone of feeling,
on the whole frame of his mind was far more calamitous than the
worst of the consequences which he anticipated would have been,
tho' realized—& his bodily health sunk under it—Sufficient that I
had the duties of a Friend to perform.—Meantime, Mrs Gillman, a
Being inexpressibly dear and valuable in my eyes, has been
evidently declining since that dreadful Fall—She is now better—
but for several months I feared the worst.—These are a specimen
only of the causes, that joined with the clamorous importunities of
my Publishers really half-stupified me—Yet day after day I formed
resolutions of writing to you—so far from forgetting you every
distress recalled you to my mind—. But I cannot pursue the subject. I will write again if I cannot come to town in a few days—as
I expect.—Think as kindly of me as you can—for I solemnly assure
you that I retain every emotion of regard and every Conviction of
your Worth & every interest in all that concerns you, that ever in
the most genial hour had place in the Soul of, my dearest Sir,

                         Your sincere tho' neglectful Friend
                                        S. T. Coleridge

1438. *To John Taylor Coleridge*

Address: J. T. Coleridge Esqre. | 65 Torrington Square
MS. British Museum. Pub. with omis. Letters, *ii. 734.*
Postmark: 8 April 1825.

Friday [8 April 1825]
Grove, Highgate—

My dear Nephew

I need not tell you, that no attention, in my power to offer, shall be wanting to Dr Reich. As a foreigner and a man of letters, he might claim this in his own right; and that he came from you would have ensured it, even tho' he had been a frenchman. But that he is a German, and that you think him a worthy and deserving man, and that his lot, like my own, has been cast on the bleak North Side of the Mountain, make me reflect with pain on the little influence, I possess, and the all but *zero* of my direct means, to serve or to assist him. The prejudices excited against me by Jeffray, combining with the mistaken notion of my German Metaphysics to which (I am told) some passages in some biographical Gossip-book about Lord Byron have given fresh currency, have rendered my authority with the TRADE worse than nothing.[1] Of the three schemes of Philosophy, Kant's, Fichte's and Schelling's (as diverse each from the other as those of Aristotle, Zeno and Plotinus, tho' all crushed together under the name, *Kantean* Philosophy, in the English Talk) I should find it difficult to select the one from which I *differed* the most—tho' perfectly easy to determine which of the three *Men* I hold in highest honor. And Immanuel Kant I assuredly do value most highly; not, however, as a Metaphysician but as a Logician, who has completed and systematized what Lord Bacon had boldly designed and loosely sketched out in the miscellany of Aphorisms, his Novum Organum—In Kant's Critique of the Pure Reason there is more than one fundamental error; but the main fault lies in the Title-page, which to the manifold advantage of the Work might be exchanged for—An Inquisition respecting the constitution and limits of the Human Understanding.—I can not only honestly assert but I can satisfactorily prove by reference to Writings (Letters, Marginal Notes and those in books that have never been in my possession since I first left England for Hamburgh, &c) that all the elements, the *differentials* as the Algebraists say, of my present

[1] See Thomas Medwin, *Conversations of Lord Byron*, 1824, p. 266: 'If he [Coleridge] had never gone to Germany, nor spoilt his fine genius by the transcendental philosophy and German metaphysics, nor taken to write lay sermons, he would have made the greatest poet of the day. What poets had we in 1795? Hayley had got a monopoly, such as it was. Coleridge might have been any thing: as it is, he is a thing "that dreams are made of".'

Opinions existed for me before I had even seen a book of German Metaphysics, later than Wolff[1] and Leibnitz, or could have read it, if I had.—But what will this avail ? A High German Transcendentalist I must be content to remain—and a young American Painter, Lesly, (the pupil & friend of a very dear friend of mine, Allston) to whom I have been in the habit for ten years and more of shewing as cordial regards as I could to a near relation, has, I find, introduced a portrait of me in a picture from Sir W. Scott's Antiquary as Dr Dusterswevil, or whatever the name is.[2]—Still however, I will make any attempt to serve Dr Reich, which he may point out and which, I am not sure, would *dis*serve him. I do not, of course, know what command he has over the English Language—If he wrote it fluently, I should think that it would answer to any one of our great Publishers to engage him in the translation of the best and cheapest Natural History in existence—viz. Oken's in three thick Octavo Volumes, containing the inorganic world, and the Animals from the Πρωτόζωα, (Animalcula of Infusions) to Man—. The Botany was not published, two years ago: whether it is now, I do not know—there is one thin Quarto of Plates.[3] It is by far the most entertaining as well as instructive Book of the Kind, I ever saw; and with a few Notes, and the Omission (or Castigation) of one or two of Oken's adventurous Whimsies, would be a valuable addition to our English Literature.—So much for this.—

I will not disguise from you, my dearest Nephew! that the first certain information of your having taken the Quarterly gave me a pain, which it required all my confidence in the soundness of your Judgement to counteract. I had long before by conversation with experienced Barristers got rid of all apprehension of it's being likely to injure you professionally. My fears were directed to the *invidiousness* of the situation, it being the notion of Publishers that without satire and sarcasm no Review can obtain or keep up a Sale—. Perhaps, Pride had some concern in it. *For* myself, I have

---

[1] Christian von Wolff or Wolf (1679–1754). A copy of Wolff's *Logic, or, Rational Thoughts on the powers of the human understanding. . . . Translated from the German*, 1770, containing annotations by Coleridge is in the British Museum.

[2] The frontispiece of the second volume of *The Antiquary* (vol. v of *Novels and Tales*, 1823) represents Dousterswivel digging for treasure in Misticot's grave, an illustration drawn by C. R. Leslie. E. H. Coleridge thought the resemblance to Coleridge 'perhaps, not wholly imaginary'. *Letters*, ii. 736 n.

[3] Lorenz Oken, *Lehrbuch der Naturgeschichte*, 3 Thle. and an atlas of plates, 1813–26. The three volumes to which Coleridge refers were the *Mineralogie*, 1 vol., 1813, and the *Zoologie*, 2 vols., 1815–16. Only one division of Oken's *Botanik* (Blüthen- u. Fruchtpflanzen) was published. It appeared in two parts, 1825–6. A copy of the *Lehrbuch der Naturgeschichte*, 1813, with annotations by Coleridge is in the British Museum.

none—probably because I had time out of mind given it up as a lost case, given myself over, I mean, as a predestined Author, tho' without a drop of true *Author* Blood in my veins—But a pride in & for the Name of my Father's House I have—and those, with whom I live, know that it is never more than in *dog-sleep*, and apt to *start up* on slight alarms. Now, tho' very sillily, I felt pain at the notion of any *comparisons* being drawn between *you* (to whom with your Sister my heart pulls the strongest) and Mr Gifford—even tho' they should be to your advantage: and still more, the Thought that so thorough a —— (supply the rest!) —— as Murray, should be or hold himself entitled to have and express an opinion on the subject. The insolence of one of his proposals to me, viz. that he would publish an edition of my Poems, on the condition that a Gentleman in his confidence (Mr Millman! I understood) was to select, and make such omissions and corrections as should be thought advisable[1]—this, which offered to myself excited only a smile in which there was nothing sardonic, might very possibly have rendered me sorer and more sensitive when I boded even an infinitesimal ejusdem farinae in connection with you.

But henceforward I shall look at the thing in a sunnier mood— Mr G. Frere is strongly impressed with the importance and even dignity of the Trust—and on the power, you have, of gradually giving a steadier and manlier tone to the feelings and principles of the higher classes. But I hope very soon to converse with you on this Subject—as soon as I have finished my Essay for the Literary Society, in which, I flatter myself, I have thrown some light on the passages in Herodotus respecting the derivation of the Greek Mythology from Egypt—and in what sense that paragraph respecting Homer & Hesiod are [is?] to be understood[2]—and when I have likewise got my 'Aids to Reflection' out of the Press—. But I have more to do—for the necessities of the day & which are *Nos*— non nobis—than I can well manage so as to go on with my own works—tho' I work from Morning to Night, as far as my health admits and the loss of my friendly Amanuensis. For the slowness, with which I get on with the pen in my own hand contrasts most strangely with the rapidity with which I dictate.

Your kind letter of invitation did not reach me—but there was one, which I ought to have answered long ago, which came while I was at Ramsgate.—We have had a continued succession of Illness in our family here—at one time six persons confined to their beds. I have been sadly afraid that we should lose Mrs Gillman, who would be a loss indeed to the whole Neighborhood—young and old.

---

[1] See Letters 1339, 1344, 1448, 1456, and 1742.

[2] Herodotus, ii. 53, but see the passage from 43 on.

But she seems, thank God! to recover strength, tho' slowly.—As
I hope to write again in a few days, with my Book, I shall now
desire my cordial regards to Mrs J. Coleridge, and with my affectionate Love to the little ones—& assure you that
    with the warmest interest of affection and | esteem I am, my
        dear John, | your sincere Friend

                                                S. T. Coleridge

1439. *To Edward Coleridge*

Address: Edward Coleridge, Esqre | —— Pattison's Esqre | Gower Street—
MS. Pierpont Morgan Lib. Pub. E. L. G. ii. 339.

                            Thursday Afternoon.—[14 April 1825][1]
My dear Nephew
    Did I, or did you, mistake the day on which I was to expect the
pleasure of seeing you with your Italian Friend? Was it Friday,
perhaps? Or perhaps, some accident has intervened, that has prevented you from coming? I had made an engagement to call on my
Publishers on Friday; but yet, if I were certain of seeing you tomorrow, I would contrive to put that off—so anxious am I to talk
with you respecting the Eton Foundation-Boys. You asked me if it
was for a *particular* friend. When I tell you, that it is for Henry
Gillman, the younger of Mr & Mrs Gillman's two Children, I might
adopt *Elia's* (C. Lamb's) words in his Letter to Southey, 'Coleridge's
more than Friend, Mr Gillman'.[2] But in every honest & moral sense
I might and I do reply—*for myself.* For the failure and thorough-
paced Rascality of Fenner & Curtis having at one stroke deprived
me of the whole amount of the Gains of my literary Labors, but
even compelled me to borrow money to buy up the Half-Copy
Rights, the remuneration of my *Author*-Labors since then is still in
reversion; and the trifles, I have been able to earn, by private
Teaching, or literary assistance, have not for the last six years
enabled me to pay half the actual expences of my maintenance.
My children have received the same kindness & more than *friendship* as myself—& all the while I know that my friend, like most
other professional men in so limited a sphere as Highgate, [is]
obliged to struggle hard in order to the performance of the duties,
he owes to his own children & his own station in Society. If at the

---

    [1] Since Edward Coleridge and his 'Italian Friend', Prati, came to Highgate
on Friday, 15 Apr. 1825, the present letter, in which Coleridge mentions their
intended visit, must have been written on Thursday the 14th. See Letters
1440–1.
    [2] See 'Letter of Elia to Robert Southey', *London Magazine*, Oct. 1823.

time, I published the Friend in Volumes, I had reason (& most
sufficing reason I had) to express what I did express in my Dedication of the Work to Mr and Mrs Gillman, what must I not say now,
after eight years' unremitted Love & Affection, and hourly occasions to experience & venerate their worth! Whatever, therefore,
you can do, & whatever interest you possess, I earnestly beseech
you to exert it for their Child, not with less warmth than if it had
been my own. I have conversed with Mr and Mrs Gillman, who have
determined to avail themselves of your kind offer, and I will take
care, that the Boy shall do no discredit to your Patronage. He is a
generous-minded & sweet-tempered Boy: and his connections and
nearest Relations are in every sense of the word highly respectable.
With such a Mother, as he has (and I have never yet in all points
seen her equal) his manners, notions and principles could scarcely
be otherwise than gentlemanly—(I use this word because Mr J. H.
Frere called him, 'a gentlemanly little Fellow'.) If you possibly can
contrive to give me an hour or two of your time either tomorrow or
Saturday, so as to see Mr & Mrs Gillman, you will give me no
ordinary pleasure—Unfortunately, I forgot to ask your address in
town—and therefore I shall dispatch a trusty Messenger with this,
to go first to Torrington Square, & then to Gower Street—I have
been this last two or three Hours with Dr Reich, who answers to
John's account of him. I have given him the best advice in my
power—viz. to give up all thought of interesting either Public or
London Publishers in German Metaphysics, except as far as he
should be engaged to write an Article (historical & critical) for
either of the two Giant Reviews—and rather to turn his attention to
the many valuable Historical Works with which the German
Literature has been recently enriched—and to their Natural
Histories, Zoological, Mineralogical &c—But I shall write to your
Cousin [brother?] as soon as I hear of his Return from the West.—

Give my kind Love to Mrs P. and assure her, I have not forgot
her nor the Epithalamium—for *her* Poet ought to feel as her Husband feels, that the recency of the Event is the smallest part of the
Interest, by which it is endeared. If Epithalamia be congratulations,
my subject will improve by keeping, and grow by compound
interest.

Be so good as to return a Line by the Bearer—whether and on
what day I may hope to see you—& believe me,

dear Edward, | with sincere regard | your affectionate Uncle
S. T. Coleridge

1440. *To Mrs. John Patteson*

Address: Mrs Pattison | —— Pattison's, Esqre | Gower Street
MS. Mrs. Phyllis Coleridge Hooper. Hitherto unpublished.

[14 April 1825][1]

My dear Niece

As I have sent a message to you in my letter to Edward, I have only to beg you to direct my Messenger where he is likely to find your Brother as I am very anxious to have an answer from him. I have been expecting him since One o'clock with an Italian Gentleman, he was to have introduced—or if he should be out of town, whether he returns this evening, & sleeps in Gower Street—If so, of course the Letter must wait for him—

But on the possibility that he may be in Torrington Square (for I forgot to enquire his address) I have given the bearer a Note to Mrs J. Coleridge—

Need I say, how highly I should be gratified by a call from you & Mr Pattison, should choice or chance lead you hitherward? You will give great delight to my excellent Friends, Mr & Mrs Gillman— & we expect the Nightingales now every evening—and you would scarcely imagine that so beautiful a Prospect should exist within 5 miles from Town as I have from my Window at this moment—For we have changed Houses, I think—since you were here.

God bless you | & your affectionate | Uncle
S. T. Coleridge

1441. *To Derwent Coleridge*[2]

Address: Derwent Coleridge Esqre. | Davenport | Devon | [in another hand] Plymouth
MS. Victoria University Lib. Hitherto unpublished fragment.
Postmark: Highgate, 15 April 1825.

[15 April 1825]

. . . if they do not hear soon or the money be applied for—The money will be in Mr Sutton's Hands—who will pay it to your

---

[1] This and the preceding letter were delivered the same day by Coleridge's 'trusty Messenger'.

[2] The present letter is written on the back of the following note which Coleridge had received from George Skinner:

Jesus Coll. Thursday
14 April, [1825]

My dear Sir,

immediately on my arrival I applied to one of the Deans of S. John's (in the absence of the Tutors) upon the subject you mentioned. The College will

Order.[1] I have this moment parted from your Cousin, Edward Coleridge, who has accepted an Assistant Master's Place at Eton— he passed the morning here with two friends whom he introduced, Sir James Stuart & Mr Woodcock[2]—and a Dr Prati, a literary German—.[3] My health is better & worse—better κατὰ ζωήν, worse κατ' ὄργανα—The House more decayed; but the rubbish of the fallen out-rooms have buttressed the walls of those that remain, so far at least as to intercept the drafts thro' the crannies.—

Mrs Gillman, I am sorry to say, is rather declining than advancing —Good God! what a Loss she will be, should it [plea]se God to take her!—My *Aids to Reflection* is on the eve of publication—. What is the most inexpensive way in which I can convey a copy to you? Who is your Plymouth Bookseller's London Correspondent? Perhaps, I could get it inclosed in his monthly Parcel—They have stayed so long that if I do not conclude, I shall lose the Post—. . .

1442. *To Richard Cattermole*

Address: To the Revd. R. Cattermole, | Secretary &c | of the Royal Society of Literature.
MS. Huntington Lib. Pub. E. L. G. ii. 338.

Grove, Highgate
26 April, 1825

Reverend Sir

At the time, when most unexpectedly I had the honor to be appointed a Royal Associate of the R.S.L., I was employed in the completion of three Works, the preparations for, and composition of, which have employed every hour during the last 20 years of my Life, that Ill-health and the exactions of that imperious Taskmaster, the ever-recurring To-Day, have allowed me to call *my own*. The first of the three, entitled 'Aids to Reflection in the formation of a manly character', is printed and on the eve of publi-

make *no difficulty* in signing the certificate, & your Son had better write forthwith to the Tutor, who will be in College in a few days.

Believe me, my dear Sir, | with sincere respect & esteem, | Your obliged,

G. Skin[ner.]

[1] Coleridge refers to the proceeds due from the Mercers' Company exhibition which Derwent had held since Lady Day 1822. Derwent was entitled to receive further payments from this exhibition after taking his degree and leaving Cambridge in Jan. 1824, but 'misinformation and mistake on the part of R. Sutton Junr' and Derwent concerning the regulations of the Company led Coleridge to abandon his efforts to obtain the money. See Letters 1614–17.

[2] Sir James Stuart was married to the Rev. Henry Woodcock's sister.

[3] Gioacchino de' Prati. See Letter 1457.

cation. The second, or the Elements of Discourse, is finished: and in preparation for the Press. Of the third and far larger and more laborious Work, on Religion in it's twofold character of Philosophy and History, under the title of 'Religion considered as *implying* Revelation, and Christianity as the only Revelation of universal and perpetual Validity', the former Half only is completed. And I owe it to my own character not to omit, that before I had received the least intimation respecting my possible election as Royal Associate, I had already entered into engagements with my present Publishers—which engagements, partly, anxiety from a deep sense of the importance of the Objects, I had in view, and the knowlege that my convictions stood in sharp and almost hostile contrast with the prevailing Opinions of the Age; partly, the Absence of a friendly Amanuensis—a heavy loss to a man, whose progress in composing with the pen in his own hand is *inversely* as his rapidity in dictating; and partly, a succession of disturbing and depressing Accidents; have rendered beyond my anticipation difficult to fulfil.

I throw myself therefore on the indulgence of the Society and entreat them to regard the Year past as a period employed in the liquidation of a debt previously incurred, and for the purpose of enabling myself with a free and disentangled spirit to discharge the duties of more recent origin henceforward.

Not, however, to leave the letter of my obligation uncomplied with, I here lay before the Society the first specimen of a series of Disquisitions[1] respecting the Nature, Origin, and distinctive characters of the Religious Institutions of Ancient Greece, the Mysteries, the Sacerdotal Cultus and the Popular Superstitions; and of the relation, in which the Philosophy, the Epic and Dramatic Poetry, and the Fine Arts of the Greek Republics stood to each of these.[2]

And I remain most respectfully, | Reverend Sir, | Your obedient Servant

S. T. Coleridge

[1] At the time he accepted his appointment as Royal Associate in 1824, Coleridge was aware of his obligation to read an annual essay before the Royal Society of Literature, but a month later he told his nephew that this obligation was 'a serious set off against the yearly £100'. In the present letter he acknowledges that he is in arrears and sends the first essay as a 'specimen of a series of Disquisitions' to follow. The title of the lecture delivered on 18 May 1825 also mentions this 'series of Disquisitions'. No further lectures, however, were delivered. (See Letters 1382, 1392, 1427, 1463, and 1606.) The present Secretary of the Royal Society of Literature informs me that several of the Royal Associates gave no lectures at all.

[2] In his lecture of 18 May 1825, *On the Prometheus of Æschylus; An Essay, Preparatory to a series of Disquisitions respecting the Egyptian in connection*

1443. *To Thomas Allsop*

Address: T. Allsop, Esqre. | 2 Blandford Place | Pall Mall
MS. Professor Earl Daniels. Pub. with omis. Letters, Conversations and
Rec. 222.
Postmark: Highgate, 2 May 1825.

30 April 1825
Grove, Highgate.

My dearest Allsop

Having disburthened myself of the main Loads, of outward
obligation at least, that pressed on me, my Essay for the R.S.L.,
and my Aids to Reflection, with other matters not so expressly
my own but having the same if not greater demands on such
quantity of time, as bodily pain and disqualification with unpre-
cludible interruptions have enabled [me] to make use of—I take
the *very* first moment of the Furlow to tell you, that I have been
perplexed both by your silence & your absence. In fact, I had
taken for granted, you were in Derbyshire: till this afternoon I
met Mr Maud, your Mineralogist, who told me he had met you
either this morning or yesterday I forget which.

Now I cannot recall any thing that can—I am sure, ought to
have given you offence—unless it were my non-performance of the
Request communicated to me by Mr Jameson—about the Borneo
Business. I was, even in the *stifle* of my *reflected* anxieties, i.e.
anxieties felt by reflection from those of others, & my *Tangle* of
Things-to-be-done, solicitous to see & talk with you. But this not
being in my power, I was obliged to act on my own judgement,
imperfect & scanty as the Data were on which it was to be grounded.

with the Sacerdotal Theology, and in contrast with the Mysteries of ancient Greece,
Coleridge said:

The objects which, on my appointment as Royal Associate of the Royal
Society of Literature, I proposed to myself were, 1st. The elucidation of the
purpose of the Greek drama, and the relations in which it stood to the
mysteries on the one hand, and to the state or sacerdotal religion on the
other:—2nd. The connection of the Greek tragic poets with philosophy as
the peculiar offspring of Greek genius:—3rd. The connection of the Homeric
and cyclical poets with the popular religion of the Greeks: and, lastly from all
these,—namely, the mysteries, the sacerdotal religion, their philosophy before
and after Socrates, the stage, the Homeric poetry and the legendary belief
of the people, and from the sources and productive causes in the derivation
and confluence of the tribes that finally shaped themselves into a nation of
Greeks—to give a juster and more distinct view of this singular people, and
of the place which they occupied in the history of the world, and the great
scheme of divine providence, than I have hitherto seen,—or rather let me say,
than it appears to me possible to give by any other process. (*Literary
Remains*, ii. 330.)

See also Coleridge's comments in *Aids to Reflection*, 1825, pp. 276–8.

And first, I had a very slight acquaintance with Mudford, consisting indeed of my having once dined with him—& 2. I had never in my life recommended any thing of which I had not at the time knowlege proportionate to my recommendation. But lastly & a 1000 times more influencive on my mind was the seeming clearness and distinctness, with which I saw the impolicy of the Article that appeared in the Paper—so utterly unlike the dignified plan, you had chalked out for yourself & have pursued in the Peak Association—I have seldom read a paragraph, that gave me so much pain.[1] —But besides this, you must not feel wounded if loving you so truly as I do, and feeling more and more every week that nothing is worth living for but the consciousness of living aright, I was *nervous*, if you will, with regard to the effect of these speculations on the frame of your moral & intellectual Being. I did not understand them enough to be able to draw the line between honorable enterprize, and a feverish spirit of Gambling. I heard of the swarm, I saw in the papers the very productivity of putrefaction in the mob of Maggots that crawled forth every succeeding day—and even Mr Chance told me, they began to be disreputable—In the mean time, you never came near me, so that I might have been able to rectify my opinions or rather to form them—& I felt and still feel, that I would gladly go into a garrett & work from morning to late night at any work, I could get money by, & more than share my pittance with you & your's than see you an Adventurer with 20,000£ at your command.—

Do not, my dearest Allsop! therefore let my perplexities derived in great measure from my unacquaintance with the facts, and to which my ever-wakeful affection gave the origin, prevent you from treating as you were wont to do

Your truly sincere

S. T. Coleridge

[1] The following paragraph appeared in *The Times* of 28 Apr. 1825:

A company is about to be formed for the purpose of carrying on mining operations in Derbyshire—a county with respect to which some peculiar mining laws exist, which seem to render them more eligible to be conducted by a company than by private individuals. In an extensive district called the King's Field, the first finder of ore of lead or other minerals, has the right of working that vein, if he thinks proper to exercise it, in whomsoever the property in the land itself may reside ; but having once declared an intention to explore its course, he cannot withdraw from the undertaking, which he must give security at the commencement to prosecute. This circumstance, and the increasing value of lead, which is the principal mineral found in that district, has led to the formation of the association alluded to, which seems to be a sufficiently prudent and useful application of English capital. It is to be called the Peak Association.

Mr & Mrs G., I am grieved to say, are neither of them *well*. And Mrs G. is very poorly.

My kindest regard to Mrs A.—

1444. *To Mrs. George Frere*

Address: Mrs. G. Frere
MS. Rush Rhees Lib., University of Rochester. Hitherto unpublished.

[Endorsed May 1825]

My dear Madam

Should it be *quite the same* whether I waited on you on Friday or Saturday, I should prefer, *Saturday*—nay, that is not exactly true: for I should all to nothing prefer going to Hamstead on Friday, and either staying at home on Saturday or remaining with you till Noon, to hear the more of Signor Rosetti's poem[1]—but our family, it seems, have been engaged to our worthy next door Neighbour, Mr Nixon, and I was included in the invitation & in the acceptance, tho' I was not aware of the circumstance.—

Still, however, if I do not hear from you, I shall conclude that Friday is the more convenient—and shall be with you at an early hour—my feelings on the point being altogether *reflected* from the anticipated feelings of others.—

Thank God! I was, when Bartlet sent up your note, putting down the last sentence of the long-lingering 'Aids to Reflection' which was to have been a small volume of Selections from Archbishop Leighton with a few notes by S.T.C. and which has ended in a few pages of Leighton and a large Volume by S.T.C.—

With my kind regards to John, and to all of your fire-side I
remain
Your and Mr Frere's | obliged & faithful Friend
S. T. Coleridge.

1445. *To Taylor and Hessey*

Address: Messrs. Taylor and Hessey | 93 Fleet Street
MS. Mr. C. Geigy-Hagenbach. Hitherto unpublished.

[Early May 1925]

Should Mr Hessey not be up—it would perhaps prevent delay if the Pacquet were opened, and retaining the first leaf of my letter to

[1] Coleridge had met Gabriele Rossetti in 1824. See Letter 1423.

Mr Hessey to send the other half with the *second* Volume of Paley[1] and the corrected Proof to the Printer. If the Printer's Office is at no great distance from Fleet Street, my Messenger, Riley, may take them: and bring back with him two Books which the Printer has, I believe—viz. the old 'FRIEND'[2] and the little Tract on Infant Baptism.[3]

S. T. Coleridge

1446. *To John Taylor Coleridge*

MS. British Museum. Hitherto unpublished.

5 May 1825
Grove, Highgate.

My dear John

Basil Montagu tells me that you are on terms of familiar acquaintance with Mr Harrison, 'the Quaker Barrister', now of Hampstead but about to settle in Highgate. If this be accurate, I should feel myself personally obliged if you would warmly—& I pledge my own experience & conscience on the safety with which you may on all accounts of professional Integrity and professional *Wisdom* no less than those of Skill and Learning—most warmly recommend Mr Gillman to him, as his medical Attendant.[4]—

[1] At the end of the *Aids to Reflection* (pp. 403–4) Coleridge inserted a passage from William Paley with the following introduction: 'In compliance with the suggestion of a judicious friend, the celebrated conclusion of the fourth [fifth] Book of Paley's Moral and Political Philosophy, cited in p. 336 of this Volume, is here transprinted for the convenience of the Reader.'

[2] On 12 May Coleridge again asked Hessey for the return of 'the old FRIEND'.

[3] William Wall's *A Conference between Two Men that had Doubts about Infant Baptism*, 1706. Coleridge quotes from this 'very sensible little Tract' in *Aids to Reflection*, 372–5.

[4] Coleridge had earlier sent a similar appeal to Dorothy Wordsworth. Her comments, in which she included a sentence from Coleridge's letter, may be quoted here. 'My dear Friend', she wrote to Mrs. Clarkson on 4 May 1825,

An unusual event, a letter from Coleridge, impels me to take the pen immediately. He begins by requesting in the most earnest language that I will use my interest with the Hoares of Hampstead, if I have any, and with Mr Clarkson, to promote an object that he has very much at heart. He then states that a Mr Harrison, a Quaker, is coming to settle at Highgate, and that he is most anxious that his friend, Mr Gilman, should be recommended to the said Mr Harrison, as his medical attendant. Now this matter, as nakedly stated to us, at this distance from Highgate, might seem of little importance; but to dear Coleridge, from his extreme earnestness, it is evident few things at this present time are of more. I will quote from his letter, and you shall judge for yourselves. But, by the bye, I must first explain that the letter (except the introductory sentence) was originally addressed to another Friend, who, he afterwards found, had no acquaintance with Mr Harrison;

I wish I could induce my Brother James with your Mother and
all of you, or at worst as many as possible to pass a day with me at
the Grove, Highgate—in this season of Nightingales! We would
dine at your own hour.—

Some years ago Mr Murray proposed to me to make a Volume
of such Tales &c as those entitled Specimens of Rabbinical Wisdom
in THE FRIEND—and offered me a fixed Sum—.[1] I found on trying
that I had not Learning enough, either in my head or in my
Library—and that the time, effort and waste of Health in going to
town from one Library to another to consult rare Books—viz.
Latin Translations of the Works in Syro-chaldaic or Rabbinical
Hebrew, would make it a dear bargain for me. But about 3 years
ago I mentioned the Subject to my friend, H. Hurwitz, the Author
of the Vindiciae Hebraicae, or Defence of the Established Version
of the Old Testament, against Bellamy & others—for which the
Bishop of London wrote a very handsome letter to Mr Hurwitz.—
He who is doubtless the first Rabbinical & Talmudic Scholar in the
Kingdom, offered to collect for me all the most interesting Tales,
Apologues, Witty Sayings &c from the uninspired Hebrew Literature—if I would give them the point, polish of style &c.—This has
now been perfected on both sides, together with a truly valuable
& interesting Essay by Mr H. on the characteristic Merits and
demerits of the Uninspired Hebrew Literature from the AEra of the
Maccabees to the 15th Century.

I have both pride enough & honesty enough to be chary of my

and Coleridge, not having time to write another letter to me, forwarded that
which had been intended for his male friend.

'I hear that a neighbour of yours is coming to settle at Highgate, and I will
venture to entreat you, in my own name, and as an act of friendship to me
personally, that you would use your interest in recommending Mr Gilman as
his medical attendant.' Coleridge then goes on to speak in high terms of
Mr G.'s medical skill, and of his excellent moral character; and states that
a Mr Snow has been recommended to Mr Harrison by one of the 'religious';
and, from what C. says, it appears that he is apprehensive of a formidable
Rival in this Mr Snow, who is favoured by certain denominations of religious
persons. And this will throw some light upon Coleridge's wish that his
Friend should attend Mr Harrison's Family. We live in a strange world.
What can be so stupid as to choose a medical adviser from any other considerations than professional skill, humanity, and integrity! To these points
Coleridge speaks decidedly in Mr Gilman's favour, and all Coleridge's
friends think highly of him. Therefore Mr Clarkson (being ever ready to
serve worthy people) will I am sure if he have the means, and can use them
with propriety do his utmost to recommend Mr Gilman to Mr Harrison.
Coleridge speaks of Mr Snow, as a man not respectable in private life—and
very ignorant—but of this part of C's communication it would be improper to
take any notice. *Later Years*, i. 200–2.

[1] See Letters 1019 and 1041.

1446]   *To John Taylor Coleridge*

good word—but how very highly I esteem the work—and especially
The Hebrew Tales, Sayings and Anecdotes, as among the very best
Books I have ever seen, for the use of *Schools*, as an *English* Book,
you will see in a day or two, in my preface to the 'Aids to Reflection'
—which only the Delay of the Printer prevents me from sending you
the *Proof* Sheet with this[1]—and at the same time the Titles of all
the different Tales, &c which I think uncommonly well-*pointed*, and
attractive.—The whole makes a Volume of about 350 Octavo
Pages: and the whole, written out and corrected, is completely
ready for the Press.—Now as I consider Mr Murray as in some sort
the originator of the Work, I told Mr Hurwitz, I thought it right,
with his consent, to offer it in the first instance to Mr Murray[2]—
which, as soon at least as you have received the prefatory Sheet of
my Work, I intreat you to take the first convenient opportunity
of doing.

God bless you! and believe me to be with high esteem & most
cordial Regard

Your affectionate Uncle

S. T. Coleridge

1447. *To J. A. Hessey*

Address: Messrs Taylor and Hessey | 93 Fleet Street   *For Mr Hessey*
MS. Harvard College Lib. Hitherto unpublished.
Postmark: Highgate, 7 May 1825.

[7 May 1825]

Dear Sir

1. ON FAITH.
2. ON THE EUCHARIST, doctrinally and historically.
3. On the PHILOSOPHY OF PRAYER.
4. On the Hebrew Prophets & the prophetic *Gift*. (not more than four pages.)
5. On the Church—& the true character of the Romish Church.
6. On the right and the superstitious Use of the Sacred Scriptures.[3]—

[1] This commendation of Hurwitz's *Hebrew Tales* formed the concluding
paragraph of the Advertisement or '*Pre*-preface' to the *Aids to Reflection*, but
on Murray's advice it was cancelled in the proof. See Letters 1448–9, 1456,
and 1460–2.

[2] Despite Coleridge's efforts, Murray did not publish the *Hebrew Tales*. See
Letters 1448–9, 1456, 1459–62, 1470–1, 1478–9, 1492, and 1494.

[3] In *Aids to Reflection* Coleridge announced his intention to publish the first,
second, third, fifth, and sixth of these disquisitions:

The author had written and intended to insert a similar exposition on the
Eucharist. But as the leading view has been given in the Comment on

(434)

All together, as far as I can guess, about 200 pages, perhaps 250. Now suppose that you had the whole in your hand within 10 days— the 6th you *have*[1]—the 1st., 2. and 4th. you may have immediately—. Now, under these circumstances (Understand me: I mean on the condition of your having the 3rd and 5th in your possession) would you recommend the publication immediately, under the Title of a Supplement?—Or under an independent Title of *Six Disquisitions*, on &c?—

Again: what do you think? *Ought* I to attach ROYAL ASSOCIATE of the R. S. L.?[2]—I have no fondness for this Bashaship with *one Tail*—(My Brother-in-law has, at least a dozen queues.) neither for

Redemption, its length induces him to defer it, together with the articles on Faith and the philosophy of Prayer, to a small supplementary Volume. (*Aids*, 1825, p. 376, 1831, p. 378.)

An Essay on the Church, as instituted by Christ, and as an Establishment of the State, and a series of Letters on the right and the superstitious use and estimation of the Bible, will appear in a small volume by themselves, should the reception given to the present volume encourage or permit the publication. (*Aids*, 1825, p. 381, 1831, p. 383.)

Only the fifth of these disquisitions appeared during Coleridge's lifetime. It was published in 1830 under the title, *On the Constitution of The Church and State, according to the Idea of Each: with Aids toward a Right Judgment on the late Catholic Bill.* The sixth disquisition, 'On the right and the superstitious Use of the Sacred Scriptures', was published by H. N. Coleridge in 1840 as *Confessions of an Inquiring Spirit.* Mention should also be made of the 'Essay on Faith' included in *Literary Remains*, iv. 425. In his letter to Tulk of 16 July 1820 Coleridge says he has 'lately written a short essay or tract on the true nature of Faith'.

[1] Writing to J. Blanco White on 20 July 1825, Coleridge said that this disquisition had been in his publishers' hands 'for more than a year'. According to Hessey, who did not return the MS. until 1826, the *Confessions* was originally intended to be a part of *Aids to Reflection* but was omitted because of its length. (See note to Letter 1480.) The opening page of the *Confessions of an Inquiring Spirit* reads:

LETTER I.

MY DEAR FRIEND,

I EMPLOYED the compelled and most unwelcome leisure of severe indisposition in reading *The Confessions of a Fair Saint* in Mr. Carlyle's recent translation of the *Wilhelm Meister*, which might, I think, have been better rendered literally, *The Confessions of a Beautiful Soul.* This, acting in conjunction with the concluding sentences of your Letter, threw my thoughts inward on my own religious experience, and gave the immediate occasion to the following Confessions.

Carlyle presented a copy of *Wilhelm Meister* to Coleridge in June 1824. See R. W. Armour and R. F. Howes, *Coleridge the Talker*, 1940, pp. 111–12.

[2] The title-page of the first edition of *Aids to Reflection* reads merely 'By S. T. Coleridge', but that of the second edition (1831) and those of the first and second editions of *The Church and State* (1830) read 'By S. T. Coleridge, Esq., R. A., R. S. L.'

the Title, nor for the Thing—tho' as to the latter my Poverty is of
a different opinion from my Self.—

> Your's, dear Sir, | very cordially
> S. T. Coleridge

1448. *To John Taylor Coleridge*

Address: John Coleridge, Esqre | 2 Pump Court | Temple
MS. British Museum. Pub. with omis. Samuel Taylor Coleridge and the English
Romantic School, *by Alois Brandl, translated by Lady Eastlake, 1887, p. 351.*

Private

[8 May 1825][1]

My very dear Nephew

I write you one Letter on 3 different Sheets—the motive for
which you will have no difficulty in decyphering.—*This* de Domino
Murray. I must love and esteem an individual in order for it to
become possible that I should quarrel with him. Ergo: I have &
have had no quarrel, with Mr M.[2]—What terms he may be on with
his conception of me, I myself can only deduce by conjectural or
tentative Logic from the *facts*: and these, of course, are the only
Data, I can supply, for you to ground an opinion on. When between 8 and 9 years ago I came from Calne to London with the ill-
starred Zapolya, written Musis et Apolline nullo[3] for the Theatre at
Lord Byron's instance, I had from change of diet, over-excitement,
agitating anxieties on poor Morgan's account, and (to *seal* all)
indiscreet attempts to stave off a coming evil; i.e. to keep up the
strength, or rather *power*, of spirits and animal motion, and to
defer the inevitable Ebb & dead Low Water, till I had come to some
settlement and certainty with regard to pecuniary matters, by
means of the Play, my Biographia Literaria, Sibylline Leaves
(then printed but not published) and the rifacciamento of THE
FRIEND (as it now is)—from all these causes I had a violent fit of
Sickness, which confined me to my bed for about 3 weeks, & *led* in

---

[1] The opening sentence of the present letter—'I write you one Letter on
3 different Sheets'—indicates that Letters 1448, 1449, and 1450 were probably
written on the same day. The second of these letters is dated 8 May 1825 and
establishes the date of the others. By 16 May Coleridge had not heard from his
nephew concerning this correspondence and reported that he had entrusted the
'pacquet' containing the 'triple Epistle, or 3 Letters' to the Highgate carrier
on Tuesday the 10th, if he did not 'mistake' the day. See Letter 1459.

[2] In reply to the letter of 8 Apr. 1825, in which Coleridge condemns Murray
and mentions the 'insolence of one of his proposals', John Taylor Coleridge
asked for a statement of the 'terms' on which his uncle stood with that publisher. The present letter was written in 'compliance' with this request. See
Letter 1456.

[3] Martial, *Epigrams* II. 89. 3.

it's consequences to my settlement at Highgate with Mr Gillman—originally intended for no more than 3 months; but which in all human probability will end only with my Life, or (which God forbid!) their Lives.—Well! while yet in London, (Norfolk Street, Strand) and in the first days of my Convalescence Mr Murray called on me, in consequence of some flashes of praise, which Lord Byron had coruscated respecting the Fragment of the Christabel. Murray urged me to publish it, and offered me 80 Pounds or guineas.—The publication was utterly against my feelings and my Judgement—But poor Morgan's Necessities, including his Wife & Sister, were urgent & clamorous: and I never yet possessed even a decent quantity of fortitude in withstanding distress in the form of persons, who, I had reason to think, loved me & who in better days (or rather what they themselves had mistaken for such) had manifested attachment to me & mine. With many a pang & many a groan, when I could groan unheard, I concluded the bargain—and gave the 80£ to Morgan—who was already Debtor rather than Creditor, on all former accounts of Board &c—. It was likewise understood by me, that Mr Murray was to be my Publisher for my Works generally—The Sale of the Christabel sadly disappointed Mr Murray. It was abused & ridiculed by the Edingburgh Review: & the Quarterly refused even to notice it. Sir W. Scott *might* have served me if he had at [that] time said only *one half* of what he has since avowed,[1] in large companies—as at Sir G. Beaumont's, Mr Rogers's, Mr Sotheby's &c[2]—all, however, persons who knew the fact almost as well as Sir W. himself.—In this mood Mr Murray expressed himself in such words, as led me, nervous & imperfectly recovered as I was, to suppose that he had no pleasure in this connection—at least, that he would have nothing to do with what he called *my Metaphysics*—which were in truth my all. At this time and under this impression I was found out by that consummated Integrity of Scoundrelism, the REVEREND Mr Curtis, who by a shilling Licence had so transmografied himself from Mr C., the Pater-noster Row Bookseller.—I never liked the man; but his pretensions to Religion were such—you should hear the particulars from Mr Gillman, who was present at the greater number of our

[1] In 1817, after *Christabel* appeared, Coleridge complained to Murray: 'With the exception of Lord Byron there was not [one] of the many, who had for so many years together spoken so warmly in it's praise who gave it the least positive Furtherance after it's publication.' See Letter 1050.

[2] Gillman records one of these later occasions: 'The late Mr. Sotheby informed me, that, at his house in a large party, Sir Walter made the following remark:—"I am indebted to Coleridge for the mode of telling a tale by question and answer. This was a new light to me, and I was greatly struck by it."' *Life*, 278.

interviews—that I literally did not *dare* disbelieve him, and his solemn attestations of Zeal & friendship. Nay, I was offended & shocked with Mr Gillman for his avowals that he thought him a hypocrite. However, let that pass. I trusted him—and lost 1100£ *clear*: and was forced to borrow 150£ in order to buy up my own Books & half-copyrights—a Shock which has kept me embarrassed & in debt (thank God! to one Person only) even to this moment.

With Mr Murray I had no intercourse, till in consequence of some conversation with Mr Tulk I proposed to him the Work mentioned in the ADVERTISEMENT, before the Preface. At the same time thro' Mr Tulk he proposed to me the Publication of my poetic Works—I waited on him—and found him all courtesy—but again and again I waited—came in on purpose from Highgate—at length (after having made that modest proposal with regard to my Poems &c, I mentioned in my letter to you)[1] it was evident, he wished to avoid an interview—and I received a note, declining the publication of the proposed Life [& Be]auties of Arch-bishop Leighton, in a very dry way, which [chagr]ined me only on account of the civilities, he & Mrs Murray had shewn to Sara Coleridge. Immediately after, Offers were made me by Taylor & Hessey to publish any Works of mine, on any terms I might wish. I made no terms but that of not risking what if lost I had no means of paying; but thought it best to try whether or no the evil day of Calumny and far more injurious Friendlessness in the shape of silent Friends had passed by—And the 'aids to reflection' is the first experiment.—Mr Tulk considered himself as having been trifled with; but nothing of the Nature of any Dispute or expressed Resentment has passed between me & Murray. I feel, that he does not like me; and my main motives for having this Work of my friend's—in which I have no pecuniary*

[1] i.e., Murray's proposal to publish Coleridge's poems on condition that Milman oversee the edition. See Letter 1438.

* Mr Hurwitz gave me 12£ for my time & trouble in carefully revising, polishing & pointing the tales—which, however, I in part repaid by giving to him the Specimens of Rabbinical Wisdom which I had myself written in the *old* Friend, & one or two others composed by me after Mr Murray had suggested the work.—Tho' as Mr Hurwitz is attached to me & knows my circumstances, it is not improbable, that he regards the market contingencies of the Book more wishfully from some view to my participation. [Note by S. T. C.]

Three of Coleridge's *Specimens of Rabbinical Wisdom, selected from the Mishna* were included in Hurwitz's *Hebrew Tales.* They had earlier appeared in the eleventh and twenty-second numbers of *The Friend.* A fourth *Specimen,* which appeared in the twelfth number of the original issue of *The Friend* (1809–10) but was omitted in the 1812 edition, was not included. By 'old Friend' Coleridge in his note obviously refers to the 1812 edition. See also Letters 1445 and 1455.

In the preface to his *Hebrew Tales* Hurwitz acknowledged Coleridge's con-

interest—offered to Mr Murray—are first (& this *really* as well as ostensibly) that Mr M. was the original Suggester of the Scheme— 2nd. the respectability of Mr Murray's Name as the Publisher—& last, that without any conscious partiality I think that the Work deserves &, if properly befriended, could not but remunerate a respectable Publisher.—

If then you would shew or read to Mr Murray my letter,[1] and the description, I have given of the Work in the Advertisement or Pre-preface to my 'Aids to Reflection', the sheet containing which I have inclosed, together with the Titles of the first sixty Tales which are so constructed as to contain the *Moral*, and as often as was possible, expressed proverbially—& hear what he says, you can do no more.—[No signature in MS.]

P.S.[2] My unfavorable Opinions or rather feelings, of μυρραι[3] originated in sundry anecdotes which Wordsworth told me, in addition to a conversation of M. himself with Wordsworth. Did you ever read Galt's *Provost*? If you have, you will understand me.[4]

1449. *To John Taylor Coleridge*

MS. British Museum. Pub. E. L. G. ii. 346.

8 May 1825
Grove, Highgate.

My dear Nephew

Some eight or nine years ago Mr Murray suggested and proposed to me the re-publication of the 'Specimens of Rabbinical Wisdom', that appeared in the original Friend, as circulated by the Post on

tributions as follows: 'Excepting the three moral Tales, so admirably translated by my esteemed friend Mr. S. T. Coleridge, and which are, by his kind permission, inserted in this Collection, I know of no similar attempt in this or in any other of the modern languages.'

[1] Coleridge refers to the next letter.
[2] This postscript is written at the top of page one of the MS.
[3] Underlined once in MS.
[4] A note which Coleridge wrote in a copy of *The Provost* may be included here:

This work is not for the many; but in the unconscious, perfectly natural irony of self-delusion, in all parts intelligible to the intelligent reader, without the slightest suspicion on the part of the autobiographer, I know of no equal in our literature. The governing trait in the Provost's character is nowhere caricatured. In the character of Betty, John's wife, or the beggar girl, intense selfishness without malignity, as a *nature*, and with all the innocence of a nature, is admirably portrayed. In the Provost a similar *self*ness is united with a *slyness* and a plausibility eminently successful in cheating the man himself into a happy state of constant self-applause. (*Coleridge's Miscellaneous Criticism*, ed. T. M. Raysor, 1936, pp. 344–5.)

stamped Sheets, with as many additional ones as would make a sizable Volume. I was pleased with the scheme, and set myself to work on it: but by the time, I had collected and re-composed two or three tales, I discovered, first that I had not Learning enough for the Task, but must depend wholly on the Latin Translations of such of the Works, Arabic or Rabbinical Hebrew, as had met with Translators. Secondly, that these Translations were very rare Books, and the most important to be found only in the British Museum. Thirdly, my state of Health & the living five miles from Town opposed almost insurmountable obstacles to such attendance on Public Libraries as would be necessary—And lastly, that the Quantity of dry reading to be fagged thro'—this hunt for needles in a score of Hay-stacks—the bodily fatigue in going, returning, & (not least) in sitting, the expence of Stages; & after all, with the knowlege that the most productive Mines were not accessible by me—rendered the sum offered (tho' quite adequate to the probable marketable Value of the Work itself; yet) inadequate to the certain toil & inconvenience, and the very questionable success of my researches.—I therefore abandoned it in despair.

Some years afterward I had the good fortune of forming an intimate acquaintance with Mr Hurwitz, the Author of the VINDICIAE HEBRAICAE, or defence of our church Translation of the Old Testament against the attacks of Bellamy & others—a Work which procured and *merited* a very handsome letter to the Author from the present Bishop of London. It is indeed a work which ought to be in the Library of every Biblical Student.—Beyond all doubt or comparison Mr Hurwitz, whom it would be no flattery to name the English MENDELSSOHN, is the first Hebrew and Rabbinical Scholar in the kingdom; and among the first in the Languages of the Hither Easts—I mean, the ancient & modern Arabic, the Syriac, Chaldaic, and Syro-chaldaic.—To him I accidentally mentioned the circumstance, and the causes & motives of my having abandoned the Undertaking—. He promised to bear it in mind, in the course of his Reading—& even to read for *the purpose*—in short, that [as] I retained no thought of doing it myself, he would endeavor to produce a Volume of the sort & character proposed—if, when finished, I would correct the work and give it whatever point, piquancy and polish of Style my readier Command of Language might enable me to give.—I promised this: and my excellent Friend (what *my* convictions concerning him are, you will find recorded in p. 205 of my 'Aids to Reflection';[1] the sheet containing

___

[1] The passage in *Aids to Reflection* reads: 'This latter and most endearing name [Fellow-christian] I scarcely know how to withhold even from my friend, HYMAN HURWITZ, as often as I read what every Reverer of Holy Writ and of

which I have inclosed together with the first Sheet) set about it, I have found, in good earnest—& made his way thro' a mass & multiplicity of Reading during the last 3 or four years, i.e. since his retirement from the School, which no one could undertake who had not leisure and easy circumstances, and few would have accomplished under any circumstances.—On my return from Ramsgate in December last he brought me the Result, which far exceeded my anticipations.—I too have fulfilled my part of the engagement, which was indeed a light and easy task.—I should be ashamed to be proud; but neither will I affect a humility, I do not feel: and whatever rank my Judgement may hold in the opinion of others, I set too high a value on my own reputation & even on *my good word* to risk the one or prostitute the other by praise beyond merit—even if insincerity were less hateful to me than it is.—I refer, however, to the concluding Paragraph of my *Pre*-preface, at present, solely for a description of the Work—and further have sent for the same purpose the Titles (purposely so constructed as to contain the Moral or Point of each Tale or Narrative, generally in the form of an epigrammatic Proverb) of about three fourths or nearly so of the Collection. The Scrap of paper containing the Titles of the Remainder I have mislaid among my Wilderness; and must give up the search *in order* to find it—for things are sure never to turn up, till I have given over looking for them.—This letter is introductory to a request, that you would state it's contents to Mr Murray. My motives for wishing the Work to be proposed to him are—first, that the Work deserves a respectable, and will, I am confident, if properly brought out, remunerate an influencive Publisher—and next, that I thought myself bound to do so, it owing it's existence to Mr Murray's Suggestion, and being in fact a realizing of his Plan & Outline.—I have only to add, that the MSS is quite ready for the Press.

We have just received a long letter from my dear Sara—and are in anxious contriving about her coming up & being with me two or three months—. But of this when I see you—.

I want very much to talk with you about the Quarterly Review —There is but one opinion that in Travels, Voyages, Geography, &c, it is immeasurably superior to the Edingb.—The same in all matters of *practical* Politics, and the actual state of things.—In Classical Learning the Quarterly is doubtless superior; but it is not my opinion only, that it *ought to be* still more so—& might so

the English Bible ought to read, his admirable VINDICIAE HEBRAICAE! It has trembled on the verge, as it were, of my lips, every time I have conversed with that pious, learned, strong-minded, and single-hearted Jew, an Israelite indeed and without guile.'

easily be. In the *star* articles, men will think according to their Parties—I who am of no party, can often read the political Essay in the Quarterly over again—which I scarcely ever can, in the Edingburgh.—On the other hand, in Political Economy the Edingburgh has the general opinion in it's favor. In my Conviction the whole pretended Science is but a Humbug. I have attentively read not only Sir James Stewart[1] & Adam Smith; but Malthus, and Ricardo[2]—and found (i.e. believe myself to have found) a multitude of Sophisms but not a single just and important Result which might [not] far more convincingly be deduced from the simplest principles of Morality and Common Sense—. But certainly in the Edingburgh Articles there is more Shew & effective Pretension.— In SCIENCE, likewise, the Ed. has been too much allowed to have the appearance of Superiority.—In interesting information as to the real products & growth of the Literature of the Day both Reviews are (me judice) equally defective.—I have for some time worked hard in Egyptian Antiquities; & if I do not delude myself, have the means of *quashing* the *deduction* at least which certain half Infidels have drawn from Champollon or what's his name's decypherings.[3] I meant the materials as stuff for Papers to the R.S.L.; but if you liked them, & thought they would be useful, they shall be at your service.

God bless you &

S. T. C.—

P.S. My Belief, grounded on no slight evidence, in addition to that of common Sense & the *Harmony* of Historical Experience, is: that all Inscriptions, Hieroglyphics, &c earlier than Moses are ancient Forgeries—that the wisest Ancients were well acquainted with these pretended Kings &c & regarded them as mere Egyptian Lies—&c &c—In short, my researches with the light of English Common Sense have rendered me a sturdy Anti-egyptian & a very sceptical Hindostanist. S. T. C.—

[1] Sir James Steuart, later Denham (1712–80), author of *An Inquiry into the Principles of Political Oeconomy*, 2 vols., 1767.
[2] David Ricardo (1772–1823), author of *Principles of Political Economy and Taxation*, 1817.
[3] J. F. Champollion (1790–1832), French Egyptologist, whose first decipherment of hieroglyphics dates from 1821. His *Précis du système hiéroglyphique* appeared in 1824.

1450. *To John Taylor Coleridge*

Address: John Coleridge, Esqre   with the first Third of the 'Aids to Reflection'.
MS. British Museum. Pub. E. L. G. ii. 343.

[8 May 1825]

My dear Nephew

I have here inclosed the first THIRD of my 'Aids to Reflection', comprizing the Prudential and Moral Aphorisms and Comments, both indeed in alliance with the Religious Principle, and so arranged as to be inobtrusively preparatory to the succeeding reflections and expositions on positive Christianity.—As soon as I can procure a complete Copy of the whole work—now in a few days, I hope— I will send it, & you will be so good as to return these.

I am aware of your many and onerous engagements: and therefore have sent this portion only, as readable *off hand*, with the exception of two or three pages at least. But if you could find an hora subseciva, so as to be able to let me know your actual impressions—first, as to the presence or absence of that which is calculated to excite an *interest*, such, of course, as can be expected in a *didactic* work professedly religious—second—as to the *style* in point of perspicuity—whether it *reads* well—you would oblige me more than I can express. You will believe me, when I say that I want no praise; but from my heart's heart, *e corculo cordis*, exactly and nakedly your *first* feeling, and *it's* judgement, not formally given but merely by striking a line with your pencil down the Margin and if it pleased or interested you, put B.—if better, BB.—if you thought it questionable or objectionable put a ? beside a line—if it read *heavy*, P.—if obscure, O.

This will be quite sufficient: for I am half in doubt whether to wish that the impression made on you should be modified even by the objects & purposes stated in the preface—it being enough for me to be certain beforehand, that you will not expect the interest of a Novel in 'Aids to Reflection'.

Had I commenced with the plan & purpose afterwards adopted, I should certainly have prefixed a chapter or series of Aphorisms on Prudence, or Good Sense and Discretion in the management of a Man's Feelings, Behaviour, Conversation, Studies &c, generally— without any direct connection with religion, the ultimate end. As it is, the Book will, of course, have few readers but such as purchase it *as* a religious Book.—

One of my principal motives for the request, I have made, is that I may have an opinion, that I can rely on, as to the effect of the aphorismatic form; whether it distracts or relieves the attention.—

The remaining two thirds of the Volume, (the philosophical and theological) are, of necessity, more continuous: and of these I can form some opinion: of the former I cannot—but am quite adrift.

I have six Disquisitions ready for the Press—as a sort of Supplement to this—the second of which was to have followed the disquisition on Baptism, and Infant Baptism; but was obliged to be left out from the length of the Volume.[1]

1. On Faith. 2. The Eucharist. 3. The philosophy of PRAYER: and the three kinds of **Prayer**, Public, Domestic, and Solitary. 4. On the prophetic character of the Old Testament: and on the Gift of Prophecy. 5. On the Church+Establishment, and Dissent— and the true character & danger of the Romish Church. 6. On the right and the superstitious use and estimation of the Sacred Scriptures: this last in a series of Letters.

In the 'Aids to Reflection' I have touched on the Mystery of the Trinity only in a *negative* way. That is, I have shewn the hollowness of the arguments by which it has been assailed—have demonstrated that the doctrine involves nothing contrary to Reason, and the nothingness & even absurdity of a Christianity without it. In short, I have contented myself with exposing the causes of it's rejection and in removing (what by experience I know to be) the ordinary obstacles to it's belief.[2]—But the positive establishment of the Doctrine as involved in the Idea, God—together with the *Origin* of EVIL, as distinguished from Original Sin (on which I *have* treated at large)[3] and the Creation of the visible World—THESE as absolutely requiring the habit of abstraction, and *severe Thinking*, I have reserved for my larger Work—of which I have fin[ished] the first Division, namely, the *Philosophy* of the Christian Creed, or Christianity true in *Idea*. The 2nd. Division will be—Xty true in *fact*—i.e. historically. The third & last will be—Xty true in *act*— i.e. morally & spiritually.[4]—

But with exception of the Trinity (the *positive* proof of)—the Origin of Evil, metaphysically examined—and the Creation—I may venture to say, that the Aids to Reflection (the latter $\frac{2}{3}$rds, I mean) with the six supplementary Disquisitions contain a compleat *System* of internal evidences. At least, I can think of no essential Article of Faith omitted.—At all events, no one hereafter can with justice complain that I have disclosed my sentiments

---

[1] See Letter 1447 n. 3.

[2] For Coleridge's comments on the Doctrine of the Trinity in *Aids to Reflection*, 1825, see pp. 151, 169–80, and 247–9.

[3] For Coleridge's discussion of Original Sin see *Aids*, 1825, p. 249 fol.

[4] For similar comments see *Aids*, 1825, pp. 151–2, where Coleridge announces hat he is 'now preparing for the Press' his *Assertion of Religion*.

only in flashes and fragments—and that no one can tell what the
Opinions & Belief are of

> your affectionate Uncle & Friend
> S. T. Coleridge—

1451. *To J. A. Hessey*

Address: For Mr Hessey
MS. Bodleian Library. Hitherto unpublished.

[*Circa* 10 May 1825]

Dear Sir
I have sent off the first Sheet, containing the Preface &c, with
the clean sheets, I had in my possession up to p. 272, to my nephew,
Mr John Coleridge—but if I recollect aright, there is a blank page,
facing some thing or other—And on this page if it be not too late
I should be glad to have the two Mottos inclosed printed[1]—i.e. if
it can be done without much trouble or delay.
I am desirous to learn your decision—as it would influence me
with regard to the attempting or not attempting the scheme concerning which I am about to ask the opinions of intelligent friends
—& the first letter I have here inclosed to you[2]—And you would
serve me much if you would shew it in confidence to such persons
as you think likely to form a sound opinion—

> Your obliged
> S. T. Coleridge—

1452. *To Thomas Allsop*

Transcript Mrs. R. L. Grigg. *Pub. with omis.* Letters, Conversations and Rec.
234.

10 May 1825

My dearest Allsop
I have been reflecting earnestly and actively on the subject of a
Metropolitan University, now in agitation:[3] and could conveniently

---

[1] Two mottoes appear on the verso of the page containing the Table of
'Contents' of *Aids to Reflection*. The first motto is from Marinus, the second
from Vico.

[2] Coleridge refers to his proposed lectures 'on the subject of a Metropolitan
University', but the 'first letter' mentioned here has not come to light. This
'LECTURE SCHEME' had been given up by 17 May. See Letters 1452-3, 1458,
1460, and 1462.

[3] The University of London had its origin in a movement initiated in 1825
by Thomas Campbell and espoused by Henry Brougham and others. The fact
that Dissenters were practically excluded from Oxford and Cambridge gave
impetus to the scheme. As the plan developed it became non-theological. The

comprize the Results in three Lectures. 1. On the History of Universities generally; the more interesting features in the History of the
most celebrated Universities in Great Britian, Germany, France
&c—Reduction of all Universities of any name, with respect to
their construction and constitution, to three Classes.—2. The
meaning of the term, University, and the one true & only adequate
Scheme of a University stated and unfolded from the Seed (i.e. the
Idea) to the full Tree with all it's Branches. 3. The Advantages,
moral, intellectual, national, developed from reason and established
by proofs of History—and lastly, a plan (& sketch of the *means*) of
approximating to the Ideal, adapted and applied to this Metropolis
—(N.B. The Plan *in detail*, Salaries only not mentioned, the particular Sums I mean.) The Obstacles—the favorable circumstances
—the Pro and Con regarding the question of *Collegiate* Universities
&c &c. That I could make these subjects not only highly interesting
but even entertaining, I have not the least doubt. But would the
Subject excite an interest of *Curiosity*? Would the anticipation of
what I might say attract an Audience of respectable Small-Clothes
and Petticoats sufficiently large to produce something more than
with the same exertion of Head & Hand I might earn in my
Garrett (to give the precise *Top*-ography of my Abode) here at
Nemorosae—alias, Houses in the Grove?—For the expence of the
Coach hire, the bodily fatigue, and (to borrow a phrase from poor
Charles Lloyd) 'the *hot huddle of indefinite sensations*' that hustle
my inward man in the Monster City and a Crown & Anchor Room
demand a +, and would an = after all expences paid but ragged
economy—unless I were certain of effecting more good in this than
in a quieter way of industry.

I wrote to Mr B. Montague for his advice. But he felt no interest
himself in the Subject, and naturally therefore was doubtful of

deed of settlement was drawn up on 11 Feb. 1826, and the college opened in
Oct. 1828 as the University of London. 'The application of "London University"
for incorporation and degree-giving powers met with bitter opposition', and it
was not until 28 Nov. 1836 that the Charter of Incorporation was granted by
William IV. Thenceforth the college was designated as University College,
London. On the same day the Charter of the University of London was signed.
Thus University College became a 'teaching body', whereas the responsibility
of the University of London was limited to 'the institution of examinations
and the conferring of degrees'. See *University of London Calendar, 1963-4*,
pp. 70–72, and *Encyclopaedia Britannica*, 1910–11, xxvii. 772–3.

King's College was founded by a body of defenders of the established order
who planned a college 'in which instruction in the doctrines and duties of
Christianity as taught by the Church of England should be for ever combined
with other branches of useful education'. A Royal Charter of Incorporation was
granted in Aug. 1829, and the college opened in Oct. 1831. In 1836 King's
College, London, was also incorporated with the University of London.

any number of others feeling any. But he promised to talk with Mr Irving about it.—On the other hand, I heard from Mr Hughes and a Mr Wilkes[1] (a clever Solicitor-sort of a man who lives in Finsbury Square, has a great sway with the Slangi, yclept the Religious Public, and (this I add *as a White-washer*) was a regular attendant of *my* Lectures), that the Subject itself is stirring up the mud-pool of the Public Mind in London with the vivacity of a Bottom-wind.

If you can find time, talk with Jameson about it—& sound as many as are likely to guess aright—& let me know your own Opinion & Anticipation above all and at all events—and as soon as possible. We dine on Friday with Mr Chance—I wish, you were with us—Indeed, if you could come up, I should feel no impropriety in going arm in arm with you: for I am sure he would be very glad to see you. Need I say that my Thoughts, wishes, & prayers follow you in all your doings & strivings—for I am evermore, my dearest Allsop,

Your's with a friend's & a father's affection & solicitude
S. T. Coleridge

My kindest remembrances to Mrs Allsop, with kisses for little Titania Puckinella. Years have passed since I heard the Nightingales sing as they did this evening, in Mr Robarts's Garden-grounds[2] —so many and in such full song—particularly, that giddy voluminous Whirl of Notes which you never hear but when the Birds feel the temperature of the Air *voluptuous*.

P.S. If I undertook these Lectures I should compose the three and write them out with as much care and polish as if for the Press —tho' I should probably make no use of the MSS in speaking, or at all attempt to recollect it—It would, relatively to my vivâ voce addresses, be only a way of pre-meditating the subject.

1453. *To J. H. Green*

Address: J. H. Green, Esqre | 46 | Lincoln's Inn Fields
MS. Pierpont Morgan Lib. Hitherto unpublished.

My dear Sir   [10 May 1825]

I have for some time past been reading and reflecting earnestly and actively on the subject of a Metropolitan University, now in

[1] Probably John Wilks (1765 ?–1854), attorney and author of *An Apology for the Missionary Society*, 1799.

[2] Fitzroy House, the seat of Lord Southampton, was occupied by Robarts the banker. It was surrounded by extensive grounds 'of a most delightfully undulating character, studded with beautiful timber'. John H. Lloyd, *The History . . . of Highgate*, 1888, p. 348.

agitation—and I could conveniently comprize the results of my meditation and researches in three Discourses—the chief contents of which would be—

a. the History and Origin of European Universities generally.

b. the more interesting facts and features in the histories of the more celebrated Universities at home and abroad—especially, the University of Paris.

c. Construction and Constitution of British & Continental universities: and reduction of the same to three *Kinds* or classes.

d. the origin and proper sense of the term, University: and the right and only adequate Frame of a University stated—i.e. an ideal University developed from the germinal Idea to the full-grown Tree of Knowlege with all it's Branches.—

e. The advantages, individual and national; moral, intellectual, and political, of a true University, deduced from reason and established by proofs of fact and historical Evidences.—

f. Cambridge and Oxford national blessings; but not true Universities. On the *collegiate* form, with the arguments pro et contra. Is a great city a proper place for a University ? Is it equally proper ? Has it any peculiar advantages ? What are the disadvantages & objections ? Which over-balances ?

g. A full Exposé of the Plan and Means of the greatest practicable approximation to the Ideal of a University at the present time—given in detail—with proof that this Plan would comprehend all the several advantages, on which all the different Parties have grounded their particular schemes—& that it is exposed to fewer Obstacles, and removes or precludes the most formidable— Conclusion. Display of the probable Consequences on the Wealth, Worth and character of the Country at large and of the Metropolis in particular.

That I could make these subjects highly interesting and even entertaining, I dare confidently promise myself. But would the Announcement of the same excite an interest of *Curiosity* ? Would the anticipation of what I might have to offer attract a sufficient number of respectable Auditors to liquidate the expences of Room, Advertisements &c—with a surplus equal to what with the same exertion of Head & Hand I should earn in my own attic by a quieter industry ? I say, *hand*: because I should compose and write out each of the three discourses, as I should do, were they then going to the Press—though probably I should make no use of the MSS. in speaking—& consider the writing as but one method of carefully *pre-meditating* my Address—and I put the query because in my present circumstances I cannot HONESTLY *give* the

time. The fatigue & painful sensations with which Public Speaking
and the Great City always oppress me, I would willingly undergo—
& willingly give or give up the pleasurable quiet of domestic Study
—if I were led to believe the affirmative to this my last question—
viz. Should I be likely to promote a useful and desirable Object ?
Should I do more good by the vivâ voce promulgation of my sentiments & the grounds of the same ?—These are the questions which
being unable to decide for myself I anxiously entreat you to
answer, to the best of your judgement and from what you know &
have observed of the *public mind* & the prevalent tone of feeling.

A single Line of, I think, you would have a sufficient Audience—
or I fear, not—would be enough and would seriously *serve*, I need
not add, oblige, my dear Sir,

Your sincere Friend & Servt

S. T. Coleridge

1454. *To Unknown Correspondent*

MS. Harvard College Lib. Hitherto unpublished.

Grove, Highgate
12 May 1825.

The first stanza of the Poem, composed in the same year[1] in which
I wrote the Ancient Mariner and the first Book of Christabel.—

> Encinctur'd with a twine of Leaves,[2]
> That leafy twine his only Dress!
> A lovely Boy was plucking fruits
> In a moonlight wilderness.
> The Moon was bright, the air was free—
> And Fruits and Flowers together grew
> On many a Shrub and many a Tree:
> And all put on a gentle hue,
> Hanging in the shadowy air
> Like a Picture rich and rare.
> It was a Climate where, they say,
> The Night is more beloved than Day.
> But who that beauteous Boy beguil'd,
> That beauteous Boy! to linger here ?
> Alone, by night, a little child,
> In place so silent and so wild—
> Has he no friend, no loving mother near ?

WANDERINGS OF CAIN, *a MSS Poem.*—

[1] Coleridge first wrote 'month' and then altered it to 'year'.
[2] These lines, which were included in a letter sent to Byron on 22 Oct. 1815,
were first published in *Aids to Reflection*, 1825, p. 383 n. See *Poems*, i. 287.

Dear Sir
Tho' it has no pretension to a place in the collection of your
phil-autographic Friend, yet at your request I send the above
scrap written in and by my own hand, and with my best respects to
Mrs P., and a kiss to the little *Kingdom-of-Heavenite* I remain
your obliged

S. T. Coleridge

1455. *To J. A. Hessey*

Address: Messrs Taylor & Hessey | 93 Fleet Street   For Mr Hessey
MS. Mr. W. Hugh Peal. Hitherto unpublished.
Postmark: Highgate, 12 May 1825.

My dear Sir   [12 May 1825]
Yes!—true enough—a pacquet has been lost—and after [de]lay
and long consultations Mrs Gillman as well as myself *appear* to
ourselves to recollect it's having been intrusted to my Nephew,
Edward Coleridge, now at Eton (He is about, by the bye, to marry
Dr Keates's Daughter, the Head-Master)[1]—and he, I suppose, over
engaged in talking with Sir James Stuart & Dr Prati forgot it—
or trusted it to a Waiter—. It is vexatious for I now recollect that
besides the letter to you the three or four pages had particularly
satisfied—However, what can not be cured m[ust] be endured—
and in order to that not thought of—
I have patched it up, so as scarcely to add a line[2]—.
The Printer has, I think, two if not three Books of mine—the Old
Friend is one—I should be glad of a complete Copy as soon as
possible—. I have not heard from you in reply to my question
respecting the Six disquisition[s.]
Your's with sinc[ere] respect

S. [T. Coleri]dge.

1456. *To Hyman Hurwitz*

Address: Hyman Hurtwitz [*sic*], Esqre | Grenada Cottage | Old Kent Road
MS. University of Pennsylvania Lib. Hitherto unpublished.
Postmark: Highgate, 14 May 1825.

My dear Sir   [14 May 1825]
I can only say, that I have written four letters, 3 of them very
long ones—that the very same day, that I procured the first proof
of my Preface (having by my Nephew's Advice waited till then) I
sent it with a Letter *to* my Nephew but written purposely for him

---

[1] Edward Coleridge married Mary Keate on 3 Aug. 1826.
[2] The missing pages were intended for the 'Conclusion' to *Aids to Reflection*.
See Letters 1456 and 1465.

to shew to Murray—I having in compliance with John Coleridge's request made him acquainted exactly with the terms on which I stood with Murray—that there had been no quarrel or dispute (I think far too meanly of him as a man to render that *possible*) between him & *me*—but that he had certainly trifled with me for a long time & at last made a proposal that I had sufficient respect for my own Standing in the literary world to consider as impertinent —viz. An offer to purchase my Poems on condition that some friend of his whom I was not to know, but who (I believe) was a third rate Poetaster by the name of the Revd. Mr Millman, [was] to omit, what he pleased, and to make what corrections and additions, *he* might think desirable—that in consequence of this I was disinclined to have any personal interview with Murray—and that my Motives for wishing the Work to be offered to *him* were really those which I assigned in the letter to be shewn to Murray—1. That the Work richly deserved an *influencive* Publisher, and if properly published & befriended would, I confidently believed, remunerate an active Publisher.—2 and principally, that I felt myself *bound* to use what influence I had with *you*, to have it offered to Murray, because in fact the origin, occasion, & idea of the Work belonged to Mr Murray, and I had myself undertaken it on his suggestion—tho' afterwards I found that to do it, as it ought to be done, the Writer must be an Oriental & Rabbinical Scholar—and that it would have fallen to the ground, had not I become acquainted with *you* & transferred both the work, and the interest in it, to the only man in the kingdom capable of executing it.—

At the same time I had a fair and corrected Copy neatly written out, entitled Chapter of Contents: or Titles of the Tales, apologues, &c and inclosed it, with my Printed Preface or Pre-preface, which both describes the Work & gives my decided Judgement of it's Worth and Value.—

My Nephew wrote to me, that he would lose no time in doing all, I had requested, and in giving any weight to it that his opinion might have with Murray—

Every day or rather twice a day I have been anxiously expecting to hear from my Nephew—& knowing that he is a man of business, I suspect that Murray has been out of town for a day or two—. However, I have again written by this post—and doubtless, shall receive an answer from him on Monday, explaining the cause of the delay—tho' I ought to say, that he who would have any thing to do with Murray, must calculate on *delays* & waverings— so much so that *in my own case* I should have given up the undoubtedly important advantage of having a Work published by Mr M. rather than submit to his smooth *courtierly* insolence—

except that in this particular instance I feel, that he is entitled to the first Offer, as far as it was in my power to procure the same to be done.—

My own work suffered a week's delay by the loss—how? is not certain; but probably by the forgetfulness of another Nephew of mine, to wh[om] (Mrs Gillman seems to recollect that) I had entrusted [a] small parcel containing about six pages of the Conclusion—. I had no copy: & was forced to compose it anew. However, the Work is now *all* printed—& I suppose will appear in the course of the Week—

I am now at leisure—and shall be happy to see you on any day next week, excepting Wednesday, when I read my Essay at the Royal Society of Literature in Lincoln's Fields, & on Friday, 20th, when I dine to meet the Bishop of London at Sir George Beaumont's—& shall take occasion to mention your work to the Bishop & read to him what I have said of it—

God bless you &

S. T. Coleridge—

1457. *To Gioacchino de' Prati*[1]

Pub. Penny Satirist, *6 October 1838, p. 2.*

Grove, Highgate, May 14, 1825.

My dear Sir,—For as we both speak from the heart, we will both in our occasional epistolary intercommunion employ the most suitable vehicle for its utterance, our mother tongue.—If ever in my life I wished to be a man of fortune, if ever I was out of humour, and malcontent with my poverty, and with the dispensations of Providence, which has made it my fate to live (in our idiomatic phrase) 'from hand to mouth', or to quote my own words from a poem published in 1795, or 1799, and which are as true now as when first written,

---

[1] Gioacchino de' Prati (1790–1863), Italian patriot and conspirator. In 1810 he received a law degree at Pavia. M. H. Fisch says, however, that he was 'better trained in medicine'. As a result of his revolutionary activities, Prati fled to Switzerland in 1816. For a time he held a teaching position in Pestalozzi's school at Yverdon. In 1823 he found political refuge in England. In Apr. 1825 he became acquainted with Coleridge, through whom he met J. H. Green. According to Mr. Fisch, it was under Green's guidance that Prati 'mastered the standard English medical and pharmaceutical treatises while in prison for debt in 1829'. From 1837 to 1846 Prati contributed a column of medical advice to the *Penny Satirist,* a radical weekly. In 1852 the Austrian authorities permitted him to return to Italy. See M. H. Fisch, 'The Coleridges, Dr. Prati, and Vico', *Modern Philology,* Nov. 1943, pp. 111–22. See also Letters 1441, 1483, 1529, 1643, and 1794.

I [un]partaking of the evil thing,
With daily prayers and daily toil,
Soliciting for food my scanty soil,[1]—&c.,

it has been since I became acquainted with you. But I am in my own country; I have many sworn friends; and I have some influence, and though (I dare affirm) disproportionate to what it ought to be, at which you will not wonder when you know that during five and twenty, I might say thirty years, I have been resolutely opposing the whole system of modern illumination, in all its forms of Jacobinism, and Legitimatism, Epicurean (in our country Pelagian) Christianity, Pelagian morals, Pelagian politics, and 'casting my bread on the waters', yet, 'after many days', I have begun to find it, and therefore, I may venture to add that I have a growing influence. Now be assured, that whatever I could do for a brother, I will do for you. Nothing shall be lost for want of *effort* on my part. But some time must elapse before I can have talked, consulted, and written to my friends,[2] though I hope *shortly* to be able to send you some present and temporary assistance. I shall read with great interest the works you have sent me, and as soon as my *Aids to Reflection* have left the printer's office in the shape of a volume, I will send you all such of my works as are not out of print.

I now write for no other purpose but that dictated by the belief that it will be a comfort to you to be re-assured that you possess one most sincere well-wisher and sympathising friend in

S. T. Coleridge.

[1] *Ode to the Departing Year*, lines 154–6, *Poems*, i. 168.
[2] In the British Museum there is a manuscript in Coleridge's handwriting headed 'Documents'. It lists several certificates and two attestations relating to Prati and concludes with the following undated statement by Coleridge himself:

It would be useless to add more attestations of the latter kind. Of many I have taken without selection the two first, that came to hand. But I ought to add, that Dr Somerville, of Hanover Square, is not only well acquainted with Dr De Prati himself, but with his family, and with the detail of the Causes that drove him from his Country without any conduct on his part that a man of honor or an English Gentleman of *any* party or political creed would consider as detracting from his respectability or moral worth.—

Dr De Prati was first introduced to me by the Revd Mr Woodcock and my Nephew, the Revd E. Coleridge, both of whom had the highest opinion of him, & I can truly add that having passed many hours with Dr Prati every week since that time, I can most conscientiously add my suffrage to his merits, and think myself the more entitled to place confidence in the estimation, I have formed, by finding it in perfect coincidence with the judgement of my friends, Mr Irving, Mr Basil Montague, Mr Green, and Mr & Mrs Gillman. [Add. MS. 34255, ff. 168–9.]

P.S.—I am more and more delighted with G. B. Vico,[1] and if I had (which thank God's good grace I have not) the least drop of *Author's* blood in my veins, I should twenty times successively in the perusal of the first volume (I have not yet begun the second) have exclaimed: *'Pereant qui ante nos nostra dixere.'*[2] By the bye, when I see you on Thursday[3] I will mention a set of articles, on which I myself for a long time had set my thoughts, a critical and biographical account of the great *revolutionists* in the intellectual world, philosophical and religious. I am pretty certain that I could dispose of them, so as to make it worth your while, and at more than a common bookseller's honorarium, to the *Quarterly Review*, and other works of extensive sale, and which would not at all prevent your afterwards collecting and publishing them in a volume. God bless you! mention my name with all respectful kindness to Mrs. ——.[4]

1458. *To J. A. Hessey*

MS. *New York Public Lib. Pub. E. L. G. ii. 342.*

[*Circa* 16 May 1825][5]

Dear Sir I thank you for your kind letter. In every two friends, I have hitherto consulted, I have found the same difference of anticipation, as in you and Mr Taylor: to whom be pleased to present

[1] Prati had recently loaned Coleridge a copy of G. B. Vico's *Principii d'una Scienza Nuova*, 3 vols., 1816 (6th edn.). The work first appeared in 1725. The motto from Vico sent to Hessey for inclusion in *Aids to Reflection* is taken from the *Autobiography*, i. 50. See Letter 1451 and note, and M. H. Fisch, 'The Coleridges, Dr. Prati, and Vico', *Modern Philology*, Nov. 1943, pp. 111–22.

In the *Theory of Life* Coleridge had earlier quoted a passage abridged from Vico's *De antiquissima Italorum sapientia*, 1710. Mr. Fisch shows, however, that the Vico passage 'was lifted, and its context adapted' from F. H. Jacobi's *Von den göttlichen Dingen und ihrer Offenbarung*, 1811. See note to Letter 1235 and M. H. Fisch, op. cit. 119–20.

[2] This saying is attributed to Donatus by St. Jerome. See *Commentarium in Ecclesiasten* 390 (Migne, Patrologia latina: Hieronymus, vol. iii, column 1019).

[3] For an account of Coleridge's conversation reported in Prati's autobiography, see M. H. Fisch, op. cit. 111 and 120–2. This autobiography was published in instalments in the *Penny Satirist* from 1837 to 1840.

[4] Giuseppina Maffei, Prati's 'unwedded companion'. See H. M. Fisch, op. cit. 112 n.

[5] In the present letter Coleridge proposes a meeting with Hessey on Wednesday before proceeding to the Royal Society of Literature, where he lectured on 18 May 1825.

my thanks. I shall take tomorrow to consider of it—when I hope
to receive a letter from the Revd. Joseph Hughes, of Battersea,
and Mr Wilkes of Finsbury Square, a constant attendant on my
former Lectures. But one of my best friends is of opinion that
should you and Mr Taylor hold it expedient to put to the Press
immediately the Six Disquisitions on Faith; the Eucharist; the
Philosophy of Prayer; the church as an institution of Christ and
as a Constituent Estate of the State, *Ec*clesia *⚓ En*clesia;[1] the
prophetic character of the Hebrew Scriptures, and the nature and
extent of the *Gift* of Prophecy, and in what respect peculiar to the
Hebrew Seers; and, last, on the right & superstitious Use & Estimation of the Scriptures—the Subjects are of such importance both in
themselves, and as forming with the AIDS a compleat System of
the Philosophy of Religion, as far as it was possible without such
abstruse reasoning as would be unintelligible to all but a Few—
And this is the question, your & Mr Taylor's answer to which I
most wished to receive.—But I shall endeavor to call on Wednesday before I go to the Royal Society of Literature.

I am DELIGHTED with the 'Superannuated Man'.[2] I have read
[it] a dozen times at least. It is worthy of Charles Lamb in his
happiest Carolo-lambian Hour: and that is saying a great deal.

I have put a slip of paper in the place; but I have marked it so
precisely on the 3rd. side of this sheet, that there can be no
mistake.—

With sincere esteem and regard | I remain, my dear Sir, your
obliged Friend & Servt

                                        S. T. Coleridge

'I stammered out a bow'—exquisite. None but C.L. could have
written that.

---

[1] See *The Church and State*, p. 52: 'If this latter [the Church of Christ] be
ecclesia, the communion of such as are called out of the world, *i.e.* in reference
to the especial ends and purposes of that communion; this other [the National
Church] might more expressively have been entitled *enclesia*, or an order of
men, chosen in and of the realm, and constituting an estate of that realm.'
Coleridge also introduces the two terms in a marginal note written in Hooker's
Ecclesiastical Polity. See *Literary Remains*, iii. 24–25. H. N. Coleridge noted the
parallel to the passage in *The Church and State.* See also *Aids to Reflection*, 1825,
p. 166 n., where Coleridge defines ecclesia as 'those who have been *called out*
of the World'.

T. J. Wise, *Two Lake Poets . . .*, 1927, p. 132, comments on the annotations
which Coleridge wrote in a copy of Hooker's *Works*, 1682. The volume is now
in the British Museum. The notes were first printed in *Literary Remains*, iii.
18–57.

[2] *The Superannuated Man* first appeared in the *London Magazine* of May
1825.

P.S. ⚹ is my usual mark for, *opposed to* or *as the antithesis of*: and ⚹ for *the contrary of*. Thus Sweet ⚹ Sour: Sweet ⚹ Bitter.[1]

1459. *To John Taylor Coleridge*

Address: John Coleridge, Esqre. | 61. Torrington Square | near Gower Street.
MS. British Museum. Hitherto unpublished.
Postmark: Highgate, 16 May 1825.

Grove, Highgate.
Monday—[16 May 1825]

My dear Nephew

I hope, that the pacquet I sent last week—Tuesday if I do not mistake—by our Highgate Carrier, and which, he assured me, should be delivered at No. 2. Pump Court, Temple before One o'clock—has not mist it's way—Be so good as to let me know by next post whether you have received it with my triple Epistle, or 3 Letters.[2] This ascertained, I should for myself feel no impatience: but my worthy friend, Mr H. from the lateness of the Season & other causes, is naturally anxious to learn the result.

I direct this to Torrington Square: because probably our afternoon (¼ before 5) 3d Post will not be delivered till after your hour of emancipation from Chambers.—

On Wednesday Afternoon, 3 o'clock, I read my Essay at the R.S.L. 61. Lincoln's Inn Fields: and on Friday I dine in South Audley Street, to meet the Bishop of London with his angel-faced Wife & Miss Hooley[3]—. Perhaps, you may find it in your power to call there—

My kindest regards to Mrs John Coleridge—and many many Loves to my dear grand-nephews.

With sincere & cordial respect and affection

I am ever your attached Uncle

S. T. C.

[1] This postscript is written at the top of the MS.
[2] Coleridge refers to Letters 1448–50.
[3] Mary Anne Howley.

1460. *To John Taylor Coleridge*

Address: John Coleridge, Esqre | 2. Pump Court | Temple
MS. British Museum. Hitherto unpublished.
Postmark: Highgate, 17 May 1825.

17 May 1825

My dear Nephew

Your approbation of 'the Aids &c' has been an inexpressible comfort to me—for indeed and indeed there are very few, painfully and depressively few, on whose heart and judgement *conjointly* I can rely.—Alas! that I had not had your note three days before—I fear, it is too late. But I am now sending off a dispatch to the Publisher to see if it be yet possible to cancel or take out the types of all the latter part of the Advertisement.—I have never received your note of Saturday—. I shall write by Post to Mr Hurwitz—& doubtless, the MSS will be sent without delay. I have them (the greater part at least) but think it right first to inform him. What Mr Murray desires, *is done*—and as popularly as Mr M. himself could wish. Indeed, the account of the Talmud is most entertaining as well as instructive—The faults & follies are neither hidden or palliated—tho' the false accusations are rebutted.—Do not think any more of the *compendious criticisms*—what you have said is what I wanted.—It is on *Friday* that I dine with the Beaumonts—who have a sincerely warm regard & respect for you—

God bless you—I am in great haste—

I have given up or rather decisively rejected the plan of giving 3 discourses on the plan of a London University vivâ voce—lest I should be supposed to advocate it—which, I am not certain (even were it my Opinion which is the contrary) that as a Cambridge Man I should be right in so doing—for dearly do I love my Alma Mater, and my worthy Aunt in fair proportion.

S. T. Coleridge

1461. *To Hyman Hurwitz*

MS. University of Pennsylvania Lib. Hitherto unpublished.

Grove, Highgate—
17 May 1825

My dear Sir

I have this morning received a Note from my Nephew, of which I inclose the *concerning* Half,[1] the other part respecting my own

---

[1] This *'concerning* Half' of John Taylor Coleridge's note is extant:
My dear Uncle—

I [You?] ought to have had my first note—so I will only say, that I wrote

Aids to Reflection.[1]—The Letter, he speaks of as having written on Saturday, I have never received—this is the third instance within the last month, and I intend to write to Mr Freeling. . . . The Two penny Post, I have before . . . by my own experience, . . . be some recent increase . . .[2] management.—

In my own case, I should not hesitate in sending the MSS to Murray; *the Tales*, at least—which, I do not doubt, will be taken as a sufficient Datum whereon to form his judgement. And meantime, you can abridge the Essay—i.e. reducing it, if I may advise, as nearly to the form in which you first read it to me as possible— and to reserve a more minute Detail for another Work, in which it would be exceedingly interesting if you could give something like critico-biographical Memorabilia of the several Hebrew Sages, who have been eminent, each in a different Age.—Three or four I can furnish you with the materials for—I wait for your answer as to sending the Tales thro' my Nephew to Murray. To morrow & Friday I shall be in town—& shall probably not return on Friday Night, or till Saturday Afternoon.—

I inclose a rough proof of my Advertisement & Preface—which were shewn to Murray, who expressed his regret that my critique had [not] been reserved till after the Publication of the Hebrew Tales &c—when by appearing in the Literary Gazette with my Name, or in some similar channel, it would have more effectually drawn attention to the Work—But the advice came too late—I have said what I believed to be the strict truth, and what with this belief I felt it my duty to say—and he is not a man after my heart, who does not prefer saying a *truth* out of place & time when the merits of a friend are in question, to the prudential slowness which involves the risk of not saying it at all. . . . [Conclusion and signature cut off.]

to you on Saturday to say that Murray will be very glad to undertake the work, and wishes to have the MS as soon as possible—till he has seen it, of course he can say nothing as to terms—He thinks a popular account of the Talmud &c should be prefixed.

I hope I will see you this week—but on Wednesday I may be in Court all day at Sittings.

Goodnight and believe me always my dear Uncle

Your affect. nephew
J. T. Coleridge

[MS. University of Pennsylvania Lib.]

[1] The part of John Tay'or Coleridge's note concerning *Aids to Reflection* was forwarded to Hessey. See next letter.

[2] MS. mutilated by removal of the conclusion and signature on the verso of the page.

1462. To J. A. Hessey

MS. Private possession. Hitherto unpublished.

17 May 1825.

My dear Sir

'Whatsoever ye do, do it in faith'! is a sound maxim of prudence as well as a positive injunction of Morality. I GIVE UP THE LECTURE SCHEME. A university in the proper sense of the term (and a Herring is a Herring, and you might as rationally talk of 'Sprats, Bantam Cocks, Pilchards, Centipedes and other species of *Lions*', as honor the various schemes, which I have seen or heard of, with the name of UNIVERSITY)—a UNIVERSITY, I say, will never be adopted and supported in the present state of 'the Metropolitan Mind'—(the phrase is in high fashion at this moment—the *Public* Mind—the *religious Mind*—&c) & I might probably give offence to my Cambridge & Oxford Friends—Besides, if I did not succeed in procuring a sufficient number of Ticket-takers for the Course, and a 100 would be but 50£, I should only expose my own lack of influencive reputation—. And it might be asked, if Mr C. has any thing useful or important to communicate, why not print it, either by itself or in the London Magazine ?—I shall therefore immediately set to work with the one yet to be written Disquisition. I quite agree with you as to the *Untakingness* of the Title[1]—& will think of some other, and am inclined to think, that I shall add a 7th— by putting together some letters, I have been composing at the earnest request of Sir Alexander Johnson,[2] the late chief Judge at Ceylon, on the Subject of Missions and Missionaries. He professed to be, and I believe *was*, deeply interested with the views, I had expressed to him in several conversations at Ramsgate—and urged me to reduce them to writing, promising that he would exert his influence in giving them publicity and effect.—And now for a *nearer* Subject. There are many, on whose *heart* and sincerity I can confidently rely: there are some, to whose sound judgement and knowlege of the World I look up: but the conjunction of Head and Heart, that would make it my duty to prefer the Possessor's judgement to my own—this I can conscientiously attribute but *to few*—And among these Few my Nephew, John Coleridge, stands foremost in my estimation. I have never found him in the wrong, in any opinion, he had permitted himself to express—Therefore, if I had fortunately received his Note (of this morning; and of which

---

[1] i.e. *Six Disquisitions*. See Letters 1447 and 1466.
[2] Sir Alexander Johnston, whom Coleridge had met at Ramsgate in 1824. See Letter 1416.

I have sent you the *concerning* half) four or five days earlier, I should not have hesitated in leaving out *the Advertisement*. As it is, I must take the consequence of my own zeal for a most worthy friend—not that I have said a syllable more than I really think— not that I could not, 'on my bible oath' as the folks say, repeat every word respecting 'the Hebrew Tales'—but because I now see that it would have [been] more expedient for my friend's interest & the reputation of his Work to have reserved my critique for a more appropriate time & place. Had the Sheet not been drawn off, the Types (I imagine) might have been taken out, from the words 'primitive church-man'.[1]—I now recollect that *You* seemed not quite to like THE ADVERTISEMENT, compared with The Preface; and were only prevented by delicacy from saying so.—But what cannot be cured, must be endured—. Few things in a small way are more mischievous than a glaringly injudicious adviser, by disposing you to hurry into the very contrary to his advice. So here—A certain Person remonstrated with me that I should cry up the work of a Jew, and an enemy to Christians—adding a degrading epithet to the word 'Jew'.—I could only answer—Would to Heaven, for your sake, that you were only half as good a Christian as this —— Jew—& sent it off in a pet of indignation.—

Your's truly

S. T. C.

1463. *To Basil Montagu*

Address: Basil Mountagu, Esqre. | at his Chambers | Lincoln's Inn Square
MS. formerly in the possession of the late M. G. D. Clive. Hitherto unpublished.

[18 May 1825]

My dear Mountagu

[Although I][2] looked at your signature but an hour or two ago in order to *see* how you spelt it, such is the ideocy of my pre-eminent Organ of Locality,[3] that to save my life I could not determine

---

[1] Coleridge's estimate of Hurwitz's *Hebrew Tales* was cancelled, and the 'Advertisement' as it appears in the first edition of *Aids to Reflection* concludes with the words 'primitive Churchman'.

[2] MS. torn.

[3] In a manuscript note Coleridge speaks of 'the little less than idiocy of that same faculty of LOCALITY, the size, prominence, and unusual developement of the significant Bump-organ of which attracted the notice and excited the admiration of Professor SPURZHEIM, who consoled me therewith for the want, or evanescence, of the Organ of Ideality or Imagination'. [British Museum, Egerton MS. 2800 f. 188.] See also H. N. Coleridge's note in *Table Talk*, 24 June 1827: 'I believe the beginning of Mr. C.'s liking for Dr. Spurzheim was

whether it was *Mon* or Moun or gu or gue—and if I went down to Mrs Gillman to see, it is odds but it would have dissolved into chaos again by the time I had reached my Attic. It is unpleasant—chiefly because it is difficult to make persons believe, that it is not affectation. But I am persuaded, that there is a division of Labor in the Factory of the Memory, and a dozen perhaps of Journeymen Memories, each clever, if clever, at it's own trade exclusively—and that my Name, Number, place and way Memory is a *natural fool*!—This is the Preface to the letter. Now the Letter itself.

My dear M. I read my Essay, Part I. this afternoon, 3 o'clock, at 61, Lincoln's Inn Fields.[1]

S. T. C.

Mr Green accompanies me: and if Mr Gillman can leave Highgate, he must be your Umbra or vice versâ. Had the former a proportionate broad-brimmed Hat, he might be the diminutive—viz. my Umbrella—Let us persuade him & Irving to get one, by way of accomodating their friends in a rainy season.[2]

1464. *To John Taylor Coleridge*

Address: John Coleridge, Esqre | 65 | Torrington Square
MS. British Museum. Pub. E. L. G. ii. 349.
Postmark: Highgate, 19 May 1825.

[19 May 1825]

My dear John

God willing, I will not fail to be with you in 65 Torrington Square, on Saturday Week, by 5 o'clock.

I inflicted the whole Essay (an hour and 25 m.) on the ears of the R.S.L., with most remorseful Sympathy with the Audience, who could not possibly understand the 10th part—. For let it's merits be what they may, it was not a thing to read to, but to *be* read *by*—

In haste for the Posta fugax—

S. T. Coleridge—

the hearty good humour with which the Doctor bore the laughter of a party, in the presence of which he, unknowing of his man, denied any *Ideality*, and awarded an unusual share of *Locality*, to the majestic silver-haired head of my dear uncle and father-in-law.'

[1] On 18 May 1825 Coleridge read his essay before the Royal Society of Literature. He had sent the MS. to Cattermole on 26 Apr. 1825. (Letter 1442.) The essay was printed under the title: *On the Prometheus of Æschylus; An Essay, Preparatory to a series of Disquisitions respecting the Egyptian in connection with the Sacerdotal Theology, and in contrast with the Mysteries of ancient Greece.* According to Wise, this 'Private Edition' of 25 copies 'was printed and circulated in the customary manner, in advance of the reading of the Essay'. (*Bibliography*, 129.) The essay was reprinted in *Literary Remains*, ii. 323–59.

[2] This paragraph is written in the address sheet of the MS.

1465. To Edward Coleridge

Address: Edward Coleridge, Esqre. | Eton
MS. Pierpont Morgan Lib. Pub. with omis. Letters, *ii. 738*.
Postmark: Highgate, 19 May 1825.

[19 May 1825]

My very dear Nephew

You have left me under a painful and yet genial feeling of regret, that my lot in life has hitherto so much estranged me from the children of the Sons of my Father, that venerable Countenance and Name which form my earliest recollections and make them *religious*. It is not in my power to express adequately so as to convey it to others, what a revolution has taken place in my mind since I have seen your Sister, and John, and Henry and lastly yourself—. Yet revolution is not the word, I want. It is rather, the sudden Evolution of a seed that had sunk too deep for the warmth, and exciting Air to reach; but which a casual Spade had turned up and brought close to the surface: and I now *know* the *meaning* as well as feel the *truth*, of the Scottish Proverb—Blood is thicker than Water.—

My Book will be *out*, on Monday next; and Mr Hessey hopes, that he shall be able to have a Copy ready for me by tomorrow afternoon, so that I may present it to the Bishop of London, whom (at his own request, Lady B. tells me) with his Angel-faced Wife & Miss Hooley I am to meet at Sir George's tomorrow at six o'clock—There are many on whose sincerity & goodness of heart I can rely. There are several, in whose Judgement and knowlege of the world I have greater trust, than in my own. But few, very few are there, in whom both co-exist, and both in that degree that I can at once adopt their sentiments as my own. And among these few John Coleridge ranks foremost. It was therefore an indescribable comfort to me to hear from him, that the first Third of my 'Aids to Reflection'—i.e. all, he has yet seen—had 'delighted him BEYOND MEASURE'. I can with severest truth declare, that half a score flaming panegyrical Reviews in as many Works of periodical Criticism would not have given me half the pleasure, nor one quarter the satisfaction.

I write now first to send you the Verses, you wished to have— and as soon as I can find time to look over my Wilderness of Papers I will transcribe or get copied some half dozen other Poems that have not been published, and send them to you—2ndly to ask whether or no—for I have no distinct recollection of it—I gave you a letter or little parcel to take to town, for me—for a letter containing 3 or 4 pages, of which I had neither copy or reproductive recollection, never reached the Publisher—which, tho' I contrived to make a sort of connection by adding a sentence or two, has however left a chasm in the reasoning of my 'Conclusion'. It is now of no consequence—& I ask, merely in anticipation of a Negative.— And lastly, with regard to little Henry, who has been fagging thro' his Grammar again, and qualifying himself to be dodged in the Propria quae maribus—of the possible use or purpose of which I profess myself profoundly ignorant. But I want now to begin with him in Latin Verse. He can scan pretty well, and is perfect both in the simple and composite feet. But I would at the same time work him in Ovid's Long and Short Verses—and should be glad, if you would let me know what part of Ovid's Works, besides the Metamorphoses, are read at Eton—whether it would be best to take the Epistles, or the Fasti, or the Tristia.—In short, any thing and every thing, you will be so good as to suggest, will make Mrs Gillman happy and grateful.—I dine, D.V. on Saturday Week, in Torrington Square—when doubtless we shall drink your health with appropriate adjuncts.—

Yesterday I had to inflict an hour and 25 minutes' Essay, full of Greek and superannuated Metaphysics, on the ears of the Royal Society of Literature—the subject being—the Prometheus of Eschylus decyphered in proof and as instance of the connection of the Greek Drama with the Mysteries. Deuce take me (as Charles Lamb says in his 'Superannuated Man') if I did not feel remorseful Pity for my Audience all the time. For at the very best it was a Thing *to be* read not to *read*.

God bless you or I shall be too late for the Post.—

Your affectionate Uncle

S. T. Coleridge

P.S. I went yesterday to the Exhibition—and hastily thrid the labyrinth of the dense huddle, for the sole purpose of seeing our Bishop's Portrait—but it did not please me. It was like and not like. My own by the same Artist is very much better: tho' even in this the Smile is exaggerated. But Fanny and your Mother were in raptures with it—while they too seemed very cold in their praises of William's.[1]

---

[1] Thomas Phillips exhibited his portrait of William Hart Coleridge at the Royal Academy in 1825. Coleridge's own portrait by the same artist was not exhibited there. (From information kindly supplied by Mr. Sidney C. Hutchison, Librarian, Royal Academy of Arts.)

1466. *To J. A. Hessey*

Address: Messrs. Taylor and Hessey | 93 Fleet Street   For Mr Hessey.
MS. New York Public Lib. Pub. E. L. G. ii. 350.
Postmark: 23 May 1825.

Grove, Highgate
My dear Sir   23 May 1825.—

Since I left you, I have been *moiling* for an appropriate and inviting Title for, and instead of, the six Disquisitions. A late Physiologist represents the nervous system as a Plant, of which the spinal Cord is the Stem and the Brain the compound Flower—and if you have ever watched a Humble-bee at a Fox-glove or a Monks-hood, visiting one Bell after another, and bustling and humming in each, you will have no bad likeness of the dips and dives I have been making into the several cells and campanulae of my Brain. Two only have occurred to me—or rather the same in two forms—both suggested by real incidents—the first, Conversations on Stainmoor (n.b. the dreariest and longest Waste-land in England) the second —[The young Chaplain and the Grey-headed Passenger: or Conversations on Shipboard—or Convers. during a Voyage to the Mediterranean—or Cabin Conversations on subjects of moral and religious interest—supplemental of the AIDS TO REFLECTION—or lastly thus—][1]

The grey-headed Passenger: or Conversations on Ship-board during a voyage to the Mediterranean, supplemental of the AIDS TO Reflection by S. T. Coleridge.—

My supposed fellow-passenger a young Clergyman, newly ordained who had subscribed [to] the 39 Articles, on the principles of Paley as mere Articles of Peace, quite satisfied in conscience that he should never preach counter to them as he should never trouble himself or his flock about them. He should keep to the *morality* of the Gospel & simply teach his Hearers to do as they would be done by.—In short, his Divinity would consist of two chapters—first, that Honesty is the best Policy; and, second, if you don't find it so here, you will hereafter. But notwithstanding this very compendious, convenient and portable faith, I find him a young man of fine intellect, and generous feelings, a good classic & an enthusiastic lover of Nature &c—The Conversations are supposed to take place during the latter half of the Voyage—the first indeed at Gibraltar—& to have been preceded by a long series of discussions, which had ended in convincing him of the hollowness of the ground on which he had hitherto stood, of the cheerlessness, vulgarity and common-place character of the mechanical philosophy, and

---

[1] Passage in brackets crossed out in MS.

Paleyian Expedience—but still more in impressing him with the superior *power* and ampler *command* given by the habit of seeking for the first principles of all living & effective truth in the constitution and constituent faculties of the Mind itself. He is roused and affected by an animated portraiture of the Life and Labors of a Minister of the Gospel, who is at the same time a Philosopher and a Christian and who finds the consummation and most perfect form of Philosophy in Christianity—and declares his determination to set about the building up of the philosophic mind in himself—but is mortified by the doubts which the Grey-headed Passenger expresses as to his perseverance in the task—and in the irritation occasioned by this unexpected Check avows his contempt and detestation of all quackery and mystery, and asks indignantly—If this Philosophy be true and important and agreeable to the Reason, Moral Being, and all the contra-distinguishing Attributes of Humanity, what should make it of such difficult acquirement for any man of education, and tolerable strength of intellect?—And with the answer to this question the Conversations commence: and after the two first that he begins to read the Aids to Reflection.

What is your judgement of this as a title, & as the *mould* of the Work?[1]—

It is singular that on my return to Highgate much impressed with the Light, you had flashed upon my mind with regard to the cure of Stammering, one of the very first sentences I met with in Giambattista Vico was the following—

'I *mutoli* mandan fuori i suoni informi *cantando*: e gli *scilinguati* pur *cantando* spediscono la lingua a pronunziare.'—i.e. Mutes or Dumb Persons send forth indistinct sounds in a sing-song: and Stammerers by chaunting gradually unloose and accustom or facilitate the tongue to pronounce freely.—A curious co-incidence—I have myself repeatedly observed that children in being taught to read begin to stutter when you prevent them from *singing* their words.—

Of course, as soon as a few Copies can be made ready, I shall be glad to receive them—

With great respect and regard | my dear Sir | Your obliged

S. T. Coleridge

---

[1] This letter concludes Coleridge's correspondence with J. A. Hessey, whose partnership with John Taylor was dissolved on 30 June 1825. Hessey continued as a bookseller in the premises in Fleet Street, and Taylor retained the publishing business which was located in Waterloo Place. In 1826 Coleridge refers to Taylor as 'my Publisher'. Except for the first edition of *Aids to Reflection*, which was published by Taylor and Hessey in May 1825, no work of Coleridge's appeared under the imprint either of that firm or of John Taylor. See *The Keats Circle*, ed. H. E. Rollins, 2 vols., 1948, i, pp. cxxxix–cxlii; and Letters 1511, 1647, and 1652.

1467. *To James Gillman*

MS. Yale University Lib. Pub. Fraser's Magazine, *January 1835, p. 54.*
According to H. B. Smith, *A Sentimental Library,* 1914, p. 59, this letter was
originally written in the fly-leaves of *Aids to Reflection,* 1825.

[May 1825 ?]

The Three Sorts of Friends

Tho' Friendships differ endless *in degree,*
The *Sorts,* methinks, may be reduced to Three:
*Ac*quaintance many; and *Con*quaintance few;
But for *In*quaintance I know only two,
The Friend, I've mourn'd with, and the Maid, I woo![1]

My dear Gillman,

The ground and 'matériel' of this division of one's friends into
Ac- Con- and *In-* quaintance was given by Hartley Coleridge, when
he was scarcely five years old. On some one asking him, if Anny
Sealy (a little girl, he went to school with) was an Acquaintance
of his, he replied very fervently, pressing his right hand on his
heart—No! She is an *In*quaintance. 'Well! 'tis a Father's tale!'[2]
—& the recollection soothes your old

Friend & *In*quaintance

S. T. Coleridge

1468. *To J. H. Green*

Address: J. H. Green, Esqre. | 46. | Lincoln's Inn Fields.
MS. Pierpont Morgan Lib. Hitherto unpublished.
Postmark: Highgate, 11 June 1825.

[11 June 1825]

My dear Friend

Mrs Green informed Mrs Gillman, that there is some one place
(in Bond-street, she believes) at which a superior sort of White
Mustard Seed may be procured. You would much oblige me if you
would let your servant procure a bottle or whatever the Vehicle
or Container may be, and bring it with you on Sunday. I am
desirous to try it myself; but I am very anxious that Mrs G. should
give it a trial—because with her it would be a *fair* trial, without
the draw-back, that every thing of the kind has in my instance.

Mr Gillman has used some two Ounces of the Sulfate of Quina in
his recent practice; but he has not found any effect beyond that of
common Bark in the ordinary doses. Pray, what is the Quina

[1] *Poems,* ii. 1012.
[2] *The Nightingale,* lines 105–6, *Poems,* i. 267.

Wine? Is it more than a decoction (or infusion?) of the Quina in Wine? And in what wine? And in what proportion of the Quina to the Wine?

Could you procure me a Copy of those Lines which a long time ago I sent to Mrs Green by you, on constancy to the *Idea* of a beloved Object—ending, I remember, with a Simile of a Woodman following his own projected Shadow?[1]—In my Supplementary Volume I should like to publish it, as a Note to the sentence, last line but 13, in p. 220 of the Aids to Reflection.[2]

In p. 223, l. 3. the following sentence might be inserted. 'It is a most important truth, but a truth of which the Fewest are aware, that all *reality* in nature, all belief in a substance existing independently of the Perceiver (as when we say, "Yes! it *is* a Tree": or "there *is* a Cloud there"—) is grounded in an act of the Understanding, not in an affection of the Sight or any other sense. The *reality* of the Image—i.e. that it is a thing and not a *thought* or

---

[1] *Constancy to an Ideal Object*, *Poems*, i. 455. E. H. Coleridge conjecturally dates the poem 1826, but the statement above indicates that it was composed earlier. See also Letter 1325. Campbell (*Poetical Works*, 172 and 632) believed the poem to have been written at Malta in 1805. The concluding lines read:

> The woodman winding westward up the glen
> At wintry dawn, where o'er the sheep-track's maze
> The viewless snow-mist weaves a glist'ning haze,
> Sees full before him, gliding without tread,
> An image* with a glory round its head;
> The enamoured rustic worships its fair hues,
> Nor knows he makes the shadow, he pursues!

* This phenomenon, which the Author has himself experienced, and of which the reader may find a description in one of the earlier volumes of the Manchester Philosophical Transactions, is applied figuratively in the following passage of the AIDS to REFLECTION:

'Pindar's fine remark respecting the different effects of music, on different characters, holds equally true of Genius: as many as are not delighted by it are disturbed, perplexed, irritated. The beholder either recognizes it *as a projected form of his own Being, that moves before him with a Glory round its head*, or recoils from it as a spectre.'—AIDS to REFLECTION, p. 220. [Note by S. T. C. in *Poetical Works*, 1829.]

The 'description' which Coleridge found in the *Memoirs of the Literary and Philosophical Society of Manchester* is reprinted by J. L. Lowes in *The Road to Xanadu*, 1930, p. 470.

[2] In an annotated copy of *Aids to Reflection* now in the Harvard College Library, Coleridge comments in a marginal note on the passage in p. 220:

This refers to a curious phenomenon which occurs occasionally when the air is filled with fine particles of frozen Snow, constituting an almost invisibly subtle Snow mist, and a person is walking with ye Sun behind his back. His shadow is projected, and he sees a figure moving before him with a glory round his head. I have myself seen it twice, and it is described in the 1st or 2d vol. of ye Manchester Phil. Transactns. (J. L. Lowes, op. cit. 471.)

sensation—is in all instances *Hypothesis*, Supposition, substantiation. This is the true import of the word, Understanding. It is the *substantiating*, substance-declaring, Power. When, however, we proceed under the influence of the Fancy, and not according to the rules of the Understanding, the Product or Result is an Hypo-*poiēsis* not an Hypo*thesis*, a Suf*fiction* not a Supposition.'

Our Hamlet, and specially our quiet Grove is crowded with Carriages, Coachmen and other such Cattle, from Mrs Cootes's Visitors.

God bless you | &

S. T. Coleridge

1469. *To John Taylor Coleridge*

Address: John Coleridge Esqre | 2 Pump Court | Temple.
MS. British Museum. Hitherto unpublished.

[13 June 1825]¹

My dear John

You must read *thro'* my next sentence before you judge me. Till your note came, I had forgot my engagement to dine with you; but the whole Saturday I was confined to my Bed, and for four days preceding to my bed-room with a dysenteric Diarrhoea—from which even at this moment I am imperfectly recovered.—But this would not yet supply a vindication of my neglect in apprising you of my illness—the fact was, I had on receiving your first note written out the day & your name on a Card and given it (as I always do on such occasions) to Mrs Gillman—to remind me of it—. Partly, perhaps, anxiety on my account might have put it out of her thoughts; but the main cause was, that a young woman, the daughter of a family in great distress, for whom Mrs G. had procured an advantageous situation, had behaved in that happy mid thing between *mad* and *wicked*, as to be suddenly returned on her poor Parents' Hands— the first tidings of which reached Highgate on the Friday.

I have now come to town, for the purpose of meeting Southey at Sir G. Beaumont's—and who sets off for Holland on Wednesday Morning—and tomorrow by or before Noon I shall take the chance of seeing you at your Chambers.—I here send a corrected Copy with a few *MSS* Notes of the Aids to Reflection. God bless you | &

S. T. C.—

---

¹ This letter, which is endorsed 'June 1825', was written a day or two before Southey left for the Continent on Wednesday, 15 June. See *Southey Letters*, iii. 489.

1470. *To John Taylor Coleridge*

Address: John Coleridge, Esqre
MS. British Museum. Hitherto unpublished.

Thursday, 16 June—[1825]

My dear Nephew

I forget my disappointment in missing you in the concern for the cause—I do most earnestly hope, that you are not a Successor of mine in 'the Fashionable'—for so, I understand, a sort of dysenteric Diarrhoea is now called. If you have any cause to complain of the behaviour of your Stomach or quae infra jacent, I can confidently recommend the White Mustard Seed—from two to four Tea Spoonfulls, twice or three times a day—to be swallowed uncrushed, without aid of any fluid, if you can do it with ease—if not, with as little water, as will suffice to wash it down the Esophagus. I have taken it now four days only—but the effect has been so unmistakeably *an* effect of the medicine, and at the same time so desirable, that I give full credit to Collins' (the Painter's) statement of his restoration to full and vigorous health by a month's perseverance in this & this exclusively.—How it acts, whether mechanically as gravel on chicken, or whether in addition to the friction any gluten is drawn from the seeds by the heat of the Stomach, I know not. Apparently, it's *Exit* is as it's Entrance—it seems to have been an uninjured Passenger thro' the dark Labyrinth. Nor during the Tour does it in any way give you notice of it's goings on—by griping, or any other symptom. It is simply aperient, without any approach to the Purgative. For the last 15 years it has been my lot to awake every morning in pain, more or less severe—and to continue in a discomfortable state of feeling for an hour or two. The first morning, after the first 3 doses of the preceding day, the Pain was manifestly much less—the second morning it was trifling—and for the two last mornings (and I made an unusually copious dinner, and drank at least a bottle of Wine at Mr Sotheby's yesterday) for the first time in 15—nay, I might say 20 years, I have awoke in perfect comfort of body, without pain, without drowsiness. Mrs Gillman has likewise received great benefit.—I could add, of my own neighbors & acquaintance, four other cases. Were it only, that it supersedes the necessity of taking medicine (aloetic, mercurial, or saline), and without leaving weakness or languor, it would be no small blessing.—

I called here, with Mr Hurwitz's 'Hebrew Tales'—As I am obliged to be home (at Highgate) by dinner, I cannot conveniently (putting the *Broil* of the Day better for Hay-making than Streetwalking) go myself to Albermarle Street—(And this being the

Wedding-day of George Beaumont & Miss Howley[1] I left South-
Audley before 9 o'clock this morning, and of course too early to
have a chance of seeing Mr Murray.)—Will you, therefore, allow
me to give you the trouble of putting the MSS into Mr Murray's
Hands—the next time your occasions lead you to Albermarle
Street?—And to let me know, when I may expect an Answer?—
I wish *very much* to have an hour's conversation with you—
especially, on the Quarterly. I have not seen the last number; but
from Mr Hallam[2] I heard that there was an article on Niebuhr.[3]
Now as Niebuhr's leading Principles & Facts are taken from Giambattista Vico,[4] if you have not introduced his Name already, it
would surely be a most desirable thing that you should give a
sketch of this most extraordinary Man's *Life* & principal Work—.
I will with great pleasure supply you with a skeleton of his great
work—The life and substance of the three Volumes, with a brief
account of the man himself, might, I doubt not, be comprized in
about two Sheets—and I will venture to say, that in the quantity
and quality of Interest, and even of *Entertainingness*, whether you
take the importance or the Originality of the Ideas, it would not
be easy to point out two sheets that could stand in competition
with it—. Whether the Reader becomes a Convert or no, is a matter
of indifference—. It is *Literary* History—and it is quite impossible,
that a Scholar, who is at the same time a man of vigorous intellect,
should read it without something like a *revolution* in his mind—
were it only from the connection of the *Heroic* History of Greece
and Rome with the *Feudal* History of Modern Europe, after the
disruption of the Western Empire—& (in perhaps a still livelier
resemblance) with the state of Society in our present Colonies in
the W. Indies.[5]—

[1] Mary Anne Howley, daughter of the bishop of London, and George How-
land Willoughby Beaumont, a cousin of Sir George Beaumont, were married
on 16 June 1825.
[2] Henry Hallam (1777–1859), historian, whose *View of the State of Europe
during the Middle Ages*, 2 vols., appeared in 1818.
[3] The first two volumes of B. G. Niebuhr's *Römische Geschichte* appeared in
1811–12. Thomas Arnold's article dealing with Niebuhr's *History of Rome*
appeared in the *Quarterly Review*, June 1825.
[4] M. H. Fisch points out that Dr. Prati 'was an intimate friend of the Swiss
philologist, J. K. Orelli, who had been the first to call attention to Vico's anticipations of Niebuhr'. 'The Coleridges, Dr. Prati, and Vico', *Modern Philology*,
Nov. 1943, p. 113.
[5] Vico was uppermost in Coleridge's mind at the conversazione at Highgate
on the evening of 16 June. 'Mr. Irving and his brother-in-law Mr. Martin and
myself placed ourselves in a chariot', notes Crabb Robinson, 'and Basil Montagu
took a seat without and we rode to Highgate, where we took tea at Mr. Gillman's. . . . Dr. Prati came in, and Coleridge treated him with marked attention.
. . . Coleridge referred to an Italian Vico who is said to have anticipated Wolf's

I can dine with you any day next week, but Thursday—Will
Tuesday suit you?—or is there any day in which you could spare a
couple of hours, at any other time?—tho' I long to see the Little
Ones, & Mrs J. Coleridge.—Of course, I speak of the Sketch of
Vico, not as an Article but as rude Materials for yourself—to be
used collectively or in different Articles according to your judgement. I am convinced, that a new splendor might be given to the
Quarterly R. in the Classic Department, on the principles of
Comparative History, analogous to the Science of Comparative
Anatomy—in short, by bringing the principles of Common Sense,
and the Canons of historical Credibility, to bear on the earlier
periods of Greece, Rome, Egypt &c—I shall be anxious to hear,
how you are—. A single Line, merely to say—'I am better'—would
be a comfort to,

my dear John, | your affectionate Friend
S. T. C.—

1471. To Hyman Hurwitz

Address: Hyman Hurwitz, Esqre | Grenada Cottage | Old Kent Road
MS. University of Pennsylvania Lib. Hitherto unpublished.
Postmark: 17 June 1825.

Lincoln's Inn Square
Mr Montague's Chambers.
16 June, ½ past 2. [1825]

My dear Friend

I promised that I would let you hear from me on Thursday—and
therefore, tho' from the debilitating effects of a downright *Broil*,
for which the Sun supplied the Fire and London Streets the
Gridiron, I can scarcely guide the pen—my hand trembles so—I will
yet perform the letter of my promise—tho' the spirit I must defer
till Saturday—. For after leaving the one half of the Bridal Party,
viz. Sir George and Lady Beaumont, the Bridgroom, and the
Bride groom's former Tutor (Dean Beresford) this morning; and
dispatched two or three necessary Calls at the West End of the
Town; I proceeded to my Nephew's Rooms (2. Pump Court,
Temple) at which I had called yesterday, & not finding him at
Chambers left a Note for him—I received the distressing informa-

theory concerning Homer (which Coleridge says was his at college). Vico wrote
Sur une nouvelle Science, viz. Comparative History. Goethe notices him in his
Life as an original thinker and great man. Vico wrote on the origin of Rome.
Coleridge drew a parallel between the West India planters and the negroes, the
subjection between them and the condition of the plebs of Rome towards the
patricians.' *Robinson on Books and Their Writers*, i. 320–1.

tion, that he had been compelled by sudden indisposition to take a Hackney Coach & return to his House in Torrington Square near Gower Street—I waited for an hour till his Clerk, who had gone with him, came back to the Chambers—and from him learnt, that the Medical Attendant had pronounced it—the *fashionable* complaint—a diarrhoea, similar (I guess) to that which had inflicted a visit on me, but did not doubt, that 48 hours *absolute quiet*, & a few tonic Aperients would set him to rights.—I could not, of course, follow him under such circumstances to any purpose— even if I had not had an engagement to be back at Highgate by 4 o'clock—but I shall on Saturday go to town by the Tottenham Court Stage, call first at Torrington Square, & then direct my Course either to his Chambers or to Albermarle Street, according as I find matters—For his Clerk will this evening deliver a hasty Note, I wrote for him—which will, I doubt not, secure full directions for me on Saturday Noon, in case I should not (as I hope, I may not) find him at home.—

God bless you | &

S. T. Coleridge

1472. *To Charles Lamb*

Transcript Coleridge family. Pub. Memorials of Thomas Hood, *ed.* Mrs. F. F. *Broderip and Thomas Hood, Jr., 2 vols., 1860, i. 16.*

[Thursday, 30 June 1825][1]

My dear Charles

This afternoon, a little, thin, mean-looking sort of a foolscap sub-octavo of poems, printed on very dingy outsides, lay on the table, which the cover informed me was circulating in our book-club, so very Grub Streetish in all its appearance, internal as well as external, that I cannot explain by what accident of impulse (assuredly there was no *motive* in play) I came to look into it. Least of all, the title, Odes & Addresses to Great Men,[2] which connected itself in my head with Rejected Addresses, and all the Smith & Theodore Hook[3] squad. But, my dear Charles, it was certainly written by you, or under you, or *una cum* you. I know none of your frequent visitors capacious & assimilative enough of

---

[1] Charles Lamb's reply of 2 July 1825 establishes the date of this letter. *Lamb Letters*, iii. 7.

[2] *Odes and Addresses to Great People*, 1825, was published anonymously. Of the 15 contributions, 5 were written by John Hamilton Reynolds, 9 by Thomas Hood, and 1 in collaboration.

[3] Theodore Hook (1788–1841), novelist, miscellaneous writer, and first editor of *John Bull.*

your converse to have reproduced you so honestly, supposing you had left yourself in pledge in his lock-up house. Gillman, to whom I read the spirited parody on the introduction to Peter Bell,[1] the Ode to the Great Unknown,[2] and to Mrs Twig [Fry]—he speaks doubtfully of Reynolds & Hood. But here come Irving & Basil Montagu.

Thursday night, 10 o'clock.—No! Charles, it is *you*. I have read them over again, & I understand why you have *anon'd* the book. The puns are nine in ten good—many excellent—the *Newgatory*[3] transcendent. And then the *exemplum sine exemplo* of a volume of personalities and contemporaneities, without a single line that could inflict the infinitesimal of an unpleasance on any man in his senses; saving & except perhaps in the envy-addled brain of the despiser of your *Lays*. If not a triumph over him, it is at least an *ovation*. Then, moreover, & besides, to speak with becoming modesty, excepting my own self, who is there but you who could write the musical lines & stanzas that are intermixed? Here Gillman, come up to my garret, and driven back by the guardian spirits of four huge flower-holders of omnigenous roses & honey-suckles—(Lord have mercy on his hysterical olfactories! what will he do in Paradise? I must have a pair or two of nostril-plugs, or nose-goggles, laid in his coffin.)—stands at the door reading that to M'Adam,[4] & the washerwoman's letter,[5] and he admits *the facts*. You are found *in the manner*, as the Lawyers say! so, Mr Charles! hang yourself up, and send me a line, by way of token and acknowledgment.[6] My dear love to Mary.

God bless you and your Unshamabramizer,
S. T. Coleridge.

---

[1] Coleridge refers to Hood's *Ode to Mr. Graham. The Aeronaut.*

[2] By Thomas Hood.

[3] See Hood's *A Friendly Address to Mrs. Fry*, IN *Newgate*: 'But I don't like your Newgatory teaching'.

[4] By J. H. Reynolds.

[5] *An Address to the Steam Washing Company: Letter of Remonstrance from Bridget Jones*, by Thomas Hood.

[6] Lamb replied as follows: 'The Odes are 4–5ths done by Hood, a silentish young man you met at Islington one day, an invalid. The rest are Reynolds's, whose sister H. has recently married. I have not had a broken finger in them. . . . Hood will be gratify'd, as much as I am, by your mistake. . . . Hood has just come in; his sick eyes sparkled into health when he read your approbation. They had meditated a copy for you, but postponed it till a neater 2d Edition, which is at hand.' *Lamb Letters*, iii. 7–8.

1473. *To Daniel Stuart*

Address: D. Stuart, Esqre | Harley Street | Portland Square
MS. British Museum. Pub. with omis. Letters, *ii. 740.*
Postmark: Highgate, 9 July 1825.

Grove
Highgate.
Friday, July (8?) 1825.

My dear Sir

The bad weather had so far damped my expectations that tho' I regretted, I did not feel any disappointment at, your not coming. And yet I hope, you will remember our Highgate Thursday Conversation Evenings on your return to town: because if you come once, I flatter myself, you will afterwards be no unfrequent Visitor. At least, I have never been at any of the Town Conversazioni, literary or artistical, in which the conversation has been more miscellaneous without degenerating into *Pinches*, a Pinch of this, and a Pinch of that, without the least connection between the subjects, and with as little interest. You will like Irving, as a companion and a converser even more than you admire him as a Preacher—He has a vigorous & (what is always pleasant) a *growing* mind: and his character is *manly* throughout.[1]—There is one thing too, that I can not help considering as a recommendation to our Evenings, that in addition to a few Ladies & pretty Lasses we have seldom more than 5 or 6 in company, and these generally of as many different professions or pursuits—. A few weeks ago we had present, two Painters, two Poets, one Divine, an eminent Chemist & Naturalist, a Major, a Naval Captain & Voyager, a Physician, a colonial Chief Justice, a Barrister and a Baronet—& this was the most numerous Meeting, we ever had—

It would more than gratify me to know from you, what the impressions are which my Aids to Reflection make on your judge-

---

[1] See *Aids to Reflection*, 1825, pp. 372–3, for Coleridge's tribute to Irving, which concludes with four lines of verse, the first two of which are adapted from *The Nightingale*:

Friend pure of heart and fervent! we have learnt
A different lore! We may not thus profane
The Idea and Name of Him whose absolute Will
Is Reason—Truth Supreme!—Essential Order!

In 1825 Irving dedicated to Coleridge his *For Missionaries after the Apostolical School, A Series of Orations*, and in elaborate terms expressed 'the gratitude of a disciple to a wise and generous teacher'. Lamb was greatly impressed by Irving's dedication and wrote enthusiastically of it to Leigh Hunt, Bernard Barton, and Wordsworth. (*Lamb Letters*, ii. 457, 464, and 468.) A copy of Irving's *For Missionaries* with annotations by Coleridge is in the British

ment.[1] The conviction respecting the character of the Times, expressed in the COMMENT on Aph. vi. p. 147, contains the Aim & Object of the whole Book. I venture to direct your notice particularly to the Note, p. 204–207, to the Note to p. 218, and to the sentences respecting Common Sense in the last 12 lines of p. 252, and the CONCLUSION, p. 377.

Lady Beaumont writes to me, that the Bishop of London has expressed a MOST favorable Opinion of the Book—and Blanco White[2] was sufficiently struck with it, as immediately to purchase all my Works, that are in Print, and has procured from Sir George Beaumont an introduction to me. It is well, it should have some one to speak for it. For I am unluckily ill off. Jeffray, by the most unprovoked and to me wholly unaccountable antipathy to me, not content with abusing what I have published, has openly avowed his determination to '*cut up*' (I use his own phrase) whatever I shall publish—& to my knowlege hired *Hazlitt* before the publication of my Lay Sermons to review them, on the ground of Hazlitt's notorious frantic hatred of me, who was Father, and Brother to him in one, and of Southey who saved him from Transportation or the Tread-mill[3]—

In the Quarterly, Gifford disliked me—& would never mention a book of mine—And now my own Nephew will not, I suppose, dare do it for fear of the charge of partiality. Add to this, careless and perhaps heartless Publishers, shy of the expence of advertising—and my recluse mode of Life, & little or no intercourse with Authors, neither reviewing myself nor courting those who do—& you will easily see, what a chance a poor Book of mine has in these days.

Such has been the influence of the Edingburgh Review that in all Edinburgh not a single Copy of Wordsworth's Works, or of any part of them, could be procured a few months ago. The only Copy, Irving saw in Scotland, belonged to a poor Weaver at Paisley, who prized them next to his Bible—& had all the Lyrical Ballads by heart—a fact, which would cut Jeffray's Conscience to the bone, if he had any. I give you my honor, that Jeffray himself told me, that *he* was himself an enthusiastic Admirer of Wordsworth's Poetry—but it was necessary that a Review should have a character.

Forgive this egotism—and be pleased to remember me kindly &

Museum. It is inscribed: 'From the Author To his dear friend & kind Instructor Samuel Taylor Coleridge.'
[1] A copy of *Aids to Reflection*, 1825, in the British Museum bears the inscription: 'To Daniel Stuart Esqre from his obliged Friend S. T. Coleridge.'
[2] See next letter.   [3] See Letter 1025 and notes.

with my best respects to Mrs Stuart—& with every cordial wish &
prayer for you & your's be assured that I am

Your obliged & affectionate Friend
S. T. Coleridge

1474. To J. Blanco White[1]

Address: Revd. B. White | 7 Paradise Row | Chelsea
*MS. in the Rathbone Papers, now on deposit in the University Library, Liverpool;
printed by permission of Mr. Reynolds Rathbone. Pub.* Life of Joseph Blanco
White, *i. 417.*
Postmark: Highgate, 13 July 1825.

Grove, Highgate
Tuesday. [12 July 1825]
Dear Sir

Twice have arrangements been made at my request by my kind
and most respected Friend & Neighbor, Mr Chance, for my introduction to you—add a third when I was to have had the pleasure
of meeting you at his house. But each time some accident intervened. I mention this, to shew you that I was beforehand with you
in my wish to be personally known to you—from the esteem, I
attached to your character & motives, and the high value, I set on
your services. I cannot say that in the pursuit of Truth I have no
interest; but my Conscience bears me witness, that I am aware of
no other but the interest of Truth itself. And this is no idle play
on words—For the rest, I am so rarely from home that it would be
ill-luck indeed if you should come & not find me. I regret, that your
distance (tho' we could procure you a comfortable bed) & health
forbid me to anticipate the pleasure, I should have in introducing
you to a few choice literary Friends, who generally pass their
Thursday Evenings here—particularly my friend, Edward Irving,
who is more earnest in his love of Truth & more fervent in his
assurance that what is *truth must* be Christianity, and more out of
all risk of the Apostolic Anathema Maranatha,[2] than almost any
man, I have met with—and with fewer prejudices, national or
sectarian. I would, he had been of our Church: which, however,

---

[1] Joseph Blanco White (1775–1841), theological writer. Born in Spain, White
was ordained a Roman Catholic priest in 1800. Afterwards he abandoned his
belief in Christianity. In 1810 he fled to England. After again embracing
Christianity, he signed the 39 Articles in 1814 to qualify himself to act as an
English clergyman. By his *Evidence against Catholicism*, 1825, and other works
he became a 'protestant champion'. In 1826 the University of Oxford conferred
the M.A. degree on him in recognition of his services to the church. In 1835 he
withdrew from the Anglican Church and adopted the Unitarian views.

[2] 1 Corinthians xvi. 22.

he has learnt to love & reverence, even by contrast with his experience of our present Dissenting Clergy—most degenerate
Successors of the Baxters, and Calamies of old.—Any time after
11 o'clock, A.M.—to the same hour P.M.—I shall be most happy to
assure you vivâ voce, that I am with unfeigned respect & regard,
dear Sir, your's sincerely,

S. T. Coleridge

1475. To Samuel Mence

Address: Revd. S. Mence.
MS. Mr. H. T. Butler. Pub. E. L. G. ii. 352.

July 13, 1825.

My dear Sir

It must (I am almost ashamed to confess it) have been more than
20 years since I had read the Εἰκὼν Βασιλική.[1] I determined therefore, after having skimmed the first 20 pages of Dr Wordsworth,[2]
to give it a careful re-perusal, before I entered on the controversy
as to it's true Author. This I have done: and tho' I cannot help
conceding to Dr Walker's argument[3] drawn from the chapter on
the Covenant more force, or at least greater plausibility than
Dr Wordsworth is disposed to allow it, it does not sensibly weaken
my total and final impression—first, that the work was written by
the King—tho' I think it probable that many passages were
composed from his recollection of the public papers, published in
his name, but as we learn from Clarendon written by himself, or
Lord Falkland.—Second, that the Book was written with the
intent & foresight (surely, a very justifiable nay laudable design!)
of conciliating the judgement and affections of his subjects, in
favor of himself—should the opportunity offer—or at all events of
his Children.—And doubtless, neither you nor I will be ashamed to
regard it as some confirmation of this conjecture, that God did
actually bless the work to this end: and that it militated more

[1] *Εἰκὼν Βασιλική, the Pourtraicture of His Sacred Majestie in His Solitudes
and Sufferings*, purporting to be the genuine work of Charles I, was published
shortly after his execution in 1649.

[2] Mr. H. T. Butler, who kindly sent me a transcript of the MS., tells me that
Coleridge's letter is enclosed in a copy of Christopher Wordsworth's '*Who
wrote ΕΙΚΩΝ ΒΑΣΙΛΙΚΗ?*' considered and answered, in Two Letters addressed
to his Grace the Archbishop of Canterbury, 1824. Wordsworth, who supports the
claim that Charles I was the author, published a *Documentary Supplement* in
1825. For a general discussion of the controversy see the review of Wordsworth's two works in the *Quarterly Review* of Oct. 1825.

[3] Anthony Walker, *A True Account of the Author of a Book entituled Εἰκὼν
Βασιλική*, 1692, attributed the authorship to John Gauden (1605–62). Walker
had been Gauden's curate at Bocking.

effectively for his Son's restoration, than all the cowardly crowned heads of Europe, and all the tumultuary Plots and Mobbings of the drinking and swearing Cavaliers.—But this second point of view, in which I look on the work, sufficiently explains the Chapter on the Covenant—and other passages in a nobler strain, which correspond better to Falkland's praeter saeculum liberality and enlargement of Principles than to Laud's Royal Admirer & Partisan; tho' God forbid! that I should scruple to believe, that Adversity, the Mother or Nurse of Reflection, might have led Charles to adopt them, as his own—negatively, at least, and as permissible when circumstances rendered it necessary or highly expedient. A man, whose object is to mediate, soften, bring together *for a time* contending parties, will naturally, and may innocently, go as far as he can—even beyond his wishes, if not beyond his intentions. The example of his Father, James I, in the best, or rather the only, good and wise book he ever wrote, addressed to himself, the year before James ascended the English Throne,[1] might not improbably have suggested the idea of the Eikon, and the whole work, style & matter, is exactly what we might expect from a man accustomed to peruse, and even to make, abstracts of Memoirs and State Papers —Results—Notes of the leading Points, &c—As to Gauden's writing it, it is hard to say what is *impossible*; but it appears to me, judging wholly from internal Evidence, next to impossible.— Alas! is it not a melancholy Reflection, that the Bishops after the Restoration, who affected to idolize this book & it's ostensible Author, should have acted throughout in direct opposition to all it's principles and counsels!!—But so it is! Experience, like the stern lanthorn of a Ship, casts it's light only on the *Wake*—on the Track already past.

Your's, with affectionate Esteem,

S. T. Coleridge.

1476. *To Edward Coleridge*

MS. *Pierpont Morgan Lib. Pub. E. L. G. ii. 355.*

[15 July 1825][2]

My dear Edward

Herewith you will receive, I trust, a Copy of the Aids to Reflection, corrected by myself and with a few Mss Notes, and a little MSS. additament in two parts, the one of which you will (should

[1] Βασιλικὸν Δῶρον, 1599, was written by James I as a guide for the conduct of his eldest son, Henry, when he became a king. Henry died prematurely in 1612.

[2] This letter was written on the day following Blanco White's first visit to Highgate on 14 July 1825. See *Life of Joseph Blanco White*, i. 418.

you ever think the Volume worth a more durable Covering) have
bound at the beginning—before the Title-page, the other at the
end.[1] The last, as an illustration of St Paul's Reasoning, I cannot
but think worthy the attention of a young Clergyman: as beyond
all rational doubt the difference between the outward Deed, and
the inward principle of responsible Action, in which consists the
difference in kind between Schemes of Ec[onom]y, social & political
—such as Paley's (mistitled) *Moral* & Political Phi[loso]phy—and
the *Science* of pure Ethics—this difference, I say, is *presupposed* in
the article of Original Sin (see p. 264) on which Article that of
Redemption is grounded and on which alone it can be supported
& rendered intelligible. But again on the doctrine of Redemption,
thus rescued from evaporation into a mere metaphor *per hyper-
bolen*, rests the faith in the Divinity of the Redeemer, and by consequence the Trinity, the Incarnation, and the characteristic
Spirituality of the Gospel Dispensation. It is not saying too much,
therefore, to say that the Rationale of, the sufficing Insight into,
the whole Organism of Christianity is grounded on the *essential*
difference between Good & Evil—but this could not be affirmed
without a contradiction, if the mere *Deeds* (in the Apostle's
Language, *Works*) were included in Good & Evil—for a *Deed*, taken
abstractedly from the Principle, is indifferent. Thus the mutilation
of the Body may be good, as the Act of a skilful Surgeon—detest-
able, as the work of an Assassin—and simply unfortunate, as the
result of an Accident, not to be foreseen. In the first, it would be
the subject of self-approval, in the second of Remorse, in the third
of Regret only. No wonder, therefore, that St Paul recurs so often
to this point; or that it colours all his reasoning. But in the present
time, it is of especial importance to a Minister of the Established
Church on two accounts, a minor & a major. First, in this alone is
found that scriptural mid-ground between Calvinism and the
Socinian Scheme, which it is the honor of our Church to have
occupied—& second, it alone can wean an infant Faith from the
History of the Revelation—it's necessary & appropriate nourishment for a time—to the more nutritious Diet of the *Religion* itself.
An able Vindication of the Miracles *may* prevent a man from becoming an Infidel—or it may puzzle an Infidel how the *History* of
Christianity can be *false*; but it will not, cannot, make a man see
and feel the *truth* of the Christian *Religion*—a truth, that compre-
hends the miracles themselves, and the conviction of which is one
(& an indispensable) *part** of the evidence of their credibility.

---

[1] The copy of *Aids to Reflection* presented to Edward Coleridge is in the
Pierpont Morgan Library.
* For to a reasonable and conscientious Man what conceivable force of

Independent of their value as means of converting the Beholders, and of drawing the world to Christianity, in the first ages, it gives the miracles a perpetual worth & interest for them that already believe, as so many Symbols and (so to say) embodyings of the great Doctrines & Duties of the Gospel. (The Conversion of Water into Wine, and the Fish with the Tribute-money in it's mouth,[1] will instance & explain my meaning—the former establishing the Bearings of Christianity on the social, the latter on the political, ties and duties of a Believer.)

Bear with my prolixity, my dear Edward! which, however, I should not have indulged, had I not received testimonies from three distinguished, no less than Zealous, Clergymen (two of these, of our own Church) that this View of Christianity first opened out to their minds the true purpose and connection of the Sacred Writings, had been as a perpetual comment on the Writings of Paul, and John, and by the inexhaustible fruitfulness of the Idea; by it's tendency to give a *practical* character to the whole of their divinity; and lastly, by it's universal intelligibility, inasmuch as, appealing to the Conscience & Experience common to all men, it's application is at once it's exposition and it's evidence; had rendered their labors in the Pulpit easy and delightful to them.—

I was asked, some few months past, and by no ordinary man, what course of Reading I would recommend as most likely to store the mind with various information & to fit it for the use & application of the knowlege acquired. I answered without hesitation— Make a point of reading a certain portion of the Scriptures, beginning from the Beginning, every day—whether a chapter, or 20 verses, or ten, must depend on the time which your other Duties permit you to allot to your private Studies—Only read with the determination to leave no means untried, that are in your power, to understand *every word*. Use as your general Help, the Critici Sacri,[2] or Pole's Synopsis[3]—to which you may add (if you can conveniently procure the Work) the Commentaries of Cocceius.[4] And by this direct your other reading—(& even in your chance

human testimony would suffice to prove the Miracles recorded in a pretended Revelation, that permitted promiscuous Concubinage, enjoined private Revenge as a Duty, & commanded Persecution? [Note by S. T. C.]

[1] John ii. 1–11, and Matthew xvii. 27.

[2] *Critici Sacri; sive Doctissimorum Virorum in SS. Biblia Annotationes et Tractatus*, ed. J. Pearson, A. Scattergood, F. Gouldman, and R. Pearson, 9 vols., 1660.

[3] *Synopsis Criticorum aliorumque Sacrae Scripturae Interpretum* [Matthew Poole or Pole], 5 vols., 1669–76.

[4] Johannes Cocceius, *Lexicon et Commentarius Sermonis Hebraici et Chaldaici*, 1669.

reading, which I by no means discourage, bear this in mind—)
Travels, Voyages, Antiquities, &c &c: as the object, you have in
view at the particular time, may suggest or require. Supposing you
to have read only three chapters a week on an average, I dare
anticipate that at the end of a year you will yourself be surprized
at the quantity and variety of information, that you will have
acquired, & which will hang together in your mind—so as literally
to become a memoria technica, by it's unity of purpose, or con-
vergence ad idem. The Hebrew Sages said—Three things were,
before the World was: the Law, Messiah and the Last Judgement.
With better taste & without a play on words, we may say—The
World was made for the Gospel, or that Christianity is the final
Cause of the World. If so, the Idea of the Redemption of the
World must needs form the best central Reservoir for all our
knowleges, physical or personal. Every fact must find it's place, as
a component point in some one or other of the converging
Radii.—

The Bishop of London has been pleased to express a MOST
favorable Opinion of my Work—in consequence of which the
celebrated Mr Blanco White procured the Volume, and a few days
after the Friend. He then procured an introduction to me from Sir
George & Lady Beaumont—& yesterday he came from Chelsea in
a Glass Coach (for he is in very infirm health) & spent the whole day
from 1 o'clock till ½ past 9 with me. It was highly gratifying to me
to find, that he had the 'Aids to Reflection' at his fingers' ends: and
it would scarcely become me to repeat the strong expressions, he
used, respecting the effect produced on his mind & views of
Christianity by the §§ phs p. 130–140, and the Disquisitions on
Original Sin & Redemption, with that on the Diversity of Reason
& Understanding.—Have you seen White's Answer to Catholic
Butler?[1]—I am not surprized, that the Bishop regards it as one of
the most momentous Works that have appeared on the subject of the
true character of the Romish Religion.—Blanco White is by general
admission a man of strong mind: and it is impossible to be with him
& not feel that he is a very good man.—He was so anxious to have
the Addenda, I intended for you, transcribed in order to be bound
in his Copy, that I let him have them—& shall bring them with me,
when I come—

[1] Charles Butler's *Book of the Roman Catholic Church: in a series of letters
addressed to R. Southey, Esq., on his 'Book of the Church'*, 1825, was, as the title
indicates, an answer to Southey's *Book of the Church*, 1824. J. Blanco White
entered the controversy with his *Practical and Internal Evidence against
Catholicism, with Occasional Strictures on Mr. Butler's 'Book of the Roman
Catholic Church'*, which appeared in May 1825. A copy of White's work with
annotations by Coleridge is in the British Museum.

And now let me conclude this prolix *Author's* Letter, & take another sheet for my immediate Business—in the mean time, may God bless you, my dear Nephew! and all with whom your happiness & well-being are or are about to be intertwined.—

S. T. Coleridge—

1477. *To Edward Coleridge*

Address: Revd. Edward Coleridge | Eton
MS. Pierpont Morgan Lib. Pub. E. L. G. ii. 359.

[15 July 1825][1]

My dear Nephew

That dear & excellent Woman, Mrs Gillman, has for the last two months or more eat, drank, woke, slept, thought, dreamed nothing but Henry Gillman & Eaton College—and in fact the greater part of my own time & anxiety has been fixed to this point—Poor Lady! it makes my very heart ache to see her, worn as she is to a Shadow—grieving and mourning not only or chiefly at the sad loss of time, the Boy had suffered, for the year or more, he was at a School in the Hamlet; but on account of the habit of inattention which had seriously weakened his power of attending, and of course of *combining*, even with his very best efforts. The consequence has been, that tho' I was indefatigable in my efforts, two thirds of the Time were consumed (but for the nearness and urgency of the Need, I should have said, well & usefully employed) in overcoming this obstacle—and had his examination been appointed for October instead of July, I should have few apprehensions of the Result—so few indeed, that I should not hesitate to give my pledge, that by the time, he returned, to become bonâ fide resident (September, I believe) what is wanting now, should be supplied to the quantum sufficit of the Form. As it was, I had no other choice but that of giving up the less necessary in order to establish him in the fundamentals—. In construing and parsing Latin, I hope, that he will be found fit to commence on equal ground with his Form-fellows any such Books, as are read in the form—Ovid, Selecta, &c. —He is quite perfect in his knowlege of prosody, and scanning of Hexameter & Elegiac Verse, and familiar with the prosody-names of all words not exceeding four syllables—and the division of all the Feet, simple or composite, into those of equal times— | $-\cup\cup$ |

[1] In the last paragraph of the preceding letter Coleridge says he will take 'another sheet' for his 'immediate Business'—a reference to the present letter. The two letters were dispatched together.

ᴗ–ᴗ | ᴗᴗ– | &c—and he understands the mechanism, or way of making verses, if you give him (as I have found it necessary to do) the English of two, four, or six Verses, pretty closely translated from an equal number of Latin Verses, that he has not seen.—But to make verses out of his own head, or to turn English Verse into Latin—for this he is not yet ripe—But I doubt not, that by September, he will be able to do this very passably.—

In his Greek he is well-grounded in his Nouns, and all the forms of the Verbs, & in the *rationale*, as well as in the technique of the formation of one tense from another—& if he were examined in the 4, 5, or 6 Chapters of Matthew, I think, that the Examiner would be satisfied from his mode of parsing, that he had not learnt them by *rote*; but was fit to go on—or if other parts, that he had not read, were set him to learn, with his Grammar & Lexicon—

But my dear Edward! the poor fellow from having been so fearfully shaken by the Hooping-Cough is nervous; & easily fluttered—& then loses his recollection & becomes confused—and he has had so many things to be learnt, & unlearnt, within a short time—that I must again intreat, that, if possible, some allowance of *Hope* may be made, for his progress during the interval between the Examination & his return in September—*for which, I* AGAIN *pledge myself.*—Briefly, for *my* sake & for the sake of his fond & anxious Mother, & for my friend, Mr Gillman, do what you can. Mr Henry Hall is the little fellow's good friend: and I promise both you & him, that you shall have no reason to regret any indulgence, it may be in your power to extend to him at his examination so that he may be put in the Fourth Form.—

Mr Gillman has procured a Wallenstein, which he begs you to accept, with his kind regards.—

I propose accompanying Henry to Eaton, & passing the two or three days there—but pray, do not think of putting yourself to any trouble or inconvenience—I shall do very well at the Inn.—Only be so good as to let me know and if possible within a day from your receipt of this, what day it is necessary, that we should be there—and any other information, you may think proper.—

Make my best remembrances to Mr Hautrey[1]—whom, should choice or chance lead him hitherto, my kind friends, Mr & Mrs Gillman, would be most happy to see—& could give him a bed—. I need not add, that this applies to yourself a fortiori.—Let me hear from you—: for you may easily suppose, that I am first anxious on my own account, as a sort of Tutor—& secondly, most anxious by sympathy with the anxiety of Mr Gillman, and his incomparable

---

[1] Edward Craven Hawtrey, D.D. (1789–1862), successively assistant master, 1814, headmaster, 1834, and provost, 1852, of Eton College.

Wife, to whom I owe so many obligations—God bless you, my dear Nephew

& your faithful Friend | & affectionate Uncle

S. T. Coleridge—

Poor Southey has been arrested on his Journey by a *Bug-bite* which has inflamed his leg & lamed him—& he fears, will prevent him from reaching Amsterdam.—

1478. *To John Murray*

Address: Mr J. Murray | Albemarle Street
MS. Sir John Murray. Pub. E. L. G. ii. 354.
Postmark: Highgate, 18 July 1825.

Grove, Highgate
Monday
18 July 1825.

Dear Sir

I am much obliged to you for your politeness in forwarding to me Mr Blanco White's interesting and most valuable Work,[1] with his gratifying Note. The Praise of such a Man, and the approbation of the Bishop of London, are Prizes in the Lottery of Literature, which I did not expect to draw.—

I was grievously disappointed in finding that my Nephew had quitted town for the Western Circuit without leaving any information for me respecting Mr Hurwitz's *Hebrew Tales*.[2] I am reduced therefore to intreat your permission to wait on you myself with Mr H— and as I am compelled to go to Eton to my Nephew, Mr Edward Coleridge, on Thursday, I have only Wednesday—or rather Wednesday—the day after tomorrow—is the latest day in my power—. I shall therefore call at Albermarle Street between One & Two—in the hopes of obtaining an interview with you personally—or (should it not be in your power to oblige me thus far) yet that you will either leave a Note for me, or at least let me hear from you by return of Post, supposing that it should not be convenient for you to receive me on the day mentioned—

I remain, dear Sir, | very respectfully | your obliged &c

S. T. Coleridge

[1] i.e. *Evidence against Catholicism*. See Letters 1476 and 1480.
[2] See Letters 1446 and 1470–1.

1479. *To Hyman Hurwitz*

Address: Hyman Hurwitz, Esqre | Granada Cottage | Old Kent Road.
MS. University of Pennsylvania Lib. Hitherto unpublished.
Postmark: 18 July 1825.

[18 July 1825]
My dear Friend

My memory perplexes me—I have appointed *Wednesday*, between One & Two—& now I am haunted, lest you should have said or understood *Tuesday*.—But on Wednesday I shall be (God permitting) at Mr Montague's Chambers before One o'clock—. On Thursday I go to Eton with little Henry Gillman—

God bless you &

S. T. Coleridge

1480. *To J. Blanco White*

Address: Revd. J. B. White | 7 Paradise Row | Chelsea
MS. in the Rathbone Papers, now on deposit in the University Library, Liverpool; printed by permission of Mr. Reynolds Rathbone. Pub. Life of Joseph Blanco White, *i. 418.*
Postmark: 20 July 1825.

July 20 1825—
Wednesday Afternoon
My dear Sir

I set off tomorrow evening with my little Protégé, Henry Gillman, for Eton; and shall return, D.V. on Wednesday next—I cannot, however, without risking a quarrel with my own feelings, defer to so long a time my acknowlegement of your Pract. & Intern. Evidence & the very kind Note that accompanied it. I am on the point of putting to the Press a small Work on the Church, in it's twofold sense—viz. as an Institution of Christ, and as a State Institution— in the latter part of which I come on the same ground with you, and tho' I cannot ascribe to the perusal of your work what had been written before it's publication, I shall feel myself induced by prudence as well as constrained by Justice, to express my sense of it's worth & value, and the delight, I have received from the unexpected confirmation of my own Convictions, in fuller terms than I may address to yourself.[1]—It is indeed delightful to me on so many points to find myself, head, heart & spirit, in sympathy with such an Intellect & such a Spirit as your's—The inclosed may perhaps amuse you on this score—tho' on a comparatively trifling subject.—But, my dear Sir! much, very much I have to *say* to you,

---

[1] See *The Church and State*, 99 n. and 156 n.

for which not worldly but Christian Discretion requires *fit* Auditor[1] & competent.—First, I thank you for the manliness with which you have opposed that current illiberal dogma, that Infidelity always arises from Vice or corrupt affections. Sunt quibus non credidisse honor est et fidei futurae pignus—One of the best men and *now* most assured Christian I know had been made an Infidel in consequence of reading Paley's Evidences.—Secondly, I venture to confess my persuasion, that the pernicious Idol of delegated Infallibility has it's *base* on a yet deeper Error common to Romish & Reformed—and I would fain shew you a series of Letters, which have for more than a year been in my Publishers' Hands, on the right & superstitious Use & Veneration of the Sacred Scriptures—.[2] God knows! if all the Books in the world were in one Scale & the Bible in the other—the former would strike the Beam in my serious Judgement—But still an infallibility wholly *objective* & without any correspondent *Subjective* (call it Grace, Spiritual Experience, or what you will) is *an absurdity*—a substanceless Idol, to which *Sensations* may be attached, but which cannot be the subject of distinct Conception, much less of a clear Idea.—But I must break off.

With fervent prayers for the strengthening of your bodily health, and for all that by adding to your happiness will extend your utility—with no every-day feeling tho' in every-day phrases, I remain,

   my dear Sir, | with affectionate Esteem & Respect | Your
      sincere Friend

                                          S. T. Coleridge.

[1] Cf. *Paradise Lost*, vii. 31: 'fit audience find, though few.'
[2] As the following letter from Hessey to John Taylor of 30 June 1826 shows, nearly another year elapsed before the MS. of the sixth disquisition was returned to Coleridge:

Simmons [the printer] has discovered among his Papers the Manuscript to which Mr Coleridge alludes. It appears to have passed thro' my hands certainly, but it was as a Portion of the 'Aids to Reflection' which was left out of that work on Account of its length. It has been lying ever since in Simmons' Desk and I am very happy it is found. I return Mr Coleridge's Letter with it. When you write to him pray make my kind regards & tell him I am very sorry for the anxiety which I have unwittingly caused him. (*The Keats Circle*, ed. H. E. Rollins, 2 vols., 1948, ii. 463–4.) See also Letter 1447.

A manuscript of the *Confessions of an Inquiring Spirit* is in the British Museum, Add. MS. 34225. According to H. StJ. Hart, who edited the work in 1956, the British Museum Catalogue 'very justly' describes this MS. as 'probably an early draft, with many slight variations from the printed edition'. The paper is watermarked 1822.

1481. *To the Gillmans*

MS. Victoria University Lib. Hitherto unpublished.

Eton—

[*Circa* 24 July 1825][1]

My dear Friends

All things equal to our wish & perhaps beyond our expectation. Henry is put in the 4th form; & tomorrow will be elected into the College—He has gone thro' his first & most important examination with success, failing only in his Verses—Even with this, Dr K. (BUT THIS MUST BE KEPT A PROFOUND SECRET) would have put him in the higher class of the form, where according to his age he should be in order to have an equal chance for King's—but on considering the matter over, I thought for reasons, that I am sure will satisfy you, that it was better to leave his rank in the 4th Form undetermined till his return—when if I can but bring up his Verses equal to his other points of Scholarship (of which I entertain no doubt, if he continue as good a boy as he has for some time been) he will be ranked in the manner most conducive to his future fortunes.—I raised the House last night by the long & loud screams & distressful Noises in my sleep—I was quite unconscious of what had occurred in the morning—I doubt not, this often happens; but at Highgate I am not so within hearing as in this small & thin-walled House— But thank God! I am rather better than usual, in my day-health—.

Henry has been so good a boy that I have promised to let him have all the tale of Eton to tell himself, what he has seen & what done—*Nothing* can *surpass* the flattering attentions that have been shewn me by the Provost, Dr Keates, Fellows &c &c—I expect to be with you again by Tuesday Night by the last stage—God bless you, my dearest Friends!—I can barely force these few minutes to fulfill my promise— . . . [Conclusion and signature cut off.]

HENRICUS ANTONIUS GILLMAN ETONENSIS sends his dutiful Love to his Father & Mother.—

P.S. I will take care, my dear Mrs G. not to forget any of your Mementos.—

---

[1] Coleridge planned to leave for Eton on Thursday, 21 July 1825, and as the present letter from that place shows, he expected to return to Highgate on Tuesday the 26th. See Letter 1480.

1482. *To Thomas Hurst*[1]

Address: T. Hurst, Esqre | Winchester House
Transcript Mrs. W. M. Sweeny. *Hitherto unpublished.*

6 Aug. 1825.

My dear Sir

Allow me to trouble you by a request, that you would desire one of your Clerks to order Nizolius's Dictionary of Phrases from Oxford. I am not sure of the exact title whether Nizolii Diction- arium Ciceronianum, or Nizolii Dictionarium Phraseologicum;[2] but I know that the work has been reprinted at the Clarendon Press.— Is there no London Bookseller, the Agent of the Oxford Press?—
Mr & Mrs Gillman beg to add their request, that the work may be procured as soon as possible: it being intended for their eldest son, who is in immediate want of it—and Mr Gillman will settle for it.—
Present my respectful compliments to Mrs Hurst, & believe me
with sincere | esteem | your obliged
S. T. Coleridge

1483. *To Gioacchino de' Prati*

MS. University of York Lib. Hitherto unpublished.

[September 1825 ?][3]

My dear Dr De Prati

Mr Gillman is confident, that, the Bile having evidently com- menced it's reflux into it's proper channels, another day or two of mild purgatives, in divided doses, will completely defecate my blood of this Yellow Alien; and that by Wednesday I may expect the Return of my own Self to it's old Lodgings, and know that I have a Head by it's *functions*, instead of *feeling* it, like a hot *Wen* on my Shoulders, as is the case now & has been for sometime past.—I talked with Mr Green last night on your, I should say our, scheme;[4]

[1] Thomas Hurst, a resident of Highgate and at this time a partner in the Longman publishing house, was ruined in 1826 by the failure of Hurst, Robinson, and Co., a firm of booksellers and publishers in which his elder brother John was a partner. Subsequently Thomas Hurst was a member of Hurst, Chance, and Co., publishers, St. Paul's Church-Yard. See Letters 1521 and n., 1540, and 1652.

[2] *Lexicon Ciceronianum M. Nizolii ex recensione A. Scoti. Accedunt phrases et formulae Linguae Latinae ex commentariis S. Doleti,* London, 1820.

[3] The references to a recent attack of jaundice in this and the next letter suggest that the two letters were written about the same time.

[4] In his autobiography, which appeared in the *Penny Satirist,* 1837–40, Prati has this to say of Coleridge and Green:

Coleridge . . . took the most lively interest in my welfare, and seeing from my conversation that I was deeply engaged in physiological and medical studies,

but while he assured me of every assistance on his part, he begged me to suspend the Subject—from the flurry that the least attempt to talk connectedly had produced—. Therefore, till Wednesday (and or Thursday I hope to *see* you here) I should be hurting myself without benefiting you, if I attempted to set about the thing in that systematic good earnest, without which I should be doing nothing.—You would hardly imagine with what effort & with how many suspensions I have been able to scribble these few lines—& with what a cold sweat my Brow is covered as I now assure you of my regard & persevering friendship—

S. T. Coleridge

1484. *To Edward Coleridge*

Address: Revd. Edward Coleridge | Eton
MS. Professor R. C. Bald. Hitherto unpublished.
Postmark: Highgate, 6 September 1825.

Tuesday afternoon [6 September 1825]
Grove Highgate—

My dear Edward

It has been no small comfort to me to follow you in spirit along the Banks of the Otter, and over the Hills & Vales adjacent, and to return with you, with the spolia opima, Otter-fatning Trout or trout-devouring Otter—Partridge & Pheasant not excluded—there being no Game-laws for the Fancy—to the social Table, the Chat, the Music, and the group of happy Faces and affectionate Hearts—and to assure myself, that from the large *In*-come of Strength and Health you have been able to spend liberally and yet lay up a stock for the ludi-magistral Post-ludium, of the ensuing three or four Months. Believe me, it was both a comfort & a frequent alleviation of the contrast, I was myself affording to these pictured Assurances.—During the fortnight that followed the five memorable Hot Days I was noticeably unwell, deprest by day, and wandering all night thro' the Swedenborgian Devildom, like a Dante all at once left by his Guide, or whose supposed Virgil had turned into Mrs Brownrigg—.[1] While I remained quiet and motionless, I had full possession of my thoughts; but as soon as I

recommended me warmly to Mr. Henry Green of Lincoln's-inn-fields, and I am proud to say, that I have found in him not only the most talented philosopher, eminent physiologist, and well educated gentleman, but a friend, a father, a counsellor, in short, a being to whom I owe not only esteem and gratitude, but filial respect and eternal obligation. (M. H. Fisch, 'The Coleridges, Dr. Prati, and Vico', *Modern Philology*, Nov. 1943, p. 122.)

[1] Elizabeth Brownrigg, murderess, was hanged at Tyburn on 14 Sept. 1767.

attempted to give them utterance, I became flurried, and lost all command over them. The cause and occasion of all this distempera- ture were at length disclosed—and on commencing my morning Shave, the only time I have the pleasure of looking at myself, I was greeted by a duplicate, in color tho' not stature, of Nebuchad- nezzar's Image—. From the hair-line of my forehead to the soles of my Feet all Gold—with some alloy of Brass or Copper for the Neck & Breast—. In short, a consummated Jaundice, and, as I shortly after found, with an entire suspension of the biliary secre- tions, in their right channels at least. Mr Gillman said nothing till he had examined me; but after he had pressed, pushed, massed, and struck various regions of my trunk without any *ish sh*, or retraction on my part, he concluded from the abruptness of the Visit that the Visitor would not stay long—and so it proved—In about eight days my skin resumed it's usual clearness; just as certain symptoms in my gums and palate indicated the discon- tinuance of the Calomel, which I took in very small doses with Jalap & extract of Hyoscyamus. The medicine & the Regimen left me weak and languid—and tho' I am *progredient*, I am still not equal to much, or any continuance of effort.—To this you must attribute my inability to look over or bring together my Scraps for you, and (which I regret) the discontinuance of my perusal of Matthai's Greek Grammar,[1] and of the Notes, I was writing—& which, I fear, partake of the unclearness in which my mind then was. I am quite sure, however, that one octavo Volume with half the number of pages would suffice to answer all the purposes, at which M. aims, and yet leave space for the numerous points which he has not noticed. I see but one difficulty—but one subject, I mean, the understanding of which and of it's Rationale requires any subtlety—and this is, the uses for which the Latins invented their Ablative Case—what I call the *border*-land between the Greek Genitive and Dative. You remember my dear Father's Quare- quale-quidditive Case?[2]—That it is the Case Absolute—and (as always occurs) the Nom. or rather the caseless word itself, in the Italian—seems to me to promise light for it's solution.—One and very important consideration in Grammar is the influence of mere analogy, or the changes effected in language by assimilation of words to the forms of most frequent recurrence, and how far the Grammarians themselves have added to this tendency. There is a

[1] A copy of A. H. Matthiae's *Copious Greek Grammar*, translated from the German by E. V. Blomfield, 2 vols., 1824, containing annotations by Coleridge is in the Huntington Library.

[2] See Letters 179 and 1658, and Chambers, *Life*, 4. The reference is to John Coleridge's *Critical Latin Grammar*, 1772.

striking instance in the German Sonnè (Sun). In the oldest German
Writings the articles are Die,=The, the bi-sexual Article, and
Dat=that, the Neuter. Accordingly, in the oldest Theotiscan[1]
Poetry Die Sonnè, the Sun, is described with male attributes, and
Die Mond with female—. But when Poets arose who used the
Ober-teut[s]ch (or South-German) which has three articles, Der,
die, and das, the words ending in è took their gender from the
article—and die Sonne became a Goddess—& in like manner the
nouns ending in d, the consonantal being the masculine termina-
tion, der Mond put on Breeches—The ignorance of this misled Horn
Tooke to a bitter sneer at Harris,[2] & to the rejection of very just
tho' imperfect Views respecting the Genders.—

And now for Business.—On what day must Henry set off for
Eton ? Will Friday do ?—Whither is he to go, on leaving the Stage?
—Tho' my Illness has been a sad loss to him, poor Fellow! yet I
trust, you will find him considerably improved—tho' if I had
had the strength and the conveniences of *flogging* him, instead of
scolding or confining, more would have been done—and yet I am
persuaded, that he is desirous to do well—but his habits of carelessness and of having recourse to others on every difficulty, i.e. on
every point, that does not present itself to him in the first moment,
hang on him still—. And tho' he is now tolerably expert in turning
words into Hex. and Pentameter, in the way of the papers, I had
from you, he is still sadly behind hand in making any either out of
his own head, or where the thoughts have not been worded so as to
contain the verse.—As it is, I should have succeeded better, had
I but thought in time of the Christ Hospital Grammar. I have sent
one with Henry—and from page 150 it does appear to me in every
respect so very superior to any other Book of Exercises, both in
the matter and the arrangement, that I cannot help expressing a
wish that you would look over it.—(Apropos.—Leighton *was* the
Boy, you so kindly noticed.[3] He related it to me with an amiable
enthusiasm; and I assure you, he does great credit to your discrimination. I do not doubt, that he will be a sound Clergyman, and a
worthy Successor of the late Bishop of Calcutta, whom he much
resembles in his person & manners.)—

Henry will take with him 1. a Dictionary. 2. Schrevellius'
Lexicon[4]—3. Gradus. 4. Pantheon—. 5. Epigrams. 6. Selecta.

---

[1] See Letter 277 and *Biog. Lit.* i. 139.
[2] J. Horne Tooke 'especially ridiculed' James Harris's *Hermes, or a Philosophical Inquiry concerning Universal Grammar*, 1751.
[3] David H. Leighton was the Senior Grecian at Christ's Hospital in 1826.
[4] The Greek lexicon by Schrevelius (Kornelis Schrevel) was published in
1670.

7. Ovid. 8. Pantheon— [9. & 10. La]tin & Greek Grammar (Eton, of course.) 11. Exercises. Are [there] any other Books, he ought to bring with him ?— His Mother (whose feelings & sentiments toward you I will not attempt to describe) would be happy, if you would determine what weekly pocket-money he ought to have—so as not to be unhappy by having less, than the Boys of his own class & age in the College generally have—& yet the less, he has, the better it will be for him, on account of his delicate digestive powers.—By the bye, is it true that in the winter time the larger College Boys take away all the Blankets from the little ones & leave them to sleep in the cold with only the coverlet ?—I cannot believe it—but poor Mrs G. has been told this, & has accordingly put up two or three warm flannel Shirts for him to put on, in case of such an event.—She proposes (if you will permit it) to send 5£ inclosed to you, for his entrances, at his Dame's, & for his Pocket-money.—I am afraid, that Mr Gillman will not be able to take him down, from the number & state of his Patients—so that I must tax your kindness to compleat the kind work, you have begun—& need I say, that tho' it will not add to the affection, I feel, it will be among the subjects that will cluster round it—. But I must hurry or lose the Post—Be so good as to write by return of Post—if (as I hope) it will find you. God bless you &

S. T. Coleridge

1485. *To Edward Coleridge*

Address: Revd. Edward Coleridge   by Henry Gillman
MS. Pierpont Morgan Lib. Pub. E. L. G. ii. 361.

7 Septr 1825[1]

My dear Edward

My own diffidence in my memory in all that regards dates, vel Loci vel Temporis, prevented me from insisting as strongly on my recollection of the words; 'but *he* must be here by the *Seventh*'—as it's distinctness would have justified—and as I could not get your letter till ¼ before 12, all is in a bustle & I have merely time & power to say, that in the course of a fortnight I shall have looked over four or five of my larger and smaller Memorandum Books, and excerp the few Pages, or References that I may want for the work in hand—& send them to you with a bag of single Scraps. In some of the Memorandum Books of old date, there are passages, which I do not mind your seeing—for the more *you* know what my mind has been as well as what it *is*, for strength and for weakness, the

---

[1] The date is written in the address sheet.

more accordant will your judgement respecting me be with my wishes—only you will read them *dramatically*—i.e. as the portrait and impress of the mood and the moment—birds of passages—or Bubbles—But I would have them sacred to your eyes.—

I will return your Matthai as well worth your valuing, as the sum total of my Lucubrations on the philosophy of Language in detailed Application to the Greek Language can make it—

Notwithstanding the exception afforded by your Father's Family, and one or two others within my experience, I am yet glad that dear Fanny has a *Girl*.—

I trust, that Henry will be a good boy to the best of the powers, Nature has endowed him with. I am sure, that he is earnestly desirous to do well; but the want of a Command over what he actually knows, and the fainting-fits of his Recollection on the very Couch of his Memory, are & for a time will be, much against him.—

Every thing, that you judge proper, will be received here with grateful assent.—God bless you & your affectionate

Uncle & sincere Friend

S. T. Coleridge—

P.S. I have engaged to translate with comments &c. Bacon's Novum Organum for Basil Montague's Splendid Edition—.[1] And Montague has undertaken to arrange an engagement with his Publisher for an Edition of Shakspear by me—These to employ the half of my time while I am bringing out the toils of my meditations, from which I do not expect ever to derive a shilling of pecuniary profit. Do what I would, I could not (to use Wesley's phrase) be shallow enough for a polite Public.[2]—

---

[1] Coleridge did not translate Bacon's *Novum Organum*, the work being subsequently carried out by William Page Wood. Montagu's edition of Bacon was published by William Pickering, 16 volumes, 1825–36. In the preface, which is dated 17 Nov. 1834, Montagu acknowledges his indebtedness to Coleridge:

> One friend the grave has closed over, who cheered me in my task when I was weary, and better able, from his rich and comprehensive mind, to detect errors, than any man, was always more happy to encourage and to commend. Wise as the serpent, gall-less as the dove, pious and pure of heart, tender, affectionate, and forgiving, this, and more than this, I can say, after the trial of forty years, was my friend and instructor, Samuel Taylor Coleridge.

[2] John Wesley, *Journal*, 25 Aug. 1771: 'O how hard it is to be shallow enough for a polite audience!'

1486. *To H. F. Cary*

Address: The Revd. F. Carey | Chiswick
MS. Pierpont Morgan Lib. Hitherto unpublished.
Postmark: Highgate, 22 September 1825.

Grove, Highgate—
Thursday [22 September 1825]
My dear Friend

I have been very ill; but I have neglected nothing except answering your & Dr Ferguson's Letters.[1] On Mr Green's return from his Trip to the Netherlands I wrote to him & spoke to him—he knows how very much any thing would gratify me that served you or your's.—Mr G. had been spoken to by or about a Mr Elliby, and had declined—or stated his intention not to take any part in the election. In consequence of this, he cannot appear *as openly* in Dr F's behalf as he otherwise would do; but possibly, nay probably, will be able to befriend him *more* effectually, on this very account.—If Dr F. will call on Mr G. (46, Lincoln's Inn Fields) any morning before 11 o'clock, Mr G. will be happy to converse with Dr F. on the Subject—and meantime advises Dr F. to call on or leave his card with, the Treasurer of St Thomas's, Mr Chapman, and to make as much interest with him by means of Friends as he can. But all this Dr F. will learn better from Mr G. vivâ voce—and will find Mr G. exceedingly disposed to further his views—Make my excuses to Dr F.—& believe me

affectionately | your sincere tho' | dejected Friend
S. T. Coleridge

1487. *To J. H. Green*

Address: J. H. Green, Esqre | Lincoln's Inn Fields
MS. Pierpont Morgan Lib. Hitherto unpublished.

[Late September 1825][2]
My dear Friend

I more than fear that there will be some trouble in the *Abridgement* Line: even should Part II. pass the ordeal of Prudence with unsinged Pinions, and not be impeached of soaring too high a pitch.

[1] Robert Ferguson (1799–1865) settled in London after taking his M.D. degree at Edinburgh in 1823. He was active in the founding of the *London Medical Gazette* in 1827. He was appointed professor of obstetrics at King's College, London, in 1831 and physician-accoucheur to Queen Victoria in 1840.
[2] The statement in the postscript indicates that this letter was written shortly before Coleridge left for Ramsgate on Wednesday, 5 Oct. 1825. See Letter 1490.

And yet as there is nothing introduced that can be justly or plaus-
ibly supposed to interfere with the instructions or principles
properly artistic of the professorial Artists, not only nothing
technical but no attempt at any canons of special Criticism, no rules
of appreciation or comparison between Picture & Picture, but
merely an assertion of the dignity, worth & value of your own
profession, and so far therefore a vindication of the Judgement of
those who attached a Professor of Anatomy to the Royal Academy,[1]
while it contains advice not only *useful* to such of the growing
Generation graphic and plastic as are capable of being advised to
any higher Object than that of House-painting, whether the
Wainscoting or the framed Canvasses that hide it, is a matter of
indifference—but likewise complimentary to the Artistic character
generally & in the Idea—and as moreover it is, under existing
circumstances, it is better to be talked of, tho' against, for having
done too much, than to escape all Talk by doing too little—for
with your mind and powers *just* enough for J.J. and B.B. is *too
little* for your self—better to be abused for a display of superiority
than decried for mediocrity—and as more—more-over, you of all
men have reason to know from your own experience, that in real
Life there is no such thing possible as a *Medium*—that no circumspection, no not even the happy privilege, you possess, of maintaining your own respectability without standing in the way of
any man's Vanity, can save a man from being abused, as long as he
possesses any thing which any other man would like to have—for
these reasons I would rather that you erred by boldness than by
fear or caution—

By the first Post of next week you will (no mortal accidents
intervening) receive what we talked about—. I am still inclined to
think, that on the subject of Expression something might be
introduced from the Supervacanea, the passage I mean, respecting
the *Ideal & Individual* without offence—I shall not, however,
suppose any such, nor make any reference—tho' something in a
humbler style, yet of similar import, would form an apposite
Winding up of the *other* Subject—the Spurzheimian, I mean—.

We have received very chearful & encouraging Accounts from
Mrs Randal of Henry and Eton. The effect fully justified the
tenderness & sympathizing tone of the Answer to his Nostalgic

---

[1] In 1825 J. H. Green was appointed professor of anatomy to the Royal
Academy, a post he resigned in 1852. During his tenure he gave six lectures a
year on anatomy in its relation to the fine arts. Two of his lectures, an introductory one, 'Beauty and Expression as the Elements of the Fine Arts', and a
second, 'The Conditions of Beauty in the Beautiful Object', were published in
the *Athenaeum* on 16 and 23 Dec. 1843.

Eruption. He expected (as I foresaw) an angry letter: & it's kindness quite overset & then calmed & comforted him.—

In about a month hence I expect to have made some progress in the Translation of the Novum Organum with Notes for B. Montague's Edition; but if I should not have done, what I at present calculate on, I shall be forced, I fear, to apply to your kindness for three or four Pound, for the payment of some small Bills which I do not like to trouble Mrs Gillman about. I say this now, to have it off my mind, lest my anxiety about it should interfere with my thoughts, to prevent me from taking the means of rendering the application unnecessary—God knows, I feel it unreasona[ble] but for that very reason, the mere notion of the thing harasses me, and I shall not be ashamed of your knowing what I had intended, if by this means I can supersede the said intention.—

God bless you &

S. T. Coleridge

P.S. On *my own* account I would rather remain at home than go to Ramsgate—

1488. *To James Gillman*

Address: James Gillman, Esqre | Surgeon | Grove | Highgate
MS. Texas Christian University Lib. Pub. with omis. Letters, *ii. 742.*
Postmark: 10 October 1825. *Stamped*: Ramsgate.

9 Octr 1825
8 Plains of Waterloo
Ramsgate—

My dear Friend

It is a flat'ning Thought, that the more we have seen, the less we have to say. In Youth and early Manhood the Mind and Nature are, as it were, two rival Artists, both potent Magicians, and engaged, like the King's Daughter and the rebel Genie in the Arabian Nights' Enternts., in sharp conflict of Conjuration—each having for it's object to turn the other into Canvas to paint on, Clay to mould, or Cabinet to contain. For a while the Mind seems to have the better in the contest, and makes of Nature what it likes; takes her Lichens and Weather-stains for Types & Printer's Ink and prints Maps & Fac Similes of Arabic and Sanscrit Mss. on her rocks; composes Country-Dances on her moon-shiny Ripples, Fandangos on her Waves and Walzes on her Eddy-pools; transforms her Summer Gales into Harps and Harpers, Lovers' Sighs and sighing Lovers, and her Winter Blasts into Pindaric Odes, Christabels & Ancient Mariners set to music by Beethoven, and in the insolence

of triumph conjures her Clouds into Whales and Walrusses with
Palanquins on their Backs, and chaces the dodging Stars in a
Sky-hunt!—But alas! alas! that Nature is a wary wily long-
breathed old Witch, tough-lived as a Turtle and divisible as the
Polyp, repullulative in a thousand Snips and Cuttings, integra et in
toto! She is sure to get the better of Lady MIND in the long run, and
to take her revenge too—transforms our To Day into a Canvass
dead-colored to receive the dull featureless Portrait of Yesterday;
not alone turns the mimic Mind, the ci-devant Sculptress with all
her kaleidoscopic freaks and symmetries! into clay, but *leaves* it
such a *clay*, to cast dumps or bullets in; and lastly (to end with
that which suggested the beginning—) she mocks the mind with
it's own metaphors, metamorphosing the Memory into a lignum
vitae Escrutoire to keep unpaid Bills & Dun's Letters in, with
Outlines that had never been filled up, MSS that never went farther
than the Title-pages, and Proof-Sheets & Foul Copies of Watch-
men, Friends, Aids to Reflection & other *Stationary* Wares that
have kissed the Publisher's Shelf with gluey Lips with all the
tender intimacy of inosculation!—Finis!—And what is all this
about? Why, verily, my dear Friend! the thought forced itself on
me, as I was beginning to put down the first sentence of this letter,
how impossible it would have been 15 or even ten years ago for
me to have travelled & voyaged by Land, River, and Sea a hundred
and twenty miles, with fire and water blending their souls for my
propulsion, as if I had been riding on a Centaur with a Sopha for a
Saddle—& yet to have nothing more to tell of it than that we had a
very fine day, and ran aside the steps in Ramsgate Pier at ½ past 4
exactly, all having been well except poor Harriet, who during the
middle Third of the Voyage fell into a reflecting melancholy, in the
contemplation of successive specimens of her inner woman in a
Wash-hand Basin. She looked pathetic; but I cannot affirm, that
I observed any thing sympathetic in the countenances of her
Fellow-passengers—which drew forth a sigh from me & a sage
remark, how many of our virtues originate in the fear of Death—&
that while we flatter ourselves that we are melting in Christian
Sensibility over the sorrows of our human Brethren and Sisteren,
we are in fact, tho' perhaps unconsciously, moved at the prospect
of our own End—For who ever sincerely pities Sea-sickness, Tooth-
ache, or a fit of the Gout in a lusty Good-liver of 50?—

What have I to say?—We have received the Snuff—for which I
thank your providential memory.—There are no one here, that we
know—saving & excepting the Joneses—. Mrs Gillman bathed
yesterday—and sends her Love—& will write in a day or two.—
We went to Margate—(Susan just this moment comes up close to

my ear, just as I was saying to Mrs G.—Is there any thing, Ma'am! that you wish me to say?—with—'Sir! will you give *my* kind love to Mr Gillman?'—Bless her!—She is a darling of a Girl. It is impossible not to love her.)—to Margate, & saw the Caverns, as likewise smelt the same—called on Mr Bailey & got the Novum Organum. In my hurry I scrambled up the Blackwood instead of a Volume of Giambattista Vɪᴄᴏ which I left on the Table in my Room, & forgot my Sponge & Sponge-Bag of oiled Silk.—But perhaps when I sit down to work, I may have to request something to be sent, which may come with them. I therefore defer it till then—
The Steels enjoy themselves, and are happy. Remember me kindly to Susan.—
I would be remembered to Hutton & Anderson: for they are House-mates. Heart-mates, I fear, they will never seek to be.—
My kind love to Eliza Nixon, and to Amelia, & to Anne—and my kind regards to Mr Nixon—& my best possible respects to Mrs Nixon, the Tree-Clip[per.] And pray, do not forget to mention me affection[ately] & cordially to Mr and to Mrs Chance—
God bless you, my dear Friend!—You will soon hear again from

S. T. Coleridge

1489. *To James Gillman*

MS. *Cornell University Lib. Pub. with omis.* Coleridge at Highgate, *by Lucy E. Watson, 1925, p. 112.*

16 Octr. 1825.—Thursday is my Birth-day—
Pray, drink my health—and take a bottle
of the Sweet Port for the purpose.—

My dear Gillman
I have nothing to say—and too short a warning to say that nothing with the accuracy, so important a subject would require. It is, I own, positively asserted by Mrs Gillman, whose deposition is confirmed by the joint attestation of Mrs Haighton Steel[1] and her Daughter, Susanna, that I was apprized some days ago of Mr Steel's intention once more to mount the long-backed Centaur, ꜱᴛᴇᴀᴍ, Offspring and First-born of the Marriage, which that famous Match-maker and Go-between, the Muse of Science, Epistemè hight, brought about, of Fire and Water—or (to speak

---

[1] According to the records at Christ's Hospital, Thomas Steel was a student there from June 1777 to June 1784. See next letter in which Coleridge speaks of him as 'an old School-fellow of mine'.

poetically) that he is to leave us by the Royal Sovereign tomorrow morning, ½ past 7.—Nay, the Deponents further declare, that I both heard, and answered.—Equally certain, however it is, that I must have heard it, as men hear in sleep, and answered as men answer in a dream.—For it came on me with a Surprize.—Yet I cannot bear that he should see you without a line in his hand from me (a Jack Ketch sort of phrase, by the bye!—tho' I trust, it will have the opposite effect to that of *holding you in suspense.*)—

The Celebrated Lignum Vitae, that imperial Duplicate of his Grace of Wellington, which used to scare the Sea-Gulls (N.B. not the She-gulls) from the crescent Garden, has disappeared from it's Pediment—whether from any dark Conspiracy, of which young Napoleon is at the bottom, can be only conjectured. Sufficient that it is gone! Mr Underwood, to whose Taste and Munificence the Crescent & the Plains of Waterloo owed this Chef d'oeuvre of Heroiglyphic Carpentry, is himself turned *wood* at the loss (Vide Baily's Dictionary)[1]—and the Ramsgate *Gibbons*, who chipped it, talks (I hear) darkly and mysteriously about Chauntry—and what things Envy may drive Artists to perpetrate.

Last night ¼ before 11 I saw the Comet. Mr Steel & myself had indeed *as good as* seen it three nights before—only *that* turned out to be the Pleiades, or (as a passer-by called it) Jack in the Bush. But the real Comet is so like it, that I should have had no great loss, tho' we had not been undeceived—It looks like a Rag torn out from the Milky Way.—

Item. That plusquam lengthy Canadian Ship, Columbus the Second, alias Baron of Renfrew, & Lignum Lignorum, passed by us close in to shore the day before yesterday—& this morning it's two Steam-pilates have contrived to lodge it snug on the Long Sands beyond Margate. Whatever it might want in length before, it will be *long enough* before it gets off from it's present Road-sted— rather an *old* Joke, Master Gillman!—

I met old Mr Minshull yesterday on the Pier—with his Daughter, who expressed to Mr Steel a wish to have her Papa introduced to me. She is an admirer of mine—a sensible pleasing young Woman— & he is very rich & lives at Kentish Town, & resides at present with Mr Divett—who can frank letters. I shall call & leave my Card tomorrow.—

I have bathed 3 times, & have found hitherto no ill consequences from increase of expectoration or any other ominous symptom— But I have a sort of rheumatism in all my left Jaw, & all the Teeth on that side are loose & moveable—and last night I picked out an

---

[1] N. Bailey, *An Universal Etymological English Dictionary*, 1721.

ancient snag from the upper gum of my right Jaw with my finger
and thumb.—What would you advise? There is no soreness either
of the Gums or the Palate. In other respects, I find no additional
grounds of Alarm, but am, indeed, I am inclined to imagine, somewhat better than usual: tho' I had a most singular dream on
Friday Night, 14 Octr, 1825—saw two strange figures, that were
talking of me. The one was a lurid blotchy Hospital-looking
Fellow, who, I seemed to know, represented the Liver—the other
a dusky red-colored naked Youth, like the colored Plates, I have
seen, . . .[1]

Mrs Gillman, I think I may say with confidence, has received
advantage already from the Sea-air, & Bathing—She *looks* better,
and is in better spirits the day thro', than I have known her for
some time back.—

And now, my dear Gillman!—I must request you to transplant
all the kind messages & remembrances from my former letter to
this—(By the bye, beg Susan not to forget to water my Geranium
in my Bed-room, & my Acorns in the Garden Pot in the Kitchen.)

God bless you!—I would that I could supply your place at
Highgate, if there were no other way of gaining you a fortnight's
Run by the Sea-shore.—This letter will cost nothing—but as soon
as I have, or shall invent, any matter worth a postage, I will write
again—& perhaps before—especially if I can flux a Frank out of
old Divel or Divet—

                                          S. T. Coleridge.

1490. *To Edward Coleridge*

Address: Revd. Edward Coleridge | Eton | near | Windsor
MS. Pierpont Morgan Lib. Hitherto unpublished.
Postmark: 19 October 1825. *Stamped*: Ramsgate.

8. Plains of Waterloo, Ramsgate—Tuesday Afternoon
                                          18 Octr 1825—.

My very dear Edward

I have just received your letter inclosed in one from Mr Gillman;
and (Deo Volente & Adjuvante) I trust to reach Eton on Friday
Evening. Mr Gillman can not leave Highgate—*must* not. It is
morally impossible. And as to Mrs Gillman's going, this seems to me
as profitless as the other is impracticable—as under our present
impressions there appears but one thing to do—namely, to go and
bring him back with me. Mrs Gillman received the sad tidings as

_____
[1] One-half of p. 3 cut out of MS.

from my intimate knowlege of her character I could have anticipated. The correctness of her Feelings, her moral High-mindedness,
could not save her from suffering keenly as a mother; but it
preserved her judgement unwarped, and the moment the first
Shock had subsided, she reverted affectionately to the distress and
vexation, that you must have suffered in having to write the letter,
and during the time in which the necessity of taking this step
became daily more evident. She sought an alleviation of the afflicting
intelligence in her habitual conviction, that the Parent, who has not
to mourn over *Want of Principle* in a child, ought to blend gratitude
to Providence with the sharpest feelings of natural grief for any lesser
infliction. Accustomed to find Comfort herself in the Consciousness of
having done her Duty, she still recurs to your attestation in Henry's
behalf—that you have discovered nothing bad in his moral nature,
and weakness & inconstancy, rather than want of Understanding.
But of this be assured, that both Parents feel undiminished
gratitude & affection to you, and the fullest confidence not only in
the kindness of your intentions but in the persistency and judicious
direction of your efforts to realize them.—After Henry's Letters,
written indeed in the paroxysm of Home-sickness but yet dis-
closing a strong presentiment of his unfitness for the Arena in which
he was to wrestle, your information did not surprize us—except
that in every transformation of fear into Certainty, of *Thought* into
Thing, there is a suddenness, that imitates Surprize, and which
no Fore-bodings can prevent.—

But I will not intrude longer on your time—as I shall so soon
have the opportunity of talking it over.—I left Highgate, tomorrow
will be a fortnight—with Mr, Mrs, and Miss Steel & Mrs Gillman,
by the Ramsgate Steam-Vessel—Mr Steel is an old School-fellow
of mine—& the Family intimate acquaintances of the Gillmans—
and very worthy people—so that we form a very comfortable
Household here.—I shall bring with me a small boxful of my
Memorata—o sia, Crudezze futuriformi e seminativi—as I must
first go to Highgate.—

May God bless you, | my dear Edward! | and your obliged and
affectionate | Uncle

S. T. Coleridge

I leave this place by the Steam-Vessel on Thursday Morning ½ past
7—My Birth-day!—But I cannot pass it better than in performing
an act of Duty to Mr & Mrs Gillman.

P.S. The only part of your information that perplexed us was of
Henry's personal uncleanliness & 'the act of *indecency*'—from his

infancy he has been bred up with such scrupulous attention to Neatness, and all the minutiæ of Modesty—And in the last Mementos, I wrote for him & which his Mother, I believe, made him transcribe into his pocket-book, the anxious retention of the habits, which he had [been] brought up in, on those points was especially urged. Can it have arisen from an abandonment of himself to Despondency?

1491. *To James Gillman*

Address: Jam[es Gil]lman, Esqre | Grove | Highgate | London
MS. Pierpont Morgan Lib. Hitherto unpublished.
Postmark: 19 October 1825.

18 Oc[tober 1825]

My dearest Gillman

I find that it will be impossible to get any letter, that you might write in answer to this, till an hour or more after the Steam Vessel sets off—Therefore I must act on my own judgement singly —& God willing, shall be with you on Thursday Evening—If the Royal Sovereign should have a fair voyage, & arrive before 4, I might dine with you—but do not wait beyond ½ past 5.—And on Friday Evening I propose to be at Eton. Tho' I by no means see the event in such sombre hues, as you in the first shock of the tidings see it; yet I perfectly agree with you in the propriety of removing Henry. Much evil & no good can come of his remaining!—Or if from conversation with Edward Coleridge & minuter information on the Spot, and my observation of Henry himself, I should gather any data for a different opinion, you may safely trust my inclination to avail myself of it, & I hope, my judgement likewise. As to Mrs Gillman's accompanying me, in whatever way I look at it, and on whatever supposition—whether of Henry's removal or continuance—I am positive in dissuading it *as worse than useless*. As it is absolutely & confessedly impracticable for you to go, there would, I feel, be almost an impropriety in *my* being not the representative of both Parents but of you only. Besides, the more quietly the whole is managed & with the least attraction of notice, the better it will be—whichever Result should be decided on. In like manner, as to Highgate.—It should be said what with sufficient truth may be said, that Henry's strength is found unequal to the hardships of the College, & that his Health had begun to be affected by it—& to give this fuller effect & for other still weightier reasons, it will be best for him to return with me at once to Ramsgate—& be under my care for the next month—during which time I shall be better able to offer you and Mrs G. a well-weighed Advice.—My dear Gillman! you have my Nephew's testimony that Henry's a Boy of *Principle*, and that there is weakness and impersistency rather than want of Intellect.—For the rest, it was an experiment—& no experiment ought to be said to have wholly failed, if it has shewn what road we are to take—tho' negatively, by demonstrating the impracticability of the Road, we should have preferred. No apprehension can be turned into a Certainty, no *Thought* returned upon us a *Thing*, without a sad'ning Suddenness that for the moment lays our powers prostrate & which no fore-bodings, however distinct, no not prescience itself can disarm of it's sting or blunt it's sharpness.—But let the Thing settle back & thin away again, into a Thought—& the Evil shrinks with it into human & bearable Dimensions.—What? if H. had been reported to you as an incurable Liar? or privy Thief?—Of Anderson I say nothing— Indeed nothing but my vexation at finding you so depressed would make me attempt *writing* any thing when in so short a time I expect to be talking with you.—I have not talked much with Mrs Gillman. She must & I doubt not will pardon me for the abruptness with which I put the negative on her going to Eton. But really the Light flashed so vividly on my mind that I should have done violence to my Conscience not to have made my words as decisive as my Convictions.—

I never remember any run of Ill Luck or what was thought such, that was not succeeded by some Compensative Occurrence or other. And at all events we will breast the waves together—Would you purchase the removal of all these mishaps at the price of a single Pang of *Remorse*?—Then stand upright, my dear Gillman! and to hear the worst, hope the best! . . . [Conclusion and signature cut off.]

I have written to E[dward.][1]

1492. *To Hyman Hurwitz*

Address: Hyman Hurwitz, Esqre | Granada Cottage | Old Kent Road
MS. University of Pennsylvania Lib. Hitherto unpublished.
Postmark: 21 October 1825.

½ past One,
Grove, Highgate—21 Octr 1825—

My dear Friend

The date of place & time of this hasty scrawl, where I have just arrived & this same moment received your letter forwarded from

---

[1] This sentence is written in the address sheet, which was mutilated by removal of conclusion and signature on the opposite side of the page.

Ramsgate, and that after I have finished this answer & taken a sandwich & a glass of Wine & water I must leave in order to return by the 3 o'clock Stage that leaves Piccadilly for Eton—that tomorrow night, if possible, but at the latest on Sunday, I shall leave Eton & hope, God permitting, to reach Ramsgate by Monday Evening if the strength of the young Charge, I shall have with me, holds out—these particulars with the interpretation, which I should not withhold from *your* confidential *Ear*, but would rather not *write* even if I had the time or tranquillity requisite—will entirely acquit me of all intentional Neglect of your concerns—. At present, I can only reply that as soon as I reach Ramsgate, i.e. from Tuesday Morning, 25 Octr—I will readily & instantly do my best endeavors to effect all, you wish—& shall therefore content myself at present with leaving you to judge whether the distance of a one day Post from London will be an impediment or not[1]—The Post leaves Ramsgate every night (Saturdays excepted) at 7 o'clock—& Letters from London arrive at Ramsgate, & may by sending to the Post office be procured by 8 in the Morning.—If this will do, I shall find a Letter from you at Ramsgate or whatever else you may wish to send by the Ramsgate Coaches which go off from Grace-church Street—I forget the name of the Inn. But I shall certainly call & stay some hours, perhaps sleep on Sunday Night at Mr Ingram's, a HATTER, in Coleman Street: where any parcel or letter will be delivered to me, if directed—'to be delivered to Mr Coleridge when he calls'—I forget the Number—but perhaps I shall be able to learn it before I put this in the Post, & will therefore take a wafer in my pocket, & keep it open—

Excuse my haste & I fear unintelligibility—

God bless you & your troubled but | most sincere Friend
                                                    S. T. Coleridge.

Do not mention any part of the Contents of this Letter to *any one*. I have borne this continued Movement from Dan to Bathsheba day after day far better than I had dared hope for—or others for me: from which you may infer the importance & urgency of my Business.—

Mr Ingram, Hatter, 26 Coleman Street

---

[1] Hurwitz had asked Coleridge to read the proof-sheets of the *Hebrew Tales*. See Letter 1494.

1493. To James Gillman

Address: James Gillman, Esqre | Grove | Highgate
MS. Harvard College Lib. Hitherto unpublished.
Postmark: 24 October 1825. *Stamped*: Windsor.

Saturday Noon. [22 October 1825]

My dear Friend

Tho' I have barely seen Henry, and till I have talked with him tête à tête can form no decisive judgement, and tho' there is no Post till tomorrow evening, I yet commence the Letter—chiefly that I may have more *time* for the writing of what is to come, when I have that only to write; but likewise that you may know the process of my mind as well as it's ultimate decision. I had, of course, a cordial reception from Edward—and after clearing a plate of mutton kidneys & half an hour's earnest conversation, I accompanied my Nephew to Dr Keates who is confined by indisposition, & tho' recovering, still very weak from a sort of bilious fever. I never remember a more perfect confirmation, than several of the facts gave, of your conjectures, tho' the most striking I obtained from Sally. It was evident (N.B. not to herself: who had drawn no such conclusion, having mentioned them only as instances of Henry's simplicity and entire confidence in her, as his comforter) that the Floggings had gratified his Vanity, & almost perhaps so as to be an object of his aspiration. What a strange child he is!—But this is an anticipation.—Edward began by entreating me to understand one thing—that *he* did not wish the Boy to be removed, on account of any trouble or the like, that he occasioned *him* (Edward) personally—that there were other Boys that gave him far more trouble—that as far as his Letter originated in any motive relating to himself, it was exclusively this—to put you & Mrs Gillman in full possession of what he could & of what he could *not*, henceforward hold himself *responsible* for.—'If his moral Being should receive a stain, more than superficial; and if his classical education should make no advance, or none, that for a moment would be considered by you as compensation for the loss of innocence, in it's two great points, Veracity and Purity; I must not be held responsible for the result. I will do all in my power to prevent it, I will spare no trouble or circumspection to bring about the contrary; but I must not be held responsible for the One, and I cannot promise the other.' No one (he continued) 'can be more thoroughly aware, than I am, that a bare six weeks, and for a *Nestling* too, could not in any ordinary case be considered even a tolerably fair Trial—and especially, when so large a part of his Faults and

Failures might, as appears from the Letters you have shewn me, be rationally attributed to the paroxysm of Home-sickness and the Exhaustion consequent both on this and on the previous state of Excitement and the Straining of his Faculties beyond their natural strength. And were the *moral* Risk out of the question, even now tho' this is *not* an ordinary case, I should think that this consideration ought to decide in favor of his remaining here—for a time, at least, sufficient to ascertain what he can or will do, when his mind is at ease, & his feelings reconciled to the change, and familiarized to the ways &c of the School & College. But he does seem to me so little capable of withstanding temptation, and still less, far far less of repelling Seduction—his facility in giving way to any impudent Boy who laughs at or scoffs him for hesitating to follow his example is so extreme—that I do feel that there is a serious *moral* Risk— both respecting his Purity of mind & act, and his *Veracity*. Hitherto, his Honesty and Adherence to the Truth have been exemplary & in some instances affecting. But how long with such childishness, and want of *Sense* (I use the word *practically* & in distinction from Talent or intellectual Capability) may this continue? I can not remove Temptation—& there are many bad Boys, from whose intimacy I can warn him but from whose neighborhood I cannot remove him.—How long, I say?—Let the following Instance shew, how far my fears are or are not groundless. A bad vulgar-minded bold Boy asked Henry to go down with him into a Butcher's yard near the College, instead of going on (as he was going) to the College. Henry resisted—did not want to go—refused—& on being again asked or bullied, went—to see a Bullock killed & *cut up*—& to receive certain anatomical demonstrations from the Butcher's Boys, as the little Rascal's (his Seducer's) premature fancy had anticipated. Poor Henry had either no, or very indistinct, notions what it was, he was to see. However, the Bullock *had* been killed & cut up before they arrived: but one of the Butcher's Lads asked Medsum (or some such name) whether he had been flogged that day—the little Vagabond answered, Yes!—"Let us see"—and he consented & let down his Trousers to shew the[m. (There] were two Butcher's Lads & a Butcher's man as the Spectators.) T[hen the] question was put to, & received the same answer from, Henry. And he too was called on, & desired to do the same, that they might compare the Floggings. Henry hesitated, &, I doubt not, was very unwilling—But on the other Boy's threatening him, that the Butchers would spurt some blood on him, he consented, and exposed his person & the marks of Shame to these Ruffians!'—

Other cases have occurred, not indeed (thank God!) of this sort but yet sad proofs of his incapability to stand out in any resolve

that his own better mind would dictate.—I do think, my dear
Gillman! that the preceding Anecdote suggests a strong additional
Ground of Objection to the practice, & above all to the frequency of
Flogging in the Public Schools. It can not but weaken the Boys'
sense of Self-respect in one of it's most efficient Supports and Consequents, reverential Modesty to their own person—& deaden the
human instinct of proud Shame, and the connection of Shame
with Nakedness.—(++)

Of Henry's goings on in point of *Learning*, & of the Symptoms of
Ability or Inability to go through with the Tasks imposed on him,
& which in a short period will increase in number & difficulty, I
can say nothing which has not been already communicated in my
Nephew's Letter to you.—Here then I conclude, for the present,
the one side of the Question. Now audi alteram partem.—Henry
came in, while we were breakfasting. Whether Sally had prepared
him, I don't know—Probably she had. He did not appear at all
agitated—so very little, that I could not help asking him—if he
was not glad to see me? Yes! very glad.—And by his manners &
conversation it was plain that he felt under no restraint or awe from
his Tutor's Presence. He looked plump & well—& tolerably neat,
according to *my* preconceptions of School-boys. He drank a basin
or large Cup of Tea & eat a roll & butter—& was obliged (he said)
to go off to attend his Master.— At ++ of this letter he came to me
in Edward's Study, according to my desire: and I have had about
an hour's Talk with him.—The result may be conveyed in few
words. The neglect of his person in washing & change of line[n] he in
part denied—it was a false charge which his Dame's Servant had
made to Sally & which his Tutor over-heard—She had said, he
neglected washing because he did not wash at his Dame's, where
they stole his Soap, but washed at Mother Stevens's where he
could do it comfortably; and in part, he laid the fault on his Dame,
whom he dislikes, and her Servants whom he detests. But that
since the Time, his Tutor had talked to him, he had given no cause
of complaint, that he was aware of, in this respect.—When I spoke
to him of the Act of Indecency, he was silent. And when I told him,
I must tell you of it but would not for the world that his Mother
should ever know the particulars, & pointed out the shockingness of
the degradation as it would appear to every pure mind, he wept.
When I charged him with the frightful silliness, the almost ideotic
childishness of being vain of his Floggings & boasting almost of
them to a Woman-servant, he was silent.—But over and over
again, he said, he was happy, very happy—was never happier any
where—wished very much to *stay* & said, his greatest difficulty &
the chief occasion of his being flogged, was his inability to learn

by heart, which he had never been accustomed to—that he could
learn Greek far easier than Latin, and Long Ovid (i.e. the Metamorphoses) tho' 40 lines, easier than Short Ovid (i.e. Epistles) tho'
but 24—but that he thought, he should get over it—& tho' he
could not say much of his Progress hitherto, yet he did think that
now he was quite comfortable, he should make way. He talked
rationally. It was one of his sensible days, at least. I gave him a
Shilling: & bid him come to me [again a]fter Church, i.e. at 4 o'clock.
It is now 3. These are the Facts [on both] sides.—

I shall decide, I thin[k, in favor of his s]taying—unless you
think no—

On the other hand, he does not seem to have any better reason
for believing that he shall be equal to his Tasks & Rank in the
School but his *feelings*. I will try to see Pattison. One bad thing
is that the Boys are all possessed with the notion of his silliness
& absurdity.

P.S. Edward expects his Brother Henry to pass by Egham on
his road from Devon to Town, and has written an urgent letter to
stop him & bring him here for a day ; & has intreated me so strongly
to stay over Monday, that I have given a half-promise to do so—
the more readily, that I may have a few lines from you in answer
to this, if you write by return of Post. I never was so perplexed &
irresolute before. The main argument for his staying till Christmas,
at least, is the ill effect, it may have on the Boy's own mind, to
think that he has been hardly used, and not allowed to have a fair
Trial: when he was eager to do so—Perhaps, too, on his Mother's
mind, & might strengthen her desire to repeat the Experiment at
the Charter House.—I will again consult Dr Keates.—

God bless you & your ever faithful S.T.C.—

1494. *To Edward Coleridge*

Address: Revd E. Coleridge | the College | Eton
MS. Pierpont Morgan Lib. Pub. E. L. G. ii. 383.

Ramsgate
Friday [11 November 1825][1]

My dear Edward

In this obdurate weather, ipso Novembre *Novembrius*, even to
monologue with you telegraphically is to enjoy a Half-holiday (for
a 'holi*hour*' will not, I suspect, pass the Mint) from the most

[1] The similarity of the opening sentence in this and the next letter suggests
that the two letters were written about the same time.

tedious Work for trifling Wage, that even an unpopular Author was
doomed to moil at—videlicet, the correction of the Proof Sheets of
another Man's Compositions, where the Composer's Errors in Stuff
and Style are to be rectified as well as the Compositor's Errata.[1]
This is far worse and the Earning still more unconscionably disproportionate to the Time and Trouble, than Translation itself—
nor should I have undertaken it but to oblige a very worthy man
and in the belief, that the work itself will do good.—The worst (i.e.
to *my* feelings) of all th[ese] necessitated tasks is, that I work at
them under the painf[ul re]flection that they are so many *Avulsions*
from the small remainder of Time that might have been devoted to
the completion of my own Works, and with my mind constantly
starting off to them like a Horse when he is passing the door of his
Stable, or the road that turns down to it.—But indeed, if they were
(as one of them actually is) ready for the Press, I see no chance of
their seeing the light otherwise than as post-humous Publications.
Warned by the unsaleableness of all that have been published, the
Booksellers are shy of risking so great an expence—I could not in
common honesty attempt to influence any but the most opulent,
the Magnates of the Trade—and among these I have no Hopers or
Admirers—and as to publishing by *Subscription*, I sicken at the
very thought of it. A Novel, or a Tour, may make it's own way—
but experience has given me bitter proof, that a Work intended to
add to the knowlege of the Reader, on subjects in which knowlege
cannot be acquired without more or less effort of Thought on the
Reader's part, will for ever remain in the Publisher's Cellar, unless
the Public are informed by some Authority that they ought to have
the Book in their Libraries. I am not silly enough to overlook the
defects of my writings, or the internal causes of their unpopular-
ness; but still it remains true, what Charles Lamb wrote to me,
some 15 months ago—'You are one of Fortune's *Ne'er-do-wells*:—
the Edinburgh Review abuses you, the Quarterly never mentions
you—Murray hates you, Gifford did not like you, and now your
Nephew is Editor, he cannot befriend you, without subjecting
himself & (as Murray will say) the Quarterly itself to a charge of
Partiality and Nepotism.'—With as full a confidence, as a Christian
dare feel respecting his own acquaintance with his own heart, I can
assert, that, if I possessed a sufficiency for the decencies and comforts of Life that are in fact necessaries if the exertion of my intel-

---

[1] Coleridge refers to the proof-sheets of Hyman Hurwitz's *Hebrew Tales;
selected and translated from the Writings of the Ancient Hebrew Sages: to which is
prefixed, an Essay on the Uninspired Literature of the Hebrews*. The work was
published by Morrison and Watt in 1826. Three of Coleridge's *Specimens of
Rabbinical Wisdom* were included in the volume. See note to Letter 1448.

lectual powers be included in *Living*, the thought of writing for
posterity alone and of benefiting my contemporaries by kindling
and inseminating the minds of a few Individuals, as I have
hitherto done in the *Nos non nobis* way of Conversation, would be
pleasurable to me. I have not a single sparkle of the Love of literary
Reputation for it's own sake. Could I be sure that the same good
would be effected by any thing, I wrote, a very trifling sum would
purchase from me the reputation of having written it.—But things
being as they are, I cannot help feeling my friendlessness in the
Literary Republic hard—& it deepens my regret in not having
entered into the Church.—

I have had but little time for reading. I have, however, gone thro'
the two Volumes of Skelton,[1] and Davison's Discourses.[2]—Skelton
was a truly *genial* Spirit—tho' his compositions are strikingly
unequal. On the subject of the Trinity he is a *Master*—and worthy
to be named with Bull and Waterland.[3] His greatest Draw back he
has in common with several other Divines of that period—the
disposition to place the favorite *Theory* of the Age on the same level
with the sacred Truths, which it was one way of *arguing* for—I will
explain myself hereafter—However, I have not seen any work from
which half a dozen powerful and useful Sermons for the great
Festivals of the Church might be more easily compiled.—

Davison's is indeed a most valuable Accession to our Theological
Literature—and eminently free from the error, I complain of in
Skelton. Nevertheless, I must confess, that the first 120 pages
excited an expectation, which the remainder of the Volume did not
quite answer—Yet understand this rather as a tribute to the
extraordinary merit of the former, than as any dispraise of the
latter.—The subject appears to me a Mine, the richest Veins of
which still remain to be opened—and with all Davison's well-
earned honors distinctly before me, I do exceedingly wish that *you*
had the same or a similar opportunity of distinguishing yourself.—
And this brings me back to my chief motive for availing myself of
an offered Frank—viz. to urge you not to forget your half-promise
to pass a few days with me at Highgate. I cannot express how great
a delight & comfort it would be to me—

[1] *The Complete Works of Philip Skelton. To which is prefixed Burdy's Life of
the author*, 6 vols., 1824. A copy of this edition with annotations by Coleridge is in
the British Museum. The annotations are printed in *Literary Remains*, iv. 258–88.

[2] John Davison, *Discourses on Prophecy; in which are considered its structure,
use and inspiration*, 1825 (2nd edn.). Coleridge's annotations are printed in
Literary Remains, iv. 385–99.

[3] See Letters 1126 and 1793, *Aids to Reflection*, 1825, p. 308 n., and *Table
Talk*, 8 July 1827. For Coleridge's marginalia in two of Waterland's works see
Literary Remains, iv. 221–58.

We leave Ramsgate at the close of next week—& as soon as I reach Highgate, I promise myself to write a more entertaining Letter than the present.—I pray God fervently for his worthy Parents' sake that Henry Gillman may be going on well—and doing his best, at least!—

God bless you, and your affectionate Uncle

S. T. Coleridge

1495. *To James Gillman*

Address: James Gillman, Esqre | Grove | Highgate | London
MS. Private possession. Hitherto unpublished.
Postmark: 14 November 1825. *Stamped*: Ramsgate.

3. Wellington Crescent
Sunday [13 November 1825]
Ramsgate

My dear Gillman

This most unramsgatish, this obdurate Weather *ipso Novembre Novembrius*—thank God! it is no longer *this*!

Old Mother Damnable on the Sky-Top
Wringing her Dish-clouts or twirling her Mop—
Or astride on her Broom-stick, a notable Roarer
With her grim duffel Cloak (*vide* Juvenal's Satires)—

Qy? Why?

Be-Trimm'd and be-flounced with it's own Rags & Tatters
Blown over her head and streaming before her
She gallop'd away, on the scent of the Booty,
      Right over the Deck
      [Of a] Goodwin sands Wreck
To stop the poor Soul that had not paid the Duty—

is gone—Exit! and makes room for a Lady-like Sky.—All our weather-sages assure us that the Weather has taken a turn, and that we shall have a Spell of the *right Ramgsate*—dry, bracing, cheerful.—In fact, so long a continuance of *wicked* bad weather is scarcely remembered here—and I know but of one thing, in compensation—namely, that tho' it put a stop to Bathing, forbad Ass-exercise, (or, interpreting the words according to the Heteröepy and Heterography of the broad Vulgar, allowed of no other) amerced all our Walks, or confined them to the Colonnade—still it produced no *retrograde* movement in Mrs Gillman's Health. It did [not] even suspend her progress; tho' it doubtless put a drag to the Wheel, and made it less than it would have been. Still, however, it is a great Comfort that she had no lee-way to make up—and judging from her Looks after her Sea-bath before Breakfast this

morning, and after her Donkey-trip with Mrs Steele and Susan to
Margate (for the purpose of calling on Mrs Westinghausen, and to
return a Volume of Bacon to the Revd Mr Bayley) and back again
—and now (untired) gone for a Walk on the Pier, I do think that a
fortnight of such weather so used and availed of would not only
make but *leave* an improvement in her strength, that would be
felt throughout the Winter. Before the bad weather visited us, she
had repeatedly rode ten and even twelve Miles, walked an hour &
half before, and again after her return—with no worse effect than
that of feeling pleasantly tired at Bed-time—and that the gloomy
damp weather, and the entire suspension of all these Befriendments
did not *undo* the good effect, but left her able to start afresh, is to
me a datum of Hope—on which I ground *my* anticipation of a
benefit greater than she has derived from her Sea-sojourn in the
two or three Autumns before this.—I regard her *strength* much
more than her *Looks*; and of course, all I have said, must be
understood relatively and comparatively.—

I will not speak of myself, for tho' I certainly feel the *commencement* of an improvement in my own health, in two points especially
and those the points, that had most disquieted & harrassed me—
& cannot deny, that I shall take the cup from my lips reluctantly,
and with a wish for a fuller draught—yet as certainly this is not my
influencing motive—and therefore I will not let it pass for such.—

Mrs Gillman, however, is prepared to return with Mrs Steele &
Susan on Thursday—and should the Day be fair, and as Captn
Major assures them will, be the case, if the Weather continue in
it's present mood, the Vessel likely to arrive at the Custom-house
Steps by four o'clock, they propose to return by *it*.—I give you my
honor, that Mrs Gillman has *discountenanced* the notion of staying
out the two months (on which I had & supposed her to have,
calculated—and the more so that my Trip and then the Weather-
luck had abridged it—a fortnight or more) from the hour that
Mr Steele's last letter came—. Neither does she think that even
tho' you wished us to stay out the time, I should be able to prevail
on Mrs Steele to leave Susan here—without which &c—for verily,
with all respect for, and due sense of, *appearances*, I can neither
think of or even look at myself without a sort of BITTER *Smile*, in
connection with the Scruple—tho' it is only one of the occasions,
in which I feel the sharpy and jagged Contrast of the wickedness of
the World & my own innocence[1]—& painfully were it only that it

---

[1] Coleridge and the Gillmans were probably aware of the 'unwarrantable
Scandal' being spread abroad by the Rev. Frederick William Franklin, master
of Christ's Hospital, Hertford, 1801–27. 'Coleridge is not returned from the
Sea', Lamb wrote to Sara Hutchinson on 25 Nov. 1824:

draws my attention to the latter as if any thing else were possible, just as if I was compelled to say to myself—No! I have not a stinking purulent ulcer under my Arm! It is not true, that my Nose is rotting off!

Mrs Gillman has been in again, to protest against my putting the question—whether if I could induce Mrs Steele to let Susan stay, you would like us to remain here another fortnight—So I let it drop—Nevertheless, I must entreat you to write by Monday Evening's Post, respecting the return by the Steam-Pacquet. You may rely on it, that if the Day did not promise and all but ensure a calm & quick passage, I should not permit them to go aboard—But if I do not finish, I shall lose the Post—. Poor dear Mr & Mrs Aders!—One day all Rain & Storm, and Mr A. ill in his Bedroom—& the next day forced by his Letters to set off again, to Town . . . [Conclusion and signature cut off.]
(O that you had this Sea before you! How gladly would I live in Horsemonger Lane Goal for a fortnight, to give you the same time in this House[1]—)

1496. *To James Gillman*

Address: James Gillman, Esqre | Grove | Highgate | London
MS. Cornell University Lib. Hitherto unpublished.
Postmark: 17 November 1825. *Stamped*: Ramsgate.

16 Novr 1825—

My dearest Gillman

On the receipt of your kind Letter, Mrs Steele having in conse-quence offered to leave Susan, and it *being* very fine, and *promising* settled, weather, it was decided that we should stay: tho' Mrs Gillman was so much affected by the kindness of your expressions

As a little scandal may divert you recluses—we were in the Summer dining at a Clergyman of Southey's 'Church of England,' at Hertford, . . . an old contemporary Blue of C.'s and mine at School. After dinner we talked of C., and F. who is a mighty good fellow in the main, but hath his cassock prejudices, inveighed against the moral character of C. I endeavoured to en-lighten him on the subject, till having driven him out of some of his holds, he stopt my mouth at once by appealing to me whether it was not very well known that C. 'at that very moment was living in a state of open a——y with Mrs. * * * * * * at Highgate ?' Nothing I could say serious or bantering after that could remove the deep inrooted conviction of the whole company assembled that such was the case! . . . My interference of course was imputed to the goodness of my heart, that could imagine nothing wrong &c. Such it is if Ladies will go gadding about with other people's husbands at watering places. How careful we should be to avoid the appearance of Evil. (*Lamb Letters*, ii. 445.)

[1] These two sentences are written at the top of page one of the manuscript.

and your goodness in so promptly acceding to the first wish expressed in her behalf, tho' (as was really the case) without her
consent, that she was more than disposed to prove her sense of it
by not availing herself of the permission, and instead of entrusting
it to my eloquence (there is no such word, escribence—in consequence, I imagine, of the scri being a *long* syllable: for really
éscrĭbence would have been an accession to our language) return to
thank you in person.—In fact, there were some tears shed, & I stood
for the moment arraigned by her feelings of *selfishness*—tho' God
knows! the only self-reference consisting in my aversion to appear
a Trifler, and retract convictions, without any conviction of their
having been formed without due grounds.—If personal wishes,
confined to my feelings of and concerning my own single Self, had
been allowed to determine the matter, or rather if I had allowed
any right of voting to such Wishes, I should not have left the
Grove: and at this moment have the Parlour & my comfortable
Bed and Book Room before my Heart's Eyes. But your Wife's
undoubted & regular advance in flesh and strength gives a warrant
to my Belief, that a longer period of *Stationariness* of her present
Winnings will be obtained by prolonging her sojourn to the close
of the Month (i.e. should the fine weather continue)—& that at the
worst, we shall all be more satisfied that the chance had been
given. I think, that she *looks* much better; but as I said before, it
is not by her Looks that I have been influenced but by the continued change for the better in her *strength*—as evinced among
other signs by her spirits flagging so much less from 5 o'clock to
½ past 10—or Bed-time.

Mrs Steel has been very good & kind, and altogether a great
Comfort—. Even on my own account I shall always think of her
with affectionate pleasure.—I wish, when you meet Mr Steel, you
would express this to him—and any little recognition on your part
of the Service, she has been to Mrs Gillman, to Mrs Steel herself—
half a score words said as *you* can say them—would be felt by her
in no common way—for she entertains a high esteem & partiality
(I cannot hit on a better word) for you.—

Poor Mrs Kaye!—I had seen a Paragraph about an eminent
City Solicitor—& had asked half a score people in Burgess's
Library, and elsewhere *who* it was, with a curiosity and interest
that I could not myself account for—but from your letter first I
learnt the Name. Good God! what a misery—and poor Caroline
Atkins—The two Lads were Pupils of Edward's, who had christened
them *Scythian* and *Arab*—but thought highly of their talents.—
It is very curious; but just after my return hither from Eton Mrs
Gillman gently remonstrated with me for the dislike, & *prejudice*,

I had taken to Mr Kaye—adding that he was an affectionate Husband, good Father, &c—& my answer (as she will tell you) was to
this purpose—that I could not help it; that I had never taken to
him but that the last time, I saw him on horse-back in the Grove,
his face or a something in it had disturbed me so, that holy or
unholy, *the Spirit* twitched me back from him—tho' doubtless I
ought to keep it to myself.—

I have written to Edward—& purpose to write again to morrow,
if I get a frank—& Mrs G. will write again to Henry.—If he can
but make *any* progress, & at the same time goes on in safety, the
Advantage cannot but be great—& tho' I am anxious, uneasy
perhaps, still I have cheering Hopes—the Child appeared to me so
much improved in his manners. I only press on Edward the
necessity of *Patience* for a time—& that he will be so good as to
bear in mind, that the reality of *any* progress, much more than the
quantity, is the thing on your heart at present.—

I have received a multiplicity of Invitations; but have refused
all, but Sir T. Gray (once) and Mr Jones (once) and a Mr Morice &
Mr Wykeham Martin each once—the third took me by surprize—
and Mr W. Martin by virtue of his famous Leeds Castle, near Maid-
stone, his lineal descent from William of Wykeham, & his having
a large *Waggon-load* of MSS consisting of Letters between Oliver
Cromwell & Sir T. Fair-fax—

But I have neither seen or heard aught of the least interest—

Pray, remember me kindly to Mr and Mrs Mence—& to Mr
Nixon, and the Lasses—and to Mr Chance & his good Lady—and
likewise to Hutton Rolandson.—Tell Susan, that Harriet & Lester
have just returned with her Mistress, Mrs & Miss Steele from King's
Gate—in high delight with their Treat. . . . [Conclusion and signature cut off.]

P.S. Mrs Westinghausen has been over here—her Plans not yet
settled—She & Charlotte are coming to dine with us—Edmund
after a most stormy voyage arrived safe at Elington &c—Susy sends
her *very* kind love to Mr Gillman—.

1497. *To James Gillman*

Address: James Gillman, Esqre | Grove | Highgate
MS. Harvard College Lib. Hitherto unpublished.
Postmark: 23 November 1825. *Stamped*: Ramsgate.

[22 November 1825]

My dear Friend

Never came letter more acceptable than your's to me this morning.—The contents of the preceding one—the afflicting symptom of

want of sense in the requests, after such a preface, particularly of
his desiring you to send some one down to him, as if my journey
had been mainly for his *amusement*; & the proof, which the prefatory confession gave, of the entire evaporation of the effect
produced by my coming, by his Tutor's solemn address to him, by
his narrow escape & the contract, which he had made and subscribed to, all gone, like so much Ether, that had but touched the
surface & left it unwet—all this weighed & preyed on *my own mind*,
and set my fears at work *composing* the Letter from Edward which
I expected to come & fancied myself reading. But on his Mother the
Facts came like a Simoom—that stifles and withers—or as if all
Hope had been pumped out of her by one stroke of the piston! She
was not agitated, nor could she shed tears; but I was downright
sick at heart with the apprehension, that all the little Capital &
Lay-up of Strength & Spirits would imperceptibly steal away like
water in the Egyptian Wine-Coolers—only a tear-drop seen now
and then on the outside, yet at the close of the day all gone—. To
her therefore Edward's Letter came with wings of Healing—There
was still a *Perch* for Hope to entálon, tho' it should hang by it's
claws with it's head downward.—She bore the gentle *censure* on
her excess of anxious Superintendence with a cheerful good grace;
and only observed (not, I must say, without some reason) that whatever portion of the Evil was attributed to this, an equal portion of
the *good* should take the same direction. The never intermitted
Over-looking, By-standing, and Admonishing, which had en-
feebled his Volition by habituating him to dependence on others,
had likewise kept the moral Will pure and rendered VERACITY a
Habit. Something too should be allowed for the *passive* strength in
bearing bodily pain—so far at least, that the punishments, he
knows himself to have deserved, have produced neither resentment,
nor a desire to get out of their reach, nor any other mark of self-
abandonment. Sad and strange as his Idleness is, it is not however
the sloth of self-despairing Baseness.—

But in simple truth, we know what the result is under $+A$; but
what it would have been under $-A$, we do not know! Therefore,
it is very difficult to determine how much or how little of the
Result is to be considered as an *Effect*—. The whole has been *cum
hôc*; but it does not follow, that the whole is *propter* hoc.—His
Idleness, the absence or great deficiency of *initiative* power, of
setting himself off on the skaits, no momentum from within, and
even when this had been supplied from without, yet no fulcrum to
renew it from—these (in their existing *degree*, at least) and in some
measure likewise his Vanity, as being the natural offspring of
conscious weakness with habits of dependency on others, in natures

that but for weakness would be *affectionate,* & which being weak are *fond*—these, I say, or rather the *degree* in which these exist in Henry, may be justly, because probably, attributed to the incessant solicitude and attendance, of which he knew himself to be the *Object.*—But the weakness itself, the Substratum of his character, the combination of intenacity with unimpressibility, the gleaminess of his intellectual powers that at once proves their existence and their feebleness—and more than all, the want of *Sense* under the evident sufficiency of memory, apprehension, & associative power —these can*not* be accidents of *Education*—these can not reasonably be accounted for by any excess of good qualities in the Instructor & Guardian. I never thought so much on any one character in my whole life as I have on Henry's—& never have been so much perplexed & baffled in my attempts to understand it.—I will not say, that I have arrived at *no* result; but that the following is the only Result, I can rest in—. First however, I must premise that by *Sense* I here mean a man's power of thinking of himself in relation to the Things and Persons, that he has to deal with, and vice versâ, the power of apprehending and looking at Things & Persons in relation to himself. Only in this way can the Self become a Subject, or the *Cir[cu]mstantia Objects;* but both would fleet on a delirium where [the] sensations are as objective as the Perceptions, and the Perceptions as subjective as the Sensations. It is only, I say, by the habit of referring a number and variety of passing objects to the same abiding *Subject,* that the *flux* of the former can be arrested, and the latter made a nucleus for them to chrystallize round. But again it is only by the habit of referring & comparing the Subject to and with the Objects, that it can be consciously known as the *same & abiding*—and before it can be *compared,* it must have been distinguished, thought of separately, and singly for itself—. There must be Reflection—a turning in of the Mind on itself. In order to be a Subject, the conscious Percipient and Appropriator of outward Objects, it must have been made itself an Object for itself— for so only can it know itself to be a *Subject* relatively to all else.— Now what is that which first induces the Individual to turn inward on himself? *Generally* expressed, it is *Sensibility.* But that is far *too* general. I am persuaded, that it is some *specific* sensibility, having it's seat and source in some special energy of the organic and organific Life—& connected with, growing with, & following the same fates with, some system of organs—not perhaps the structure, but yet with the functions and functional developement. —Now the peccatum radicale in Henn is, I am persuaded, Want of Sense, arising from the lateness in the developement of the *conditions* of Sense—whether from a fault in the Germ, which I do

(517)

not think probable, or from some nipping Frost or Blight in early
Spring, God knows!—Now the practical conclusion, I would draw,
is simply—Patience, fed by the Consolation which the good points
of his character supply—and Hope directed toward the revolution,
that his Body and bodily Life will sooner or later undergo—satisfied in the interim, that all enfeebling Causes are removed, & that
by virtue of the contrary Influences and Excitants his manners, and
automatic volitions will imperceptibly be prepared for, & perhaps
accelerating, the change—I was to have said a great deal for Mrs G.
& about our coming—& how a good *two thirds* of our daily weather
is fine & delightful here—but I must write again—God bless you &
                                                            S. T. C.

We have rain, generally, from about 5 in the afternoon, till 8, 9,
or even the greater part of the Night—but delighful Mornings &
days. Yesterday was one of the only two *reprobate* days, we have
had. Mrs Gillman enjoined me to tell you, how very thankful she
is for your kindness in so immediately sending Edward's Letter.—
Susan sends her *very* kind love.—

1498. *To George Skinner*

Transcript Coleridge family. Hitherto unpublished.

                                                   22 Novr 1825
                              3 Wellington Crescent, Ramsgate
My dear Sir
    I feel so much confidence in your kindness that I will not hesitate
to tell you that it would be a long story to explain the first causes &
occasions of this lamentable weakness, this great but self-punishing
fault—in periods of Sickness & depression I have such a nervous
dread of Letters, that had I not a better and wiser self than myself
I might lose every friend I possessed and see the explanation before
my eyes in a pile of unopened Letters. When therefore I feel myself
unwell and my spirits depressed, I entreat Mr & Mrs Gillman to
open the letters, and *make* me answer them.—That my trust in
them is absolute and yet only commensurate with my Obligations,
and that I have not knowingly a recess of my heart or a thought in
it which I would not wish layed open to them, will perhaps but half
excuse this transfer of duties—the other half of the excuse must
be, that it is the lesser of two evils. You will not therefore wonder
that on leaving Highgate for a sojourn by the Sea side—I entreated
Mr G. to open my Letters, and inform me of such as required an
answer—and that it is in this way that I have learnt of your very
kind invitation. How gladly would I have availed myself of it had

it been in my power! But I am obliged to remain here till the 1st of December, and then I return with the expectation of a Visit from my Nephew, the Revd E. Coleridge of Eton.—As soon however as I can summon my thoughts, I mean to write to you & show you that you have been often in the thoughts of

My dear Sir . . . [No conclusion or signature in transcript.]

1499. *To Edward Coleridge*

Transcript Coleridge family. Hitherto unpublished.

Tuesday Noon.—[6] Dec. 1825

My dear Edward

Since the receipt of your kind & to me most exhilarating letter, one interruption after another has *punctuated* my answer from a semi-colon to a full stop. Long & short —— — ? ! !! — and blank interspaces sufficient for the division of chapters. Instead therefore of attempting to finish my reply *seriatim* to the different topics started in your's, and which has already reached the beginning of the second side of a second sheet—tho' if I can find it in my heart to make you pay double postage, or should procure a frank, you will receive it on Thursday Morning—I have decided on sending a sort of Dwarf Trumpeter before—with the *necessaries* for the interim.—Without therefore repeating my gladness at the thought of seeing you, I shall simply say that all days & hours will be convenient, with the single exception of Friday next—which I am obliged to devote to my excellent friend, Mr Green of Lincoln's Inn Fields on a matter of great & pressing importance to him in his present harrassing Contest with Envy, Hatred, and Malice in the persons of Sir Astley Cooper & his two Nephews, Mess. Bransby Cooper & Key, with Farce, Falsehood, and Fatuity as their Train-bearers.[1]

[1] In Jan. 1825 Sir Astley Cooper resigned the lectureship in anatomy and surgery which he had shared with Green at St. Thomas's Hospital. His understanding was that his nephews Bransby Cooper and Aston Key were to succeed him. Green acquiesced, but the authorities at St. Thomas's appointed another man to the joint lectureship in anatomy proposed for Bransby Cooper. Sir Astley thereupon induced Guy's Hospital to found a separate medical school, with his nephews as lecturers in anatomy and surgery. St. Thomas's claimed the valuable specimens which Cooper had deposited there to illustrate his lectures. This led to a quarrel. In 1825 Green published a pamphlet, 'Letter to Sir Astley Cooper on the Establishment of an Anatomical and Surgical School at Guy's Hospital', in which he gave the legal aspects of the case but left the way open for friendly relations in the future between himself and Bransby Cooper and Aston Key.

Poor dear Miss Lamb is under her sore periodical Visitation—
and Charles himself very unwell.—I foreboded, and I more than
fear too truly, that his emancipation from the India House would
not add to his Happiness. Blanco White is, you know, a Vale-
tudinarian, & by a very interesting letter I have received from him
with Doblado[1] & his 'Poor Man's Preservative against Popery',
which had for me all the charm of Novelty and I even think pleased
me more than the original Work,[2] [I learn that he] is very infirm
and weather-daunted. But the moment, I hear from you, what day
(alas! why must I say *day*—I have no liking for your singular
numbers! I want Daniel's 'a time and two times and half a time'[3]—
and here is a comfortable Bed and Bed-room for you, and Mr & Mrs
Gillman to worship as well as welcome you—Every additional
hour, you spent here, would really confer a week of genial Sensation
on these warm-hearted and affectionate people, both intensive in
the present enjoyment & extensive in their after-recollections.)—
I will set about it in good earnest with Irving, White, and the
unique Charles.—

It so happens, that on Thursday Mr & Mrs Gillman have the
offer of a rich Friend's carriage, which could fetch Henry from the
Piccadilly Coach-place—and I am instructed to ask you, whether
there would be any *impropriety* in requesting of Dr Keate his permission for Henry to leave Eton on Thursday—whether *you* deem
it right and advisable. For if you entertain the least *doubt* on the
subject, they would not think of it. By return of post be so good as
to give me two or three lines. I do not ask for more—knowing how
busy you must be.

And now I must conclude—yet I cannot do it without transcribing or rather abridging one part of my letter—viz. respecting
the Quarterly. When I wrote, I was in the atro-caerulean Mist of
the hell-blue Spirits (let the epithet pass for a Germanism, hell-blau
or clear blue)—but even then any complaint of John was leagues
off from my thoughts. Not only myself, but Charles Lamb, meant
the term 'ill-luck' in it's simplest & strictest sense.[4] He placed him-

[1] *Letters from Spain. By Don Leucadio Doblado*, 1822. For Coleridge's
annotations in a copy of this work see *Notes, Theological, Political, and Miscellaneous. By Samuel Taylor Coleridge*, ed. Derwent Coleridge, 1853, pp. 131–5.
[2] After his *Evidence against Catholicism* appeared in 1825, Blanco White was
induced by 'a sense of duty in regard to the poorer classes' to write *The Poor
Man's Preservative against Popery*. The work was published in 1825. See *Life
of Joseph Blanco White*, i. 230. A copy of this work with annotations by Coleridge is in the British Museum.
[3] Revelation xii. 14: 'for a time, and times, and half a time'. Daniel vii. 25
reads: 'a time and times and the dividing of time'.
[4] See Letter 1494.

self in John's situation, and judged by what would regulate his own decision. Silent as the Quarterly on every occasion had been respecting me, any Review, that could at *any* time have served me, would inevitably be attributed by a large party to the change in the Editors—Read under such an impression it could do *me* no good—and might injure the Review, & certainly would expose John to censure or suspicion.—Such were my inmost convictions— and such too would have been the advice, I would give, even at this moment. You are aware, my very dear Nephew! that neither my feelings nor my judgement have ever been thoroughly reconciled to this Editorship[1]—and only appeased by the almost implicit confidence I have the habit of feeling in John's strength & sanity of judgement. The pleasure with which I heard of his professional success was sensibly increased by the hope, that stress of business would with the motive remove the ability to continue in that honorable but invidious situation—for which likewise a *dash* of the party-coloured Devil is almost a necessary qualification—and if I shrunk from the very fancy, that Murray had the *power* of saying to John—Why did you do so?—with how much stronger & quicker aversion must I not recoil from the thought that Murray should have a *right* to say it?—All Walter Scott's reputation with my Contemporaries would not compensate for the knowledge that such a thing had happened, & on my account—For I very, very much love, esteem, & prize your Brother.— . . . [No conclusion or signature in transcript.]

1500. *To Edward Coleridge*

Transcript Pierpont Morgan Lib. Pub. Letters, ii. 744.

Thursday Midnight [8 December 1825][2]

My dear Edward

I write merely to tell you, that I have secured Charles Lamb and Mr Irvine to meet you, & wait only to learn the day for the endeavour to induce Mr Blanco White to join us. Will you present Mr & Mrs Gillman's regards to your Brothers, Henry and John— & that they would be most happy if both or either could be induced to accompany you?

I have had a very interesting conversation with Irvine this evening on the present condition of the Scottish Church, the spiritual arteries of which, yea, the very Aorta, he describes as in a

---

[1] See Letters 1395, 1438, and 1502.
[2] The transcript is endorsed 'Decbr 9th 1825', the date on which the letter was received.

state of Ossification. The greater part of the Scottish Clergy, he complains, have lost the *unction* of their own Church without acquiring the erudition and accomplishments of ours—Their sermons are all dry theological arguing & disputing, lifeless, pulseless —a rush-light in a fleshless skull.

My kindest Love to your Sister and kisses, prayers, and blessings for the Little one—

[S. T. Coleridge.]

I almost despair of John's coming; but do persuade Henry if you can. I quite long to see him again.

1501. *To J. Blanco White*

Address: Revd. Blanco White | Paradise Row | Chelsea.
MS. in the Rathbone Papers, now on deposit in the University Library, Liverpool; printed by permission of Mr. Reynolds Rathbone. Pub. Life of Joseph Blanco White, *i. 422.*
Postmark: Highgate, 12 December 1825.

Grove, Highgate
Monday Afternoon [12 December 1825]

My dear Sir

On my return from my two months' *Maritimate* at Ramsgate I found Doblado, the Poor Man's Preservative & your very kind and interesting letter. For all three receive my cordial thanks. The first I had never read tho' often heard of. I began it an hour before dinner—resumed it after tea, i.e. 7 o'clock—and when I heard the clock strike 2, thought it was time to undress—and did so, save and except my drawers & dressing gown, but could not lay the Book down till I had finished the last page just as it struck three. I need not say, it was a delightful work; but I should be ungrateful if I did not avow that both directly and by suggestion it has been a most instructive one to me.—The Poor Man's Preservative—to repeat the words I used in a note to my Nephew—had all the charm of Novelty for me. I am not certain that it did not please me even more than the original larger Volume. But probably, the constant lively sense of the great present utility of the Preservative, and the excellent management of the Dialogue, bribed my Judgement a little.—The fashionable *French* Modesty has for many years supplied a subject of indignant contempt & complaint with me—. To morrow I purpose to send a small parcel to you, with Hurwitz's 'Vindiciae Hebraicae', a work which passed under my hands—and of which the Author (the person spoken of in my Aids to Reflection, p. 205) respectfully entreats your acceptance. In a passage, that I have marked by a slip of Paper (and which Mr Hurwitz has introduced with a compliment[1] that shews him to have contemplated my character thro' the famous '*Amici* Reflecting-Microscope'[2] that is said to magnify a million times) you will find the echo of your sentiments—But for this & other topics I must refer you to the Letter which I shall inclose in the parcel—For the proper and immediate purpose of the present Scrawl is to say—that my Nephew, the Revd. Edward Coleridge, of Eton, a most sincere Lover and Admirer of your's, is with his Brother, Henry (who accompanied his Cousin, the Bishop, to Barbadoes), to spend the day with us on Thursday next.—They both anxiously wish for a personal introduction to you—and tho' my knowlege of your ill-health and that you are, not without good cause, weather-daunted, make my hopes burn very dim, yet I cannot help *trying*—so far as to assure you in my own name, my Nephews', and Mr and Mrs Gillman's, that you would confer an especial delight on us all, if you would join the party. We shall dine at an early hour—about 4: and a well-aired Bed & Bed Room with a Fire in it will be prepared for you.—Oblige me with a single Line by the return of Post—and let it be, Yes! if *that* be possible with *safety*. But if you are convinced, that you could not come but at a hazard, I retract my request, and tho' the *Wish* will survive, yet it shall be swallowed up in a larger, as Jonas in the Whale, to be cast on shore again, sub dio in a more genial Season.—I shall miss the Post, if I do not hasten to repeat that

with unmixed Esteem and cordial | regard I am, my dear Sir, |
        Your obliged Friend

S. T. Coleridge

[1] The 'compliment' to which Coleridge refers reads as follows:

A celebrated author, to whom the following may justly be applied, '*Vir in divinis Scripturis eruditissimus, & in secularibus nobiliter doctus, carmine excellens, & prosa, eloquio, disertus, sensu profundus, ingenio subtilis, assertione nervosus, vita & conversatione sanctissimus apparuit*'—has recommended the Bible as the STATESMAN'S MANUAL. (*Vindiciae Hebraicae*, 76.)

[2] G. B. Amici (1786–1863), Italian astronomer and microscopist.

1502. *To John Taylor Coleridge*

Address: John Coleridge, Esqre | 2 Pump Court | Temple
MS. British Museum. Pub. with omis. E. L. G. ii. 363.
Postmark: Highgate, 20 December 1825.

> Grove
> Highgate
> Monday Night—or (bless me! Two o'clock)
> Tuesday Morning. [20 December 1825]

My dear John

Derwent not having hitherto fulfilled his promise of transmitting to me an Exposé of the state of his feelings and opinions respecting the momentous points of Religion, Revelation, and the grounds and obligations of the moral Law—I can only hope, that his convictions have undergone a considerable change since my last conversation with him on the Subject. Heaven knows! the Skin was so flimsy and adhered so loosely to the body of his Faith, that he might have sloughed half a dozen such by this time, and yet not have excreted that which is to be succeeded by wings and eyes. I trust in God, that he has been hitherto but the Larva of his real and final Self. But in what period of his Catterpillerage he at present is, he has, as aforesaid, not afforded me the means of ascertaining or even of conjecturing. Assuredly, however, all that you have stated may be said of him with strictest truth; and with some addition, I think, on the score of interesting Manners and Talent above par.— So much (or rather so little) on the one side—& not more is it in my power to judge with respect to the other side—namely, whether *if* he were fit for the situation, the situation be desirable for him. And on this subject I should have been glad if you had intimated your own opinion, or given me some notion of what the duties and what the emoluments or other advantages of the Chaplaincy+Secretariate are—should Derwent have the offer. I cannot write to him till Wednesday's Post for a very strange-sounding reason—viz. my ignorance of his exact address since he left Davenport, neither of which leaving nor of it's motives has he communicated any thing to me—& tho' in a Letter from his Mother to Mrs Gillman there is a Mr Lowndes of Backfastleigh mentioned, I do not know where Backfastleigh is, or whether it be a Town or a Gentleman's Seat, or what title to pre- or af-fix to Mr Lowndes's name.[1] But on Wednesday Noon I shall be able to learn all this from Mr Poulton,

---

[1] According to Mrs. Coleridge, Derwent was 'first classical assistant at the large establishment at Buckfastleigh'. See *Minnow among Tritons*, ed. Stephen Potter, 1934, p. 94 (letter misdated).

20 December 1825   [1502

Henry Gillman's Latin and Writing Master, who saw Derwent at
Mr Lowndes's—which Mr P. mentioned to me on his return from
Devonshire—but I supposed him to have met with your Brother,
James Duke Coleridge,[1] Mr P. having by mistake spoken of Der-
went as the *Revd* Mr Coleridge.

Tho' I am ignorant of the particular occasions and motives that
influenced you in your relinquency of the 4rly,[2] which I first learnt
from Edward, yet I trust that in rejoicing at the event I was not
out of tune or sympathy with your own judgement and feelings.
There are those—and indeed I do not consciously flatter when I
add that I believe you to be one—who have in themselves an
Antidote to all poison and can breathe Malaria with ruddy cheek
and Eyes undimmed. But I cannot persuade myself, that the
Business of Reviewing, and the Habit of procuring, sanctioning and
becoming both morally and ostensibly responsible for anonymous
Criticism on the works of Contemporaries are not unfavorable to
sanity of Judgement and Delicacy of Feeling—the Pulse in those
Minor Morals, which are perhaps most friendly to the spiritual
growth of the *entire* Man.—I have found in Seneca and even in
Lord Bacon as poor a play on words and compensated by a less
weighty meaning than in the maxim—that a man may retain a
character of Integrity and yet have lost integrity of character.
To write a silly book and to be fooled by unwise friends into publishing it, may be declared a misdemeanour in the mildest Court of

---

[1] James Duke Coleridge (1789–1857), eldest son of Colonel James Coleridge.
[2] After serving as editor of the *Quarterly Review* from Dec. 1824 to Nov.
1825, John Taylor Coleridge was replaced by J. G. Lockhart. Mrs. Coleridge
bluntly stated the circumstances in a letter to Poole: 'You know, I presume,
that J. T. C. is no longer Editor of the Quarterly—his business in the Law
encreased rapidly, but he had *not* intended to resign the Edi[tor]ship for a year
to come. Mr M[urray] proposed his resigning in favour of Mr Lockhart.' See
Minnow among Tritons, ed. Stephen Potter, 1934, p. 97 (letter misdated).
'Were I to look to my own interests only', John Taylor Coleridge wrote to
Murray on 19 Nov. 1825, 'perhaps it would have been better that my retreat
should have been delayed till a more *ostensible* change had taken place in my
professional rank. . . . Upon due reflection you have satisfied your mind that
Mr. Lockhart's conduct of the *Review* is likely to be more beneficial to your
interests than mine. . . . I shall therefore certainly not interfere with your
forming a permanent arrangement with him. . . . I have now only one more
observation to make. . . . I own I think that so many and such full formed
reports of my retreat should not have been suffered to get into circulation
before the circumstances were disclosed to me. . . . I might have been spared
. . . the mortification of contradicting rumours which I was bound in justice to
you to regard as unfounded, but which now appear to have been circulated on
good authority. . . . I still think that the moment the report was in circulation,
I was entitled in courtesy and justice to have been fully informed of your
wishes. This is the only unpleasant part in the transaction.' Lord Coleridge,
The Story of a Devonshire House, 1905, pp. 286–8.

(525)

Criticism; but to be made permanently ridiculous, and to have a Wife, a Sister, a Daughter know it, does seem to me a punishment unconsciously disproportionate to the offence. When I met poor Dibdin just below Middle Row, and saw him bursting, swelling, throbbing with the pain of inflammation, I could not refrain from sympathizing with his sufferings—And when Mr Benson said at your House—He richly deserved the Lash—I said to myself—It may be so; but still I would not have had one, whom *I* loved & esteemed, the Beadle.[1]—At all events, it is an *invidious* office—and never compleatly off the mind—and I am heartily glad that you have done with it. One motive of a selfish complexion works a little with me. I want sadly to take counsel with and of you respecting my own literary operations—and I can now do this without any disturbing force from the thought that I might excite a painful wish in your mind of doing what could not be done without imputation—Yet if I know myself, I can truly declare that all, I ever wished to see in a Review was a fair account of the Work, I had written—how far it had the character of originality, and how far the less doubtful merit of truth & importance.—I wanted no disquisitions on myself or my genius—but a fair statement of my objects, and of my Arguments—& to be set right where the Reviewer conceived me to have gone wrong.—

My kind Love to Mrs John—& Love & Blessings to my dear Grand-nephews—and be assured that I am with most affectionate regard & esteem your Kinsman & Friend

S. T. Coleridge

1503. *To Derwent Coleridge*

Address: Derwent Coleridge, Esqre | Revd M. Lowndes | Backfastleigh Devon [Readdressed in another hand] J. H. Macaulay Esq. | Plymouth
MS. Victoria University Lib. Hitherto unpublished.
Postmark: 21 December 1825. *Stamped*: Ashburton.

[21 December 1825]

My dear Derwent

God knows! it not only gives me a sharp *stitch* at particular moments, but is a perpetual aching and dull pain at heart, that what with the tangle & endless Cat-crad[l]e of petty embarrassments, which I turn & twist round and round to get rid of, as in a dyspeptic dream, wasting my time and power on other men's

---

[1] *The Library Companion, or the Young Man's Guide and the Old Man's Comfort in the Choice of a Library*, 2 vols., 1824, the only one of T. F. Dibdin's works 'which was fully (and very severely) reviewed at the time of its publication'. *D.N.B.*

affairs in order to procure immediate supplies, and the decreasing
proportion of the 24 hours that I can work in, to any good for the
day, and without loss and harm to the morrow—for like many
others I find myself decaying before I ever felt myself ripe—the
necessary conditions of any, however trifling, *proceeds* from any
works, that I can, or can endure to, write & publish being precluded in my instance by the unlucky accident, that the Dispensers
of Publicity are divided into those who mention my Books only
to abuse them, and those who to avoid the imputation of partiality
and nepotism never mention them at all—in short, what from being
always behind hand, on *my* part—and no lack of disturbing forces
on the other—I go on from month to month as if I had no Sons in
the world, never hearing *of* you or Hartley without a compounded
or biforked Sting of grief and shame that I never hear *from* you.—
But enough of this—neither can I now enter into the detail of the
baffled Efforts I made at the Goldsmiths' & Mercers' Companies
respecting your exhibitions[1]—or the evident Languor of the
Suttons, since Mr Gillman's manly but too prominent opposition to
the factious & vindictive attack on Mr Mence & the Trustees of
the Highgate School—I write at present in consequence of a Note
received yesterday from your Cousin, John Coleridge—The new
Bishop of Quebec having conversed with Mr Tateham[2] respecting
his Chaplaincy & Secretariate, Mr T. recommended *you* to him—
& the Bishop called on John Coleridge, intimating however that
there was a negociation going on with some one else (in short,
John's Note is remarkably scanty, in particulars). John described
you, as correct in conduct, well-informed & fond of Literature; but
professed his ignorance as to your views or intentions of taking
orders—and asks me if I knew whether there had been any change
in opinions—I replied, that I took for granted, you had, like myself at your time of life, sloughed half a dozen skins since I last conversed with you: but whether you had excreted that which was to
be succeeded by wings & eyes; or whether you had already come
forth, like

> fresh Clarion, ready dight
> That to his journey did himself address
> And with good speed begin to take his flight[3]—

I could not positively say—but expressed my regret that he had
not given me any data for judging whether if you were suited to the

[1] See Letters 1395 and 1441.
[2] Ralph Tatham (1778–1857), tutor at St. John's College, Cambridge, 1814–
30. In 1838 he became master of the college; subsequently he served two terms
(1839–40 and 1845–6) as vice-chancellor of the University.
[3] Spenser, *Muiopotmos*, lines 145–7.

situation, the situation was desirable for you—in present emolument or future prospects.—So, my dear *Larva*! if you are still in your Caterpillage—or (as my Wishes would bribe me to hope) my dear IMAGO vera Derwentî, et ipse Derwentus! if you think it worth your inquiry, write to John about it.—

Knight's Magazines *uncut* look me reproachfully in the face; but I have put this down third in my list of promised performances—and as my friend, Mr Green, will not be here on Sunday next, I have set aside that for the regular reading of them—at all events, of all I suppose your's.[1]—Would to God, I could see you for a week or so! —Poor as I am, I would gladly frank you to & fry [*sic*].—If you will tell me WHERE to send them, by what vehicle &c, I will send you two or three Copies of the 'Aids to Reflection'—one of them much corrected and with some MSS additions in my own hand—And it is possible that if you would take the trouble of correcting the others, & making the transcript of the MSS comments, the presenting them to some one or other might be taken as a compliment. Over all the few good results of the publication I place the acquaintance and friendship of Mr J. Blanco White—the Spaniard—who has inflicted a deeper wound on Antichrist & his scarlet Prima Donna than they have received since our Revolution. —Yesterday I received the following Sonnet from him, which with exception of 'widen'd in his view' I think a noble production—and from a Spaniard born & bred an extraordinary one—. He is a Scholar—an exquisite Musician, both as Composer & Performer—and from my soul I believe, a thoroughly good Man.

Night and Death
a Sonnet
dedicated to S. T. Coleridge, Esqre. by his sincere Friend,
Joseph Blanco White.

Mysterious NIGHT! when the first man but knew
Thee by report, unseen: and heard thy name,
Did he not tremble for this lovely frame,
This glorious Canopy of Light and Blue?
Yet, 'neath a curtain of transparent Dew,
Bathed in the rays of the great setting F[lame,]
Hesperus with the Host of Heaven came,
And lo! Creation widen'd in his View!   Qy.
Who could have thought what darkness lay [concealed]
Beneath thy beams, O Sun! Or who could f[ind,]

---

[1] *Knight's Quarterly Magazine*, 1823–4; continued as the *Quarterly Magazine*, 1825. Along with Derwent Coleridge the contributors included H. N. Coleridge, T. B. Macaulay, De Quincey, and Sidney Walker.

While Fly, and Leaf and Insect stood reve[aled,][1]
That to such endless orbs thou mad'st us blind!
Weak Man! why to shun Death this anxious strife?
If Light can thus deceive, wherefore not Life?[2]

Henry is come home for his Holidays from Eton (you know, he is a little Colleger, under Edward Coleridge's protection) much improved.—Mrs Gillman's health has been greatly benefited by her Sojourn at Ramsgate—and they both desire their kind regards to you!—God bless you my dear Boy! & your anxiously affect. Father

S.T.C.

P.S. I shall dine on Saturday with Mr J. Hookham Frere.[3] Let me hear *from* you. John Coleridge's address—No. 2. Pump Court, Temple. I like your cousin Edward much—& the more, the more I see of him— . . .[4]

[1] MS. torn.
[2] For a version of this sonnet as revised by Blanco White in 1838 see *Life of Joseph Blanco White*, iii. 48.
[3] After several years' absence in Malta, Frere returned to England in Sept. 1825 and remained there for a year. *John Hookham Frere*, 270.
[4] One sentence heavily inked out in MS.

DATE DUE
